The Baha'i Communities of Iran
1851–1921

Volume 2: The South of Iran

Other books by Moojan Momen

The Babi and Baha'i Religions 1844–1944: Some Contemporary Western Accounts. George Ronald, 1981.

Studies in Babi and Baha'i History, vol. 1 (ed.) Kalimat Press, 1982.

(With Juan R. Cole) *From Iran East and West* (eds.) Studies in Babi and Baha'i History, vol. 2. Kalimat Press, 1984.

An Introduction to Shi'i Islam: The History and Doctrines of Twelver Shi'ism. Yale University Press; George Ronald; Oxford University Press, 1985.

Selections from the Writings of E.G. Browne on the Babi and Baha'i Religions (ed.) George Ronald, 1987.

Studies in Honor of the Late Hasan M. Balyuzi, ed. Studies in the Babi and Baha'i Religions, vol. 5. Kalimat Press, 1988.

The Works of Shaykh Ahmad al-Ahsa'i: A Bibliography. Baha'i Studies Monograph, no. 1, Newcastle, 1991.

Scripture and Revelation, (ed.) George Ronald, 1998.

The Phenomenon of Religion: A Thematic Approach. Oneworld, 1999 (reprinted as *Understanding Religion: A Thematic Approach.* Oneworld, 2009).

The Baha'i Faith and the World's Religions, (ed.) George Ronald, 2003.

(With Wendi Momen) *Understanding the Baha'i Faith.* Dunedin Academic Press, 2006.

Baha'u'llah: A Short Biography. Oneworld, 2007.

The Baha'i Communities of Iran, 1851–1921. Volume 1: The North of Iran. George Ronald, 2015.

Shi'i Islam: A Beginner's Guide. Oneworld, 2016.

The Baha'i Communities of Iran
1851–1921

Volume 2: The South of Iran

by
Moojan Momen

George Ronald
Oxford

George Ronald, *Publisher*
Oxford
www.grbooks.com

*A catalogue record for this book is available
from the British Library*

ISBN 978–0–85398–630–0

Cover design: Steiner Graphics

For my parents
Gloria (Iman) Momen and Sedratollah Momen

MAP OF IRAN

CONTENTS

Map of the Provinces of Kashan, Isfahan and the Central Provinces

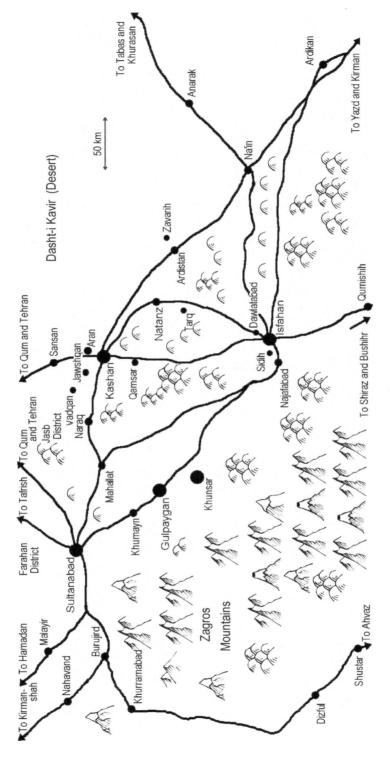

ILLUSTRATIONS

INTRODUCTION

This book is the second volume of a history of the Baha'i communities of Iran over the period from 1851 to 1921. The Babi movement, founded by Sayyid 'Ali Muhammad, who took the title the Bab (1819–50), was the immediate predecessor to the Baha'i Faith and had caused religious and social turmoil in Iran from its beginning in 1844. This book begins with the events of the period immediately after the execution of the Bab in 1850 and the end of the Babi upheavals in Iran in 1852 when the shah gave orders for the extermination of the Babi community. Thousands of Babis had been killed in the period 1848–52, leading to a period of confusion and decline in the Babi community. A number of people put forward claims to the leadership of the community, but during the period 1851–63, one of these, Mirza Husayn 'Ali Nuri, who took the title Baha'u'llah (1817–92), emerged as the effective leader of the community. He then put forward the claim to be the figure whom the Bab had promised and indeed to be the messianic figure who is promised in all religions. Thus was founded the Baha'i Faith.

The period covered by this book stretches across the leadership of the Baha'i community by Baha'u'llah and his son and successor 'Abdu'l-Baha ('Abbas Effendi, 1844–1921). Coincidentally and conveniently, the end point of this period, 1921, corresponds with two changes that were of great importance to the Baha'i community, one external and one internal. The internal change was the death of 'Abdu'l-Baha in 1921 and the start of the leadership of Shoghi Effendi, who quickly formalized and systematized an administrative framework within the Baha'i community which had only been embryonic during the time of 'Abdu'l-Baha. From this time onwards, it became the administrative institutions rather than learned or influential individuals who were in authority in the Baha'i community. The year 1921 also witnessed a great external change, which began with a *coup d'état* that marked the effective end of the Qajar dynasty and first brought to power the man who would in 1925 be crowned as Reza Shah. He was able to impose a strong centralized government upon Iran, thus changing radically the framework within which the Baha'i community operated in ways that were both beneficial and detrimental to the Baha'i community.

The reader should refer to the Introduction to the first volume for a more detailed historical account of the leadership of the Baha'i Faith and the conditions in Iran during this period as well as for a review of the literature on the subject of this book. This information will not be repeated here, except to set out a few brief historical facts that the reader may need to contextualize references that occur in the text.

Baha'u'llah's successive exiles were from Tehran to Baghdad in 1853, to Istanbul and then Edirne in 1863, and finally in 1868 to 'Akka, where he died in 1892. 'Abdu'l-Baha lived in the Haifa–'Akka area until his death in 1921, except for a period from 1910 to 1913, when he moved to Egypt and from there made two journeys: the first to Europe in 1911 and the second to North America and Europe in 1912–13. Until 1918, the Haifa–'Akka area was under Ottoman rule. It was then administered by Britain under a League of Nations mandate. During the period covered by this book, the shahs of Iran were: Nasiru'd-Din Shah (r. 1848–96), Muzaffaru'd-Din Shah (r. 1896–1907), Muhammad 'Ali Shah (r. 1907–9) and Ahmad Shah, whose reign was effectively ended by a coup in 1921; he was forced into exile in 1923, although he was not formally deposed until 1925. Also frequently mentioned in the course of this book are two internal movements of opposition to the Baha'i leaders. Baha'u'llah's half-brother, Mirza Yahya Azal (1831–1912), claimed leadership of the Babi movement. Most Babis (probably more than 95 per cent) followed Baha'u'llah but a small number followed Azal and became known as 'Azalis' or 'Azali Babis'. This group strongly opposed the Baha'is and caused problems in a number of places. Similarly, during the leadership of 'Abdu'l-Baha, his half-brother Mirza Muhammad 'Ali (1852–1937), challenged his leadership. The number following Mirza Muhammad 'Ali was even fewer than those following Azal and probably totalled no more than a few hundred in the whole of Iran. Nevertheless, the episode caused problems for the Baha'i community.

Notes for the reader

This section is more or less identical to the one in the first volume. Throughout this book it has been convenient to refer to four general periods of time which correspond to social and political developments both in Iran and within the Baha'i community:

a) *The Babi Period (1844–52)* This precedes the period that the present book deals with but of course is very important for the development of the Baha'i community in that the Babi movement is the immediate predecessor of the Baha'i Faith.

b) *The Ministry of Baha'u'llah (1853–92)* This period begins with Baha'u'llah assuming effective although not formal leadership of the Babi community, continues with his founding and development of the Baha'i community, and ends with his passing. As well as marking a distinct period in Baha'i history, it can also be thought of in terms of Iranian history as a period when the old Qajar autocracy reigned supreme and unchallenged.

c) *The Ministry of 'Abdu'l-Baha (1892–1921)* As well as marking a distinct period of leadership in the Baha'i community, this era in Iranian history marked the emergence of political unrest culminating in the granting of the Constitution of 1906 and the subsequent decline in the Qajar dynasty until its overthrow in a *coup d'état* in 1921.

d) *The Ministry of Shoghi Effendi (1922–57)* or the modern period (1922–79). This period saw the institutionalization of the Baha'i community in Iran with its affairs coming under the control of an elected national spiritual assembly. The period corresponded with the strong centralizing and authoritarian government of Reza Shah, who effected many changes in Iran, although some of these changes were reversed after his overthrow in 1941. This period is after the events described in the present work, although, inevitably, reference is made to it. Occasionally some events occurring shortly after 1921 are described insofar as they reflect the chaotic administration of the Qajar period rather than the more organized centralized Pahlavi regime.

The transliteration of Persian and Arabic words has been kept to a minimum in this book. Words and place names that have come into the English language are given in the form in which they have become widely used, even when this does not exactly conform to Persian usage or the transliteration system adopted in this book (e.g. dervish, Tehran, etc.). For all other names (including Baha'i, Baha'u'llah and 'Abdu'l-Baha), the form of the Baha'i transliteration system is maintained but diacritical marks are not used. The full transliteration of names in accordance with the system universally used in Baha'i books can be found in the Index and Bibliography (this system is derived from a system adopted by the Tenth International Congress of Orientalists held in September 1894 at Geneva and approximates to the system used by the Encyclopaedia of Islam and the International Journal of Middle Eastern Studies).[1] Many Persian and Arabic words and phrases can be found in the Glossary (pp. 455–464) and are fully transliterated there but not in the main text of the book. Others, appearing less frequently and for which there are no straightforward English equivalents, are explained and transliterated in the text. In general, the different elements of Arabic names and titles of individuals and book titles are separated (e.g. Zill us-Sultan). However, in the case of given names, the two parts are fused together (e.g. 'Abdu'llah and Nasiru'd-Din). A number of translation conventions are used throughout the book: for example the words 'propagate', 'spread' and 'teach' are used to translate the term '*tablígh*' in Persian; similarly 'teacher' or 'travelling teacher' are used for '*muballigh*'; 'cleric' is used for a member of the '*ulamá*', 'tablet' is used to translate *lawḥ* (the word usually used for works of Baha'i scripture), etc. Baha'i terminology in English is explained in the Glossary.

Each town or village that has been described is, wherever available, ascribed a population for the years 1905 or 1914 and 1951 or 1956. The population for 1905 is derived from *Gazetteer of Persia*, compiled by MacGregor and others in the Intelligence Branch of the Quarter-Master General's Department, and published in India between 1885 and 1905; and that for 1914 is derived from the *Gazetteer of Persia*, prepared in four volumes by the General Staff, Headquarters, and published in India in 1910–18. However, it should be noted that the population figures in these two gazetteers were culled from data published over several decades and can be thought of as mainly representing figures for the last part of the 19th century and the first decade of the 20th. Most of the *Gazetteer of Persia*, 1910–18, is reproduced with additional material in Adamec, *Historical Gazetteer of Iran*, in four volumes published in 1976–89. Many entries in these gazetteers and other sources give only the number of houses or families in a town or village. In such cases, a factor of five has been used to calculate the population. Where available, for the larger towns and cities, population figures from the 1956 census have been given, mainly taken from Bémont, *Les Villes d'Iran*. Where this is not available, for some towns and for the villages, population figures have been taken from Razmara and Nawbakht, *Farhang-i Jugráfiyá'i-yi Iran*, the figures for which appear to relate to counts that were done mainly in 1330/1951 (although the

---

1   For a full description of this transliteration system, see the section on transliteration in any of the *Baha'i World* volumes, up to volume 20, for example, 20:1053–65.

date 1328/1949 is also mentioned in places). Where these volumes do not contain a population figure, the modern data given in Adamec, *Gazetteer of Persia*, which appear to relate to the 1966 census, are used. For the provinces and larger cities, brief descriptions of geography, climate, agriculture and trade are given and these are largely also drawn from the three gazetteers noted above, as well as several other sources. For the larger towns and cities, population figures for 1868 are also given. These are drawn from a report by the British diplomat Ronald Thomson.[2]

Iran has had several different patterns of geographical administrative division over the past 150 years. In the present book the provinces that were traditional in the late 19th century have been used. Even so, there were frequent changes in the boundaries of the provinces and the areas ruled by the provincial governors. Since it was necessary to allocate towns to particular chapters, for the purposes of this book the provincial boundaries shown in a map published in the *Harmsworth Universal Atlas* published in London (Amalgamated Press, London, c. 1900, pp. 111–12) have been used (see map on p. vi) since these appear to correspond best to the usages in the various historical sources. A list of the abbreviations of books frequently cited in the footnotes is given at the beginning of the Bibliography. Where dates are only known according to the Islamic lunar Hijri calendar (AHQ), they are given thus 1321/1903, where the first date is the Hijri lunar year and the second is the first of the two Common Era years in which that Hijri year falls (unless 1 Muharram falls in December, in which case the following year is given). Hijri solar years (AHS) have been converted into the first of the two Common Era years in which they fall, except in the Bibliography where both Hijri solar and Common Era years are given.

---

2   See Issawi, *Economic History* 28.

ACKNOWLEDGEMENTS

I wish to acknowledge the help given by numerous people in this project which has taken over 25 years to complete and I apologize to those whom I have omitted, of which there must be many. I am grateful to the following who have provided oral or written information regarding specific localities (these contributions are recorded in the footnotes): Hasan Balyuzi, Hasan Afnan, Ata Agah, Cyrus Agahi, Cyrus Ala'i, Vahid Bihmardi, Yahya Jafari, Manuchehr Khodadad, Anthony Lee, Jalal Mahmudi, Heshmat Moayyad, Heshmatollah Mohammad-Hosseini, Servat Mokhtari, Fariba Nadimi, Azizu'llah Purshafi-Ardestani, Hasan Rahimi, Farham Sabet, Ashraf Sha-habadi, Hassan Songhorabadi, Zibandih Shams-Isfandabadi, Ali Tavangar, Khadijih Ulfat, and Bahiyyih Varqa. More general assistance has been given by Iraj Ayman, Shapour Rassekh, Abu'l-Qasim Afnan, Payam Afsharian, Arash Abizadeh, Bijan Masumian, and Ruhu'llah Mehrabkhani. Many also helped me to track down the photographs in this volume. Some of the material in this book was presented on the 'Tarikh' email list and I benefited from the discussions there. My abiding gratitude must always go to the late Hasan Balyuzi who first enthused me and guided me in my research into the history of the Baha'i community. I would also like to record my thanks to my wife Wendi Momen (who edited this book on behalf of George Ronald) and the other members of my family who have supported me over the years.

A number of my papers were preliminary to or drawn from the research that produced this book. Among these were the articles on Iran prepared for the Baha'i Encyclopedia project, 'Preliminary Survey of the Baha'i Community of Iran', and 'Persecution and Resilience: A History of the Baha'i Religion in Qajar Isfahan' (see Bibliography for details).

The picture on p. 156, chapter 12, is by Rug Connoisseur. The picture on p. 423, chapter 19, is by Diego Delso. [Both CC BY-SA 4.0 (https://creativecommons.org/licenses/by-sa/4.0)].

ISFAHAN

The central provinces of Iran were often referred to in the Qajar era as 'Iraq-i 'Ajami (Persian Iraq, as distinct from the Ottoman province of Iraq, which was called 'Iraq-i 'Arabi, Arabic Iraq). However, this area was also often split into numerous governorships of individual towns and there was an ever-shifting pattern of administration. In this chapter we will deal only with the area immediately around Isfahan, which was always directly administered from Isfahan.

The province of Isfahan is situated on the high semi-arid plateau of central Iran. Despite the dry conditions, there was, with the help of irrigation, much agriculture in the province, producing wheat, tobacco, cotton and fruit. The southwest of this area was dominated by the Bakhtiyari nomadic tribe. Although Ardistan was sometimes considered part of this province, in this book it is placed under Kashan (see maps at Frontispieces 1 and 2).

Isfahan

The city of Isfahan is situated in the centre of Iran (430 km south of Tehran and 485 km north of Shiraz) and was, in the 17th century under the Safavid dynasty, the capital of the country. In 1868 it was reckoned to be the third largest city in Iran, with a population of 60,000 (with 2,000 Christians and 1,500 Jews).[1] A census in about 1881 gave a total of 75,000.[2] By 1914 its population is estimated to have been 80,000 and by 1956 was 254,700. The city has the finest architectural monuments of Islamic Iran and has been famous as a centre of the textile trade and of many crafts. In the late Safavid period Isfahan had been the residence of the leading religious authorities of the Shi'i world and even in the Qajar period it retained something of its pre-eminence, being regarded as the leading centre of Shi'i scholarship within Iran for at least the first half of the 19th century.

No satisfactory history of the Baha'i Faith in Isfahan has been written. When, in the 1920s, on the instructions of Shoghi Effendi, histories of the various towns and provinces of Iran were being written, a history of Isfahan was composed by an unknown author and completed in late 1930 but it is mainly a series of biographies and is only 71 pages long. There are also two memoirs from the early period, one by Aqa Husayn 'Ali Nur, covering events in Isfahan from about 1874 until 1879 when the author fled to Tehran; the second is the memoirs of Aqa Muhammad Ja'far Kharazi-furush Thabit Isfahani (edited by his son 'Abbas Thabit), recording events from when he became a Baha'i in Isfahan in 1296/1879 until 1907, when he migrated to Tehran. Both of these have been published (see Bibliography).

The Babi period

Isfahan and the surrounding villages were Babi strongholds, as evidenced by the fact that some ten per cent of the participants at Shaykh Tabarsi were from the area.[3] The Bab was in Isfahan from October 1846 to March 1847. Since he was staying for part of the time in the house of the Imam-Jum'ih, many of the clerics and theological students of the city took the opportunity to meet him and some were favourably impressed. It was in this house that the Bab wrote his Commentary on the Qur'anic Surih of Wa'l-Asr for the Imam-Jum'ih and his treatise on the specific prophetic

---

1   Thomson, cited in Issawi, *Economic History* 28; although Abbott in 1850 was giving an estimate of 75,000 with 300 Jews (Amanat, *Cities and Trade* 125, 127).

2   Afḍal ul-Mulk, *Safar-namih-yi Isfahan* 74. See also Walcher, *Shadow* 28–30.

3   Momen, 'Social Basis' 164.

mission of Muhammad (*Nubuvvat-i Khāss*) for the governor Manuchihr Khan, who was to become his most prominent follower. A considerable number of converts were made, some from among the most influential sectors of the population.

In December 1851, after the execution of the Bab, Sayyid Basir Hindi came to Isfahan promulgating his claim to leadership of the Babis (see p. 80 and vol. 1:6). His ecstatic states and rousing speeches stirred the Babi community. Shaykh Isma'il, who had been a religious student and had become a Babi, began to enter ecstatic states and declared that he was the return of the Prophet Muhammad and that Aqa Muhammad Qasim Aba-duz (cloak-maker), who had converted him, was the return of the Imam 'Ali. He then declared himself to be 'He whom God shall make manifest'. A number of the Babis in Isfahan accepted this claim and even Mulla Baqir Tabrizi, the Letter of the Living, who was in Isfahan at this time, said that he had been promised by the Bab that he would meet 'Him whom God shall make manifest' and that perhaps this was he. One day, Shaykh Isma'il instructed Aqa Muhammad Qasim to make a public announcement of his claim in the main bazaar of the town. These two and two others who were with them were arrested along with about a hundred others, although not all of these were Babis. Shaykh Isma'il was declared insane but the other three arrested in the bazaar were publicly executed. The others arrested were mulcted of as much money as could be obtained from them and released.[4]

During the time that Baha'u'llah was in Baghdad a number of the Babis of the Isfahan area, such as Mirza Muhammad 'Ali Nahri (see p. 17) and Mulla Zaynu'l-'Abidin of Najafabad (known to Baha'is as Zayn ul-Muqarrabin), made the journey to Baghdad, met Baha'u'llah and returned enthused. This resulted in an upsurge of Babi activities. One consequence of this was that in about 1861 the governor Khanlar Mirza Ihtisham ud-Dawlih ordered the arrest of five of the Babis of the town, one of whom was released after a short time because he declared he was not a Babi. After they had spent two months in prison, the governor ordered the execution of the two more senior of the prisoners, Mulla 'Ali Sabbagh and Aqa

---

4   Afnan, *'Ahd-i A'la* 480, 483–4, 543 (the text of the letter on p. 484 is missing a segment of the original letter, as shown on p. 543, which makes it clear that the latter part of the original refers to events in Isfahan); ZH 4:34–6; Browne in ['Abdu'l-Baha], *Traveller's Narrative* 2:331; Nicolas, *Sayyed Ali Mohammed* 430; *Ruz-Namih-yi Vaqayi'-yi Ittifaqiyyih*, no. 48, 9 Rabi' I, 1268, p. 3.

2. Muhammad 'Ali Salmani

Muhammad Javad Kharrat. The other two had their ears and noses cut and were led around the streets and bazaar before being released.⁵ One of these latter two was Muhammad 'Ali Salmani (1835–after 1903, see fig. 2), who was later to visit Baha'u'llah in Baghdad and accompany him to Edirne; he also lived in 'Akka a while before finally going to Ashkhabad.⁶ One of Azal's main supporters in Isfahan, Mirza Hadi Dawlatabadi, converted many but, as in Naraq and Kashan (see pp. 82 and 122–3), several of these, such as Aqa 'Ali Nur (d. c. 1294/1877)⁷ and Aqa Muhammad Kazim (see p. 15), went to Baghdad and returned as supporters of Baha'u'llah.

The beginnings of the Baha'i community

The foundations for the conversion of the Babis of this area to the Baha'i Faith were laid through those Babis who visited Baha'u'llah during his exile in Baghdad. In addition, in 1861 Sayyid Muhammad, the uncle of the Bab, arrived in Isfahan on his way to Shiraz with the Kitab-i Iqan which Baha'u'llah had composed for him in Baghdad. This book was read enthusiastically by the Babis and attained such a status that supporters of Azal tried to insinuate that it was really composed by him. It is not clear who was the first to announce Baha'u'llah's claim in Isfahan. It may have been Nabil Zarandi who arrived there in late 1866.⁸ It may be, however, that

5   ZH 4:217 gives the date of this event as 1276/1859. But since Salmani remembers it as a year of famine, around 1861 would be more correct, and this accords better with the dates when Khanlar Mirza was governor; Salmani, *My Memories* 7–10; Ishraq-Khavari, *Rahiq-i Makhtum* 2:673–4; Dhuka'i-Bayda'i, *Tadhkirih* 2:188.
6   Salmani, *My Memories*; ZH 6:176–89; Balyuzi, *Baha'u'llah* 227–30, 260, 325, 330, 483.
7   ZH 6:191.
8   Rafati, 'Nabil' 35.

prior to this, Mirza Ja'far Yazdi stayed in Isfahan on his way to Yazd where he is known to have announced Baha'u'llah's claim. Most of the prominent Babis of the area became Baha'is; such persons as Zayn ul-Muqarrabin, Haji Sayyid Javad Muharrir (scribe, who had been with the Bab on pilgrimage in 1844 and had become a Babi at that time,[9] d. 1312/1894), Mirza Ashraf of Najafabad, Mirza Muhammad 'Ali Nahri, Mirza Haydar 'Ali Ardistani, Aqa 'Abdu'l-Hamid (the son of Mulla Ja'far Gandumpakkun, the first Babi in the city) and others (see below for more on some of these individuals).

Another Babi who became a strong supporter of Baha'u'llah was Aqa Sayyid 'Abdu'r-Rahim Isfahani (c. 1808–91), who was from a Tabriz merchant family resident in Isfahan and was himself a cloth-dealer. He had been the agent of the prominent Isfahan cleric Sayyid Muhammad Baqir Rashti (Shafti), administering some of his village properties in the Pir Bakran area to the west of Isfahan, and after this had studied under Shafti and earned a living as a scribe and oculist. He had met Mulla Husayn Bushru'i when the latter visited Isfahan in about 1843 at the behest of the Shaykhi leader Sayyid Kazim Rashti, had met the Bab in Isfahan (and acted as a scribe for him) and most of the leading Babis at Badasht and Shaykh Tabarsi. Mulla Husayn Bushru'i ordered him to leave Shaykh Tabarsi and teach the Babi religion, which he did in Mazandaran and elsewhere until he returned to Isfahan, where he was arrested by the deputy governor Chiragh-'Ali Khan in about 1852 and only freed on the intervention of his daughter and the Imam-Jum'ih. He had met Baha'u'llah and Azal in Tehran, and Haji Mirza Haydar 'Ali Isfahani records that even before Baha'u'llah had openly declared his mission, 'Abdu'r-Rahim was interpreting the Bayan and the books of the Bab to say that Baha'u'llah was 'He whom God shall make manifest' promised by the Bab. He was given the title Ismu'llah ur-Rahim (the name of God the Merciful) by the Bab and this was confirmed by Baha'u'llah. He travelled around Iran teaching the Baha'i Faith for some 20 years.[10]

Since the early Baha'i community of Isfahan emerged as conversions of most of the Babi community, it closely resembled the latter in its social structure. Analyses of the Babi community have indicated that in Isfahan the Babi religion had spread mainly through merchants and the

---

9 Anon, Tarikh Amri Isfahan 1–3.
10 Isfahani, *Bihjat us-Sudur* 25 (trans. *Delight* 10–11); Anon, Tarikh Amri Isfahan 4–11; Rahmani Najafabadi, 'Sharh-i Ahval'.

3. Mirza Husayn Mishkin Qalam

bazaar network of retailers and craftsmen.[11] The persecutions of 1848–52 had brought this growth to a halt but during the late 1850s there was a resurgence of activities, as described above, such that the community began to increase again. By the early 1870s it was even becoming noticeable to outsiders. Rev. Robert Bruce, a British missionary of the Church Missionary Society resident in Isfahan, wrote in 1874: 'The sect of Baabis which is now increasing in Persia is that called Bahai.'[12] Much of this increase was among the same class of merchants, retailers and craftsmen, as indicated by the names of the converts: Sayyid 'Ali Zargar (goldsmith), Haji 'Ali Chini-furush (seller of porcelain) and his brother Aqa Muhammad Ibrahim Tunbaku-furush (tobacconist), Mirza Muhammad Hasan Qannad (confectioner, d. 1325/1907), Aqa Muhammad Rahim Tajir (merchant), Aqa Muhammad Husayn Tunbaku-furush (tobacconist) and Haji Muhammad Rida Tajir (merchant).[13]

Among those who became Baha'is in the 1860s was Mirza Husayn Mishkin Qalam (1812–6 December 1912, see figs. 3 and 95), the son of the merchant Haji Muhammad 'Ali Isfahani. He was a Sufi of the Ni'matu'llahi order and a pre-eminent calligrapher; his skill in this was recognized by the shah, who gave him the name Mishkin Qalam[14] and sent him to tutor the heir-apparent in Tabriz. It was on his way back from a trip to Isfahan to see his wife and family that he met Sayyid Mahdi Dihaji and heard of the Baha'i Faith. He was so enamoured of this discovery that he left everything and set out for Baghdad. Baha'u'llah had already left for Edirne; so after spending some time in Baghdad he went on. In Aleppo the governor Jevdet Pasha was so taken by his calligraphy that he persuaded him to remain. In mid-1867 Nabil Zarandi came to Aleppo and talked with Mishkin Qalam such that he came to full belief in Baha'u'llah and left with Nabil for Edirne. Mishkin

11   See in particular the Babi participants at Shaykh Tabarsi in Momen, 'Social Basis' 162 and comments relating to Isfahan in Amanat, *Resurrection* 339–63.
12   Letter of 19 Nov. 1874, cited in Momen, 'Early relations' 63.
13   Nur, Tarikh 18–20; ZH 6:172–4.
14   'Qalam' means pen. The adjective 'Mishkin' means 'musk-like'. In English, musk is chiefly known for its fragrance but in Iranian culture it is known for both its fragrance and the blackness of the musk grains.

Qalam was exiled with Azal to Cyprus in 1868. His family from Isfahan travelled to 'Akka in about 1882 and Mishkin Qalam moved to 'Akka in 1886, later spending periods of time in Egypt, Bombay and Damascus.[15]

Also converted at this time was Mirza Asadu'llah Isfahani (d. 1343/1924), who was from the famous Nuri clan of government officials to which Baha'u'llah also belonged. He eschewed the family career to become a cleric studying at the Madrasih Kasihgaran in Isfahan. Then in 1278/1861 he became a Babi and travelled throughout Iran propagating the Babi and then the Baha'i Faith until 1294/1877, when he settled in Tehran. He was one of the first to promote the establishment of Baha'i institutions during travels through Iran in 1880–2, based on his understandings of the Kitab-i Aqdas: *majlis-i shawr* (*mahfil-i shawr*, assemblies of consultation), *mashriqu'l-adhkar* (communal dawn prayers and buildings for these) and *mahall ul-barakah* (communal Baha'i funds). He then settled in 'Akka but undertook a number of journeys to propagate the Baha'i Faith in Iran in 1303/1885, 1306/1888 and 1312/1895. In 1882 he married Gawhar, a daughter of Mirza Muhammad 'Ali Nahri (see pp. 17–18), thus becoming the brother-in-law of 'Abdu'l-Baha. In 1898 he was commissioned by 'Abdu'l-Baha to transport the remains of the Bab from Iran to 'Akka. In 1900 he was asked by 'Abdu'l-Baha to undertake a mission to America where he was responsible for trying to counter the activities of Ibrahim Kheiralla, who had defected to the side of Mirza Muhammad 'Ali. Here also he was instrumental in establishing Baha'i institutions. It appears that he replaced Kheiralla's fallacious teachings about the Baha'i Faith with his own idiosyncratic interests in dream interpretation and soothsaying. He returned to Haifa in 1902. Later, he accompanied 'Abdu'l-Baha on his journeys in the West. After their return, however, his son, Dr Aminu'llah Fareed, who had caused 'Abdu'l-Baha numerous problems during the journeys to the West by soliciting money from western Baha'is, left for Europe and North America in 1914 against 'Abdu'l-Baha's wishes. Mirza Asadu'llah joined him in London and both father and son were expelled from the Baha'i community.[16]

In about 1870 a number of students at the theological colleges in Isfahan

---

15 ZH 5: 294, 6:154–8; ['Abdu'l-Baha], *Traveller's Narrative*, 2:380, 382, 388–9; Ishraq-Khavari, *Nurayn* 72–83; Balyuzi, *Eminent Baha'is* 271–2; Sharifi, 'Mishkin Qalam'; Momen, 'Cyprus Exiles' 85, 86, 87; Dihaji, Risalih 182.

16 ZH 6:165–7; 8b:1138–9; Peter Smith, 'American Baha'i Community' 112–13, 168. In a letter to Zill us-Sultan, Mirza Asadu'llah calls himself 'Mahallati' (Yad-dasht-ha 100).

became Baha'is. Word spread among the clerical community about these conversions and the new converts had to disperse and hide, with Mulla Kazim Talkhunchihi (see p. 77) and Mirza 'Ata'u'llah Siraj ul-Hukama (see pp. 288–9) returning to their home towns, Aqa Sayyid Zaynu'l-'Abidin (d. 1911, see fig. 4)[17] hiding in the Isfahan area, and his brother Mirza Abu Turab Jarrah leaving for Tehran.[18] The nephew of the latter two, Ahmad Sohrab (1891–1958, see fig. 164), left Isfahan shortly after their home was raided and looted in the events of 1903 (see pp. 38–41). He travelled to Haifa from where 'Abdu'l-Baha sent him to Cairo to obtain an education. He was then sent to the United States to assist Mirza Abu'l-Fadl Gul-paygani. He remained there and was 'Abdu'l-Baha's translator during his journey to the West in 1912–13. In later years, however, while living in the United States, he rebelled against the authority of Shoghi Effendi and was expelled from the Baha'i community in 1930.[19]

Another who became a Baha'i was Mirza Asadu'llah Vazir Shah-shahani (1264/1848–1336/1917, see fig. 5), a descendant of Fath-'Ali Khan I'timad ud-Dawlih, a famous minister from the Safavid period. He became a Baha'i through the afore-mentioned Mirza Asadu'llah Isfahani in 1291/1874 and married the latter's sister, Aminih Khanum. In 1292/1875 he visited Baha'u'llah in 'Akka and, in about 1878, he joined the tax office of Isfahan under Mirza Habibu'llah Ansari Mushir ul-Mulk. After Mirza Habibu'llah was dismissed from his post in 1308/1890, Mirza Asadu'llah was appointed to the post of Vazir of Isfahan with responsibility for government finances in the Isfahan province. Despite the fact that he was well known to be a Baha'i, that he used to hold regular Baha'i meetings in his house and that he provided accommodation for travelling Baha'i teachers, he was so powerful and well respected in the town that the enemies of the Baha'i Faith were unable to harm him. When Samsam us-Saltanih entered Isfahan in January 1909 with his Bakhtiyari tribesmen at the start of the

---

17   ZH 6:192, 8a:140.
18   B. Agah, 'Sharh-i Ahval' 189.
19   ZH 8a:140–3; *Ministry of Custodians* 90. The main cause of Sohrab's expulsion was his antagonism towards the Baha'i administration being established by Shoghi Effendi. He had formed, together with Julie Stuyvesant Chanler, the New History Society in 1929, which was promoting the Baha'i Faith, but he refused to allow the Baha'i administration to have oversight of the organization. In 1930 the Caravan of East and West was formed to prepare children and youth to join the New History Society. Both organizations are now defunct. After his expulsion Ahmad Sohrab joined forces with other opponents of Shoghi Effendi, including Azalis and the family and supporters of Mirza Muhammad 'Ali.

4. Sayyid Zaynu'l-'Abidin Isfahani   5. Mirza Asadu'llah Vazir Isfahani

counter-coup against Muhammad 'Ali Shah, he had urgent need of funds to pay his troops but the town's treasury had been drained by the previous governor. Mirza Asadu'llah Vazir was summoned and threatened with imprisonment and torture unless he found some money. Mirza Asadu'llah had no choice but to take on a personal debt of 20,000 *tumans* in order to satisfy Samsam us-Saltanih. Following the overthrow of Muhammad 'Ali Shah there was a two-year period in which everything was in confusion. The parliament failed to make any decisions about stipends and pensions and so the ministry of finance was unable to give Mirza Asadu'llah any instructions. The delay was causing great distress to those who depended on these stipends and pensions and so Mirza Asadu'llah decided to borrow more money in order to pay them. Then troops arrived in Isfahan with an order from Samsam us-Saltanih in Tehran that they should be given money. Once again Mirza Asadu'llah had to borrow money in order to do this. Eventually his debts stood at some 160,000 *tumans* (£30,000 in the money of the time; £3,000,000 or US$3,850,000 in the money of 2018[20])

---

20   Issawi, *Economic History* 345 (note that Issawi gives the conversions in *qirans*; 10 *qirans* is 1 *tuman*); Officer, 'Five Ways to Compute the Relative Value of a UK Pound' and Officer and Williamson, 'Computing "Real Value" Over Time' (accessed 31 Oct. 2019). Most merchants in Iran at this time had net assets well below this figure (see Floor, 'The Merchants' 123).

and there was no sign of the government repaying him. He went to Tehran and found only chaos there and had to resign himself to the financial loss, which effectively ruined him. Despite this enormous reversal of fortune, he is reported to have remained composed and dignified.[21]

The struggle for power in Isfahan and the persecution of 1874

In the early period of Baha'u'llah's ministry there was comparatively little pressure against the Baha'is in the city. There were three major clerical families in the city. The Khatunabadi family of sayyids were hereditary Imam-Jum'ihs in the town and thus controlled the Jum'ih (Friday) Mosque. They were at this time headed by Mir Sayyid Muhammad Sultan ul-'Ulama, who had hosted the Bab for the first part of the latter's stay in Isfahan and had been impressed by him. The second influential family was that of the deceased Sayyid Muhammad Baqir Shafti (d. 1844), who had been one of the most powerful clerics of the previous generation in Iran, one of the wealthiest men in the country and had dominated Isfahan, building the large Sayyid Mosque in the Bidabad quarter. Although his eldest son Sayyid Asadu'llah (1227/1812–74) was not the powerful figure his father had been, the wealth of the family ensured him influence and importance. He was in general a moderating force in the city. He had probably met Mulla Husayn Bushru'i when the latter came to ask for his father's endorsement of Sayyid Kazim Rashti in 1843. He had refused to sign a decree (*fatwa*) drawn up by the other clerics of the city in 1846 condemning the Bab to death. In addition, his cousin Shams ud-Duha, who had been brought up in his home after her parents died and was thus effectively his foster sister, was a Shaykhi, then a Babi and then a Baha'i and was open and effective in her promotion of her religious beliefs (see pp. 17–19).[22] The third major clerical family of Isfahan was the Masjid-Shahi or Najafi family, often also called the Aqayan-i Masjid-i Shah. Shaykh Muhammad Baqir

---

21   ZH 6:167–8, 8a:125–6; Tarikh Amri Isfahan 53–8. On Mirza Asadu'llah being well known to be a Baha'i, see Jamalzadih, *Sar u Tah* 101–2. See also the story of an encounter between Mirza Asadu'llah and Aqa Najafi, in which the latter used the threat of denouncing the former as a way to avoid paying taxes (Malikzadih, *Tarikh-i Inqilab* 1:73).

22   For his refusal to condemn Mulla Husayn Bushru'i and the Bab, see DB 97–8, 209; for an account of his moderation, see Majd ul-Islam, *Tarikh Inhilal Majlis* 195–8. For a biographical account of him, see Hirzu'd-Din, *Ma'arif ar-Rijal* 1:94–8.

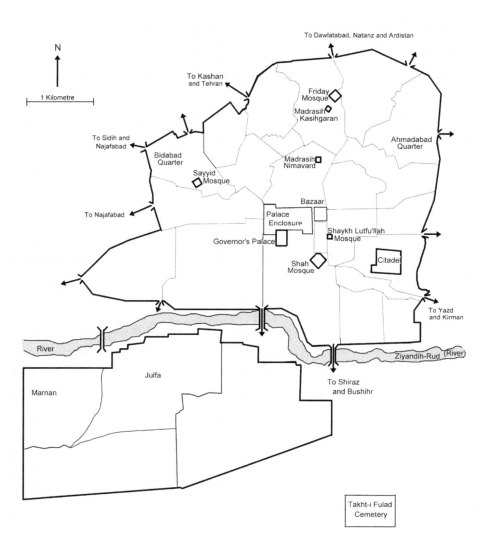

N

1 Kilometre

To Dawlatabad, Natanz and Ardistan

To Kashan
and Tehran

Friday
Mosque

Madrasih
Kasihgaran

To Sidih and
Najafabad

Ahmadabad
Quarter

Bidabad
Quarter

Madrasih
Nimavard

Sayyid
Mosque

Bazaar

To Najafabad

Palace
Enclosure

Shaykh Lutfu'llah
Mosque

Governor's Palace

Citadel

Shah
Mosque

To Yazd
and Kirman

River

Ziyandih-Rud (River)

Julfa

To Shiraz
and Bushihr

Marnan

Takht-i Fulad
Cemetery

6. Map of Isfahan in the 19th century (based on the map drawn by Pascal Coste in 1840).
This shows the quarters and gates of the walled city of Isfahan to the north of the river and
the Christian quarter (Julfa) and other areas south of the river. Some of the buildings and
localities named in the text are shown.

(1235/1819–83, called by Baha'u'llah 'the Wolf', see fig. 7),[23] and his son
Shaykh Muhammad Taqi Aqa Najafi (1846–1914, called by Baha'u'llah 'the
Son of the Wolf', see fig. 16)[24] controlled the Shah Mosque (Masjid-i Shah)
and the Shaykh Lutfu'llah Mosque as well as building a new mosque, the
Masjid-i Naw, and were implacable enemies of the Baha'i community.[25]

The year 1874 was to be a momentous one for Isfahan. In that year
a number of events occurred which were to set the social and political
dynamics of the city for the rest of the century and at the same time tip
the balance against the Baha'is. In February 1874 the death occurred of
Sayyid Asadu'llah Rashti, who had acted as a moderating force among the
city's clerics. And at this time the Imam-Jum'ih Mir Muhammad Sultan
ul-'Ulama was very ill and died in September. He was succeeded as Imam-
Jum'ih by his brother Aqa Mir Muhammad Husayn but it took some time
for him to build up a power base. This left Shaykh Muhammad Baqir
Najafi, or Masjid-Shahi, and his son Shaykh Muhammad Taqi Aqa Najafi
as the pre-eminent powers among the clerics of Isfahan for the rest of the
century. Both father and son used their power in Isfahan to extort large
amounts of money from the citizens as religious taxes. No merchant, trader
or craftsman was safe unless he had made a substantial contribution to
their coffers. One of their most lucrative actions was to hoard grain during

---

23 For a biographical account of him, see Habibabadi, *Makarim* 3:1007–10;
     al-Amin, *Mustadrakat* 7:260–1, no. 444; Walcher, *Shadow* 43–7. His mother
     Nasmih Khatun was the daughter of Shaykh Ja'far Kashif ul-Ghita, one of the
     foremost *mujtahids* of Najaf in his time.

24 For a biographical account of him, see Habibabadi, *Makarim* 5:1662–6; Walcher,
     Shadow 48–50 and *passim*, see Index.

25 On Isfahan in the 19th century, see Walcher, *Shadow*; on these mosques, see
     Walcher, 'Face of the seven spheres, Part 2'. In his translation of the Bab's book,
     Livre de Sept Preuves (57–8n), Nicolas relates the following story which dem-
     onstrates well the degree of Aqa Najafi's hatred of the Baha'is – he was even
     willing to distort the religion of Islam rather than see any advantage to Baha'is.
     Concerning the Muslim dawn prayer for the fast, Nicolas writes, 'The Imam
     Baqir [the fifth Imam of the Shi'is] has said that this prayer is the loftiest of
     prayers because it contains the greatest name of God – Baha! The Muslim world
     naturally remained in agreement with this until the day when someone drew
     the attention of Aqa Najafi, the *mujtahid* of Isfahan, to the fact that in it was
     precisely the name of the *Man Yuzhiruhu'llah* [Him whom God shall make
     manifest] promised by the Bab. Aqa Najafi prohibited the saying of this prayer
     from that time on.' Baha'u'llah responded to this, in the *Epistle to the Son of the
     Wolf* (140) addressed to Aqa Najafi, by urging him to recite this dawn prayer
     which begins: 'O my God! I beseech Thee by Thy most glorious light (*bahā'ika
     bi-abhāihi*), and all Thy lights (*bahā'ika*) are verily glorious (*bahiyyun*).'

7. Shaykh Muhammad Baqir Najafi,
called by Baha'u'llah 'The Wolf'

8. Zill us-Sultan (Sultan Mas'ud Mirza,
Governor of Isfahan) in about 1882

times of famine and then sell it to a starving population at grossly inflated prices.[26] When the mayor of Isfahan (*ra'is-i baladiyyih*), Haji Muhammad Ja'far, protested that people were dying of hunger and they had tons of grain in storage, they accused him of being a 'Babi' and had him executed.[27] The power that they wielded in Isfahan can be judged by the fact that according to one source, Aqa Najafi had a following of some 5,000 students and others to whom he paid an income,[28] let alone those who might follow his orders as a religious obligation. Even the governor would have difficulty mustering that level of support in the city.

In May of the same year, 1874, Sultan Mas'ud Mirza Zill us-Sultan (1850–1918, see fig. 8) became governor of Isfahan, which he was to

---

26 For Shaykh Muhammad Baqir during the famine of 1871, see ZH 6:140; for Aqa Najafi in 1871, see Ha'iri, *Shi'ism* 110; for Aqa Najafi during the famine of 1893, see Algar, *Religion and State* 220, and Bakhash, *Iran* 287 (Malikzadih, *Tarikh-i Inqilab* 1:129 probably also relates to this episode). Despite their wealth, they were well known for not paying any taxes (see Malikzadih, *Tarikh-i Inqilab* 1:73).

27 Malikzadih, *Tarikh-i Inqilab* 1:129; Malikzadih does not state that the execution was on the accusation of being a Babi but this is implied in the fact that the episode is placed in a section under the subtitle 'Babi-kushi' (Killing Babis); this is also how Ha'iri has interpreted this (*Shi'ism* 110).

28 Malikzadih, *Tarikh-i Inqilab* 1:72.

remain for the next 33 years (until 1907). Although he was the eldest son of Nasiru'd-Din Shah, he was excluded from the succession because his mother was not of the royal family. This circumstance stuck in his craw. It became his life's ambition to overturn the succession and gain the throne. From his power-base in Isfahan, he tried to extend his area of control gradually, persuading his father, partly through handsome bribes, to give him authority over province after province. By the 1880s he ruled over most of the southern half of the country. In addition he was trying to gain allies who would help him in his quest. He tried to persuade the British to back his claim to the throne, pointing out that the crown prince, as governor of Adharbayjan, had come under the influence of the Russians. By the end of this decade, however, his fortunes were in decline. Nasiru'd-Din Shah became aware of his plotting and in February 1888 he was stripped of all his governorships except Isfahan. When the shah was assassinated in 1896, the British refused to give him any support and so he was unable to make any play for the throne. During this time, however, Zill us-Sultan had amassed a considerable fortune, some of which was in property in the Isfahan area and some of it in the British-owned bank.[29]

For most of his time as governor of Isfahan, especially in the later years, Zill us-Sultan was engaged in a titanic struggle for control of the town with Shaykh Muhammad Baqir and Aqa Najafi. At stake was the ability to gain wealth and power by controlling endowments and dominating the merchants, traders and craftsmen of the city, and thus determining whether these citizens gave of their money for government taxes or for religious ones. Whoever was able to exert power in the city would be the person to whom the local merchants, traders and craftsmen would turn to settle disputes and in return would be the recipient of emoluments and gifts. In the struggle for control of the city, the Baha'is were often caught in the middle. The clerics would raise a disturbance against the Baha'is as a way of discomfiting Zill us-Sultan, demonstrating their power and the weakness of the governor (and also the implicit threat that if merchants did not pay their religious taxes, they would be denounced as Baha'is). Nor was power and wealth the only issue at stake between the governor and the clerics. It was widely known in Isfahan that Zill us-Sultan had succeeded in seducing Shaykh Muhammad Baqir's wife and had regular liaisons with her, while on one occasion in 1877 he succeeded in tricking and violating

---

29   Sayyah, *Khatirat* 278; Adamec, *Gazetteer* 1:254.

another lady who had sought sanctuary in Shaykh Muhammad Baqir's home from the prince's advances.[30] This was such a cause of shame to Shaykh Muhammad Baqir that for a time he left Isfahan and travelled to Mashhad. Even there, however, he did not cease to be a cause of trouble for the Baha'is (vol. 1:156–7).

The governor and the clerics were not, however, always on opposite sides. Sometimes, if a wealthy Baha'i came to their attention, their avarice would surmount their enmity and they would sink their differences in order to gain whatever they could from denouncing him as a Baha'i. According to Baha'i accounts, this is what happened in the first major episode of Baha'i persecution that occurred in Isfahan. Perhaps fittingly, this episode occurred right at the start of the new era for Isfahan, within a few days of the arrival of Zill us-Sultan in 1874. Although the episode started with the persecution of the Shaykhis of Isfahan (probably in connection with a visit to Isfahan of the Shaykhi leader Muhammad Karim Khan Kirmani[31]), it soon moved in an anti-Baha'i direction. There were five brothers, sons of Haji Abu'l-Hasan Shushtari. Two of them, Aqa Muhammad Sadiq (d. 1303/1885) and Aqa Muhammad Ja'far, had already left for Khurasan at this time and three remained in Isfahan: Aqa Muhammad Kazim (d. 1892; he had seen the Bab as a ten-year-old boy and had in 1279/1862 gone to Baghdad to meet Azal and returned from there a follower of Baha'u'llah); Aqa Muhammad Baqir and Haji 'Abdu'l-Husayn (d. 1308/1890). They were wealthy merchants and their house was a centre of Baha'i activities in Isfahan. Zill us-Sultan and Shaykh Muhammad Baqir conspired to strip them of their wealth. The governor first ordered the telegraph office, the postal service and the city gate-keepers to allow no Baha'i or any message from a Baha'i to leave Isfahan. They then arrested the three brothers. According to the report of the British missionary, Rev. Bruce, Shaykh Muhammad Baqir had compiled a list of a hundred (or possibly

---

30 Nava'i, 'Abbas Mirza Mulk-Ara 114–15.

31 Zill us-Sultan, Khatirat 1: 385. Interestingly, in these pages (Khatirat 1:383–6), Zill us-Sultan strives to exonerate Shaykh Muhammad Baqir and blame Mir Muhammad Husayn for this episode, but the account by Rev. Bruce and the Baha'i sources make it clear that, at least with regard to the Baha'is, Shaykh Muhammad Baqir was the main instigator and Zill us-Sultan was covering up the actions of his co-conspirator. It is also clear that Zill us-Sultan was antagonistic towards Muhammad Ibrahim Khan Nuri Saham ud-Dawlih (Khatirat 2:457), who acted vigorously to protect the victims (BBR 271–2).

four hundred) Baha'is and now ordered these to be arrested,[32] perhaps to conceal the fact that the three brothers were the true target of the conspirators. In any case, advantage was taken of the situation for some to be accused of being Baha'is who had no connection with the new religion, either because their accuser had a grudge against that person or because one of the government officials (*farrashes* and *darughihs*) saw an opportunity to extort money. About 20 or so Baha'is were arrested (including most of the list of Baha'i traders and craftsmen given on p. 6) and the rest of the Baha'is either fled the city or took refuge in the telegraph office. Realizing that they could not send anything from Isfahan, the Baha'is managed to smuggle one of their number out of the city. He hurried to Kashan with three letters addressed to the shah and other officials. He managed to send them from there and the situation was alleviated.[33] Shaykh Muhammad Baqir was eventually summoned to Tehran to account for the disturbance he had caused but he was not punished in any way and so he returned on 16 April 1878 with an enhanced reputation.[34]

---

32   BBR 270–1.

33   There are seven accounts of this episode. One (Nur, Tarikh Isfahan 1–8) writes of the arrest of the three brothers only and gives no date. The second (Nicolas, *Massacres* 16–17) gives a list of seven of those arrested, which appears to include the three brothers but does not give a date for this. The third (ZH 6:169–70) also describes the arrest of the brothers and others in 1294/1877 (although here five brothers are named but it appears from Nur, Tarikh Isfahan that the other brothers were in Quchan at this time). The fourth (BBR 269–73) writes of the arrest of 20 or more Baha'is in 1874. The fifth source (ZH 6:286) gives the date as 1292/1875, describes the arrest of the three brothers and their father and four others. The sixth source (Tarikh Amri Isfahan 13–14, 16–17) also refers briefly to this episode in relation to the three brothers. The seventh source (Yazdi, *Tarikh 'Ishqabad* 411–12) indicates the date of this episode was 1878. It may be that these were two separate episodes (a general arrest in 1874, including the three brothers, and a further arrest of the three brothers in 1877) but since in the story as given in the first, second and fifth sources, a Baha'i was smuggled out of Isfahan to convey a petition to the shah and telegraphed from Kashan (albeit this individual is named differently in the sources), since both the first and fourth sources refer to Baha'is going to the Isfahan telegraph office, and since the first, second, fifth and sixth sources record that Mulla Kazim of Talkhunchih was arrested on this occasion, I have chosen to treat the seven accounts as referring to the same episode and have dated this from the contemporary account in BBR 269–73. See also Walcher, *Shadow* 119–20.

34   The date of return is in a report of 23 Apr. 1878, in FO 248 348. Walcher's account of this is somewhat confused, saying in one place that Shaykh Muhammad Baqir went to Tehran then Mashhad for four years in 1874 and in another that he was sent to Tehran and pardoned in 1876 but she acknowledges this confusion in a footnote (*Shadow* 47, 120, 376 n. 163).

Eventually the three brothers left Isfahan for Khurasan.[35]

Jamal Burujirdi arrived in Isfahan shortly after this episode and began to encourage the Baha'is to flee to Russia and seek the protection and assistance of that government to right their wrongs. Mirza Hasan Nahri (see p. 18) wrote to Baha'u'llah reporting this and Baha'u'llah forbade any such action.[36] The next episode of persecution in Isfahan was the execution in Isfahan of Mulla Kazim of Talkhunchih (see p. 78).

The Nahri family

Among those Babis who became Baha'is were the Nahri family whose ancestor Sayyid Muhammad Tabataba'i was from Zavarih and had gone to India where he had married into a very wealthy family. His son, Sayyid Mahdi, moved to Najaf where he expended his great wealth on pious benefactions, including the building of a canal (*nahr*) to bring water to Najaf, hence the family name became Nahri.[37] While there he became a follower of Shaykh Ahmad al-Ahsa'i. Eventually he decided to return to Iran and settled in Isfahan. Here he married a relative of the wife of Sayyid Muhammad Baqir Shafti, the most powerful cleric in Isfahan, with whom he had three sons. The older two were Mirza Muhammad 'Ali (d. 1275/1858) and Mirza Hadi (d. 1848). The latter was a favourite of Shafti, who had married him to his niece Khurshid Bigum (d. 1893), who was given the title Shams ud-Duha by Baha'u'llah (she had been orphaned as a child and was raised in the home of the *mujtahid*). The two brothers and Shams ud-Duha went to Karbala where they studied under the Shaykhi leader Sayyid Kazim Rashti. Here the two brothers met the Bab during the Bab's stay in Karbala in about 1842, and when they heard of the Bab's claim in 1844, they set off for Shiraz but arrived after the Bab had left for pilgrimage. They met Mulla Husayn Bushru'i, however, who convinced them of the

---

35 According to ZH 6:170 and Yazdi, *Tarikh 'Ishqabad* 412, it was after the 1874 episode but, according to Tarikh Amri Isfahan 17, it was only after the execution of the Nahri brothers in 1879 that these three brothers were eventually compelled to leave Isfahan for Sabzivar and then Ashkhabad but Aqa Najafi blocked attempts by Haji 'Abdu'l-Husayn to sell his property.

36 ZH 6:308.

37 It is possible to speculate that Sayyid Mahdi was the agent of the Nawab of Awadh (Oudh): either Asif ud-Dawlih, who sent the money for the construction of the Hindiyyah Canal which brought water from the Euphrates to Najaf and Karbala (opened 1803) or of Ghaziyu'd-Din Haydar, who sent money for its repair in 1817. See Litvak, *Shi'i Scholars* 128, 130, 137.

9. Munirih Khanum, wife of 'Abdu'l-Baha

truth of the Bab's claims. The two brothers were present at the conference of Badasht in 1848 but as they were returning from this, the Babis were attacked at Niyala and Mirza Hadi died as a result of injuries he received. Mirza Muhammad 'Ali had three daughters and a son, the most famous of whom was his eldest daughter Fatimih who was given the title Munirih Khanum (see fig. 9) and became the wife of 'Abdu'l-Baha.[38]

The youngest brother of Mirza Muhammad 'Ali and Mirza Hadi was Mirza Ibrahim, who was not at first a Babi. He became the agent of the Imam-Jum'ih and it was as a result of this that he held a dinner for the Bab in his house on one occasion (the governor of Isfahan had asked the Imam-Jum'ih to be the Bab's host). He had three sons and a daughter, of whom the most famous are the elder two sons: Mirza Muhammad Husayn (usually just called Mirza Husayn, 1251/1835–79, see fig. 10) and Mirza Muhammad Hasan (usually just called Mirza Hasan, 1252/1836–79, see fig. 10). These two were converted by their uncle Mirza Muhammad 'Ali Nahri and the three went to Baghdad in 1273/1856 where they met Baha'u'llah. Mirza Muhammad 'Ali is reported to have recognized Baha'u'llah as 'He whom God shall make manifest' prophesied by the Bab. After the death of his first wife, Mirza Ibrahim married Khurshid Bigum Shams ud-Duha, the widow of his brother, and she converted him to the Baha'i Faith.[39]

As we have seen, Shams ud-Duha was married to one of the Nahri brothers, Mirza Hadi, and accompanied him to Karbala and became a Babi. She became one of a circle of prominent Babi women who gathered around Tahirih and the widow of Sayyid Kazim Rashti in Karbala.

38 Ishraq-Khavari, *Nurayn* 11–52; Amanat, *Resurrection* 340–4.
39 Ishraq-Khavari, *Nurayn* 55.

10. *Left*: Mirza Hasan Nahri (Sultan ush-Shuhada, King of Martyrs);
Right: Mirza Husayn Nahri (Mahbub ush-Shuhada, Beloved of Martyrs)

She accompanied Tahirih to Baghdad and again on her expulsion to Iran.
She then returned to Isfahan. Despite her close links with a leading religious family of Isfahan, Shams ud-Duha began to teach the Baha'i Faith
enthusiastically. Her daughter Fatimih Bigum married Mirza Hasan, the
second son of Mirza Ibrahim Nahri, and their home became a centre of
Babi and later Baha'i activities. While Mirza Hasan served male guests
in the outer apartments (*biruni*) and spoke to them of the new religion,
Shams ud-Duha and her daughter entertained female guests in the inner
apartments (*andarun*) and taught them about the Babi and Baha'i religions. Shams ud-Duha, as described above, married Mirza Ibrahim after
her first husband's death and converted him. She continued to teach the
Baha'i Faith openly despite the fact that her first husband had been killed
as a Babi in 1848 and her son-in-law was executed as a Baha'i in 1879 (see
pp. 20–2). She became well known throughout Isfahan as a Baha'i and
was even known as the 'Fatimih of the Baha'is' or as 'Fatimih, the Baha'is'
Lady of Light', in reference to the Prophet Muhammad's daughter. On one
occasion she was arrested and beaten unconscious by the governor Zill us-
Sultan himself and was only saved from death by the intervention of her
brother, who was not a Baha'i. Because of her notoriety, her brother was
eventually forced to transfer their residence to Mashhad. Here too Shams
ud-Duha taught the Baha'i Faith and rallied the Baha'i women until it

evoked such an uproar that her brother was forced to return with her to Isfahan.[40]

After the death of Mirza Ibrahim, it was his son Mirza Hasan who took over his father's role as commercial agent to Mir Muhammad Sultan ul-'Ulama, the Imam-Jum'ih. The two brothers prospered as businessmen, establishing connections with the trading empire of the Afnan family (see p. 254); they were at the same time the backbone of the Baha'i community of Isfahan, their homes being a meeting place for the community. When Baha'u'llah was exiled to 'Akka, these two brothers were the first to establish contact with him by telegraph there and to send much needed money to alleviate the severe conditions under which the exiles were being held.[41] During the famine of 1871 they assisted both Baha'is and non-Baha'is by purchasing and distributing food.[42] Because of their activities, they became well known in the town as Baha'is and consequently earned the enmity of Shaykh Muhammad Baqir, but as long as they were under the protection of the Imam-Jum'ih, he was unable to move against them.

When Mir Muhammad Sultan ul-'Ulama died in September 1874, it was Mirza Hasan who ensured that Sultan ul-'Ulama's brother, Mir Muhammad Husayn (d. 1881, called by Baha'u'llah 'Raqsha', the She-Serpent, see fig. 11), would become his successor as Imam-Jum'ih, despite the opposition of Shaykh Muhammad Baqir. Mirza Hasan continued in his role as the Imam-Jum'ih's commercial agent. The new Imam-Jum'ih had incurred debts to obtain his position and was, moreover, living beyond his means; he was continually authorizing Mirza Hasan to make payments on his behalf. In the course of time the Imam-Jum'ih became indebted to him to the sum of 18,000 *tumans* (£6,600 in the money of the time; £858,000 or US$1,370,000 in the money of 2018[43]). After seeing how

---

40 'Abdu'l-Baha, *Memorials* 175–85; ZH 3:97–9, 6:142–4; Arbab, *Akhtaran* 1:68–72.

41 Blomfield, *Chosen Highway* 67.

42 Tarikh Amri Isfahan 24.

43 Using conversion given by C.J. Wills (BBR 275; cf conversion in Issawi, *Economic History* 344) and tables in Officer, 'Five Ways to Compute the Relative Value of a UK Pound' and Officer and Williamson, 'Computing "Real Value" Over Time' (accessed 31 Oct. 2019). If an average earnings index were used to calculate the present-day equivalent figure, it would be about seven times as much. There are various figures cited for the amount of the debt. The lowest is 12,000 *tumans* (Nicolas, *Massacres* 18). I have selected the figure of 18,000 to which two contemporary sources attest – the telegraph company doctor in Isfahan, Dr Wills (BBR 275) and Nur (Tarikh 13). Anonymous (Tarikh Isfahan

easily the execution of Mulla Kazim Talkhunchihi was accomplished (see p. 78), the Imam-Jum'ih, urged on by his brother-in-law Mirza Sulayman Mulla-bashi (who wanted to take over the position of Mirza Hasan as the Imam-Jum'ih's financial agent), conceived of a plan to join with Shaykh Muhammad Baqir the Shaykh ul-Islam in denouncing the brothers as 'Babis', thus putting himself in the position of being able to rid himself of his vast debt and even of appropriating some of their wealth. Shaykh Muhammad Baqir also relished the opportunity to make trouble for Zill us-Sultan. Zill us-Sultan did not oppose the two clerics, fearing trouble in the town if they were to raise the rabble against the 'Babis' and, in any case, he also stood to gain financially from destroying the brothers. The birthday of the Prophet Muhammad fell on 11 March in 1879, Mirza Husayn and the youngest brother, Mirza Isma'il, went to greet the Imam-Jum'ih and were detained by him and sent to the governor. Mirza Hasan was at the house of another cleric and was also arrested. Precious goods, items of furniture and jewellery were carted away from their houses by the donkey-load. Officials also went round arresting as many other prominent Baha'is as they could find, looting their houses and businesses.[44] Mirza Isma'il was released after a few days.[45] Representations were made in the presence of Zill us-Sultan by the merchants of the city, including Johannes Collignon, the agent in Isfahan of the Dutch firm Hotz and Co., and in a letter from Rev. Robert Bruce, a British missionary in Isfahan, and Ernst Hoeltzer, a German who worked for the telegraph department.[46]

A report was sent by the Imam-Jum'ih to Mulla 'Ali Kani in Tehran requesting that the shah be asked for permission to have the brothers

24) states the sum owed was 30,000 *tumans*, of which 12,000 was on the books and could be disputed, but 18,000 *tumans* of this was based on documents that the Imam-Jum'ih himself had signed and were indisputable.

44 Ishraq-Khavari, *Nurayn* 95–9, 237, 258–63, 272–8; Anonymous, Tarikh Isfahan 26–9; Nur, *Khatirat* 11–17; Balyuzi, *Eminent Baha'is* 33–7.

45 Abu'l-Fadl Gulpaygani (quoted in Ishraq-Khavari, *Nurayn* 262) states that Mirza Isma'il dissimulated and recanted his faith in order to obtain his freedom and this is supported by Charles Wills, a British physician who was resident in Isfahan at this time (Wills, *Land of the Lion and Sun* 154–6; BBR 274–6), but according to Ishraq-Khavari (*Nurayn* 85–8), his wealthy and influential Muslim father-in-law forged his name on a letter of recantation and this resulted in his being freed. According to three other accounts, he was set free by Zill us-Sultan in order to go and collect the debts owed to his brothers and bring the money to the prince (Anonymous, Tarikh Isfahan 26; Nur, *Khatirat* 17; Fadil Mazandarani quoted in Ishraq-Khavari, *Nurayn* 278).

46 Wills, *Land of the Lion and Sun* 154–6; Stack, *Six Months* 2:30; BBR 274–6.

11. Mir Muhammad Husayn Imam-
Jumʻih, called by Baha'u'llah 'Raqsha',
the She-Serpent

12. Haji Sayyah Mahallati at the time of his
arrest in 1891, see pp. 367–8

executed and meanwhile Zill us-Sultan was urging them to recant their
faith as a way of saving themselves. When a message arrived from Tehran
to the effect that the brothers should be sent there, the Imam-Jumʻih
became alarmed. He realized that should the brothers be sent to Tehran,
their innocence would be established and the plan would go awry. Therefore in conjunction with Shaykh Muhammad Baqir, he organized that the
bazaar in Isfahan be shut down and a mob descend upon the house of the
governor. Zill us-Sultan remonstrated with them but to no avail. Eventually he asked for a *fatwa* and 60 clerics of the city signed one decreeing
the death of the two brothers.[47] They were executed in secret on 17 March
1879.[48] The two leading clerical instigators of their deaths did not live
long enough, however, to enjoy the fruits of their plot. Mir Muhammad
Husayn the Imam-Jumʻih was banished to Mashhad in August 1880 and
died there in July 1881 of a disease that caused a foul-smelling abscess on

---

47   Among the clerics who signed the decree apart from the Imam-Jumʻih and
      Shaykh Muhammad Baqir were Sayyid Jaʻfar Bidabadi, Mulla Baqir Fisharaki
      and Mirza Muhammad Hashim Chaharsuqi (Anonymous, Tarikh Isfahan 29).
48   Ishraq-Khavari, *Nurayn* 99–118, 263–5, 278–83; Anonymous, Tarikh Isfahan
      29–32; Nur, *Khatirat* 30–1; Balyuzi, *Eminent Baha'is* 37–40. Nur also includes
      mention of the Baha'i women going to the Isfahan telegraph office and the dis-
      patch of someone to Kashan to send a telegram from there (Nur, *Khatirat* 18–21,
      30), but in comparing it with the original manuscript, it is clear that this passage
      belongs to the account of the 1874 episode and should not have been placed
      here.

his neck, while Shaykh Muhammad Baqir was forced into exile to Najaf and died in 1883. The two brothers were designated by Baha'u'llah the King of Martyrs (Sultan ush-Shuhada, Mirza Hasan) and the Beloved of Martyrs (Mahbub ush-Shuhada, Mirza Husayn).[49]

In the aftermath of the Nahri executions

This episode of the execution of the Nahri brothers brought about a temporary change in Zill us-Sultan's attitude towards the Baha'is. He perceived that their courage and determination might be a useful asset in his schemes to gain the throne and so, for a short time, he became friendly towards them. When he went to Tehran in 1882–3, he contacted the Baha'is there and tried to help them (vol. 1:27, 45).[50] He even sent Haji Sayyah Mahallati (Haji Muhammad 'Ali, c. 1836–1925, see fig. 12), his henchman, to 'Akka in 1885 to try to enlist the support of Baha'u'llah, who refused, however, to countenance any such schemes.[51] For a time after this Zill us-Sultan continued to try to enlist the support of the Baha'is. A number of letters from Baha'u'llah to Haji Mirza Haydar 'Ali in Isfahan from the period 1888–9 exist, warning him not to trust Haji Sayyah or Zill us-Sultan.[52] After this time Zill us-Sultan reverted to his inimical attitude

---

49 From the titles given to them by Baha'u'llah and from the fact that Shoghi Effendi lists Mirza Hasan Sultan ush-Shuhada but not his brother as one the Apostles of Baha'u'llah (BW 4:108–9), it may be inferred that the younger brother is regarded as the more important of the two.

50 Mirza Isfahani, Yad-dasht-ha 94, 96.

51 See Baha'u'llah's account in Ishraq-Khavari, *Ma'idih Asmani* 4:124–34, 156. See also ZH5:370 and n. Habibu'llah Afnan reports Baha'u'llah's account of this meeting with Sayyah and his rejection of Zill us-Sultan's offer of freedom for the Baha'is in exchange for assistance with overthrowing the shah; Afnan, *Khatirat* 53. See also Sayyah, *Khatirat* 278–81; although there is no mention of travelling to 'Akka in these memoirs, it would have been a short journey from Egypt which was the starting point of a ten-month tour of Europe (and 'Akka may even have been his first stop on this tour). Similarly, he conceals the fact in these memoirs that he was working for Zill us-Sultan but this was well known to his contemporaries, see I'timad us-Saltanih, *Ruz-namih* 591, 751; Bamdad, *Tarikh* 3:426. It is probable that, since these memoirs were written after the Constitutional Revolution, Haji Sayyah wished to remain quiet about his association with Zill us-Sultan, who was much reviled as a Qajar despot in the liberal circles in which Haji Sayyah moved. On his Azali connections, see Bayat, *Revolution* 67–8 (this may also be why I'timad us-Saltanih calls him a Babi, *Ruz-namih* 87).

52 Baha'u'llah urged the Baha'is not to have any dealings with Zill us-Sultan, as he was not to be trusted, and to be prudent and wary in their interactions with Haji

13. Aqa Husayn 'Ali Nur

towards the Baha'is and indeed was, by the early 1900s, supporting and giving money to a number of Azalis to advance his schemes of gaining the throne.[53]

Mirza Asadu'llah Isfahani was in Isfahan in 1881 on the occasion of the second anniversary of the execution of the two brothers. He records going to the house of the brothers for a day dedicated to elegies (*marāthī*) of them and the chanting of tablets of Baha'u'llah. At this time the Baha'is were gathering only in small numbers because of the pressure upon them.[54] Owing to the danger to them, the family of Mirza Hasan the King of Martyrs, as well as Shams ud-Duha and her daughter, migrated to 'Akka in 1885–6, where one of Mirza Hasan's sons, Mirza Jalal, married Ruha, a daughter of 'Abdu'l-Baha. 'Ali Muhammad Varqa was sent from Yazd to Isfahan as a prisoner in about 1883 (see p. 366). Since at this time Zill us-Sultan was still hopeful of gaining the throne and was hoping for the support of the Baha'is to achieve his aims, the Baha'is of Isfahan were able to arrange for his release, especially since Zill us-Sultan's confidant, the above-mentioned Haji Sayyah, had previously been saved from execution in Tabriz by Varqa's father-in-law.[55]

Following the execution of the two brothers in 1879, a number of the most active Baha'is of Isfahan fled to Tehran and other places, some such as Aqa Husayn 'Ali Nur (see fig. 13), his brother Aqa Hasan 'Ali and Ustad Muhammad Ibrahim Najjar (a grandson of a famous cleric Aqa Muhammad Bidabadi) leaving immediately.[56] Others, such as the above-mentioned merchant Haji Muhammad Rida (see fig. 14), left after a further bout of persecution in 1302/1884, during which his brother was

Sayyah, since it was such interactions in Tehran in 1883 that led to the arrest of Baha'is in Tehran, Mazandaran and Gilan and the execution of Mirza 'Ali Jan Mahfuruzaki (vol. 1:35–50, 293–5, 332–4); ZH 5:370–1n; ZH 5:370–1; Isfahani, *Bihjat us-Sudur* 197, 227.

53 Bayat, *Revolution* 211, 221.
54 Asadu'llah, Yad-dasht-ha 52, 56.
55 MH 1:257–62; Balyuzi, *Eminent Baha'is* 78–80; Varqa, 'Sharh-i Ahval' 23–4; Malmiri, *Tarikh Yazd* 48–9.
56 Nur, *Khatirat Muhajirati* 40–1; Nur, Tarikh 16–17; Yazdi, *Tarikh 'Ishqabad* 258–60.

arrested and beaten in order to ascertain his whereabouts. He spent some time in the hills around the town but when his family informed him it was still not safe to return, he left for Tun and then Yazd. From there he visited Baha'u'llah in 'Akka before settling in Ashkhabad.[57] His murder as a Baha'i in Ashkhabad in 1889 had many consequences, including a famous trial which was the first occasion anywhere that those who persecuted the Baha'is were punished, despite the efforts of the Muslim clergy in Iran and the Iranian government to have the charges dismissed.[58]

Mirza Abu'l-Fadl Gulpaygani visited Isfahan in about May 1885, staying until about September 1886. The letters he wrote from Isfahan reveal a community that had not recovered from the 1879 episode. The level of activity in the community was low. When, in about August 1886, a number of Baha'i prisoners were brought to Isfahan from Yazd (see p. 367), for example, Gulpaygani experienced the greatest difficulty in getting the Isfahan Baha'is to support their co-religionists even to the extent of sending food to them in prison (in Iran at this time, unless relatives or friends sent food, prisoners were in danger of dying of starvation or of poisoning from the small amounts of rotten food provided). Gulpaygani personally had to take food to the prisoners. The Baha'is were also in a poor state financially, since apart from the two executed brothers, many of those who had fled Isfahan were among the merchants and richer members of the community, who were most exposed to extortion from the governor and the local clerics. Eventually the prisoners were released.[59]

With the help of Gulpaygani and Haji Mirza Haydar 'Ali Isfahani, who also lived in and visited Isfahan frequently from about 1885 onwards, the community was gradually revived and became more self-confident. It was in Isfahan on 28 February 1888 that one of the Baha'is of this town, Mirza Javad, a relative of Mishkin Qalam, was courageous enough to introduce

---

57 ZH 6:147–8; Yazdi, *Tarikh 'Ishqabad* 224–37; Usku'i, Tarikh Adharyjan, MS A, part 2:22; MS B 91. He had been living in Sabzivar for a time after fleeing Isfahan following a previous episode of persecution and had then also lived in Tun (see Rahmani, 'Amr-i Baha'i' 304–5) before returning to Isfahan. He should not be confused with Aqa Muhammad Rida Arbab Isfahani, son of Haji Muhammad Kazim Isfahani, who also lived in both Sabzivar and Ashkhabad (vol. 1:161–2).

58 *Tarikh 'Ishqabad* 237–57; Rabbani, 'Haji Muhammad-Rida'; Momen, 'Baha'i Community of Ashkhabad' 283–4; BBR 296–300; Shahvar et al., *Baha'is of Iran, Transcapsia and the Caucasus* 2:49–56.

59 Gulpaygani, *Rasa'il* 363, 367, 371–2; Mehrabkhani, *Gulpaygani* 108–10.

14. Haji Muhammad Rida Isfahani   15. Haji Mirza Haydar Ali Isfahani

himself to E.G. Browne as a Baha'i, thus initiating Browne's contact with
the Baha'i community that was to lead eventually to his visit to 'Akka to
meet Baha'u'llah.[60]

During this visit to Isfahan, Browne met Haji Mirza Haydar 'Ali Isfahani (1250/1834– 27 August 1920, see figs. 15 and 95). Haydar 'Ali was
the son of a Shaykhi of Isfahan and had been brought up in the circle
of Haji Mirza Muhammad Karim Khan Kirmani, the Shaykhi leader, in
Kirman (see p. 424). He came, however, to despise the Shaykhi leader
and left Kirman for Isfahan where he heard of the Babi Faith and was
converted. After reading the Kitab-i Iqan in 1862 he became attracted
to Baha'u'llah, and after visiting Baha'u'llah in Edirne in 1867 he became
an ardent follower. He was arrested as a Baha'i in Egypt in the winter of
1867–8 and exiled to the Sudan for some 11 years. He was freed in about
1879 by General Gordon, who was then governor of Khartum and the
Sudan. He spent three months visiting Baha'u'llah in 'Akka, after which he
returned to Iran in 1880. He then spent the next 20 years travelling around

---

60   Browne, *Year* 223. Mirza Javad's name is given in the handwritten diaries on
     which the book is based, in a list, at the end of volume 4, of those he met in Iran.

Iran spreading the Baha'i Faith until, in 1900, he went to Haifa where he remained until he died. The following is Browne's description of him in Isfahan in 1888:

> He was a grave, earnest-looking man of about forty-five years of age, as I should guess; and as he sat opposite to me sipping his tea, I had plenty of time to observe his countenance attentively, and to note the combination of decision, energy, and thoughtfulness which it expressed. His manners were pleasing, and his speech, when he spoke, persuasive. Altogether he was a man whom one would not readily forget, even after a single interview, and on whose memory one dwells with pleasure.[61]

Later in the same year as Browne's visit to Isfahan, there occurred the next major episode of persecution. This episode marks the end of the period of time when Zill us-Sultan was friendly towards the Baha'is in the hope of obtaining their support.[62] Mirza Ashraf was from a sayyid family of Bushruyih who had been born in Najafabad. He had studied with the prominent clerics of Isfahan and obtained a certificate of *ijtihad* from Mirza Muhammad Hashim.[63] He moved to Abadih during the persecutions in Najafabad in 1864 (see pp. 61–4) and lived there for many years (and thus was known as Abadihi), helping to found a Baha'i community there (see pp. 288–9). When he became too well known as a Baha'i in Abadih, he travelled to India, in about 1884, and lived in Bombay for a time. He then returned to Abadih but was forced to leave and had been living in Isfahan for about two years at this time. He was active in spreading the Baha'i Faith in Isfahan and among those whom he converted were some of the staff of Zill us-Sultan's private apartments (*andarun*). These included Mirza 'Ali Khan Navvab, the Munshi Agha-bashi (secretary of the head eunuch), and Aqa Mirza Aqa, a young servant in the *andarun*. The latter was caught one day by the head eunuch making a copy of the Kitab-i Iqan. Zill us-Sultan was alarmed that 'Babis' had penetrated his private apartments and ordered the boy tortured until he revealed who had converted him. The Baha'is were

---

61   Browne, *Year* 229; Browne, *Selections* 28–9; for biographical information on Haji Mirza Haydar 'Ali Isfahani, see his autobiography, *Bihjat as-Sudur* (partly translated as *Stories from the Delight of Hearts*); ZH 6:158–65; MH 1:9–92; Balyuzi, *Eminent Baha'is* 237–50.

62   See statement to this effect from Baha'u'llah in a Tablet often called the Tablet to *The Times* of London; Ishraq-Khavari, *Rahiq-i Makhtum* 1:284.

63   Isfahani, *Bihjat* 230.

16. Aqa Najafi (Shaykh Muhammad
Taqi, called by Baha'u'llah 'the Son of
the Wolf')

then tricked into revealing Mirza Ashraf's home and he was arrested. A number of clerics were brought to interrogate him. Only Aqa Najafi was prepared to give a decree of death but that was enough for Zill us-Sultan. He obtained permission from Tehran and ordered the execution of Mirza Ashraf, which was carried out on 23 October 1888 and his body burned afterwards.[64]

When in February 1888 Zill us-Sultan was stripped of all his governorships except that for Isfahan, this greatly affected his power and prestige. It allowed Aqa Najafi to regain the upper hand in the affairs of Isfahan and there was no better way to assert this than to initiate a campaign against the religious minorities of the city, Christians, Jews and Baha'is. The Christians were difficult to take on, living as they did in a separate quarter across the river and being under the powerful protection of all the European powers. Even when he was attacking Christians, however, Aqa Najafi would often combine this with an attack on the Baha'is, as, for example, when he attacked the British missionary Dr Robert Bruce by declaring he would have him killed for protecting the Baha'is.[65] Since a campaign against Christians ran the risk of a severe punishment from the central government, Aqa Najafi tried a campaign against the Jews in the summer of 1889, introducing severe restrictions on the activities of Jews in the city and making them wear a distinctive badge. By 1889, however, even the Jews were obtaining a measure of European protection. On his European tour the shah had given assurances to delegations of European Jews, and Drummond Wolff, the British minister in Tehran, was urging the shah to improve conditions for Jews. And so

---

64   'Ali Aqa (later Muvaqqar ud-Dawlih) in ['Abdu'l-Baha], *Traveller's Narrative* 2:404–6; Anonymous, Tarikh Isfahan 32b–35b, 36; Isfahani, *Bihjat* 231; KD 1:486; Ishraq-Khavari, *Muhadirat* 684; Abadihi, *Vaqayi' Abadih* 230–2; Mudarris, *Tarikh Najafabad* 215–21.
65   BBR 280.

Aqa Najafi was told in strong terms to rescind his decree.[66] He therefore
turned his attention to the Babis and Baha'is of the Isfahan area, who were
a far easier target. Attacking them was less likely to cause any problems for
Aqa Najafi, especially as Zill us-Sultan had by now despaired of obtaining
any assistance from the Baha'is in his efforts to gain the throne and was
no longer friendly towards them. There ensued the campaigns against the
Baha'is of Najafabad and the Babis of Sidih which went on from 1889 to
the end of the century and beyond (see pp. 49, 65–71).

Despite such persecution, the Baha'i Faith was spreading in Isfahan.
Among the important Baha'is of Isfahan towards the end of the 19th
century was Mirza Ja'far Hadioff (Rahmani, d. 1352/1933), who although
originally from Jahrum and Shiraz, became a Baha'i in Isfahan, migrated
to Ashkhabad in the 1880s and became an important merchant there. He
built the Eastern Pilgrim House in Haifa in 1909.[67] Another important
Baha'i was Mirza Mahmud Khan Afshar (d. 1313/1895). He was the editor
of the main newspaper in Isfahan, *Farhang*, which had been founded under
the auspices of Zill us-Sultan and was published until 1890. He had corresponded with Baha'u'llah since the 1870s but it was not until he visited
Baha'u'llah in 'Akka in the summer of 1888 on his way back to Iran from
France that he was converted. He was addressed by Baha'u'llah as Mirza
Maqsud and was the recipient of a well-known Tablet of Baha'u'llah, the
Lawh-i Maqsud (Tablet of Maqsud). His son, Mirza Muhammad Khan
Farhang ul-Mamalik (d. 1339/1920), was also a Baha'i.[68] At about this
time, some 50 families of the Ahl-i Haqq religious community became
Baha'is through Mirza 'Abbas-Quli, Ghulam-Rida Khan and Mirza
Muhammad Khan.[69]

The years of the ministry of 'Abdu'l-Baha

After the death of Baha'u'llah, the writings of 'Abdu'l-Baha began to spread
among the Baha'is. Aqa Najafi spoke from the pulpit saying that he had
hoped that this movement would be extinguished with the death of its

---

66   See Tsadik, *Between Foreigners*, esp. 137–48; Walcher, *Shadow* esp. 112–17. It is
     ironic that when Shi'i clerics wanted to move against Jews, they invariably revived
     regulations that were first introduced by a person they regard as an illegitimate
     ruler, the second caliph 'Umar.
67   ZH 6: 998–9; 8a:573–4.
68   ZH 5:365n; 6:192, 8a:136; Browne, *Press and Poetry* 121–2.
69   Isfahani, *Bihjat* 227; ZH 6:195.

founder but the writings of 'Abbas Effendi ('Abdu'l-Baha) were just as brazen and defiant and compelling as those of his father and that, since the king was no longer countering this movement, it fell to the clerics to carry out this duty and to save Islam.[70] However, the religion continued to spread.

By the end of the 19th century leadership of the Baha'i community had fallen to the sons of the first generation. Two brothers, Aqa Sayyid Mahdi 'Alaqiband (d. 1343/1924) and Aqa Sayyid Hadi 'Alaqiband (d. 1352/1933), sons of the above-mentioned Sayyid 'Abdu'r-Rahim, had a shop near the Ashraf gate where they sold lace and silk. This became the communications centre for the Baha'is of Isfahan in respect of letters from and to 'Abdu'l-Baha and Baha'is in other parts of Iran.[71] Haji Mirza 'Ali Muhammad Sayf udh-Dhakirin (d. 1926), the son of the above-mentioned Haji Sayyid Javad Muharrir, received an Islamic religious education and made a living as a preacher and *rawdih-khan*. In the midst of his discourse he would, however, allude to the Baha'i Faith.[72] Another leading Baha'i was Mirza Muhammad Sadiq (d. 1920), the son of Mirza Husayn Mahbub ush-Shuhada.[73]

Among the prominent Baha'is was the *mujtahid* Haji Mir Sayyid 'Ali (1277/1860–1350/1931), named Fadil Isfahani, who was the son of a Baha'i named Mirza Habibu'llah Isfahani. Fadil Isfahani had obtained an Islamic religious education and certificate of *ijtihad* in Isfahan and had begun to teach at the Madrasih Kasihgaran there. Aqa Najafi and the other clerics discovered he was a Baha'i and forced him out. He moved to Tehran where he began to teach at the Madrasih Imamzadih and later at the Madrasih Sipahsalar. Eventually Mirza 'Ali Naqi Sani' ul-Mamalik, an administrator at the *madrasih*, discovered that Haji Mir Sayyid 'Ali was a Baha'i and he had to migrate to Mashhad. He lived there for a time and then in Ashkhabad. In 1312/1894 he visited 'Abdu'l-Baha in 'Akka and was asked to move to Tabriz. Here again he was able to propagate the Baha'i Faith among the clerical class and succeeded in converting Mirza Isma'il Mamaqani, the son of Mulla Muhammad Mamaqani (the Shaykhi cleric who had been present at the trial of the Bab, vol. 1:378). Haji Mir Sayyid 'Ali then lived in Tehran and Isfahan for periods of time and taught Arabic at the Tarbiyat school.[74]

---

70 ZH 5:32–3.
71 ZH 8a:122–3.
72 ZH 8a:123.
73 ZH 8a:121–2.
74 ZH 8a:136–8; Usku'i, Tarikh Adharbayjan - MS A, Part 1, Section 1:11–12; Ghani, *Yad-dasht-ha* 1:73.

Prelude to the 1903 persecution of the Baha'is

17. Malik ul-Mutakallimin

During the time that Mirza 'Ali Khan Amin ud-Dawlih was prime minister (June 1897–June 1898), he curbed the powers of Aqa Najafi and the Baha'is of Isfahan had a relatively peaceful interlude. After Amin ud-Dawlih's fall, however, Aqa Najafi was determined to restore his authority. Majd ul-Islam Kirmani has described how he was among a group of religious students summoned to Aqa Najafi's presence. Aqa Najafi told them that his standing in the town had declined during the period that Amin ud-Dawlih was prime minister and that in order to restore his authority in the town, it was necessary to catch a number of people drinking alcohol and whip them and to kill a few 'Babis'.[75] As a result, a persecution of the Baha'is of Isfahan and Najafabad (see pp. 37–8, 67–70) was initiated and this also became a thread that led to the persecution of 1903.

Another factor that contributed to the persecution of 1903 was the activities of a number of individuals who were initially drawn to the Baha'i community as a vehicle for social reform. They formed the core element of a group among Isfahan's intelligentsia calling for reform. In a book by Sayyid Muhammad 'Ali Jamalzadih, the son of one member, this group is called the Progress Society (Anjuman-i Taraqqi),[76] while Mahdi Malikzadih, the son of another member, lists a similar group of individuals without giving the group a name.[77] They advocated social reform, planned for the founding of a modern school, criticized the conservative clerics, and read and discussed the reform newspapers that were being published outside Iran such as *Habl ul-Matin*.

A leading member of the Progress Society was Mirza Nasru'llah Bihishti Malik ul-Mutakallimin (1861–July 1908, see fig. 17), a skilled orator (*va'iz*), *rawdih-khan* and musician, who was born in Isfahan. He travelled to India in 1882 but had to leave after a quarrel with the Isma'ili leader,

---

75   Majd ul-Islam, *Tarikh Inhilal Majlis* 209–10.
76   Jamalzadih, *Sar u Tah* 102; Yaghma'i, *Sayyid Jamal Va'iz* 2; see also Jamalzadih, *Khatirat* 23.
77   Malikzadih, *Zindigi-yi Malik ul-Mutakallimin* 63–4, cited and described in Nabavi Razavi, *Tarikh Maktum* 227–35.

18. Sayyid Jamalu'd-Din Va'iz

the Aga Khan, over a book on reform and liberty that he had written and published. He returned to Isfahan in 1886 and was very vocal in his calls for reform, as well as setting up a modern school. It is said that his skill at oratory and his consequent ability to attract large crowds caused the clerics of Isfahan to become jealous. They wrecked his school before it could open and forced him out of Isfahan in 1895. He lived for a time in Tabriz and Tehran before being invited back to Isfahan by Zill us-Sultan in 1896. Here he resumed his activities in the circle of reformers and founded a school. The enmity of Aqa Najafi and other clerics forced him to leave again in early 1903. Up until this time he was actively participating in the Baha'i community and when he left in early 1903 for Shiraz, he began to propagate the Baha'i Faith there until expelled later in the year for doing this (see p. 278).[78] While he was in Shiraz he permitted his home in Isfahan to be used to house the prominent Baha'i Mirza Hasan Adib when he came to Isfahan in 1903.[79] Having been expelled from Shiraz as a Baha'i and regarding the situation in Isfahan as hopeless after the anti-Baha'i persecution of 1903, Malik ul-Mutakallimin moved to Tehran.[80]

A second member of the Progress Society was Sayyid Jamalu'd-Din Va'iz (1863–1908, see fig. 18), who was from a family of the Jabal 'Amil in today's Lebanon, was born in Hamadan but is generally known as Isfahani. He was an eloquent preacher and used to attend meetings at the home

78 On Malik ul-Mutakallimin's life, see Malikzadih, *Tarikh-i Inqilab* 1:156–65; Yaghma'i, *Sayyid Jamal Va'iz* 77–8, 301; Bayat, *Revolution* 61–2; Afari, *Revolution* 46–7; Nazim ul-Islam, *Tarikh Bidari* 3:260; Majd ul-Islam, *Tarikh Inhilal Majlis* 284; Bamdad, *Tarikh* 4:346–8; Nabavi Razavi, *Tarikh Maktum* 217–68. On his later being a 'Babi'/Azali, see Browne, *Materials* xix, 221; 'Alaqiband, Tarikh 58, 88.

79 ZH 8a:170; Majd ul-Islam, *Tarikh Inhilal Majlis* 214.

80 See the letter Malik ul-Mutakallimin wrote to Mirza Asadu'llah Vazir in Malikzadih, *Tarikh-i Inqilab* 1:161–5. The chronology given here is confirmed by the contemporaneous narrative given in *Vaqayi'-yi Ittifaqiyyih* 707–8, although it contradicts somewhat Malikzadih's chronology (*Tarikh-i Inqilab* 1:158–61) which has Malik ul-Mutakallimin coming to Shiraz after he had settled in Tehran.

of Mirza Asadu'llah Vazir and so became
known as a Baha'i. This enabled the clerics
of the town to prevent him preaching in
Isfahan and so he would travel to Tabriz
and elsewhere to earn his livelihood.
When the anti-Baha'i outburst occurred in
Isfahan in 1903, he was in Tabriz and was
advised not to return to Isfahan, and so he
moved his family to Tehran.[81]

A third member of the Progress
Society was Shaykh Ahmad Majd ul-Islam
Kirmani (1871–1923, see fig. 19), who
was born in Kirman and came to Isfahan
in 1890. He was accused of being a Babi
and left for Tehran in 1901. His exact relationship with the Baha'i community is not
clear. There is no evidence that he associated with the Azalis in Kirman. In Isfahan
he probably associated with the Baha'is;

19. Shaykh Ahmad Majd ul-Islam
Kirmani

and in Tehran he joined the Azalis circles, playing an important role in the
Constitutional Movement and editing *Nidā-yi Vaṭan*, one of the reformist
newspapers.[82] One Baha'i writing in about 1910 describes him as basically
a free-thinker (*lā madhhab*) and that among the Azalis he called himself an
Azali and among the Baha'is, a Baha'i.[83]

A fourth member of the Progress Society was Mirza Ahmad Khan Fatih
ul-Mulk (see fig. 21), a recent Baha'i convert, who would be among the
Baha'is who took sanctuary in the Russian Consulate and who would host
Laura Barney and Hippolyte Dreyfus when they came to Isfahan (see p. 42).
He was a military leader who was at this time the Iranian foreign office
agent in Isfahan and later a supporter of the Constitutionalist Movement.

---

81 On Sayyid Jamal's life, see Jamalzadih, *Sar u Tah* 97–104; Jamalzadih, *Khatirat*
21–4; Malikzadih, *Tarikh-i Inqilab* 1:165–8; Bamdad, *Tarikh* 1:255–7; Bayat,
Revolution 62–6; Afari, *Revolution* 46; Yaghma'i, *Sayyid Jamal Va'iz*. On his being
an Azali in later years, see 'Alaqiband, Tarikh 58, 88. The prominent *mujtahid*,
Sadr Isfahani of Najaf, was his uncle.
82 Biographical Introduction by Mahmud Khalilpur in Majd ul-Islam Kirmani,
Tarikh Inhilal Majlis, pp. *ta-yih*; Bayat, *Revolution* 62–3, 66, 168; Afari, *Revolution* 45–6; Yaghma'i, *Sayyid Jamal Va'iz* 78–9.
83 'Alaqiband, Tarikh 375–6.

He was elected in 1909 as a member for Isfahan of the second Iranian parliament.

Two other members of the Progress Society who were Baha'is were Aqa Muhammad Javad Sarraf (money changer ; see fig. 20) and Mirza (Sayyid) 'Ali (or 'Ali Naqi) Khan Lashkarnivis (army accountant), who were wealthy, propertied individuals and established with Malik ul-Mutakallimin the first school in Isfahan run on modern lines, teaching such subjects as science and English. Mirza 'Ali Khan, who had attended the Dar ul-Funun in Tehran (the first modern school and college in Iran), was the headmaster. This school was immediately opposed by Aqa Najafi and the conservative clerics of the city and they succeeded in closing it down.[84] Also named as members of the Progress Society were Sayyid 'Abdu'l-Vahhab Imami, Mirza Ahmad 'Alam and Haji Sayyid 'Ali Jinabzadih.[85] Among those cited by Malikzadih as being among the circle of these reformers were Baha'is such as Mirza Asadu'llah Vazir (see pp. 8–10), Muhammad Husayn Mirza Mu'ayyid us-Saltanih, head of the post office in Isfahan (see pp. 198–9) and Mirza Mahmud Sadr ul-'Ulama, who became a Baha'i in 1904 (see p. 57).

Among the activities of this society was to establish, in August 1898, a company to encourage the revival of local crafts that had suffered owing to the flood of cheaper foreign imports. Furthermore, this was the first company in Iran to be owned by shareholders.[86] Also important was the writing and publication in 1318/1900 by the first four of the above list of a scathing satire on the corruption of Zill us-Sultan and Aqa Najafi called *Ru'ya-yi Sadiqih*.[87] Another associate of this group was Mirza Asadu'llah

---

84   These two members of the Progress Society and founders of the modern school are named by Jamalzadih as Aqa Muhammad Javad Sarraf and Sayyid 'Ali Naqi Khan in one source (*Sar u Tah* 100, 102) and by the same writer as Aqa Javad Sarraf and Mirza 'Ali Khan in another (*Khatirat* 23). It is almost certain that these two are the two Baha'i converts who were sought by Aqa Najafi in 1903, the first being arrested and beaten on Aqa Najafi's orders, while the second escaped (see p. 38). The main difference between the accounts is that the occu-pation of the second is described as *lashkarnivis* by Jamalzadih and as *sarraf* in the Baha'i sources. He may well have had both occupations.

85   This list of members of this society is drawn from Jamalzadih, *Sar u Tah* 102 and Yaghma'i, *Sayyid Jamal Va'iz* 2.

86   Malikzadih, *Tarikh-i Inqilab* 1:137–8; Yaghma'i, *Sayyid Jamal Va'iz* 5.

87   Yaghma'i, *Sayyid Jamal Va'iz* 12. While most authors attribute the writing of this work to just the first three, Malizadih (*Zindigi* 64) says that Ahmad Khan Fatih ul-Mulk also had a hand in the writing of this work.

Khan Na'ini, who was secretary to the Russian consulate in Isfahan and arranged for the manuscript of this book to be smuggled out of Isfahan and published in Russia. He was known as, and probably was, a Baha'i.[88]

The important point is that of the nine known members of the Progress Society, five (Malik ul-Mutakallimin, Sayyid Jamalu'd-Din Va'iz, Mirza Ahmad Khan Fatih ul-Mulk, Aqa Muhammad Javad Sarraf and Mirza 'Ali Khan) were publicly known to be members of the Baha'i community.[89] A sixth member, Majd ul-Islam Kirmani, was publicly known as 'a Babi' but whether he was a member of the Baha'i community at this time is not clear, while at least three others of their close associates listed by Malikzadih were Baha'is. Furthermore, it is clear that the activities of this society greatly angered both Aqa Najafi (in their ridicule of him in *Ru'ya-yi Sadiqih* and their establishment of a modern school) and Zill us-Sultan (in their ridicule of him in *Ru'ya-yi Sadiqih* and their call for social and political reform). This, together with the rapid spread of the Baha'i Faith among the educated sections of the population of Isfahan, explains the heightened anxiety of the clerics of the city, headed by Aqa Najafi, and their desire to reassert their religious authority on the situation in Isfahan – a desire that resulted in the 1903 persecution described below. At the same time, it explains the lack of action on the part of Zill us-Sultan in reacting to that persecution.[90]

---

88 Afary, *Revolution* 45–7; Bayat, *Revolution* 63–4. Iranian Foreign Office documents show that Na'ini was regarded as a 'Babi' by the people of Isfahan (Sadeghian, 'Minorities and Foreigners' 118). Afary and Bayat regard him as an Azali but this is because of their assumption that Malik ul-Mutakallimin and Sayyid Jamal Va'iz were Azalis at this time whereas the evidence presented here suggests that they were moving in Baha'i circles while in Isfahan and only later became Azalis in Tehran. Further evidence that Na'ini was a Baha'i comes from the fact that Na'ini later facilitated (and, according to some accounts, instigated) the Baha'is taking sanctuary in the Russian consulate in 1903, see pp. 38–41.

89 They used to gather together with well-known Baha'is and attend meetings at the home of Mirza Asadu'llah Vazir and this became known in the town (Malikzadih, *Tarikh-i Inqilab* 1:73, 161; Jamalzadih, *Sar u Tah* 101–2).

90 Indeed it explains the vehement hatred of Zill us-Sultan towards Sayyid Jamalu'd-Din Va'iz demonstrated in an episode related by the latter's son, Muhammad 'Ali Jamalzadih, who records that his father was expected back from a trip to Tabriz when the 1903 episode broke out. As his father was known throughout the town as a Baha'i, his mother sent him to a relative and neighbour, Haji Mirza Abu'l-Qasim Qadi, to ask whether it was safe for his father to return to Isfahan. But this man said that he had been present at the court of Zill us-Sultan the previous day when the prince had held up a pen sharpener and declared that he was waiting for Sayyid Jamalu'd-Din to return when he would tear apart his flesh with that very implement (Jamalzadih, *Sar u Tah* 101).

Of the above-mentioned social activist members of the Progress Society, three of them – Malik ul-Mutakallimin, Sayyid Jamalu'd-Din Va'iz Isfahani and Majd ul-Islam Kirmani – moved to Tehran, the first two as a direct result of the anti-Baha'i persecution in 1903. All three then joined the Azali circle in Tehran and became major figures in the Constitutional movement, the first two being killed by Muhammad 'Ali Shah after his coup in 1908. Because of their connections with the Azalis in Tehran, it has been assumed that they were Azalis in Isfahan also. However, there is no evidence that they associated with Azalis while in Isfahan and all the evidence shows that they associated with Baha'is and were either Baha'is or close Baha'i sympathizers while they were there. It is likely that in Tehran this group's increasing involvement with anti-government action gradually estranged them from the Baha'i community (who had clear instructions from the Baha'i leaders not to engage in such activity) and they found the Tehran Azali circle more aligned with their desire for direct political action.

Then in August 1902 the prominent Baha'i, reformer, preacher, religious scholar and Qajar prince Shaykh ur-Ra'is had come to Isfahan from Shiraz (see p. 278, fig. 20 and vol. 1, fig. 51 and pp. 128–31). Zill us-Sultan went off on a hunting trip to avoid meeting him and the clerics of Isfahan, warned of Shaykh ur-Ra'is's arrival by their colleagues in Shiraz, determined to prevent him from settling and making a base in Isfahan. They announced that the Shaykh was a 'Babi' and all those who attended his lectures stood to be accused of being 'Babis'. Shaykh ur-Ra'is was, however, an eloquent and charismatic figure and was soon drawing to himself large crowds. Nicolas, who was in Isfahan at this time and thus an eyewitness, states that more than 10,000 people were in the crowds that flocked to hear Shaykh ur-Ra'is, although this seems an exaggeration.[91] Among those who frequented his meetings and helped to organize them were two new Baha'i converts, the above-mentioned Aqa Muhammad Javad Sarraf and Mirza 'Ali Khan (see footnote 84). Aqa Najafi and the other clerics were not pleased that a new religious leader was reducing their congregations, much less that this figure was preaching reform and was reported to be a Baha'i. They put pressure on Zill us-Sultan, who, apart from the annoyance that the Baha'i reformers had caused him, was probably also somewhat unhappy that another member of the Qajar

---

91   Nicolas, *Massacres* 13; ZH 7:158–9.

20. Shaykh ur-Ra'is (seated in centre with cane in hand) and
Aqa Muhammad Javad Sarraf (standing behind him to the right)

royal family was rising to prominence in his city. After about a month
of pressure, Shaykh ur-Ra'is left Isfahan. All this Baha'i activity was too
much for Aqa Najafi, however, and so he determined on action against
the Baha'is. He got his men to raid the home of one Baha'i, Mirza 'Ali
Muhammad Sayf udh-Dhakirin, to look for incriminatory evidence and
also put out the rumour that Aqa Muhammad Javad Sarraf – who, as
mentioned above, had already incurred Aqa Najafi's wrath by starting a
modern school in Isfahan and organizing Shaykh ur-Ra'is's meetings –
had been seen drinking wine.[92]

Shortly afterwards, Mirza 'Azizu'llah Khan Varqa, a prominent Baha'i,
came to Isfahan and large crowds attended his meetings; but Aqa Najafi did
not act because Varqa was secretary and translator at the Russian Discount
and Loan Bank and Aqa Najafi did not want to take on the Russian government.[93] Following this, some of Aqa Najafi's men tried to arrest Mirza
'Ali Muhammad Talavih when it was discovered that a book he had left

---

92   Nicolas, *Massacres* 13–14; Majd ul-Islam, *Tarikh Inhilal Majlis* 210–12; KD
      96–9; ZH 7:158–9, 8a:214–15.
93   Majd ul-Islam, *Tarikh Inhilal Majlis* 212–13.

21. Mirza Ahmad Khan Fatih ul-Mulk

with a bookbinder was a Baha'i book, the *Fara'id* of Abu'l-Fadl Gulpaygani, but he went into hiding and then fled the town.[94]

The siege of the Russian consulate, 1903

The most important episode in the Baha'i history of Isfahan during the ministry of 'Abdu'l-Baha was the 1903 affair at the Russian consulate. This event had its origins both in the disturbed national political situation (the agitation of reformers against the reactionary prime minister Amin us-Sultan) and in local politics as described in the preceding section, which had left both Zill us-Sultan and Aqa Najafi seething with rage against the Baha'is, who were perceived by the former as advocates of reform of the sclerotic Qajar polity and by the latter as rivals for the religious leadership of Isfahan.

On 20 May 1903 two prominent Baha'i teachers, Mirza Hasan Adib[95] and Shaykh Muhammad 'Ali Qa'ini, arrived in Isfahan. Husayn Khan Saham us-Saltanih (see pp. 86, 139–40) informed Aqa Najafi of their arrival and the latter tried to intercept them. But Mirza Asadu'llah Vazir managed to arrange for them to be brought into the city without detection and housed in the home of Malik ul-Mutakallimin (who was himself in Shiraz at this time), where the Baha'is met with them in secret. Three days later, a prominent Baha'i, Haji Muhammad Isma'il Sarraf, died. Knowing that both Aqa Muhammad Javad and Mirza 'Ali Khan would be at the funeral, Aqa Najafi sent men to seize them. They managed to arrest Aqa Muhammad Javad and brought him to the Shah Mosque before Aqa Najafi, who ordered that he be whipped for his supposed drinking of wine the previous year.[96]

---

94   Nicolas, *Massacres* 22–4 (trans. BBR 382); Majd ul-Islam, *Tarikh Inhilal Majlis* 214–15; Dawlatabadi, *Hayat-i Yahya* 1:318; ZH 7:159.
95   The date of his death was given incorrectly in vol. 1:116. It should be 3 Aug. 1919.
96   Nicolas, *Massacres* 24 (trans. BBR 382–3); Majd ul-Islam, *Tarikh Inhilal Majlis* 215–16; BBR 377; Dawlatabadi, *Hayat-i Yahya* 1:318; ZH 7:159–60; Jamalzadih, *Sar u Tah* 23; Sadeghian, 'Minorities and Foreigners' 111.

The Baha'is met and decided that they had to act to try to prevent a recurrence of this type of arbitrary persecution by the Islamic clerics. Since appealing to Zill us-Sultan himself had had no effect in previous years, another way had to be found. A common way of drawing attention to a perceived injustice in Iran at this time was to take sanctuary in a holy place, the embassies or consulates of foreign governments or in the telegraph office (from where a telegraph could be sent to the shah). Representatives were sent to both the English and Russian consulates. Mirza Hasan Adib had a previous acquaintance with the Russian acting consul Baronovski and wrote to him personally while Mirza Asadu'llah Na'ini, the secretary of the consulate who was probably a Baha'i (see pp. 34–5), encouraged the Baha'is to come to the Russian consulate. Baronovski agreed to help. And so the Baha'is decided to take sanctuary in the Russian consul-ate. At first some 200 of them gathered there but Baronovski, apparently seeking to build up the episode for his own purposes, said that he could not do anything unless more Baha'is came to take refuge. Since at the same time Aqa Najafi had given orders that all Baha'is were to be attacked and arrested, more Baha'is streamed into the consulate on 26 and 27 May, their numbers eventually reaching 600, according to an unsigned report in the British consular archives, and 4,000, according to Nicolas, who was in Isfahan at this time.[97]

Baronovski tried to get Zill us-Sultan to act decisively but the latter stated that with the troops at his disposal and with no clear instructions from Tehran, he could do nothing. Furthermore, a forged telegraph was made public, appearing to come from the prime minister to Aqa Najafi, giving him permission to do as he thought fit in the matter. The situation reached a climax on 28 May, with a large crowd surrounding the Russian consulate and threatening to storm it. Zill us-Sultan sent word to Aqa Najafi that he would hold him responsible and that he must disperse the mob. Aqa Najafi went in person to the area around the Russian consulate and told the people to go home. Baronovski, his resolve having weakened at the sight of the mob outside his walls, then told the Baha'is that they had to leave.[98]

---

97   BBR 377–81; Nicolas, *Massacres* 24–5 (trans. BBR 383–4); Majd ul-Islam, *Tarikh Inhilal Majlis* 216–17; Dawlatabadi, *Hayat-i Yahya* 1:318; ZH 7:160–2; Ishraq-Khavari, *Nurayn* 222–4; Sadeghian, 'Minorities and Foreigners' 108.

98   Nicolas, *Massacres* 25–6 (trans. BBR 383); Majd ul-Islam, *Tarikh Inhilal Majlis* 217; BBR 377–9; Dawlatabadi, *Hayat-i Yahya* 1:318; ZH 7:162; Sadeghian, 'Minorities and Foreigners' 111–12.

Many of the street ruffians had remained in the vicinity of the Russian consulate, however, and as the Baha'is came out in small groups towards evening on 28 May and on the morning of 29 May, they were attacked and robbed. One elderly Baha'i, Sayyid Abu'l-Qasim Marnani (Marnan was a small village on the southwest margin of the town of Isfahan which was eventually swallowed up within the town as it expanded), a landowner and prominent citizen of the town who had become a Baha'i in 1290/1873, was so badly beaten that he died, and many other Baha'is were severely injured.[99]

The opportunity was taken, as usual, to extort money from numerous Baha'is and even from some individuals who were not Baha'is, on the threat of accusing them of being Baha'is. All the clerics of Isfahan took part in this opportunity to make money, including Haji Mirza Hashim the Imam-Jum'ih; Haji Aqa Sidihi; Aqa Nuru'llah, the brother of Aqa Najafi; and Aqa Munir, the son of Jamal Burujirdi. On 2 June, two brothers, Haji Muhammad Hadi Khayyat and Haji Muhammad Husayn Khayyat, who were well-known merchants and who may have been Azalis but kept their beliefs hidden under a strict outward show of Islamic orthodoxy, were arrested on the orders of Sayyid Abu'l-Qasim Zanjani, a local *pish-namaz* (prayer-leader) who owed them over a thousand *tumans*. He took them before Aqa Najafi, who declined to order their death as there was no evidence against them and they denied the charge. Zanjani was, however, unwilling to let his quarry go and imprisoned them in his own house. He obtained a *fatwa* from Aqa Munir, the son of Jamal Burujirdi, and they were taken to the middle of the Maydan-i Shah, one of the largest public squares in the world, where a large mob that filled this square to overflowing hacked the two to pieces and mutilated and burned their bodies. In the aftermath of this, Aqa Najafi pointed to the connection of these two brothers with the Azali leaders, the Dawlatabadi family, and tried to organize an attack on the Dawlatabadi family home but this failed. Only one of the Islamic clerics made efforts to protect the Baha'is during this episode and that was Shaykh Muhammad Hasan 'Arab Shaykh ul-'Iraqayn.[100]

---

99 Nicolas, *Massacres* 26–7 (trans. BBR 384); Majd ul-Islam, *Tarikh Inhilal Majlis* 217–19; BBR 377–9; Dawlatabadi, *Hayat-i Yahya* 1:318–19; ZH 7:162–3. Malikzadih is probably writing about this same man (although he calls him Sayyid-i Marbini) when he states that Aqa Najafi had his students tear the Sayyid to pieces because he wanted the old man's land, which adjoined his own (*Tarikh-i Inqilab* 1:129).

100 Nicolas, *Massacres* 27–8 (trans. BBR 385); Majd ul-Islam, *Tarikh Inhilal Majlis*

Although orders were given for a military force to be sent to Isfahan and Yazd under Nasr us-Saltanih to restore order, in the event only 300 troops under Huzhabr us-Saltanih arrived. And although orders were issued for the arrest of the clerics involved in this episode, Zanjani fled to Iraq before he could be arrested and Zill us-Sultan acted to prevent Aqa Najafi and Haji Mirza Hashim the Imam-Jum'ih being taken to Tehran, as he feared that if that occurred they would convince the authorities of his culpability and the fact that he had profited from the episode by extorting money.[101]

The overall effect of the 1903 episode was to put an end to the advances being made by two interconnected movements that had been gaining momentum in Isfahan and which both the senior clerics, such as Aqa Najafi, and the governor, Zill us-Sultan, detested and feared. The first was the increasing number of Baha'i converts among the intelligentsia and emerging middle class of Isfahan, the minor clerics (such as Malik ul-Mutakallimin and Sayyid Jamalu'd-din Va'iz), minor government officials (such as Mirza Muhammad Khan Lashkarnivis and Mirza 'Ali Khan Lashkarnivis), military figures (such as Mirza Ahmad Khan Fatih ul-Mulk), merchants (such as Mirza Ja'far Hadioff) and financiers (such as Aqa Muhammad Javad and Haji Muhammad Isma'il Sarraf). The second of these two movements was the call for social and political reform that was gaining ground in Isfahan. Although one can distinguish these two groups conceptually, they were in practice composed of largely the same individuals. And so although the outward form of the episode was an outburst of anti-Baha'i persecution, in fact the overall and intended result was the suppression of both movements.

220–3; Dawlatabadi, *Hayat-i Yahya* 1:319–20. The famous Iranian author Muhammad 'Ali Jamalazadih witnessed this episode as a child and records in his memoirs the fanaticism of the crowd that witnessed and took part in this (*Sar u Tah* 97–101; *Khatirat* 23). Other accounts of the Russian Consulate episode include Anonymous, Tarikh Isfahan 40–50; BBR 364, 376–85; ZH 7:163–4, 166–8; KD 2:96–102. 2:96–102. For Zill us-Sultan's account of this episode, see Sadeghian, 'Minorities and Foreigners' 111–12. For 'Abdu'l-Baha's description and comments on this episode, see *Makatib* 3:126–30 (trans. as Rabbani, "Abdu'l-Baha's proclamation' 57–9 and [Isfahani], *Bahai Martyrdoms*). Shaykh ul-'Iraqayn was one of those in the circle of the reformers (Malikzadeh, *Zindigi* 64–5) and probably a covert Babi or Baha'i, see Nabavi Radavi, *Tarikh Maktum* 231–2.

101 Majd ul-Islam, *Tarikh Inhilal Majlis* 225–6.

Events in Isfahan after the 1903 episode

During and following the 1903 episode at the Russian consulate, numerous Baha'is were forced to leave Isfahan. Most, including the above-mentioned Sayf udh-Dhakirin and Mirza Muhammad Khan Lashkarnivis, settled in Tehran but some fled to other places, such as Aqa Sayyid Mahdi and Aqa Sayyid Hadi who went to Abadih. According to one source, the number of Baha'is who had to leave Isfahan was some 400, although some returned after a time.[102] It is difficult to know how many Baha'is there were in Isfahan at this time. Although there may have been as many as 4,000 Baha'is who crowded into the Russian consulate in this episode, many of these were from Najafabad (Najafabad at this time had 2,000 to 3,000 Baha'is so it is unlikely that any more than a few hundred men would have come to Isfahan). Majd ul-Islam Kirmani puts the number of Baha'is in Isfahan at this time at 600[103] but that is probably an under-estimate and may represent only those who were publicly known as Baha'is. Also such numbers given by Iranian historians often refer only to the number of adult males. In the latter case, Kirmani's figure would indicate a total Baha'i population of about 3,000 (or about four per cent of the population of Isfahan). In 1906 Hippolyte Dreyfus, the first French Baha'i, and Laura Barney, an American Baha'i (and later Dreyfus's wife), visited Isfahan and were entertained by Mirza Asadu'llah Vazir and Fatih ul-Mulk.[104]

The unsettled conditions in the country over the first two decades of the 20th century led to much insecurity and the opportunity for the enemies of the Baha'is to make trouble for them. There were numerous examples of petty harassment and the murder in 1909 of Haji Haydar (see p. 71). During this period there was a contest for religious leadership of Isfahan between Aqa Najafi and his younger brother, Aqa Nuru'llah (1861–1927, see fig. 22), the latter having taken a more prominent role in the Constitutional Revolution and having orchestrated the downfall of Zill us-Sultan in 1907. After Aqa Najafi's death on 4 July 1914, Aqa Nuru'llah became the undisputed religious leader of Isfahan and was just as opposed to the Baha'is as his brother had been.[105] Then in 1920, during a visit to Isfahan by the

---

102 Anonymous, Tarikh Isfahan 46; ZH 8a:122–3.
103 Majd ul-Islam, *Tarikh Inhilal Majlis* 214.
104 ZH 8b:1194.
105 For some details on the competition between Aqa Najafi and his brother, see Walcher, *Shadow* 48–55.

Baha'i teacher Mirza Munir Nabilzadih, the Baha'i graves in the town cemetery, Takht-i Pulad (or Takht-i Fulad), were attacked by a mob instigated by Aqa Rida Mujtahid. Although the mob was at first restrained, later the governor, the Bakhti-yari leader Sardar Jang, who was in the hands of the religious leaders of the town, visited the site and ordered that a plat-form that had been built over the graves of the executed Nahri brothers (see pp. 17–23) should be destroyed. After this, several other Baha'i graves in the vicinity, including those of Mirza Asadu'llah Vazir and Mirza Mahdi, were desecrated.[106]

22. Aqa Nuru'llah (Shaykh Muhammad Mahdi)

Keith Ransom-Kehler, who had been sent to Iran by Shoghi Effendi to try to persuade the Iranian government to lift its restrictions on the Baha'i community, died in Isfahan in 1933 while on a tour of the country. She was buried next to the graves of the Nahri brothers. Shoghi Effendi referred on several occasions to these three graves and they became a site frequently visited by Baha'is.

As the above description shows, there were two main periods of growth of the Isfahan Baha'i community, each terminated by a major persecution that led to the migration of many of the most important Baha'is away from the town. The first of these was a period of expansion in the 1860s and 1870s which was brought to an end by the execution of the two Nahri brothers in 1879, subsequent to which many leading Baha'is emigrated. The second period of expansion occurred in the 1890s and came to end with the episode of the Russian consulate in 1903, after which again many of the leading Baha'is emigrated. Some of these migrants from Isfahan, as noted above, went to Khurasan, some to Abadih and some to Ashkhabad, but most went to Tehran, while a considerable number joined the Baha'i

---

106 Anonymous, Tarikh Isfahan 66–7; BBR 437–9; MH 5:254; ZH 7:322; Ishraq-Khavari, *Nurayn* 65–8. Sardar Jang had in fact sided with the royalist forces and against his fellow-tribesmen in the Revolution but had been forgiven by the Bakhtiyari leadership after their victory in 1909.

leadership in 'Akka.[107] Each of these two waves of migrations left the town's Baha'i community weakened and depleted and it was some time before activities resumed their previous level. There were, however, many more episodes of persecution than these two. Indeed, if one adds together the persecutions in both the town itself and the surrounding villages, then in the period from 1852 to 1920 there was a major episode of persecution on average every two to three years.

Azalis of the Isfahan area

Isfahan and the surrounding area was one of the few places in Iran where an appreciable number of the Babis became Azalis, including a number of leading Babis such as Mulla Rajab-'Ali Qahir and his brother Mulla 'Ali Muhammad Siraj. Their sister Fatimih Khanum (d. 1916) had been the temporary wife of the Bab when he was in Isfahan. When the Bab was hidden by the governor of Isfahan Mu'tamid ud-Dawlih in his private palace, the Imarat-i Khurshid, in order to protect him from the clerics of Isfahan, it became necessary for someone to attend to the household chores in the Bab's apartments. Fatimih Khanum was chosen for this. Because of the laws of Islam governing society in those times, it was not possible for an unrelated man and woman to be alone together. Therefore it seems likely that the Bab entered into a temporary marriage (*sighih*) arrangement in order to allow this, rather than a full marriage.[108]

Mulla Rajab-'Ali Qahir, Mulla 'Ali Muhammad Siraj, Fatimih Khanum and a fourth figure, Sayyid Muhammad Isfahani (d. 1872), all migrated to Baghdad in the 1850s and joined forces with Azal there. Azal married Fatimih Khanum in Baghdad and after a short time gave her in marriage to

---

107 Momen, 'Patterns of Exile' 34.
108 Afnan, *Ahd-i A'la* 218–22. Afnan confirms that this was a *sighih* marriage. He also records that Sayyid Muhammad 'Ali Jamalazadih, the son of Sayyid Jamal Va'iz Isfahani (see pp. 32–3), had told him that his father had heard from the Azali leader Haji Mirza Yahya Dawlatabadi that the second wife of the Bab had told him that she had been brought to the governor's palace and went into the room where the Bab was busy writing. He had asked her to be seated and then carried on writing. After a time she grew tired and left the room and went to another room and slept. She had said that that was the totality of her interactions with the Bab during the whole of her time with him. This would seem to confirm the idea that this was a *sighih mahramiyyat* (temporary marriage excluding sexual contact) arrangement, made to allow her to do the household chores in the Bab's apartments.

Sayyid Muhammad Isfahani, actions
which Baha'u'llah repeatedly decries
in his writings. When Baha'u'llah and
Azal were sent on to Istanbul and
Edirne, Sayyid Muhammad accompanied the party but the others
remained in Karbala, where, according
to Azali accusations, the two brothers were killed in a dispute with the
Baha'is in about 1867.[109]

Another prominent Azali of the
Isfahan area was Haji Mirza Hadi Dawlatabadi (1253/1837–17 Nov. 1908;
see fig. 23 and 1:102). He was born
to a wealthy family of the village of
Dawlatabad (see pp. 54–6), who were
descendants of a prominent Shi'i cleric,
Qadi Nuru'llah Shushtari. He married

23. Haji Mirza Hadi Dawlatabadi

Khatimih Bigum, a granddaughter of the prominent Isfahan philosopher
and cleric Mulla 'Ali Nuri. He became a Babi in the 1850s and in 1866 was
in Kazimayn in Iraq on his way to Mecca when Baha'u'llah's claim became
known. He was in close contact with Mulla Ja'far Naraqi, the Azali propo-
nent in Kazimayn, and himself became a follower of Azal, supporting the
latter financially and by writing a book, *Fasl ul-Kalam*, in support of his
claim. Dawlatabadi received a full religious education, at first in Isfahan,
and then in spring 1873 he went to Iraq where he completed his education
and received a certificate of *ijtihad* from Mulla Zaynu'l-'Abidin Mazandarani. He returned in early 1877 to Isfahan and set himself up as a religious

---

109 Browne, *Materials* 199, 220; 'Izziyyih Khanum, 'Tanbih an-Na'imin', Browne
    manuscripts F. 60, Cambridge University Library 128. According to Browne,
    the Baha'i who killed Qahir was one Nasir the Arab. If this accusation is correct,
    then this is presumably the same fiery individual who also was implicated in the
    murder of Mirza Ahmad Kashani (see p. 95) and who some years later came to
    'Akka intending to deal with the Azalis there and had to be prevented from car-
    rying out his plan by Baha'u'llah's firm instructions for him to leave; Browne,
    Mate-rials 53–4; Shaykh Ahmad Ruhi and Mirza Aqa Khan Kirmani, *Hasht
    Bihisht* as summarized by Browne in ['Abdu'l-Baha], *Traveller's Narrative* 2:359;
    Balyuzi, *Baha'u'llah* 323–5 and n. For an example of Baha'u'llah's words concern-
    ing the marriages of Fatimih Khanum to Mirza Yahya and Sayyid Muhammad
    Isfahani, see *Epistle* 176–7.

authority in the Ahmadabad quarter of the city. He had a great deal of wealth and had influence in Isfahan and especially in Dawlatabad. He was, to a certain extent, protected by Zill us-Sultan, no doubt in the hope that he might become a counter to Shaykh Muhammad Baqir among the clerics of Isfahan. A number of people were converted to the Babi religion through him. His Babi beliefs became generally known, however, and in late 1880 he was forced to leave Isfahan for Mashhad and Tehran. He then returned to Isfahan in 1882 (presumably because Shaykh Muhammad Baqir was by that time in exile). In 1303/1885 he went on pilgrimage to Mecca and visited Azal in Cyprus with his two sons. At this time Azal appointed him his successor. On his return to Isfahan in 1887, however, he faced the combined opposition of the clerics, under the leadership of Aqa Najafi, and the governor Zill us-Sultan, who was trying to mulct him of his wealth. Succumbing to these pressures, he ascended the pulpit and openly declared his renunciation of the Bab as well as cursing 'Cyprus and the one who lives there'. In 1888, when the execution of Mirza Ashraf occurred (see pp. 27–8), he was again under pressure and again publicly recanted. However, even this did not suffice to relieve the opposition to him, which became so great that he migrated from Isfahan in late 1888, arriving in 1889 in Tehran, where he remained until his death (vol. 1:102).[110]

Since Dawlatabadi died before Azal, the latter appointed Dawlatabadi's second son, Haji Mirza Yahya Dawlatabadi (Jan. 1863–27 Oct. 1939, see fig. 24), to be his successor.[111] Yahya Dawlatabadi had studied at Najaf while his father had been there from 1873, had returned to Isfahan with him in early 1877 and had been forced to leave Isfahan along with his father in 1880–2. On his return to Isfahan he joined the circle of Azalis, in particular Shaykh Ahmad Ruhi and Mirza Aqa Khan Kirmani (see p. 429), who were promoting social change. After going on a trip to Mecca and Cyprus and spending some time in Najaf in 1886–8, Yahya finally left Isfahan in 1889 and settled in Tehran, where he studied under Mirza Hasan Ashtiyani (no doubt partly because he needed the protection of this powerful *mujtahid* against those who were accusing him of being a Babi). He was a prominent supporter of the Constitutionalist movement and is also well known as an educator, founding a number of schools. He sought British protection at the time of Muhammad 'Ali Shah's coup in 1908 and

110 Bamdad, *Tarikh* 6:289–91; Dawlatabadi, *Hayat,* vol. 1 *passim*; ZH 6:287–8, 8a:505–6; Walcher, *Shadow* 118–21.
111 ZH 6:290.

24. Haji Mirza Yahya Dawlatabadi (right) and
his brother Mirza 'Ali Muhammad Dawlatabadi (left)

worked for the Germans against the British during World War I, before
again courting the British after the war.[112] He attended the Universal Races
Congress in London in 1911 and gave a paper. He had no sons, however,
and he appears to have refrained from appointing a successor to the leadership of the Azalis. He is reported to have announced before his death
that the successorship is now suspended for 300 years and after that time,
the king of the Bayan will appear.[113] Shaykh Hadi's other son, Mirza 'Ali
Muhammad Dawlatabadi (c. 1868–1345/1926, see fig. 24), was also an
Azali and active in Tehran during the Constitutional Revolution.

In addition to these figures in Isfahan, a number of the leading Babis in
the surrounding villages, such as Mulla Isma'il Sabbagh in Sidih and Mulla
Muhammad Baqir Mujtahid in Tar, became supporters of Azal, resulting
in significant Azali communities in some villages to the north of Isfahan,
such as Sidih (see pp. 49–50); Dawlatabad (see p. 55); Tar, Tarq and Kishih
(see pp. 144–5).

Lastly, among the Azalis of the circle of Dawlatabadi was a certain
Mirza Yahya Isfahani. In about 1891 he went to Bombay on a mission
from Dawlatabadi to print some Azali texts there. Here he met Mirza
Husayn Khartumi (Shirazi), who took him to Baha'i meetings, and he professed to have become a Baha'i, although Mirza 'Azizu'llah Jadhdhab, who
met him there, doubted his sincerity. Khartumi himself was at this time

112 Bamdad, *Tarikh* 4:437–8; Abbas Amanat, 'Dawlatabadi, Seyyed Yahya' in *Encyclopædia Iranica*.
113 MH 9:85.

25. Mulla Isma'il Sabbagh Sidihi (later known as Mirza Mustafa Katib)

covertly advancing the cause of Mirza Muhammad 'Ali. Mirza Yahya went on to 'Akka and met 'Abdu'l-Baha and then settled in the port of Jeddah in Arabia in about 1892, where he married the daughter of Mirza Husayn Lari, a wealthy Baha'i merchant who was the Iranian vice-consul there. Here he began to promote the rebellion of Mirza Muhammad 'Ali, with much vituperation of 'Abdu'l-Baha, until his death in 1898. Because his death followed upon a message to him from 'Abdu'l-Baha to the effect that, if he did not repent, then the vengeance of God would follow, the supporters of Mirza Muhammad 'Ali accused the Baha'is of killing him. His father-in-law, however, described in a letter that he was called to Mirza Yahya's house and found that he was bringing up blood. He called a physician and a ruptured blood vessel in the lung was diagnosed. He died a few days later. In those days, this was not an uncommon cause of death from pulmonary tuberculosis.[114]

Sidih

Sidih (pop. 44,000 in 1951) is composed of three large villages: Furushan, Varnusfadaran and Khuzan, situated 12 kilometres west of Isfahan, north of the road to Najafabad. It is situated on the ruins of an ancient city. It appears that the Babi community in this area was started by Mulla Zaynu'l-'Abidin of Najafabad, who converted a number of the people of the village in the 1850s. Among those whom he converted was Mulla Isma'il Sabbagh (dyer, d. 1339/1920, see fig. 25) of Varnusfadaran.

---

114 Browne, *Materials* 154–67, which contains 'Abdu'l-Baha's tablet to Haji Mirza Husayn Lari (also at 'Abdu'l-Baha, *Makatib* 1:267–72). Jadhdhab calls him Sayyid Yahya, see ZH 8a:1152–7n.

When the split between Baha'u'llah and Azal
occurred, most of the Babis of Sidih appear to
have remained Babis or become Azalis.[115] Some
of these Azalis, including Mulla Isma'il, converted to Christianity in 1871 for a time (but
the reason for this may well have been to obtain
relief from the famine that afflicted Iran in that
year).[116]

26. Mirza Sulayman Khan
Shirazi Rukn ul-Mulk, deputy
governor of Isfahan

In the summer of 1889, at the same time
as he instigated a persecution of the Baha'is of
Najafabad, Aqa Najafi also moved against the
Sidihi Babis and Azalis. Some 30 of the men
went to Tehran to plead for justice and returned
with assurances from the shah. Despite this, however, when they returned
to Isfahan, Aqa Najafi refused to let them return to their homes. The
Sidihis occupied the telegraph office, sending petitions to the shah. Eventually the deputy governor, Mirza Sulayman Khan Shirazi Rukn ul-Mulk
(1254/1838–1912, see fig. 26), arranged for the Sidihis to be taken to their
homes under military escort, but as they arrived in February 1890, a mob of
some 2,000, led by Mir Sayyid 'Ali the Imam-Jum'ih, fell upon them. The
military escort was dispersed by threats and seven of the Azalis had their
throats cut and their bodies burned. A Muslim historian makes the following comment on this episode: 'The Inquisition of medieval Europe had
been reborn in Iran in the nineteenth century only somewhat worse, more
severe and more brutish.' A great affront to the authority of the shah had
occurred and everyone waited to see what the consequence would be. The
shah launched an enquiry and Aqa Najafi was summoned to Tehran[117] but
nothing further came of this. Aqa Najafi was in fact treated well in Tehran
and was soon back in Isfahan stirring up trouble.[118]

---

115 Zayn ul-Muqarrabin wrote a lengthy letter to Mulla Isma'il Sabbagh trying to
     persuade him of the truth of Baha'u'llah's claim but Mulla Isma'il wrote an even
     lengthier rebuttal. Cambridge University Library, Browne manuscripts F.64.
116 Momen, 'Early relations' 57–63.
117 See text of telegram summoning him in Safa'i, *Asnad Barguzidih* 124–6; the
     tone of the telegram is very accommodating and respectful. Quotation is from
     Bamdad, *Tarikh* 6:263n. See also I'timad us-Saltanih, *Ruznamih* 684, 697, events
     related to 8 Rajab and 15 Ramadan 1307.
118 BBR 284–9; Dawlatabadi, *Hayat* 1:88–9; Welcher, *In the Shadow* 133–7; De
     Vries, *Babi Question*, 27–30.

27. Aqa Sayyid Isma'il Sina (left) and Aqa Sayyid Mahmud Nayyir (right)

During this episode Mulla Isma'il Sabbagh had his ear cut off by Zill us-Sultan and was forced to flee first to Tar near Natanz and then to Tehran where he changed his name to Mirza Mustafa and became a scribe, eventually providing Prof. E.G. Browne with many of his Babi and Azali manuscripts.[119] From statements made at this time, we may conclude that there were about 200 Babis or Azalis in Sidih.[120]

In the 1870s a number of literate young men, who were mostly from the Furushan village of Sidih, had formed a literary circle of mystics and poets in the village. There are differing accounts of how the group became Baha'is and the following is one of these.[121] The group decided to search

---

119 Balyuzi, *Browne* 34–5n3; Bamdad, *Tarikh* 6:264–5.
120 This is based on the fact that the 40 men who were driven out of Sidih are described as 'heads of families' (BBR 284). Forty families would be approximately 200 persons.
121 There are two main accounts, one by Sina and the other by Na'im, but they differ in important details. The account given here is that of Sina (quoted in ZH 6:225–32 and MH 1:107–11) because it is a first-hand account (Na'im was not on the trip to Tabriz) and also because the account given by Na'im and written by Mirza Muhsin Na'imi ('Tarjumih Hal Hadrat-i Na'im') is already available in English, being the basis for the account by Balyuzi (*Eminent Baha'is* 129–36). Although the date for the conversion of Nayyir and Sina in Tabriz is given as 1292/1875 in ZH 6:225, this is evidently a mistake as it is given as 1297/1880 in the same account quoted in MH 1:107 and concurs with the date of 20

for the true spiritual path among all the paths that existed. It was the custom for a party of the sayyids of the area to travel throughout Iran, attending to their business affairs and collecting the *khums* religious tax that Shi'is pay to descendants of the prophet. Several of this literary circle belonged to an extended family of sayyids in the village and they decided to use these journeys as an opportunity to look also for the true spiritual path. They made three trips to Khurasan without any success and then in the course of a journey that several of them made to Adharbayjan in late 1880, they were introduced to the Baha'i Faith by Mirza Asadu'llah Tafrishi and Mirza 'Inayatu'llah 'Aliyabadi in Tabriz and became much attracted to the religion. This group included two brothers, Aqa Sayyid Mahmud Nayyir (1262/1846–1327/1909, see fig. 27) and Aqa Sayyid Isma'il Sina (Nov. 1848–1336/1917, see fig. 27), who were from a much respected family of sayyids (descended from Imam Musa) and clerics of Furushan. They had received a clerical education and wore clerical garb. Also on that journey was a cousin, Mirza Mahmud, and a more distant relative, Haji Sayyid Mirza of Khuzan village (who set off immediately from Tabriz for 'Akka). Those in the literary circle who became Baha'is included other relatives of these two brothers and some three or four others, including Haji Muhammad Taqi of Furushan (who was illiterate and yet was able to debate successfully with senior clerics), Aqa Mirza Rida Manzar (Mirza Mahram, d. 1914) and Aqa Ghulam-'Ali (d. c. 1321/1921, father of the future Hand of the Cause Jalal Khazeh).[122]

Mirza Muhammad of Furushan, who took the pen-name of Na'im (Apr. 1856–14 March 1916, see fig. 28), was another member of this group and a neighbour of Nayyir and Sina. His father was a farmer but had given his only son a clerical education. In 1871, however, when there was a severe famine in Iran, Na'im had married and been forced to turn to farm work to support himself and his family. After a time, because he had established a reputation for honesty and piety, his maternal cousin Haji Mulla Hasan, a major merchant of Isfahan, entrusted his agricultural and trading activities in Sidih to Na'im. Na'im had not been on the above-mentioned trip to Adharbayjan but when Sina wrote to him of what had happened in Tabriz, he began to investigate for himself. Thus it was that he was drawn

---

Dhu'l-Qad'ih 1297 (24 Oct. 1880) in the poetry of Na'im quoted by Na'imi ('Tarjumih Hal Hadrat-i Na'im' 26; although it is given as 1298/1881 in a prose account by Na'im, ZH 6:266).

122 MH 1:120–1; ZH 6:276–9; 'Ala'i, *Mu'assisih* 686–7.

28. Mirza Muhammad Na'im

to the Azali Mulla Isma'il Sabbagh to find
out about the new religion. He was much
attracted to the writings of the Bab that he
was given but did not think much of Azal's
works. When Nayyir and Sina returned in
1881 and shared with him the writings of
Baha'u'llah, he left the Azalis and joined
the Baha'is.[123]

At first Haji Mulla Kazim, one of the
clerics of the village, tried to persuade the
converts to revert to Islam but he found
himself defeated in argument. Then in
1883 when the Baha'is were being persecuted in Tehran and elsewhere, Mir Sayyid
'Ali Bahr ul-'Ulum and Mir Sayyid 'Ali
the Imam-Jum'ih wrote to Shaykh Muhammad Baqir in Isfahan complaining of the activities of these young men in converting others in the
village. The deputy governor Rukn ul-Mulk sent men to arrest five of the
Baha'is including Nayyir, Sina and Na'im. Their houses were looted and
burned and they were severely beaten and taken off to Isfahan. At this time
Na'im and two other Baha'is were led through the streets and bazaar with
rings through their noses and their faces blacked (a traditional humili-
ating punishment).[124] Although Shaykh Muhammad Baqir was insisting
on their death, Rukn ul-Mulk decided to free them after a time. Life in
Sidih became very difficult, however, and they could hardly emerge from
their homes. Bahr ul-'Ulum forced Na'im's wife to divorce her 'infidel'
husband and she took their three children and all of his money with her.
About four years later, in March 1887, the men were again arrested and
suffered greatly. As a result of this, later that same year, Nayyir, Sina, Mirza
Mahram and Haji Muhammad Taqi decided to leave for Tehran, setting
off with only the clothes they stood up in and suffering greatly on the way.
Na'im joined them in 1310/1892.[125]

123 Na'imi, 'Tarjumih Hal Hadrat-i Na'im', 21–4; Balyuzi, Eminent Baha'is 130–2;
     Mu'ayyad, 'Na'im Sidihi' 35–6.
124 Malmiri, Khatirat 122–3; Baha'i, Istintaqiyyih MS B 103; according to the latter
     account, there were four arrested in Sidih and brought to Isfahan and after their
     release they went for a time to Tehran before returning to their homes.
125 Some accounts indicate that Nayyir, Sina, Mirza Mahram, Haji Muhammad
     Taqi and Na'im all migrated to Tehran in 1310/1892 (ZH 6:244), suffering

In Tehran the refugees settled in the Hayat-i Bagh (vol. 1:31) and earned a meagre living by transcribing the writings of Baha'u'llah for other Baha'is and educating their children. Nayyir and Sina's wives and children remained for a time in Sidih but they were subjected to continuous harassment and attacks and eventually joined their husbands in Tehran in about 1313/1895. Nayyir and Sina travelled to various parts of Iran, such Khurasan (1307/1889 and 1311/1893 with Mirza Mahram and 1314–17/1896–9), Yazd and Kirman (1308/1890, 1312/1894 with Mirza Mahmud Zarqani and 1314–17/1896–9), Fars (1313/1895 with Zarqani) and Kirmanshah (1317/1899), propagating the Baha'i Faith. In about 1899, however, 'Abdu'l-Baha instructed them to remain in Tehran and to teach the Baha'i Faith from the Hayat-i Bagh complex there (vol. 1:94–5).[126] Other members of the family of Nayyir and Sina, including their mother and sister and their wives[127] and children all distinguished themselves in various ways: for example their sister Shirin Jahan Bigum (pen-names Sayyidih and Faniyyih Sidihi, 1267/1850–?21 April 1913), an accomplished poet, became a Baha'i in Isfahan in 1887 as a result of the persecution of her brothers and moved to Tehran in 1313/1895;[128] Sina's daughter Bakimih, known as Mu'allimih Khanum (1296/1879–?) was a prominent Baha'i teacher of girls both in Tehran (1324–34/1906–15) and then in Ashkhabad;[129] Sayyid Jalal, son of Sina (d. Aug. 1925), attended the classes of Sadr us-Sudur (vol. 1, fig. 40) and became a teacher of the Baha'i Faith, travelling throughout Iran and to Ashkhabad until his death in the Mazandaran village of Kafshgar-kala in the course of these travels.[130]

Na'im was later able to obtain employment teaching Persian at the

---

much and staying at Dawlatabad on the way. However, it seems more likely that only Nayyir, Sina, Mirza Mahram and Haji Muhammad Taqi migrated in 1304/1886, while Mirza Na'im migrated in 1310/1892 (ZH 6:269). This is because it seems certain that at least one of them was in Dawlatabad in 1310/1892 on his way to Tehran (ZH 6:284) and it does not seem that this was Nayyir, Sina or Mirza Mahram because they are recorded as having gone on a trip from Tehran to Khurasan in 1307/1889 while Nayyir and Sina travelled from Tehran to Yazd and Kirman in 1308/1890 (ZH 6:245–6). Thus these must already have migrated to Tehran before 1310/1892.

126 For biographies of Nayyir and Sina, see ZH 5:331, 6:224–51, 8a:329–38; MH 1:93–172; Gulpaygani, *Rasa'il* 393–4; Dhuka'i-Bayda'i, *Tadhkirih* 2:218–31.

127 ZH 8a:337–9.

128 Dhuka'i-Bayda'i, *Tadhkirih* 3:154–66.

129 ZH 8a:341–2.

130 ZH 8a:339–40; Rastigar, *Sadr us-Sudur* 62–3.

British embassy in Tehran. After the death of Sadr us-Sudur in 1907, Na'im took over the classes that Sadr us-Sudur had started for learning how to teach the Baha'i Faith to others. As well as much first-class poetry, Na'im wrote several apologetic works, including one for E.G. Browne and one in reply to the Sufi leader Safi 'Ali Shah.[131] His son, 'Abdu'l-Husayn Na'imi (vol. 1, fig. 39), also worked for the British embassy, while his daughter, Mahbubih, married a prominent Baha'i of Tehran, Mirza Muhsin Khan Na'imi Dabir Mu'ayyad.[132] After settling in Tehran, Mirza Mahram moved eventually in 1315/1897 to Bombay where he countered the activities of the supporters of Mirza Muhammad 'Ali and travelled extensively propagating the Baha'i Faith. In particular, he met with Ghulam-Ahmad, the founder of the Ahmadiyyih or Qadiyani religious community, and informed him of Baha'u'llah's claim.[133]

Dawlatabad

Dawlatabad is a village 15 kilometres north of Isfahan (pop. 8,117 in 1951). A short time after the execution of the Bab in 1850 a dervish first brought the religion of the Bab to the village.[134] Then in 1270/1853, Sayyid Ja'far Yazdi, who had been a companion of Vahid Darabi, came to the village as a preacher and reciter of the stories of the Imams and remained for a time propagating the new religion in secret. A number of people became Babis, including Mulla Muhammad Bakhtiyari, who farmed his own land and had a shop in the village; Mulla Muhammad 'Ali Isfahani, who ran a *maktab*; and his brother Mulla Muhammad Baqir. As the number of Babis grew, the Muslim clerics in the village began to protest. The *kadkhuda* tried to extort money from Mulla Muhammad Bakhtiyari and when that failed, he sent his men to the latter's home where Sayyid Ja'far was staying and the Babis were meeting. As a result, Mulla Muhammad and Sayyid Ja'far fled the village. Mulla Muhammad was able to return after a while, although thenceforth he was constantly being harassed and his home and shop were attacked from time to time.[135]

---

131 For a biography of Na'im, see Na'imi, 'Tarjumih Hal Hadrat-i Na'im'; ZH 5:331, 6:263–76, 8a:362–4; MH 3:114–71; Mu'ayyad, 'Na'im Sidihi'; KD 2:192; Dhuka'i-Bayda'i, *Tadhkirih* 4:479–556; Balyuzi, *Eminent Baha'is* 129–41.
132 KD 2:192; Dhuka'i-Bayda'i, *Tadhkirih* 3:486n.
133 ZH 6:278–9; ZH 8b:1152.
134 Muhajirin, *Muhajirin Dawlatabadi* 19–20.
135 ZH 6:281; Muhajirin, *Muhajirin Dawlatabadi* 19–20.

In 1866 Mirza Ja'far Yazdi[136] came to the village surreptitiously and invited the Babis to a meeting in Isfahan at the home of Muhammad Sadiq, son of Mulla Ja'far Gandumpakkun. Some 15 of the Babis of the village attended. At this meeting, Mirza Ja'far read out some of the writings of Baha'u'llah and announced the latter's claim to be 'He whom God shall make manifest'. Mulla Muhammad Bakhtiyari immediately accepted while the rest remained Babis and Azalis. After a time, Baha'u'llah wrote to Mulla Muhammad instructing him to teach the Babis of Dawlatabad about his claims. At the same time, letters arrived from Azal cursing Mulla Muhammad. After a time, Mulla Muhammad managed to convince most of his own family as well as Mulla Muhammad 'Ali Isfahani and his brother Mulla Muhammad Baqir and their families and also a few other Azalis in the village of the truth of the Baha'i Faith. The Azalis were led by Mirza Hadi Dawlatabadi (see pp. 45–6) who was a cleric of a prominent rank among the clerics of Isfahan.[137]

Many Baha'is came to Dawlatabad to try to convert the Azalis there, including Aqa Sayyid 'Abdu'r-Rahim Isfahani and his sons; Sina, Mirza Ashraf, Abu'l-Fadl Gulpaygani, Haji Mirza Haydar 'Ali Isfahani, Sayyid Husayn Mahjur, Na'im and others.[138] Mirza Abu'l-Fadl writes that he went several times to Dawlatabad from Isfahan in about 1885. On some occasions he met with one or two Azalis and on one occasion with some 20. One evening the house was full of people and some Muslims were even observing the proceedings from neighbouring rooftops. Some of the Azalis of Dawlatabad also visited Mirza Abu'l-Fadl in Isfahan.[139] As a result of these proceedings a few of the Azalis converted to the Baha'i Faith. In 1308/1890 two of the sons of Mulla Muhammad Bakhtiyari were among a group who left to visit Baha'u'llah in 'Akka. They took with them a third brother, Aqa 'Abdu'llah, who was an Azali and married into one of the

---

136 ZH 6:278–9 states that this was Sayyid Ja'far Yazdi who had spread the Babi religion in 1853 returning to Dawlatabad but Aqa Sayyid Ja'far appears to have died before Baha'u'llah's open declaration of his mission (see Malmiri, *Khatirat* 30) and it was Mirza Ja'far Yazdi who passed through this area at this time and had been commissioned by Baha'u'llah to announce his claim. Family tradition among the Baha'is of Dawlatabad states, however, that it was Haji Mirza Haydar 'Ali Isfahani who first brought the claim of Baha'u'llah to Dawlatabad (Muhajirin, *Muhajirin Dawlatabadi* 22–3), but this seems unlikely as that would not have occurred until about 1880, owing to Isfahani's imprisonment in the Sudan.

137 ZH 6:280–1.

138 ZH 6:281–2.

139 Mihrabkhani, *Gulpaygani* 116–18.

leading Azali families of Dawlatabad; he intended to go from 'Akka to Cyprus to meet Azal. Haji 'Abdu'l-'Azim, the son of Mulla Muhammad 'Ali Isfahani, also accompanied them. When Aqa 'Abdu'llah reached 'Akka and met Baha'u'llah, however, he was convinced of the truth of the Baha'i position and decided to forego his trip to Cyprus.[140] Aqa 'Abdu'llah also asked for a commentary on the words 'Bismi'llah ar-Rahman ar-Rahim'. Baha'u'llah asked 'Abdu'l-Baha to write this and when the pilgrims returned from 'Akka, they challenged the Azalis to ask Azal for a commentary on the same words for comparison. When the commentary of Azal arrived, comparing it with 'Abdu'l-Baha's served to confirm them in the Baha'i Faith.[141]

In about 1310/1892 when Na'im was forced to leave Sidih (see p. 52), he stayed for a time with the Baha'is of Dawlatabad. But his stay and the return of the above pilgrims from 'Akka resulted in a stirring up of hostility among the Muslims of the village.[142] Finally, in 1312/1894, a group of the Muslims in the village went to Isfahan to lay a complaint against the Baha'is and a group of Baha'is also went to Isfahan to defend themselves. Despite the efforts of Mirza Asadu'llah Vazir, the situation deteriorated. Aqa Najafi actively urged the persecution of the Baha'is. Some 25 of the villagers were imprisoned by the Imam-Jum'ih, nine of these were Baha'is and the rest were probably Azalis. They were due to be executed but were freed by a well-wisher two days before their execution. The Baha'is decided that they could not return to the village and so after paying the *kadkhuda* of the village to look after their families, they left for Tehran. Over the next few years until about 1897 the rest of the Baha'is of the village also left for Tehran and the Azalis were expelled from the village. Because of their flight from their homes, 'Abdu'l-Baha addressed these Baha'is in his letters as Muhajir or Muhajirin (emigrant, emigrants), which they adopted as their family names.[143] Mulla Muhammad Bakhtiyari's great-grandson, Rahmatu'llah Muhajir, was appointed a Hand of the Cause by Shoghi Effendi in October 1957.

---

140 ZH 6:282; Muhajirin, *Muhajirin Dawlatabadi* 26–35.
141 ZH 6:282–3; Muhajirin, *Muhajirin Dawlatabadi* 27–33.
142 ZH 6:284; this account says that it was Nayyir, Sina, Mirza Mahram and Na'im who came to the village in 1310 but for reasons stated in note 125 above, it would appear that Nayyir, Sina and Mirza Mahram probably visited in the course of their migration in 1304 and that in 1310 it was only Na'im.
143 ZH 6:284; Muhajirin, *Muhajirin Dawlatabadi* 35–42.

Other villages

Firaydan (Faridan) is a district some 100 kilometres west of Isfahan, beyond Najafabad, where there were many Georgian and Armenian villages as well as Bakhtiyari tribesmen. Although there is said to have been a certain Muhammad Taqi Bayk from this area who met the Bab and became a follower, nothing much is known about him.[144] The first to become a Baha'i in the area was Ja'far-Quli Khan Chadgani Mu'azzam ul-Mulk, a military officer who had witnessed the interrogation of the Nahri brothers by Zill us-Sultan in 1879 and been much affected by their courage and steadfastness. He became general (*sartip*) of the Firaydan regiment and helped the Baha'is whenever he could.[145] Several of the notables and landowners in the area, such as Allahvirdi Khan and, in the time of 'Abdu'l-Baha, Mu'azzam ul-Mulk's brother Mufakhkham us-Sultan,[146] became Baha'is as well as some prominent clerics, such as Aqa Sayyid Mahdi Imam-Jum'ih (who was converted by Mirza Asadu'llah and Haji Mirza Haydar 'Ali Isfahani),[147] and later Haji Shaykh Muhammad 'Ali and Mirza Mahmud Sadr ul-'Ulama (Sadr ul-Ahrar, d. 1346/1927), who became a Baha'i in Isfahan in 1322/1904, had to flee the wrath of Aqa Najafi, returned to Firaydan and later lived in Tehran and Isfahan again.[148]

Luhrasb Khan, a notable of the Firaydan area, became a Baha'i in the early 1910s. Through his efforts a large number of people in the area became Baha'is, including all the inhabitants of two villages that he owned, Qal'ih-Murgh (pop. 400 in 1940s, 40 km west of Najafabad) and Hillab (pop. 200 in 1940s, 3 km northwest of Qal'ih-Murgh).[149] There were also Baha'is in other villages of the area such as Nanadgan. Luhrasb Khan had had enemies before he was a Baha'i and in 1334/1915, after he had become a Baha'i, one of his enemies, Amir Khan, decided to try to kill him. This was not an easy task as this was a lawless period in Iran's history and every notable had an armed retinue. One night a shot was fired at a figure in

---

144 Mazandarani, *Asrar* 4:446.
145 Abadihi, Tarikh Abadih, MS B 57; Ishraq-Khavari, *Nurayn* 108.
146 Mazandarani, *Asrar* 4:446.
147 Mazandarani, *Asrar* 4:446.
148 ZH 8a:169; Mazandarani, *Asrar* 4:446; Ishraq-Khavari, *Ganjinih* 185n; this latter source gives the date of his death as about 1325 AHS/1946.
149 Interview with Mr Cyrus Ala'i, who had visited these two villages in the 1940s, in London, 26 Dec. 2005.

the dark but killed Nuru'llah Firdawsiyan, a Baha'i employee of Luhrasb Khan, instead.[150]

In the village of Riz (33 km southwest of Isfahan; pop. 11,308 in 1951), the *kadkhuda*, Haji Muhammad Hashim Rizi became a Baha'i. He was arrested in December 1877.[151] In the time of 'Abdu'l-Baha a number of new Baha'i communities arose in the villages around Isfahan. In the village of Gaz (later known as Jaz, 18 km north of Isfahan; pop. 9,903 in 1951), Haji Na'ib Gazi became well known as a Baha'i and suffered numerous beatings and other persecutions.[152] There was a general uprising against the Baha'is in the village in 1920 at the instigation of the local clerics. Some of the people of the village also went into Isfahan and created an uproar there, encouraging some of the criminal elements of Isfahan to come to the village and assist them against the Baha'is. Most of the Baha'is fled and their houses were looted. Some of them were captured in Isfahan and elsewhere and were beaten and mulcted of money. The clerics decreed that they could not return to the village and so they were forced to migrate to Qumm, Tehran and elsewhere, although some did eventually manage to return to the village.[153] In nearby Khurzuq (17 km north of Isfahan; pop. 5,016 in 1951), a Baha'i community arose under the leadership of Mulla Ramadan. As in Gaz, there was an uprising against the Baha'is in 1920. Some of the Baha'is were imprisoned and had to pay to be released, while others were forced to leave the village and migrate elsewhere. Since it was winter when this happened, some of those leaving the village died on their way.[154]

There were also small Baha'i communities in many of the other villages in the Isfahan area.[155] Once the *Baha'i World* volumes first began listing a directory of Baha'i communities around the world, the volume for 1940–4 listed all the local assemblies in Iran, indicating that the Isfahan district had the highest number of local assemblies (28) of any area in that country and the second highest number of localities where Baha'is resided (72).[156]

---

150 Mudarris, *Tarikh* 113.
151 Nicolas, *Massacre des Babis* 17.
152 ZH 8a:134.
153 BBR 451 (citing Public Record Office, FO 248 1279, file 'Bahais', papers 13 and 14); ZH 7:322.
154 ZH 7:322, 8a:134.
155 See, for example, the list of recipients of a tablet of 'Abdu'l-Baha living in various villages, in ILMA 52:130–2.
156 *Baha'i World* 9 (1940–4) 674.

Najafabad

Najafabad (pop. 15,000 in 1918;[157] 30,400 in 1956) is a small town some 26 kilometres west of Isfahan on the road towards Hamadan and Kirmanshah. The town was constructed in the Safavid period when Isfahan was the capital of Iran. In 1613 Shah 'Abbas I had gathered a large amount of money and jewels to be sent to be sent to the shrine of Imam 'Ali at Najaf, which at that time lay in Ottoman domains. The foremost religious figure of the period, Shaykh Baha'i (1547–1622), realizing that Iran could not afford the loss of such a large amount of wealth, came to the shah and told him that he had had a dream of the Imam 'Ali who had told him that Najaf had enough wealth at present and that the shah should spend the money on the construction of a town called Najafabad near Isfahan. The shah assented to this and the town was constructed according to the plan and under the supervision of Shaykh Baha'i. Grain was grown in the area and it was famous for grapes that were sold to the Armenians of Isfahan for wine-making until this was prohibited by Aqa Najafi in the 19th century.

The Baha'i community in the town had its origins in the Babi period. When the religion of the Bab began to spread among the people of Isfahan in about 1846 during the residence of the Bab in that city, a number of Najafabadis also became Babis. There was one Najafabadi Babi killed at Shaykh Tabarsi and three among the Babis killed in Tehran in the aftermath of the attempt on the life of the shah in 1852.

In the first half of 1852 Mirza Sulayman-Quli Nuri, who was a skilled Babi orator known as Khatib ur-Rahman (the orator of the All-Merciful), came to Najafabad and took up residence in the home of Mulla Ahmad, who led prayers in one of the mosques of the town (Masjid-i Maydan, now Masjid-i Jami'). Since Sulayman-Quli was a person of learning, he was invited to address the people from the pulpit of Mulla Ahmad's mosque. The latter was so delighted with the oration given that he introduced Sulayman-Quli to Mulla Zaynu'l-'Abidin, a *mujtahid* and leading religious figure in the town.[158] The latter, who later received the title of Zayn ul-Muqarrabin

---

157 KD 1:394; the figure of 150 houses and 1,000 inhabitants given by the *Gazetteer of Persia, 1910–18*, is clearly an error.

158 I am here following the account given by Zayn ul-Muqarrabin himself quoted in Zayn, 'Khatirat Hayat' 1:7–9 and ZH 6:196–7. Mudarris (*Tarikh* 52) gives a slightly different story saying that Sulayman-Quli openly preached of the end of the time of Islam and coming of the promised Imam and Mulla Ahmad was unable to answer him and therefore turned to Zayn ul-Muqarrabin for help. Khatib ur-Rahman was related to Baha'u'llah on his mother's side.

(1818–1903, see figs. 30 and 95) from Baha'u'llah, had studied at the shrine cities of Iraq until 1253/1837 when his father had summoned him to return and take over his functions of religious leadership while he went on pilgrimage to Mecca. But his father had died on this pilgrimage and he had remained as imam of one of the main mosques in the bazaar of the town, the Masjid-i Aqa Muhammad. He had been visiting Karbala in 1844 and had heard of the claim of the Bab but nothing had come of it then. Zayn ul-Muqarrabin agreed to allow Sulayman-Quli to speak from the pulpit of his mosque. After this he spoke at length with Sulayman-Quli, who told him of the claims of the Bab and converted both him and Mulla Ahmad. Zayn ul-Muqarrabin had a very prominent and influential position in the town and soon some one hundred others had become Babis in Najafabad. Word of the conversions spread alarm among the clerics and a complaint was made to the deputy governor of Isfahan, Chiragh-'Ali Khan Siraj ul-Mulk (he was from Zanjan and had witnessed the Zanjan upheaval of 1850). He sent officials to bring Zayn ul-Muqarrabin to Isfahan where he was questioned but gave satisfactory answers.[159]

Zayn ul-Muqarrabin then visited Baghdad. On his first visit, which must have been in about 1855, Baha'u'llah was absent in Sulaymaniyyih and, having failed to meet Azal, Zayn ul-Muqarrabin returned towards his home town disappointed. As he approached the town however, he heard that the Babis in Najafabad were being persecuted and that the mob was looking for him in particular, so he turned back to Baghdad. In this episode, a *mujtahid* in Najafabad, together with some of the sayyids and clerics, had initiated a persecution of the Babis, had arrested some of them and sent them to Isfahan where Chiragh-'Ali Khan had imprisoned them. The clerics obtained a *fatwa* for the death of the prisoners from Aqa Muhammad Hadi, a *mujtahid* of Isfahan. At this point, Chiragh-'Ali Khan was dismissed and a new governor, Hamzih Mirza Hishmat ud-Dawlih, was appointed. He interrogated the prisoners and as no one could establish their unbelief (*kufr*), he freed them.[160]

By the time Zayn ul-Muqarrabin had retraced his steps to Baghdad, Baha'u'llah had returned and Zayn ul-Muqarrabin met him and became devoted to him. He returned to Najafabad but the further episode of persecution in 1864 detailed below caused him to leave again. In 1867–9 he was in Yazd and Khurasan where he assisted in converting the Babi community

159 ZH 6:196–215; Mudarris, *Tarikh* 53–4; KD 1:391–2.
160 ZH 6:202; Mudarris, *Tarikh* 53–4; KD 1:393.

into the Baha'i community and then he headed for Baghdad where he settled and occupied himself transcribing the tablets of Baha'u'llah. In 1870 he was the leading figure among the Baha'is exiled from Baghdad to Mosul by the Ottoman government. Here he was entrusted by Baha'u'llah with many important tasks such as asking Baha'u'llah the questions regarding the Kitab-i Aqdas which, when answered, formed the text of the Questions and Answers appended to this book. He was also responsible for transcribing the tablets arriving from 'Akka and sending these on to the Baha'is in Iran. In 1885 he moved to 'Akka where he continued this work.[161] The tablets transcribed by Zayn ul-Muqarrabin are regarded by Baha'is as authentic and accurate.

Another of those converted while Mirza Sulayman-Quli was staying at the home of Mulla Ahmad was Mulla Qasim (d. 1328/1910). After two years, his wife, who was educated and learned, also became a Babi and she was quite fearless about confronting even the religious leaders in the town with the claims of the Babi and later the Baha'i Faith. These two converted many others to the Baha'i Faith and faced much opposition. On one occasion Mulla Qasim was arrested and taken off to Isfahan, while his house was looted. He was released after two months in prison.[162]

A major persecution of Babis in Najafabad began in 1864. Shaykh Muhammad Baqir (the Wolf) of Isfahan plotted with Mulla Rahim, a *mujtahid* of Najafabad, to have Mirza Nasru'llah, the brother of Dabir ul-Mulk, who was the deputy governor of Isfahan acting for Jalal ud-Dawlih (a son of Nasiru'd-Din Shah, d. 1868), take action against the Babis of the town, offering him a bribe of 10,000 *tumans* for his assistance. The latter sent men to Najafabad on the pretext of tax collection to bring as many of the Babis to Isfahan as possible, with the help of the *kadkhuda*, Kalb-'Ali. Many of the Babis, including Zayn ul-Muqarrabin, realized that this was a trick and went into hiding, but nevertheless the stratagem succeeded in bringing about the arrest of many Babis. Then one of the residents of Najafabad offered to identify more of the Babis of the town and a mob went round the town arresting them and pillaging their houses. The arrested Babis were taken in chains to Isfahan. There were more than 80 Babis in all imprisoned in Isfahan.

---

161 Autobiographical account of Zayn ul-Muqarrabin in Zayn, 'Khatirat Hayat' 1:5–31. This autobiographical account is included in ZH 6:195–215 and MH 5:412–72; see also Mudarris, *Tarikh* 53–67; KD 1:393–4.
162 ZH 8a:154; Mudarris, *Tarikh* 68.

In Isfahan the Babis were brought one by one before Shaykh Muhammad Baqir and residents of Najafabad would testify that they were Babis. There was a danger that all these Babis might be executed. But Mirza Muhammad Baqir Ha'i (the husband of Zayn ul-Muqarrabin's sister, see fig. 31) intervened by going to another of the *mujtahids* of Isfahan, Haji Muhammad Ja'far Mujtahid Abadihi, and obtaining a *fatwa* that the testimony that was being given was motivated by malice and not disinterested (as those giving testimony were the same people who had looted the property of the accused). Shaykh Muhammad Baqir had previously obtained evidence against one of the Babis, Habibu'llah, a young man who had travelled to Baghdad and met Baha'u'llah. He was executed at the insistence of Shaykh Muhammad Baqir, two others had their ears cut off, and others were tortured and led around the town. At this time news arrived of the dismissal of the governor and so it was decided that 15 should remain imprisoned in Isfahan, 18 sent in chains to Tehran and the rest fined and set free. As those who were to be sent to Tehran were about to leave, Shaykh Muhammad Baqir insisted on the execution of one of them, Ustad Husayn ibn 'Ali Khayyat, who was hung upside down for a whole day at the entrance to the bazaar at the north end of the main square of the town, the Maydan-i Shah, in the hope that it would make him recant. He was begging to be put out of his misery so piteously that some of the onlookers piled up some bricks so that he could reach them and rest on them. But a cleric came along and kicked the bricks away. One of the executioners who was looking on commented, 'We executioners are notorious among the people for our hard-heartedness but if the Imam Husayn had fallen into the hards of these clerics, they would have cut his head off quicker than Shimr.'[163] When he would not recant, Ustad Husayn Khayyat was taken down, but he was executed a few days later. One of those sent to Tehran, Ustad Husayn Chitsaz, died at Kashan on the way there and another, Mulla 'Ali Rida, died in prison in Tehran. Those who returned to Najafabad from Isfahan, some 60 or more in all, were bastinadoed and then given over to the mob gathered in the main square of the town (see fig. 29) to be beaten and abused in various ways, as a result of which several died.[164]

After five months the prisoners in Tehran were released and allowed home. Upon their arrival in Najafabad, Mulla Rahim wrote to the new governor,

---

163 Shimr was the man who killed the Imam Husayn, the third Shi'i Imam, at Karbala in 680 AD and then decapitated him.

164 ZH 4:342–4.

29. Najafabad:
public square
where Baha'is were
beaten in 1864

30. Zayn ul-
Muqarrabin (portrait
by Ethel Rosenberg)

31. Mirza or Mulla Muhammad Baqir Ha'i Najafabadi   32. Haji Haydar Najafabadi

Amir Aslan Khan Majd ud-Dawlih,[165] saying that the Babis were plotting
a rebellion and that a situation similar to what had happened in Zanjan
(where the Babi upheaval in 1850 had occurred during Majd ud-Dawlih's
governorship) was likely to arise. This alarmed the governor sufficiently to
have all 15 of the Babis who had returned from Tehran arrested again and
thrown into prison where the other Babis still languished. After a time, in
September 1864, Haji Mulla Hasan, a distinguished elderly Babi and uncle
of Zayn ul-Muqarrabin, and two others were taken from the prison and
publicly executed. The remaining Babis were sent back to Najafabad where
they had rings put through their noses and were led through the town and
beaten. Several, both from among the prisoners and other Babis from the
town, such as Isma'il and 'Abbas 'Ali, were killed. The body of 'Abbas 'Ali was
thrown out into a ditch outside Isfahan for public display. At the request of
Fath-i A'zam of Ardistan, however, Mir Sayyid Muhammad Imam-Jum'ih
of Isfahan sent his men and, in defiance of Shaykh Muhammad Baqir and
Aqa Najafi, they recovered the body and buried it. Some of the prisoners
had noses or ears cut off and then the survivors were all released. According
to some accounts this persecution of the Babis went on for two years and
according to others for five.[166]

The above-mentioned Mirza Muhammad Baqir Ha'i was imprisoned for a time in 1882. A report from this time states that the Baha'is
of Najafabad were constantly being arrested, beaten and fined and were
in a state of great humiliation.[167] Another Baha'i of Najafabad who was
executed in Isfahan in 1888 was Mirza Ashraf (see pp. 27–8).

One of the main instigators of the persecution of the Baha'is over a few
decades from the late 1880s onwards was Fath-'Ali Khan Yavar (major),
who had command of the troops stationed at Najafabad. He lost no
opportunity to harass the Baha'is and to extort money from them. He was
supported by a local notable, Aqa Muhsin, and, of course, by Aqa Najafi
in Isfahan. Since Najafabad was largely unprotected from depredations
by bandits and tribesmen, most homeowners, including the Baha'is, had

---

165 The governor is named as 'Isa Khan in KD 1:400.
166 In the main this follows the account in ZH 4:339–44 and Mudarris, *Tarikh*
     69–76; however KD 1:390–404 and Malik-Khusravi, *Tarikh* 3:355–6 give
     slightly different details. Both Mudarris and Malik-Khusravi date this event
     as 1285/1868 but the diplomatic despatches in BBR 268–9 make it clear this
     episode was in 1864. See also ZH 6:204–5; Walcher, *Shadow* 118–19; Sa'idi,
     'Tarikh' 58; Nabil, *Mathnavi* 45–6.
167 Asadu'llah Isfahani, Yad-dasht-ha 86, 96–7, 100, 108–9.

guns in their houses and were ready to use them if attacked. Furthermore, most of the Baha'is lived in the Panj-Jubih quarter. It was only such considerations that prevented Fath-'Ali Khan from doing more against the Baha'is.[168] Fath-'Ali Khan's wife was the daughter of Haji 'Ali Adhari. Her brother Haji Ibrahim, her sister Fatimih and her sister's husband, Haji Haydar (see fig. 32), became Baha'is. Haji Haydar was a man of wealth and influence, owning property in Najafabad. In one source he is described as the *kadkhuda* of the Baha'is,[169] which presumably meant *kadkhuda* of the Panj-Jubih quarter. His six sons-in-law and all their families also became Baha'is. Since Fath-'Ali Khan and Haji Haydar, although related to each other, had a disagreement over ownership of some land, this personal disagreement added to the enmity that Fath-'Ali Khan had towards the Baha'is. Fath-'Ali Khan went to Aqa Najafi and obtained a *fatwa* for the death of Haji Haydar. This was sent to Zill us-Sultan but the latter responded that Haji Haydar was a man of wealth and influence and could not just be executed. He therefore sent some men to Najafabad and had Haji Haydar arrested and imprisoned. A combination of the Baha'is and Haji Haydar's other influential friends managed to obtain his release however. Frustrated in his purpose, Fath-'Ali Khan instigated some of the criminal elements in Najafabad to kill Haji Haydar. As a consequence, Haji Haydar was reduced to remaining in his house and only leaving with armed guards. Despite this, he was shot at on one occasion when he left his house with his son to go to the public baths but the four shots that were fired all missed.[170]

There was a further episode of persecution in 1889. Near Najafabad were two small villages Malikabad (5 km west of Najafabad; pop. of 573 in 1953) and 'Aliyabad (5 km southwest of Najafabad; pop. 411 in 1925[171]). In both these villages a substantial Baha'i community arose and Fath-'Ali Khan Yavar instituted persecutions against them. He sent word to Aqa Najafi, who then told the governor of Isfahan, Zill us-Sultan, who owned these two villages, that all the Baha'is in these two villages should be killed

---

168 Mudarris Janimi, 'Tarikh Amri Najafabad' 23.
169 BBR 431.
170 Mudarris Janimi, 'Tarikh Amri Najafabad' 23–4; Mudarris, *Tarikh* 83–4.
171 Razmara and Nawtash, *Farhang Jughrafiya* 10:137 states this village is 50 kilometres west of Najafabad but the map in this volume clearly shows the village about five kilometres southwest of Najafabad – with no village of that name at 50 kilometres west of Najafabad. The Baha'i account also agrees with the figure of about five kilometres (one *farsakh*), ZH 8a:162.

and their property divided between the governor and the Muslims of the village. When the Baha'is of these villages heard of this they left their homes and sought sanctuary here and there. A mob from Najafabad instigated by Fath-'Ali Khan and stirred at the prospect of booty, set off for the two villages and looted the houses of the Baha'is of goods which were said to be valued at 50,000 *tumans* (although this seems a very large sum for the goods that villagers might have possessed). In the course of this looting, one Baha'i woman was killed by a stone that was thrown at her as she was defending her child. After she had been buried, the clerics instigated the mob to dig up her remains and burn them. This caused an altercation between the Muslims and the Baha'is which appears to have spread to Najafabad itself. According to Mr Preece, the Assistant Superintendent of the Indo-European Telegraph Department in Isfahan, the Baha'is were 'stoned and their women and children were maltreated, their houses broken into, their goods stolen, crops destroyed and houses wrecked, three of their number were taken prisoner and sent into Ispahan . . . About 1000 of them took refuge in flight, some 300 coming in here, and distributed themselves about the place, seeking refuge (bast) in such places as the stables of the Prince and Mushir ul-Mulk and the Persian and English Telegraph offices; about 200 have gone up to Tehran and 500 have fled to the hills.' Preece wrote to Zill us-Sultan asking him to intervene so that the Baha'is would leave the telegraph office. Hasan Khan Farrash-bashi (head footman) of Mushir ul-Mulk came and after some going backwards and forwards, the three imprisoned Baha'is were released and the Baha'is in the telegraph office were induced to return to Najafabad. Hasan Khan went to Najafabad, fined some of the people 200 *tumans* and recovered what he could. However the Baha'is of the two villages were never able to return to their homes and were forced to eke out a living in other localities wherever they could find shelter.[172]

The British Christian missionary Rev. Charles Stileman spent a week with the Baha'is of Najafabad in April 1893 and wrote an account of this. He writes of having dinner with the 'chief exponent of Behai principles' at Najafabad. This was probably Mirza or Mulla Muhammad Baqir Ha'i (sometimes called Mirza Baqir Ha'i, 1820–1917; see fig. 31) who had become a Babi in the days when Mirza Sulayman-Quli was in Najafabad. Stileman writes: 'The man who sat immediately opposite me . . . had been

---

172 BBR 280–4; ZH 8a:162–4; Mudarris, *Tarikh* 85; d'Allemagne, *Du Khorassan* 145; Walcher, *Shadow* 118–23.

imprisoned for six months, beaten, and then mutilated by having part of his ears cut off. The man who sat on my left hand told me that his own father was murdered for being a Behai. But one and all declare that they will die rather than renounce their faith, and though very many have been killed, I have not yet heard of one who has abjured his faith.'[173]

As noted above, after the fall of Amin ud-Dawlih in mid-1898, there was an upsurge of persecutions. The years from 1899 until 1901 were turbulent ones for the Baha'is of Najafabad. On 9 April 1899, at the instigation of Aqa Najafi and on the orders of Zill us-Sultan, Muhammad Husayn Khan Sartip Sidihi accompanied by Na'ib 'Abdu'r-Rahim Sidihi and 12 horsemen were sent to Najafabad. They looted the house of Mirza Baqir Ha'i, destroying what they could not remove. The local policeman (*dabit*) Mustafa Khan and Fath-'Ali Khan Yavar (who was said to have been the person who initiated this episode by reporting to Aqa Najafi that Ha'i had numerous Baha'i books in his possession) assisted them. Other Baha'i houses were also looted. Eventually they took Ha'i, who was some 80 years old at this time, off to 'Azizabad, a village belonging to Zill us-Sultan. At the same time, Haji Baqir, the above-mentioned husband of Zayn ul-Muqarrabin's sister, who was a wealthy and influential resident of Najafabad, was also arrested and taken to Isfahan. The Baha'is of Isfahan informed the Hands of the Cause in Tehran that there was a danger that he might be executed. The Hands asked Susan Baji (vol. 1:34–5, 252) to address a plea to the shah, which was successful and Haji Baqir was freed but not before he had paid a considerable fine.[174]

Some 300 of the Baha'is of Najafabad then walked *en masse* to Isfahan, where they first went to the Persian Government Telegraph Office to send a complaint to the shah. The official at the telegraph office refused to send their message so they then went to the English Telegraph Office in the Christian Julfa quarter of Isfahan. Mr McIntyre, who was in charge of the office, wrote to Zill us-Sultan who replied that he could not openly defy Aqa Najafi without the support of the central government to whom he had sent a report. Dr Minas Aganoor, the acting British Consul in Isfahan

---

173 Stileman, 'Week with the Babis' 516. Ha'i was very friendly with the British missionaries in Isfahan and even worked for them for a time. See also *Bible Society Monthly Reporter* (Feb. 1888) 46–7.

174 BBR 426, 428; Mudarris Janimi, 'Tarikh Amri Najafabad' 16–17. The printed version, Mudarris, *Tarikh*, 90 differs considerably from the manuscript. Although the latter is said to be based on an account by Ha'i himself, the former accords better with the account in BBR.

wrote: 'The open and fearless way that they confess their belief and express their determination that their position must be made clear, once for all, is quite unusual for a body of a religious sect to do, in Persia.'[175] Eventually, in mid-April, word came that Ha'i should be sent to Tehran (where he remained for a year in prison before being released). The Najafabadis camped out at the telegraph office refused, however, to move until they received assurances that the government would protect them. But Zill us-Sultan had only received vague instructions to look into the matter from Tehran and considered that he could not act to protect the Baha'is unless he received specific instruction from Tehran to do so, otherwise he would be accused by Aqa Najafi of being a Baha'i himself. By the middle of June 1899 the Najafabadis were desperate and were casting about for a resolution of their problem. The acting British Consul Dr Aganoor reported that the British missionary Rev. St. Clair Tisdall had told him that the Baha'is did not want to appeal to the Russians but that if their calls for justice went unheard, they might be forced to do this.[176]

It appears that for several years from 1899 to 1912 there were frequent occasions on which the Najafabadi Baha'is would go to the telegraph office to send telegrams of complaint to the shah and the government to seek justice for injuries they had sustained. There were some seven occasions on which groups of 40 or more of them even proceeded to Tehran in order to pursue the matter, on each occasion remaining there from one to six months.[177]

On one occasion, after Fath-'Ali Khan Yavar and Aqa Najafi had succeeded in getting Zill us-Sultan to imprison Haji Haydar for nine months, the Baha'is again sent petitions to Muzaffaru'd-Din Shah and succeeded in having Haji Haydar released. At about the same time in June 1901, one of Yavar's men burned down the door of the house of one of the Najafabad clerics, Sayyid Husayn Pishnamaz, and on the next day spread abroad the rumour that this had been done by a Baha'i. Immediately a large crowd gathered and set off angrily, with trumpets and horns blowing, for Isfahan to protest to Aqa Najafi and the governor. At a caravanserai on the way, the mob captured a Baha'i, Ghulam-Rida, and dragged him for miles, beating him until he was dead (see fig. 33).[178] Immediately upon his release Haji

---

175   BBR 427.
176   BBR 426–9.
177   Mudarris, *Tarikh* 98.
178   ZH 7:134; BBR 430; Faizi, *Bih Yad Dust* 143–4.

33. Caravanserai between Isfahan and Najafabad where
Ghulam-Rida was captured by a mob in 1901

Haydar led a group of a hundred Najafabadi Baha'is to Tehran in July 1901.
On this occasion, as their previous petitions for protection had not been
successful, they tried sending their petition through the British minister
to Tehran 'as a last resort'. On 4 August 1901 this petition was forwarded
to the prime minister Amin us-Sultan 'in a purely unofficial and private
manner' to present to the shah.[179] An outbreak of cholera, however, threw

179 ZH 8a:159–60; BBR 430–2.

the capital into chaos and the Najafabadis were forced to return, losing five of their number to the disease as they returned.[180]

There were many Najafabadi Baha'is among those who took sanctuary in the Russian Consulate in Isfahan in 1903 (see pp. 38–41) and there was an attack on the Baha'is of Najafabad itself during this episode. It is reported by one source that some Najafabadi Baha'is were killed.[181] One of the Baha'is killed at about this time was Hasan Zaynu'l-'Abidin, who was shot by one of the town ruffians, Isma'il, son of Hasan, at the instigation of Fath-'Ali Khan Yavar. When the Baha'is tried to bury the body, a mob of 2,000 came to the cemetery, intending to burn the body. They seized it but then a Baha'i, Haydar Tupchi (gunner), who belonged to Zill us-Sultan's forces, and another Baha'i, Ni'matu'llah, attacked the mob and dispersed them, allowing the body to be buried. Then the mob counter-attacked and the two Baha'is had to barricade themselves in a shop. The mob was about to bring the house down on top of them when a few government forces arrived and took the two Baha'is to the governor's house, where they were imprisoned for six months.[182]

On about 30 March 1905 Haji Kalb-'Ali, a son-in-law of Haji Haydar, who had already survived one attempt to stab him to death in Isfahan, was shot dead as he returned home. When Zill us-Sultan tried to arrest the murderers, he was prevented by the religious leaders in Najafabad and by Aqa Najafi.[183] It must have been shortly after this that the prime minister of the time, Sultan Majid Mirza 'Ayn ud-Dawlih, refused to accept a petition from the Najafabadis. Since they had already tried presenting their petition through a foreign legation in Tehran, without success, the Najafabadis tried a different ploy. Two of the Baha'is, brothers Aqa 'Ali and Aqa Nasru'llah Janimi, who had gone to Tehran, went on to Ashkhabad where they presented their grievances to the Russian government. They asked that the Russian government take their land in Iran in exchange for land in Russian territories where they could carry on their lives without living in fear of such 'blood-thirsty tyrants' as Aqa Najafi and Zill us-Sultan. The governor of Ashkhabad replied, one suspects from ulterior

180 ZH 8a:159–60; Mudarris Janimi, 'Tarikh Amri Najafabad' 26–7 is presumably referring to the same episode although it dates this to 1322/1904; see also Mudarris, *Tarikh* 98–9.
181 BBR 381, 384.
182 ZH 7:226–7.
183 BBR 432; ZH 8a:156–7. ZH 7: 262 and Mudarris, *Tarikh* 100–1 suggest a date of March 1908 but the evidence of BBR 432 refutes this.

political motives,[184] that the quickest way to bring their plight into prominence and gather support for their cause would be to give interviews to the newspapers. This was done and the reports reached Europe. Muzaffaru'd-Din Shah, who was on his third trip to Europe at this time, was asked about these reports. He immediately telegrammed to Iran that the case of the Baha'is must be settled at once. This gave the Baha'is some temporary relief.[185]

During these years when the Constitutional Revolution occurred, the enemies of the Baha'is in Najafabad accused the Baha'is of supporting the Constitutionalists and thus the Baha'is suffered harassment from the anti-Constitutionalists.[186] Another episode in 1906 saw Haji Haydar go to Tehran to try to seek redress. While he was there, in June 1906, the pressure was building on the shah and Prime Minister 'Ayn ud-Dawlih to grant reforms. Haji Haydar was arrested along with some of the reformers and he was fined 150 *tumans* before being released.[187]

Then in 1909, Fath-'Ali Khan Yavar, having been frustrated so many times before in encompassing the death of Haji Haydar, finally succeeded in his goal. Haji Haydar, realizing that he could never live at peace in Najafabad, had moved to Isfahan, but even here he could not escape the vengeful spirit of Fath-'Ali Khan. As he was riding along the street on 8 November 1909, he was surrounded by five men who shot at him until they had killed him. Although the guilt of Fath-'Ali Khan was known to all and the country was under a new government which was committed to establishing constitutional law, the murderer was in fact protected by Najaf-Quli Khan Samsam us-Saltanih, the Bakhtiyari governor of Isfahan, and his brother, Haji Khusraw Khan Sardar Zafar.[188] Other Baha'is were murdered in Najafabad: Muhammad Ja'far Sabbagh in January 1910 (shot to death near his home as he returned from a Baha'i meeting at night) and, on 20 September 1910, Rajab-'Ali Sarraf.[189]

---

184 For a background to the situation at this time, see Browne, *Persian Revolution* 108–19, esp. 111; the Russian government probably wanted to put pressure on the shah in order to counter British influence.
185 Mudarris Janimi, 'Tarikh Amri Najafabad' 24–6; cf. Mudarris, *Tarikh* 98–9.
186 Mudarris Janimi, 'Tarikh Amri Najafabad' 32.
187 Kirmani, *Tarikh Bidari* 188.
188 BBR 432–4; Mudarris, *Tarikh* 104; ZH 7:267 gives the date as 24 Oct. 1909 but BBR is based on a contemporary telegram.
189 Mudarris, *Tarikh* 100–3; ZH 7:276, 8a:161–2. ZH 7:243 suggests that the murder of Rajab-'Ali occurred in 1907.

Shortly after 1892 'Ammih Bigum (1863–1905), the daughter of Haji Muhammad Baqir and a niece of Zayn ul-Muqarrabin, had started a small traditional school (*maktab*) for both boys and girls and two other women also established *maktabs*, Hajiyyih Khanum Rahmani (c. 1881–1967), and Bibi Jan Makhmurih (c. 1839–1935), who set up her *maktab* in about 1895.[190] In about 1908 the Local Spiritual Assembly of Najafabad decided to construct a building that would act as both a travellers' hospice (*musafir-khanih*) and a modern school. The school was ready in about two years when, in 1328/1910, the Baha'is invited Aqa Mirza Hashim Salmanpur, who was the son-in-law of Shaykh Salman (see p. 246), to come from Isfahan and be the teacher at the school.[191]

The clerics of Najafabad considered the news of the opening of the school as an affront and one day they gathered a mob together in the south of the town to march to the Panj-Jubih quarter and pull the school building down. One of the Baha'is, Mirza Nasru'llah, was working in the local finance office and just at this time a number of the local elders were in his office in connection with paying taxes. When one of his workers came and informed him that a mob was heading towards the school, Mirza Nasru'llah told him in a loud voice to distribute arms among the Baha'is and to tell them to barricade the Baha'i quarter and to fire on the mob if anyone tried to enter. The elders present were sufficiently alarmed by this that they hurried off and dispersed the mob.[192] On the day of 'Ashura (commemoration of the martyrdom of Imam Husayn), the procession of mourners and self-flagellators again tried to enter the Baha'i quarter and attack the school. The Baha'is armed themselves and manned the barricades at the entrance to their quarter. The procession halted and after an hour during which two Baha'is went over and talked with them and offered them drinks and sweets, the rabble returned to their own area of the town.[193]

In 1335/1916 there was a famine throughout the region and times were hard for the Baha'is of Najafabad. The operation of the school was suspended for a time. Then Mirza Fadlu'llah Nuri was asked to come to the town and to be the teacher. Up to this time the Baha'is had been accustomed to burying their dead in the town cemetery according to Muslim customs and rites. Nuri remonstrated with them over this, saying

---

190 Mudarris, *Tarikh* 176–7.
191 Mudarris Janimi, 'Tarikh Amri Najafabad' 28–9.
192 Mudarris, *Tarikh* 108–9.
193 Mudarris, *Tarikh* 109.

that a Baha'i should be buried according to Baha'i law. In January 1917 Haji Kalb-'Ali Kaffash (cobbler), a well-known Baha'i who had visited Baha'u'llah in 'Akka in 1878, died and was buried according to Baha'i rites. After his burial a thousand-strong mob broke into his grave and disinterred his coffin, pulled out the body and re-interred it without the coffin, as is Muslim custom. A few days later Turab Khan, another Baha'i died, and again the mob broke into the grave and pulled out the body, this time intending to burn it. The Baha'is managed to retrieve the body and took it off for safe-keeping elsewhere. Upon hearing this, the clerics of Isfahan issued a *fatwa* forbidding all Muslims from selling goods to or buying them from the Baha'is or allowing Baha'is into the public baths. Instead of defending the Baha'is, the authorities arrested 32 of them and extorted a large amount of money from them. The Baha'is of Najafabad protested to the governor of Isfahan, Akbar Mirza Sarim ud-Dawlih (1885–1975), a son of Zill us-Sultan who was in general favourable to Baha'is and had met 'Abdu'l-Baha in Paris. He freed the imprisoned Baha'is and after negotiations with 'Amu Aqa 'Ali, the nephew of Zayn ul-Muqarrabin and the leader of the Baha'i community, it was decided that the Baha'is should have their own separate cemetery.[194]

In 1337/1918 a young Baha'i called Ni'matu'llah was shot dead with impunity in broad daylight in the bazaar of the town by a group of street ruffians.[195] In July 1924 it was rumoured that on the day of 'Ashura the whole town would rise up against the Baha'is and kill them all. However, with the murder of Major Robert Imbrie in Tehran on 18 July (vol. 1:104), the government instructed that firm steps be taken to prevent any similar problems elsewhere and as a consequence the threat was removed.[196]

Until 1924 the classes of the Baha'i school were held in the Baha'i Travellers' Hospice and only went up to the fourth elementary year. When the Baha'i teacher (*muballigh*) Nuru'd-Din Mumtazi visited Najafabad that year, he persuaded the Baha'is there to build a separate school building to house six classes.[197] In 1928 a girls' school was also built and Thabitih Sadiqi came from Tehran to be its head, while her sister Saniyyih was *nāzim*

194 ZH 8a:164–6; Mudarris Janimi, 'Tarikh Amri Najafabad' 35–7; Mudarris, *Tarikh* 114, 123–4.
195 Mudarris, *Tarikh* 125.
196 Mudarris, *Tarikh* 130. Here the episode is dated Aug. 1922 but I have changed this to 1924 since that was the year of Imbrie's murder.
197 Mudarris, *Tarikh* 137–8.

(administrator).[198] Eventually there was both a boys' school and a girls' school situated next to each other. Each had about 100 to 150 pupils up to the sixth elementary class. A few Muslims also attended the school.[199]

The Baha'is lived mainly in the Panj-Jubih Mahallih (quarter) in the northeast of the town.[200] The name of this quarter, Panj-Jubih (five water channels), refers to the fact that five channels from the *qanat* bringing water to Najafabad went to this quarter, while six went to the neighbouring Shish-Jubih quarter, where a small number of Baha'is also lived.[201] In 1889 the British missionary in Isfahan, Rev. Robert Bruce, who was in close touch with the Baha'is in Najafabad, stated there were 2,000 Baha'is in Najafabad.[202] A Baha'i source gives the population of the town in 1918 as 15,000 inhabitants, of whom 3,500 were Baha'is (i.e. 23 per cent of the population).[203]

Chahar Mahal and Bakhtiyari country

Chahar Mahal is the area (now a separate province) to the southwest of Isfahan over which the Bakhtiyari nomadic tribe roamed. In one of his writings dated April 1882, Baha'u'llah expresses a desire that one of the Baha'is should teach in the Bakhtiyari tribal areas.[204] It is recorded that during the month that Varqa was in prison in Isfahan in about 1883 (see p. 24), his fellow-prisoner was Iskandar Khan Bakhtiyari, son of Husayn-Quli Khan Ilkhani (chief) of the Bakhtiyari tribe, and that he was converted to the Baha'i Faith.[205] Haji Muhammad Ibrahim of Qumishih, who met the Bab in Murchihkhurt and was resident in Isfahan, is described as being a Bakhtiyari. He travelled to 'Akka and became a steward in the household of Baha'u'llah, becoming known as Nazir (supervisor).[206] Apart from this, there were no Baha'is among the Bakhtiyari tribespeople until the

---

198 Mudarris, *Tarikh* 140–2; interview with Servat Mukhtari (daughter of Saniyyih Sadiqi Mukhtari), Bristol, 5 Jan. 2006.
199 Telephone interview Dr Ali Tavangar, 10 Oct. 2004.
200 Mudarris Janimi, 'Tarikh Amri Najafabad' 29; telephone interview with Dr Ali Tavangar, 10 Oct. 2004.
201 Telephone interview Dr Ali Tavangar, 10 Oct. 2004.
202 BBR 283; one report states that the Baha'is of the town claimed there were 5,000 Baha'is there in 1899 (BBR 427) but this is probably an overestimate.
203 KD 1:394.
204 Rafati, *Payk* 96.
205 MH 1:259–62; Malmiri, *Khatirat* 42–3; Varqa, 'Sharh-i Ahval' 23–4; Balyuzi, *Eminent Baha'is* 78–80.
206 ZH 6:191.

time of 'Abdu'l-Baha. Then the Sufi Baha'i Haji Tavangar Qazvini travelled through the Bakhtiyari country and confirmed Iskandar Khan's belief and converted a few others. From that time onwards the number of Baha'is in this area increased and included Mirza Asghar Khazan (1296/1879–1940), a distinguished Bakhtiyari poet, who converted a number of people.[207]

A certain Aqa Hasan of Burujin (120 km south of Isfahan; pop. 3,000 in 1914; 9,383 in 1951) was a travelling salesman of small goods (*pilihvar*). In the course of his travels he was in Shiraz at the time that Aqa Murtada Sarvistani was executed in 1892 for being a Baha'i (see p. 269). This excited his curiosity and so he journeyed on to Sarvistan where he was introduced to the Baha'i Faith by a blind Baha'i and attended a meeting. He then attended more meetings in Abadih and became a Baha'i. He returned to his home town and spoke of the Baha'i Faith to his business partner, Aqa Ghulam-Husayn Asifi (1861–1931). The two of them then went on a selling journey together and, after speaking to the Baha'is in Abadih and Bavanat, Asifi also became a Baha'i. He became a simple but very effective teacher of the Baha'i Faith and succeeded in converting many people in Burujin. His activities caused an uproar among the clerics and he was forced to leave the village. After wandering for a time, he settled in Dastgird (pop. 700 in 1914, 1,505 in 1951; 43 km west of Burujin). Here he remained despite persecution by the clerics and the Bakhtiyari chiefs of the area, and he succeeded in converting many in the area.[208] Aqa Mirza Mahdi (c. 1875–1949), the son of a farmer of Burujin, was a prolific poet with the pen-name Shariq. After spending some time farming, he set off in about 1895 in search of a medical education, going to Isfahan, Khurasan, Ashkhabad and Bukhara. In Ashkhabad he encountered the Baha'i Faith and was converted. He returned to Burujin in 1908 and after a time working as a doctor and dentist there, he passed the state medical examinations in 1932 and was employed by the Ministry of Health in 1935 as the public health officer for the district of Lurdigan (Lurdijan) in Chahar Mahal.[209] Another Baha'i poet of Burujin was Yazdanbakhsh (1874–1930), who had the pen-name Yazdan and was a travelling pedlar

---

207 ZH 8a:143; Dhuka'i-Bayda'i, *Tadhkirih* 2:114–33.
208 MH 8:371–93; two slightly different accounts of the conversion of Aqa Hasan and Asifi are given here, the first from an account compiled by the Baha'i Local Spiritual Assembly of Dastgird dated 1967; and the second as a result of Sulaymani's own investigations in 1971.
209 Dhuka'i-Bayda'i, *Tadhkirih* 2:232–46.

in the area and later a shopkeeper in Burujin.[210]

A tablet of 'Abdu'l-Baha addressed to 13 Baha'is in the town of Burujin in 1920 might indicate a Baha'i population of 120 if these are assumed to be heads of families. In 1967 there were 150 Baha'is in Dastgird.[211] Fadil Mazandarani, writing in the late 1930s, records the number of Baha'is in the Burujin area as being 300 of the 14,000 inhabitants. In the Filard area 70 kilometres south of Burujin, he records 10 Baha'is in the village of Mal-khalifih (pop. 418 in 1955); 35 Baha'is in Amara (pop. 45 in 1955); and 36 Baha'is in Girdab (pop. 126 in 1955).[212]

Qumishih and Talkhunchih

Qumishih (now called Shahrida) is a small town situated on the road from Isfahan to Shiraz (83 km south of Isfahan; pop. 27,215 in 1951). The Baha'i community here dated from the time of the Bab's overnight stay near the town while on his way from Shiraz to Isfahan. Although the clerics of the town had closed the gates and prohibited anyone from contacting the Bab, four of the town's residents – Haji Sabz-'Ali, Haji Amru'llah, Ghulam-Rida and Karbala'i Muhammad Sadri – went out by night, met with the Bab and were converted. Mulla Baqir, the son of the Imam-Jum'ih of Qum-ishih, was converted by Nabil Akbar Qa'ini in Najaf and met Baha'u'llah in Baghdad but did not reside in Qumishih after this.[213] The community is recorded as being weak and few in numbers in the time of 'Abdu'l-Baha but some prominent Baha'is, such as 'Andalib and Haji Tavangar, visited the town and a number of the residents were converted. A Baha'i named Rida-Quli Nikubin of Isfahan was the postmaster in the town from 1918 onwards and through his efforts and those of 'Andalib, Sayyid Muham-mad Baqir Javid (1891–1950), the son of Mirza Hasan Maftun Sayyid ul-Mashayikh, a Sufi shaykh, became a Baha'i in 1919 and his wife Qamar Sultan Javid (d. 1984) became one shortly afterwards.[214]

---

210 Dhuka'i-Bayda'i, *Tadhkirih* 4:392–7.
211 MH 8:384, citing report of Baha'i Local Spiritual Assembly of Dastgird.
212 ZH 8a:147.
213 Balyuzi, *Baha'u'llah* 135–6.
214 ZH 8a:168; Sadiqzadih, Nufudh va Paydayish Amr dar Shahrida, 15–33. Accord-ing to a letter dated 27 Aug. 1950 from Muhammad 'Ali 'Aqda'i, secretary of the Local Assembly of Qumishih/Shahrida, there were only three residents who went out to meet the Bab: Karbala'i Muhammad, Ghulam-Rida and Asadu'llah; quoted in Labib, Majmu'ih-yi Musavvar 373–7.

34. Walls and gate of Qumishih

A large village in the vicinity of Qumishih is Talkhunchih (40 km northwest of Qumishih; pop. 5,714 in 1951). Mulla Kazim was one of the clerics of this village who had studied in Isfahan, had reached the status of *mujtahid* and was residing in the Madrasih Gul-Bahar of Isfahan. He and a number of his fellow students had become Babis (see pp. 7–8), in his case through contact with Sayyid 'Abdu'r-Rahim in about 1870. Mulla Kazim had, however, been so enthusiastic in spreading his new beliefs that a complaint was made about him to Shaykh Muhammad Baqir, who issued a decree for his death. Mulla Kazim was forced to leave Isfahan for his home village for a time. When he returned to Isfahan, he was arrested in the 1874 persecution of the Baha'is (see pp. 15–16). After this Mulla Kazim went to Shiraz and then to the Madrasih Dar ush-Shafa in Tehran for a time. At the end of 1877 Mulla Kazim returned to Talkhunchih where he debated the truth of the Baha'i Faith with Sayyid Husayn Mujtahid and other religious leaders of the village. Eventually these religious leaders complained to Shaykh Muhammad Baqir in Isfahan and he induced Zill us-Sultan to send officials to arrest Mulla Kazim. He was arrested together with another Baha'i, Sayyid Aqa Jan, and taken to Isfahan. Here Mulla

Kazim was brought before Shaykh Muhammad Baqir. It appears that the latter taunted Mulla Kazim by stating that there was no mention of the Bab and Baha'u'llah in the Qur'an, to which Mulla Kazim replied that there was equally no mention of Muhammad in the Gospels. Enraged, Shaykh Muhammad Baqir demanded Mulla Kazim's execution from Zill us-Sultan. Mulla Kazim was eventually executed in public, while Sayyid Aqa Jan was beaten severely and his ears were cut off.[215] Although various dates have been given, it is likely that this execution occurred on 13 February 1879.[216] Another cleric from this village, Mulla Salih, was a Baha'i who ran a traditional school (*maktab*) in Isfahan. On one occasion, probably in about 1903, he was beaten severely by a mob and had to leave the town for a time.[217]

Sometime, towards the end of the 19th century, the Baha'i Faith spread to Dihaqan (18 km west of Qumishih, pop. 7,000 in 1951) when a Baha'i visited the village and left two Baha'i books with his host, Haji Hashim, who subsequently became a Baha'i. He was opposed, however, by the people of the village and even by his own family and it was not until decades later that a Baha'i travelling teacher came to the village and two individuals became Baha'is, Ni'matu'llah Mithaqi and Hidayatu'llah Agah. Further conversions followed and by the 1920s there were about 40 Baha'is in the village.[218]

---

215 Nicolas, *Massacre des Babis* 15–18; BBR 273–4; Ishraq-Khavari, *Nurayn* 218–21; Bassett, *Persia* 51–2; Tarikh Amri Isfahan 12–16; Nur, Tarikh Isfahan 9; B. Agah, 'Sharh-i Ahval' 189. Mazandarani (ZH 8a:505) appears to confuse Sayyid Aqa Jan of Talkhunchih who had his ears cut off in this episode with the Azali Mulla Isma'il Sabbagh of Sidih, who also had his ears cut off and took the name Mulla Mustafa (see p. 49). Charles Wills (*Land of the Lion and Sun* 154) who was in Isfahan at this time and saw Mulla Kazim being led to prison, states that Mulla Kazim was betrayed by his wife.

216 ZH 5:241; Ishraq-Khavari, *Nurayn* 219. Wills (*Land of the Lion and Sun* 154) who was in Isfahan suggests a similar date, stating that it was only a few days after this execution that the Nahri brothers were arrested; see p. 21). Nicolas gives a date of December 1877 (*Massacres* 17) but this seems unlikely as Shaykh Muhammad Baqir was in Khurasan until at least November 1877 (vol. 1:156–7). ZH 6:286 gives the date of this event as 1295, which began on 5 January 1878. Browne states that Mirza Yahya Azal claimed that Mulla Kazim was an Azali (['Abdu'l-Baha], *Traveller's Narrative* 400). This is refuted not only by Baha'i historians but also in the account by Nicolas, who was in Isfahan a few years after Mulla Kazim's execution. Nicolas's account concludes with a tablet from Baha'u'llah in honour of Mulla Kazim (Nicolas, *Massacres de Babis* 17).

217 Ishraq-Khavari, *Nurayn* 225–6.

218 Memoire by Maryam Mithaqi and oral interview by telephone with Dr Amanu'llah Missaghi on 11 April 2020.

11

KASHAN

The province of Kashan is situated south of Tehran and Qumm and north of Isfahan on the central plain of Iran to the west of the central desert (Dasht-i Kavir). The climate is dry and agriculture dependent on irrigation. In the 19th century, tobacco and cotton were the main crops. The area also had numerous mulberry trees for the production of silk. Qumm was sometimes part of this province and sometimes a separate one; it is considered in volume one of this book. Ardistan is included in this province although it was sometimes part of Yazd and sometimes part of Isfahan. (See map at Frontispiece 2.)

Kashan

The city of Kashan lies some 200 kilometres south of Tehran, in the centre of Iran at the place where the road from Tehran divides with one branch going towards Isfahan and the other to Yazd. Its population was estimated to be 30,000 in 1850,[1] 30,000 in 1905 and 46,000 in 1956. It is on the high plateau that occupies most of central Iran and at the western edge of the country's great central desert. The city of Kashan was famous for its

---

1   Abbot in Amanat, *Cities and Trade* 75, 121; Comte Sercy, the French envoy in 1839–40, also gives a figure of 30,000 (cited in Naraqi, *Tarikh Ijtima'i-yi Kashan* 253); Thompson (1868, in Issawi, *Economic History* 28), however, gives only 10,000.

brass and copper wares, its earthenware and decorative mosaics (which are known in Persian as *kāshī* after the town) and was also a centre of silk and velvet manufacture. In 1889 Lord Curzon described it as 'one of the most dilapidated cities in Persia. A more funereal place I have not yet seen. Scarcely a building was in repair, barely a wall intact.'[2]

The Babi period

The message of the Bab was first brought to Kashan in 1844 by Mulla Husayn Bushru'i. The Bab stayed in the town for three days (20–3 March 1847) as a guest of Haji Mirza Jani. A strong Babi community grew up here. During the 1850s, when the Babi community in most towns had still not fully recovered from the persecutions of 1848–52, Kashan was a leading centre of Babi activity. The most learned and one of the most active in propagating the new religion in the area was Mulla Ja'far Naraqi, who was a respected religious leader and teacher in Kashan and Naraq. He became a Babi and was soon well known as such (for more details on him see under Naraq below).[3]

Perhaps because it was such an active community at this time, Kashan was the scene of major struggles for the leadership of the Babi movement following the execution of the Bab in 1850. Sayyid Basir Hindi arrived in Kashan in June 1851, and Shaykh 'Ali 'Azim arrived at about the same time. They had clashed in Tehran over the leadership of the Babi community and they did so again in Kashan. In a letter written to his brother Haji Muhammad Isma'il Dhabih in Najaf, Haji Mirza Jani in Kashan states that Basir laid claim to the 'station of the Husayni secret (*maqām-i sirr-i Ḥusaynī*, i.e. to be the return of the Imam Husayn)' and was entering ecstatic trances and revealing verses. Then 'Azim arrived uttering words of anger and Haji Mirza Jani tried to mediate between the two. Eventually, after five months, 'Azim returned to Tehran and calm returned. Following this, Basir and Haji Mirza Jani went to Isfahan (see p. 3). After their return, Haji Mirza Jani accompanied Basir to Sultanabad.[4] Some years

---

2   Curzon, *Persia* 2:14–15.
3   Bamdad, *Tarikh* 6:219–22.
4   Afnan, *'Ahd-i A'la* 480, 483–4, 543; [Kashani], *Nuqtatu'l-Kaf* 258–60 (trans-
      lated in Hamadani, *New History* 390–3). It may be that the main confronta-
      tion between 'Azim and Basir in Tehran (vol. 1:6) in fact occurred in Kashan.
      However, it is likely that there was a clash in Tehran since Haji Mirza Jani's letter
      confirms that Basir had put forward his claim in Tehran prior to his arrival in

later another leading Babi, Mulla Hashim Kashani (Naraqi), put forward a claim to be 'He whom God shall make manifest', promised by the Bab, but he later visited Baghdad and withdrew his claim in favour of Baha'u'llah.[5] Haji Mirza Musa Qummi and Nabil Zarandi also promulgated their claims to be 'He whom God shall make manifest' in Kashan and Naraq before later withdrawing them in favour of Baha'u'llah.[6]

When the Babi leadership was centred in Baghdad in the 1850s, a large number of Kashanis went to that city. Some stayed on while others returned. Owing to this close connection with Baghdad, the consequences of the schism between Baha'u'llah and Azal manifested themselves earlier in Kashan than elsewhere. Indeed, it would appear that there was already a split among the Kashanis even before the division between Baha'u'llah and Azal had come into the open (which did not occur until the Edirne period). Mulla Ja'far was a strong supporter of the leadership of Azal and he encouraged many of the most active Babis in the Kashan area to visit Baghdad and meet him. He was, however, let down by the fact that when these people went to Baghdad, Azal refused to see them and once they had met Baha'u'llah and read his writings, they returned as his adherents. The first of those to whom this occurred was Haji Mirza Kamalu'd-Din Naraqi (see below under Naraq). This also happened, however, to Aqa Muhammad Hasan and to Haji Muhammad Yazdi, whom Mulla Ja'far sent to Baghdad with letters of recommendation to Azal but who returned saying, 'no one other than *Ishān* (Baha'u'llah) is the centre of this Cause'.[7] Similarly, Aqa Muhammad 'Ali Pushtibaf or Makhmalbaf (velvet-maker, d. 1315/1897) and Aqa Sha'ban-'Ali Charmibaf (Pushtibaf, who was known as 'Amu Sha'ban and as the 'Gabriel of the Babis' and who suffered a great deal of persecution, d. 1327/1909[8]) were sent to Baghdad by Mulla Ja'far to see Azal but were refused an audience. They then met Baha'u'llah and returned to Kashan determined to counter the efforts of Mulla Ja'far. Aqa

Kashan and 'Azim appears to have followed Bashir to Kashan and was angry on arrival. Haji Mirza Jani wrote a history of the Babi religion shortly before his execution in Tehran in 1852. E.G. Browne published *Nuqtatu'l-Kaf* as this history of Haji Mirza Jani. However this attribution is doubtful, see p. 180, n. 6; Balyuzi, *Browne* 62–88; and BBR 34n.

5 Natiq Isfahani, 'Tarikh Amri Kashan' 2, 4–5; ZH 4:24, 192; Balyuzi, *Baha'u'llah* 131.
6 ZH 4:179–80.
7 Natiq Isfahani, 'Tarikh Amri Kashan' 6–7. *Ishān* is a term of respect.
8 ZH 6:652–4; Rayhani in Amanat, 'Negotiating Identities' 297–8; Amanat, *Kashan* 48–9.

Muhammad 'Ali, in particular, met with the remaining Babis of Kashan and persuaded them of the truth of Baha'u'llah. He became known, however, as a Baha'i, and although he was a wealthy and prominent individual in the town, owning a factory for making velvet with designs on it and being connected with the government, he was subject to persecution, being imprisoned on one occasion and, on another, having his house stoned by a mob, incited by a preacher named Sayyid Hasan. He spent a year and half in hiding and eventually was forced to move to Tehran in about 1886. He was the progenitor of the Majidi family.[9] Another early Babi who visited Baha'u'llah in Baghdad and then became one of the pillars of the Babi, and later the Baha'i, community was Aqa Husayn 'Amu Zaynal.[10]

Shams-i Jahan Khanum of Tehran (vol. 1:32–3) stayed two months in Kashan in about 1858 on her way back from Baghdad, where she had become a follower of Baha'u'llah. She reports that the only two persons she met in the Kashan area who were, like her, followers of Baha'u'llah, were Kamalu'd-Din Naraqi and 'Ibrahim', who had written poetry about Baha'u'llah. This would seem to indicate that the other five mentioned above (apart from Kamalu'd-Din Naraqi) who journeyed to Baghdad and became followers of Baha'u'llah, did so after about 1858. The 'Ibrahim' that Shams-i Jahan mentions is almost certainly Mirza Muhammad Ibrahim Kashani, who was given the name Khalil by Baha'u'llah and wrote poetry under the pen-name of Mansur. He had visited Baghdad and then returned to Kashan. Later he returned to Baghdad with his family and was among the exiles from Baghdad to Mosul. After his release from there, he went to 'Akka. Baha'u'llah instructed him to move to Haifa and set up as a coppersmith there, in order to look after the pilgrims who came from Iran and to act as a centre of communications.[11] There was another Muhammad Ibrahim of Kashan who moved to Baghdad and accompanied Baha'u'llah

---

9   ZH 6:651–4; 8a:383; Amanat, *Kashan* 298–9.
10   Amanat, *Kashan* 270–1. The disagreements between followers of Baha'u'llah and Azal in Kashan during this time became so heated that Baha'u'llah forbade Kashani Babis coming to Baghdad for a period of two years in order to calm the atmosphere, ZH 4:197–8.
11   'Abdu'l-Baha, *Memorials* 81–2; Dhuka'i-Bayda'i, *Tadhkirih* 3:173, 192, 341–52; ZH 6: 662–3. Dhuka'i-Bayda'i believes that this man is the Ibrahim mentioned by Shams-i Jahan Khanum. It may, however, be that she was referring to a Muhammad Ibrahim 'Arab, who is reported to have started to compose poetry after visiting Baha'u'llah in Baghdad (Amanat, *Kashan* 48), but it would appear that his visit to Baghdad was after 1861 and so too late to have been the person whom Shams-i Jahan met.

in all stages of his exile. He was called Muhammad Ibrahim Nazir Kashani (d. 1920) but he is unlikely to be the person indicated by Shams Jahan as he is not mentioned as having been a poet.[12] Other Babis who moved to Baghdad and subsequently were companions-in-exile of Baha'u'llah were Mirza Mahmud Kashani (d. 1912, see fig. 95), who moved to Baghdad in about 1858, and Mirza Husayn Ashchi (d. 1927, see fig. 36).[13]

36. Aqa Husayn Ashchi Kashani

Many other Babis travelled to Baghdad during this period,[14] including Mirza Mahdi Kashani (in 1861) whose sister, Gawhar Khanum, became the third wife of Baha'u'llah. Their father, Mirza Ahmad Rawdih-khan, was known as Mirza Ahmad Chap on account of having been the first person to bring a printing press to Kashan. Mirza Mahdi remained in Baghdad copying the writings of Baha'u'llah in his excellent calligraphy. He and his sister stayed in Baghdad when Baha'u'llah left and they were among the Babis exiled to Mosul in 1868. When Midhat Pasha passed through Mosul in 1869, however, he freed them and they went to 'Akka.[15]

---

12 'Abdu'l-Baha, *Memorials* 94–5. He should not be confused with another individual with the title 'Nazir' who was resident in 'Akka: Haji Mirza Abu'l-Qasim Nazir Isfahani (see fig. 95), who had held some minor governorships in Iran, such as Miyandu'ab where he became a Baha'i (vol. 1:416). He then lived for seven years in 'Akka and was sent on missions to India in 1884–5 (with Mirza Muhammad 'Ali Ghusn-i Akbar, see Momen, 'Jamal Effendi' 57–9) and to Istanbul in 1888–9 (see Balyuzi, *Baha'u'llah* 396–8). In the time of 'Abdu'l-Baha, however, he refused to cut his links with Mirza Muhammad 'Ali and was expelled from the Baha'i community. He then returned to Tehran.

13 'Abdu'l-Baha, *Memorials* 39–41; Kashani wrote a treatise of 142 pages in support of 'Abdu'l-Baha and refutation of Mirza Muhammad 'Ali; Anonymous, 'Risalih-yi Istidlaliyyih-ye Aqa Mirza Mahmud Kashani'.

14 Natiq Isfahani (Tarikh Amri Kashan 6–10) lists five who travelled in 1860 and the names of some 12 others; however, ZH 6:624–95 lists many more than this and Amanat, (*Kashan*, 47) lists 61.

15 ZH 5:514–15 and n. On Gawhar Khanum, see Maani, *Leaves* 251–8.

37. 'Isa Khan Biglarbigi, governor of Kashan

The beginning of the Baha'i Faith in Kashan

It was probably Haji Amin who first brought news of Baha'u'llah's claim to Kashan, although Munib (see pp. 92–3) and Nabil Zarandi passed through Kashan at this time (the latter in about December 1866) and may also have been instrumental in this. Some families were divided by the split between Baha'u-'llah and Azal. Haji Mirza Jani, who was the host of the Bab during the latter's stay in Kashan, was among the Babis executed in 1852. His brother Haji Muhammad Isma'il became an ardent follower of Baha'u'llah; while another brother, Mirza Ahmad Kashani, followed Azal (see p. 95). After Mulla Ja'far was expelled from the Kashan-Naraq area (see p. 123) and other followers of Azal such as Mirza Ahmad had also left, there is little further mention of an Azali presence in the area.

During the early years of the reign of Nasiru'd-Din Shah after the fall of Mirza Taqi Khan Amir Kabir, Kashan fell into lawlessness. One reason for this was that the Prime Minister, Mirza Aqa Khan Nuri, had been exiled in Kashan for almost three years during the reign of Muhammad Shah. When he subsequently came to power, a number of the notables of Kashan, who had become his close friends during his exile, felt that they had *carte blanche* to do whatever they liked in the town. The townspeople were at the mercy of whoever could assert his power, whether from among the local notables or from the street louts and roughs. Occasionally matters would become so grave that a force of soldiers would be sent from Tehran to restore order but they would return after a short time and the situation in Kashan would revert to its former condition. This state of affairs continued even after the downfall of Mirza Aqa Khan Nuri.[16]

---

16 Naraqi, *Kashan dar Junbish Mashrutih* 16–17; Khusravi, *Tughyan-i Nayib-bin* 77; Darrabi (*Tarikh Kashan* 244) also alludes to this state of affairs.

In 1279/1862 there was an outburst of persecution of the Babis when some of the local religious leaders pressed the governor of the town, 'Isa Khan Biglarbigi (see fig. 37), to arrest a number of the town's leading Babis. These Babis were beaten, fined, imprisoned and their houses looted. Five of them, including Haji Muhammad Isma'il Dhabih, were then marched to Tehran in chains and imprisoned. Two of these, Pahlavan Rida and Aqa Muhammad Ibrahim Hamami, died in prison in Tehran (vol. 1:11–12 and n).[17]

Mulla Muhammad Mujtahid Naraqi (1215/1800–1297/Jan. 1880) was head of the Madrasih Sultani and son of one of the leading clerics of the reign of Fath-'Ali Shah, Mulla Ahmad Naraqi.[18] He had met Mulla Husayn Bushru'i in 1844[19] and was the uncle of the above-mentioned Babi, Haji Mirza Kamalu'd-Din Naraqi. He was not himself a Babi or Baha'i but he did protect this community on some occasions. In 1287/1870, however, Mulla Muhammad fell out with some of his Babi neighbours. He wanted to extend his own property, and in order to put pressure on his neighbours, he began to denounce them as Babis. The son of this Babi household, who became known as Shah Mirza, went to Naraqi and argued with him over his actions. Naraqi ordered the young man seized and bastinadoed severely. When the young man's mother came to protest this, he cursed her and denounced her as a Babi also.

The persecution of his family reached a point at which Shah Mirza felt he had little recourse but to rise in armed rebellion. It appears that he was probably already a leader of one of the factions in the town[20] and he soon had a large number of people following him, helped no doubt by the severe famine that raged throughout Iran shortly after his rebellion began, reducing people to desperation. Shah Mirza seized government property

---

17 Natiq Isfahani, Tarikh Amri Kashan 10–12; Malik-Khusravi, *Tarikh* 3:349–50; ZH 4: 247–8, 6:626 dates this event as 1278/1861.

18 Farrukhyar, *Mashahir-i Kashan* 172–3; Habibabadi, *Makarim* 2:555–6.

19 Mulla Husayn Bushru'i, as he passed through Kashan, met Mulla Muhammad Naraqi but was unable to convince him of the truth of the Bab's claim. Sipihr, *Nasikh ut-Tavarikh* (1:1011) states that Mulla Muhammad was hostile to the message brought by Bushru'i but Baha'i sources indicate that his feelings were mixed (ZH 6:678).

20 Naraqi, *Kashan dar Junbish Mashrutih* 18, names him as a leader of one of the street gangs (*luti-gari*) that was suppressed in 1280/1863 by Muhammad 'Ali Khan Musaddiq ud-Dawlih Ghaffari. Khusravi, *Tughyan-i Nayibbin* 99, describes him as a veteran rebel leader in 1285/1868 (see also p. 77). On *luti-gari*, see Floor, 'The lutis'.

and taxes (including the tax of the province of Fars that was being taken through Kashan to Tehran), gave a receipt for it in his name and distributed it among his followers. Although this rebellion had little to do with the Babis (apart from a number of his relatives, Shah Mirza's followers were Muslim townspeople), it was reported to the shah that several thousand Babis had come out in rebellion in Kashan and that they might even attack Tehran. So the shah sent Mustafa-Quli Khan Saham us-Saltanih, who was the commander of the 'Arab tribal levy and was responsible for the security of the roads between Yazd, Kashan and Isfahan, against the rebels.[21] The latter brought his men from Isfahan to Kashan and established a base there to begin operations against the rebels. Many of the town's criminal elements (*ashrār va awbāsh*) were recruited to his forces and were thus able to continue their criminal activities but now under government protection. They extorted money from anyone they could under the pretext of gathering government or religious taxes, and when someone died they would invade the deceased's house and effectively loot it.[22] Saham us-Saltanih was a great enemy of the Babis and Baha'is (see p. 125 and pp. 130–1). Because he had been told that the rebels were Babis, he began by seeking out the Babis of the area. He descended on Mazgan and arrested Shaykh Abu'l-Qasim Mazgani (see pp. 130–1), accusing him of assisting the rebels, and looted the houses of the Babis of that village and of Qamsar.[23]

At this point, Haji Mirza 'Ali Akbar Naraqi, who had returned to the area from having met Baha'u'llah at 'Akka, and some other Baha'is met with Shah Mirza. They spoke to him about Baha'u'llah and how Shah Mirza's actions of armed rebellion were against the new teachings now being promulgated by Baha'u'llah.[24] Shah Mirza was persuaded to end his rebellion and disperse his followers. Shah Mirza himself left town but some of his followers were arrested and punished. Saham us-Saltanih, having failed to capture Shah Mirza, turned his attention to the Babis and Baha'is

---

21 ZH 5:136–9. Mustafa Quli Khan 'Arab 'Amiri Saham us-Saltanih (d. Tehran, 1306/1888) was from Ardistan and was governor of Yazd (in 1304/1886) and Kashan as well as having military command of the roads between Yazd, Kashan and Isfahan. He was a wealthy landowner and noted for his cruelty and tyranny (Bamdad, *Tarikh* 4:117). He and his sons, Intizam ul-Mulk and Husayn Khan Saham us-Saltanih, were great enemies of the Baha'is (ZH 5:142n).

22 Naraqi, *Kashan dar Junbish Mashrutih* 23.

23 ZH 5:139–40; Amanat *Kashan* 37–8.

24 ZH 6:685; for the instructions Baha'u'llah sent regarding this matter, see Mazandarani, *Asrar* 4:186–7.

of Naraq, arrested 17 of them and led them off to Tehran for execution (see pp. 125–6).[25]

In 1874 there was a famine in Kashan. About this time there was an upsurge in Baha'i activities in Kashan because the Baha'is there heard of the efforts of Sayyid Jamal Burujirdi to bring the teachings of the Baha'i Faith to the attention of the shah. This resulted in a general movement against the Baha'is and some 24 of them fled to Tehran. They went first to the village of Sansan, where a local notable, Aqa Muhammad Big, was a Baha'i and he helped them to get to Tehran. Aqa Sayyid 'Ali Ursi-duz (shoe-maker) was, however, captured and taken before Mulla Muhammad Mujtahid Naraqi, who told them to let the man go. They took him home but beat him and looted his house. Aqa Sayyid 'Ali and five other Baha'is were then arrested by the governor Mirza Humayun, taken to Tehran where they languished in prison for three and a half years before being set free.[26] Those Baha'is of Kashan who were already in Tehran tried to make an appeal to the shah regarding the prisoners and were also imprisoned until the end of the year, when all the Kashani prisoners were freed (vol. 1:21–3).[27]

Haji Mirza Haydar 'Ali Isfahani writes that when he visited Kashan in the 1880s he found that the Baha'is were very poor because many of them were weavers by trade and at that time the market for hand-woven cloth was very weak. This was partly because more European cloth was being imported and partly because demand changed from the more expensive, higher quality velvet (*makhmal-bāf*) that was woven in Kashan to a cheaper cloth (*mishgī-bāf*) that was woven by the tribal peoples.[28] He states that nevertheless the Baha'is were united and helped each other and the destitute. He describes in particular Haji Ghulam-'Ali Mari (c. 1839–1351/1936), a

---

25 Although the Baha'i sources seem to indicate that the rebellion of Shah Mirza lasted only a short time after it began in 1870, there are indications that it went on for some six or more years. In accounts of the rebellion in ZH 5:136–8, there are references to the famine in the area which occurred in 1874 and to the appropriation by Shah Mirza of taxes that were sent from Fars by Mu'tamad ud-Dawlih, who became governor of Fars in 1876.

26 Natiq Isfahani, Tarikh Amri Kashan 12 and ZH 5:209–10 and 6:667 give the date of this episode as 1290/1873. However the existence of a report from the French minister Mellinot establishes the date of this episode as 1874, BBR 255–6. This report states that a dozen Babis had been arrested and may also refer to the arrest of some Baha'is of Naraq at this time (see previous paragraph).

27 ZH 5:210–12, BBR 225–6.

28 Naraqi, *Tarikh Ijtima'i* 275–7.

simple weaver who was skilled at teaching the Baha'i Faith using humour and analogies and whose house in the Sar-Pullih quarter was a place where Baha'is and enquirers met in the evenings and visiting Baha'is were lodged. He also visited the villages around Kashan as a *rawdih-khan*, successfully teaching the Baha'i Faith. He moved to Tehran in later years and is the progenitor of the Makhmalbaf family.[29]

There was another family who took the surname Makhmalbaf. They were the descendants of two brothers, Sayyid Baqir and Sayyid Rida. These two brothers decided to take it in turn to perform the pilgrimage to the shrines in Iraq. First Sayyid Rida went and on the way back he visited Baghdad where he met Baha'u'llah and became a Babi. Unknown to him, in the meanwhile, his brother, left behind in Kashan, had become a Babi also. When Sayyid Rida returned home each brother tried, gradually and with great caution, to make the other aware of the new religion until they suddenly realized what had happened. Sayyid Baqir's daughter Bisharat Khanum was a devoted Baha'i. She not only guided her Muslim husband, Mirza Husayn 'Ala'i, to the Baha'i Faith by arranging for Baha'i teachers to talk to him, but also helped him give up his addictions. When her husband was dismissed from his government position because of his faith, she took on various menial occupations to provide for the family. Out of this meagre income, she saved sufficient to send small amounts of money regularly to the Baha'i leadership. When she died about a kilogram of receipts for donations to Baha'i funds, some for only pennies, was found among her effects.[30]

Although Mulla Muhammad Naraqi was to some extent protective of the Baha'is, after his death in January 1880 religious leadership in Kashan fell into the hands of clerics such Mulla Habibu'llah Darvazih-Isfahani (c. 1262/1846–1922, who had been a Babi and had reverted to Islam as a result of persecution and a beating he received at the hands of Sayyid Husayn Mujtahid Kashani),[31] and Mirza Fakhru'd-Din

---

29   Isfahani, *Bihjat* 192 (trans. *Delight* 96–7); ZH 8b:665; Amanat, *Kashan* 284–8.
30   Amanat, *Kashan* 301–4.
31   Rayhani in Amanat, 'Negotiating Identities' 252. For the date of death I am here assuming this Mulla Habibu'llah was Mulla Habibu'llah ibn 'Ali Madad Kashani (Farrukhyar, *Mashahir-i Kashan* 75–7 and Tihrani, *adh-Dhari'ah* 7:271), who wrote a refutation of the Babi religion in 1867 entitled *Rujum ush-Shayatin fi Radd ul-Mala'in* (*adh-Dhari'ah* 10:164, no. 305). However there also appears to have been a Mulla Habibu'llah Mujtahid in Kashan in 1903–20 who was friendly towards the Baha'is; see Dhuka'i-Bayda'i, *Tadhkirih* 1:242–3, 4:39n and MH 4:253–4, 442. This may have been a different individual or it could be the same person who changed his attitude (note that as late as 1906, a Mulla

Naraqi[32] (given name Abu'l-Qasim, 1252/1836–1319/1901), who was a son of Mulla Muhammad Naraqi. These two *mujtahids* were inimical to the Baha'is.

In late 1881 Mirza Asadu'llah Isfahani visited the town, urging the Baha'is to adopt the practice of paying Huququ'llah. While he was there a tablet from Baha'u'llah came for him encouraging the Baha'is to adopt the practice of consultation. Following the receipt of this, Isfahani gathered nine prominent local Baha'is to form an assembly of consultation, as ordained in the verses of the Kitab-i Aqdas relating to Houses of Justice being established in each locality, and urged that all community affairs should be referred to this body.[33]

In 1882 one of the clerics of the town began to harass two of the Baha'is, Aqa Muhammad Ja'far and Aqa Muhammad Hashim, mainly in the expectation of monetary gain. He tried to get the former expelled from the town, and when this did not succeed, he went to the governor Muhammad Hasan Khan Anis ud-Dawlih and said that these two owed him money, that they were 'Babis' and should be arrested. Muhammad Ja'far and his sons went into hiding but Muhammad Hashim was arrested. The wife of the latter went bravely before the governor and said that if Mulla Baqir could show evidence of a debt, they would gladly repay it but, when summoned, Mulla Baqir could not do this. The governor ordered Aqa Muhammad Hashim released but said that unless he recanted his faith within the next 24 hours, he would be expelled from the town, and so he left for Isfahan.[34]

Apart from the Haji Mirza Jani mentioned above, there was another Haji Mirza Jani (called Kuchik – junior – to differentiate him from the above-mentioned man, who was called Buzurg – senior) who became a Babi and subsequently a Baha'i. He was the head of a top-ranking Kashan merchant family called the Tabrizis (because they originally hailed from that town).[35] A generation later, the head of the family, Haji Muhammad Husayn Turk (Lutf), visited Baha'u'llah in 'Akka and upon his return in spring 1886, Mulla Habibu'llah, without even enquiring into the matter or questioning him, raised a storm about this, declaring him an unbeliever

---

Habibu'llah was persecuting Baha'is; see under Qamsar).
32 Farrukhyar, *Mashahir-i Kashan* 173–4.
33 Asadu'llah Isfahani, Yad-dasht-ha 72. This body does not appear to have continued for long.
34 Asadu'llah Isfahani, Yad-dasht-ha 104–6.
35 See Darrabi, *Tarikh Kashan* 236.

38. Mirza Mahdi Khan Vazir Humayun   39. Mirza Aqa Jan Khadimu'llah (Katib)
            Ghaffari

and proclaiming a *jihad*. A report was sent to the shah and Haji Muhammad
Husayn also went to Tehran to put his case. The shah, knowing such clerics
well, gave Haji Muhammad Husayn a cloak of honour and the title Amin
ut-Tujjar and ordered that Mulla Habibu'llah be reprimanded and expelled
from Kashan. The deputy governor of Kashan was sympathetic to the cleric
and, on his advice, urged the clerics of Kashan to send petitions to the shah
to allow Mulla Habibu'llah to stay; petitions which the shah granted. In later
years, Haji Muhammad Husayn was chairman of the Baha'i Local Assembly
of Kashan.[36] Another prominent citizen of Kashan who became a Baha'i was
Sayyid Muhammad Saray-dar (owner of a caravanserai).[37]

Mirza Mahdi Khan Vazir Humayun Ghaffari (Qa'im-Maqam, Vazir
Makhsus, Ajudan Makhsus, 1282/1865 – 1336/1917, see fig. 38), the son
of Farrukh Khan Amin ud-Dawlih Minister of Court (d. 1288/1871), was
closely connected to the courts of three successive shahs, Nasiru'd-Din,
Muzaffaru'd-Din and Muhammad 'Ali. He was a courtier and had the ability
to make people laugh by his clowning and jokes. He was at court from the

36   Gulpaygani, *Kashf ul-Ghita* 42–4; Gulpaygani, *Rasa'il* 90–1; the author was in
     Kashan at this time and a witness to these events. See also Rayhani (in Amanat,
     'Negotiating Identities' 162–3, 303–6) who says that Muhammad Husayn was
     being harassed by another merchant and this is what caused him to go to Tehran
     and obtain the title of Amin ut-Tujjar.
37   Rayhani in Amanat, 'Negotiating Identities' 228 and n.

age of 13 and in 1305/1887 was made Nasiru'd-Din Shah's private secretary. The following year he accompanied the shah on his tour of Europe and in 1893 he was given responsibility for dealing with the debts of the Royal Bank, which he dealt with very efficiently. In 1898 he was put in charge of the post office. He was implicated in a plot against the government in 1901 and exiled but returned in 1902 and accompanied Muzaffaru'd-Din Shah to Europe in that year. From 1903 he was governor of Zanjan. During this time he was hostile to the Baha'is (on one occasion, he sent officials to Jasb to beat Mulla Ghulam-Rida and Aqa Mir Jasbi) but he stood up to the clerics and started a modern school in Zanjan. He became a Baha'i while governor of Sultanabad in 1322/1904 through Haji Mu'nis Qazvini (see fig. 84 and vol. 1:486), Haji Tavangar and Mulla Mirza Aqa Taliqani. There is a difference of opinion as to whether he supported or opposed the Constitutional Movement but it is said that he was instrumental in getting Muzaffaru'd-Din Shah to sign the Constitution. He then retired to his house in Vadqan, near Kashan, where he became very bold in his open advocacy of the Baha'i Faith. He was advised by 'Abdu'l-Baha to be cautious. However, after a time he came to Tehran and again began to teach the Baha'i Faith openly. When he left to visit 'Abdu'l-Baha in Egypt in early 1910 this fact was announced in the newspapers.[38] When this news reached his family, his mother sent his older brother, Abu'l-Qasim Khan Mukhtar us-Saltanih (Nasir Khaqan, d. sometime between 1914 and 1917), in pursuit to prevent the visit and save the family's honour. Thus Mukhtar us-Saltanih met 'Abdu'l-Baha in Ramleh and became a Baha'i there (on their mother, Ashraf ud-Dawlih, see p. 141).[39]

Important Kashani Baha'is outside Kashan

A number of Baha'is of Kashan played an important role in Baha'i history but not in Kashan itself. These include Mirza Aqa Jan Khadimu'llah (original name 'Abdu'llah; d. Muharram 1319/May 1901, see fig. 39), who was

---

38   KD 2:181–3; Rastigar, *Sadr us-Sudur* 30–1; Balyuzi, *Baha'u'llah* 290n; Bamdad 4:172–5; *Sharafat*, no. 39 (Rajab 1317) 1–4; Darrabi, *Tarikh Kashan* 542; Churchill, *Persian Statesmen and Notables* 88; MH 9:315; Khoshbin, *Taraz Ilahi*, 1:339–41; MH 9:315; Isfahani, *Bihjat* 331–2; Rayhani in Amanat, 'Negotiating Identities' 298–9 and n, 300–3; Amanat, *Kashan* 276–8. 'Abdu'l-Baha writes of him in *Makatib* 3:429.

39   Khoshbin, *Taraz Ilahi*, 1:341–2; Isfahani, *Bihjat* 331–2; KD 2:182; Rayhani in Amanat, 'Negotiating Identities' 299–300.

from a prominent family of makers and traders of soap. One day in his shop he was selling soap to an old lady who asked him to be true in his weighing of the soap. He replied that he never did anything that was not in accord with the truth. Then the old lady, who was a Babi, said, 'If you are speaking the truth, then why is it that it has been some time that the True One has appeared and yet you have not recognized him?' After this Mirza Aqa Jan investigated the Babi religion and was converted. He travelled to Baghdad in 1853 and was credited by Baha'u'llah as being the first to believe in him. He became Baha'u'llah's secretary and personal assistant in Baghdad, Edirne and 'Akka. Many of the Baha'is wrote to Mirza Aqa Jan to ask him to mention their names to Baha'u'llah and to ask questions. Baha'u'llah's reply would be dictated as though it had been written by Mirza Aqa Jan. A short while before Baha'u'llah's passing, however, he fell from Baha'u'llah's favour when he was asked whether the writings that were in his name were his or Baha'u'llah's and he did not answer, creating doubt in people's minds. After the passing of Baha'u'llah, he was threatened with death by Mirza Muhammad 'Ali but 'Abdu'l-Baha took Mirza Aqa Jan into his own home for five years. Then on 30 May 1897, at a commemoration of Baha'u'llah's passing at Bahji, he suddenly stood up and began to speak to the gathering in favour of Mirza Muhammad 'Ali's claims. After this he lived in one of the rooms of the shrine of Baha'u'llah until his death in 1901.[40]

Another prominent Baha'i of Kashan was Mirza Aqa, who was given the titles Ismu'llah ul-Munib and Ismu'llah ul-Munir by Baha'u'llah. He was severely beaten and almost killed by his father when he found out that his son had become a Babi but his father eventually consented to his departure for Baghdad, where he met Baha'u'llah. During the time Baha'u'llah was in Baghdad, Munib was engaged in transcribing the writings of Baha'u'llah and acting as a courier. Baha'u'llah thought very highly of Munib and especially of his abilities as a writer. On one occasion, while speaking of the steps he had taken to conceal himself in the days before he had openly proclaimed his mission, Baha'u'llah compared Munib with Mirza Yahya Azal. Nabil attributes the following words to Baha'u'llah:

---

40   ZH 6:644–51, 7:11–16; Mazandarani, *Asrar* 1:20–1, 3:170–96; Ishraq-Khavari, *Muhadarat* 1:448–55. For an account by one of the supporters of Mirza Muhammad 'Ali, see Muhammad Javad Qazvini in Browne, *Materials* 87–9. There is evidence in the writings of the Azali Mirza Aqa Khan Kirmani that immediately after the passing of Baha'u'llah, Mirza Aqa Jan was plotting in support of Mirza Muhammad 'Ali (see Balyuzi, *Idvard Giranvil Birawn* [Edward Granville Browne, Persian trans.] 56).

. . . in accordance with divine wisdom, the tongues of several individuals were enabled to speak in a wondrous manner so that people's attention should be diverted in various directions and no one should become completely aware of the focal point prematurely. One of these individuals was Munir, whose words were to be preferred to those of Yahya [Azal] . . . [The Bab] had urged notable Babis to educate Yahya and we spent many years occupying Yahya with writing out the words and verses of God. He would write in our presence and we would encourage him. We would correct what he wrote. He began to lay the foundations for his writing from the age of 20 but there were always errors in the form and meaning of what he wrote. But Munir, without our teaching him anything, wrote wondrous words and with no need for any corrections. If Yahya had had an iota of justice within him, the existence of Munir would by itself have been sufficient proof for him. For he had seen during the days in Baghdad and Edirne that his [Munir's] words are, with no training, pure [spiritual] power. And, according to the testamentary instructions of the Bab to Yahya, if, during his days, one like him were to appear, then he should hand over the Cause to him. And yet he [Yahya] witnessed one who was greater than him [i.e. Munir] and still did not hand over the Cause to him.[41]

From Edirne, Baha'u'llah sent Munir to travel around Iran and Iraq and he was one of the most important of those who promulgated the claim of Baha'u'llah to the Babi communities. He then rejoined Baha'u'llah in Edirne and was sentenced to be deported with Baha'u'llah to 'Akka but he died when the ship carrying them docked at Izmir.[42]

Apart from Mirza Aqa Jan Khadimu'llah and Mirza Aqa-yi Munir, many other Kashanis chose to migrate to be with Baha'u'llah in Baghdad and later to accompany him on the various stages of his exile. Indeed, Kashanis were among the largest contingent of those accompanying Baha'u'llah – for example, more than a quarter of those sent with Baha'u'llah and his family from Edirne to 'Akka were Kashanis and they formed the largest contingent from any town.

One Baha'i who originated from Kashan was Sayyid Faraju'llah Kashani, who became a successful merchant in Cairo. It is not known how he

---

41   ZH 5:25–6. The reference to the testamentary instructions of the Bab to Mirza Yahya appears to be a reference to the Tablet of the Bab to Azal to be found in ILMA 64:95–102, this passage on p. 97.

42   ZH 6:640–4.

became a Baha'i but he was the maternal uncle of both Sayyid Nasru'llah Munzavi (see p. 143) and Mirza Ahmad Chap (see p. 83). In 1900 he took over the running of a Persian newspaper, *Thurayya*, published in Cairo, which had been started in 1898 by Mirza 'Ali Muhammad Khan Shaybani. In 1903 he moved the newspaper to Tehran and it became one of the principal publications advocating reform, leading up to the Constitutional Revolution in 1906. Finally, in 1909 he moved the newspaper to his hometown of Kashan, setting up the first newspaper press there.[43]

40. Haji Muhammad Isma'il Dhabih Kashani

Another prominent Baha'i of Kashan was Sayyid Ahmad Va'iz (1270/1853– 1333/1914), the son of Sayyid Hashim, a prominent cleric in Kashan. Sayyid Ahmad received clerical training and became a well-known preacher and *rawdih-khan* in both Kashan and Tehran. Indeed, his skill and eloquence were so widely regarded that he came to the attention of Muzaffaru'd-Din Shah, who gave him the titles Lisan ul-Islam and Fakhr ul-Va'izin and presented him with a jewelled cane. While living in Tehran he also published, in 1911, a satirical newspaper called *Mizan*, which was broadly supportive of the reform movement. He was also a poet (with the poetic name Khavari) and a book of his poetry called *Kitāb-i Maḥmūd*, written in condemnation of opium, was published in Tehran in 1911. He tried to keep his allegiance to the Baha'i Faith concealed but nevertheless it became widely known and was even acknowledged by his son, Sayyid Mahmud Fakhr (Sadr ul-Va'izin), who was an enemy of the Baha'i Faith.[44]

Other Baha'is who came from Kashan but played important roles in Baha'i history elsewhere included Haji Muhammad Isma'il (1237–Sha'ban 1298/1821– July 1882, see fig. 40; the above-mentioned brother of Haji

---

43 Fadil Mazandarani, *Asrar al-Athar* 2:190–1; Fadil Mazandarani, *Amr va Khalq* 3:346; Browne, *Press and Poetry* 66–7; Amanat, *Kashan* 118–20.

44 Dhuka'i-Bayda'i, *Tadhkirih* 1:315–23; Amanat, *Kashan* 128–9; Browne, *Press and Poetry* 144.

Mirza Jani), who was given the names Dhabih (sacrifice) and Anis (companion) by Baha'u'llah and who became a Babi as a result of meeting the Bab in Kashan. He then met Baha'u'llah in Karbala in 1851 and again in Baghdad 1858 and became his follower. He was among the Babis arrested in Kashan in 1279/1862 and was imprisoned for two years in Tehran (vol. 1:12 and n). He arrived in Edirne in 1868 just as Baha'u'llah and his companions were being arrested and deported but he managed to see Baha'u'llah in Gallipoli. He took up residence in Tehran in 1873 and became well known as a Baha'i, being arrested and imprisoned there in 1874 (vol. 1:22–3), in 1877 (vol. 1:25–6) and in 1880 (vol. 1:26). He then moved to Tabriz in 1881, where he died.[45] His half-brother Mirza Ahmad Kashani, however, took a different course. He also met the Bab in Kashan and fled the town following Haji Mirza Jani's execution in 1852. He moved to Baghdad where he set up as a merchant. An altercation with Malikzadih Khanum (the mother of Anushirvan Khan 'Ayn ul-Mulk), a Qajar princess, led the Iranian consul in Baghdad, Mirza Buzurg Qazvini, to arrest him and he was only saved from deportation to Iran by Baha'u'llah's intervention. He migrated with Baha'u'llah from Baghdad to Istanbul and Edirne but became increasingly associated with Azal and Sayyid Muhammad Isfahani, despite Baha'u'llah's words addressed to him in the important Persian Tablet of Ahmad. When Baha'u'llah severed his ties with Azal in March 1866, Mirza Ahmad returned to Baghdad and joined the Azali circle there in their conflict with the Baha'is, during the course of which he was killed by Nasir (also known as Haji 'Abbas) shortly after his arrival.[46]

Ustad Husayn Na'lband Kashani was taught the Baha'i Faith by Aqa Sayyid 'Ali Ursi-duz. Following the persecutions in 1874 these two moved to Tehran, where Ustad Husayn became a very successful teacher of the Baha'i Faith (vol. 1, fig. 15 and pp. 16, 31–2). Khurshid, the daughter of Ustad Husayn, married Sayyid Habibu'llah, the son of Sayyid 'Ali and they established a family that later took the surname Quds Jurabchi, while the

---

45   ZH 6:624–38; Amanat, *Resurrection* 344–8. Asadu'llah Isfahani states he died in February 1882 and implies it was in Tehran (Yad-dasht-ha 87). Amanat, *Kashan* 106–12.

46   ZH 4:260, 279, 318–19, 329, 330n, 351, 353, 362, 370; 5:9; Balyuzi, *Baha'u'llah* 157, 202, 220, 231, 323 and n; ['Abdu'l-Baha], *Traveller's Narrative* 332. The Persian Tablet of Ahmad can be found at Baha'u'llah, *Majmu'ih* 315–30 (partly translated in *Gleanings*, nos. 152–3, pp. 322–9). For his role in the writing of the *Nuqtatu'l-Kaf*, see p. 180, n6.

sons of Ustad Husayn established families that took the surnames Ittihad and Ihsani.[47]

Another who was very similar to Ustad Husayn in having no formal learning but being a very effective teacher of the Baha'i Faith was 'Amu 'Ali 'Askar Kashani (c. 1840–1326/1908) who became a Babi in the 1850s when he was aged 25, and then became a Baha'i. After visiting Baha'u'llah in 'Akka he became an enthusiastic teacher of the Baha'i Faith, converting many in Kashan and Abyanih (see p. 145). This subjected him to such persecution that he was forced to moved to Tehran where he again converted many (vol. 1:51).[48] There is also mention of Ustad Hasan Babi, who was an architect and a builder in Tehran. He became the chief builder of the shah and was responsible for such edifices as the Gulistan Palace, the Grand Hotel, the Sipahsalar Mosque and the 12 gates of Tehran.[49]

Mirza 'Abdu'r-Rahim Khan (d. c. 1894) was from a notable Kashan family who were known as Darrabi since they were in charge of the royal mint (ḍarrāb-khānih). He had seen the Bab during the latter's stay in Kashan and became a Babi in 1866 through Mirza Faraju'llah and his family, who were bakers in Kashan and eventually became bakers to the shah in Tehran.[50] Mirza 'Abdu'r-Rahim Khan was later a Baha'i but kept his faith secret and kept his distance from the Baha'i community, although he was in communication with Baha'u'llah. He moved to Tehran in 1880, rose to become counsellor (mustashar) in the new-style police department that had been set up in the fashion of European gendarmeries and he became known as kalantar. He wrote a history of Kashan entitled Mirat ul-Qasan (which was subsequently published as Tarikh-i Kashan[51]) for Manekji Sahib, the agent of the Zoroastrians of India in Tehran. The Darrabi family was among the elite of Kashan. Mirza 'Abdu'r-Rahim Khan's wife Khadijih's first marriage had been to Muhammad Ibrahim Khan Ghaffari, another very prominent family of Kashan whose nephew was the above-mentioned minister

47   Amanat, Kashan 335–9.
48   ZH 6:656–7; Haji, quoted in Ishraq-Khavari, Muhadarat 2:1121–6; Amanat, Kashan 392–3.
49   Marzieh Gail (The Baha'i Magazine, vol. 24, no. 11, Feb. 1934, pp. 348–50) translates an article about this man that she states is from 'Abdu'l-Baha's Memorials of the Faithful. However, there is no such article in the present editions of Memorials of the Faithful. I have assumed that this man is the same person as Ustad Hasan Banna Kashi who was arrested in the 1883 episode in Tehran (vol. 1:32, 37), although the article does not say he is from Kashan.
50   Gail, Arches of the Years 22, 28.
51   See Bibliography.

Farrukh Khan Amin ud-Dawlih – and two of the sons of this first marriage (Nizamu'd-Din Khan Muhandis ul-Mamalik and Zaynu'l-'Abidin Khan Sharif ud-Dawlih) married two daughters of Ihtisham ul-Mulk, a Qajar prince who was governor of Kashan (see pp. 130–1). One of Mirza 'Abdu'r-Rahim Khan's daughters married into the Lisan ul-Mulk Sipihr family, another very influential Kashan family. These relatives were not Baha'is but Mirza 'Abdu'r-Rahim Khan's two sons were. His elder son was Husayn-Quli Khan Kalantar, who was chamberlain to Muzaffaru'd-Din Shah when the latter was governor in Tabriz.[52] The second son, 'Ali-Quli Khan Nabil ud-Dawlih (c. 1879–1966, see fig. 71), learned English and French at the Dar ul-Funun School. The two brothers frequented the *zūr-khānihs* (gymnasia) in Tehran and the older brother was converted to the Baha'i Faith by Ustad Ghulam-Husayn Kashi, a wrestler, while the younger was subsequently converted in about 1895 after speaking with Nayyir and Sina. When Haji Mu'nis Qazvini (see fig. 84), a Baha'i dervish, was in Tehran, he enthused 'Ali-Quli Khan so much that he gave up his life in high social circles in Tehran and took up the life of a wandering dervish. Eventually, hearing that 'Abdu'l-Baha needed Baha'is who could translate between English and Persian for the new American Baha'is, he left for 'Akka, where he served as secretary to 'Abdu'l-Baha for a year in about 1900, then accompanied Mirza Abu'l-Fadl Gulpaygani to America in 1901 as his translator. He settled in America (where he was known as Ali Kuli Khan) and married the American Baha'i Florence Breed, the first marriage between Iranian and American Baha'is. He was Iranian consul in Washington from 1907, then *chargé d'affaires* at the Iranian embassy in Washington 1910–14, minister at the Conference of Versailles 1918–20, minister at Istanbul 1921, minister of the court of the crown prince 1921–3 and Iranian minister to republics in the Caucasus 1923–4, after which he returned to the United States. He was active in translating Baha'i scripture into English.[53]

Kashan was also an important centre for the diffusion of the Baha'i Faith. It was in Kashan that the first Zoroastrian was converted (see pp.

---

52 Gail, *Arches of the Years* 29.
53 BW 14:351–3; Gail, *Summon Up Remembrance* and *Arches of the Years*; ZH 8a:490–1. Compare Gail's account of 'Ali-Quli Khan's time at the Istanbul embassy (*Arches* 187–93) with the hostile account of Khan-Malik Sasani (*Yad-bud-ha* 293–5), whom 'Ali-Quli Khan replaced and who then did his best to undermine 'Ali-Quli Khan's position by intrigue and by denouncing him as a Baha'i to the Turkish authorities.

100–1). It was from the Kashan area that Aqa Muhammad Javad and Aqa Muhammad Baqir Naraqi moved to Hamadan and thus established the Baha'i community there as well as initiating the conversion of Jews in the town (see pp. 181, 183). Many Baha'is from the Kashan area moved to Tehran and in particular established the Baha'i Faith in the villages to the south of Tehran (see pp. 141, 143–4 and vol. 1:105).

Baha'i women of Kashan

There were a number of women who were literate and learned and actively promoting the Baha'i Faith in Kashan. The first was the maternal aunt of the above-mentioned Haji Mirza Jani, Bigum Kuchik Khanum, who became a Babi at the time of the Bab's stay in Kashan. She was very active in spreading the Baha'i Faith, especially among women. She was subject to much persecution for this and eventually had to move to Ardistan. Her daughter Khadijih Bigum, known as Mirza Baji Khanum Kashaniyyih, was also a prominent and effective teacher of the Baha'i Faith both in Kashan and later in Tehran, as well as being a teacher in Baha'i schools. The latter's daughter Malikih Khanum (Mirza Khanum) became headmistress of the Tarbiyat School for girls.[54]

Among the Baha'i women's circle of Kashan were Malik Sultan Khanum (d. 1300/1882), daughter of Haji 'Ali Akbar of the prominent Tabrizi merchant clan in Kashan, who was learned and a teacher of the Baha'i Faith,[55] and Agha Bigum, daughter of Aqa Muhammad Ja'far of the same Tabrizi clan, who never married and devoted herself to promoting the Baha'i

---

54   ZH 3:393, 6:672; Amanat, Baha'iyan-i Furqani 347–8; Amanat, *Kashan* 327–8. Dhuka'i-Bayda'i (*Tadhkirih* 1:309–14) was shown by 'Abbas Iqbal Ashtiyani, a famous Iranian historian, a manuscript in his library of Hadiqat ush-Shu'ara, a compilation of poets of the 13th Islamic century by Mirza Ahmad Divan-bigi Shirazi. In this was the story of Khadijih Kashaniyyih, daughter of Haji Muhammad Sadiq, a prominent cleric of Kashan. According to the account by her husband, Mirza Nasru'llah Kashani, the Bab stayed in the house of her father in Kashan one night and during that night Khadijih listened from behind the curtain to the conversation. During this she became so moved that she rushed into the room unveiled and fell at the feet of the Bab. For the rest of her life she was a believer and assisted the Baha'is as much as she could. Dhuka'i-Bayda'i identifies her as Bigum Kuchik Khanum, the aunt of Haji Mirza Jani, but it is difficult to confirm this identification.

55   Natiq Isfahani, Tarikh Amri Kashan 54–5; Isfahani states that at the end of her life she gave all her wealth to the Baha'i Faith.

Faith. Together with her mother, Hajiyyih Khanum, and two sisters, she visited Baha'u'llah in 'Akka.[56]

Sahibih Khanum, known as Hajiyyih 'Ammih Khanum, first heard of the Bab from her husband Haji Mulla 'Ali Akbar who had been a fellow-pilgrim of the Bab. Her husband had not been interested but she was attracted and sent her black slave Shirin to investigate. After meeting Haji Mirza Jani, both Sahibih Khanum and Shirin became Babis and then Baha'is, despite the resolute opposition of Sahibih Khanum's husband. She raised her six sons and two daughters as Baha'is (the Muhtadi family) and even visited 'Akka on the pretext of a pilgrimage to Mecca. When people became aware of this journey, however, there was a commotion in Kashan and she had to move to Tehran. She was the sister of the above-mentioned Mirza Ahmad Rawdih-khan and it may have been through her that this man and his children became Baha'is. The name by which she is known, Hajiyyih 'Ammih Khanum ('Ammih means paternal aunt), refers to her family relation to Mirza Ahmad's daughter, the third wife of Baha'u'llah, Gawhar Khanum. Similarly, her two daughters, Khadijih Sultan and Bigum Sultan, were known among the Baha'is as 'Ammih Ghazi Buzurg and 'Ammih Ghazi Kuchik (the elder cousin and the younger cousin) respectively (vol. 1, fig. 32).[57]

Natiq Isfahani mentions three other similar women: Khatun Jan Khanum (who was literate and learned and accompanied Agha Bigum to 'Akka and remained there for four years as a teacher for the girls in Baha'u'llah's family, d. 1303/1885); Gawhar Khanum (daughter of Mirza Ahmad Yazdi to whom the Arabic Tablet of Ahmad was written); and Zaynat Khanum (daughter of Aqa Muhammad 'Ali Qamsari). He then writes: 'There were many women believers in Kashan and the surrounding area who in steadfastness and devotion had stolen a march on the men.'[58]

In later years, Nazanin Khanum, the wife of Mirza Faraju'llah Big (Farid), bravely took food to any Baha'is who were in prison. On one occasion as she walked along the street, she saw a mob attacking a Baha'i and beating him severely. She hurried over and shouted to the mob that she

---

56 Natiq Isfahani, Tarikh Amri Kashan 53–4.
57 Arbab, *Akhtaran* 1:116–18; Isfahani, *Bihjat* 326; ZH 6:655–6; Amanat, Baha'iyan-i Furqani 126–7; Amanat, *Kashan* 376–7. Haj 'Ammih Khanum's grandson Mirza Fadlu'llah (Faydu'llah) Subhi Muhtadi, however, left the Baha'i Faith in the spring of 1928 and became a hostile and vitriolic enemy of it; see EIr under 'Sobhi'; Hafizi, *Memoirs* 2:118.
58 Natiq Isfahani, 'Tarikh Amri Kashan' 54–5.

41. Kaykhusraw Khudadad

was also a Baha'i and so the mob left the man they were attacking and started beating her.[59]

Zoroastrian conversions

'Abdu'r-Rahim Darrabi's history of Kashan, completed in 1288/1871, states that there were some 20–30 Zoroastrian merchants from Yazd in Kashan, who had not brought their families and who lived in caravan-serais.[60] The first Zoroastrian convert was in the time of the Bab and was a merchant in Kashan. It appears that his name was Suhrab Kavus (or Pur-Kavus),[61] although other names are given for him in some sources.[62] He had witnessed an episode in 1265/1849, when the governor of Kashan, 'Abbas 'Ali Khan Turk, punished a Babi, Muhammad Rida Makhmalbaf, a merchant who had met the Bab in Mecca.[63] The latter had had his property looted, been bastinadoed and led through the streets with his clothes torn off him so that the people could spit on him and beat him. Since Suhrab knew the man to be a moral and upright person, he was moved to make enquiries about the new religion and eventually converted.[64]

The first Zoroastrian to become a Baha'i is generally reckoned to have been Kaykhusraw Khudadad (1266/1849–1344/1925, see fig. 41). It has

---

59   Amanat, *Kashan* 272–3.

60   Darrabi, *Tarikh Kashan* 245.

61   Sifidvash, *Pishgamanan* 21–3; Faridani, *Dustan-i Rastan* 33–4. 'Abdu'l-Baha refers to this conversion in *Traveller's Narrative* 1: 33–4.

62   He has been variously named as Mihraban Bahman (ZH 3:395n; 6:841) from the Rishbuzi family and Bahman Pur-Kavus (ZH 3:395n).

63   ZH 3:395n; Sifidvash, *Pishgamanan* 21–3; Faridani, *Dustan-i Rastan* 33–4; Amanat, *Kashan* 36, 42–3. He is however named as Muhammad Baqir in ZH 6:841–2 and as Aqa Mahdi Kamranibaf in Natiq Isfahani, Tarikh Amri Kashan 4; the date is given in Natiq Isfahani, Tarikh Amri Kashan 4. It is possible that this may have been the Haji Baqir Makhmalbaf who visited Baha'u'llah in Istanbul (Balyuzi, *Baha'u'llah* 204) or the Sayyid Rida mentioned on p. 88.

64   ZH 3:395n; this episode is related in ['Abdu'l-Baha], *Traveller's Narrative* 2:33–4, without however naming the individuals involved.

been stated that the latter observed an episode when a Baha'i was dragged through the streets and killed by a mob in Kashan and this caused him to investigate the religion and become a Baha'i.[65] This account is so similar to the previous account of what occurred to Suhrab Kavus that one must suspect that an error of transmission has occurred and the event that occurred to the first Zoroastrian to convert to the Babi religion has been mistakenly transferred onto the first Zoroastrian to become a Baha'i – although it may refer to the execution of Shaykh Abu'l-Qasim Mazgani in 1870 (see pp. 130–1).[66] Since other accounts state that Kaykhusraw Khudadad was related to Suhrab Kavus,[67] it is possible that he came to know about the Babi and Baha'i Faiths through the latter. Even if they were not related, the Zoroastrian merchants in Kashan were, as indicated above, a small, closely-knit community.[68]

Some years later a certain Zoroastrian named Bahram came to work for Khudadad. On two previous occasions Bahram had heard people speak of the Babis' bravery before death and this had made him curious about the religion, but he had no idea that his employer was a Baha'i. Then, in 1879, a message arrived that clearly upset his employer. When Bahram pressed Khudadad about this, the latter explained that the message had contained news of the execution of the King of Martyrs and the Beloved of Martyrs in Isfahan (see pp. 21–3). After this Bahram investigated the new religion. He moved to Yazd in about 1882 and became a Baha'i in 1885; he was responsible for the conversion of many Zoroastrians there. Because of his great learning he became known as Mulla Bahram and he later took the surname of Akhtar-Khavari (see p. 371 and fig. 144).[69]

Jewish conversions

A British report from 1868 states that there were 750 Jews in Kashan.[70] 'Abdu'r-Rahim Darrabi's history of Kashan, completed in 1288/1871,

---

65 Faridani, *Dustan* 37; Taherzadeh, *Revelation of Baha'u'llah* 3:269.
66 Both 'I. Sefidvash (*Pishgamanan* 59) and Faridani (*Dustan* 37) state that Kaykhusraw became a Baha'i in 1299/1881 but this cannot be correct if the eyewitness story ('I. Sefidvash, *Pishgamanan* 58) indicating that Kaykhusraw was already a Baha'i in 1879 is correct.
67 'I. Sifidvash, *Pishgamanan* 58.
68 Although Faridani (*Dustan-i Rastan* 37), in view of the difference in age between them, considers it unlikely that they were even resident in Kashan at the same time.
69 Faridani, *Dustan-i Rastan* 37.
70 Report from Thompson in Issawi, *Economic History* 28, 32.

states that there were between 300 and 400 houses of Jews in Kashan (approx. 1,500–2,000 persons).[71] A Jewish report from 1907 states that Kashan had been an important centre for Jewish intellectual life in Iran in the 18th century, becoming known as 'little Jerusalem', and that there were, in 1907, some 2,000 Jews (350 families).[72]

It is said that when the Bab was in Kashan he was visited by two of the prominent Jews of the town, Hakim Harun (d. c. 1885) and Mulla Musa. While it may just be family legend that both were impressed by the Bab and became secret converts,[73] certainly the former impressed the Christian missionary Rev. Henry Stern by his openness to other religions,[74] while the latter, in later years, encouraged his daughter to remain with her Baha'i husband when she was under pressure to divorce him (see pp. 109–10). Many descendants of these two became Baha'is.[75] Hakim Harun's son Nahuray, who had accompanied his father to meet the Bab, was invited to Tehran by Nasiru'd-Din Shah to become his personal physician, converted to Islam, received the title Nur ul-Hukama and became known as Nur Mahmud (1238/1822–1317/1899). Although he did not become a Baha'i, he played an important role in Baha'i history (vol. 1, fig. 19 and pp. 56, 63) and most of his children became Baha'is.[76]

The first Jew of Kashan to become a Baha'i was Haji Ilyahu Kahin (named 'Abd-i Husayn by Baha'u'llah), who was among the first wave of converts in Hamadan in 1296/1879. He was from a family of Shirazi Jewish Kohens who had migrated to Kashan. He was probably the first Jewish convert to visit Baha'u'llah, in 1298/1881. He was charged with taking the Baha'i Faith to the Jews of Iran and he wrote from 'Akka to the Jews of Kashan with proofs of the new religion. He then returned to Kashan, married his cousin and became a physician. After a short time, however, he moved to Qumm and then to Tehran, where he was responsible for setting off a wave of conversions (vol. 1:57–8). After visiting Sangsar and

---

71 Darrabi, *Tarikh Kashan* 245.
72 *Bulletin d'Alliance Israélite Universelle*, no. 32 (1907) 72–6.
73 Thabiti, *Varithan* 30–1. It should be noted, however, that there was evidently some early interest among the Jews of Kashan in the Baha'i Faith. In 1878 Haji Mirza Kamalu'd-Din forwarded to Baha'u'llah two questions from a certain Hakim Hizqil Hayyim, see Mazandarani, *Amr va Khalq* 2:197–8.
74 Stern, *Dawnings*, 254–60; Amanat, 'Negotiating Identities' 109; Amanat, *Kashan* 391.
75 Tulu'i, 'Hashim Sajid'; Geula, *Iranian Baha'is* 76–7.
76 Amanat, 'Negotiating Identities' 96–7; Amanat, *Kashan* 389.

42. Aqa Yahuda   43. Jahan Khanum

Shahmirzad, he set out for 'Akka again and on this occasion Baha'u'llah seems to have commissioned him to travel through various lands, including Egypt, in dervish attire propagating the Baha'i Faith. He visited 'Akka after the passing of Baha'u'llah. It appears he then returned to Egypt and no further information is available about him.[77] He was therefore not long in Kashan as a Baha'i.

There is some discrepancy among the sources as to the first Jewish resident in Kashan to become a Baha'i. Some say this was Aqa Yahuda (see fig. 42), who was converted in Hamadan in 1306/1888. He returned to Kashan and set up as a silk merchant. He disclosed his new beliefs to a few people but was met with great hostility. Some Jews complained to the Islamic clerics about him and the Shaykhis of the town attacked his house but did not find him. He was forced to flee to Hamadan, where he remained for two years. He then returned to Kashan but was again subjected to harassment. Baha'i meetings were held in his house at which conversions were made, including his wife, Jahan Khanum (see fig. 43), the youngest daughter of

---

77 ZH 6:674–6; Amanat, 'Ahibba-yi Kalimi' 67–8; Amanat, *Kashan* 288–90; Rayhani appears to have had differences with him and does not have a high opinion of him, calling him a thief (Amanat, 'Negotiating Identities' 191, 201–5).

44. Rayhan Rayhani

the above-mentioned Hakim Harun. On one occasion he was beaten so severely that he suffered permanent giddiness and weakness. The physicians of the town were unable to cure him and so he went to Tehran, where he died in 1325/1907.[78] According to other accounts, the first Jewish Baha'i resident in Kashan was a butcher, Aqa Shlomo Qassab (d. 1322/1904), who first became a Muslim and then a Babi. Not much is known of him.[79]

Mirza Rayhan Rayhani (1280/1863[80]–1949, given name Rubin, see fig. 44) was just seven years old when his father died and he went to live with an aunt whose husband was a rabbi. They took Rayhani to Tehran. After a period back in Kashan he went to Tehran where he lived with the above-mentioned prominent Jewish physician Hakim Nur Mahmud. It was in this house that he heard of the Baha'i Faith and after five years of wavering committed himself (vol. 1:56). He was a pedlar of goods in the villages around Kashan and was skilled at teaching the Baha'i Faith. Because of his outspokenness, he was much persecuted. He writes in his memoirs of being confined to his house on several occasions for periods of up to three weeks, and of times

---

78 ZH 6:676–7; Amanat, *Kashan* 309–10; Geula, *Iranian Baha'is* 131–2.
79 Amanat, 'Abna Khalil' 39–40; Amanat, *Kashan* 94–5.
80 Various dates have been suggested for the birth of Rayhani. Mehrdad Amanat ('Negotiating Identities' 132; *Jewish Identities* 121) gives 1859; Musa Amanat (*Kashan* 254) gives 1270/1854; and Fadil Mazandarani gives 1278/1861. However, Rayhani in his memoirs states he was seven years old when he witnessed the execution of Shaykh Abu'l-Qasim Mazgani, which occurred in 1287/1870, hence the date of birth given above. This date of birth is further confirmed by the fact that Rayhani remembers that there was a cholera epidemic at this time (which led to the death of his father) and a severe famine the following year (Rayhani in 'Negotiating Identities' 179–80). A cholera epidemic struck Iran in 1870–1 and a severe famine began in 1871. However, Rayhani later says that he had turned ten years old in 1288 when the famine struck (Rayhani in 'Negotiating Identities' 181), so it could be that he was born in 1278/1861.

45. Mulla Musa   46. Khajih Rabi'

when all his goods were confiscated. His wife, known simply as 'Khanum' became the first Jewish woman in Kashan to become a Baha'i and, during the 1901 episode of imprisonment, brought the prisoners food and communications from their families.[81]

Another early convert was Il'azar (Haqnazar) who is said to have been the first Jew in Kashan to become a merchant (*tājir*), this being an occupation prohibited to Jews previously.[82] In early 1306/late 1888 Mirza Abu'l-Fadl Gulpaygani visited Kashan. During his stay a meeting was arranged in the home of Haqnazar between him and three of the senior Jewish religious leaders in Kashan, the most learned of whom was named Mordecai (Mulla Murad). Mirza Abu'l-Fadl tried to persuade them that the prophecies in the Hebrew Bible should be interpreted figuratively but they insisted upon a literal interpretation. Finally Mirza Abu'l-Fadl declared that the Bible states that the meaning of the scriptures is sealed up until the time of the end and so any interpretation of the Jewish religious leaders has no

81 Rayhani's memoirs are translated in Amanat, 'Negotiating Identities' 179–320; summary in Amanat, *Jewish Identity* 119–46; see also ZH 8b:707–12; Amanat, *Kashan* 254–7.

82 It is not clear when Haqnazar became a Baha'i but Amanat suggests that he met Baha'u'llah during a business trip to Baghdad (*Kashan* 218).

validity. At a result of this meeting several more Jews converted.[83] Two of
the learned Jews present at this meeting were the brothers Mulla Rabi' (d.
Tehran, 1910) and Mulla Sulayman (Shalum, d. Tehran 1351/1932), sons
of Rubin Shirazi, and they became Baha'is. Mulla Rabi' was a supervisor
in the mint and was arrested in the 1901 episode and beaten so severely
on the orders of Musa, the *kadkhuda* of the Jewish quarter, that it affected
him gravely. He moved to Tehran and died a few years later.[84] Mulla Sulayman became a Baha'i together with his following of 700 to 800 people,
but after the persecutions a year later, refrained from being open about his
beliefs and eventually returned to being a Jew. He later moved to Tehran
and became one of the leading rabbis there, although on account of his
Baha'i brothers, he never spoke against the Baha'i Faith from the pulpit
and sometimes indirectly guided people towards it.[85]

The persecution that caused Mulla Sulayman to waver in his faith
occurred in about 1889. A certain Darvish Qasim composed anti-Baha'i
songs and would lead mobs around the city streets singing them. The Jews
of Kashan took up these songs and would sing them. Rayhani says he was
afraid to go out of his house for three weeks. Then a diphtheria epidemic
broke out, killing hundreds, which put an end to this episode.[86]

Members of three separate families came together to form the Muttahidih trading company and they later all took the surname Muttahidih.
This company had offices in Kashan, Tehran, Rasht, Anzali, Hamadan and
Kirmanshah. Two of the partners were Mirza Ishaq (d. Tehran, 1934) and
Mulla Musa (d. 1909, see fig. 45 and vol. 1:356), the two younger brothers
of the above-mentioned Mulla Rabi' and Mulla Sulayman. On one Sabbath
in about 1903 when the Jews of the town were praying that they would not
remain heedless on the Promised Day, Mulla Musa announced in a loud
voice that the Promised One had come but that it required a hearing ear
and a pure heart to discern this. The Jewish rabbis were incensed at this
and took counsel together under the leadership of Mulla Shamu'il. They
decided to complain to the governor and Mulla Musa was arrested and

---

83   Gulpaygani, *Mukhatarat* 187–9; Mihrabkhani, *Gulpaygani* 159–60; Rayhani
     in Amanat, 'Negotiating Identities' 211–12. See also the account in Amanat,
     Kashan 40–1, 218, 221 (on this last page Haqnazar is named Hizqiya rather than
     Il'azar).
84   ZH 8b: 702–3; Amanat, *Kashan* 237–9.
85   ZH 8b:712–13; Rayhani in Amanat, 'Negotiating Identities' 154, 214; Amanat,
     Kashan 239–40.
86   Rayhani in Amanat, 'Negotiating Identities' 253–5.

threatened with death but he refused to recant. He asked the governor that
the rabbis be brought to debate with him but they only replied that he
had broken the Sabbath laws. The Baha'is eventually managed to get him
freed but he continued to be persecuted: he was robbed by his partners
and a servant of Mirza Fakhru'd-Din Mujtahid Naraqi broke some of his
teeth. He was eventually forced to flee to Lahijan where he was murdered
in 1909.[87]

The founder and driving force behind the Muttahidih company was
Khajih Rabi' (Muttahidih, 1283/1866 – 22 June 1918, see fig. 46), the
eldest of five sons of Mulla Isma'il. He was given the title Khajih by the
prime minister Amin us-Sultan and was one of the leading merchants of
Kashan. He was the prime mover in the establishment of the Baha'i school
in Kashan and distributed food to the poor during the famine of 1917–19.
The other brothers were also merchants but lived in Hamadan, Tehran and
elsewhere: Haji Yusif (Munfarid 1881–1949), Mirza Hashim (Yarshatir
1887–1934), Mirza Ishaq (Nuru'd-Din Mumtazi 1896–1960) and Mirza
Ya'qub (Muttahidih, who was the company representative in Kirmanshah
and was assassinated there in 1921, see p. 226 and fig. 85).[88] Yet another
partner in the Muttahidih company who took the surname Muttahidih
was Mirza Yusif. For a time he was the company representative in Rasht
and when the company was dissolved in 1918 after the death of Khajih
Rabi', Mirza Yusif moved to Tehran where he became a successful dealer
in antiques.[89]

Despite the hostility of the Jewish leadership, the Jewish Baha'i community grew. There were a number of factors that contributed to this but
one account mentions in particular the meetings that were held by the
Baha'is: the spiritual atmosphere, the chanting of prayers and scriptures
and the talks giving proofs and explanations. The number of young Jews
becoming Baha'is became a cause of concern to some of the elders of the
Jewish community such as Mulla Ishaq (Kashan's leading rabbi), Hakim
Ilyas (a brother of Hakim Nur Mahmud) and Aqa Musa, the *kadkhuda* of
the Jewish quarter. In about 1901 they went to the governor Muhammad
Ja'far Khan, who was married to the shah's sister, with a complaint that the

---

87 ZH 7:227, 8b:713–15; Amanat, 'Negotiating Identities' 155. These sources all
    give the date of the killing of Mulla Musa as 1323/1905. Amanat (*Kashan* 242,
    483 n23) states that the grandchildren of this man give the date of 1909.
88 Amanat, *Kashan* 296.
89 See vol. 1, p. 348; Amanat, *Kashan* 297–8.

converts had been disrespectful to the holy prophets. They also bribed the governor, promising him that he would also be able to collect large fines from the Baha'is, and so he ordered the arrest of six of the recent converts and put them in prison. Unfortunately, at that time none of the more influential members of the Baha'i community, who could have intervened, were in town. So two of the Jewish Baha'is, Hakim Faraju'llah and Mirza Rayhan, went before the governor and asked the reason for the imprisonment of the Baha'is. They were also thrown into prison. Mulla Rabi', who arrived in the town at this time, was also arrested. The Baha'is informed Mirza Khalil Arjumand (the Baha'i son of Hakim Ibrahim Shalum and nephew of the above-mentioned Nur Mahmud, vol. 1:58–9) in Tehran of the situation and he went to Mirza Nasru'llah Khan Mushir ud-Dawlih, the Minister for Foreign Affairs, who sent a telegraph asking for a report. The governor replied that the Jewish leaders had come to him and said that many of their people had become Baha'is and that if this was not checked, there would be no more Jews. Mushir ud-Dawlih is reported to have commented that he was not at all worried about the disappearance of the Jewish religion. Orders were sent to Kashan but the governor ignored them until a telegram arrived from the shah himself whereupon the governor fined the Baha'is and set them free.[90]

A prominent Jewish Baha'i was the above-mentioned Hakim Faraju'llah (d. 1324/1906), whose maternal uncle Mulla Yahuda was among the foremost Jewish religious leaders in Kashan. Although at first a silk merchant, he learned medicine from his brother-in-law Hakim Harun. He is reported to have studied other religions as a result of a dying wish of his father. As a result he embraced Christianity, and then, having learned

90   ZH 7:139–40; 8b:706–7, 710–11 gives the date 1319/1901 for this episode; Natiq Isfahani (Tarikh Amri Kashan 18–21) gives the date given as 1318/1900. Some elements from Natiq have been incorporated into this account. ZH 8b:711 suggests that Rayhani got himself arrested deliberately so as to be with the recent Jewish converts in prison and support them; Rayhani's own account (in Amanat, 'Negotiating Identities', 223–33), only partly supports that assertion. Amanat (*Kashan* 100–1, 225) suggests both Rayhani and Hakim Faraju'llah got themselves arrested deliberately, gives the date as 1318/1901 and names the first two of the Jewish elders who went to the governor as Rabbi Ilyas and Aqa Yahuda Jalumashi. Rayhani and Nughaba'i ('Tarikh-i Iqbal' p. 12) state that the episode occurred in 1322/1904. The reason that Arjumand went to the Minister for Foreign Affairs was that the affairs of the religious minorities, in this case Jews, had been made his responsibility (see Tsadik, *Between Foreigners* 78–9, 105–6, 186).

47. Hakim Ya'qub Birjis   48. Hashim Sajid

Arabic, studied the Islamic scriptures and the Mathnavi of Rumi, he converted to Islam. He became a Baha'i after attending the above-mentioned
meeting between Mirza Abu'l-Fadl Gulpaygani and the Jewish rabbis in
1888 and started to propagate this religion among his co-religionists. He
was one of the Jewish Baha'is imprisoned in 1901.[91] Another physician was
Hakim Ya'qub Shams ul-Hukama (Birjis, c. 1872–1924, see fig. 47), who
studied medicine with his maternal grandfather, Hakim Nur Mahmud,
and maternal uncle, Hakim Ayyub (c. 1860–1905, a Baha'i, vol. 1:56),
who were very eminent physicians in Tehran, and became a Baha'i there.
Hakim Ya'qub returned to Kashan where he practised in Nushabad and
later in Kashan itself until his death. His paternal cousin Mulla Ishaq was
the above-mentioned leading rabbi of Kashan who was much opposed to
the Baha'is.[92]

Mulla 'Ashur, son of Ibrahim Kahin, was a silk merchant who became
a Baha'i while on a business trip to Naraq in 1300/1882 and then took the
name Hashim Sajid (1275/1858–1352/1933, see fig. 48). He was called
Ghayur (zealous) by 'Abdu'l-Baha. He was bold in his advocacy of the
Baha'i Faith and his breaking the laws of the Sabbath roused the wrath
of the Kashan Jews. His wife, Maryam Khanum, came under pressure to

---

91 ZH 8b: 705–6; Amanat, *Kashan* 223–6.
92 ZH 8b:703; Amanat, 'Negotiating Identities' 290 and n; Amanat, *Kashan*
    212–13.

divorce him but was dissuaded from doing so by her father Mulla Musa (see p. 102). She too eventually became a Baha'i. In 1307/1889 Hashim Sajid moved to Sultanabad (see p. 160). In 1314/1896 he returned to Kashan and was on his way back to Sultanabad with his family when the Jews of Kashan raised a complaint against him and he was arrested at Naraq and returned to Kashan. The governor of Kashan released him after a time and he settled in Naraq. Later he moved back to Sultanabad, where he continued to teach the Baha'i Faith until finally he moved to Tehran.[93]

Another silk merchant was Murad Amanat (d. 1949), who came from a very religious family. Because he had a pleasant voice and a good knowledge of the Hebrew scripture, he was a cantor in the synagogue. He was much influenced by Mulla Ilyahu Kahin, who was a Karaite (Qara'i, a sect of Judaism that holds only to the Torah and rejects the interpretation of the scripture by rabbis and the oral tradition that is contained in the Talmud and Midrash) and held to the truth of Jesus and Muhammad as prophets. Amanat became a Baha'i during a business trip when he came into contact with the Jewish Baha'is of Hamadan. He then set about converting his family and business associates. He lived for a time in Hamadan and subsequently in Rasht, and finally in Tehran.[94]

'Abdu'l-Mithaq Mithaqiyyih (original name Mirza Ilyas, 1890–1981), who was a son of the above-mentioned Aqa Yahuda and Jahan Khanum, became a Baha'i while staying in Hamadan. He returned to Kashan when his father fell ill and continued the latter's business, trading in connection with the Muttahidih Company. He was in Rasht for three years and then in Kirmanshah, where he was subjected to such harassment that the governor asked him to leave (Mirza Ya'qub Muttahidih who replaced him as representative of the Muttahidih Company was assassinated shortly afterwards). Mithaqiyyih went to Hamadan before returning to Kashan, where he became a member of the local spiritual assembly. Some time after 1921 he moved to Tehran where he was also a member of the spiritual assembly and contributed financially to important community projects. In particular, in 1940 he built and donated to the Baha'i community the Mithaqiyyih Hospital, which became, after the closure of the Baha'i schools, the only

93 ZH 6:679a, 8b:704–5; Tulu'i, 'Hashim Sajid'; Amanat, *Kashan* 258–60. He is called Mirza Hashim 'Natars' (fearless) on account of his open teaching of the Baha'i Faith by Rayhani (in Amanat, 'Negotiating Identities' 192, 196–7). He may have converted to Islam at one stage and this may have been why he took the name Hashim (see Amanat, *Kashan* 259).

94 Amanat, *Kashan* 203–7.

Baha'i institution to which the Iranian public had access. In later years he also donated sums for the purchase of Baha'i properties and endowments in Africa and elsewhere.[95] Aqa Haqnazar (Shayan, d. 1933) was a prominent merchant of Kashan and his business had branches in Sultanabad and Hamadan. It was during a business trip to Hamadan that he first heard of the Baha'i Faith and he was then taught the new religion by Khajih Rabi'.

A large number of the Jews of Kashan became Baha'is. In addition to those named above were the progenitors of such notable families as the Tawfiq, Mahir, Khavari, Tulu'i, Yusifiyan, Yazhari and Malakuti families. In general, however, the Jewish women were much slower than the men to convert,[96] although once they were Baha'is they were tenacious in their faith and often were able to bring up their children to be Baha'is even in the face of opposition from Jewish husbands.[97] In many ways, women such as the above-mentioned Jahan Khanum Mithaqiyyih (the wife of Aqa Yahuda), who was literate and talented and firm in her religion and a much-loved aunt to six or more Baha'i families,[98] were responsible for forging the links that maintained the unity and cohesion of the Baha'i community. The first marriage between a Baha'i of Muslim background and a Baha'i of Jewish background in Kashan did not occur until 1934, when Ibrahim Shirvani (d. 1996), a convert from a strict Muslim family, married 'Atiyyih (d. 1999), the daughter of Rayhan Rayhani.[99]

Later events in Kashan

An interesting comment is made by Haji Mirza Haydar 'Ali who visited Kashan some time in the mid-1890s. He states that 'the friends came from many different backgrounds: Jewish, Christian, Zoroastrian and Muslim. But one could not tell them apart. Their unity was like water and rose water: once mixed, it is impossible to distinguish one from the other.'[100] This unity of the Baha'is of Kashan, despite the differences in

95 ZH 8b:700–2; BW 18:779–81; Geula, *Iranian Baha'is* 133–5; Amanat, *Kashan* 311–14.
96 Rayhani states that in about 1900 his wife was the only Jewish woman to have become a Baha'i; Amanat, 'Negotiating Identities' 225.
97 Anthony Lee, unpublished research, personal correspondence, 10 Mar. 2000.
98 Amanat, *Kashan* 310–11; although when first married she had been greatly opposed to the Baha'i Faith (Roshan Mavaddat in *Baha'i World* 18:779).
99 Amanat, *Kashan* 129.
100 Isfahani, *Bihjat* 309 (trans. *Delight of Hearts* 135); translation slightly amended.

their backgrounds, is borne out by the following story. General meetings of the whole Baha'i community were held, as elsewhere in Iran, on Friday afternoons. But after a time it became clear that the Jewish Baha'is who had businesses were continuing to work until late afternoon on Fridays, following the pattern of the other Jewish businesses in the town. There-fore, the general Baha'i meetings were moved to Saturday afternoons.[101]

In 1313/1895 the governor Muhammad Hasan Khan Anis ud-Dawlih ordered the Baha'i Mir 'Abdu'l-Baqi Sabbagh (dyer) to be arrested and for all of the hair on his head, even his eyebrows, to be shaved off. His turban, which was the sign of his being a descendant of the Prophet Muham-mad, was removed and he was beaten, tortured and thrown into prison for several days. He died a few days after his release as a result of the injuries he received. He was buried but after 30 days, at the instigation of Mulla Habibu'llah, the body was dug up and beaten further.[102]

In about 1902 a Baha'i, Aqa Mir Jasbi (vol. 1:106, 513), came to Kashan acting on behalf of Mirza Khalil (Arjumand). While carrying out his business he ran foul of some of the clerics, who started a campaign against him and soon brought the fact that he was a Baha'i into it. At the instigation of Haji Mirza Fakhru'd-Din Mujtahid Naraqi, the governor Hisam Lashkar arrested Aqa Mir Jasbi and four of the Kashan Baha'is. A number of Baha'is, including women, went to the government telegraph office to send petitions to the government in Tehran but the telegraph office refused. So they proceeded to the English telegraph office where they barricaded themselves inside in protest at these arrests. The people of the town were stirred up by the clerics, surrounded the telegraph office and began to throw stones at it. All the while the telegraph office was sending reports of the situation to Tehran. Orders for the release of the prisoners and the punishment of the wrong-doers came from Tehran. The governor was anxious not to allow this situation to continue and so he freed the

---

101 Amanat, 'Ahibba-yi Kalimi' 51–2.
102 Natiq Isfahani, Tarikh Amri Kashan 15–16; ZH 7:46–7. Rayhani describes this
     episode (in Amanat, 'Negotiating Identities' 252–3) and states that the relatives
     of Mir 'Abdu'l-Baqi went to Sayyid Husayn Mujtahid Kashani and said that
     Mir 'Abdu'l-Baqi had recanted before death and thus they obtained a *fatwa* for
     his burial. Mulla Habibu'llah (who was not a *mujtahid* at this time) objected
     saying, 'The recantation of a Babi is not acceptable.' Sayyid Husayn responded
     by saying, 'I still have in my library your Mathnavi [written in support of the
     Babi Faith while Mulla Habibu'llah was still a Babi] and so your recantation is
     not acceptable either.'

prisoners and banished Aqa Mir Jasbi from the town. But the town was in turmoil for about a month over this episode and several Baha'is were beaten.[103] This incident also bears witness to the unity between the Jewish Baha'is and the Muslim Baha'is in the community in that although all of the imprisoned Baha'is were Muslim Baha'is, Jewish Baha'is participated in the occupation of the telegraph office.

Among the prominent Baha'is of Kashan was Nur-'Ali Shaybani Nusrat ul-Mamalik (pen-name Adhar, 1298/1881–1937), who was a poet and the son of one of the well-known poets of Kashan, Fathu'llah Khan Shaybani.[104] The Shaybani family was one of three important families of notables in Kashan who competed with each other for power and influence, the others being the Ghaffari and Sipihr families (see pp. 96–7). The father of Nur-'Ali died when he was young and the family was living in Tehran. When he was 16 years old and living in Tehran, Nur-'Ali was introduced to the Baha'i Faith by a Baha'i shopkeeper, Fathu'llah Isfahani, and was convinced after meeting Nabil Akbar Qa'ini. He was employed in a number of government posts, being in charge of the post office and subsequently of the police and the tax office in several towns before he was dismissed because of his being a Baha'i. He then retired to Kashan, where he lived until his death. He composed a history of the Baha'i Faith called the Baha'-namih, in the same poetic style as the Shah-namih of Firdawsi.[105]

Another poet, the perfumer and pharmacist Mirza Masha'u'llah Laqa'i (1868–1928, see fig. 49), was converted through the efforts of his Baha'i neighbour, Mirza Hashim Kisih-gir (tobacconist), who taught the Baha'i Faith to many and whose house in Kashan was a place where many travelling Baha'i teachers stayed. Laqa'i in turn taught the Baha'i Faith to many others and became well known as a Baha'i. On one occasion, Mirza Fakhru'd-Din Naraqi stopped outside his shop and ordered the 30 students who were accompanying him to attack Laqa'i. Hearing of a need for Baha'is in Qumm in 1908, he tried to move there but he was so well known as a Baha'i that the camel-drivers in the caravan that he joined to go

---

103 Natiq Isfahani, *Tarikh Amri Kashan* 22–3; Rayhani in Amanat, 'Negotiating Identities' 261 (who states that the person in charge of the English telegraph office was an Armenian Baha'i); (ZH 7:220–1) and Amanat, (*Kashan* 236) date this episode to 1321/1903.

104 On Fathu'llah Khan Shaybani see Darrabi, *Tarikh Kashan* 392; Farrukhyar, *Mashahir-i Kashan* 79.

105 Dhuka'i-Bayda'i, *Tadhkirih* 3:1–16; ZH 8b:666–71 (this source gives his date of birth as 1301/1883); Amanat, *Kashan* 123–5.

49. Mirza Masha'u'llah Laqa'i

to Qumm publicized his being a Baha'i upon their arrival in the town. Thereupon he was beaten and only saved from death by the governor 'Abbas Mirza I'tidad ud-Dawlih, who sent his footmen to rescue Laqa'i from the mob, arranged for him to be treated for his injuries and then sent him out of the town. Laqa'i went on to Tehran. He returned to Kashan in 1920 where he later donated the houses that the community used as their Baha'i centre (*hazirat ul-quds*) and girls' school.[106]

Another talented Baha'i of Kashan was Ustad 'Abbas 'Ali Haqiqi (1888–1963), who became a Baha'i in 1917. He was a skilled weaver of cloth, carpets and of gold brocade and played a great part in the revival of the craft of weaving gold brocade in Iran. In 1920 he was invited to Tehran to help establish a workshop for this craft in a national academy for crafts (*hunaristān*). Although uneducated, he was an effective teacher of the Baha'i Faith.[107]

Mirza Muhammad Azurdigan (1282/1866–1321/1903) was from a very religious family and owned a cloth-weaving factory. He became a Baha'i in 1310/1896 through one of his Baha'i employees and his brothers turned against him. In 1896 they went to Aqa Mir Muhammad 'Ali Mujtahid and obtained a *fatwa* decreeing their brother's death. On the strength of this they went to the governor, who ordered Mirza Muhammad's arrest. He was beaten and severely bastinadoed and thrown into prison. After a time, however, the governor freed him and exiled him from the town. He went to Tehran where he established himself as a weaver.[108] Other influential Baha'is included Mashhadi Muhammad, the *darughih* (police chief)[109]

---

106 ZH 8b:673–85; Dhuka'i-Bayda'i, *Tadhkirih* 3:267–310; Dadrisan, 'Laqa'i Kashani'.

107 Amanat, *Kashan* 235–6.

108 ZH 8b:671–3.

109 Rayhani in Amanat, 'Negotiating Identities' 239–40.

and Sayyid Muhammad Karavansaray-dar (owner of a caravanserai, who also had control of the bean and grain market and of the production of bread in Kashan).[110]

From about 1907 onwards, with the general disorder caused by the Constitutional Revolution, the coup of Muhammad Shah and the uprising against the latter, Kashan came increasingly under the grip of a gang (*luti-gari*) leader called Na'ib Husayn Kashi (see fig. 50). He had briefly been associated with Shah Mirza (see pp. 85–6) in earlier years but had then gone to Karbala and Tehran (where

50. Na'ib Husayn Kashi
(seated in centre)

he had been in the service of the mother of the shah and had received the title of Na'ib) before returning to Kashan. Once his sons had grown to an age that they could support him, Na'ib Husayn began to grow in power in the town. At first, he had been friendly towards the Baha'is, especially as Sayyid Muhammad Karavansaray-dar was his sponsor and Na'ib Husayn's son Amir Khan had business relations with Khajih Rabi'. His eldest son, Masha'u'llah Khan, had even expressed an interest in attending Baha'i meetings, although this had been avoided by the Baha'is because of his bad reputation. Later, when Na'ib Husayn and Masha'u'llah Khan inclined towards Sufism, they turned against the Baha'is and even persecuted them, driving some Baha'is from their homes, killing the wife of Arbab Aqa Mirza Nushabadi and causing the death of others.[111] Among the events that also occurred during this period was the murder of a young Baha'i, Aqa Mahdi Khadim, by a mob in the streets in about 1912, but this does not appear to have been related to Na'ib Husayn's activities.[112]

Na'ib Husayn was used at first by the government to suppress rebellion but he soon came out in open rebellion against the government. He was opposed by Mulla Habibu'llah Mujtahid and for a time the two divided the town, each despoiling an agreed part of it with their gangs. For much of a period of about ten years (about 1909 to 1919), Na'ib Husayn was the *de facto* ruler of an area of Iran which extended from Kashan north to Qumm, eastwards to Natanz and Ardistan, and at times even further

---

110 Rayhani in ibid. 228 and n, 240–1.
111 Rayhani in ibid. 282–3, 293–4.
112 ZH 7:301–2; Amanat, *Kashan* 236.

eastwards as far as Tabas and southwards to Yazd. Eventually, during the prime ministership of Vuthuq ud-Dawlih, Masha'u'llah Khan was brought to Tehran and executed and Na'ib Husayn himself was hunted down in the hills around Kashan, arrested and executed in 1919.

Sharply varying accounts of Na'ib Husayn can be found. Some historians such as Hasan Naraqi describe Na'ib Husayn as nothing more than a bloodthirsty brigand who terrorized a large part of Iran. Muhammad Rida Khusravi, on the other hand, describes Na'ib Husayn as a people's hero who opposed the Russian and British hegemony over Iran. He states that Na'ib Husayn's reputation has been deliberately besmirched in the official reports and by those officials who have written their memoirs because Na'ib Husayn stood up to the Qajar 'kleptocracy' which controlled the country and which Na'ib Husayn repeatedly outwitted and humiliated. Hasan Naraqi's account is, however, undoubtedly coloured by the fact that Na'ib Husayn was responsible for the murder of his brother, while Muhammad Rida Khusravi appears to be infected by a romanticism not dissimilar to the writings of the Marxist historian Eric Hobsbawn about social bandits such as the Sicilian mafiosi.[113]

Despite their widely differing views about Na'ib Husayn, these two authors are agreed that his associate Rajab-'Ali Bakhtiyari was indeed nothing more than a robber and a brigand, whose actions when he raped the women and terrorized the Baha'is in Naraq (see p. 129) were typical of his actions elsewhere. They differ, however, in that Naraqi considers Bakhtiyari to have been a henchman and ally of Na'ib Husayn,[114] while Khusravi maintains that the government had deliberately tried to destroy Na'ib Husayn's reputation by linking him to Bakhtiyari whereas in fact Na'ib Husayn opposed the actions of Bakhtiyari.[115] The Baha'i accounts seem for the most part to support Naraqi in their negative assessment of Na'ib Husayn and their linking of Bakhtiyari to him.[116] One reason for the

---

113 See Hobsbawm, *Bandits*.
114 Naraqi, *Kashan dar Junbish Mashrutih* 151–5.
115 Khusravi, *Tughyan-i Nayibbin* 286–7.
116 See Natiq Isfahani, Tarikh Amri Kashan 45–6, 48–9; ZH 8b: 664–5; KD 2:255. However, for a more neutral assessment of Na'ib Husayn, see 'Alaqiband (Tarikh 425–30, 465–71) who considers that Na'ib Husayn was pushed into some of his actions by government misdeeds. Rayhani (in Amanat, 'Negotiating Identities' 284) states that, in the days when Na'ib Husayn and Mulla Habibu'llah divided the town between them, people preferred to be summoned before Na'ib Husayn rather than Mulla Habibu'llah Mujtahid.

differences in opinion about Na'ib Husayn may be the fact that while he mulcted and robbed many people of their money, he was always consider-ate towards the people of Kashan itself.[117]

In late 1919–early 1920 a travelling Baha'i teacher (*muballigh*), Mirza 'Abdu'llah Mutlaq, was visiting Kashan when the Islamic Council (Hay'at-i Islami) of the town asked him to come to a debate in the Madrasih Sultani. He asked for certain conditions such as the presence of the police to main-tain order but this was refused. Later a number of the clerics of the town led by Sayyid Ahmad Darivalluni and Mulla Baqir Masgar, together with a mob, came to a meeting that Mutlaq was to address. They made objections and tried to disrupt the meeting but Mutlaq demonstrated the falseness of what they were saying. Then Na'ib Lutfu'llah Munajjimi and Mirza Yahya Khan, the head of the gendarmerie, arrived and the clerics were unable to cause the disruption they had planned. The general disorder in the town, however, forced Mutlaq to leave.[118] Kashan was also visited by Hippolyte Dreyfus, Laura Clifford Barney and Madame Lacheney in 1906 and by Martha Root in 1930.[119]

Baha'i institutions and community life

Being on the main road between Tehran and the south of Iran, Kashan was visited by most of the well-known travelling Baha'i teachers (*mubal-lighs*) at one time or another. In January–February 1909 Mirza Mahdi Akhavan Safa, one of these teachers, came to the town and during his visit formed the Baha'i Local Spiritual Assembly of Kashan.[120] It consisted from the start of Baha'is from both Jewish and Muslim backgrounds. As noted above, general meetings of the whole Baha'i community were initially held on Friday afternoons but were eventually moved to Saturday afternoons. At these meetings one or more of the learned Baha'is or visiting Baha'i teachers would give a talk, following which tea would be served. There would also be the recital of Baha'i prayers and Baha'i poetry as well as songs and music from men and women.[121]

While he was visiting Kashan in early 1909, Mirza Mahdi Akhavan

---

117 See in particular 'Alaqiband Tarikh 466–7.
118 MH 4:133–44; Natiq Isfahani, Tarikh Amri Kashan 31; Rayhani in Amanat, 'Negotiating Identities' 263–4.
119 Natiq Isfahani, Tarikh Amri Kashan 31.
120 Amanat, *Kashan* 85.
121 ibid. 88–90.

Safa also spoke to the Baha'is about the importance of education. A traditional *maktab* had been started in the home of the above-mentioned Khajih Rabi'. The *maktab* teacher had been Hakim Faraju'llah, but he had died in 1905. During this visit Akhavan Safa re-established this *maktab* and it was taught by Aqa Muhammad Isma'il, known as Arbab, who had been a Shaykhi before becoming a Baha'i. Then in 1327/1909 Aqa Mirza Ruhu'llah Khadim Mazgani came from Tehran and reorganized the school along modern lines, setting up several classes according to ability and appointing teachers and assistants. The school was named the Vahdat-i Bashar School (School of the Unity of Humanity) by 'Abdu'l-Baha. A large number of Baha'i and Jewish children started to attend the school. Mirza Ruhu'llah also established classes in the Baha'i community for propagating the Baha'i Faith and moral education classes for the Baha'i children.[122]

In 1328/1910 Natiq Isfahani (see pp. 151–2) was passing through Kashan. The Baha'is of Kashan persuaded him to remain and teach in the school, and when Mirza Ruhu'llah left in 1329/1911, he became headmaster. In the same year the school moved from the house of Khajih Rabi' to a new, larger building in the Rangrizan district. In 1331/1912–13 one of those hostile to the Baha'is obtained a copy of *Durus ud-Diyanah* (by Shaykh Muhammad 'Ali Qa'ini) which had been in the hands of one of the pupils of the school. Those opposed to the Faith proclaimed that this book was against the *shari'ah* and was being taught at the school and they demanded the school be closed. But the Baha'is asked the central government to give the school official recognition and this was granted.[123] In 1332/1914 a secondary class was added to the six primary classes.[124] In March 1917 Fa'izih Khanum (vol. 1:81–3) came to Kashan and remained for a year and three months. She found that there was a Baha'i boys' school but no girls' school since the girls were expected to be weaving carpets. She consulted with the local Baha'i assembly and a house was rented and furniture obtained so that she could start a school, to which some 32 girls – Baha'is, Muslims and Jews – came. During the day she also gave classes for the Baha'i women and in the evenings to the Baha'i men. She converted several people during this visit including a Mulla Abu'l-Qasim of Abyanih (see p. 146) with whom

---

122 Natiq Isfahani, Tarikh Amri Kashan 25–6; Arbab, 'Khanih-yi muqaddas' *Payam Badi'* 87 (1990) 38–42; ZH 7:276; Amanat, *Kashan* 146–7, 153–7, 225. On Arbab Muhammad Isma'il, see also Rayhani in Amanat, 'Negotiating Identities', 275–6.

123 Natiq Isfahani, Tarikh Amri Kashan 26–7; ZH 7:301.

124 Mazandarani, *Asrar* 5:283.

she spoke unveiled.[125] It appears that the school then fell into abeyance for a time but was restarted in 1921 owing to the efforts of a visiting Baha'i teacher, Mirza Munir Nabilzadih, and Masha'u'llah Laqa'i and progressed greatly after Maryam Natiqi (née Afsahi, wife of 'Ata'u'llah Natiqi, the head of the boys' school) became head.[126]

Burials were a continuing problem for the Baha'is because the Muslim religious leaders would not allow the Baha'is to be buried in the town cemeteries. One practice that became common was for people to be buried in the grounds of their own homes. In Ramadan 1339/May 1921 Aqa Muhammad Ibrahim (known as Nam, 'wet', because his occupation was to wet and package tobacco leaves; he had been one of the Baha'is imprisoned in 1902) died and was buried in the general cemetery. A crowd of Muslims emerged from the mosque of Mulla Habibu'llah Mujtahid, went to the cemetery, dug up the corpse and dragged it around the streets of Kashan, finally dumping it in the Jewish cemetery. The Jews also rejected the body and it was finally buried at Mikhchal, a property owned by some Baha'is.[127]

In 1339/1920 'Abdu'l-Hamid Mirza Mawzun took over as head of the school. In 1921 there was an attempt to organize an attack on the school. Sayyid Ahmad Darivalluni, who was now leader of one of the political parties in Kashan, had ill-feelings against the Baha'is after he had been worsted in a discussion with Mirza 'Abdu'llah Mutlaq the previous year; Mahdi 'Abdu'r-Rasul, the head of education in the city, was hostile; and the governor Sardar Ashja' Tabrizi was weak and ineffective. The Baha'is appealed to the authorities in Tehran and eventually orders came that the name and staff of the school should be changed. The minister of education at this time, Sayyid Husayn Qummi, had complied with the wishes of the enemies of the Baha'is. As a result, the school was shut down and the school's name-board was taken down by the local official of the Ministry of Education. When word of this reached 'Abdu'l-Baha, he wrote directly to the prime minister Qavam us-Saltanih, protesting that these people have the word 'civilization' on their lips but their actions are tearing out the roots of civilization. The prime minister sent orders instructing that the school be opened again with the same name and the same staff.[128] Later

---

125 Fa'izih, untitled treatise 196–209.
126 Amanat, *Kashan* 163.
127 Natiq Isfahani, Tarikh Amri Kashan 24; ZH 7:322; memoirs of Mirza Rayhan Rayhani (from an electronic file of a typescript provided by Mr Ehsan Reyhani); Amanat, *Kashan* 315–16.
128 Natiq Isfahani, Tarikh Amri Kashan 27–8; Faizi, *'Abdu'l-Baha* 319–21;

(before 1925) 'Ata'u'llah Natiqi took over as headmaster, followed by 'Ali Muhammad Nabili in 1928 and, after three years, 'Abbas Mahmudi (son of Mahmud Vadqani, see fig. 57 and p. 141). By this time the school was considered the foremost school in Kashan and the children of many of the notables of the town, such as the Ghaffari and Shaybani families, and even the children of religious leaders, such as the Thiqat ul-Islam and Shari'atmadari families, attended. In the latter part of 1932 there was another attempt by the local education ministry officials to close down the school; it was finally closed by the authorities in December 1934 as part of the general shutdown of the Baha'i schools.[129]

The Dutch writer and traveller Maurits Wagenwoort, who was interested in the Baha'i community of Iran, records that when he visited Kashan in 1905 it was reported to him that the Baha'i community of Kashan was more than a thousand strong at this time (and therefore about three per cent of the population of the town), of whom a hundred were Jews who had become Baha'is (out of a Jewish pop. of 1,000).[130]

Naraq

Naraq is a large village on the road between Kashan and Mahallat (70 km west of the former and 30 km east of the latter; pop. 3,000 in 1914; 2,504 in 1955). It became famous during the early 19th century owing to the residence there and in Kashan of Mulla Ahmad Naraqi, one of the most important clerics of the reign of Fath-'Ali Shah. It is situated in the hills near Kashan and thus many of the notables of Kashan repaired to the village in the summer months.

The Babi religion was introduced to Naraq in 1844 when one of the leading clerics of the village, Mulla Muhammad Ja'far Naraqi (usually called just Mulla Ja'far, d. 1869, see fig. 51) became a Babi. His father, Mulla Muhammad Qasim, was a son-in-law of the famous Mulla Ahmad Naraqi, mentioned above.[131] Mulla Ja'far had studied at Najaf and Karbala,

Ishraq-Khavari, *Sharh-i Tawqi' Naw-Ruz 113* 34–5; Ishraq-Khavari, *Muhadarat* 1:526–9; ZH 7:324.

129 For details of the shut-down of the school in Kashan, see MH 9:331–8.
130 Cited in De Vries, *The Babi Question* 71.
131 ZH4:171, 6:679 states Mulla Ja'far was married to the daughter of Mulla Ahmad; Bamdad, *Tarikh* 6:219 states it was a granddaughter. According to Mulla Ja'far's son, Sharif Kashani (Tarikh-i Ja'fari 2–3), he was first married to a daughter of Mulla Ahmad and when she died, he married a granddaughter.

obtaining the rank of *mujtahid*, and
had also been a student of Sayyid Kazim
Rashti. He then settled in Kashan
where he established himself as a religious leader and teacher. He appears to
have spent part of every year in Naraq
and was Imam-Jum'ih in one of the
mosques there. He was a Shaykhi and it
was presumably on account of this that
he met Mulla Husayn Bushru'i (who
was on his way north from Shiraz) in
Kashan in 1844 and thus became a
Babi.

51. Mulla (Muhammad) Ja'far Naraqi

Mulla Ja'far then returned to Naraq
and was successful in converting a substantial number of the people of the
village over the years. His most important convert was Haji Mirza Kamalu'd-
Din (d. early 1882), whose father, Mulla Muhammad Taqi, was the third
son of the famous Mulla Ahmad Naraqi.[132] Kamalu'd-Din was married to
Munirih (known as Sayyidih Khanum), a granddaughter of Mirza Abu'l-
Qasim known as Mirza-yi Qummi. Both of these ancestors, Mulla Ahmad
Naraqi and Mirza-yi Qummi, had been among the top-ranking clerics of the
reign of Fath-'Ali Shah.[133] Kamalu'd-Din's conversion was in late 1269/1853
and because he then openly began to proclaim his new faith to the people of
the village, Mulla Ja'far encouraged him to travel immediately to Baghdad
to meet with Mirza Yahya Azal whom Mulla Ja'far strongly supported. But
Mirza Yahya would not meet Kamalu'd-Din and only gave a very inade-
quate reply to his request for a commentary on a verse of the Qur'an (3:93).
Baha'u'llah, however, gave a reply (Lawh-i Kull ut-Ta'am, Tablet of All Food)
that satisfied Haji Mirza Kamalu'd-Din, who returned to Kashan a follower
of Baha'u'llah.[134] His wife also became a Babi and later a Baha'i and was
named Umm Nur (Mother of Light) by Baha'u'llah.[135] Kamalu'd-Din also
converted his two sisters Agha Bigum and Jahan Khatun, as well as a number
of the residents of Naraq. With these relatives and converts, he made a
further trip to Baghdad to see Baha'u'llah.[136]

---

132 Darrabi, *Tarikh Kashan* 284.
133 For brief biographies of these two see Momen, *Shi'i Islam* 318, 319.
134 Furughi, *Sharh Vaqayi'* 6–7; ZH 6:678–85.
135 Amanat, *Kashan* 328.
136 Furughi, *Sharh Vaqayi'* 7.

52. Mirza Muhammad Mahdi Sharif Kashani (son of
Mulla Ja'far Naraqi)

Another prominent citizen of Naraq who became a Babi and travelled to Baghdad was Mirza Mustafa Naraqi. He remained there for some time, becoming a follower of Baha'u'llah. He then returned to Naraq for a while before setting out again to visit Baha'u'llah. He arrived in Istanbul just as Baha'u'llah was leaving for Edirne and so only had a brief interview with him before being instructed to return to Iran. He then lived for a time in Qazvin and Tabriz, copying the writings of Baha'u'llah. He was arrested in Tabriz and executed there on 11 January 1867 (vol. 1:365–6).[137] A third notable of the village to convert was Haji Mirza 'Ali Akbar Naraqi. After the execution of the Bab, Mulla Ja'far had started to tell the Babis of Naraq to do reprehensible deeds. When 'Ali Akbar had challenged him as to whether these were the instructions of the Bab, Mulla Ja'far had replied that they were the orders of Azal, the Bab's successor, and that Azal had said that everything that had previously been forbidden was now allowed. 'Ali Akbar then left for Baghdad to visit Azal and find out for himself. He managed to find Azal's residence but Azal refused to meet with him. Eventually 'Ali Akbar met with Baha'u'llah and returned to Naraq as his follower.[138]

In the mid-1850s, after the execution of the Bab, both Nabil Zarandi and Haji Mirza Musa Qummi were in Naraq propagating their claims to be *Man Yuzhiruhu'llah* (He whom God shall make manifest) among the Babis of the village and distributing their poetry, thus leading to divisions

---

137 'Abdu'l-Baha, *Memorials* 148–50; Samandar, *Athar* 207–8; Ishraq-Khavari, *Muhadarat* 1:335–8.
138 As recounted by Mirza 'Ali Akbar's son Mirza Muhammad Taqi Badi' ul-Mamalik to Qabil Abadihi ([Tarikh Amr] 78–9).

among the Babis. Meanwhile Haji Mirza Kamalu'd-Din, upon his return from Baghdad, had led an upsurge in Babi activities, with both he and Mulla Ja'far preaching the new religion from the pulpit. This led to uproar among the clerics of Naraq and Kashan, led by Mulla Rida Va'iz Yazdi. Mulla Ja'far tried to deflect this attack by denying his adherence to the Bab from the pulpit but it only temporarily quieted the situation. The governor of Kashan, 'Isa Khan Biglarbigi, reported the matter to Tehran. Eventually, on 8 January 1860, many of the Babis of Naraq were arrested and their homes looted. Mulla Ja'far and his son Mirza Muhammad Mahdi Sharif Kashani (d. 1922, see fig. 52) were arrested and exiled to Iraq, where they settled in Kazimayn and continued to support Mirza Yahya Azal against Baha'u'llah.[139]

Haji Mirza Kamalu'd-Din was asked by the people to replace Mulla Ja'far as Imam-Jum'ih in Mulla Ja'far's mosque in the village. After about a year, Haji Mirza Kamalu'd-Din suddenly, in the middle of leading prayers, decided he could no longer conceal his true beliefs in this way and walked out of the mosque. Haji Mirza Kamalu'd-Din then tried to convert his uncle Mulla Muhammad Naraqi, who was one of the leading clerics of Kashan (see p. 85). He did not convert but was usually protective of the Babis and later the Baha'is in Kashan and Naraq.[140] Then Mulla Ja'far returned and tried to live unobtrusively in Naraq but once again his enemies stirred up the population and again the governor sent reports to Tehran. The shah wanted to send troops to Naraq to tear the place apart but the village was the fief (*tuyūl*) of the shah's sister 'Izzat ud-Dawlih (see fig. 53). In addition, Khan Baba Khan, the maternal uncle of the shah, was married to the sister-in-law of Mirza Mahmud Naraqi, Kamalu'd-Din's brother. These two women intervened strongly and managed to persuade the shah that reports from Naraq had been exaggerated. Although Mulla Ja'far had been sufficiently frightened to go to Kashan and publicly repudiate the Babi religion in front of Mulla Muhammad Naraqi, the shah neverthe-less decided to exile him to Iraq, where he again settled in Kazimayn in

---

139 ZH 4:181–2. Baha'u'llah states that Mulla Ja'far had, at about this time, ordered every Babi to pay over one-fifth (*khums*) of their wealth to him (*Athar Qalam A'la* 7:234–5) and Sayyid Mahdi Dihaji asserts that he had put forward a claim to be 'Him whom God will make manifest' (Dihaji, *Risalih* 69). For 'Abdu'l-Baha's assessment of Mulla Ja'far, see Ishraq-Khavari, *Ma'idih Asmani* 5:265–6.

140 ZH 6:678, 679–80n, 681; however, according to one account (Furughi, *Sharh Vaqayi'* 10–11) he did on one occasion order the severe beating of Haji Mirza Kamalu'd-Din.

53. 'Izzat ud-Dawlih

early 1862. When Baha'u'llah left Baghdad in 1863, Azal entrusted his wife Maryam (Qanitih) and son Mirza Nuru'llah to Mulla Ja'far before himself leaving Baghdad. In 1286/1869 the Persian consul in Baghdad, Mirza Buzurg Qazvini, arrested Mulla Ja'far and brought him and his son Mirza Husayn (Sharif Kashani) and Azal's son Mirza Nuru'llah back to Iran with him. Mulla Ja'far fell ill in Kirmanshah and was eventually transferred to prison in Tehran, where he died on 18 July 1869. He is generally thought to have been poisoned or strangled.[141]

Shortly after Mulla Ja'far's exile from Naraq, during the month of Ramadan (March 1862), one of the Babis of Naraq was discussing religious matters and said that the laws of fasting had been changed. To prove the point he ate some fruit that he had just purchased. The crowd seized him and took him to the governor's residence. His brother, who tried to rescue him, was taken as well. Haji Mirza Kamalu'd-Din sent a messenger to ask for the release of the two Babis and the messenger was arrested, as were Kamalu'd-Din himself and his brother Mirza Mahmud when they went to take the matter up. A mob descended on the Babi houses but found their way blocked by six Babis with guns in their hands, led by Haji Mirza 'Ali Akbar, the above-mentioned notable of the area. A commotion ensued and the mob was dispersed. The next day the *kadkhuda*, who was friendly towards the Babis, intervened. He went to the governor and spoke to him in such a way that he took fright and fled the area in women's clothing. The Babi captives were released. The governor, however, sent reports to Tehran of what had happened and warned that if the Babis of Naraq were not suppressed they would take over the area. The government there sent a force to take control of Naraq. Haji Mirza 'Ali Akbar, as soon as he heard of this development, sent his family off to Hamadan, where his father lived, and later joined them there. But his father was opposed to the new religion and threw them out, so they went on to Baghdad.[142]

---

141 ZH4:142–3; Bamdad, *Tarikh* 6:219–22.
142 The account of this episode from 1860 to 1862 is drawn mainly from ZH 4:178–84, Bamdad *Tarikh* 6:219–22, Furughi, *Sharh Vaqayi'* 4–5. However, the latter part of the account in ZH 4:185 appears to conflate with the later episode in 1873–4.

It was Haji Amin (see pp. 413–14) who brought news of Baha'u'llah's claim to Kashan and Naraq. Despite Haji Mirza Kamalu'd-Din's experience in Baghdad and possibly because of the strong influence of Mulla Ja'far in the area, it took a month of arguing before Kamalu'd-Din and his brother accepted Baha'u'llah's claim.[143] After this, however, within a short time and despite the influence of Mulla Ja'far and his support of Azal, most of the Babis of Naraq became Baha'is. Haji Mirza Kamalu'd-Din gradually converted many in the village to the Baha'i Faith, including some prominent citizens, such as Aqa Muhammad Kazim Nazim ut-Tujjar.[144] The Baha'is of the village eventually numbered more than a hundred in the time of Baha'u'llah (i.e. three to four per cent of the population of the village).[145]

After the rebellion of Shah Mirza (see pp. 85–7) in the 1870s was over and because Mustafa-Quli Khan Saham us-Saltanih had failed to capture Shah Mirza himself, Saham us-Saltanih descended upon the village of Naraq, which was known to contain many Baha'is. He arrested Haji Mirza Kamalu'd-Din, his brother Mirza Mahmud, Aqa Muhammad Javad, Aqa Nasru'llah, Haji Muhammad Taqi and some other Baha'is of the village. He was particularly after Mirza 'Ali Akbar and swore on the Qur'an that he only wanted to speak with him, but when Mirza 'Ali Akbar came to speak, Saham us-Saltanih arrested him also. The family of Mirza 'Ali Akbar, who were prominent merchants, came to Saham us-Saltanih to intercede for him and he collected a large sum of money from them and more money from other relatives of the prisoners. Then on the evening before he was due to release the prisoners, he incited some of the village rabble to enter a local shrine, Imamzadih Shah Sulayman, damage it, burn the Qur'an there and kill some of its doves. The next day he gave out that the Baha'is had done this. The mob was thus raised to a fever pitch and they, together with the troops, fell upon the houses of the Baha'is, arresting and looting. Since many of the men had already fled, it was mainly women and children who were arrested.[146]

Eventually in about 1873 or 1874, some 17 Baha'is, including Mirza 'Ali Akbar, his brother Aqa Muhammad Mahdi, Kamalu'd-Din and his brother Mirza Mahmud, were sent to Tehran in chains, accused of being accomplices of Shah Mirza. The mother of Mirza 'Ali Akbar, who was also

---

143 Information from Mrs Bahiyyih Varqa, a granddaughter of Mirza Mahmud Naraqi, at interview on 1 Sept. 1980, at her residence in London.
144 Furughi, *Sharh Vaqayi'* 7–8.
145 ZH 6:678.
146 ZH 5:140–3.

a Baha'i, took decisive action. She hurried off to Tehran and through her connections (she was related to Mirza Ja'far Vazir and other notables) was able to gain an audience with the shah's sister 'Izzat ud-Dawlih, to whom she tearfully recounted the depredations caused by Saham us-Saltanih. Through 'Izzat ud-Dawlih, the mother of Mirza 'Ali Akbar was able to gain an audience with the shah and put her case to him and 'Izzat ud-Dawlih also pleaded for the prisoners. In the meantime, Haji Mirza Kamalu'd-Din and the other arrested Baha'is also arrived in Tehran. The shah sent orders that the Baha'is, who were awaiting their fate in the caravanserai adjacent to the city square where public executions were held (Maydan Pa-Qapuq), should be sent instead to the 'Anbar (royal prison) for further investigation of the matter. Saham us-Saltanih, whom 'Izzat ud-Dawlih had accused of being responsible for the destruction in Naraq, took sanctuary in the shrine of Shah 'Abdu'l-'Azim and had to give the shah a large bribe to ensure his freedom. Eventually after nine months, through the further intervention of 'Izzat ud-Dawlih, the Baha'i prisoners were released. They returned to Naraq but faced much hardship as their properties had been destroyed, they were boycotted by the local tradesmen and excluded from the public baths. Consequently many of them migrated elsewhere.[147]

Haji Mirza Kamalu'd-Din continued to live in Naraq. He suffered much persecution, including one night when Mirza Muhammad 'Ali

---

147 ZH 5:143–4. The same author appears to be referring to this episode also in ZH 4: 185, except that there it is doves in the Imamzadih that are killed instead of a Qur'an burned, and it is the wife of Mirza Mahmud and her sister who take the matter up with 'Izzat ud-Dawlih but the involvement of Saham us-Saltanih and mention of 17 prisoners being sent to Tehran in both accounts make it likely that both are accounts of the same episode. Furughi, *Sharh Vaqayi'* 4–5 confirms that it is the same episode by saying that both doves were killed and a Qur'an was burned in this episode. Possibly referring to this same episode, Furughi, *Sharh Vaqayi'* 10 indicates that Mustawfi ul-Mamalik intervened to obtain their release. Another account that is possibly referring to this episode (Amanat, *Kashan* 328) states that Munirih Khanum, the wife of Kamalu'd-Din Naraqi, went to see Mahd-i Ulya, the mother of Nasiru'd-Din Shah, and succeeded in winning her over to make an intervention with the shah (in which case this episode must have occurred before 1873 when Mahd-i Ulya died). It is of course possible that all of these interventions occurred one after the other over a period of time. This episode could also be the basis of the report from the French minister in December 1874 to the effect that a dozen Babis had been arrested in Kashan and sent to Tehran, where they were imprisoned, interrogated and eventually set free (BBR 249–50). But it is more likely that this report refers to arrests in Kashan at this time, see p. 87.

Shaykh ul-Islam of Naraq organized an attack on his house, during which
one of his children was killed.[148] Haji Mirza Kamalu'd-Din's brother Mirza
Mahmud (d. 1308/1890) moved to Tehran and then to Sa'in-Qal'ih in
Adharbayjan (vol. 1:422–3) before returning to Tehran. His sons Mirza
'Ata'u'llah Sani' us-Sultan (d. 1944), who worked in the customs department, and Mirza Nasru'llah Khan Muhaqqiq ud-Dawlih were among the
most prominent Baha'is of Tehran.[149]

During the 1860s and 1870s, partly because of the persecutions in
Naraq, many Baha'is moved out of the village and some of these moved
to the west of Iran where they formed a network of merchants from
Hamadan to Adharbayjan. Among these were the above-mentioned Aqa
Muhammad Javad Naraqi and his brother Aqa Muhammad Baqir Naraqi,
two merchants who were neighbours of Haji Mirza Kamalu'd-Din. Aqa
Muhammad Javad became a Babi in Naraq and together with Haji Mirza
Kamalu'd-Din was responsible for many conversions. Although he was
already married according to Islamic custom, his marriage was renewed
by Baha'u'llah with a Babi oration while the couple were visiting Baghdad.
The couple then moved to Hamadan, where they settled and he converted
his brother. In Hamadan these two brothers were responsible for instigat-
ing the conversion of Jews to the Baha'i Faith (see pp. 181, 183). They
continued to maintain homes in Naraq and visited frequently. They owned
the Haji Mahdi Caravanserai in Naraq and had built a mosque and water
cistern as public benefactions in the village.[150] When Haji Amin and Mirza
Asadu'llah Isfahani visited Naraq in late 1881 they met with and converted
a few Azalis.[151] Among other travelling Baha'i teachers who came to Naraq,
Qabil Abadihi was particularly successful in his efforts.[152]

The persons who initiated most of the persecution of the Baha'is of
Naraq were Shaykh Abu Turab Mahallati and his son Shaykh Muhammad, both residents of Mahallat. Na'ib Husayn, the *kadkhuda* of Naraq
(not to be confused with Na'ib Husayn, the rebel mentioned above), was
beholden to Shaykh Abu Turab because each year he had to go to Mahallat to obtain a continuance of his post and needed to curry favour with
Shaykh Abu Turab to ensure this. Each year Shaykh Abu Turab used to

148 Furughi, *Sharh Vaqayi'* 8–10; Information from Mrs Bahiyyih Varqa (see note
    143 above).
149 ZH 6:685–7; Varqa, 'Khandan-i Varqa' 52–3; Furughi, *Sharh Vaqayi'* 12.
150 Furughi, *Sharh Vaqayi'* 8–9; ZH 6:687–9.
151 Asadau'llah Isfahani, Yad-dasht-ha 66.
152 Furughi, *Sharh Vaqayi'* 18–19.

send his son, Shaykh Muhammad, to Naraq for *rawdih-khani*. Shaykh Muhammad was in fact ignorant and illiterate but everyone deferred to him because of Na'ib Husayn. During the whole two month period that he was in Naraq, he used to curse and rant against the Baha'is in his preaching. He got the Baha'is banned from the public baths and boycotted by traders; some Baha'is were beaten at his instigation. These problems continued for the Baha'is until Shaykh Muhammad's early demise.[153]

Na'ib Husayn, the *kadkhuda* of Naraq, assisted Shaykh Muhammad in his depredations of the Baha'i community. 'Alaqiband writes that during the 15 years that he had lived in Tehran he had seen on numerous occasions Baha'i families from Naraq who had been deprived of homes and possessions by this man, come to Tehran to try to seek justice. They would obtain a decree and return, only for the same to occur again a few years later.[154] One of these occasions was in 1903 when, following the anti-Baha'i pogrom in Yazd, some of the residents of Naraq obtained a decree for the death and destruction of the Baha'i community of the village from clerics in Kashan. They showed this to Shaykh Muhammad Mahallati, who then preached against the Baha'is from the pulpit. The situation became so dangerous that most of the Baha'is fled the village for Jasb from where some of them went on to Qumm; some tried to return to Naraq but had to flee again. From Qumm they telegraphed the government in Tehran and obtained instructions from the shah to the governor of Kashan that they were to be safely returned to Naraq. They went with these instructions to the governor in Kashan. He was prepared to carry them out but some of those hostile to the Baha'is insisted that first six of the leading Baha'is should go before Mirza Fakhru'd-Din Naraqi and recant their faith. Therefore the Naraqi Baha'is went to Tehran to petition the government again. They were there six months. Meanwhile, some of the people of Naraq tried to have the properties of the Baha'is confiscated so that they would be permanently excluded from the village. But a number of the leading opponents either fell ill or died (this may be related to an outbreak of cholera in the Kashan area in 1904[155]) and the Baha'is were able to return. Na'ib Husayn the *kadkhuda* had attached himself to Zill us-Sultan and whenever there was any danger to his position, he would pay a bribe to Zill us-Sultan to use his influence to remove the danger. Na'ib Husayn the *kadkhuda* was eventually killed by Na'ib Husayn Kashi

153 ibid. 23–37.
154 'Alaqiband, Tarikh 426–7.
155 Amanat, *Kashan* 412.

the rebel (see pp. 115–17) in December 1908 in Jawshqan (see p. 142).[156]

In 1918 there was general disorder throughout the country and the central government was weak. In the Kashan and Qumm area, Na'ib Husayn Kashi had seized power. In the late summer of this year, Rajab-'Ali Firaydani Bakhtiyari (see p. 116),[157] an outlaw who was in league with Na'ib Husayn Kashi entered Naraq with some 400 men and took over the village. Rajab-'Ali took up residence in the house of Aqa Fadlu'llah Mu'avin ut-Tujjar, the son of the above-mentioned Muhammad Javad Naraqi and a prominent Baha'i merchant of the village, who had been a trader in Adharbayjan for some years (vol. 1:419, 424) and then returned to Naraq in 1914. Rajab-'Ali wanted a wife while he was in Naraq and he had set his sights on the daughter of Mu'avin ul-Mamalik, a notable of the village who was absent at the time. Mu'avin ul-Mamalik's wife 'Udhra Khanum promised her to him if he would kill Mu'avin ut-Tujjar. Rajab-'Ali's men raided and looted the houses of the village. Over a hundred women and girls of the village were forcibly married and raped. Some of the enemies of the Baha'i Faith in Naraq, and especially Aqa Muhammad Mujtahid, incited Rajab-'Ali and his men to attack the Baha'is. They began extorting money from them, demanding 1000 *tumans* from Mirza Muhammad 'Ali Furughi and 500 *tumans* from Mu'avin ut-Tujjar. They tortured Mu'avin ut-Tujjar by branding him, demanding that he recant his faith, and broke Furughi's teeth. Then they took these two to their base in the village of Siniqan, where on the orders of Rajab-'Ali (and probably because Rajab-'Ali had promised this to 'Udhra Khanum), Mu'avin ut-Tujjar was shot dead. Rajab-'Ali then proceeded to Qamsar (see pp. 133–4).[158]

From various indications, it is possible to estimate that the number of Baha'is in Naraq was about a hundred in 1920 but had been higher previously and many had migrated as indicated above.

156 ZH 7:225–6; 'Alaqiband, Tarikh 426–7.
157 Naraqi, *Kashan dar Junbish* 149, 151–2. He is variously described as being from the Lur or Bakhtiyari tribe. His seal read 'Rajab 'Ali Chahar-Lang' (Naraqi, *Kashan dar Junbish* 153). All these designations are correct since the Chahar-Lang is a sub-section of the Bakhtiyari, who are in turn a section of the Lur tribe. See also Faizi, *'Abdu'l-Baha* 297, which states that he was a Bakhtiyari from Firaydan. Na'ib Husayn Kashi was also of the Lur tribe (see Khusravi, *Tughyan-i Nayibin* 81).
158 ZH 7:319–20 states that it was Masha'u'llah Khan, son of Na'ib Husayn Kashi, who took Mu'avin ut-Tujjar to Siniqan and killed him there, but preference has been given to the account of Furughi (*Sharh Vaqayi'* 38–43), who was an eyewitness. See also Faizi, *'Abdu'l-Baha* 297–8; KD 2:253–4.

Qamsar and Mazgan

Qamsar is a large village in the hills (31 km south of Kashan; pop. 3,113 in 1914, nearly 4,000 in 1951), famous for its rose water. Nearby were the mines from which was obtained the lapis lazuli that makes the azure, ultramarine or cobalt-blue pigment of the tiles for which Kashan was famous. The upper part of the village, where most of the Baha'is lived, is only two kilometres from the small village of Mazgan to the southwest. Sayyid Basir Hindi was one of the first to preach the Babi religion in the villages of Qamsar and Mazgan in 1849 and several were converted.[159]

In Qamsar, Sayyid 'Abdu'r-Rahim (or Mir 'Abdu'r-Rahim) was one of those converted by Sayyid Basir. He was a much respected religious leader in the village and was well known for curing people. He travelled to Baghdad and met Baha'u'llah and became his follower. He in turn converted about one hundred of the people of Qamsar.[160] His brother Sayyid Ibrahim Mir-Husayni, who was also a religious leader in the village, was another prominent convert.[161]

In Mazgan (a small village of about 100 people), Shaykh Abu'l-Qasim (1792–1287/1870) was the leading religious authority, a well-known figure whose opinions were held in great respect even in the town of Kashan itself. He would be invited to the larger nearby villages such as Qamsar to preach, especially during the commemorations of the martyrdoms of the Shi'i Imams and during the month of Ramadan. He became a Babi, through Sayyid Basir Hindi,[162] and later a Baha'i. Meetings were held at his home to which people came from Mazgan and Qamsar and he succeeded in converting everyone in the village of Mazgan and many in other villages to the Baha'i Faith. He left his position of religious leadership and fell into great poverty, being forced to collect bramble for firewood as a means of livelihood. In about 1862 he was arrested and sent to Tehran. After a time he was freed and returned to his home.

As mentioned above, during the rebellion of Shah Mirza in 1287/1870, Shaykh Abu'l-Qasim was again arrested by the troops of Saham us-Saltanih and handed over to the governor of Kashan Jalalu'd-Din Mirza Ihtisham

---

159 KD 1:438–9.
160 Natiq Isfahani, Tarikh Amri Kashan 32; Vujdani, 'Athmar Shish Shajar'; Amanat, *Kashan* 423. His descendants took the surname Vujdani.
161 Amanat, *Kashan* 422–3.
162 ZH 3:93–4; DB 589–90 (Shaykh Abu'l-Qasim is called Shaykh-i Shahid, the martyred Shaykh, here).

ul-Mulk (117th son of Fath-'Ali Shah, who was governor of Kashan from
1868 to 1871, d.1872). He was beaten severely and thrown into prison,
then taken before Mulla Muhammad Naraqi, who refused, however, to
issue a death sentence against him. Eventually, through the intercession of
Mirza 'Abdu'llah Qamsari, one of the notables of the area who was friendly
towards the Baha'is and protected them on a number of occasions, he was
released. But 'Isa Khan (the brother of Fathu'llah Khan Shaybani from one
of the leading families of Kashan and in charge of the telegraph office)[163]
complained to the government and a further order was sent to Ihtisham
ul-Mulk for Shaykh Abu'l-Qasim to be put to death. Officials were sent to
arrest Shaykh Abu'l-Qasim but Mirza 'Abdu'llah had warned the Baha'is
and Shaykh Abu'l-Qasim could not be found, despite their harassing and
even torturing people in the area. Eventually they bribed someone in
Qamsar who through trickery found out where the Shaykh was hidden
and revealed this to the officials. Shaykh Abu'l-Qasim was taken off to
Kashan and publicly executed outside the governor's office (*divān-khānih*)
in 1287/1870.[164]

The men of Mustafa-Quli Khan Saham us-Saltanih descended a further
time upon the Baha'is of Mazgan. When they arrived in the village,
however, Mirza 'Abdu'llah had again warned the Baha'is and the men had
fled into the hills. So the soldiers looted some of the houses and harassed
some of the women. They managed to arrest three of the men and three
women (one of whom they beat severely) and took them to Qamsar in
preparation for taking them to Kashan. But Mirza 'Abdu'llah and his wife
interceded for them and they were released, although the houses of the
Baha'is of Qamsar were looted.[165]

In 1896, after the assassination of Nasiru'd-Din Shah, Aqa Zaynu'l-
'Abidin, the *kadkhuda* of Mazgan and a Baha'i, was surrounded by some
Sayyid ruffians in Kashan, beaten, taken off to the house of Aqa Sayyid
Hasan Imam and accused as a Baha'i of being party to the assassination of
the shah. When he refused to recant his belief, he was sent to the governor
of Kashan 'Abbas Mirza I'zaz ud-Dawlih, where he spent 40 days in an

---

163 Darrabi, *Tarikh Kashan* 392–3.
164 Natiq Isfahani, Tarikh Amri Kashan 13–14; ZH 5:137–40; KD 1:438–40; see
     also 'Abdu'l-Baha's words on Shaykh Abu'l-Qasim and his son Shaykh 'Ali Akbar
     Mazgani in *Memorials of the Faithful* 104–5. On the history of the Babi and
     Baha'i religions in Mazgan, see Munjadhib, Mukhtasari.
165 Natiq Isfahani, Tarikh Amri Kashan 34–5; ZH 6:691.

underground prison and was released after the Baha'is paid a fine for him.[166]

After the death of Mirza 'Abdu'llah Qamsari, who had been their great protector, the persecution of the Baha'is in this area increased. A number of the notables of the village combined to harass the Baha'is. In 1901 a few of the Baha'is went to Kashan and telegraphed Muzaffaru'd-Din Shah seeking relief from their oppression. The government sent back a telegram to the governor Muhammad Ja'far Khan in their favour. This sparked off an even greater uproar in the village and a delegation of villagers was sent to Kashan while the people prepared to attack the Baha'is. Ten of the Baha'is hurried to Kashan to try to obtain protection for the community. The authorities, on this occasion, extended their help to the Baha'is, settled the disturbance and dispersed the mob. However, the enemies of the Baha'i Faith in Qamsar did not let matters go: they harassed the Baha'is and banned them from the mosque and public baths. Thus some of the Baha'is were forced to bathe in their own homes and some to go to Mazgan and use the baths there. Eventually, on 'Abdu'l-Baha's instructions, the Baha'is of Qamsar built their own more hygienic baths. At about this time one of the notables of Qamsar, coming upon Bibi Jan Khanum, one of the Baha'i women, on the road between Qamsar and Mazgan, beat her so severely that she died a few days later. An official was sent to investigate this but returned after receiving a suitable bribe from the murderer.[167]

Since Qamsar was up in the hills, many of the leading personages of Kashan repaired to this village during the summer season. The arrival of such people as Aqa Nizam Pusht-Mashhadi and Mulla Habibu'llah Mujtahid was sometimes used by the enemies of the Baha'is as a way of initiating an attack. On one occasion, Aqa Nizam Pusht-Mashhadi, who was from a prominent family of clerics of Kashan, was persuaded to arrest four of the Baha'is and had them bastinadoed and imprisoned. It was only when 50 of the Baha'is took refuge in the telegraph office and sent petitions to Tehran that the men were released.[168] In 1324/1906, when Mulla Habibu'llah was visiting Qamsar in the summer, some people accused the Baha'is of Mazgan of cursing the clerical class. Mulla Habibu'llah sent his son Aqa Mahdi and a crowd of people to Mazgan where they seized Aqa Zaynu'l-'Abidin, the *kadkhuda* of the village, and brought him before Mulla Habibu'llah. After he refused to recant, he was beaten and sent to

---

166 Natiq Isfahani, Tarikh Amri Kashan 35–6; ZH 7:95.
167 Natiq Isfahani, Tarikh Amri Kashan 36–7; ZH 7:140–1.
168 Natiq Isfahani, Tarikh Amri Kashan 37–8; ZH 7:141.

the deputy governor of Qamsar, Habibu'llah Khan Fini. The latter imprisoned the *kadkhuda* and sent men to Mazgan to arrest four other Baha'is,
whom he also imprisoned in his house. Some of the women of Mazgan
came before Mulla Habibu'llah and asked why their husbands were being
treated thus. Mulla Habibu'llah asked them whether they were Baha'is.
They answered, 'If God accepts us as such,' whereupon the son of Mulla
Habibu'llah beat them with his water pipe (*qalyan*) until it was smashed to
pieces and others also attacked them. Eventually the imprisoned men were
released after having a large fine extorted from them.[169] As a result of such
persecutions, some of the Baha'is of these two villages migrated to Tehran.

Some of the people of Qamsar tore up a Qur'an and then accused
a Baha'i, Mir Muhammad 'Ali, of this action. Realizing his life was in
danger, he fled to Tehran, where his family later joined him. His son, Mirza
Habibu'llah Samimi (d. 1941), attended the classes of Sadr us-Sudur and
from 1906 began to travel and teach the Baha'i Faith. After a few years he
settled in Barfurush and later Nishapur and started a business but continued to teach the Baha'i Faith actively.[170] Another who left for Tehran as a
result of persecutions was Ustad 'Ali of Mazgan, who had become a Baha'i
through Shaykh Abu'l-Qasim. In Tehran he settled in a house adjacent to
the Hayat-i Bagh (vol. 1:31, 94–5) in the Sar Qabr Aqa district, where
his home became the location for the lessons of Sadr us-Sudur. His son
Mirza Nasru'llah (d. 1928) spent four years in 'Akka in the 1890s serving
in the travellers' hospice, hence 'Abdu'l-Baha addressed him in a tablet as
Khadim (servant) and he took this as his surname. In Iran he made a living
by selling cloth. In 1952 Mirza Nasru'llah's son Zikrullah Khadem was
named a Hand of the Cause by Shoghi Effendi.[171]

In December 1918 Qamsar was subjected to the same sort of attack
by Rajab-'Ali Bakhtiyari as at Naraq (see p. 129). The houses of all the
Baha'is were targeted by his men and looted. A group of 40 riders attacked
Mazgan and, after looting many houses, captured seven of the Baha'is.
They were tortured by branding and threatened with execution but refused
to recant their faith. Five of these Baha'is were then taken off to Qamsar
in the hope of extorting more money from the Baha'is there. In Qamsar,
one of them, Aqa Mandih-'Ali, was shot and killed and Aqa Husayn 'Ali
Qamsari (Azadih), who tried to help him, was saved only because the gun

---

169 ZH 7: 244–5.
170 Rastigar, *Sadr us-Sudur* 59, 63–4; MH 4:26–7, 38–41; Amanat, *Kashan* 426–7.
171 'Ala'i, *Mu'assih* 612–3; Amanat, *Kashan* 433.

jammed; the rest were beaten and set free. The Muslims of Qamsar at first accounted Rajab-'Ali a true Muslim and urged him on in his persecution of the Baha'is. But when he had finished with the Baha'is, he meted out the same treatment to the Muslims of the village, looting their houses and raping the women. Eventually government troops arrived and chased Rajab-'Ali's men to near Gulpaygan where they killed many and captured others, taking them to Tehran where they were executed. Rajab-'Ali himself escaped capture but was then killed by one of his own men and his son was also killed shortly afterwards.[172]

In 1924–5, following the general attacks in other parts of Iran after the murder of Major Robert Imbrie in Tehran (vol. 1:104), the people of Qamsar attacked Aqa Rida, who had recently become a Baha'i. He was thrown into the river by a mob headed by Aqa Ahmad, the son of a local cleric, after which he was tied to a tree and beaten. He was then dragged through the streets and publicly tortured. The house of another Baha'i, Aqa Nasru'llah, was attacked and he and his wife, who had given birth only the previous evening, were beaten and left for dead.[173]

Aran

Aran is a small town (pop. 4,377 in 1296/1879[174]; about 4,000 in 1914 and 10,000 in 1951; 12 km northeast of Kashan) which has gradually merged with the neighbouring village of Bidgul. Aqa Muhammad Isma'il Siya (d. 1308/1890, his name indicates he may have been a descendant of black slaves) was the first to become a Babi there in about 1270/1853, having been converted by Arbab Aqa Mirza Nushabadi (Munzavi, see p. 137). He used to teach the Baha'i Faith as he peddled small items in the town and the surrounding villages, despite being subjected to much abuse and beatings. Two other Baha'is, Muhammad Qabili and Aqa Murtada Hamadani, came to the town (the latter in 1283/1866) and converted people, resulting in a large community.[175]

---

172 Natiq Isfahani, Tarikh Amri Kashan 40–2; KD 2:254–5; ZH 7:319–20; Faizi, 'Abdu'l-Baha 298–9; Rayhani in Amanat, 'Negotiating Identities' 293; Amanat, Kashan 428, 431–2.

173 Report of Baha'i persecutions in Iran compiled in the USA as a press release.

174 Mudarrisi-Tabataba'i, Qumm-namih 296–7.

175 Natiq Isfahani, Tarikh Amri Kashan 48; Fadil Mazandarani names the first Baha'i of Aran as Mashhadi Isma'il, who may be the same as Aqa Muhammad Isma'il Siya, and the second Baha'i as Mashhadi Qasim, who may be the Ustad Abu'l-Qasim mentioned in the next paragraph (Asrar 1:17).

Mirza Rayhan Rayhani (see pp. 104–5 and fig. 44), one of the Jewish Baha'is of Kashan, settled in Aran in the 1890s, having set up as a dealer in cloth. The other Jews in the town agitated against him, and Iftikhar ush-Shari'ah, who was a cleric and the leading notable of Aran, is said to have asserted that he would not allow a single Baha'i in the town. Among those who taunted Rayhani was a group of ten young linen-sellers (*karbās-furūsh*) in the bazaar. Eventually one of them, Ustad Abu'l-Qasim, was persuaded in 1906 to go to a Baha'i meeting at the home of Arbab Aqa Mirza in Nushabad at which Mirza 'Ali Akbar Rafsanjani and Tarazu'llah Samandari were speaking. He was converted and was the cause of the conversion of over a hundred others, including the nine other linen-sellers. Meetings were then held in the house of Ustad Muhammad, who had become a Baha'i in Kashan. On one occasion 50 people attended a meeting there at which Mirza Mahdi Akhavan Safa spoke. Eventually one of the Baha'is, Aqa Ramadan 'Ali, purchased the house of Iftikhar ush-Shari'ah and used it to hold Baha'i meetings.[176]

The number of Baha'is in Aran continued to increase. Mirza 'Ali Muhammad Bayda'i (Adib, 1881–1934, see fig. 54) was from a family of poets of the town and himself became a noted poet both of Iran and of the Baha'i community. He became a Baha'i while studying in Kashan in 1322/1904 and returned to Aran, holding meetings in his home and converting many. This incurred the enmity of his relative, Mulla Muhammad Mujtahid Shaykh ul-'Ulama, who eventually succeeded in forcing him to move from Aran to Kashan, where he worked in the justice and later the tax offices there.[177] His brother Ni'matu'llah Dhuka'i-Bayda'i (1903–86, see fig. 55) was also a poet and wrote a four-volume biographical dictionary of the Baha'i poets of the first Baha'i century.[178] Another poet to become a Baha'i through Bayda'i was Mulla Muhammad Hasan (Diya'i), who died in 1918 aged 45 as a result of a beating he received at the hands of the servants of Masha'u'llah Khan, the son of Na'ib Husayn Kashi.[179]

Mirza Mahdi Akhavan Safa who visited the town in March 1911 states that in contrast to his previous visit two years before when everything had

---

176 Rayhani describes this and implies that he settled in Aran in the 1890s but elsewhere in his memoirs he seems to say that it was after an episode of persecution in Kashan in about 1902 (in Amanat, 'Negotiating Identities' 232–3, 245–8, 251). A similar story is told in ZH 8b:709–10 but the first of those converted is called Aqa Lami' (Aqa Ramadan 'Ali) rather than Ustad Abu'l-Qasim.

177 Dhuka'i-Bayda'i, *Tadhkirih* 1:84–162; ZH 8b: 686–99; Amanat, *Kashan* 125–7.

178 Amanat, *Kashan* 127–8.

179 ZH 8b: 690; Amanat, *Kashan* 415.

54. Mirza 'Ali Muhammad Bayda'i (Adib)   55. Ni'matu'llah Dhuka'i-Bayda'i

to be done furtively, the Baha'i Faith was being taught quite openly in the town and up to 20 people who were not Baha'is attended the meetings at which he spoke. No one dared to oppose the Baha'is on account of the protection of one of the notables of the town, Na'ib 'Ali, who was not however a Baha'i.[180] Later the Baha'is of the town suffered at the hands of the men of the rebel Na'ib Husayn Kashi (see pp. 115–17), and Ustad Abu'l-Qasim was thrown into ice-cold water in the winter of 1918–19. He became sick and left for Tehran where he died, although he was still a young man. Also, Masha'u'llah Khan looted the entire crop of a Baha'i landowning farmer, Aqa 'Ali Muhammad, forcing him and his family to leave for Tehran, where he also soon died. Another Baha'i, Aqa Mahdi, was killed.[181]

The Baha'is of Aran established a local spiritual assembly. In 1332/1914 Arbab Aqa Mirza Muhammad Rida Fallah Arani (1302/1884–1961) established a small *maktab* in his home for teaching the children of the village. As the numbers grew, the school moved to a disused mosque and Mulla 'Ali Akbar Arani (d. 1336/1917), a leading cleric of the town who was converted by his nephew Mirza Mahmud Furughi (d. 1933), began to help with the

---

180 MH 4: 50–4.
181 Rayhani in Amanat, 'Negotiating Identities' 294; ZH 7:320.

teaching.[182] Although the school was closed for a time owing to the opposition of the clerics, in 1921 it was reorganized on a more modern basis, moved to the home which Furughi had vacated when he moved to Kashan, and named the Ma'rifat School.[183] The school for girls was held in the *hazirat ul-quds*. The schools later had a separate building and eventually consisted of five primary classes.[184] Natiq Isfahani, writing in 1930, states the number of Baha'is in the town was 200.[185] Fadil Mazandarani, writing in the 1950s, states their number was 500 (about five per cent of the population).[186]

Other villages around Kashan

The Baha'i community in Nushabad (4 km west of Aran; pop. 3,654 in 1296/1879;[187] 5,250 in 1950) arose in the early 1890s with the conversion of Aqa Mir Muhammad 'Ali Munzavi (known as Arbab Aqa Mirza), who was from a prominent Kashan family of sayyids and owned land near Nushabad which he farmed. He in turn converted several others in the village. He was subjected to much persecution. On one occasion it is reported that his death was ordered by Haji Sayyid Muhammad, but when a mob of some 6,000 came to carry it out, he stood on top of the tower of his house with a gun and no one dared approach. While he was away from home in 1918, his wife, who was also a Baha'i, was shot dead by men of the rebel Na'ib Husayn (see pp. 115–17). He himself was so deeply affected by this that he died a few days later.[188] Another Baha'i was a young man named Sayyid Isma'il Basir. When his father found out that he had become a Baha'i, he ordered some men who were digging wells nearby

---

182 ZH 8b: 690, 718–19; Dhuka'i-Bayda'i, *Tadhkirih* 1:92–5. According to Amanat (*Kashan* 414–15), Mulla 'Ali Akbar's introduction to the Baha'i Faith was through his desire to put his friend Bayda'i right and his conversion was following a meeting with Muhammad Natiq in Kashan. Amanat (*Kashan* 415–16) states Mirza Mahmud's conversion was following his meeting with local Baha'is, but Mazandarani asserts that, following this introduction, he was converted during a trip to Qazvin (ZH 8b:718–20).

183 Dhuka'i-Bayda'i, *Tadhkirih* 3:203–13; Vathiqi, Tarikhchih 43–9.

184 ZH 8b: 718–19.

185 Natiq Isfahani, Tarikh Amri Kashan 48.

186 *Asrar* 1:17. In 1951, there was a general attack by the Muslims of the town upon the Baha'is and one Baha'i was killed (Ishraq-Khavari, *Taqvim* 207–8).

187 Mudarrisi-Tabataba'i, *Qumm-namih* 296.

188 ZH 7:36, 315, 8b:664–5; KD 2:255; Natiq Isfahani, Tarikh Amri Kashan 45–6; Rayhani in Amanat, 'Negotiating Identities' 243, 293–4; Amanat, *Kashan* 412.

to suspend him in a well until he recanted. But after they had suspended him, Sayyid Isma'il said to the men that they could do to him what had been done to his ancestor (meaning Imam Husayn) and he would not be affected. And so they let him go.[189] Another who was suspended in a well to make him recant was Aqa Gul Muqanni-bashi (chief digger of wells and *qanats*). He remained under such pressure that eventually he left with his family for Tehran.[190] Another Baha'i who was forced to leave the village was Muhammad Ramadan 'Ali, whose father issued a *fatwa* for his death and whose wife was forcibly married off to another.[191] A Baha'i community arose in the village but on account of the severe persecution they experienced, some 20 left the village and migrated to Tehran and elsewhere and only a small, weak community was left.[192]

One of the most prominent Baha'is from this village was Mirza Hasan Rahmani Nushabadi (1891–2 February 1962, see fig. 56). His father, Lutf-'Ali, had died shortly after receiving a severe beating from one of the enemies of the Baha'is in the village, Sayyid Radi. His mother, Halimih Khatun, had also died when Mirza Hasan was aged 12. Despite this, Mirza Hasan managed to scratch together an education. From 1910 to 1914 he accompanied Mirza Mahdi Akhavan Safa of Yazd, one of the travelling Baha'i teachers (*muballighs*), as he travelled around Iran. In between trips he would teach at various Baha'i schools around the country. From 1914 onwards he began to travel on his own around Iran as a *muballigh*. His expenses from 1916 to 1939 were paid by Mirza Aqa Khan Qa'im-Maqami (see pp. 160–1 and fig. 64). There were few parts of Iran that he did not visit (he also visited India and Singapore in 1958) before he fell ill. He was the author of several books and responsible for converting many to the Baha'i Faith (vol. 1:265–6).[193]

Yazdil (11 km west of Aran; pop. 1,200 in 1950), which is close to Nushabad, also had a Baha'i community. Arbab Muhammad Rida and his son-in-law Arbab 'Ali Rabbani, notables and landowners in the village, were Baha'is.[194]

---

189 Natiq Isfahani, Tarikh Amri Kashan 46; Amanat, *Kashan* 410.
190 Natiq Isfahani, Tarikh Amri Kashan 46; Amanat, *Kashan* 412–13; his descendants took the surname Vahman.
191 Amanat, *Kashan* 413; his descendants took the surname Ramadani.
192 Natiq Isfahani, Tarikh Amri Kashan 46; Amanat, *Kashan* 410.
193 MH 6:92–167; ZH 8b:699–700; *Akhbar Amri* year 41, no. 3–4 (June–July 1962) 206–9; Amanat, *Kashan* 411–12.
194 Amanat, *Kashan* 419–20.

Fin (about 6 km west of Kashan; pop. 2,175 in 1296/1879;[195] 4,300 in 1950) is an area of great natural beauty with plentiful water and many trees, for which reason it was a favourite place to which the people of Kashan would repair for recreation. It is famous as the place to which Mirza Taqi Khan Amir Kabir, the first prime minister of Nasiru'd-Din Shah, was exiled and where he was killed on the shah's orders. Haji Mulla Husayn (d. 1322/1904, Tehran) was a religious leader and notable of the village. He became a Baha'i and, after having concealed his belief for a number of years, on 10 Muharram 1310/5 August 1892, when the people of the village were commemorating the martyrdom of Imam Husayn, he ascended his pulpit and announced that since Imam Husayn had now appeared (i.e. Baha'u'llah had come), they should put away the accoutrements of mourning and lay out a joyful feast. He then began snapping his fingers as though for a dance. The congregation turned on him and pulled him from the pulpit and began to beat and kick him. He managed to get away from the mob but had to leave the village.[196] Fa'izih Khanum records that Fin was a favourite place for the Jews of Kashan to gather in the summer months and that she addressed a large gathering of them in 1918, after which three men and three women became Baha'is.[197]

In several other villages to the north and northwest of Kashan there were communities of Baha'is. Aqa Muhammad Big, who ran a shop and caravanserai in Sansan (some 37 km north of Kashan on the road to Qumm), had been the host when the Bab stayed in the village on his way north in March 1847. He became a follower of the Bab and later a Baha'i. He converted members of his family and was host for many Baha'is passing through the village. In 1311/1893 Aqa Najafi was passing through Kashan on his return from a pilgrimage to Mashhad. The accusation that Aqa Muhammad Big was a Baha'i was brought up and Aqa Najafi wrote to Mirza Hasan Ashtiyani in Tehran asking for instructions to be sent for Aqa Muhammad Big's execution.[198] On Aqa Najafi's instructions, Husayn Khan Saham us-Saltanih continued to press for action until eventually the governor of Kashan, Muhammad Hasan Khan Anis ud-Dawlih, ordered Aqa Muhammad Big's arrest. He was being taken to Isfahan to be examined by Aqa Najafi when the latter sent word to the soldiers taking him

---

195 Mudarrisi-Tabataba'i, *Qumm-namih* 282–5.
196 Natiq Isfahani, Tarikh Amri Kashan 15; ZH 7:33.
197 Fa'izih, untitled treatise 205–7.
198 Safa'i, *Namih-ha-yi Tarikhi* 64–5.

56. Mirza Hasan Rahmani Nushabadi   57. 'Abbas Mahmudi

that Aqa Muhammad Big should not be brought to Isfahan but put to death immediately. The soldiers tortured him, burnt all the hair on his head, drowned him and then burnt his body at Murchihkhurt, about 50 kilometres north of Isfahan. One of the Baha'is of Murchihkhurt recovered the body and brought it to Isfahan for burial. Although Aqa Muhammad Big's son went to Tehran to try to obtain justice, when interrogated, Saham us-Saltanih denied any wrong-doing saying the old man died of natural causes on the way.[199]

Aqa Muhammad Big told Hasan the miller (*asiyaban*) in Sansan of his belief and converted him in 1847. This Hasan was from Vadqan (Vadgan, 45 km northwest of Kashan; pop. 194 in 1296/1879;[200] 900 in 1950). He returned to his home village to spread the word of the message of the Bab. The first to become a Babi in Vadqan was Mulla 'Abdu'l-Hadi (d. before 1868), a cleric who was also a landowner and farmer. He succeeded in converting many in the village and, although attacked by the Muslims, the Babis prevailed. He was succeeded as the leader of the Babis

---

199 Natiq Isfahani, Tarikh Amri Kashan 16–18; ZH 6:669, 7:45; MH 9:310–11; Amanat, *Kashan* 262–3.
200 Mudarrisi-Tabataba'i, *Qumm-namih* 314.

in Vadqan by his son Mirza Mahmud (d. 1337/1918). When Baha'u'llah announced his claim, Mirza Mahmud accepted this and brought all the Babis in the village into the Baha'i Faith.²⁰¹ Haji Mirza Kamalu'd-Din also taught the Baha'i Faith in this village and sent his son Aqa Nuru'd-Din there regularly. There was eventually established a community of some 60 Baha'is in the time of Baha'u'llah (about 30 per cent of the village). Other travelling teachers who visited the village included Ibn Abhar, Mirza Aqa Rahmaniyan, Mirza Mahdi Akhavan Safa, Tarazu'llah Samanadari, Mirza 'Ali Akbar Rafsanjani, Qabil Abadihi and Mirza Baba Khan Avihi. The son of Mirza Mahmud, 'Abbas Mahmudi (October 1896–?, see fig. 57), taught the children in the Baha'i villages to the south of Tehran from 1918 to 1922 (vol. 1:105–6) and then was a teacher and later headmaster of the Vahdat Bashar School, 1922–34. He became a full-time *muballigh* from December 1940, travelling mostly in the southern half of Iran from Kirmanshah in the west to Zahidan in the east, until ill health forced him to cease this role in 1971.²⁰²

Because several of the Baha'is of the village were very influential (especially after Vazir Humayun settled in the village, see pp. 90–1), there was little opposition to the Baha'i Faith there and the numbers reached 200 at one stage during the time of 'Abdu'l-Baha. Fa'izih Khanum came to the village and converted Vazir Humayun's mother, Ashraf ud-Dawlih, and the two daughters of his brother Mukhtar ud-Dawlih in 1917.²⁰³ Natiq Isfahani reports, however, that because of famine and the depredations of the followers of Na'ib Husayn (see pp. 115–17), many moved away from the village and the numbers dropped to a little more than 60 by the time he was writing his history in 1930.²⁰⁴ Vazir Humayun purchased a house to be a Baha'i school in the village and this was later the *hazirat ul-quds*; later still, when a new, larger *hazirat ul-quds* was built, this building became the Baha'i public baths.²⁰⁵

Haji Muhammad Taqi Navvab, who was an uncle of Haji Mirza Jani, had met the Bab in Kashan and become a Babi. He had property in the large village of Jawshqan (24 km northwest of Kashan; pop. 556 in 1296/1879;²⁰⁶ 2,900 in 1950) which he visited frequently. In the course of

201 'Abbas Mahmudi in MH 9:309–12.
202 MH 9:309–52.
203 Fa'izih, untitled treatise 194–204.
204 Natiq Isfahani, Tarikh Amri Kashan 48–9; MH 9:309–12.
205 MH 9:315.
206 Mudarrisi-Tabataba'i, *Qumm-namih* 310.

his visits he converted a number of the residents of the village. Although he himself pulled away from the new religion as a result of the split with Azal,[207] those whom he converted, such as Mulla Muhammad Ja'far, did not. By the beginning of the 20th century regular meetings were being held and some villagers were converting. Among those who converted were Haji Shaykh Husayn Khurasani, who was known as Shams ul-Va'izin, a popular preacher in the mosque of the Imam-Jum'ih of the village. In 1903 there was a general upheaval against the Baha'is of Jawshqan, when the cleric Aqa Sayyid Hasan Imam of Kashan (see p. 131) was visiting the village. He had Shams ul-Va'izin thrown out of the mosque and other Baha'is arrested and beaten to make them recant. The Baha'is of Jawqshan took refuge in the nearby small village of Fathabad where most of the inhabitants were Baha'is. As the mob from Jawshqan approached the village, a few shots were fired from Fathabad. Although no one was hurt, this was enough to frighten the mob and disperse them. Then the Baha'is returned to Jawshqan and took a uncompromising stance, carrying arms and threatening to retaliate if attacked. They even prevented Aqa Sayyid Hasan from preaching in the mosque. This effectively drained the enthusiasm of their opponents and the turmoil gradually subsided. Realizing that they had contravened the Baha'i teachings in the actions they had undertaken, the Baha'is of Jawshqan and Fathabad wrote to 'Abdu'l-Baha asking for forgiveness, which was granted. Shams ul-Va'izin later resumed his preaching in the mosque at the invitation of Mulla Muhammad 'Ali Shari'atmadar.[208]

In 1908 there was a further episode when Na'ib Husayn Naraqi (see pp. 127–8) with a hundred horsemen was sent by the government against Na'ib Husayn Kashi (see pp. 115–17) who had a stronghold in the hills around Jawshqan. Naraqi announced that when he had taken care of Kashi, he would attack the Baha'is. The Baha'is were very fearful of this but during the night two of Kashi's men slipped into Jawshqan and killed Naraqi. Naraqi's men then retreated.[209] At this time one of the leading Baha'is of Jawshqan was Arbab Fadlu'llah (Rawhani), a wealthy landowner. His Baha'i wife was Mah-Liqa Khanum, daughter of Mulla Muhammad

---

207 When Nabil Zarandi visited in the spring of 1862, Navvab sent a message that if he was going to create turmoil as he had on his previous visit then Navvab would leave with his family in order to save themselves, MH 10:567.

208 Natiq Isfahani, Tarikh Amri Kashan 50–2; ZH 7:223–4; 'Andalib vol. 8, no. 31 (Summer 1989) 49. 'Abdu'l-Baha is said to have commented that, on occasions, the Jawshqani language is also necessary.

209 MH 4:556–7.

'Ali Shari'atmadar.[210] Fadil Mazandarani writing in the 1930s estimated the number of Baha'is in Jawshqan to be a hundred.[211]

In Fathabad (near Jawshqan; pop. 45 in 1296/1879[212]) Aqa Mir Muhammad 'Ali (d. 1349/1930) had become a Baha'i in 1294/1877 and converted many of his relatives and others in the village and in Jawshqan and Nushabad. He was eventually forced to leave for Tehran, where he took up residence in the village of Diya'abad (vol. 1:106) and was much respected by its inhabitants.[213] Also among the Baha'is of Fathabad were the seven sons of Mir 'Abdu'l-Wahhab Munzavi, a prominent family of sayyids and landowners, who were all gifted poets. Four of them lived in Fathabad, among them Sayyid Husayn, who was also an excellent calligrapher but died young, and Sayyid Radi, who, although a Baha'i, kept distant from community activities so that suspicion did not fall on him. Another brother, Sayyid Nasru'llah, lived in Kashan and his home was a centre of Baha'i activities. They had a sister, Fatimih Khanum, who was also a poet.[214] Eventually all the inhabitants of this village were Baha'is. Later, in about 1910, during the rebellion of Na'ib Husayn, the Baha'is of Fathabad were again subject to persecution and several of them left for Tehran.[215]

A wealthy landowner from the villages around Kashan was Arbab Aqa Baba of Mushkan (30 km northwest of Kashan; pop. 1,051 in 1951). He also managed the properties of Vazir Humayun (see pp. 90–1). Another landowner in this village was Haji Husayn of Vadqan. He was opposed to the Baha'i Faith but his sons, who were sent to manage his properties in Mushkan, became Baha'is. Mirza Rayhan Rayhani taught the Baha'i Faith here and, gradually, a Baha'i community developed.[216]

Thus as a result of persecutions and particularly of the depredations of Na'ib Husayn Kashi, many of the Baha'i villagers of the Kashan area

210 Amanat, 'Negotiating Identities' 284 and n; Amanat, *Kashan* 401–2. They were driven out of Jawshqan in 1950 after a conflict with a local cleric, Shaykh 'Ali Akbari. Their son was Qudratu'llah Rawhani, a member of the National Spiritual Assembly of Iran killed in 1981 by the government of Islamic Republic of Iran.

211 Mazandarani, *Asrar* 3:59.

212 Mudarrisi-Tabataba'i, *Qumm-namih* 127.

213 ZH 6:692–4; ZH 8b:717–18.

214 ZH 8b: 686; Asadu'llah Isfahani, Yad-dasht-ha 68; Amanat, *Kashan* 115–17.

215 Rayhani in Amanat, 'Negotiating Identities' 242–3; MH 4:557.

216 Rayhani in Amanat, 'Negotiating Identities' 286–7; Amanat, *Kashan* 409–10, 439.

moved to the villages owned by Sayyid Nasru'llah Baqirof, to the south of
Tehran (vol. 1:105–6). From Jawshqan alone a hundred Baha'is migrated
to these villages.[217]

Natanz and the surrounding villages

Natanz is a small town situated between Kashan and Isfahan (74 km southeast of Kashan; pop. 3,000 in 1905 and 4,000 in 1951). The importance of
this area for Babi and Baha'i history lies not so much in the town itself but
in a number of small villages to the southwest of the town. These consisted
of Tarq (32 km southwest of Natanz; pop. 1,500 in 1914, 4,430 in 1951);
Tar (7 km northwest of Tarq; pop. including surrounding hamlets about
600 in 1914; 1,590 in 1951) and Kishih (5 km north of Tarq; pop. including surrounding hamlets about 300 in 1914; 1,200 in 1951).[218]

One of the religious leaders of this area, Mulla Muhammad Baqir Mujtahid Tari, had been a Shaykhi and subsequently a Babi. Through him
most of the inhabitants of Tar and many in Kishih and Tarq were converted. When the division between the Baha'is and Azalis occurred, Mulla
Muhammad Baqir became one of the foremost proponents of Azal in Iran.
In 1889, when Mirza Mustafa the Azali was forced to flee from Sidih (see
pp. 48, 50), he took refuge with Mulla Muhammad Baqir in Tar and there
is some evidence that other Azalis from Isfahan also took refuge there.
Gradually, however, some of the Azalis from this area became Baha'is. In
Kishih, the two brothers Mulla Habibu'llah and Mulla Valiyu'llah converted from being Azalis to being Baha'is and gradually many other Azalis
in Kishih became Baha'is, such that Baha'is formed the majority in the
village.[219] A rough estimate would be that there were about 160 Baha'is in
Kishih out of a population of less than 300.[220] In Tar, however, the Azalis
did not convert.

---

217 Natiq Isfahani, Tarikh Amri Kashan 45; MH 9:315–31; Rahmatu'llah Afsahi in
     Amanat, *Kashan* 403, also 407–8.
218 Very rough approximates of populations have been formed from the figure of
     300 houses in Tarq and the tax revenues given in the *Historical Gazetteer* 1:650–
     1. Unfortunately the tax revenues clump together the villages of Tarq, Tar and
     Kishih with their surrounding hamlets.
219 ZH 8a:169–70; Mazandarani, *Asrar* 5:32–3.
220 The estimate of about 160 Baha'is comes from the list of 32 heads of families in
     the time of 'Abdu'l-Baha in Mazandarani, *Asrar* 5:32–3. The figure of 160 is also
     mentioned in *Century of Light*, p. 8

Fadil Yazdi records his visit to this area in about 1921. By this time most of the Azalis of Kishih had become Baha'is but the whole village of Tar was still Azali. One of the learned Azalis of Tar, Shaykh 'Ali, had inclined to the Baha'i Faith shortly before his death and Fadil Yazdi together with Mirza Muhammad Kishihi and the Shaykh ul-Islam of Tarq visited Tar to take part in his memorial meeting. Yazdi states that he met with Shaykh Muhammad Rafi' (see fig. 58), the Azali leader in Tar, who told him that the Azalis of the village held no meetings. Although Shaykh Muhammad

58. Shaykh Muhammad Rafi' Tari

Rafi' remained an Azali, his brother Shaykh Muhammad Tahir and about 50 of the Azalis of the village became Baha'is as a result of a series of meetings held at this time, although many of these must have later left the village or reverted to being Azalis since there were only a few Baha'is in Tar in later years.[221] In 1928 Sayyid Hasan Mutavajjih visited the area and again met with Shaykh Muhammad Rafi'. He found the latter to be smoking tobacco and partaking of opium. When Mutavajjih protested that this was against the explicit laws of the Bayan, the Shaykh replied that the day for the implementation of those laws had not yet arrived.[222]

Abyanih is a small, isolated town high in the hills to the south of Kashan (35 km west-northwest of Natanz; pop. 1,200 in 1914; 2,000 in 1951). Amu 'Ali 'Askar of Kashan (see p. 96), after he had visited Baha'u'llah in 'Akka, became so enthused that he decided to tell his relatives in Abyanih about the Baha'i Faith. He first went to Aqa Shaykh Husayn, the senior cleric of the town, and spoke to him about the new religion. He accepted this immediately as the fulfilment of a 40-day period of austerity and prayer he had undertaken in his desire to meet the promised Qa'im and which had ended the previous night in a dream of the Imam 'Ali. This man

---

221 MH 7: 361–6; email communication from Dr Cyrus Agahi, 10 Nov. 2005.
222 MH 6:84–5.

taught others the Baha'i Faith, including most of his sons, who included
Mulla Muhammad Husayn, the *kadkhuda* of the town.[223] Fa'izih Khanum
writes of a certain Ghulam-Rida who had been arrested, stripped of his
wealth and expelled from this town as a Baha'i on the orders of Mulla
Abu'l-Qasim and was living in Kashan in 1917. This Mulla Abu'l-Qasim
came to Kashan in this year and Ghulam-Rida challenged him to meet
and debate with Fa'izih Khanum. After much discussion, the cleric was
converted and returned to Abyanih where he assisted the Baha'is.[224] Eventually, a local spiritual assembly was formed there.

Ardistan

Ardistan is a small town situated on the road between Yazd and Kashan
(88 km northwest of Na'in, 126 km southeast of Kashan and 160 km
northeast of Isfahan; pop. 10,000 in 1914, 8,264 in 1953). It is known as
the birthplace of Anushirvan the Just (d. c. 579) of the Sasanian dynasty,
one of the most loved kings of Iran. In the 19th century it was described as
consisting of six *mahallihs* (quarters) spread over a large area with cultivation of wheat, barley, cotton and opium intervening between them, such
that it could almost be said to consist of six separate villages. The area is
also famous for its pomegranates, carpets and knitted goods. Being close
to the great central desert of Iran, water is scarce and is carried by *qanats*
from the nearby hills. One *mahallih*, Bab ur-Raha in the northeast part of
the town, was populated predominantly by Baha'is.[225]

The first person from Ardistan to become a Babi was Mulla 'Ali Akbar
Ardistani (originally from Zavarih, see p. 153), who was descended from
Fadlu'llah Ahmad Pir Jamali (d. 879/1474), the founder of the Pir Jamali
Sufi order[226] and who was a grandson of Mulla Muhammad Sadiq Ardi-
stani (Pulavi, d. 1134/1721), one of the foremost mystical philosophers
of his time.[227] Mulla 'Ali Akbar was a pupil of Mulla Sadiq Muqaddas

---

223 Amanat, *Kashan* 441–2.
224 Fa'izih Khanum, untitled treatise 197–200. Ghulam-Rida may be the same as
　　the individual named Ghulam-Rida Khunsari (Amanat, *Kashan* 442), who was
　　driven out of Abyanih, in which case he was later living in Ardistan.
225 MH 6:324.
226 Sa'idi, Tarikh 24–5, 51 and Appendix 2; Haqiqat, *Tarikh* 629–31.
227 Muhammad-Husayni, *Tarikh Qumm* 56; Muhammad-Husayni, *Hadrat-i Bab*
　　206–7; Tihrani, *adh-Dhari'ah*, vol. 4, p. 334, no. 1467; Suha, *Tarikh Hukama*
　　27, 32 (this latter source gives his date of death as 1113/1701).

Khurasani (vol. 1:122–3) and became a Babi following immediately upon his teacher in 1844. He and Mulla Sadiq were among four persons who were the first Babis to be persecuted in Iran, an episode which occurred in Shiraz in 1845 (see p. 249). After this he came to his home town with Quddus and Mulla Sadiq Muqaddas and they succeeded in converting many.[228] Some seven Babis of Ardistan participated in the Shaykh Tabarsi episode including, according to one source, Mulla 'Ali Akbar himself.[229] He and Mirza Haydar 'Ali were the only ones from Ardistan to survive this episode. Mulla 'Ali Akbar lived on in Ardistan and also spent two years in Tabriz in about 1858–9.[230]

When Zaynab Bigum heard in 1844 that Mulla Husayn Bushru'i was propagating a new claim in Isfahan in the Madrasih Nimavard (see fig. 59), which had been built in 1117/1706 by her ancestor, Amir Muhammad Mahdi Hakim ul-Mulk,[231] she hurried there with her two sons. It may be that, since she was a Shaykhi, she had met Mulla Husayn on his previous stay in Isfahan. She and her two sons became Babis, as did later her husband, Mirza Muhammad Taqi Zavarihi.[232] Zaynab Bigum's brother Mirza Muhammad Sa'id Zavarihi was a renowned poet with the pen-name Fada', who was at the court of Manuchihr Khan Mu'tamad ud-Dawlih. Although Mirza Muhammad Sa'id probably cannot be considered a Babi, he was very sympathetic to the Bab, whom he almost certainly met in Isfahan and to whom he addressed some questions which elicited a response.[233] One of Zaynab Bigum's sons, Mirza Muhammad, was killed at Shaykh Tabarsi but her other son, Mirza Haydar 'Ali Ardistani (d. 1323/1905), survived and was a prominent citizen and landowner in the area who lived in the Bab ur-Raha quarter of Ardistan. He was later in the retinue of

---

228 ZH 3:103; Malik-Khusravi, *Tarikh* 2:191–4.
229 Malik-Khusravi (*Tarikh* 2:193–4) comments that the only source that names Mulla 'Ali Akbar as a participant and survivor of Shaykh Tabarsi is Isfahani, *Bihjat* 46–7. Nabil, *Narrative* 421.
230 Samandar, *Athar* 179–80, 287; ZH 6:526.
231 Hunarfar, *Athar Tarikhiyyih Isfahan* 679–82; according to Muhammad-Husayni, (*Hadrat-i Bab* 816), this lady and her brother were also descendants of Pir Jamali (in addition to Mulla 'Ali Akbar).
232 Muhammad-Husayni, *Hadrat-i Bab* 206; Muhammad-Husayni, *Tarikh Qumm* 56. On this family see Muhammad-Husayni, 'Tarikh-i Ardistan'.
233 Muhammad-Husayni, *Hadrat-i Bab* 482, 816–17; this source states that Mirza Muhammad Sa'id's son, Mirza 'Ali Muhammad, became a Babi and was killed in the Shaykh Tabarsi episode; he is named in DB 421, but not by Malik-Khusravi in *Tarikh*.

59. Madrasih Nimavard, Isfahan

Farhad Mirza Mu'tamad ud-Dawlih.[234] The whole family converted others in Ardistan and several of these converts succeeded in meeting the Bab in Isfahan. Zaynab Bigum also organized meetings in the village of Marbin (33 km south of Ardistan; pop. 1,000 in 1953), which belonged to her father. Quddus taught the Babi religion to many people there.[235] In early 1850 Vahid Darabi also visited Ardistan, where one of his sisters lived.[236]

Over the years Zaynab Bigum continued holding large meetings at her property in Marbin, resulting in the conversion of many, including two notables of the area who were sayyids and wealthy landowners and who became major proponents of the Baha'i Faith in Ardistan. The first of these was Mirza Fath-'Ali, who was the son of the sister of Mirza Haydar 'Ali and who was named by Baha'u'llah 'Fath-i A'zam' (d. sometime after 1873). In 1279/1862 he led a group of 17 Babis from Ardistan on a visit to Baha'u'llah in Baghdad and became a firm follower.[237] The second was Mirza Rafi'a (d.

234 ZH 3:103, 8a:166–7; Malik-Khusravi in *Tarikh* 1:193–4 (this source gives his date of death as 1319/1902); Muhammad-Husayni, *Hadrat-i Bab* 481–4.
235 Muhammad-Husayni, *Hadrat-i Bab* 462.
236 ZH 3:467.
237 ZH 6:220.

1306/1888). Also among those converted were Aqa Muhammad 'Ali Naddaf and Fatimih Khanum, a married couple whose sons were later to become the leading Baha'is in Qumm.[238] With all these prominent Babis being ardent supporters of Baha'u'llah, even before he laid claim to any station, and some such as Fath-i A'zam being openly dismissive of the leadership of Azal,[239] it is not surprising that all the Babis of this area became Baha'is.

As a result of the teaching of these prominent Baha'is, almost the whole of the Bab ur-Ruha quarter of Ardistan became Baha'is.[240] There was, however, some opposition to the Baha'is in Ardistan. In 1881 a certain Haji Mirza Muhammad 'Ali, who had been antagonistic to the new religion for some time, began a campaign. He sent a report to the government that a number of 'Babis' were active in the town. As a consequence, officials were sent to arrest them. The Baha'is learned of this and most fled to the hills while some made for Tehran. Two of them were arrested at Natanz on their way to Tehran. They had to make a payment of 400 tumans before they were set free.[241] During the famine which affected Ardistan badly in 1888, Fath-i 'Azam distributed grain from his storehouses to both Baha'is and the rest of the population.[242] Evidence of the open teaching and the gains being made by the Baha'i Faith in Ardistan in the 1890s is found in the anxiety expressed in a letter written by Aqa Najafi to Mirza Hasan Ashtiyani, the pre-eminent cleric in Tehran, in about 1893:

> At this time, a group from the damned Babi sect, may a thousand curses be upon them, have rebelled in the village of Ardistan which is close by Isfahan and are openly occupied with mischief and with spreading their infidelity. People are openly reading Babi books.
>
> A few days ago, a large number of sayyids and believers of that area came to Isfahan complaining of the heavy burden of Babi unbelief [in their area] . . . I ask that an order be issued by the government authorities that some of the leading Babis of Ardistan who are the repositories of unbelief and the originators of mischief and corruption should, in accordance with the Holy Law that should be obeyed, be tried before the clerics of Isfahan

238 Muhammad-Husayni, *Hadrat-i Bab* 482.
239 When Shaykh Salman brought writings of Baha'u'llah and Azal from Baghdad, Fath-i A'zam honoured those of Baha'u'llah and paid no attention to those of Azal, ZH 6:220.
240 ZH 3:103, 6:220–1, 8a:166.
241 Asadu'llah Isfahani, Yad-dasht-ha 94.
242 Sa'idi, Tarikh 58.

and executed so that the fire of this mischief may be extinguished and the Muslims of that area be relieved of the hardship of unbelief and occupy themselves with prayers for that holy being, his highness the shadow of God [i.e. the shah]. I do not ask for anything more.[243]

When Haji Mirza Haydar 'Ali Isfahani had visited Ardistan in the 1890s, he had found that almost all the Baha'is were illiterate.[244] In about 1901, when Shaykh 'Abdu'l-Husayn Avarih, who had been driven out of his home town of Taft, came through Ardistan, the Baha'is there persuaded him to stay in Ardistan and start a traditional school (*maktab*) for the Baha'i children of the village, funded by Fath-i A'zam.[245] However, this lasted for only three years, and in 1929, when Mirza Muhammad Thabit-Sharqi visited the town, he found that there were only two Baha'is there who could read and write. So he brought his own 13-year-old daughter, who had completed her secondary education, to the town to begin to teach the Baha'is there.[246] Fath-i A'zam also funded a Baha'i meeting place in the town, which was at first called a *mashriq ul-adhkar*.[247]

The next generation of Ardistan's Baha'is included Sayyid (or Mirza) 'Abdu'l-Husayn Ardistani (Rafi'i, vol. 1, fig. 40), son of Mirza Rafi'a, who dedicated a building in the town to Baha'i use, calling it at first the *mashriq ul-adhkar* and later the *hazirat ul-quds*. He lived part of the time in Tehran and attended the classes of Sadr us-Sudur (vol. 1:98). He also accompanied Fadil Mazandarani when, on the orders of 'Abdul-Baha, Mazandarani made a journey to Iraq in 1910 to acquaint the leading Shi'i clerics there about the Baha'i Faith (vol. 1:310) and after this, he accompanied Fadil to Egypt, India and throughout Iran until 1912.[248] Another son of Mirza Rafi'a was Mirza Aqa Majd (Majd us-Sadat), who became a very prominent local figure, able to extend his protection to the Baha'i community. On one occasion in 1324/1906, when Mirza Aqa Majd was away from Ardistan, the local clerics, on the instigation of Aqa Najafi, initiated a persecution of the Baha'is of the town. During this episode Aqa Sayyid Shahab, the son of Mirza Fath-'Ali Fath-i A'zam, and his son Nuru'd-Din were forced to migrate to Tehran, although his wife, Agha Bigum (1878–1964), the daughter of Mulla 'Ali

---

243 Safa'i, *Namih-ha-yi Tarikhi* 64–5.
244 Isfahani, *Bihjat* 304.
245 ZH 8a:167; 8b:961–2.
246 MH 6:324.
247 ZH 8a:167.
248 ZH 8a:167; MH 7:83–107.

Akbar Ardistani, remained behind in Ardistan for some years.[249] When
Mirza Aqa Majd returned, he seized the leading local cleric and put him
in a cage. The other clerics came and asked that their colleague be released,
promising never to raise another outcry against the Baha'is.[250]

The years of World War I were particularly chaotic in Iran as a whole and
in the Isfahan area in particular. Aqa Nuru'llah was striving to take over the
reins of clerical power in Isfahan after the death of his brother Aqa Najafi
in July 1914. One way of doing this was to launch a campaign against Jews
and Christians and, in particular, against Baha'is. German and British agents
were also competing for power and influence throughout Iran. Dr Pugin, the
German Consul in Isfahan, was in league with Aqa Nuru'llah and the other
major clerics in Isfahan and stirring up unrest was convenient to his purposes. In Ardistan at this time the deputy governor was Chiragh-'Ali Khan
Sawlat ul-Mulk (Sardar Sawlat) Bakhtiyari, son of Zaygham us-Saltanih and
son-in-law of Saham us-Saltanih (see p. 86). He had caused great suffering in the town by quartering his Bakhtiyari troops on the populace and
extorting sums of money from all. At the instigation of Aqa Nuru'llah, he
arrested Sayyid 'Abdu'l-Husayn Rafi'i and a large number of other Baha'is of
Ardistan. Sayyid 'Abdu'l-Husayn's father-in-law held British Indian citizenship and appealed to the British minister in Tehran, who intervened with the
government and the governor of Isfahan. A large sum of money was extorted
from the Baha'is and they were then set free.[251] Owing to the depredations
caused by Chiragh-'Ali Khan and by raiding tribesmen, many citizens of
Ardistan, including Baha'is, left for Tehran and other cities.

One of the Baha'i travelling teachers (*muballighs*) who emerged from
this area was the poet and scholar Shaykh Muhammad, who wrote poetry
under the name Natiq and became known as Natiq Isfahani (or Ardistani
or Nayistani, 1880–1936, see fig. 60) of Naysiyan (48 km south of Ardistan; pop 2,556 in 1951).[252] His father was a cleric of the village and Shaykh

---

249 Sa'idi, Tarikh, 60–3.
250 Telephone interview with Mr Heshmatollah Mohammad-Hosseini, 17 Oct.
     2004.
251 BBR 434–7; The British government handbook, *Tribes and Personalities of
     Western Persia* (109) states that Chiragh 'Ali Khan had married the daughter of
     the chief landowner of Ardistan and calls him a 'highwayman'.
252 Although he himself states in an autobiographical account (MH 3:285) that
     he is from Naysiyan, he is usually called Nayistani in Baha'i sources. There is
     a village called Nayistanak 30 km east of Naysiyan on the main road between
     Ardistan and Na'in and that may be the cause of the confusion.

60. Shaykh Muhammad Natiq Isfahani
(Ardistani or Nayistani) of Naysiyan

Muhammad received a formal religious education in Isfahan and began to preach and perform religious duties in the village after his father's death. In the months of Muharram and Safar, he used to go to Zavarih and preach. During the third of these journeys, in early 1904, he was given a book to read which was a refutation of the Babi and Baha'i Faiths by Aqa Diya'u'd-Din 'Iraqi (1861–1942), who was in later years the leading cleric of the Shi'i world and resident in Najaf. He found himself agreeing with the Baha'i proofs given in this book and finding fault with the refutations made by the author.[253] He investigated further in Islamic books of traditions and eventually in 1906, after meeting Tarazu'llah Samandari and Mirza 'Ali Akbar Rafsanjani in Isfahan, became a Baha'i. He taught the Baha'i Faith to his younger brother, Mirza Muhammad 'Ali Shayiq Natiq (d. 1953), who was for many years a teacher at the Baha'i school in Hamadan.[254] Shaykh Muhammad Natiq returned to his home to try to convert his older brother and father but they refused to accept the Baha'i Faith, although his brother-in-law did later become a Baha'i. After a time Natiq became well known as a Baha'i and had to leave his home village and return to Isfahan. There too his fame as a Baha'i grew and it became too dangerous for him to stay, so he left, heading for Tehran, in late 1909. On the way, however, he was persuaded to remain in Kashan and teach at the Baha'i Vahdat Bashar school there. He remained in Kashan until 1923 (except for a 15-month journey which included a visit to Haifa). Then he moved to Hamadan where he also taught at the Baha'i Ta'id School for four years. After this he travelled to various parts of Iran as

253 According to Sa'idi (Tarikh 64), Natiq was first made aware of the Baha'i Faith when a Baha'i asked him a question during one of his journeys to Zavarih. In a family biography of Mulla Rida Shahriyar, he is credited with converting Natiq (Shahriyari, 'Nufudh-i Amr', part 1, p. 21).

254 Dhuka'i-Bayda'i, Tadhkirih 3:44–50.

a *muballigh* until 1933, when a financial downturn in the economy of the country caused problems for the Baha'i funds and a number of the full-time travelling *muballighs*, including Natiq, could no longer be supported by the national Baha'i fund. Shortly after this he was struck by ill health caused by rheumatic heart disease and so he remained in Tehran until his death in January 1936.[255]

Haji Mirza Haydar 'Ali Isfahani states that the number of Baha'is in Ardistan in the early 1890s was some 2,000 or 3,000 (about 20–30 per cent of the population of the town).[256] As described above, many Baha'is were forced to leave and this presumably is the reason why Fadil Mazandarani puts the number of Baha'is in the time of 'Abdu'l-Baha at only 300.[257] In about 1935 there were some 350 to 400 Baha'is in Ardistan, more than 300 in the Bab ur-Raha quarter and the remainder distributed in the rest of town, especially in the Ramiyan and Fahrih districts. This represented about four per cent of the town's population. The Baha'is owned a public bath in the Bab ur-Raha quarter which was highly regarded on account of its cleanliness (it had shower facilities rather than a communal trough) and was used by city officials and professionals such as doctors and teachers.[258]

Zavarih

Zavarih is a small town (17 km northeast of Ardistan; pop. 6,000 in 1914, 5,400 in 1953), in which a large number of descendants of the Prophet Muhammad are resident. There was a Babi community, all of whose members became Baha'is. The most important of these were Aqa Sayyid Isma'il Dhabih (d. c. 1858) and his cousin Aqa Sayyid Husayn Mahjur (d. 1306/1888). Aqa Sayyid Isma'il Dhabih was a poet who had met the Bab in the house of the Imam-Jum'ih of Isfahan when he was a student at the Madrasih Kasihgaran and become a Babi. He then converted his cousin. These two began to teach the new religion in Zavarih and a number of people converted. This aroused the wrath of the *kadkhuda* and the sayyids of the town and they were forced to leave for a time (during this period both of them met and converted Mulla Muhammad Nabil Zarandi).[259]

---

255 MH 3:382–416; ZH 8a:147–53; Dhuka'i-Bayda'i, *Tadhkirih* 3:392–409;
     Ishraq-Kavari, *Hamadan* 121–3; Nadiri, 'Sharh'.
256 Isfahani, *Bihjat* 273, 304.
257 ZH 8a:166.
258 Interview with Mr Azizu'llah Purshafi-Ardestani at his home on 9 Oct. 2004.
259 DB 168, 435–9.

61. Mulla Rida 'Aba-baf
Shahriyar

They returned, however, and soon there was a flourishing Babi community.[260]

The Babis of Zavarih all followed Baha'u'llah when he put forward his claim. Among those who became Baha'is was Haji Sayyid Isma'il, the Imam-Jum'ih, who used to travel by night with armed companions to the home of Fath-i A'zam in Ardistan in order to increase his knowledge of the Baha'i Faith and then return in time to perform the dawn prayers in his mosque. Another cleric of Zavarih who converted was Mirza Muhammad Hasan Ardistani.

One of the residents of Zavarih, Haji 'Ali Akbar, met Baha'u'llah in Baghdad on his way to pilgrimage in Mecca with his father and was converted, although his father was not. Out of fear of his father, who was a very strict Muslim, Haji 'Ali Akbar did not tell him or anyone else about his conversion. Nevertheless, his wife's brother, Mulla Rida 'Aba-baf Shahriyar (d. 1916, see fig. 61), noticed a difference in him and after one year of pleading with him finally caught him breaking the fast of Ramadan and demanded to know the reason for the change in him. So Haji 'Ali Akbar told him and he accepted immediately. Mulla Rida enthusiastically spread the Baha'i Faith and converted his wife Khatun and his family. He had brought the skill of cloak-weaving (*'aba-bafi*) to the town. He would invite people to his house to learn the skill and would teach them the Baha'i Faith as he did so. In this way he converted some one hundred people over a 20-year period. In the time of 'Abdu'l-Baha he became the leading Baha'i of this town. He was asked by 'Abdu'l-Baha to travel to Kishih, Tar and Tarq in order to teach the Azalis there, which he did on the pretext of buying wool and selling *'abas*. Baha'i travelling teachers, such as Nayyir, Sina and Akhavan Safa, came to Zavarih and greatly increased the depth of knowledge of the Baha'is of the town.[261]

---

260 On Sayyid Isma'il, see ZH 6:221–2, Ishraq-Khavari, *Rahiq-i Makhtum* 1:619–23; Gulzar, untitled history 1–3; on Sayyid Husayn, see ZH 6:221–3.

261 Shahriari, 'Nufudh-i Amr - Part 1'. In this account it is stated that Mulla Rida Shahriyar was the first Baha'i of the town and converted Sayyid Isma'il Dhabih. However, this cannot be correct as Mulla Rida was converted while Baha'u'llah

When the persecutions in Yazd and Isfahan erupted in 1903, some 5,000 of the people of the village, led by Sayyid Abu Turab Imam-Jum'ih, arose against the Baha'is and marched on the quarter where they lived, which was called the Pusht-i Mashhad quarter. One Baha'i, named 'Arab 'Ali (Faris) who had been a follower of Na'ib Husayn Kashi before he became a Baha'i, decided, however, that he was not going to allow a general massacre to occur and fired from his rooftop, hitting the Imam-Jum'ih in the leg, which was enough to disperse the mob.[262]

Another episode of persecution occurred in the early days of World War I when, as mentioned above, Sawlat ul-Mulk Bakhtiyari, deputy governor for the area, arrested some of the Baha'is of Ardistan. Immediately the rumour went around the town that Mulla Rida was to be arrested as well. The Baha'is advised Mulla Rida to flee but he refused, saying he had been prepared for such a day for a long time. One of Sawlat's officers, Haybatu'llah, came to Zavarih with men and began to persecute and beat Mulla Rida. Several times Mulla Rida's house was attacked, as a result of which his daughter-in-law, Mardiyyih Khanum, fell sick and died. Several times he was tied to a horse and forced to run alongside it, being thus dragged most of the 17 kilometres to Ardistan. On one of these occasions, for example, one of Sawlat's men, Aqa 'Ali Aqa Khan, came to Zavarih and arrested Mulla Rida and another Baha'i, Mulla 'Ali. They were tied to a tree and beaten before being taking off to Ardistan again. Here again they were beaten and tortured with the *ishkilak* (pieces of wood placed between the fingers and squeezed). When the officers saw that the Baha'is would not recant they returned them to Zavarih. On another occasion the people of Zavarih were instructed to bring firewood as it was intended to burn Mulla Rida alive. His persecutions and beatings were so intense that on one occasion he tried to cut his own throat as a way of ending them. Eventually he fell ill and died on 8 December 1916.[263]

---

was in Baghdad and Dhabih was already a Babi during the lifetime of the Bab, as described above. Indeed, in another account it is stated that Mulla Rida studied at the *maktab* run by Sayyid Husayn Mahjur and also participated at the *ta'ziyih* (dramatic performance of the martyrdom of the Imam Husayn) directed by him. The latter had realized Mulla Rida's potential and taught the Baha'i Faith to him (ZH 6:223–4, 8a:168; Yazdi, *Manahij ul-Ahkam* 1:219). Shahriari partially corrects this in his later article, 'Nufudh-i A'in-i Baha'i'. See also Gulzar, untitled history 3–8, which gives substantially the same story as Shahriari, although it does not say that Mulla Rida was Haji 'Ali Akbar's brother-in-law.

262 ZH 7:218, 8a:168–9; KD 2:176; Shahriari, 'Nufudh-i A'in-i Baha'i' - part 1, 45.
263 Shahriyari, 'Nufudh-i Amr - Part 2'; Gulzar, untitled history 8–9.

12

CENTRAL PROVINCES
(SULTANABAD, GULPAYGAN AND MAHALLAT)

This chapter deals with an area in central Iran where there were a number of governorships. The governors were sometimes appointed by the central government and sometimes the area was under one person, such as Zill us-Sultan, who then appointed the governors. (See map at Frontispiece 2.)

Sultanabad (Arak, 'Iraq)

The town of Sultanabad (260 km southwest of Tehran, 240 km northwest of Isfahan, 130 km northeast of Hamadan; pop. 7,000 in 1914 and 59,000 in 1956) at times acted as the capital of a small province. It had been created as a garrison town in 1808 but had grown into an important centre for carpet-weaving and the carpet trade. From 1883 the Manchester firm of Messrs Ziegler and Company directed much of the carpet-weaving to their specifications, using designs adapted from traditional Persian designs for the European market. They had large premises in the town staffed mainly by Germans and Swiss. Being a new town, Sultanabad was relatively free of the conservative and discriminatory policies of towns elsewhere. As distinct from other towns, for example, Jews could trade in the bazaar.

There appears to have been a Babi community in Sultanabad from an early date. Sayyid Basir Hindi passed through the town in 1851 and debated with the clerics there.[1] All the Babis of the town pledged their allegiance to Azal in the years after the execution of the Bab. During the 1850s a number of them travelled to Baghdad. Some, such as Mirza Mahmud

63. Aqa Muhsin
Mujtahid Araki

Hakim and Sayyid Abu'l-Fadl, established contact with Sayyid Muhammad Isfahani and Mulla Rajab-'Ali Isfahani and returned confirmed in their allegiance to Azal, while others, such as Mulla Ibrahim Mulla-bashi, Ustad Husayn, Aqa Abu'l-Qasim and Karbala'i Rahmatu'llah returned as supporters of Baha'u'llah. There was tension between the two groups but eventually most of the Babis of the town became Baha'is.[2] Karbala'i Rahmatu'llah, one of the notables of the town, was particularly active in teaching the new religion after his return from Baghdad and converted some 70 persons in Sultanabad as well as others in nearby villages such as Upper and Lower Hamzihlu and Malikabad and in the town of Malayir.[3]

Aqa Muhsin Mujtahid (1246/1830–1324/1906, see fig. 63) was the leading cleric of Sultanabad and he became one of the largest landowners and wealthiest people in Iran, eventually gaining so much power that he was able to dictate what happened in the town. It is difficult to be certain of his views on the Baha'i Faith since in the early years he is reported to have been a friend of Mulla Ibrahim Mulla-bashi and therefore protective of the Babis, although in later years (about 1896) he plotted the murder of 'Ali-Quli Khan, who was a Baha'i in the employ of the governor. It may be, however, that Aqa Muhsin's enmity towards 'Ali-Quli Khan was for other reasons since he

1   DB 590.
2   ZH 6:345.
3   ZH 4:337–8.

was generally protective of religious minorities and even allowed the Jews to trade in the bazaar.[4] Several of those around Aqa Muhsin, such as his close companion Haji Sayyid Abu'l-Fadl, his steward Aqa Muhammad Hasan Dihdashti as well as his personal servant, were Baha'is and he was given a copy of the Kitab-i Iqan by Mirza Hashim Sajid, one of the Jewish Baha'i converts of Kashan who had moved to Sultanabad (see p. 160).[5]

Haji Sayyid Muhammad Baqir Mujtahid (Hujjat ul-Islam) was particularly opposed to the Babis but was unable to do much because of Aqa Muhsin's protection. On one occasion, two of the learned Babis of the town, Mulla Ibrahim Mulla-bashi, who had authored a number of books on philosophy and was tutor to the son of the governor Firuz Mirza Nusrat ud-Dawlih, and Mulla Muhammad 'Ali, who was imam of one of the local mosques, spoke to Haji Sayyid Muhammad Baqir Mujtahid about the new religion and gave him two writings to compare – one the Sahifih-yi Sajjadiyyih, a collection of the prayers of the fourth Shi'i Imam Zaynu'l-'Abidin written in red ink, and the other some of the prayers of the Bab written in black. Since Haji Sayyid Muhammad Baqir knew that the Babis wrote the writings of the Bab in red, he confidently wrote words of condemnation on the back of the Sahifih-yi Sajjadiyyih and words of praise on the back of the writings of the Bab, thus exposing his own ignorance.[6]

In early 1864 the meetings of the Babis were infiltrated by a certain Mulla 'Ali who claimed to be interested in the new religion. Together with Haji Sayyid Muhammad Baqir Mujtahid, they hatched a plot against the Babis. Mulla 'Ali obtained the Bayan of the Bab from Mulla Muhammad 'Ali and took it to Aqa Muhsin Mujtahid, complaining of the heresy of Mulla Muhammad 'Ali. Aqa Muhsin Mujtahid asked Mulla Muhammad 'Ali to come to his house and the conspirators summoned other leading Babis, including Mulla Ibrahim, to the house of Aqa Muhsin Mujtahid in his name. Then, while Mulla Ibrahim was engaged in conversation with Aqa Muhsin, Haji Sayyid Muhammad Baqir Mujtahid suddenly entered

---

4   ZH 4:338; Gail, *Summon Up Remembrace* 84–5; Amanat, 'Negotiating Identities' 143. On this cleric, see Bamdad, *Tarikh Rijal* 3:203–4 and al-Amin, *A'yan ush-Shi'ah* 9:45, no. 97. However, it may be that his tolerance of the Jews was associated with the fact that most of the Jewish merchants rented their offices in his caravanserai (Amanat, *Kashan* 259).

5   ZH 8a:273; Amanat, 'Negotiating Identities' 196–7; Amanat, *Kashan* 259–60. He also protected Mirza Hashim Sajid when the latter was exposed as a Baha'i among his circle of students (ZH 6:679a).

6   ZH 4:338.

and killed Mulla Ibrahim with a knife; he then went on to stab to death Mulla Muhammad 'Ali and Karbala'i Rahmatu'llah with his own hands and with the help of a mob he had brought with him. Some 20 or 30 Babis were arrested by the governor and four of them were killed in the governor's dungeon: Usta Mahmud Kashani (a pea-parcher), Karbala'i Haydar Kabuli (a furrier), Mirza Hasan (a surgeon) and Mirza Ahmad Tafrishi; the rest were set free after two weeks. At about this time, Sayyidih Fatimih Bigum, who came from a Babi family of sayyids of Tafrish, was arrested. She had been married to Mirza Ma'sum Mujtahid, and, although she had had children by this husband, he divorced her because she refused to give up her beliefs and was spreading them. During this episode she was arrested and sent to Tehran, where she was strangled in the shah's private apartments.[7] Some of the Babis of the town fled, two of them, Aqa Abu'l-Qasim and Aqa Faraj, went to Edirne and then accompanied Baha'u'llah to 'Akka.[8] In the 1860s Haji Mirza Haydar 'Ali Isfahani spent a short time in Sultanabad teaching the Baha'i Faith and was beaten badly such that it took him some time to recover.[9]

Jani Khanum, the daughter of the above-mentioned Sayyidih Fatimih Bigum, was married to Mulla Husayn Rawdih-khan Kashani, a much-respected cleric of Sultanabad. She managed to convert her husband and he became well known as a Baha'i. In 1298/1881 a mob attacked his house and took him with them to the governor's house. On the way they soaked him in

---

7   There is a large discrepancy in the dates given for this event in various sources. Ishraq-Khavari gives the date as 1915 (*Taqvim* 150), Avarih gives sometime between 1296/1878–9 and 1298/1880 (*Kavakib* 2:241), Fadil Mazandarani gives 1280/1863 (ZH 4:337–9), 'Abdu'l-Baha implies a date between 1863 and 1868 (*Memorials* 172) and Browne gives 1278/1861–2 (*Year* 562n, the date is given explicitly in Browne's handwritten diary, p. 443). An Iranian author who is not a Baha'i, Ibrahim Dihgan, gives a date of 1278 but appears to be merely following Browne in this, *Tarikh-i Arak* 187. There is also a poetical account of this episode in *Mathnavi Nabil Zarandi* 43–4. This does not give a date but its position in the book implies a date between 1864 and 1866. I have chosen to go with the date of early 1864 (late 1280), which I have obtained from Mazandarani (ZH 4:342), who relates this episode to the Najafabad upheaval in 1864 (see BBR 268–9). If 1278 or 1280 are correct, the governor at this time was Firuz Mirza Nusrat ud-Dawlih. There is also some discrepancy in the accounts of what happened. I have based the above mainly on the account given by Browne (*Year* 562–3) since it is based on the recollections of an eyewitness informant. See also ZH 6:348.

8   'Abdu'l-Baha, *Memorials* 170–2; ZH 6:345.

9   Isfahani, *Bihjat* 24; MH 1:17.

64. Mirza Aqa Khan Qa'im-Maqami

wine and then accused him before the governor of being drunk. The governor ordered him to be bastinadoed and after this the mob dragged him through the streets, beating him until he was dead. Jani Khanum then married the brother of her late husband, Mirza Hasan, and converted him also.[10]

According to one source, in the 1890s the Baha'i community of Sultanabad included Baha'is from Armenian Christian and Zoroastrian as well as Muslim backgrounds.[11] At about this time a number of Jewish Baha'is from Kashan and Hamadan moved to Sultanabad to set up trading offices. The first of these, in 1307/1889, was the above-mentioned Hashim Sajid (Mulla 'Ashur Ghayur, see p. 109 and fig. 48), who was fearless in his teaching of the Baha'i Faith and converted many in the town and the surrounding villages (some 300 according to one account). He was the first Jewish Baha'i in Sultanabad to open his shop on a Saturday. There were conversions from among the Jewish merchants in the town and in particular from among their apprentices from about 1900 onwards.[12]

One of the prominent Baha'is of this town in the time of 'Abdu'l-Baha was Mirza Aqa Khan Qa'im-Maqami (1868–Jan. 1954, see fig. 64), a great-grandson of Mirza Abu'l-Qasim Farahani Qa'im-Maqam, who had been a friend of Baha'u'llah's father and the first prime minister of Muhammad Shah. Mirza Aqa Khan's father Bahlul Khan was taught the Baha'i Faith by Shaykh Muhammad 'Arab Baghdadi but did not convert although he was sympathetic. Qa'im-Maqami himself was born and raised in one of the villages of the Farahan area and was converted after meeting Sayyid Asadu'llah Qummi and some of the Baha'is of Sultanabad, including the

10   ZH 5:257–8, 6:345; the Rawshan-Damir family are descended from them.
11   Gail, *Summon Up Remembrance* 84.
12   See story of Sifidvash (vol. 1:507); Rayhani in Amanat, 'Negotiating Identities' 192; ZH 6:679a; Amanat, *Kashan* 96, 97–8.

above-mentioned Mirza Hashim Sajid. His cousin Habibu'llah Khan Ihtisham Nizam was also converted at this time. Mirza Aqa Khan suffered much because of his conversion and lost most of his wealth, such that he had to work as a painter to earn a living. As a result of a dream, however, he began to mine a nearby hill and prospered, becoming one of the wealthiest citizens of Sultanabad. Later he obtained the franchise for the postal and transport business from Sultanabad to Hamadan and as far as the Iraq border. Although he came to own many villages and had a large complex of houses in Sultanabad, he himself lived and dressed very simply. He frequently went in

65. Sayyid Aqa Nuru'd-Din Mujtahid Araki (known as Aqa Nur)

disguise among the poor of the town and distributed money to them. Qa'im-Maqami was bold in talking about the Baha'i Faith and openly ate food during Ramadan to show he was not a Muslim anymore. His position and wealth in town protected him and also protected the Baha'is to a large extent. His forthright teaching of the Baha'i Faith also attracted many to the religion, although some of these joined more for material benefit and the Baha'i community called these 'Qa'im-Maqami Baha'is'. On one occasion, however, during the governorship of Abu'l-Fadl Mirza 'Adud us-Sultan (a son of Muzaffaru'd-Din Shah, governed 1901–3), he was arrested with two other Baha'is, Mulla Mirza Aqa Taliqani and Aqa Sayyid Taqi Khalajabadi, because of their open teaching of the Baha'i Faith, and Sayyid Aqa Nuru'd-Din Mujtahid Araki (known as Aqa Nur, 1278/1861–1923, see fig. 65) issued a *fatwa* for their death. The governor had the latter two bastinadoed but a friend intervened for Qa'im-Maqami. Qa'im-Maqami moved to Tehran in about 1916 but continued to assist the Baha'is of Sultanabad. In the winter of 1918–19, for example, he held a large gathering at his house in Tehran for the notables and clerics of Sultanabad who were in Tehran at that time. 'Adud us-Sultan the governor, Haji Sayyid Ahmad Mujtahid and Haji Sayyid Muhammad Mujtahid (two sons of

Aqa Muhsin) and Haji Mirza Muhammad 'Ali Khan Mujtahid were all present and Mirza Mahmud Furughi gave a talk about the Baha'i Faith and answered their questions.[13]

In 1904 the governor of the town, Mirza Mahdi Khan Vazir Humayun (see pp. 90–1), was converted during the visit to the town of two Baha'i dervishes, Haji Mu'nis and Haji Tavangar, as well as by the efforts of Mulla Mirza Aqa Taliqani. Qa'im-Maqami purchased some land which included the site where the bodies of the Baha'is killed in 1864 were buried and this land was also used for building a Baha'i centre and travellers' hospice (*musāfir-khānih*). In 1909 Qa'im-Maqami brought to Sultanabad to be a tutor for his children Mirza Nasru'llah Rastigar, who was one of those who had studied in the classes of Sadr us-Sudur (vol. 1:97–8) and was in the process of becoming a skilled Baha'i teacher.[14] At this time, a number of other travelling Baha'i teachers, including Mirza Yusif Vujdani, Muhammad Rida the son of Sina, and a group of Baha'i dervishes, including Haji Mu'nis and Haji Tavangar, arrived in the town and were accommodated in the Baha'i travellers' hospice. Mirza Mahdi Akhavan Safa visited in September 1911. He reported meeting Shaykh Ruhu'llah, one of the *mujtahids* of the town who had become a Baha'i.[15] On one occasion after the death of the above-mentioned Aqa Muhsin Mujtahid in 1906, Sayyid Aqa Nuru'd-Din Mujtahid Araki plotted that on a particular day his followers would close the bazaar and initiate an attack on all the Baha'is of the town. Having been forewarned by sympathizers, however, the Baha'is fled the town until the governor was able to restore order.[16] Later, Mirza Ibrahim Faridiyan and his son escaped the mob by hiding in an oven.[17]

Sultanabad is best known in Baha'i history for an episode that occurred during a time of general disorder throughout Iran, with British and Russian forces on one side and German and Turkish forces on the other competing for control of the country. In this disorder and shortly after Russian forces had gained control of Sultanabad, a group of people decided that the anarchic conditions were a good opportunity to make an attack on the Baha'is. Mirza 'Ali Akbar was a prosperous merchant of the town and the son of the above-mentioned Mulla Husayn. He was well known as a Baha'i

---

13   Nushabadi, 'Qa'im-Maqami'; ZH 8a:267–78; Tulu'i, 'Hashim Sajid' 57.
14   Rastigar, *Sadr us-Sudur* 79–80; Bayda'i, *Tadhkirih* 3:471.
15   MH 4:59–61; Rastigar, *Sadr us-Sudur* 80–1.
16   Thabiti, *Varithan* 119–20.
17   ibid. 120.

66. The murdered bodies of Mirza 'Ali Akbar Sultanabadi and his four sons
(including a 40-day-old baby)

and had been summoned before the clerics of the town on several occasions (most recently in March 1914, when Mirza Hasan Niku, who was
staying with him, had spoken out against the clerics). Then on 22 February
1916, incited by clerics such as Sayyid Aqa Nuru'd-Din Mujtahid Araki,
four men entered his house by night and killed all the occupants by cutting
their throats or their abdomens: Mirza 'Ali Akbar, his wife Maryam (a
daughter of the above-mentioned Mulla Ibrahim Mulla-bashi), his wife's
14-year-old sister, and the four sons of the family ranging in age from 12
years to a 40-day-old baby (see fig. 66).[18]

The murder of this family was in itself sufficiently horrific but the

18 Avarih, *Kavakib* 2:241–7; ZH 7:308–9; Nushabadi, 'Qa'im-Maqami' 25–26.
    Various Iranian historians have tried to dismiss the religious nature of this attack.
    Dihgan, *Tarikh-i Arak* 221 states that Mirza 'Ali Akbar's murder was nothing to
    do with his being a Baha'i but was rather due to a commercial dispute with an
    Armenian who owed him money and that the murder was done by the latter's
    servant and two Russian cossacks. This seems unlikely in that there would then
    be no reason to kill the entire family, including Mirza 'Ali Akbar's wife's sister.
    The religious nature of the attack is confirmed in the account by one of the stu-
    dents of Sayyid Aqa Nuru'd-Din Araki; see Ayatu'llah Shaykh Muhammad 'Ali
    Araki in Ustadi, *Yad-Namih* 436–7.

effect was heightened by the publication in newspapers in Iran of a photograph of the dead bodies. The governor, Abu'l-Fadl Mirza 'Adud us-Sultan (1882–1922), was pressured to find the culprits. Later that year this governor was replaced by Sultan-Junayd Mirza Mu'tamad ud-Dawlih, who was acquainted with and friendly towards the Baha'i Faith. Qa'im-Maqami also made great efforts in identifying and tracking down the murderers and having them arrested and the prime minister, Muhammad Vali Khan Tunukabuni, even appointed a Baha'i, Ahmad 'Ali Khan Shahriyari, as head of the police (*nazmiyyih*). But because of the opposition of the clerics and the war-time conditions, the matter was not pursued and the arrested men were released.[19]

A short time after this the wife of Mirza Mahdi Khan Askaroff Mutarjim us-Sultan was murdered in Mashhad Dhulfabad (see p. 170). When the murderer was arrested and brought to Sultanabad through the efforts of Qa'im-Maqami and his cousin Ihtisham Nizam, he was sentenced to death. The clerics raised an uproar and closed the bazaar, saying that in a Muslim country, a Muslim cannot be executed for killing a Baha'i and a man cannot be executed for killing a woman.[20]

Then in May 1920 there was a concerted effort by the clerics of the town, led by Sayyid Aqa Nuru'd-Din Mujtahid, to attack the Baha'is. The most prominent Baha'is of the town, such as Mutarjim us-Sultan, escaped their clutches and so they turned their attention to a humble and defenceless Baha'i, Isfandiyar known as Haji 'Arab from the village of Chaqasiyah, who worked in a shop in Sultanabad. He had been so affected by the murders of Mirza 'Ali Akbar's family in 1916 that he had picked up the body of the baby and walked through the streets of Sultanabad distraught, shouting, 'O Muslims, even if you accuse Mirza 'Ali Akbar of renouncing his religion, this little baby had not done any wrong.'[21] Since then Haji 'Arab had been a marked man. The opportunity to attack him came when he went to a neighbouring shop with some paper to obtaining kindling for a fire. The owner of that shop asked him whether he realized that the paper he was burning was a page from the Qur'an and Haji 'Arab replied that since he was illiterate, he had no idea what he was burning. This shop-owner, who

---

19   Rastigar, *Sadr us-Sudur* 342–4; Nushabadi, 'Qa'im-Maqami' 26–8.
20   Nushabadi, 'Qa'im-Maqami' 28.
21   ZH 8a:278–9; some Iranian accounts say that Haji 'Arab was a town-crier, *jārchī*, but this may have been because of this episode, when he walked through the streets shouting.

was inimical to the Baha'is, went to Sayyid Aqa Nuru'd-Din Mujtahid and swore a statement to the effect that Haji 'Arab had burned the Qur'an. The clerics of the town whipped the mob into a frenzy and by the time that word had circulated in the town and an angry mob took to the streets, it was being said that Haji 'Arab had entered a mosque and burned a whole Qur'an there. Haji 'Arab had meanwhile gone into hiding in the house of one of the Baha'is in the nearby village of Husaynabad, so the mob turned on the governor, Sardar Humayun, and attacked and looted his house. Many of the Baha'is fled the town while some armed themselves and took up positions at the houses of Qa'im-Maqami and of his cousin Ihtisham Nizam such that the mob did not dare attack. Telegrams were sent to the prime minister, Vuthuq ud-Dawlih (1873–1951), who ordered that Haji 'Arab be found and the matter investigated. Troops were sent to the surrounding villages such as Khalajabad and Shahabad where they beat some of the Baha'is and questioned them. Eventually they found Haji 'Arab in Husaynabad, brought him to the town and threw him into prison. Sardar Humayun, who knew Haji 'Arab was innocent, tried to let the matter settle at this point by doing nothing, but when the month of Ramadan came, Sayyid Aqa Nuru'd-Din Mujtahid did not appear at his mosque. People took this as a sign that he was displeased and took to the streets once more. They sent a telegram to Tehran and Vuthuq ud-Dawlih sent orders that Haji 'Arab be executed, even though there had not as yet been a trial. At a farcical trial, Haji 'Arab maintained his innocence and repeatedly asked that a witness be brought who had actually seen him do this act. Despite the fact that no witness could be found, Haji 'Arab was hanged in the town square on 21 May 1920 and his body left there for two days.[22]

It is stated that, prior to his execution, Haji 'Arab was brought before the senior cleric in Sultanabad, Shaykh 'Abdu'l-Karim Ha'iri-Yazdi (who in later years was one of the leading clerics, *marja' ut-taqlid*, of the Shi'i world and was known as Ayatu'llah Ha'iri-Yazdi, see fig. 67). He refused to condemn Haji 'Arab him on the evidence presented and when he was executed anyway the next day, Shaykh 'Abdu'l-Karim was angry, closed down his teaching circle and left the town to proceed to Mashhad on

---

22 ZH 8a:278–80; Avarih, *Kavakib* 2:249–51; BBR 444–6; ZH 7:321; see also Dihgan, *Tarikh-i Arak* 225; on Sayyid Aqa Nuru'd-Din Mujtahid Araki's role, see Ayatu'llah Shaykh Muhammad 'Ali Araki in Ustadi, *Yad-Namih* 436. It is reported that later Araki moderated his attitude towards the Baha'is; Nushabadi, 'Qa'im-Maqami' 24.

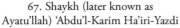

67. Shaykh (later known as   68. Mirza Taqi Khan Qajar Bahin-A'in
Ayatu'llah) 'Abdu'l-Karim Ha'iri-Yazdi

pilgrimage. During the course of his journey he passed through Qumm and was invited to move there, thus eventually re-establishing Qumm as a major Islamic teaching centre.[23]

Despite these persecutions, Mirza Taqi Khan Qajar Bahin-A'in (vol. 1:76, see fig. 68) was fearless in spreading the Baha'i Faith in the town. He had moved to Sultanabad nine months after the murders of Mirza 'Ali Akbar's family in 1916 and remained until early 1920. During this time the town was under the governorship of one of the Bakhtiyari khans who was sympathetic to the Baha'is. Bahin-A'in wrote to each of the clerics of the town either to come to his house and find out about the Baha'i Faith or he would come to theirs. They declined to respond to his challenge and complained to the governor. Undeterred, Bahin-A'in sent them through the post a treatise of Baha'i proofs that he had written and, when there was no response, he went to their houses.

In about 1919 'Abdu'llah Mutlaq, one of the Baha'i travelling teachers, arrived in Sultanabad, having travelled with and befriended Haji Shaykh Hasan Najafi, the son of Mulla Muhammad Sharabiyani one of the leading clerics of Najaf. Mutlaq persuaded Najafi to stay with Mirza Taqi Khan and

---

23 Amanat, *Kashan* 341; account given on the authority of Masha'u'llah Ihsani, who had been a student of Ha'iri-Yazdi at this time and had witnessed the episode. This episode is confirmed by Husayn Khumayni, great-grandson of Ha'iri-Yazdi and grandson of Ayatu'llah Khumayni (Quchani, 'Pidar'), and appears in standard biographies of Ha'iri-Yazdi such as in the Persian-language Wikipedia.

that night Mutlaq and Bahin-A'in spoke together, with Mutlaq pretending to be angry with Bahin-A'in when he started to bring forward Baha'i proofs. As a result of the conversation, Najafi was converted. Bahin-A'in also went with Mutlaq to the houses of some of the *mujtahids*. The result was an uproar in the town and the speedy departure of Mutlaq.[24]

Because of its central location, many prominent Baha'is passed through the town and some stayed, for varying lengths of time. In addition to those mentioned above, these included Mirza Abu'l-Fadl Gulpaygani (1887),[25] Nasru'llah Rastigar (1909),[26] Qabil Abadihi (in about 1901, with Mirza Nasru'llah Rawshan),[27] Sayyid 'Abbas 'Alavi (1924),[28] Muhammad Tahir Malmiri (c. 1925),[29] Mirza Muhammad Thabit Maraghihi (1933)[30] and Mirza Hasan Rahmani Nushabadi (1916 and in 1934–5 for 18 months).[31]

In March 1924 the leading Ayatu'llahs, Na'ini and Isfahani, who had left Najaf and repaired to Qumm in the summer of 1923 in protest at the British Mandate in Iraq, were allowed to return to Najaf. They passed through Sultanabad on the way. Their arrival coincided with the arrival in Sultanabad of a group of Baha'i villagers from the Farahan area, protesting at the behaviour of some gendarmes who had been sent to arrest the travelling Baha'i teacher (*muballigh*) Sayyid 'Abbas 'Alavi. These gendarmes had gone from one village to the next, beating and harassing the Baha'is and extorting money from them. The arrival of these two groups coincided also with the night of 15 Sha'ban when Shi'is celebrate the birth of the Twelfth Imam. This was a night on which the Shi'is of Sultanabad traditionally harassed Baha'is whom they said denied the Twelfth Imam. On this particular night, the presence of the Ayatu'llahs and of the Farahan villagers inflamed passions to a greater extent and several of the villagers as well as some of the Baha'is of Sultanabad were attacked and beaten. Rumours circulated in the town of a general attack upon the Baha'i centre (*hazirat ul-quds*), and the Baha'is were in great fear. But over the next few days, the Ayatu'llahs left and calm returned to the town.[32]

---

24   MH 4:128–30; 9:468–72.
25   Mihrabkhani, *Gulpaygani* 158.
26   Bayda'i, *Tadhkirih* 3:471.
27   ZH 8a:588–9.
28   MH 6:220–4.
29   Malmiri, *Khatirat* 202.
30   Bayda'i, *Tadhkirih* 3:247.
31   Bayda'i, *Tadhkirih* 3:247; MH 6:97–8, 102.
32   MH 6:220–4.

Villages around Sultanabad

Farahan is the name given to an area on the road north from Sultanabad, where much of the carpet-weaving for which Sultanabad was famous was actually done. There were numerous Baha'is in one of the villages of this area, Shahabad (53 km north of Sultanabad; pop. 991 in 1950). The first Baha'i there was Mulla (Muhammad) Husayn Shahabadi, who became a Babi in Tafrish through Mulla 'Abdu'l-Ghani Kukani (see p. 173), returned to his home village of Shahabad and converted many, some of whom visited Baha'u'llah in Baghdad.[33] The conversion of so many in the village caused an uproar among the clerics of Sultanabad and in about 1889 the Baha'is were summoned to appear before one of them, Aqa Diya. This is almost certainly Aqa Diya'u'd-Din 'Iraqi (1861–1942), who would later that year move to Najaf and eventually become the leading cleric (*marja' ut-taqlid*) of the Shi'i world. However, the Baha'is defended themselves well before the cleric and, with the help of the governor of Sultanabad, Mirza Muhsin Khan Muzaffar ul-Mulk, were set free. Nevertheless, the clerics of Sultanabad issued a decree for the death of Mulla Husayn and this was confirmed by Mulla Ahmad Amirihi, a *mujtahid* and prayer-leader of Amirih (87 km northeast of Sultanabad; pop. 416 in 2006), who was then very much opposed to the Baha'i Faith. Years later, in the time of 'Abdu'l-Baha, however, Mirza Husayn Tabib (physician) Shahabadi sent him a letter and a copy of the Kitab-i Aqdas. Mulla Ahmad returned the book with his objections noted in its margins and at the same time issued a decree stating that Mirza Husayn was a heretic and should be killed. Instead of fleeing, Mirza Husayn rode straight to Mulla Ahmad's house and asked to see him. Mulla Ahmad was surprised but agreed. They stayed up all night while Mirza Husayn answered each of Mulla Ahmad's objections and by the end, Mulla Ahmad was converted. He immediately resigned his position as imam of the mosque in Amirih and called upon anyone who was interested to visit him at his house and hear about the Baha'i Faith. As result of this, most of the villagers became Baha'is.[34] Mulla Ahmad wrote a number of polemical works.

---

33 ZH 6:346; Ja'fari, 'Pavaraqi' 2–3.

34 Ja'fari, 'Pavaraqi' 3. Tavangar ('Yadi') records what appears to be the same story with different details; here it is Mirza Hasan Tabib of Shahabad who sends Baha'u'llah's Kitab-i Aqdas to Mulla Ahmad Amirihi, who then debates with Mirza Hasan for two days and subsequently becomes a Baha'i. KD (2:186–7) records the story with yet another variation: Mirza Hasan Tabib of Shahabad as the teacher and the cleric is named Mulla Muhammad Hashim Amirihi

Also in the Farahan area was Khalajabad (35 km north of Sultanabad; pop. 487 in 1950), where Aqa Sayyid 'Ali, the son of the owner of Khalajabad, heard of the Baha'i Faith from Mirza Husayn Khalajabadi and was finally converted by Mirza 'Ali Akbar Naraqi when the latter visited the village. In 1876 the ownership of Khalajabad changed and there was an outburst of persecution from the new owner's agent in the village, 'Abbas-Quli Khan.[35]

Mirza Mahdi Tabib, who visited Shahabad and Khalajabad in the 1880s, stated that some two-thirds of the population of these villages were Baha'is.[36] In the early 1890s Muhammad Baqir Khan, the *kadkhuda* of Khalajabad, was a Baha'i.[37] Mirza Mahdi Akhavan Safa visited Shahabad in July–August 1911 and mentions that there were some 25 or so Jewish Baha'is there and he was invited to the home of two of them, Harun Shalum and Haji Yahuda. While he was there, some 200 *tumans* were raised towards the building of a school in the village and a site identified for the school and a Baha'i centre.[38] Mirza Hasan Nushabadi visited the Baha'i communities of this area in 1916 and spent three months in Khalajabad.[39] Mazandarani gives the number of Baha'is in Shahabad in the time of 'Abdu'l-Baha as 400.[40] It appears that, with the exception of one or two families of Muslims, the whole of the population of Khalajabad were Baha'is and about two-thirds of the population of Shahabad.[41] There was a Baha'i-owned public baths in Khalajabad.[42]

Another of the villages of this area is Mashhad Dhulfabad (3 km west of Shahabad). Mirza Mahdi Akhavan Safa visited some of the Baha'is there in August 1911, staying at the house of Karbala'i Muhammad.[43] Mirza

---

(d. 1917), a *mujtahid* who had been trained in Najaf and was imam of the mosque in Amirih.

35 Mihrabkhani, Namih-yi Zindigi 9–10.
36 Mirza Mahdi Tabib, 'Tarikh Hamadan va Rasht' 17.
37 ZH 6:679a.
38 MH4:56–8.
39 MH 6:97–8.
40 ZH 8a:281.
41 Estimates from Dr Heshmat Moayyad, who taught the children in Khalajabad for a year in about 1944 (interview by telephone, 19 August 2008). Mihrabkhani writes that during his visit in 1945, of the 40 families in Khalajabad all but three or four were Baha'is (Namih-yi Zindigi 10). Sulaymani writing in 1968 states that, with a few exceptions, all the people of Khalajabad were Baha'is (MH 6:221).
42 Interview with Ashraf Shahabadi, in Acuto, Italy, 3 July 2005.
43 MH 4:58.

Mahdi Khan Askaroff Mutarjim us-Sultan (see fig. 69) was the son of a Yazd Baha'i, Aqa 'Ali 'Askar Nassaj. The family had migrated to Ashkhabad in October 1889 and Mirza Mahdi, who was a merchant, had later moved to Alexandria in Egypt, from where he frequently visited 'Akka in the time of Baha'u'llah and 'Abdu'l-Baha. He then went to Italy, Bukhara and Samarqand. Because of the unsettled conditions in Central Asia, he returned to Iran in 1913, married Bahiyyih Khanum, the daughter of Ustad 'Ali Aqa Shishihgar, and settled in Mashhad Dhulfabad where he owned an estate and farmed. In the course of his travels he learned Arabic, French, Russian, Italian, and the Ottoman, Caucasian and Turkmenistan dialects of Turkish as well as knowing Persian and Zoroastrian Dari. Thus when Iran was engulfed by invading Russian, Ottoman and English forces during World War I, he was employed by the Iranian army as a translator and given the title of Mutarjim us-Sultan (translator of the king). One day in the summer of 1916 when Mutarjim us-Sultan was absent on business, one of his servants who was very prejudiced against the Baha'is attacked and killed his wife. Everyone was so appalled at this action that the wife of the murderer, who had been the victim's servant, reported her husband to the authorities and he was executed.[44] There was also a murder of another Baha'i woman, the wife of Mirza Rida-Quli Farzanih, at about this time in the Farahan area, but it is not clear in which village and at what date.[45]

There were also a number of Baha'is in some of the other villages of the area such as Shazand (Idrisabad), Husaynabad, Varqa and Nizam-abad.[46] Many of these villages were owned by a Baha'i, Mirza Aqa Khan Qa'im-Maqami (see pp. 160–2), and so the Baha'is there were protected. In most of these villages local spiritual assemblies were established. Because no other education was available, schools were established in the 1940s

---

44 Avarih, *Kavakib* 2:247–8; Yazdi, *Tarikh 'Ishqabad* 180, 34; ZH 7:309–10. Dihgan (*Tarikh-i Arak* 227) gives the name of the murdered woman as Sakinih, the daughter of Hasan Aqa Ashghali. He gives the date as 1924 and says that it was at first thought that Shaykh Isma'il Mashhadi had killed the woman because she was a Baha'i and he was an opponent of the Baha'is. He was arrested and taken to Hamadan but was later released after the intervention of the clerics. He maintains that later it transpired that the real culprit had been Muhammad 'Ali Khanjini, a thief – but this author tends to polemicize (see note 18).

45 ZH 7:310.

46 ZH 8a:281; MH 4:130; Tavangar, 'Yadi'. In 1911 Mirza Mahdi Akhavan Safa visited several of the Baha'is of Husaynabad at the home of Karbala'i Ramadan (MH 4:57). Nizamabad was a residence of Mirza Aqa Khan Qa'im-Maqami (MH 4:58–9).

69. Mirza Mahdi Khan Askaroff Mutarjim us-Sultan   70. Mirza Nasru'llah Tafrishi

by the National Spiritual Assembly of Iran in Shahabad, Khalajabad and Shazand.[47]

Tafrish is the name given to an area to the northeast of Sultanabad in a valley surrounded by the Zagros mountains. This name has now also been given to the main town in that area, which used to be called Tarkhuran (64 km northeast of Sultanabad and 70 km southwest of Savih; pop. 5,750 in 1951). A large proportion of the residents of the town were sayyids. This was also one of the main centres of rug- and carpet-weaving for which this region was famous and which was undertaken by women in their own homes. There was a considerable Babi community here but little is known about its beginnings and development. It appears that Mulla 'Abdu'l-Ghani (see p. 173) of the nearby village of Kukan may have been the first Babi in the Tafrish area and he converted Mulla Hasan Pishnamaz, the prayer-leader and Imam-Jum'ih of the mosque of Tarkhuran.

In the 1850s Haji Mirza Musa Qummi had declared himself to be the figure of *Man Yuzhiruhu'llah* (He whom God shall make manifest) expected by the Babis, and he found acceptance among the Babis in this

---

47   Interview with Ashraf Shahabadi, in Acuto, Italy, 3 July 2005; Tavangar, 'Yadi az Baha'iyan' 25.

area. In his meetings, one side of the room would be served tea and the other side cups of wine. Eventually the people of Tafrish fell upon him, stole everything he had and expelled him. He then travelled to Baghdad with two of the Babis of the area, Mirza Nasru'llah Tafrishi (see fig. 70) and Aqa 'Azim, met Baha'u'llah and renounced his own claim in favour of Baha'u'llah.[48] This Mirza Nasru'llah was the son of Mirza Hashim and was later a secretary in the Foreign Office in Tehran (he died in Edirne). His brother, Mirza Rida-Quli Tafrishi (d. 'Akka, 1873) sided eventually with Azal; another brother Mirza Faraju'llah (vol. 1:72–3) was loyal to Baha'u'llah; their sister Badr-i Jahan was married to Mirza Yahya Azal; another sister, Hajir, married Jamal Effendi (vol. 1:72–3). Mirza Asadu'llah Tafrishi (vol. 1:371), who was later in Tabriz, may have been the oldest of these siblings who introduced them to the Baha'i Faith.[49] Aqa 'Azim went on from Baghdad to Edirne as a servant of Mirza Nasru'llah and Mirza Rida-Quli, but broke away from Mirza Rida-Quli when he sided with Azal in 'Akka.[50] Shukru'llah, son of the above Mirza Nasru'llah, went from 'Akka to Tehran and worked in the post office, while his brother Mirza Fadlu'llah remained in 'Akka.[51]

A number of the most important Babis of Tafrish moved away from the town. Often it is not clear whether they moved because of persecution or because Tafrish, like Nur in Mazandaran, the above-mentioned Farahan and the nearby villages of Gurkan and Ashtiyan, had a tradition for the notables of the area to become educated and go to Tehran to enter the service of the Qajar state as government officials (secretaries and accountants), with some rising to become ministers and governors. Mulla Hasan Pishnamaz was forced to flee to Tehran with his son Mirza Muhammad 'Ali Mustawfi (vol. 1:73).[52] Mirza Muhammad Husayn Munajjim-bashi became a Babi, visited Baha'u'llah in Baghdad, and then, with his son Dr Muhammad Khan Munajjim, moved to Tehran where he became Munajjim-bashi (head astronomer) to the government, despite being well known as a Baha'i (vol. 1:15, 25, 72).[53] Aqa 'Abdu'r-Rasul Qummi (vol. 1:503) settled in the Tafrish area with his brother and their family. Aqa 'Abdu'r-Rasul migrated to Baghdad for a time but his son Aqa Baqir returned from Baghdad to

---

48   ZH 4:24, 192–3, 193n; Mu'ayyad, *Khatirat* 1:120.
49   ZH 6:451.
50   'Abdu'l-Baha, *Memorials*.
51   ZH 6:452.
52   ZH 6:346, Bayda'i, *Tadhkirih* 3:353.
53   ZH 6:346–7.

Tafrish. After a time, however, he became well known as a 'Babi' and was expelled from the area.[54] Other prominent Baha'is of this area were: Mirza Hasan Buzurg (d. 1878), a son-in-law of Sayyid 'Ali Majd ul-Ashraf, one of the notables of the area; Mirza Hasan Buzurg's sons Mirza Sayyid Taqi Mu'avin ul-Mamalik (vol. 1:332) and Mir Sayyid 'Ali Muhammad; Mirza Hasan Buzurg's son-in-law Mirza Hasan Aqa Tafrishi (d. 1323/1905, vol. 1:367, 371, 462), who took part in the transfer of the remains of the Bab from Tabriz to Tehran and was in later years in charge of the customs department in various parts of Iran; the latter's sons, Sayyid Shukru'llah Mutarjim ud-Dawlih and Aqa Sayyid 'Ali;[55] and Aqa Lutfu'llah and his son Haji Faraju'llah Tafrishi, who moved to Edirne where the former died and the latter accompanied Baha'u'llah to 'Akka, and finally moved to India.[56]

Other prominent Baha'is were from Tafrish but it is not clear whether they became Baha'is in Tafrish or after they moved from there: Mirza Nasir Tafrishi, who taught the Baha'i Faith in Sa'in-Qal'ih and was later chief steward to the governor of Sawj-Bulagh (vol. 1:422) and Aqa Sayyid Hasan Tafrishi (p. 223). In the case of other Baha'is from this area, it is clear that they became Baha'is after they left Tafrish: Mir Sayyid 'Abdu'llah Intizam us-Saltanih (vol. 1:78), who was converted by the above-mentioned Muna-jjim-bashi in Tehran (see p. 172); Mirza 'Abdu'r-Rahim Tafrishi, deputy governor of Abhar was converted there by Ibn Abhar (vol. 1:498–9); Mirza Muhammad 'Ali Khan Baha'i was from a famous Tafrishi family which had moved to Tehran (vol. 1:75); and Mirza Sayyid Shukru'llah Khan Rawhani (poetic pen-name Azadi, 1866–1939), poet and government official, became a Baha'i through Sadr us-Sudur in Tehran.[57] Mirza Hasan Nushabadi visited Tafrish and taught the Baha'i Faith there in about 1916.[58]

Kukan is a small village (1 km northeast of Tafrish; pop. 120 in 1951), where the above-mentioned Haji Mulla 'Abdu'l-Ghani (1814–78), a leading cleric of the area and a poet (with the poetic name Dharrih), became a Baha'i and converted others in the village. His son Mirza Yahya Khan Sarkhush (1277/1860–1338/1919) was second secretary in the British Legation in Tehran and an accomplished and published poet.[59]

---

54   ZH 6:593.
55   ZH 3:216, 6:347–8.
56   'Abdu'l-Baha, *Memorials* 75–6.
57   Dhuka'i-Bayda'i, *Tadhkirih* 1:13–17.
58   MH 6:97.
59   ZH (6:249, 8a:401) gives Mulla 'Abdu'l-Ghani's residence as Gurgan, but

The village of Gurkan (Garakan, Gulkan; 18 km southwest of Tafrish; pop. 2,178 in 1951) was another place that had a tradition of producing educated government officials, among which were some who became Baha'is after they left this area: Mirza Ibrahim Gurkani Ibtihaj ul-Mulk (vol. 1:338–9); Mirza 'Ali Khan Gulkani Dabir Humayun (vol. 1:144–5); and Mirza Abu'l-Hasan Mustashar Daftar Gurkani (vol. 1:128).

In the Khalajistan area, south of Savih, west of Qumm, a small Baha'i community arose; the most famous Baha'is of the area were Hakim Baba Jan and Sayyid 'Ali. There were also Baha'is in Qahan (60 km west of Qumm; pop. 601 in 1914, 1,335 in 1951), where Sayyid Mirza Aqa Vakil ur-Ru'aya was a prominent Baha'i, and in the Quhistan area.[60]

Gulpaygan, Khunsar and Mahallat

Gulpaygan is an important centre of religious studies in the central regions of Iran (180 km northwest of Isfahan, 106 km southeast of Sultanabad; pop. 20,000 in 1914, 22,000 in 1951). The surrounding area is good farmland where grain and fruit are grown. Some Babis came from this town, including Sayyid Muhammad, who was named Fata' ul-Malih (the fair youth) by Tahirih and accompanied her on her journey from Baghdad to Iran, and was then instructed by her to return to his hometown. He later lived in Tehran, acting as a tutor to families of the nobility, as a result of which he was able to interest Shams-i Jahan Khanum in the new religion and enabled her to meet with Tahirih (vol. 1:32). Nabil met him in Tehran.[61] In the 1860s Haji Mirza Haydar 'Ali Isfahani spent a short time in Gulpaygan teaching the Baha'i Faith.[62] Haji Muhammad of Ghawghih near Gulpaygan was a Baha'i who acted as Baha'u'llah's courier, carrying mail to and from 'Akka.[63]

A number of important Baha'is came from Gulpaygan and the

Bamdad (*Tarikh* 6:294) and Ja'fari ('Pavaraqi' 1–2) have Kukan and I have preferred the latter as Ja'fari is a descendant of Kukan Baha'is. A tablet of 'Abdu'l-Baha in 1921 to the Baha'is of this village lists 11 names which, if it is assumed they are the heads of families, would indicate a total of about 50 Baha'is in the village.

60   ZH 8a:661.
61   DB 285–6; Dhuka'i-Bayda'i, *Tadhkirih* 3:168–70.
62   MH 1:17.
63   Avarih, *Kavakib* 1:447. Ghawghih does not appear on maps. It may be that Qurghan or Gughad (12 km to the west and 4 km to the east of Gulpaygan respectively) is meant.

71. Mirza Abu'l-Fadl Gulpaygani and 'Ali-Quli Khan Nabil ud-Dawlih
in the United States of America

surrounding area, although their main contribution to the spread of the
Baha'i Faith did not occur in this region. Among these was Mirza Muhammad known as Mirza Abu'l-Fadl Gulpaygani (called Mirza Abu'l-Fada'il by
Baha'u'llah and 'Abdu'l-Baha, see fig. 71). He was from a prominent family
of clerics of the area. His father, Mirza Muhammad Rida Shari'atmadar,
was a religious leader in the town and his mother, Sharafu'n-Nisa, was
closely related to the Imam-Jum'ih there. Altogether, his extended family
included among its ranks some 50 of the clerics of Gulpaygan and
Khunsar. Following the death of his father and his being deprived of his
inheritance by his brothers, Abu'l-Fadl left Gulpaygan in October 1873 for
Tehran, where he encountered the Baha'i Faith and became a Baha'i. He
never returned to Gulpaygan and an account of the rest of his life is given
elsewhere (vol. 1:15–17). Mirza Abu'l-Fadl's brother Mirza Hidayatu'llah
(d. 1333/1912) was a *mujtahid* who lived in Gulpaygan and was inimical
towards Abu'l-Fadl and the Baha'i Faith. However, his son, Mirza Muhammad Ja'far Hidayati, who was also a *mujtahid* of Gulpaygan, became a
Baha'i.[64] In about 1929 Aqa Mirza Haji Aqa Rahmaniyan visited Gulpaygan, where he met about 40 Baha'is, led by Hidayati, who was also
acting as a cleric leading prayers in a mosque. He remarks that they had
little knowledge of the Baha'i Faith.[65]

---

64   Mihrabkhani, *Gulpaygani* 22; ZH 8b:1129.
65   MH 4:577–8; the leading Baha'i is called Aqa Shaykh Ja'far and is undoubtedly

72. Sayyid Mahdi Gulpaygani

Sayyid Mahdi Gulpaygani (1280/ 1863–1928, see fig. 72) was the son of Sayyid Abu'l-Qasim, the Imam-Jum'ih of Gulpaygan and closely related to Mirza Abu'l-Fadl. He was educated in Sultanabad and Isfahan and while he was in the latter place, Mirza Abu'l-Fadl talked to him but failed to convince him. The Baha'is of Isfahan, however, kept in touch with him. Eventually, as a result of conversations with Haji Mirza Haydar 'Ali Isfahani, he became a Baha'i in about 1892. In 1311/1893 he moved to Ashkhabad where he worked for a time as an editor of a newspaper and then as a secretary in a business, but mainly teaching in the Baha'i school there. In 1900 he married a Baha'i from Kirman. The Baha'is in Merv invited him there, where he worked as a teacher in the Baha'i school. After the Bolshevik revolution, the Baha'is of Ashkhabad launched a weekly magazine *Khurshid-i Khavar* (Sun of the East) and Sayyid Mahdi was invited back to Ashkhabad to run this.[66]

Curzon states in 1892 that three-quarters of the Jews in Gulpaygan had become Baha'is (one contemporary estimate of the Jewish population was 1,200).[67] Since there appears to be no descendants of these among the Baha'i families of Iran, it must be assumed that either this report was false or that these converts largely reverted to Judaism.

Mirza Muhammad Ja'far Hidayati, as he is described as a nephew of Mirza Abu'l-Fadl.

66 MH 3:9–51; Yazdi, *Tarikh 'Ishqabad* 558–61; Dhuka'i-Bayda'i, *Tadhkirih* 2:333–48; Mihrabkhani, *Gulpaygani* 251–3. There is some contradiction in the sources in that they state that Sayyid Mahdi's father was Sayyid Abu'l-Qasim, Imam-Jum'ih of Gulpaygan. But Sayyid Mahdi is said to be the maternal cousin of Mirza Abu'l-Fadl Gulpaygani, whose mother is said to be the sister of Mir Sayyid Hasan, Imam-Jum'ih of Gulpaygan (Mihrabkhani, *Gulpaygani* 21) and one would therefore expect that the latter was the father of Sayyid Mahdi Gulpaygani. It may be that Mir Sayyid Hasan and Sayyid Abu'l-Qasim were brothers who were successively Imam-Jum'ihs of Gulpaygan.

67 Curzon, *Persia* 1:500; estimate of Jewish population of Gulpaygan from *Gazetteer of Persia* (1905).

In Khunsar (170 km northeast of Isfahan; pop. 10,000 in 1905, 12,000 in 1951), the Babi religion was established by Haji Mulla Muhammad (d. 1327/1909), son of Mulla Muhammad Rida Mujtahid. He was studying in the shrine cities of Iraq when, in 1845, news reached him of the proclamation of the Bab at Mecca. He returned to Khunsar and began to preach in his father's mosque about the fulfilment of the prophecies of Islam. News of his preaching reached the governor, Ihtisham ul-Mulk, in Gulpaygan, who summoned him there and imprisoned him. However, through the intervention of his father and friends, he was released. He was forced eventually to flee to Tehran where he established himself in the Sar Qabr Aqa quarter.[68] In 1864, following persecutions in Najafabad, a Babi who ran a butcher's shop in Khunsar was killed together with his son.[69] A small Baha'i community subsequently arose in Khunsar. In about 1903 a Baha'i peasant farmer, Aqa 'Ali, was killed in a horrific manner. Some people followed him out to a field where he was working and held him down while stones were thrust down his throat until he suffocated.[70]

Mahallat is situated 26 kilometres west of the main road between Qumm and Isfahan (265 km southwest of Tehran; pop. 12,500 in 1951). It is likely that there was a Babi community here, since there were four Mahallatis among the defenders at Shaykh Tabarsi, one of whom, Mulla Mirza Muhammad Mahallati, survived the episode.[71]

One of the Baha'is from Mahallat became an important government official. Mirza Khan I'tidad ul-Vuzara Mahallati was postmaster in a number of different localities (see p. 436).[72] E.G. Browne met him in Kirman and describes him as 'a kindly-looking man, past middle age, with a grey moustache and the rank of colonel (*sartip*).'[73]

---

68   ZH 3: insert before p. 105; ZH 8a:375.
69   ZH 4:344.
70   Avarih, *Kavakib* 1:488; ZH 7:135. The latter source gives two other accounts of his death and says that he was a resident of Najafabad who was visiting his home town of Khunsar. There is another account of his death at ZH 7:250 related to the year 1907.
71   Malik-Khusravi, *Tarikh* 1:447, 2:289–91.
72   ZH 6:694–5.
73   Browne, *Year* 470; Isfahani, *Bihjat* 250.

13

HAMADAN

This province lies on the eastern flanks of the Zagros mountains. Rain and river water were plentiful and grain was grown. The majority of the population in the cities are Iranians with the rural areas being largely Turkish-speaking. The province is situated astride the important trade route between Baghdad and Tehran. Many pilgrims also passed through Hamadan province on their way to the shrine cities of Iraq.

Hamadan

Hamadan is one of the most ancient cities of Iran. In the 7th century BCE it was the capital of the empire of the Medes (Ectabana). In the 19th century it was famed for its tanneries and, in the last part of that century, it became an important centre for trade in western goods, especially textiles, entering Iran from Baghdad. The city was dominated politically and socially by the leading members of the Turkish Qaraguzlu tribe. Its population was said to have been 30,000 in 1868,[1] 50,000 in 1905 (of whom a quarter were Turks),[2] and 99,909 in 1956. The second decade of the 20th

1   Thomson cited in Issawi, *Economic History of Iran* 28.
2   *Gazetteer of Persia* 2:213; the total agrees with a Russian source, Sobotinskii

century was a particularly difficult period for the city as it was caught up in Salar ud-Dawlih's attempt to support Muhammad 'Ali Shah (1911–12) and was occupied successively by Russian, Ottoman and British forces during World War I.

During the third decade of the 20th century, Shoghi Effendi asked each Baha'i community to compile its history. It appears that in 1929 the Local Spiritual Assembly of Hamadan turned to 'Abdu'l-Hamid Ishraq-Khavari, who had become a Baha'i just three years before and had only recently moved to Hamadan, to perform this task. He completed it in 1930 and it has recently been published as *Tarikh Amri-yi Hamadan*. There are also a number of memoirs of the early Baha'is of the city such as Haji Mirza Yuhanna Hafizi and Mirza Mahdi Tabib Hamadani. In a recent history written by 'Abdu'llah Abizadih there is reference to other memoirs such as those of Aqa Jan Shakuri and 'Ali Firuz.

The first Babis in Hamadan were probably Haji Mulla Yusif of the nearby village of Garih-Chaqih who became a Babi after meeting the Bab in Mecca in 1844 and then returned and converted his brother Mulla Aqa Baba who lived in Hamadan itself and who was killed, together with his son Mulla 'Abdu'llah, at Shaykh Tabarsi.³ Tahirih spent some time in Hamadan in about 1273/1847 and stayed at the home of Mulla Aqa Baba. Tahirih is said to have debated with both Jewish and Muslim scholars and to have succeeded in converting a number of people. These included two Qajar princesses, Hajiyyih Khanum, the wife of Mahmud Khan Nasir ul-Mulk, head of the powerful Qaraguzlu tribe and later the Persian envoy in London and Minister for Foreign Affairs;⁴ and Shams-i Jahan Khanum, a daughter of Muhammad 'Ali Mirza Dawlatshah, who appears to have become a Babi and later a Baha'i. Shams-i Jahan Khanum tried to convince her brother Tahmasb Mirza Mu'ayyid ud-Dawlih about the truth of the new religion, and although he did not become a convert, he did become friendly to the Baha'i Faith.⁵

(1913), cited in Issawi, *Economic History of Iran* 34.

3   Samadani, 'Aghaz Amr' .

4   ZH 6:703; Ishraq-Khavari, *Hamadan* 28–9; her name appears to have been Hajiyyih Safiyyih Sultan Khanum and she was a daughter of 'Abbas Mirza, the son of Fath-'Ali Shah and thus a sister of Muhammad Shah (see http://royalark.net/Persia/qajar10.htm; accessed 29 Sept. 2019).

5   Gulpaygani, *Kashf ul-Ghita* 105, ZH 6:412–13 and n, 441. http://royalark.net/Persia/qajar5.htm (accessed 29 Sept. 2019; this website states that this latter woman was a Baha'i and died in Tabriz). She should not be confused with a Qajar

Also converted by Tahirih were two Jewish rabbis, Mulla Bakhaj (vol. 1:56) and Mulla Il'azar (Lalihzar), a learned Jew who secretly invited Tahirih to his home (although his father, Mulla Ilyahu, then asked her to leave because of the danger her presence posed for them) and was convinced of the truth of the religion of the Bab through her discourse. He later worked for the French Legation in Tehran and assisted Gobineau in his research. However, his enemies began to accuse him of being a Babi and he was forced to flee to Baghdad where he met Baha'u'llah and where he remained until his death in 1298/1881.[6] Another converted by Tahirih was a Jewish woman named Tamar. She later visited Baha'u'llah in 'Akka and her daughter Maryam was also a Baha'i.[7] In later years Hakim Ilyahu, a Jewish rabbi and physician, whose son Hafiz us-Sihhih became one of the first Jewish Baha'is of Hamadan, described for Mirza Abu'l-Fadl Gulpaygani how he had been present when Tahirih had debated with a number of Muslim clerics from behind a partition in the room in the presence of the governor. She had answered all their objections and silenced them all except for a Shaykhi cleric who, finding no answer to her powerful arguments, resorted to abuse and vilification, at which the governor terminated the proceedings.[8] Mention should also be made of Mirza Muhammad 'Ali Tabib Zanjani who had left Zanjan in 1851 after the Babi upheaval there and lived in Hamadan throughout the 1850s, meeting Baha'u'llah when

---

princess of the same name who lived in Tehran (vol. 1:32–3, 33n). Mu'ayyid ud-Dawlih was governor of Fars at the time of the second Nayriz upheaval and acted harshly towards the Nayrizi prisoners (BBR 149–51). In later years however he was favourable towards the Baha'is (vol. 1:121, 232).

6   ZH 6:702–3; Hafizi, Tarikh Zindigi 10–12, 36 (Memoir 1:10–12, 33); Ishraq-Khavari, Hamadan 30n). According to Nicolas (Le Bab 200n), Mulla Ili'azar translated passages of Sipihr's Nasikh ut-Tavarikh which Gobineau then used as the basis of his writings about the Bab in Les Religions. Mulla Ili'azar also assisted Gobineau with a translation of Descartes' Discourse on Reason into Persian (Guftar dar Ravish; Gobineau, Religions 97–8; Sarkar, Esther's Children, pp. 140, 420). He is a different person from the Hakim Lalihzar who was the father of Hakim Aqa Jan (see p. 183). In Baghdad and Kazimyan in about 1866, there were a number of people who were strong supporters of Mirza Yahya Azal including Mulla Ja'far Naraqi and Mirza Hadi Dawlatabadi. There they were joined by Mirza Ahmad Kashani, the pro-Azal brother of Haji Mirza Jani. It is possible that it was here and at this time that the Nuqtatu'l-Kaf was written by these supporters of Azal, based on Haji Mirza Jani's history, and then transmitted by Mulla Ili'azar to Gobineau from Baghdad.

7   Nughaba'i, 'Tarikh-i Iqbal' 14; Habibi, Very Brief Story.

8   Gulpaygani, Kashf ul-Ghita 105; Ishraq-Khavari, Hamadan 28–9n. Hakim Ilyahu is different from Mulla Ilyahu mentioned a few sentences previously.

he passed through and becoming a strong supporter of him. He returned to Zanjan where he was executed as a Baha'i (vol. 1:453–4).[9]

The number of Babis remained static, however, and the individual converts were seldom in touch with each other. There was thus no Babi community in Hamadan until 1280/1863 when two brothers, Aqa Muhammad Javad (d. 1318/1900) and Aqa Muhammad Baqir (d. 1336/1917), merchants of Naraq, migrated from Kashan to Hamadan. Their homes provided a centre for the propagation of the Baha'i Faith in the city and a base for visiting Baha'is.[10] Another early Baha'i migrant from Naraq to Hamadan was Sayyid Ahmad Naraqi. His wife, Sakinih Khanum, is described by Ishraq-Khavari as 'one of the wonders of her age and one of the rarest among women' for her piety and devotion.[11] Since the city is on the road between Tehran and Baghdad, Edirne and 'Akka, there was a steady stream of visiting Baha'is such as Haji Mirza Haydar 'Ali Isfahani in 1867 and Haji Amin in 1878. Although Sayyid Muhammad Isfahani, a partisan of Azal, had stayed in Hamadan for a period in about 1862, almost all the Babis in the city accepted Baha'u'llah and there is only mention of a few individual Azalis in later years.[12]

Aqa Muhammad Baqir Hamadani, known as Nabil Musafir (Nabil the traveller), a merchant, was a native of Hamadan and an early Babi who became a Baha'i and later lived in 'Akka for a time. Nabil Zarandi records meeting in Asadabad in 1283/1866 two young Jewish brothers who were merchants and who had been so impressed by the honesty and fair dealing of Nabil Musafir that they became Baha'is as a result. Once their conversion became known however, both Jews and Muslims combined against them and they were driven out of Hamadan and went to Asadabad.[13] The Baha'i community of Hamadan remained small, however, until the 1880s. Writing of the Baha'i community just before the large increase in the 1880s, one source states that there were no more than 20 Baha'is in Hamadan, and he names 14 men and two women, and of these at least eight were not natives of Hamadan.[14]

---

9   ZH 6:319–20; MH 10:549, 558.
10   MH 4:450–1; Ishraq-Khavari, *Hamadan* 40, 103.
11   Ishraq-Khavari, *Hamadan* 37–8n.
12   Ishraq-Khavari, *Hamadan* 49, 374.
13   ZH 6:706, 707–9n.
14   Hafizi, Tarikh Zindigi 22 (*Memoirs* 1:21).

Jewish conversions

The Jews of Hamadan form the oldest and historically the most important Jewish community in Iran. The biblical figures Esther and Mordecai are said to be buried here and there has been a considerable Jewish settlement of the area since at least the 4th century. The Jews spoke their own dialect, Judaeo-Hamadani, but, as distinct from other Jewish communities in Iran, they were not confined to a particular Jewish quarter in the city. According to the listing of Thompson, a British diplomat, in 1868, the Jews of Hamadan were the largest Jewish community in Iran and numbered 2,000. The 1883 the Jewish traveller Neumark gave their number as 5,000 (ten per cent of the city's population),[15] which agrees with the estimate in the *Gazetteer of Persia* (1905) and with the figures published by the Alliance Israélite Universelle (1902–13).[16] By 1952 their numbers had shrunk to about 3,000 through migration mainly to Tehran. Dr Polak (d. 1891) described the Jewish community of Hamadan thus in about 1860:

> The Jews earn their living by all kinds of gold- and silver-work, in which they are as clever as the Caucasians; by glass-cutting, silk-weaving, dealing in old clothes and in skins. Many of them are masons, blacksmiths, tailors, and shoemakers; some practise medicine, which they study according to the works of Avicenna, who is buried at Hamadan. They live under great difficulties, because they are considered as outcasts; they are constantly exposed to the caprices of the governor, who uses every pretext to plunder them . . . Should a Jew appear in the street dressed decently, or on horse-back, the spectators are indignant at him for daring to appear like a true believer. Should he, on the contrary, be dressed miserably, he is followed by a crowd of young rascals, who throw mud and stones at him.[17]

The position of the Jews in Hamadan changed towards the end of the 19th century. Hamadan became a hub for the trade in English cloth and clothes (via Basra and Baghdad) and it was Jewish merchants making use of their

---

15   Levi, *Tarikh Yahudiyan Iran* 3:663.
16   *Gazetteer of Persia* 2:213; The *Bulletin d'Alliance Israélite Universelle* gives various figures of between 5,000 and 6,000 in the years 1902–13 (see for example, 3rd series, no. 27 (1902) 145; no. 28 (1903) 136; no 29 (1904) 109, etc.).
17   From *Archives Israélites*, 1865, pp. 440ff., cited in *Jewish Enclopedia* (published 1901–1906), p. 188, see http://www.jewishencyclopedia.com/view_page.jsp?artid=153&letter=H&pid=0 (viewed 3 September 2006).

connections in Baghdad and Manchester who monopolized this trade and became very wealthy and influential.[18]

Hakim Masih of Tehran (vol. 1:12) is regarded as the first Jewish Babi and Baha'i but the above account shows that there were Jewish Babis (and later Baha'is) in Hamadan from 1847. However, the main expansion began in 1875. The above-mentioned Aqa Muhammad Baqir Naraqi maintained friendly relations with several Jews of Hamadan, in particular his physician Hakim Aqa Jan (c. 1830–81, see fig. 74), who was learned in medicine and a rabbi as well, being of Cohen decent. He was the son of Il'azar Kahin (d. 1887), known as Hakim Lalihzar, who was in turn the son of Hakham Harun, one of the senior rabbis in Hamadan. Naraqi surprised Hakim Aqa Jan by accepting an invitation to go to his house and partaking of food there in disregard of the norms of Shi'i Islam which regarded food touched by Jews as unclean. When the wife of Naraqi fell ill in about 1875, he brought in Hakim Aqa Jan to treat her. Jewish physicians were highly regarded by Iranians but also treated with contempt as they were regarded as ritually unclean. They carried out their professional activities with great trepidation for if they made an error and a Muslim patient of theirs died, it was possible that they would be killed and all their property appropriated by the relatives of their patient and even for the houses of all the Jews to be looted as well. Aqa Muhammad Baqir broke all customs in offering the Jewish physician tea on his arrival. During the course of his treatment of the patient, Hakim Aqa Jan made an error in his prescribing and Aqa Muhammad Baqir's wife's condition deteriorated suddenly. Hakim Aqa Jan was fearful of the consequences but Aqa Muhammad Baqir reassured him, saying that he realized that he had tried his best and that the mistake was an honest one. The wife recovered and Hakim Aqa Jan was so impressed with the kindness with which Aqa Muhammad Baqir had treated him that he asked him about his religious beliefs. Aqa Muhammad Baqir spoke a little about them and this aroused the interest of Hakim Aqa Jan to such an extent that he involved two others in his investigation of the Baha'i Faith, his maternal cousin Hakim Rahim who is better known by his later title of Hafiz us-Sihhih (superintendent of public health, see fig. 74), and the latter's maternal cousin Aqa Ha'im (Hizqil or Ezekiel Hayyim). All three eventually became Baha'is.[19]

---

18   Floor, 'Merchants' 122.
19   Hafizi, Tarikh Zindigi 21–2 (Memoirs 1:20–1); Gidney, History 466–7; ZH 5:234, 6:703–4; M. Amanat, 'Kayfiyat-i Iqbal - 1' 20–1; Thabiti, 'Sharh-i Hal'; Ishraq-Khavari, Hamadan 40–5; ZH 5:234–6; Baha'i World 9:613–14.

The three Jewish converts were in a difficult situation, very different from what would have been the case had they converted to Islam, as
small numbers of Jews did. If they had converted to Islam, they would
have taken on the social identity of Muslims and had a socially-accepted
and defined place. But the Baha'i community had no social identity in
Hamadan and indeed numbered, as mentioned above only about 20 individuals, all bearing a Muslim identity. To exist in a traditional society, it is
necessary to assume some social identity but there was no social identity
which they could easily take on. There were two choices open to them.
They could declare their Baha'i belief and take on the Muslim social identity of the other Baha'is; but since the Jewish community knew nothing
of the Baha'i Faith, this would be regarded as conversion to Islam and be
treated with great opprobrium in the Jewish community, resulting in their
ostracization. They would also be in great danger, for were the Muslims to
find out they were Baha'is, they would be regarded as having converted to
and apostatised from Islam and that was punishable by death. The alternative was to retain their Jewish social identity, but this was becoming very
difficult because of the rising tide of opposition from the Jewish religious
leaders and would impede their efforts to teach the Baha'i Faith to their
co-religionists.

At this time, a third option opened itself to the three Jewish converts,
which they took. Pastor Shim'un, a Nestorian of Urumiyyih who had
converted to Protestantism, had arrived in Hamadan in November 1875,
sent from Urumiyyih by the American Presbyterian Missionary Board to
set up a mission to the Armenians in and around Hamadan.[20] The three
converts saw this as an opportunity to give themselves a socially recognized space within which they could signal to the Jewish community their
change of status without suffering the opprobrium of being considered
converts to Islam. As they had become Baha'is, they saw no problem with
acknowledging the truth of Christ and studying the Bible with Shim'un.
The three Jewish converts then began to have religious conversations with
their family and acquaintances, especially younger individuals, and bring
these to the Bible study classes as a way of breaking the hold of traditional
Judaism on them. Once these were convinced of the truth of Christ in the
Bible study classes, the three converts would take them to private study

---

20   See the reports that led up to the founding of this mission in *The Missionary
     Herald* 66 (1870) 374–7; also Bassett, *Eastern Mission* 174–5.

sessions and teach them the Baha'i Faith as a natural progression.[21] The
Jewish rabbis asked the converts to desist from contacts with Shim'un but
Hafiz us-Sihhih defeated them in debate and this caused even more people
to start coming to the Bible study classes. The Baha'is found that those
Jews who were sufficiently dissatisfied with their own religion to enquire
about Christianity were the most suitable persons to whom to introduce
the Baha'i teachings.[22] Gradually, a growing group of Jewish converts to
the Baha'i Faith emerged and their faith was confirmed by travelling Baha'i
teachers such as Ibn Asdaq, who visited Hamadan in 1878, and Shaykh
Muhammad 'Arab of Baghdad in 1881 (he returned in early 1889).

Hakim Aqa Jan converted his own extensive family, including his wife
Tuba Khanum, his father (Hakim Lalihzar), eight sisters, two brothers
and all of their respective families. Then in about 1878 Hakim Aqa Jan
proclaimed the new religion openly in one of the synagogues of the city
where he himself was among those who carried out part of the ritual and
read the Torah. One Saturday he stood up and asked, 'Have I not served
you until now? Have you observed anything from me except truthfulness
and sincerity?' All those present acknowledged that this was so. And so he
continued, 'Today I bring you glad tidings and that is the good news of the
appearance of the promised Messiah. I have found through investigation
of the matter that the appearances of Jesus Christ and Muhammad were
truly from God and that now is the day of the appearance of the Lord of
Hosts and the Day of the Lord (Adonai).' It is reported that the congregation rose up and ejected him from the synagogue, but the stir caused by
his words resulted in about 15 people, mostly physicians and merchants,
investigating the new religion and becoming Baha'is.[23]

---

21 Hafizi, Tarikh Zindigi, 22–3 (*Memoirs* 1:21–2); KD 2:156–7. According to
    Gidney (*History* 466) and Waterfield (*Christians in Persia* 116), these three and
    another named 'Dr Moosa' (Hakim Musa, the brother of Hafiz us-Sihhih) were
    baptised by the American missionary James Bassett in 1878.
22 Hamadani, Tarikh Hamadan 13–14; Hafizi, Tarikh Zindigi, 23 (*Memoirs* 1:21–2).
23 Amanat, 'Kayfiyat-i Iqbal - 2', p. 22. Hakim Aqa Jan's words in the synagogue are
    given somewhat differently in Mirza Mahdi Tabib Hamadani (Tarikh Hamadan
    1): 'O Jews! That Messiah that Moses prophesied, that promised one whom the
    whole world is expecting, the light of his reality has enveloped the East and the
    West. He has appeared to you and it is incumbent upon all of you to believe
    in him. Whoever wishes for evidence, let him come forward and I will prove
    this from the Torah.' According to MH 4:454, however, Hakim Aqa Jan only
    asserted the truth of Jesus and Muhammad and then invited those interested in
    hearing more to come to his house. Thabiti (*Varithan* 41–2) gives a longer form
    of the speech, agreeing in content with Hamadani.

74. Hakim Aqa Jan (*left*); Hakim Rahim (Rahamim, later known as
Mirza 'Abdu'r-Rahim Khan) Hafiz us-Sihhih (*right*)

75. Da'i Rubin

76. Haji Mahdi Arjumand

Opposition to the activities of the Jewish Baha'is came from the more conservative elements in the Jewish community, and especially the Jewish rabbis. As early as about 1880, some of the Jews became upset at the disregard shown by Haji Yari (d. 1337/1918) to a Jewish festival (Ilanut, the festival of the trees) and prevented the Baha'is from entering the synagogue. A large number of Jews went to the house of the governor, Allah-Quli Khan Ilkhani, and were shouting and complaining in the outer apartment. As it happened, Hafiz us-Sihhih was treating the governor and came out to see what was happening. Fearing that if the Muslim crowd that had gathered by this time were to hear the accusation of 'Babism', it would pose a mortal danger to the Baha'i converts, he addressed the Muslims, accusing the Jews of being after Muslim blood. The Muslims then attacked and dispersed the Jewish crowd. The next day, another delegation of Jews went to the governor, complaining, 'A group from among us have become irreligious and have become the enemies of God and the prophet and of the king. They have become Babis.' The governor was in his inner chambers and sent one of his functionaries out to ascertain the cause of the commotion. They stated that: 'A number from among us have begun to make fires and buy things on Saturdays and to eat the food of the Muslims.' The functionary replied, 'If a person be cold, why should he not warm himself by building a fire? . . . if he be hungry, should he not buy something to eat? . . . You say that the food that Muslims eat is unclean. You fools! Have you come as a crowd to the governor's house to tell him that Muslim food is to be forbidden?'[24]

This episode demonstrates a weakness in the position of the Jewish rabbis. By becoming Baha'is, these Jews were now believers in the prophethood of Muhammad and no longer considered Muslim food to be impure. This created a limit to what the rabbis could achieve. On one occasion a group of the Jewish Baha'is were being pressured by a rabbi to return to Jewish customs and practices. When they resisted this, the rabbi said, 'If you do not do as we say, we will kill you all.' Da'i Rubin, one of the Baha'is, retorted with an implicit threat: 'It is a much-esteemed command to us that we do not harm anyone. If it were not for this, we would be able to have

---

24   The episode is recounted with some variations in Hamadani (Tarikh Hamadan 10–12); Hafizi, Tarikh Zindigi 26–7 (*Memoirs* 1:22–3); ZH 6:713; Ishraq-Khavari, *Hamadan* 44–5. It is probably in relation to this episode that, according to Gidney (*History* 466), Hafiz us-Sihhih was so badly beaten in the streets that his arm and ribs were broken.

all of you killed within a week.' He was asked, 'How would you do that?'
Da'i Rubin replied, 'We would take some of your books to the *mujtahid*
and translate for him those passages where your rabbis have refuted and
attacked Christ and Muhammad. Then see what will happen to you.'[25]

Da'i Rubin (see fig. 75), son of Aqa Yahuda, was learned in the Torah
and Jewish traditions, became one of the earliest Baha'i converts and
married a sister of Hakim Aqa Jan. He was head of the guild of *'alaqibands*
(dealers in thread and lace) and an influential person in the city. Because
of this he was able to protect the Baha'is to some extent.[26] It even happened that some of the Jews who had suffered injustice pretended to be
Baha'is in order to gain the protection of figures such as Da'i Rubin and
Hafiz us-Sihhih (who together with his father were considered the premier
physicians in Hamadan) and consequently attended Baha'i meetings; some
then became devoted Baha'is, while others reverted to Judaism when they
no longer needed help.

In early 1880 Hakim Aqa Jan and Hafiz us-Sihhih made a trip to
Tehran to try to spread the Baha'i Faith among the Jews there (vol. 1:56).
After his return, Hakim Aqa Jan ceased his work as a physician and occupied himself with spreading the Baha'i Faith. He died of dysentery on
17 December 1880.[27] Following Hakim Aqa Jan's death, Hakim Rahim
(Hebrew: Rahamim, later known as Mirza 'Abdu'r-Rahim Khan, 1844–27
December 1942, see fig. 74), known as Hafiz us-Sihhih, became the leader
of the group. He was one of the leading physicians in Hamadan and had, in
1873, even been summoned to the court of the Crown Prince Muzaffaru'd-
Din Mirza in Tabriz. Fadil Mazandarani states that he converted to Islam
while in Tabriz, but his own son's memoirs do not mention this.[28] On his
return to Hamadan, he was highly sought after and was physician to many

---

25   Hamadani, Tarikh Hamadan 6–7; ZH 6:707–8.
26   Hafizi, *Memoirs* 1:168–75; Geula, *Iranian* 187–90. He was the progenitor of the
      Shakib family.
27   Shim'un in *The Gospel in All Lands* 3 (Jan.–Jun. 1881) 175–6; reprinted in
      Wilson, *Persia* 254–5.
28   ZH 6:705–6; Hafizi, Tarikh Zindigi 18–19 (*Memoirs* 1:19–20). He was in any
      case very interested in Sufism and its poetry (*Memoirs* 9; ZH 6:708–9). Accord-
      ing to Hafizi, when the above-mentioned Mulla Lalihzar died in Baghdad, Hafiz
      us-Sihhih was invited to go there and take up his medical practice. He there-
      fore had several extended stays there during which he outwardly converted to
      Islam in the 1880s in Samarra in the presence of Mirza Hasan, Mirza-yi Shirazi
      (*Memoirs* 1:180) and acquired Ottoman citizenship (*Memoirs* 1:74). M. Amanat
      (*Jewish Identities* 174–88) discusses Hafiz us-Sihhih's multiple identities.

of the notables of the city and area, in particular, the leading members of the Qaraguzlu tribe. He was appointed Public Health Officer for the city and given the title Hafiz us-Sihhih in 1897.[29]

In the course of about two years a considerable group of people became outwardly Christians but inwardly Baha'is in this manner. Shim'un was delighted to find a group of Jews who acknowledged the truth of Christ and were content to study the Bible. He wrote glowing reports to his superiors with the result that in 1881 Rev. James W. Hawkes was sent to Hamadan to be followed the next year by several more Americans.[30] The Jewish Baha'is assisted Hawkes to set up a primary school which was begun in the home of Da'i Rubin. Some of the children of the Jewish converts began to attend this school as well as some Armenian children. After two years the school moved to the home of Dr Hawkes, and Da'i Rubin's home was used for Baha'i meetings, although at first the Christian missionaries also preached there occasionally.[31]

In October 1881 Rev. Joseph Lotka was sent by the British mission-ary organisation, the Church's Ministry among the Jews. On one occasion, Lotka went on an outing to the Alvand mountains with six of the young Jewish Baha'is. Upon their return they were arrested by the governor 'Abdu's-Samad Mirza 'Izz ud-Dawlih (1843–1929). While Lotka was released and tried unsuccessfully to raise a complaint with the national government, the Baha'is were bastinadoed and fined.[32] In about 1881 one of the first group of Jewish converts, Aqa Ha'im, whose clock-making business was not going well, took employment with the missionaries. He then stopped teaching the Baha'i Faith and tried to get the other Jewish converts to stop attending Baha'i meetings. But other Jews continued to join the Baha'i Faith.[33]

In about 1883, Shim'un, realizing that the reason that this group of Jews appeared to accept the position of Jesus was on account of their acceptance of the Baha'i teachings and not on account of the efforts of the

---

29 His father was the Hakim Ilyahu, who is described above as having met Tahirih, and he himself was a nephew through his mother of Mulla Ila'zar (Lalihzar), who had been converted by Tahirih (see p. 180). His life is documented in detail in the memoirs of his son, Yuhanna Hafizi (Tarikh Zindigi, translated as *Memoirs*); see also Thabiti, *Varithan*, 94–104; Geula, *Iranian* 109–11.

30 Wilson, *Persia* 251–2; Gidney, *History* 465–7; Waterfield, *Christians in Persia* 136.

31 Hafizi, Tarikh Zindigi 24 (*Memoirs* 1:53); ZH 6:705.

32 Gidney, *History* 467–9; Hafizi, Tarikh Zindigi 24–5 (*Memoirs* 1:53–4); Water-field, *Christians in Persia* 116.

33 Hafizi, Tarikh Zindigi 25 (*Memoirs* 1:53, 167–8).

missionaries, asked the converts whether they were Christians or Baha'is. All except Aqa Ha'im said they were Baha'is and most stopped attending the Christian services, although there was not a complete separation at this time. There were now about 50 Jewish converts to the Baha'i Faith.[34]

While it may be thought that the Baha'is sought the protection of the powerful European nations by associating with the Christian missionaries, at times, the tables were unexpectedly turned and it was the Baha'i converts who were protecting the missionaries. After a complaint was filed by elders of the Jewish community in September 1881, two of the converts were arrested (the pretext for their arrest varies in different sources) and Pastor Shim'un, who was still protecting them at this time, was arrested and was being prepared for the bastinado when Hafiz us-Sihhih intervened on his behalf. Pastor Shim'un was then forced to flee Hamadan for a time.[35]

The Jewish traveller Neumark's comments on his visit to Hamadan in 1883 indicate that the Jews who were being converted to the Baha'i Faith included some of the most distinguished and observant members of the community. He lists Mi'ir Haji Il'azar (probably Haji Mahdi Arjumand, see pp. 191, 193), Hakim Abraham, who was a teacher and *shofet* (judge or magistrate), Mulla Rabi Yihziqal, Mulla Yahuda the son of Mulla Hakham and Hakim Musa, the latter two being described as religiously observant individuals.[36] Both Jewish and Baha'i accounts agree that it was the Jewish physicians in the city in particular who converted.[37]

Matters with the Christian missionaries came to a head during the visit to Hamadan of Mirza Abu'l-Fadl Gulpaygani in 1887–8. His visit was of particular significance in view of his extensive knowledge of the Jewish holy books and traditions[38] and while in Hamadan, he wrote a treatise of Baha'i proofs for Jews, the *Risalih-yi Ayyubiyyih*.[39] The Jewish Baha'is invited Pastor Shim'un and his son-in-law, Dr Sa'id Khan Kurdistani,

34 Hafizi, Tarikh Zindigi 25 (*Memoirs* 1:54).
35 Wilson, *Persia* 252–3; J. L. Potter in *The Gospel in All Lands* 4 (Jul.–Dec. 1881) 262–3. This may be the episode related at Hafizi, *Memoirs* 1:55.
36 Levy, *Tarikh Yahud* 3:657.
37 See for example the comments in *Bulletin d'Alliance Israélite Universelle*, 3rd series, no. 25 (1900) 79; Abizadih (Vaqayi' 152) lists 20 males and one female (Sarkar Hakim Khanum, the sister of Hafiz us-Sihhih) traditional physicians (*hakims*) who became Baha'is. This list is not complete however as it omits at least Mirza Yahya 'Amid ul-Atibba.
38 See comments about the importance of Gulpaygani in Fischel, 'The Bahai Movement and Persian Jewry', 52–3 and *idem*, 'The Jews of Persia', 154–5.
39 Mihrabkhani, *Gulpaygani* 385–6.

a Kurdish Sunni Muslim who had converted to Christianity, to meet Gulpaygani. There ensued a lengthy meeting during which neither side succeeded in persuading the other of their views.[40] The visit of Gulpaygani deepened the knowledge of the Jewish converts about the Baha'i Faith and made them confident enough to state their faith openly. Several more Jewish physicians became Baha'is at this time.[41] This episode marked the final parting of the ways for the Jewish Baha'is and Christian missionaries and after this there was a great deal of antagonism and disdain expressed by the Christian missionaries towards the Baha'is, with bitter words such as 'falsehood', 'deceitful' and 'hypocrites' being used by the missionaries.[42] Among the Christians of Hamadan who were very antagonistic towards the Baha'is were the above-mentioned Dr Sa'id Kurdistani who collected a large amount of anti-Baha'i material and passed this on to William Miller, an American missionary, to use in his book attacking the Baha'i Faith, and a Jewish convert to Christianity, Dr Daniyal Khan, who also wrote against the Baha'is and later translated Avarih's attack on the Baha'is into English for the missionaries.[43]

In November 1887 there was an episode when a Jewish rabbi went to the governor with false accusations after two Jewish Baha'is, Aqa Yusif and Aqa Ishaq had purchased a house from a Muslim.[44] In 1888 a rabbi named Mulla Rabi' (or Rafi') Hakham complained to the government official in charge of the Jews who had recently arrived that the Baha'i converts were breaking Jewish law. The official had Haji Mahdi Arjumand (1861–1941; a learned Jewish Baha'i convert; see fig. 76) arrested and ordered that his hair be shaved in accordance with Jewish law. He wanted to imprison him

---

40   Mihrabkhani, *Gulpaygani* 135. The biography of Kurdistani, Rasooli and Allen, *Dr Sa'eed of Iran*, does not mention this episode.
41   Hafizi, Tarikh Zindigi 52 (*Memoirs* 1:31–2, 156–9).
42   See, for example, the statement made by Samuel Wilson, American missionary to Iran, in Wilson, *Baha'ism*, p. 201: 'A striking example of this religious dissimulation is seen in Hamadan. There about two-and-a-half percent of the Jews have accepted Baha as the Messiah. But many of these continue in the outward forms and associations of the Jews. Others profess to be Christians, and were protected as such by the Shah's government. After a decade or two it became evident that they were hypocrites, cloaking Bahaism under the Christian name.' There is also the accusation made in 1913 by Miss Annie Montgomery, an American missionary of Hamadan (ibid. p. 201, n.1): 'This sect of Moslems, thirty years ago, were afraid to appear to be what they really were, they exercised the privilege of falsehood their deceitful faith grants them, and called themselves Christians.'
43   MH 9:110–15; Hafizi, *Memoirs* 1:56–62.
44   ZH 5:367–8n.

and to bring other Baha'is for the same treatment but the Baha'is resisted this and sent petitions to Tehran, resulting in Arjumand's release.[45]

In 1308/1890, instigated by Sharif ul-Mulk (see p. 197), a group of Jews, accompanied by some rabbis who had come from Jerusalem, went to the governor 'Abdu's-Samad Mirza 'Izz ud-Dawlih, complaining that the Jews who had converted to the Baha'i Faith had discarded the Torah and were breaking their customs and laws. They asked that either the converts be compelled to comply with their laws or be expelled from among them. The governor ordered a group of people to look into the matter and it was decided to convene a gathering in the main synagogue to which the Baha'i converts were summoned to answer the charges. They came and their spokesman, Da'i Rubin, addressed the Jewish rabbis saying: 'We have not and never will in any way oppose the text of the Torah but we will not go along with the innovations that you have introduced which are contrary to the law of Moses. This is why you are displeased with us. We regard you as contravening the principles laid down in the text of the Torah . . .' After some further discussion, it was decided to refer the matter to the district council (majlis-i baladiyyih), upon which sat 12 of the notables and merchants of the city under the chairmanship of an appointee of the governor. The Baha'is sent Da'i Rubin to represent them and the chief rabbi of Hamadan came to represent the Jews, accompanied by one of the rabbis who had come from Jerusalem. The chairman of the council, Mirza Taqi Khan Qa'im-Maqami, asked the Jews what their accusation was. 'These people have left the religion of Moses, such that they no longer observe the sacredness of the Sabbath day and they partake of unclean food and drink.' 'And what do you consider to be unclean food and drink?' asked the chairman. The representative of the Jews explained that: 'Any animal that Muslims have slaughtered and any cheese or yoghurt that they have made is unclean for Jews, but these people will not abstain and eschew them.' The chairman became very angry at these words of the Jews which implied that Muslim food was unclean and he ordered the Jews be expelled from the meeting.[46] In this same year the previously-mentioned Haji Yari began to open his shop on the Sabbath. The Jews were incensed at this and wanted to attack him but were prevented by the governor.[47]

---

45   ZH 6:716; Ishraq-Khavari, *Hamadan* 71; MH 4:457.
46   ZH 5:429–30; Ishraq-Khavari, *Hamadan* 77–9; Geula, *Iranian* 187–8.
47   Ishraq-Khavari, *Hamadan* 80 (see p. 262 for Baha'u'llah's comment on this); ZH 6:713.

The spread of the Baha'i Faith among the Jews continued apace. Converts would bring their friends to the Saturday meetings and these, particularly the young, would be attracted by the modernity of the Baha'i Faith and the simplicity and lack of rituals of the Baha'i meetings. When these young converts married they would often convert their spouses also. In 1897 there was a series of debates between Haji Mahdi Arjumand and Dr George Holmes (1841–1910), an American missionary doctor, which alternated between the residences of Dr Holmes and Arjumand on Saturdays over a period of more than a year. The proceedings of these debates formed the basis of a book of Baha'i proofs published under the name *Gulshan-i Haqa'iq*. Arjumand was a nephew of Hakim Aqa Jan and earned a living as an assayer of gold.[48] A Jewish observer, Bassan, the head of the Alliance school (see p. 207), writes in 1901 of the 'frightening progress' of the Baha'i Faith among the Jews of the city and states that the two most active teachers were Da'i Rubin and Mi'ir Rafi'a (Haji Mahdi Arjumand).[49]

The opposition by the rabbis and more conservative elements in the Jewish community was not totally without detrimental impact on the converts, however. On several occasions, on the complaint of the Jews of the city, the Jewish Baha'is were arrested and fined.[50] A cloth-seller named Aqa Ishaq (Isaac), who opened his shop on a Saturday, was set upon when he went to the Jewish public baths and died as a result of the injuries he received. During World War I, when Hamadan was occupied by Russian forces (spring–summer 1916), the Jews persuaded one of the Russian soldiers to attack Aqa Ibrahim 'Attar, one of the Jewish converts, who had opened his chemist-perfumery shop on a Saturday. The latter suffered a severe blow to the chest. He was taken home, where he died.[51]

One of those who was most active in teaching the Baha'i Faith to the Jews was Sayyid Hasan Hashimizadih (vol. 1, fig. 40). He lived in Hamadan from about 1912 to 1921. Although a Baha'i from a Muslim background

---

48 Arjumand, *Gulshan-i Haqayiq* 3. For a biography of Arjumand, see MH 4:447–67; Iraj Ayman, 'Haj Mihdi Arjmand'; Hafizi, *Memoirs* 1:180–3.
49 Report of Bassan to Alliance Israélite Universelle, dated 5 December 1901; archives of Alliance Israélite Universelle, Paris (I am grateful to Dr Daniel Tsadik for a copy of this document).
50 ZH 5:430.
51 Amanat, 'Kayfiyat-i Iqbal - 3', no. 216, p. 31; Ishraq-Khavari, *Hamadan* 148, 341–2; Sabeti, *Varithan* 133–5. Abizadih, *Vaqayi'* 60, 65 states that the Russian soldier who beat Mirza Ibrahim was himself a Jew angry that Mirza Ibrahim had converted and was opening his shop on a Saturday but implies that the episode occurred in Malayir.

and, indeed, a Sayyid, a descendant of the Prophet Muhammad, he lived for part of his stay in Hamadan in an area in which many Jews lived and he became known as 'Sayyid-i Jud-ha' (Sayyid of the Jews). The elders of the Jewish community became alarmed at the large number of young Jews congregating in his house and becoming Baha'is and they went to a *mujtahid* of Hamadan, asking him to give a *fatwa* for the death of Sayyid Hasan, if not for the sake of the Jewish youth, then at least for the sake of the Muslim youth who were also converting. The *mujtahid*, however, summoned the neighbours of Sayyid Hasan and asked them what they had observed. One neighbour remarked on the beautiful sound of Sayyid Hasan's voice when he recited Arabic prayers for two hours before dawn each day. When he heard this, the *mujtahid* dismissed the Jews.[52]

The conversion of Jews to the Baha'i Faith occurred throughout the last decades of the 19th century and into the early decades of the 20th. These conversions were noted by Jewish travellers to the area. Ephraim Neumark, a Polish Jew who had migrated to Palestine, visited Hamadan in 1883. Even at that early date in the conversions, he noted that of the 800 families of Jews in the city, 150 families had become Baha'is (18 per cent) and controlled three synagogues.[53] Since he estimated the Jewish population of Hamadan as 5,000,[54] this would mean about 940 Baha'is. And there were, of course, many further conversions after 1883. Writing of his visit to Iran in 1935, Dr Abraham Jacob Brawer, a Ukrainian Jew who had migrated to Jerusalem, stated that of the 8,000 Jews in Hamadan, a quarter (2,000) were Baha'is.[55] Many of these Jewish Baha'i families intermarried and the chart on p. 195 is an attempt to show, in a very simplified way, the inter-relationships of some of the persons mentioned in the text of this book and the families descended from them. The chart omits many siblings of those shown.

Conversions among the Muslims of Hamadan

The Jews were not, however, the only ones entering the Baha'i community in Hamadan. A number of Muslim traders and merchants also became Baha'is,

---

52   Mehrangiz Vahid-Tehrani, Memorandum on Sayyid Hasan Mutavajjih, pp. 19–20, cited in Momen, *The Ayman/Iman Family*, pp. 47–8; Abizadih, Vaqayi' 138–40.
53   Ephraim Neumark quoted in Levy, *Tarikh-i Yahud Iran*, 3:657.
54   ibid. 3:663.
55   Quoted in Netzer, 'Conversion' 248.

Chart showing relationships of some of the principal Jewish Baha'is in Hamadan and lines of familial descent

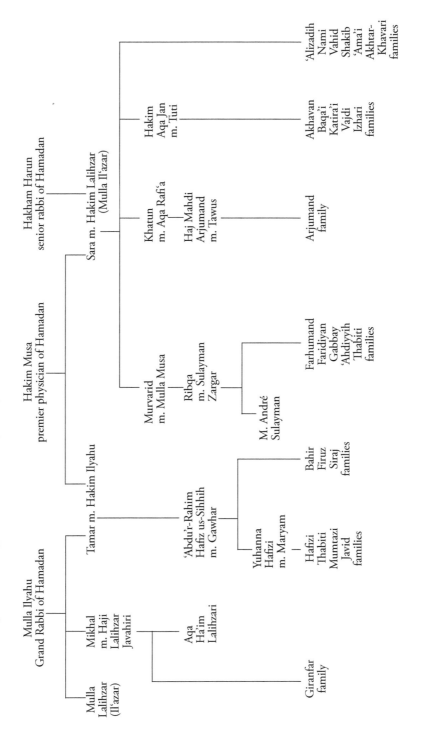

77. Feast held at the house of Hafiz us-Sihhih to celebrate an engagement, 1925. At the top, the man seated on the left in dark clothes is Hafiz us-Sihhih; to the right of him is his wife Gawhar and to the right of her is their eldest son Yuhanna Hafizi. Also in the picture are other members of the Hafizi, Bahir, Siraj, Faridiyan, Firuz and Iftikhar families.

such as Aqa Muhammad Baqir Karbas-furush (seller of thick cotton cloths) and Aqa Muhammad 'Ali Bulur-furush (seller of crystalware) Hisari. These were harassed by the townspeople and the last-named in particular suffered great financial loss as his merchandise was repeatedly stoned and broken.[56] In March 1880 some 12 of these Baha'is from a Muslim background were arrested by the governor, 'Abdu's-Samad Mirza 'Izz ud-Dawlih. This was at the instigation of one of the main enemies of the Baha'is in the city, Mirza Ahmad Sharif ul-Mulk, who was the leading merchant (ra'is ut-tujjār) of Hamadan and the steward of the governor (pīshkār) for a time. It appears that he was a Shaykhi or possibly an Azali. The Baha'is were kept in prison, tortured with the ishkilak (pieces of wood placed between the fingers and squeezed) and only released upon the intervention of Zaynu'l-'Abidin Khan Amir Afkham, the head of the Qaraguzlu tribe, who sent off telegrams to Tehran, bypassing the Hamadan telegraph office that had been blocked to the Baha'is. Orders came from Mustawfi ul-Mamalik and Nasir ul-Mulk (see p. 179) in Tehran that the Baha'is were to be released and the money taken from them returned.[57]

There were also some Muslims from Hamadan who became Baha'is but whose main importance for Baha'i history lay in what they did elsewhere. Haji Ghulam-Husayn, known as Haji Qalandar (d. Baku, 1327/1909), became a Baha'i before 1291/1874. He travelled throughout Iran and the Ottoman Empire in dervish attire and taught the Baha'i Faith. He earned his living as a craftsman in inlaid work. He had lived in India for 32 years and also knew Indian medicine. Through one or other of these means he could earn his living as he moved from one town to another teaching the Baha'i Faith. He played an important role in bringing a number of Sufis into the Baha'i Faith and was also instrumental in converting Zoroastrians in Yazd.[58] The other person was Sayyid Ahmad Hamadani Sadr us-Sudur (1285/1868– April 1907), who was first introduced to the Baha'i Faith in Hamadan in 1898 by one of the Jewish converts, Hakim Musa, who was

---

56 ZH 6:706, 7:130; Ishraq-Khavari, *Hamadan* 100–1.

57 ZH 5:258–9; Ishraq-Khavari, *Hamadan* 48–53. According to the latter source an Azali, Haji Mahdi Naraqi, was also arrested with the Baha'is. Presumably this is the same episode that is described in KD 2:155, although some of the names are different. On Sharif ul-Mulk, see Ishraq-Khavari, *Hamadan* 218. Avarih calls Sharif ul-Mulk a Shaykhi (KD 1:155) while Fadil Mazandarani is reported to have met with him and thought that he was an Azali (Ishraq-Khavari, *Hamadan* 374). See also Hafizi, *Memoir* 1:120.

58 ZH 6:710–11; 'Amid ul-Atibba, 'Tarikh', 21–4.

attending him as a physician, but Sadr us-Sudur did not become a Baha'i until after his move to Tehran (vol. 1:97–8).[59] Sadr us-Sudur's maternal uncle was Mirza Husayn Hamadani (d. 1299/1881),[60] who was also related to Rida Khan Turkaman, one of the Babis killed at Shaykh Tabarsi. He was a skilled calligrapher and secretary and entered the employ of one of the notables of Tehran, accompanying Nasiru'd-Din Shah on his first tour of Europe in 1873. On his return, he spent some time in Istanbul and then was one of the Baha'is imprisoned in Tehran in 1874. On his release, he entered the employ of Manikji Sahib, the Zoroastrian agent in Tehran, who asked him to write a history of the Babi movement. The result was the *Tarikh-i Jadid* (*The New History*), which E. G. Browne translated into English. He had planned to go on to write a history of Baha'u'llah as well but died in Rasht before he could do so.[61]

Mirza Abu'l-Fadl Gulpaygani's visit in 1887–8 was important for Muslim conversions as well as Jewish ones. He had, as was his practice in other places, first come to Hamadan unannounced and taken up residence in one of the religious colleges of the city, hoping to speak with the clerics and students there. He was, however, spotted by Aqa Shalum, a Baha'i who had met him in Tehran and who pressed him to move to his house. This proved too small for the visitors who now flocked to see him and he transferred to the house of Hafiz us-Sihhih. Eventually, however, in order to have better access to Muslims, he moved to the Haji Fadlu'llah Caravanserai, where all could come and meet him. A complaint was made eventually to the governor Sultan Ahmad Mirza (also known as Muchul Mirza) 'Adud ud-Dawlih (d. 1901) who ordered the arrest of Gulpaygani. After a time, the governor ordered Gulpaygani to be expelled from Hamadan.[62] After a few months in Kirmanshah and Kurdistan (see pp. 221, 236), Gulpaygani returned to Hamadan for a few months.

Among those who became Baha'is at this time was Muhammad Mahdi Mirza Mu'ayyid us-Saltanih, who was a son of Tahmasb Mirza (a grandson of Fath-'Ali Shah). He was a Shaykhi and very learned (he had indeed begun studies at a religious college). He remembered having been taken as a child

---

59   Rastigar, *Sadr us-Sudur* 21–8; Ishraq-Khavari, *Hamadan* 97–9; Hafizi, *Memoirs* 1:153–6.
60   Rastigar, *Sadr us-Sudur* 20–1.
61   Gulpaygani, *Rasa'il va Raqa'im* 82–4 (trans. *Letters and Essays* 76–8); Balyuzi, *Browne* 67–9; Hamadani, *Tarikh-i-Jadid* xxxvii–xli.
62   Ishraq-Khavari, *Hamadan* 67–9; Mihrabkhani, *Gulpaygani* 132–44, 153–6; Hafizi, Tarikh Zindigi 55–6 (*Memoirs* 1:156–8).

by his aunt, the above-mentioned Shams-i Jahan Khanum, to visit Tahirih. Mu'ayyid us-Saltanih's son Muhammad Husayn Mirza Mu'ayyid us-Saltanih (1855–1920) was also a Baha'i, who went on to occupy important government positions, including being Superintendent of the telegraph office in Isfahan (1895–97) and in Shiraz (1897–1905) and later governor of 'Arabistan (Khuzistan, 1920).[63] In general, the powerful Qaraguzlu tribe protected the Baha'is to whatever extent they were able, perhaps due to the influence of Hajiyyih Khanum (see p. 179). Then in the late 1890s Ghulam-Rida Khan Ihtisham ud-Dawlih Afkhami (1879–1921), son of Amir Afkham Hisam ul-Mulk (the most influential and wealthiest chief of the Qaraguzlu tribe and governor of Kirmanshah) became a Baha'i. On one occasion in 1909 he ordered armed guards to protect the *hazirat ul-quds* when it was about to be attacked by a mob. He became a son-in-law of Muzaffaru'd-Din Shah (marrying Qamar us-Saltanih, sixth daughter of the shah, in 1895) and governor of Hamadan in the 1920s. Also converted in about 1908 were the two sons of Mulla Yusif, the first Babi of the area (see p. 179), Hashim who took the surname Samadani (d. 1972), and Sha'ban who took the surname A'zami.[64]

Persecutions in Hamadan

The Baha'is and Jews of Hamadan were often caught up in the political manoeuvring for power that went on in the city between the governor and various clerics, each trying to assert his power over the other. Among the religious leaders of Hamadan was Mulla 'Abdu'llah Burujirdi Hamadani, known as Akhund (c. 1823–16 Oct. 1896), a *mujtahid* who was fanatical in his views. An Iranian historian states that he would do anything, including persecute Baha'is, Shaykhis and Jews, if it would result in the elevation of his status and importance in the city.[65] There were a large number of

---

63 ZH 8a:426–7, 215; MH 7:85; Mihrabkhani, *Abu'l-Fadl*, p. 136, 141, 384 (old ed.); Hafizi, Tarikh Zindigi 56–7 (*Memoirs* 1:158–9).

64 Gail, *Summon Up Remembrance* 83. Martha Root's visit to Hamadan was during his governorship and he met her. His father assisted the 12 Baha'is who were arrested in 1880 (Ishraq-Khavari, *Hamadan* 127, 172). Hafizi (*Memoirs* 1:286–90, 324) writes of Ihtisham ud-Dawlih's protection of Baha'is but does not say he was a Baha'i. On Samadani and A'zami, see Ishraq-Khavari, *Hamadan* 370–1.

65 Bamdad, *Tarikh* 6:145–6; see also Ishraq-Khavari, *Hamadan* 266. Hafizi states that Mulla 'Abdu'llah had close dealings with Mirza Hadi Dawlatabadi, the Azali leader, and stayed at his house when he went to Tehran (Tarikh Zindigi, 66, *Memoirs* 63, 68; see also Ishraq-Khavari, *Hamadan* 82n). Indeed, Hafizi confidently states that Mulla 'Abdu'llah was an Azali (*Memoirs* 89). For Mulla

Shaykhis in Hamadan. Mirza Muhammad Baqir Hamadani (Jandaqi, 1239/1823–1319/1901) had been sent by Karim Khan Kirmani to head the Shaykhi community in Hamadan. After the death of Karim Khan in 1871, Hamadani had considered himself to be the most knowledgeable and therefore Karim Khan's rightful successor. He had therefore separated from the Kirman Shaykhi leadership.[66] In 1295/1878 Mulla 'Abdu'llah decided to assert his authority against the Shaykhis of the city. He decreed that the Shaykhis were *najis* (unclean) and thus should not be allowed to drink water from the fountain in the courtyard of the Jami' mosque as this would render it unfit for Muslims. This led to a riot in the city and the governor Haji Abu'l-Qasim Dhu'r-Riyasatayn exiled Mulla 'Abdu'llah to Tehran for two years.[67]

In September 1892, some people complained to Mulla 'Abdu'llah that the Jews were wearing the same clothes as Muslims and riding around on horses such that it was becoming difficult to tell Jews from Muslims. Discerning an opportunity to exert his power in the city, he decreed that all the Jews of the city should wear a patch of red cloth to distinguish them from the Muslims, should not ride horses and obey some 19 other regulations. The governor Sayf ud-Dawlih (see p. 228) opposed him and this led to rioting and commotion in the city. The Jewish Baha'is were also caught up in this, some of them deciding to go along with wearing the patch, while a few asserted that, since they now believed in the Prophet Muhammad, there was nothing to prevent them from taking Muslim names and appearing as Muslims. Thus at this time Hakim Rahim Hafiz us-Sihhih became known as Mirza 'Abdu'r-Rahim and his son Hizqil became Mirza Yahya (he later took the name Yuhanna given him by 'Abdu'l-Baha, see fig. 77).[68]

'Abdu'llah's relationship with the Jews, see Tsadik, *Foreigners* 155–74, Sahim, 'Jews of Iran' 294–302.

66 Bamdad, *Tarikh* 6:209–11; Ishraq-Khavari, *Hamadan* 273.

67 Qaraguzlu, *Hagmatanih ta Hamadan* 422–3 dates this event to 1315/1897–8 but that was a later different riot against the Shaykhis, see p. 202. I have followed the dates given by Hafizi (Tarikh Zindigi 63–6, *Memoirs* 63) who was an eyewitness to this episode.

68 Hamadani, Tarikh Hamadan 21–2; Abizadih, Vaqayi' 170–1; Hafizi, *Memoirs* 1:64; see also Sahim, 'Jews of Iran' 293–302; Levy, *Tarikh* 3:756–8; Tsadik, *Foreigners* 155–74; Ioannesyan, *Development* 32–5. Shahvar et al., *Baha'is of Iran, Transcapsia and the Caucusus* 1:125–7. When this type of ruling was enforced the Jews were usually required to wear a yellow patch (called *'asali*) on their clothes. It is not clear why Mulla 'Abdu'llah decreed a red patch during this episode (see p. 29 n66). Mirza Yuhanna Hafizi, like his father, had Ottoman citizenship.

A group of 30 Jews, including a number of Jewish Baha'is, were trapped by the mob in the telegraph office as they tried to appeal to the central government for help. They were forced to convert to Islam as the only alternative to death. During this episode, a number of the Jewish Baha'is, including Haji Yari and Hakim Iliya (the brother of Hakim Aqa Jan), were also arrested and taken before both Mulla 'Abdu'llah and the governor. They were told to renounce the Baha'i Faith but refused despite being beaten, imprisoned and fined. Haji Yari's son Habibu'llah had burning coals placed on his tongue.[69] As a result of this episode, Mulla 'Abdu'llah was summoned to Tehran, where he was feted by the people and eventually returned in triumph to Hamadan.[70]

Other episodes of persecution by the Muslims of the city include Mulla 'Abdu'llah's imprisonment and fine, in about 1893, of the above-mentioned Haji Yari, who had been trying to convert a Muslim to the Baha'i Faith.[71] In about 1894 Mirza Mahdi Tabib was caught in the power struggle between two of the *mujtahids* of Hamadan. He was one of the Jewish Baha'is who was allowing people to think that he was a Muslim. Unfortunately, his strategy backfired on him in that some Muslims who were his patients insisted on marrying him to a Muslim girl, despite his several attempts to get out of this. After a time, however, he managed to convert his wife to the Baha'i Faith. One day, when he went to the baths, one of the men of Haji Aqa Muhammad, a *mujtahid* of Hamadan, said that he should not go to the baths again because as a Baha'i he rendered the water impure. On another day, the same man attacked him in the market and beat him severely. When Mirza Mahdi went to see the *mujtahid*, the latter refused to see him and sent a message to the governor that he should be punished. The governor fined Mirza Mahdi. Then the neighbours of Mirza Mahdi, indignant at

69 Hafizi, *Memoirs* 1:64–7; Shahvar, 'Oppression of Religious Minority groups' 235–6. Shahvar has published one account that states that this episode began when a group of Jews were caught enjoying themselves and drinking alcohol and were taken before Mulla 'Abdu'llah. Hafizi's account supports this. The Jewish historian Habib Levy (*Tarikh* 3:761; *Jews of Iran* 445) states that four of these forced converts to Islam – Mirza Mahdi Lalihzari, Hakim Tahir, Hakim Rahim and Mulla Ibrahim – then became Baha'is and the first two devoted their lives to spreading the Baha'i Faith; but in fact all four of these were already Baha'is and Hakim Rahim was not among those in the telegraph office.

70 Qaraguzlu, *Hagmatanih ta Hamadan* 422, 431; Tsadik, *Foreigners* 169–74; Hafizi, Tarikh Zindigi 66 (*Memoirs* 68).

71 Hafizi, Tarikh Zindigi 64–5 (*Memoirs* 1:77–8); ZH 6:714; Ishraq-Khavari, *Hamadan* 82 dates this event to 1893.

the treatment that he had received, went to another *mujtahid*, Aqa Sayyid Muhammad, and complained to him. He saw this as an opportunity to exert his power in the city and sent one of his men, first to Haji Aqa Muhammad, saying that if he continued with this enmity towards Mirza Mahdi, he, Aqa Sayyid Muhammad, knew how to deal with him; and second to the governor, demanding that Mirza Mahdi's money be returned to him.[72]

In 1896, in the confusion after the assassination of Nasiru'd-Din Shah, when it was being said that it was the 'Babis' who had done this, Haji Abu Talib Nahavandi, a Baha'i merchant in the Hamadan bazaar was shot but survived. Later in September of the same year, some of the street roughs in the employ of the above Haji Aqa Muhammad Mujtahid demanded protection money from Mirza Ya'qub, eldest son of Hafiz us-Sihhih, and when he refused to pay, the Muslim clerics and Sharif ul-Mulk concocted an accusation that he had had an illicit relationship with a Muslim woman. They took this accusation and the fact that he was a Baha'i to Hasan 'Ali Khan Garrusi who had been sent to Hamadan with troops to quell disturbances. He peremptorily ordered Mirza Yaq'ub's execution and the men he sent to seal and guard Hafiz us-Sihhih's house looted it instead.[73]

In February 1898 there was a further riot in Hamadan against the Shaykhis, this time instigated by two newly-arrived clerics, Sayyid Fadil Dizfuli (d. 1347/1928) and Sayyid Muhammad Burujirdi (known as Sayyid Najafi), who instigated their followers to eject Mirza Muhammad Baqir, the Shaykhi leader, from the Mirza Taqi Mosque, in which he had tried to establish himself. The Shaykhis were then surrounded in the home of Mirza Muhammad Baqir and one of the Muslims was injured by a shot fired by Shaykh Muhammad Baqir's son-in-law. During the riot that followed and in the ensuing weeks of disorder, some of the opponents of the Baha'is took the opportunity to attack them; some of their houses and businesses were looted and destroyed.[74] The governor during this time

---

72   Hamadani, Tarikh Hamadan 28–9.
73   Hafizi, Tarikh Zindigi 64–5 (*Memoirs* 78–82); Ishraq-Khavari, *Hamadan* 85–7; Abizadih, Vaqayi' 57–9. A somewhat different account is given in Thabiti, *Varithan* 97–8 and in ZH 7:102. This episode is also in a report from Dr Holmes to Mr Tyler, dated 25 September 1896 in *Papers relating to the Foreign Relations of the United States* 483.
74   ZH 6:715, 717, 718, 7:109, 8b:886; Hafizi, Tarikh Zindigi 113–22 (*Memoirs* 1:120–7); Ishraq-Khavari, *Hamadan* 88–92. As a result of this episode, Mirza Muhammad Baqir left Hamadan and relocated to Na'in; Bamdad, *Tarikh* 6:209–11.

was Abu'l-Hasan Khan Fakhr ul-Mulk (1862–1926) who was weak and ineffective.

Fakhr ul-Mulk was replaced by Mirza Muhsin Khan Muzaffar ul-Mulk who was deputy governor of Hamadan for the period 1898–1900. Baha'i and Azali accounts state that he was an Azali.[75] He sent spies into the Baha'i meetings and then in 1316/1898, he had twelve Baha'is who were attending the funeral of Ribqa (or Rayqa) Khanum, the wife of Aqa Sulayman Zargar (goldsmith, one of the earliest of the Jewish Baha'i converts), arrested, imprisoned, and in addition Haji Yari and Da'i Rubin were beaten. The homes of Baha'is were attacked and looted and other Baha'is harassed in the streets. The wife of Aqa Yusif Hayyim, who was in labour at the time, died, it is said, of fright. The governor demanded 1,000 *tumans* to set the prisoners free and eventually settled for 400. The above-mentioned Aqa Muhammad 'Ali Bulur-furush was arrested but as he had no money to pay the governor, he was paraded around the streets of the city and then exiled from it, so he migrated to Tehran.[76]

In 1903 there was a great deal of agitation against the Baha'is in the city when news of the anti-Baha'i pogrom in Yazd reached Hamadan in about August. The governor, Nusratu'd-Din Mirza Salar us-Saltanih (b. 1882–1954, a son of Nasiru'd-Din Shah), had made himself unpopular with the city's clerics by slighting and ignoring them. They saw this as a chance of showing the governor that they were a force to be reckoned with. They shut the mosques and put a mob onto the streets harassing the Baha'is.[77] During that summer 'Ali Akbar Khan, a Baha'i dealing in second-hand goods, was, while on a visit to a local shrine, shot by one of his fellow dealers out of jealousy for his commercial success and on the justification of that he was a Baha'i. He survived the shooting for a few hours and ordered his brother not to pursue his killer because Baha'u'llah had written that the true lovers would be in such a state of detachment and

---

75 Bamdad, *Tarikh* 3:212–14; Ishraq-Khavari, *Hamadan* 278. Hafizi (*Memoirs* 1:278-9, 304), Mirza Mahdi Tabib Hamadani (*Tarikh Hamadan* 82), and Nabavi Razavi (*Tarikh Maktum* 204–5), agree that Muzaffar ul-Mulk was an Azali and that he was the father-in-law of Mirza Yahya Dawlatabadi. Haydar 'Ali Usku'i states that later in life in Tabriz he became a Baha'i (Ishraq-Khavari, *Tarikh Hamadan* 128n).

76 Abizadih, Vaqayi' 185; Hafizi, *Memoirs* 1:232–4; Ishraq-Khavari, *Tarikh Hamadan* 92–5; ZH 7:121, 8b:886, 891.

77 Report of Bassan to Alliance Israélite Universelle, dated 23 August 1903; archives of Alliance Israélite Universelle, Paris (I am grateful to Dr Daniel Tsadik for a copy of this document).

love that they would kiss the hand of their would-be murderer.[78]

In 1322/1904 Sayyid Muhsin Mahallati Sadr ul-Ashraf (1288/1871–1962), who was the steward of the governor Nusratu'd-Din Mirza Salar us-Saltanih, arrested four of the prominent Jewish Baha'is and demanded for their release that 1,000 *tumans* be paid to the governor and 200 *tumans* to himself. The Baha'is refused to pay this much and the demand was reduced to 250 *tumans*, which the Baha'is agreed to pay. Then the governor began arresting other Baha'is and Haji Mirza Mahdi Mujtahid (who had instigated the whole episode in league with Sadr ul-Ashraf) demanded 400 *tumans* to intervene on their behalf. Eventually, some of the Baha'is took sanctuary in the telegraph office and began to send telegrams to Muzaffaru'd-Din Shah. Orders came from the shah in favour of the Baha'is, those in prison were released and the money paid out by the Baha'is was returned to them.[79]

In 1908 a travelling Baha'i teacher, Haji Va'iz Qazvini was having so much success in propagating the Baha'i Faith in Hamadan that Shaykh Baqir Bahari (1277/1860–1913), a leading local cleric, arranged for a mob to attack the house where Qazvini was staying, although he had already left by the time of the attack.[80] The servant of Bahari was responsible for beating and thus causing the death of a Baha'i, Karbala'i Muhammad Hadi Dawlatabadi (of Malayir), who was a pea-parcher and a successful propagator of the Baha'i Faith, being responsible for the conversion of the Ahl-i Haqq leader Sayyid 'Azim.[81]

The period from 1907 to 1911 was very disturbed politically. Abu'l-Fath Mirza Salar ud-Dawlih (see fig. 81), a younger brother of Muhammad 'Ali Shah, arose in rebellion against the shah at first, but later, when Muhammad 'Ali Shah had been deposed in 1909, he rose against the Constitutionalist government in support of Muhammad 'Ali Shah in 1910; and when Muhammad 'Ali Shah was defeated in 1911, he continued the rebellion in his own name. Many of the reactionary and conservative Muslim clerics

---

78   Ishraq-Khavari, *Hamadan* 110–11; ZH 7:226; Hafizi, Memoirs 1:187–9. Regarding kissing the hands of their would-be murder, see note by Rafati in Ishraq-Khavari, *Hamadan* 295; cf. Baha'u'llah, *Gems of Divine Mysteries* 28.

79   Hafizi, *Memoirs* 1:246–50; Abizadih, Vaqayi' 181; Ishraq-Khavari, *Hamadan* 112–14; ZH 6:710, 715–16, 7:244, 8:884; Geula, *Iranian* 189–90; on Sadr ul-Ashraf, see Bamdad, *Tarikh* 3:200–3; Hafizi, *Memoirs* 2:301–3.

80   MH 5:133–4; Ishraq-Khavari, *Hamadan* 315; on Bahari, see Bamdad, *Tarikh* 6:55–6. The Jews were also persecuted by Shaykh Baqir in 1908, see *Bulletin d'Alliance Israélite Universelle*, 3rd series, no. 33 (1908) 88–93.

81   Ishraq-Khavari, *Hamadan* 330.

backed Salar ud-Dawlih and this meant that he was inimical to the Baha'is. When his forces were approaching Hamadan in 1911, the enemies of the Baha'is saw this as a chance to attack and burn the Baha'i *hazirat ul-quds*, the Baha'i schools and Baha'i homes in the city. The Baha'is appealed to Ihtisham ud-Dawlih, who had sided with Salar ud-Dawlih. He sent men to protect some of the Baha'i properties while the Baha'is paid for some armed men to protect other properties and the attack did not materialize.[82] Despite this, however, one Baha'i, Aqa Hasan, had his head shaved and was beaten (this compelled him to leave Hamadan and migrate to Tehran), and several other Baha'is were arrested and beaten.[83] Once Salar ud-Dawlih had been driven out of Hamadan in 1911, the deputy governor of Hamadan, Muzaffar ul-Mulk (see p. 203) was antagonistic to the Baha'is and had one active Baha'i, Sayyid Baqir Dallal, beaten.[84] He was, however, subordinate to the governor of Kirmanshah, 'Abdu'l-Husayn Mirza Farmanfarma, who protected the Baha'is as far as he could.[85]

In 1914 a young Baha'i of Hamadan, Mirza Fathu'llah Bulur-furush, son of Haji Shukru'llah, was murdered in the village of Darrih-Murad-Bayk where he had a garden and was teaching the Baha'i Faith.[86] In 1919 a number of Muslims led by a *rawdih-khan* named Sayyid 'Abbas formed a society called the Da'vat-i Islami (Islamic Propaganda). They would gather together the rabble and criminal elements of the city and set them against the Baha'is.[87] In April 1921 a crowd roused by the Da'vat-i Islami society came to the house of Sayyid Hasan Mutavajjih on the pretext of enquiring about the Baha'i Faith and then proceeded to attack him. He was only saved from death by the intervention of the police chief, who was friendly towards the Baha'is, but his pregnant wife, Ma'sumih Khanum, died some 25 days later as a result of the episode.[88]

---

82   ZH 7:287–8; Hafizi, *Memoirs* 1:324.
83   ZH 7:301.
84   ZH 7:288.
85   Ishraq-Khavari, *Hamadan* 135.
86   Ishraq-Khavari, *Tarikh Hamadan* 147; ZH 7:307. Abizadih (Vaqayi' 55–6) states this episode occurred in 1273 AHS/1894.
87   MH 9:109–10; Ishraq-Khavari, *Hamadan* 155, 352–3.
88   Vahid-Tehrani, Memorandum on Sayyid Hasan Mutavajjih, pp. 33–7; unpublished memorandum by 'Ali Firuz and Shakiri, cited in Abizadih, Vaqayi' 66; both cited in Momen, *Ayman/Iman Family* 50; MH 6:65–79; Ishraq-Khavari, *Tarikh Hamadan* 155. Abizadih states that the death of Ma'sumih Khanum was caused by bleeding in pregnancy set off by the attack, while Ishraq-Khavari states the cause of death was severe headaches caused by the attack.

Baha'i institutional developments in Hamadan

In 1898, while Haji Amin was visiting Hamadan, a consultative assembly was formed which later became the local spiritual assembly. This assembly took over the administration of the affairs of the Baha'i Faith in the city and in due course appointed a number of committees, including ones for children's classes, the advancement of women, propagation of the Baha'i Faith, and general services. The Baha'i community of Hamadan also established a Baha'i fund which was at first called the *shirkat-i khayriyyih* and later the *ṣandūq-i khayriyyih*.[89]

Initially, it was very difficult for the Jewish Baha'is (known as the Kalimi Baha'is) and Muslim Baha'is (known as the Furqani Baha'is)[90] to be seen to be entering each others' houses. The Jewish Baha'is therefore held their meetings at the house of Da'i Rubin and the houses of other Jewish Baha'is while the Muslim Baha'is held theirs in a Baha'i centre in the Tut-Qumi-ha quarter in the north of the city. When Da'i Rubin's finances went into decline, he was forced to rent out his home. Thus in about 1902 the Local Spiritual Assembly of Hamadan began to plan a *mashriq ul-adhkar* (house of worship) in a location where all could gather. Land was purchased in the Mukhtaran quarter near the Qashuq-tarashan mosque. Work on the building was begun in 1320/1902 but the Jews complained to the governor, which delayed the work such that it took two years to complete. At one stage in 1903, when there was a general anti-Baha'i movement throughout Iran, it seemed as though the building might be attacked but the governor prevented this. Later this building was called the *hazirat ul-quds*.[91] The Local Spiritual Assembly of Hamadan also rented two houses specifically for the propagation of the Baha'i Faith where meetings and classes could be held.[92] Later, in 1906, 'Abdu'l-Baha wrote to the Baha'is of Hamadan stating that they were to cease making any distinction between

---

89 Ishraq-Khavari, *Hamadan* 95, 106, 354; Abizadih, Vaqayi' 87–95, 135, 148–9; Hafizi, *Memoirs* 1:165.

90 Kalimi relates to Kalim (interlocutor) and refers to Moses speaking with God; Furqani relates to the Furqan, a name for the Qur'an found in the Qur'an itself.

91 Hafizi, Tarikh Zindigi 153–4 (*Memoirs* 1:245–6); Abizadih, Vaqayi' 115–17; Ishraq-Khavari, *Hamadan* 105–6; account of the schools by Habibu'llah Thabiti, enclosed in Abizadih, 'Nigahi bi Vaqayi'' between pp. 114 and 115; tablet of 'Abdu'l-Baha cited in Abizadih and also given in full in *Makatib* 4:127–8. KD 2:157.

92 Abizadih, Vaqayi' 129–31.

Furqani and Kalimi, and to regard themselves simply as Baha'is.[93]

The Alliance Israélite Universelle, a Jewish organization in Paris established to assist and protect Jews around the world, set up a school for boys and girls in Hamadan in 1900. The Jewish Baha'is contributed 600 *tumans* to the building of the school and many of the children of the Jewish Baha'is enrolled, since the American missionaries running another school had become very hostile to the Baha'is and were pressurizing them to convert. After a time, however, problems arose at the Alliance school. In 1902 some of the Baha'i children were denied access to it as a way of countering criticism of the school among the Muslim population. The headmaster, Yizthak Bassan (b. 1873), a Bulgarian Jew, insisted that the Baha'i children at the school attend synagogue and follow Jewish customs. The Baha'is withdrew their children in protest and matters improved temporarily.[94] When in 1908 Ya'qub Muttahidih, a Baha'i child, was punished for being absent on Ridvan, a Baha'i holy day, the Baha'is of Hamadan decided to

78. Monsieur André Sulayman

establish their own school. The Ta'id School for boys was inaugurated in October 1908, first in the homes of some of the Baha'is and later in new, purpose-built classrooms on the site of the *hazirat ul-quds*. The Mawhibat School for girls was opened in 1327/1909. The schools were officially recognized by the government in 1331/1913. Mirza 'Abdu'llah (the son of Aqa Sulayman Zargar), a Baha'i, had been educated at the Alliance school, completed his education in France and adopted the name Monsieur André Sulayman (1889–1926, see fig. 78). He ran the Baha'i schools from 1913, introducing modern western educational methods. He dressed and groomed himself in an elegant and fashionable European style. During his tenure enrolments at the schools increased from 150 to 300. In 1919

---

93 'Abdu'l-Baha, *Makatib* 3:510–11; Thabiti, *Varithan* 57–8.
94 Hafizi, Tarikh Zindigi 164 (*Memoirs* 1:250–1); *Bulletin d'Alliance Israélite Universelle*, 3rd series, no. 27 (1902) 65; Ishraq-Khavari, *Hamadan* 105.

he returned to Paris, where he died. Fadil Shirazi (see p. 341) came from Tehran to run the boys' school while his wife ran the girls' school.[95] The schools attracted some opposition, especially from the Alliance school, where the attendance had dropped by about 100 boys and 100 girls. Two female teachers from the Alliance school made an unsuccessful attempt to close down the Baha'i schools by appealing to the governor.[96]

The schools, as elsewhere in Iran, became an important symbol for the Baha'is of the city, being their only public institution. It was a source of pride for the community that many of the dignitaries of the city attended the school end-of-year festivals. The adjacent Baha'i centre (*hazirat ul-quds*) was a focus of the Baha'i activities in the city and a reading-room with a library was established in 1908.[97] It became a favourite place to gather for the many young people, both Muslims and Jews, who were being attracted to the Baha'i Faith at this time. The Baha'i youth also put on plays and had a cycling club.[98] Indeed, some of the most active propagation of the Baha'i Faith was carried out among the Jewish youth of the city in the 1910s and 1920s. Later, in 1939, a youth committee was established.[99] Baha'i moral education and religious training classes were started in 1912.[100] A large number of committees ran these various activities, including a schools' committee, a library committee, a committee for teaching the Baha'i Faith and a committee for deepening knowledge of the Baha'i Faith.

M. Bassan, the headmaster of the Alliance Israélite Universelle school, joined the rabbis in leading the opposition to the Jewish Baha'is. In 1901, for example, he wrote in a report that the best way of halting the conversions to the Baha'i Faith was to prevent what he called 'mixed marriages' (*les marriage mixtes*) between Jews and Jewish Baha'is. He stated that he had succeeded in obtaining a promise from the rabbis of the city not to issue a *ketubah* (marriage contract) or to bless such marriages (although later in the report he stated that while he was away, the rabbis failed to carry out their promise). He also tried to prevent Jews from attending the

95 Abizadih, Vaqayi' 102–14; Hafizi, *Memoirs* 1:250–1, 350–2; Ishraq-Khavari, *Hamadan* 116–25, 128–33, 304–5, 343; ZH 7:262.
96 MH 4:459, Abizadih, Vaqayi' 105. Figures for the Alliance school are given in *Bulletin d'Alliance Israélite Universelle* (see 3rd series, no. 28 (1903) 202; no. 33 (1908) 162; no. 35 (1910) 233).
97 Abizadih, Vaqayi' 141–2; Ishraq-Khavari, *Tarikh Hamadan* 126, 310–11.
98 Momen, *Ayman/Iman Family* 89–91, 165.
99 Abizadih, Vaqayi'.
100 Ishraq-Khavari, *Hamadan* 146; Abizadih, Vaqayi' 143–7.

Saturday meetings held by the Jewish Baha'is at which they attempted to convert Jews. Bassan wrote to the president of the Alliance to instruct its Tehran representative, Mr Levy, to ask the Iranian government to expel the most active Baha'is, Da'i Rubin and Haj Mahdi Arjumand, stop the Saturday meetings and prevent mixed marriages (a request that Levy had already declined and which it appears the Alliance president also declined).[101]

Also in 1329/1911 the Jews of Hamadan decided to build a second public baths for themselves. Because the wealth of the Jewish Baha'is of the city was greater than that of the Jews themselves, they called on the Jewish Baha'is for financial assistance. The income from the first baths went, after the payment of a government tax, to help the Alliance school so the Baha'is agreed to help, provided part of the income also went to the Baha'i schools. The Jews would not agree to this and a contentious meeting ended in disarray. The Jews then forbade the Baha'is to use their baths. But even before this in 1909, the Baha'is had already begun the process of buying land for baths to be built according to the specifications of the Kitab-i Aqdas. However, the Jews, fearing losses to their own bath-houses, managed to get the construction of this bath-house halted. Then they blocked the attempt by the Baha'is to purchase a disused Muslim bath-house for a number of years.[102]

From the above it can been seen that the Baha'is of Hamadan had over the years incurred the enmity of the Christian Protestants, the Jewish religious leaders and the Muslim clerics. These would appeal to outside authorities against the Baha'is. One day in 1911, some of the children from the Jewish Alliance school came to the Ta'id school and were mocking and disparaging the children there who were practising for the Naw-Ruz (New Year) celebrations. The custodian of the school chased them away and blows were exchanged. As a consequence of the ill-feeling that had arisen, the Jews telegraphed the French Embassy in Tehran asking it to take action against the Baha'i schools. The French Embassy intervened with the Ministry of Education. At this time in 1911 the minister of education was 'Ali-Quli Khan Sardar As'ad Bakhtiyari (d. 1918), who had met 'Abdu'l-Baha in Paris a short time before. He protected the Baha'is from this attack. A little

---

101 Report of Bassan to Alliance Israélite Universelle, dated 5 December 1901; archives of Alliance Israélite Universelle, Paris (I am grateful to Dr Daniel Tsadik for a copy of this document).

102 Hafizi, Tarikh Zindigi 201 (*Memoirs* 301–4, 316–19); Abizadih, Vaqayi' 182–3; Ishraq-Khavari, *Hamadan* 134–5; see also ZH 7:288, which relates this to the anti-Baha'i sentiment roused by Salar ud-Dawlih's rebellion. See also Shahvar, *Forgotten Schools* 104–5, 168–70.

later at the Naw-Ruz celebrations, 'Abdu'l-Husayn Mirza Farmanfarma, who
was governor of Kirmanshah and had jurisdiction over Hamadan as well,
watched a display of the various schools in Hamadan. He praised the display
of the Baha'i Ta'id School compared to that of the others.[103]

Another attempt to disrupt the functioning of the Baha'i schools
occurred in about 1913, when the local government education officer
insisted on the school employing Haji Aqa Sunquri to monitor the teaching of religion in the school. He proved to be so disruptive, openly abusing
the Baha'i Faith and inciting the Muslim pupils in the school to do the
same, that he was dismissed by the headmaster M. André at the request
of the school committee.[104] When the forces of Germany and its allies triumphed in the early years of World War I, many of the Jews and Muslim
in Hamadan, who knew of Baha'u'llah's prophecy in the Kitab-i Aqdas of
defeat for Germany, mocked the Baha'is and alluded to dire consequences
when these forces triumphed in Iran as well. Complaints about the Baha'i
schools were made to the heads of the Ottoman, Russian and British
troops that successively occupied the city during World War I but none of
these was successful, and indeed both the Ottoman commander 'Ali Ihsan
Big and the Russian commander General Baratof visited the Baha'i school
and expressed approval of it.[105]

When Aqa Ishaq died in 1915 (see p. 193), the Jewish rabbis refused
to allow his burial in the Jewish cemetery. This forced the Baha'is to think
of obtaining a cemetery of their own and some land was purchased for a
Baha'i cemetery.[106] Then in 1916 Jews and Muslims combined to attack
the cortege and try to prevent the burial of the Jewish Baha'i physician
Mirza Aqa Jan Iravani in the newly-acquired Baha'i cemetery, protesting
that burial in a coffin was against the laws of both Judaism and Islam.[107]

A Mahfil-i Tahdhib (Assembly for Edification) functioned from 1918

---

103 Hafizi, *Memoirs* 1:302–8; Abizadih, Vaqayi' 105–6; Ishraq-Khavari, *Hamadan*
     135. Sardar As'ad was in Europe for one year from June 1911 for eye treatments;
     Bakhtiyari, *Khatirat* 5.
104 Hafizi, *Memoirs* 1:376–7; ZH 7:302–3; Ishraq-Khavari, *Hamadan* 162–3.
105 Hafizi, *Memoirs* 1:377–9, 389–90.
106 Amanat, 'Kayfiyat-i Iqbal - 3', no. 216, pp. 31–2; Ishraq-Khavari, *Hamadan*
     148; Abizadih, Vaqayi' 65, 182; ZH 7:310. There had been an earlier episode
     when a Baha'i had died in 1911 and burial had been refused. At that time Hafiz
     us-Sihhih had purchased some land outside city for a cemetery but problems had
     arisen with this and other land was purchased (Hafizi, *Memoirs* 1:92–4; Ishraq-
     Khavari, *Hamadan* 137–9).
107 Ishraq-Khavari, *Hamadan* 347–8.

to 1923 to serve the Baha'i community, distribute Baha'i literature and send out teachers of the Baha'i Faith. For this purpose, it collected funds from many Baha'i communities such as Kirman, Sultanabad, Kirmanshah and Baghdad and from individual Baha'is and Baha'i-owned companies. It financed some 15 Baha'i travelling teachers.[108]

In 1922, at the time when several major Shi'i clerics were passing through Hamadan in exile from Iraq, the most senior of them, Ayatu'llah Sayyid Abu'l-Hasan Isfahani (1284/1867–1946) asked the authorities to close the Ta'id School. The authorities deflected this by appointing a number of non-Baha'i teachers to the school. One of those appointed wreaked havoc in the school and had to be dismissed.[109] In 1934, as part of the general government move against the Baha'i schools, these two schools were closed.

Many prominent Baha'i teachers visited Hamadan including Mirza Yusif Vujdani, who was in the service of the governor 'Adud ud-Dawlih around 1891–2 and came again in 1315/1897;[110] Mirza Mahmud Zarqani in 1897;[111] Ishraq-Khavari, who visited twice in about 1918;[112] Mutlaq, who spent some months in Hamadan about 1919 and visited again in 1931 on his return from Haifa;[113] and Martha Root and Keith Ransom-Kehler, two prominent American Baha'i women who, after their deaths, were named Hands of the Cause by Shoghi Effendi. Large meetings were held for them in Hamadan, the first in January 1930 and the second in the summer of 1932.[114]

Such was the expansion of the Baha'i community in Hamadan that the city went from having one of the lowest numbers of Baha'is in proportion to its population in 1877 to having one of the largest for an Iranian city by 1907. Although all such figures are guesses based on poor data, an estimate for the number of Baha'is in Hamadan in 1907 would be 5,000 and this would be about ten per cent of the population of the city. Fadil Mazandarani estimated the number of Baha'is in the city in 1921 to be 6,000.[115]

---

108 Ishraq-Khavari, *Hamadan* 157–8; ZH 7:320.
109 Ishraq-Khavari, *Hamadan* 161–2.
110 MH 2:57–60, 101.
111 MH 8a:564.
112 MH 4:355–70.
113 MH 4:127, 206.
114 Ishraq Khavari, *Rahiq-i Makhtum* 2:287–8, quoting *Akhbar Amri* of Day 1308 Sh. MH 6:263–4; Ishraq-Khavari, *Hamadan* 171.
115 *Star of the West*, 12/4 (17 May 1921) 75.

Villages around Hamadan

Baha'i activities in the other towns and villages of this area were often the result of the conversion of people from that place in either Hamadan or Kirmanshah and their subsequent efforts to spread the religion among their family and friends in their home town or village. The Baha'i Faith also spread from one village to the next.

In the years from about 1881 onwards, the Baha'i Faith was spread into the villages to the north of Hamadan. Probably the first village in which it spread was Buyukabad (50 km northeast of Hamadan; pop. 1,500 in 1914) before 1881 but we do not appear to have the details of how this occurred. A letter from 'Abdu'l-Baha addressed to some 16 heads of families in the village would indicate that there were at least 60 Baha'is in the village. The foremost Baha'i of Buyukabad was Mahmud Bayk Buyukabadi. He was then responsible for much of the early spread to other villages, assisted by such travelling Baha'i teachers as Haji Mirza Haydar 'Ali Isfahani, Ibn Asdaq and Muhammad Khan Baluch. Buyukabadi began to visit Husaynabad (50 km northeast of Hamadan; pop. 842 in 1950) in about 1881 and Karbala'i Javad became the first Baha'i there. Soon there was an active Baha'i community led by Mulla Taqi.[116] Na'ib Hadi Khan Husaynabadi from this village, who had become a Baha'i in 1881, then began to spread the Baha'i Faith to other nearby villages in 1303/1885. Among these was the village of Mirza Kandi where Karam Big became a Baha'i in 1886. The head of the village sent Karam Big and some of the other Baha'is to Mulla Mahdi of Chupuqlu, the leading religious authority in the area (Chupuqlu is a village 18 km west of Husaynabad and 45 km north of Hamadan; pop. 205 in 1951). He interrogated Karam Khan and wrote a certificate of the soundness of Karam Big's Islam. Since Karam Big observed that Mulla Mahdi was a just and open-minded person, he talked to him about the new religion and gave him Baha'u'llah's Kitab-i Iqan which resulted in the conversion of Mulla Mahdi. When this became known, the people of the area stopped using his services and he fell on hard times, being forced even to sell his furniture in 1898. The owner of Chupuqlu gave Mulla Mahdi an ultimatum to declare himself a Muslim or leave the village. Consequently Mulla Mahdi left for Hamadan, where he became a teacher and prospered.[117]

Ibn Asdaq, accompanied by Mirza Mahdi Tabib Hamadani, visited

---

116 MH 2:66–7; ZH 6:720; Ishraq-Khavari, *Hamadan* 54–5n.
117 ZH 5:358; Ishraq-Khavari, *Hamadan* 65.

Amzajird, a Turkish-speaking village (15 km north of Hamadan; pop. 435 in 1950) that was half Ahl-i Haqq ('Aliyu'llahis, or as they prefer to call themselves Yarsan) and half Twelver Shi'i, and debated with a *mujtahid* there in about 1881.[118] Then Davud-Quli Beg, one of the leaders of the Nasiriyan division of the Ahl-i Haqq of the area, and Mirza Gul-Muhammad became Baha'is in 1882 through the teaching of Mahmud Bayk Buyukabadi.[119] Subsequently, Muhammad Hasan Sultan was converted while guarding Mirza Abu'l-Fadl Gulpaygani in prison in Hamadan in 1887.[120] As a result, many others of that religious community also became Baha'is including 'Abbas Big Mushtaq, one of the notables of the village. Three Baha'i Sufi dervishes, Haji Mu'nis, Haji Yuqadih Hamadani and Haji Musadih Isfahani (see fig. 84) also taught the Baha'i Faith in the village until expelled by Amir Tuman, the owner of the village.[121] The Baha'is were at first much opposed in the village and entry to the public baths was denied them. Gradually, however, they became established and eventually built a Baha'i centre (*hazirat ul-quds*) in 1900 (before the Baha'is of Hamadan had one) and a public bath with showers. In 1930, when Martha Root visited Hamadan, the Baha'i *kadkhuda* (headman) of this village wanted to invite her to the village, but Mirza Haydar 'Ali Usku'i, who was visiting, pointed out that their Baha'i centre was too small and too old to be suitable to receive such a guest. So, with the help of Usku'i, they built a new Baha'i centre.[122] Although they remained a minority in the village, the Baha'is became confident enough to be quite open about their religious adherence.

Karbala'i 'Ali Akbar (d. 1917), who became a Baha'i in 1888, was the first and most active of the converts in the village of Lalihjin (18 km north of Hamadan; pop. 5,410 in 1951) and gradually a Baha'i group built up.[123] In 1921 there was an outburst of persecution in this village instigated by two clerics. A number of the Baha'is were beaten and the wife of one of the Baha'is, who was not herself a Baha'i, was forced to divorce her husband and marry a Muslim.[124]

The Baha'i Faith had been brought to the village of Bahar (20 km

---

118 Hamadani, Tarikh Hamadan 7–9.
119 ZH 5:346; MH 2:67; Ishraq-Khavari, *Hamadan* 60–1.
120 MH 2:67; Mihrabkhani, *Gulpaygani* 140; Ishraq-Khavari, *Hamadan* 69 and n.; Thabiti, *Varithan Kalim* 55; Hafizi, *Memoirs* 1:157–8.
121 ZH 6:555–6.
122 MH 5:208–9; Abizadih, Vaqayi' 226–8; Ishraq-Khavari, *Hamadan* 60–3.
123 ZH 5:373; Abizadih, Vaqayi' 242–3; Ishraq-Khavari, *Hamadan* 72–4.
124 Ishraq-Khavari, *Hamadan* 159–60; ZH 7:324.

northeast of Hamadan; pop. 1,500 in 1914 and 9,615 in 1956) by Aqa
Muhammad Shir-'Ali Zanjani (d. 1325/1907), who had fled Zanjan after
the Babi upheaval of 1850–1 and settled in Bahar. In about 1889 he introduced one of the notables of the village, Shaykh Ahmad Khan (d. late 1930),
to the Baha'i Faith and the latter was converted by Haji Mahdi Arjumand
in Hamadan. After this there were many other conversions, mainly through
Shaykh Ahmad Khan.[125] In about 1894 the owner of the village, Husayn-
Quli Khan Diya' ul-Mulk, obtained a *fatwa* from Mulla 'Abdu'llah Burujirdi
and arrested several Baha'is. After mulcting them of their money, he released
them, but the populace had been aroused and also attacked them.[126] Two
of the clerics of Bahar feigned an interest in the Baha'i Faith and obtained a
copy of the Kitab-i Iqan from Shaykh Ahmad Khan. They took this to Mulla
'Abdu'llah along with false accusations against the Baha'is of the village. Mulla
'Abdu'llah asked the owner of the village, Diya' ul-Mulk, to expel the Baha'is.
This created an uproar in the village and a few of the Baha'is were arrested
but released after paying fines.[127] A *hazirat ul-quds* and traveller's hostel was
built in 1910 and a local assembly established in 1917. In 1917 there was
a further attack on the Baha'is of the village and money was extorted from
some of them but this attack was quelled by Diya' ul-Mulk.[128]

In Dinarabad, a Turkish-speaking village (pop. 560 in 1950) not far
from Amzajird, Mirza 'Abdu'l-Husayn Khan and his son Shir-'Ali became
Babis after hearing about the martyrdom of the Bab from some of the
Hamadani soldiers who were involved in that. They were prominent
landowners and also from the Ahl-i Haqq religious community. Mirza
'Abdu'l-Husayn Khan had then become a follower of Timur (see p. 234).
After becoming a Baha'i, Mirza 'Abdu'l-Husayn Khan was imprisoned for
a time. He then left everything he owned to his son and set off on wandering in dervish attire teaching the Baha'i Faith in towns and villages.[129]

Rida-Quli Khan was from a notable Ahl-i Haqq family which owned
the village of Khanbaghi in the district of Mihraban (60 km northwest of

---

125 ZH 5:395–6, 6:720; MH 2:66–7; Abizadih, Vaqayi' 239–41; Ishraq-Khavari,
     Hamadan 75–6.
126 ZH 7:46.
127 Ishraq-Khavari, *Hamadan* 107–8. In this source, this episode is stated to have
     occurred in 1902, but Mulla 'Abdu'llah was dead by that time. So either it
     occurred at an earlier date, probably between 1894 and 1896, or it was not Mulla
     'Abdu'llah that was involved.
128 Ishraq-Khavari, *Hamadan* 135, 152–3; ZH 7:315.
129 ZH 8b:882–3; Abizadih, Vaqayi' 175; Ishraq-Khavari, *Hamadan* 55n.

Hamadan; pop. 680 in 1951). He became a Baha'i on a trip to Hamadan in 1316/1898 after an encounter with Mirza Yusif Siraj ul-Hukama (son of Mirza Nasru'llah Tabib and a son-in-law of Hafiz us-Sihhih), who took him to meet Hafiz us-Sihhih and Mirza Mahdi Arjumand. Rida-Quli Khan then returned to his village with Mirza Yusif on the pretext that the latter would attend Rida-Quli Khan's father as a physician. The two then taught the Baha'i Faith to Rida-Quli Khan's two brothers, Najaf-Quli Khan and Haydar-Quli Khan, and eventually to about 20 people in the Mihraban area, including some notables such as Haji Nasru'llah Khan, Mulla Sadiq and Aqa Sayyid Mahdi Qavam ush-Shari'ah. When his father died, Rida-Quli Khan inherited his title of Sultan as he was chief of the Tupkhanih (artillery) of Diya' ul-Mulk. When his artillery unit accompanied the forces of Diya' ul-Mulk to Khuzistan, he also converted a number of the people in that force including Mirza Mahdi Khan Sar-rishtih-dar. The clerics declared him a heretic and that his life and property were forfeit. He was murdered shortly after this in 1321/1903 in Hamadan just as he was preparing to depart with his soldiers for Tehran: it was said he was going to be sent to Yazd to quell the anti-Baha'i pogrom there.[130]

Mirza 'Ali Muhammad Khan Sar-rishtih-dar (vol. 1:78) is reported to have visited Hamadan in about 1908 and to have then gone to one of the villages in the area and talked to an Ahl-i Haqq religious leader, 'Ali Ashraf Khan. As a result the latter acknowledged that the Baha'i Faith fulfilled the prophecies of several Ahl-i Haqq leaders of the past including Qushchi-Ughli. His brother and several others also became Baha'is. Unfortunately the name of the village is not given.[131]

---

130 Hafizi, Tarikh Zindigi 110–11 (Memoirs 1:162–5); Raf'at, 'Rida-Quli Khan'; Ishraq-Khavari, Hamadan 95–7, 109–10; ZH 7:226. KD 2:157–8 and Faizi, 'Abdul-Baha 157–8 state that Rida-Quli Khan became a Baha'i in Tehran through Haji Mirza 'Abdu'llah Sahih-furush who was also of the Ahl-i Haqq. 'Abdu'l-Baha named him Sarvar-i Shuhada (leader of the martyrs).
131 MH 3:502–3; Dehqan, 'Notes' possibly refers to this episode.

14

KIRMANSHAH AND KURDISTAN

These two provinces lie in the Zagros mountains on the west border of Iran. There is more rainfall here than in much of the rest of Iran and cereals are grown in the valleys between the mountain ranges that run northwest to southeast. Kurds are the majority of the population in both the provinces of Kirmanshah and Kurdistan. In Kurdistan, they are mainly Sunnis, but as one proceeds south towards Kirmanshah, there is an increasing number of Ahl-i Haqq ('Aliyu'llahis), a Shi'i sect that is regarded by orthodox Shi'is as extremist and heretical; they prefer to call themselves Yarsan.

Kirmanshah

Although the town of Kirmanshah existed in Sasanian times, it may well have been at some distance from the present town. There is little mention of the town until about the 18th century when it became an important border town. It grew to major importance in the early 19th century when Fath-'Ali Shah's eldest son, Muhammad 'Ali Mirza, was governor there. The Shaykhi leader Shaykh Ahmad al-Ahsa'i resided there and Muhammad 'Ali Mirza gave him ownership of some villages in the area. After the death of Muhammad 'Ali Mirza in December 1820, however, the town declined for some 50 years. It increased in prosperity towards the end of the 19th century. In the period from 1911 to 1918 the town suffered greatly through constantly changing hands, firstly, as a result of the rebellion of Salar ud-Dawlih (see p. 204) and then in World War I as Ottoman, Russian and British forces fought over it. It was estimated to have a population of 30,000 in 1868, 40,000 in 1905, 60,000 in 1914 and 125,439 in 1956.[1] The number of Jews in the town is given as 250 in 1868 and 1884, 750 in the *Gazetteer of Persia* (1914), but 1,400 in the *Bulletin* published by the Alliance Israélite Universelle in 1904.[2] The nobility of the town consisted mainly of Qajar princes, descended from Muhammad 'Ali Mirza, and the leaders of the powerful Qaraguzlu tribe. The majority of the population were Kurds, who were mostly of the Ahl-i Haqq religious community, although many had been pressured into becoming orthodox Twelver Shi'is. Most of the merchants in the town worked as commission agents for merchants in Hamadan or Baghdad, but there were also merchants from Kashan, Isfahan and Yazd settled in the town carrying out trade with their home towns. Much of the wealth of the town came from the estimated 100,000 pilgrims that passed through annually on their way to the shrine cities of Iraq (in addition to the 7,000 corpses on their way for burial at Karbala).[3] Crops in the vicinity included rice, grain and cotton.

There appear to be no Baha'i histories of Kirmanshah. The memoirs of Habib Mu'ayyad contain a little information but, for the most part, the following account has had to be compiled from more general secondary sources.

Baha'u'llah spent one month in Kirmanshah in 1851 and a few days again on his way to Baghdad in 1853; Mirza Ahmad Katib (Mulla 'Abdu'l-Karim Qazvini, the Bab's secretary) and Nabil Zarandi spent several months in Kirmanshah in 1267/1851; and Mirza Muhammad 'Ali Tabib Zanjani spent periods of time in the town from about 1850 until at least the early 1860s. A certain merchant, Ghulam-Husayn Shushtari, was resident in Kirmanshah during both of Baha'u'llah's sojourns in the

---

1   For 1868, Thomson cited in Issawi, *Economic History of Iran* 28. A Russian source, Sobotinskii (cited in Issawi, *Economic History of Iran* 34), gives 50,000 for 1913.

2   Thomson cited in Issawi, *Economic History of Iran* 32; Levy citing Neumark, *Tarikh Yahud* 3:662; *Gazetteer of Persia* 2: 371; *Bulletin d'Alliance Israélite Universelle* no. 29 (1904) 109 (the same figures are given in the *Bulletins* for 1909 and 1913).

3   *Gazetteer of Persia* 2:370–1.

80. Mirza 'Abdu'llah Ghawgha

81. Salar ud-Dawlih (Abu'l-Fath Mirza)

82. Habib Mu'ayyad

town and 'Abdu'llah Kafsh-furush Qazvini during Baha'u'llah's second visit. There is reference to the arrest and sending to Tehran of a certain Mulla 'Ali Asghar Babi during the governorship of Imam-Quli Mirza 'Imad ud-Dawlih, a son of Muhammad 'Ali Mirza (governor 1268/1851–1292/1875).[4] Among the claimants to authority in the Babi community after the Bab was Mirza 'Abdu'llah Ghawgha (see fig. 80), who lived in Kirmanshah until his death in 1289/1872.[5] Despite these initial activities, there were few conversions and the small group in Kirmanshah consisted mainly of individuals from other parts of Iran, most of whom had fled there to escape persecution.[6]

Owing to the presence in Kirmanshah for periods of time of such persons as Sayyid Muhammad Isfahani and Mulla Ja'far Naraqi during the 1850s and 1860s, many of the Babis in Kirmanshah became followers of Mirza Yahya Azal. One of the most prominent members of the community here was Shaykh Muhammad Mudarris, who had first become a Babi after hearing Tahirih speak as she passed through Kirmanshah. He had studied in Iraq and was sent back to Iran in about 1869 when Mulla Ja'far Naraqi was also expelled from Kazimayn. Shaykh Muhammad Mudarris remained in Kirmanshah as a prominent religious scholar, teaching in Madrasih 'Imad ud-Dawlih in the town. When the split between Baha'u'llah and Azal became an issue locally, each side claimed him as their own. Eventually he was asked to make his opinion clear and he sided with Baha'u'llah. His son Shaykh 'Ali was also a Baha'i.[7]

In about 1864 Haji Mirza Haydar 'Ali Isfahani spent a short time in the town teaching the Baha'i Faith.[8] A number of Baha'is from other parts of Iran also settled in Kirmanshah such as Aqa Muhammad Sarraf Isfahani (d. 1305/1887), whose home became the focus of Baha'i activity, Aqa Qasim Bulur-furush Qazvini and Aqa Muhammad Isma'il Tajir Isfahani.[9] In a letter dated dated April 1882, Baha'u'llah expresses a desire that one

---

4   Sipihr, *Nasikh at-Tavarikh* 1:1179; Sultani, *Tarikh* 3:340.
5   Bamdad, *Tarikh* 6:148. Imam-Quli Mirza 'Imad ud-Dawlih, governor of Kirmanshah, was a follower of Ghawgha (see talk of 'Abdu'l-Baha in *Khitabat* 2:77), as was Darvish Sidq 'Ali (vol. 1:485–6) in 1858 (ZH 4:193n).
6   ZH 3:405.
7   ZH 6:695; Mazandarani, *Asrar* 5:25–6; however, Baha'u'llah may be referring to this individual in a letter written in about 1886, stating that Shaykh Muhammad had turned away from the Baha'i Faith and had fallen out with his son over this, ILMA 27:494–5.
8   Isfahani, *Bihjat* 37–9; MH 1:17.
9   ZH 6:693.

of the Baha'is should teach among the tribal peoples in the Kirmanshah area.[10]

In early 1881 the Jewish Baha'i physician Hafiz us-Sihhih of Hamadan visited Kirmanshah and converted his relative Hakim Yari (d. 1883 or 1884). Eventually some 80 of the Jews of the town converted. If Neumark's estimate of 250 Jews in Kirmanshah in 1883 is correct, this would constitute the conversion of more than 30 per cent of the Jews of the town.[11]

One of these Jewish Baha'is, Haji Khudabakhsh (1853–1941), a merchant, moved for a time to Sahnih to escape persecution. His eldest son, Murad, was killed there (see p. 233), and Haji Khudabakhsh returned to Kirmanshah. Many of the Baha'is travelling to and from 'Akka and Haifa would stay in his homes in Kirmanshah and in Sahnih. In about 1911, when Abu'l-Fath Mirza Salar ud-Dawlih (1882–1954, see fig. 81) seized the town in an attempt to restore his brother Muhammad 'Ali Shah to the throne, he unleashed a wave of persecution against the Baha'is. Khudabakhsh was seized and beaten severely such that he sustained permanent injuries to his tongue.[12] Another of his sons was Dr Habib Mu'ayyad (1888–1971, see fig. 82), who graduated from the Syrian Protestant College (American University) in Beirut in medicine (1907–11), spent three years in Haifa and Abu Sinan (1911–14) and was a leading Baha'i of Kirmanshah before moving to Tehran, where he was for many years on the National Spiritual Assembly of Iran. He wrote a memoir of the years he spent in Beirut and Haifa (*Khatirat-i Habib*).[13]

The spread of the Baha'i Faith in Kirmanshah was, however, hampered by three factors: the opposition of an active group of Azalis who had taken it upon themselves to counter everything the Baha'is did (including trying to turn away new converts); the opposition of Shaykh Shihabu'd-Din, a powerful Ahl-i Haqq leader in the town; and the enmity of a number

---

10 Rafati, *Payk* 96.

11 Hafizi, Tarikh Zindigi 36 (*Memoirs* 36); Ishraq-Khavari, *Hamadan* 69. According to ZH 6:695, Haji Yari was visiting Hamadan from Kirmanshah when he was introduced to the Baha'i Faith by Hafiz us-Sihhih and converted. Neumark, cited in Levy, *Tarikh Yahud* 3:662.

12 ZH 8:747–9; Mu'ayyad, *Khatirat* 2:349–52; S. Mu'ayyad, 'Hajj Khudabakhsh'; the latter source implies a date of 1878 for Khudabakhsh's conversion (p. 75) but this is probably an error. Regarding Salar ud-Dawlih, see BBR 458–9.

13 BW 15:501–3. Abu Sinan is a Druze village to the north of 'Akka to which 'Abdu'l-Baha evacuated the Baha'i communities of Haifa and 'Akka during the first years of World War I, see Rabbani, ''Abdu'l-Baha in Abu Sinan'.

of governors including Zaynu'l-'Abidin Khan Qaraguzlu Hisam ul-Mulk Amir Afkham (gov. 1888–91, 1896–7 and 1905–7) and Hasan 'Ali Khan Garrusi Amir Nizam (d. 1899; gov. 1891–6).[14] A number of the notables of the town such as the two brothers Husayn Khan Kalbi Mu'in ur-Ru'aya (assassinated 1911) and Hasan Khan Mu'avin ul-Mulk (d. 1948) and their families were also strongly opposed to the new religion.[15] Baha'u'llah wrote, in a letter of December 1886 addressed to Haji Amin, that the Baha'is in Tehran should consult together and determine upon an appropriate person to send to Kirmanshah who could both settle some disputes that had arisen among the Baha'is and bring the Baha'i Faith to the attention of the notables in that area in a suitable manner.[16]

As a consequence of the difficult conditions, a number of Baha'i teachers who came to Kirmanshah, such as Sayyid Jamal Burujirdi and Mulla Sadiq Muqaddas, were not able to do much. Mirza Abu'l-Fadl Gulpaygani, who spent three months in the town in 1887–8 (perhaps as a direct result of the letter of Baha'u'llah mentioned above[17]), found the Baha'i community there to be still small. In a letter written in Kirmanshah he states that he found the conditions there for the Baha'i Faith were more difficult than in any of the other towns he had visited. He states that although the number of Azalis in the town at that time was not more than five or six individuals, they had introduced such doubts and falsehoods among the population that it was impossible to raise the matter of the Baha'i Faith among the ordinary people without hearing from them objections that had been put into their heads by the Azalis. He writes that most of his time in the two months he had been in the town up to that point had been spent countering these falsehoods.[18] In another letter he compares the Baha'i situation in Kirmanshah unfavourably with that in Hamadan at that time.[19] Gulpaygani himself was unable to stay in the town for long. He had two open debates with Shaykh Shihabu'd-Din, after which he had to go into hiding

---

14 Mihrabkhani, *Gulpaygani* 145–9, (new ed.); ZH 8b:745–6.
15 MH 8b:746; on this family, see Sultani, *Tarikh* 4:1263–88.
16 ILMA 27:494–5.
17 Gulpaygani writes that Ibn Asdaq, who may well have been in Tehran when Baha'u'llah's letter arrived, had gone to Kirmanshah and then to Hamadan and asked Gulpaygani to go to Kirmanshah. Gulpaygani, *Rasa'il va Raqa'im* 406; ZH 6:368.
18 Gulpaygani, *Rasa'il va Raqa'im* 406.
19 Mihrabkhani, *Gulpaygani* 153.

83. Iqbal ud-Dawlih (Mirza
Muhammad Rida Ghaffari)

in the town and eventually left.[20]

Over the years the Azali opposition faded away[21] and the Baha'i population grew. After about 1897, moreover, the governors of the town were less inimical to the Baha'is. The town was visited by many travelling Baha'i teachers (*muballighs*), including Sayyid Asadu'llah Qummi and Qabil Abadihi in 1898[22] and Mirza Yusif Khan Vujdani and Mirza Musa Hakim-bashi (Hakim Ilahi) Qazvini in 1901.[23] During this latter visit, Aqa Sayyid Rustam, an Ahl-i Haqq leader, and Khudamarut Khan, a notable of the Kurdish Sanjabi tribe, were converted. Hakim-bashi, who appears to have stayed on in the town for a time, succeeded in establishing the local assembly there. However, eventually, Mu'in ur-Ru'aya threatened Hakim-bashi, forcing him at first to go into hiding and then to leave the town.[24] Sina visited Kirmanshah in 1899 and again in 1904 for two years. During the first visit, he faced opposition from a local preacher (*va'iz*), Mirza Muhammad Rida Hamadani. Mirza Muhammad Khan Ghaffari Iqbal ud-Dawlih (c. 1848–1923, see fig. 83), who was governor from 1898 to 1902, was friendly towards the Baha'i Faith and a poet and mystic. One of his closest confidants, Aqa 'Abdu'l-Karim Mahut-furush, was a Baha'i (he was the person who had first interested Mirza Abu'l-Fadl Gulpaygani in the Baha'i Faith). On account of his closeness to the governor, he had gained the title Qavam Divan. Iqbal ud-Dawlih ordered the expulsion from Kirmanshah of the above-mentioned preacher, who went on to Tehran and died there shortly thereafter. Aqa 'Abdu'l-Karim introduced Sina to the governor and they spent many sessions together exchanging poetry.[25] At the same time as

20   Mihrabkhani, *Gulpaygani* 145–9; ZH 6:366–7.
21   Mazandarani, *Asrar* 5:26.
22   MH 2:210.
23   ZH 8b:746.
24   ibid.
25   MH 1:147–8; ZH 6:247–8; 8a:331–3.

84. Six Baha'i dervishes. *Left to right*: Haji Yuqadih Hamadani, Haji Tayfur Isfahani, Haji Mu'nis Qazvini, Haji Musadih Isfahani, Haji Tavangar Qazvini, unknown

Sina's second visit, Haji Mu'nis Qazvini (see fig. 84) arrived with a group of Baha'i dervishes and they recited Baha'i poetry openly in the bazaar. This aroused opposition in the town and a shot was fired by one of the family of Mu'avin ul-Mulk at Haji Mu'nis, wounding him.[26] In 1898 the remains of the Bab passed through Kirmanshah, as they were being taken by Mirza Asadu'llah Isfahani to 'Akka; they were placed in the home of Mirza Muhammad Sarraf Isfahani.

Mirza Ishaq Khan Haqiqi (1282/1865–1358/1939), son of Mirza Buzurg Khan the vazir of Kirmanshah, became a Baha'i in about 1894 after meeting with Baha'is such as Aqa Sayyid Hasan Tafrishi and Fath-'Ali Bayk Tabib, who were resident in Karand where he was governor, and later conversing with some of the Baha'i teachers who passed through Kirmanshah.[27] This man later held a high position in the customs in the area, which was administered by the Belgians, rose to an important position in the Ministry of Finance and Provisions and was a prominent member of the Baha'i communities in Kirmanshah and Tehran.[28]

---

26   ZH 6:746–7.
27   In particular Sayyid Asadu'llah Qummi, ZH 8b:749–50; according to MH 1:147–8, however, Haqiqi did not become a Baha'i until 1904, through Sina.
28   ZH 8b:749–51.

In 1909, just as the opposition to Muhammad 'Ali Shah was building up around the country, a severe persecution of the Jews broke out in Kirmanshah. A Jew who owned a sock factory and who had been converted to Christianity by the American missionaries beat one of his apprentices, a Muslim boy who was from a family of sayyids. Two days later the boy died, probably from a cause unrelated to the beating. Some of the ruffians in the town, however, used this as an excuse to raise a commotion. On 27 March 1909 they dragged the body of the dead boy around the town and stirred up a mob which then attacked the Jewish quarter. The entire quarter was looted and sacked, several houses were burned and a number of Jews killed. Since, as mentioned above, a large proportion of the Jews of the town were Baha'is, these were among those who suffered on that day. The governor failed to act decisively to suppress the rioters when the trouble first began and he then tried to make amends by ordering that all the looted property be returned. Then, as the British consul in Kirmanshah Captain Lionel Haworth reported on 7 April 1909, 'there was a further rumour that an attack was to be made on the Jews, this time, on their lives not their property. A large number of the more important Jews in Kermanshah, and in Hamadan also, are Babis. In returning the stolen goods, amongst other things, a picture of the Bab appeared, and it was this that appears to have excited some of the Hooligans in the bazaar.'[29] On this occasion the British and Russian consuls made strong representations to the governor. A guard was posted around the Jewish quarter and further trouble was averted.[30]

In 1910 Fadil Mazandarani and Sayyid 'Abdu'l-Husayn Ardistani came to Kirmanshah on their way to Iraq, where 'Abdu'l-Baha had sent them on a mission to inform the leading clerics of Shi'i Islam about the Baha'i Faith (vol. 1:310). At a meeting held for them by the Baha'is in Kirmanshah, a group photograph was taken. A little later this photograph fell into the hands of the enemies of the Baha'i Faith. Since Mu'avin ul-Mulk and his brothers were in charge of Kirmanshah at this time, all those in the photograph who could be identified were arrested. A Baghdad Jew who was trading in Kirmanshah, Mirza Musa (who later took the surname Banani), was arrested by mistake for his brother, whom he strongly resembled and who was in the photograph. His brother was a Baha'i but Mirza Musa was

---

29   Haworth to Barclay No. 8C, 11 Apr. 1909: FO 248 968, in BBR 369. The picture is likely to have been of 'Abdu'l-Baha.
30   Sultani, *Tarikh*, 3: 504–7.

not. Mirza Musa observed the conduct
of his fellow-prisoner Aqa Ha'im Ishaq
Abrar (1868–1927), who was kind to him
and who refused to deny his faith despite
being tortured. This led Mirza Musa to
investigate the Baha'i Faith and become a
Baha'i. He was later to become one of the
most prominent Baha'is of Iran and was
designated a Hand of the Cause.[31]

In 1906 Mirza Mahdi Akhavan Safa
and Mirza Habibu'llah Samimi visited
Kirmanshah[32] and the former visited again
in the winter of 1914–15 together with
Mirza Hasan Nushabadi. After they had
been in the town a while during the latter
visit, there was an uproar that resulted in
their expulsion from the town. In fact,
one of the prominent Baha'is, Sayyid
Faraju'llah, who was Mirza Aqa Khan

85. Mirza Ya'qub
Muttahidih

Qa'im-Maqami's agent for postal services in Kirmanshah and had become
chairman of the local assembly, was secretly in league with Azalis and had
stirred up this commotion. Qa'im-Maqami, who was informed about this
by 'Abdu'l-Baha, dismissed him but did not disclose his misdemeanours.[33]
In 1918–19 'Abdu'llah Mutlaq stayed for almost a year. He extended the
range of meetings that the Baha'is were holding (adding meetings for the
propagation of the Baha'i Faith and other meetings for learning how to
do this, as well as Nineteen Day Feasts and deepening meetings) and converted many people.[34] Mirza Muhammad 'Ali Khan Baha'i spent three
years in Kirmanshah from about 1919.[35]

The years of 1911–21 were difficult ones for the general population, as
indicated above, but also for the Baha'is. Dr Mu'ayyad records, for example,
how shortly after his return to the town in 1915 leaflets were distributed
around the town showing him with his head cut off and threatening him

31   Sadiqiyan, 'Sharh-i Hal-i Jinab-i Ha'im Ishaq Abrar'; Harper, *Lights* 339.
32   ZH 6:747; MH .
33   Nushabadi, 'Qa'im-Maqami' 25–6.
34   MH 4:125.
35   MH 8:366–8.

with this fate if he did not leave the town.[36]

One of the most notable events in the Baha'i history of Kirmanshah was the public assassination of Mirza Ya'qub Muttahidih (see fig. 85), one of five Kashani Jewish brothers who had become Baha'is in Kashan (see p. 107). He had moved to Kirmanshah to run a branch of his brother's business, the Muttahidih Company. Although only 25 years old, he had become a successful merchant and one of the leading Baha'is of the town. In 1920 some of the Muslim religious leaders had excited a public agitation against the Baha'is, and in order to quell the disorder, the governor, Akbar Mirza Sarim ud-Dawlih, a son of Zill us-Sultan, had had one Baha'i beaten and had sent Mirza Ya'qub out of the town. Mirza Ya'qub returned with the governor's permission but on 23 January 1921 was shot dead in the middle of the day in Amin ul-Mamalik Street, one of the main streets of the town near the bazaar, by Javad, the son of the above-mentioned Mu'in ur-Ru'aya. The *fatwa* for Mirza Ya'qub' s death had been given by the *mujtahid* Haji Sayyid Husayn Ha'iri (Karbala'i). The other local Baha'is were harassed and many had to go into hiding. Although instructions were sent from Tehran that the assassin should be arrested and sent to Tehran, the governor was too weak to do this and nothing happened.[37]

Malayir and Tuysargan

Malayir (also called Dawlatabad, pop. 4,500 in 1915 and 21,100 in 1951) is situated 65 kilometres southeast of Hamadan on the road to Sultanabad (Iraq); Tuysargan (pop. 15,000 in 1951) is situated 40 kilometres south of Hamadan. Although much closer to Hamadan, both these towns were in the province of Kirmanshah. As well as his history of Hamadan, 'Abdu'l-Hamid Ishraq-Khavari wrote a history of the Baha'i community in these two towns, which he completed in 1346/1927. In addition, 'Abdu'llah Abizadih deals with these two towns in his written history of Hamadan.

---

36   Mu'ayyad, *Khatirat* 2:380.
37   Mu'ayyad, *Sharh Shahadat*; Mu'ayyad, *Khatirat* 2:398–403; KD 2:258–61; BBR 446–50; MH 8:366–8; ZH 7:323–4; Faizi, *'Abdu'l-Baha* 300–2; Guy, 'Jewish Martyr'. Mu'ayyad (*Sharh Shahadat* 77) mentions one other Jewish Baha'i of Kirmanshah who was killed on account of his faith, Aqa Baba Jan Gawhari, but I have been unable to find out anything about the circumstances of his death. When Tarazu'llah Samandari visited the town in January 1941 he had meetings which at least 80 men attended. Thus the Baha'i population of the town was probably at least 400 (Khoshbin, *Taraz Ilahi* 1:541).

Karbala'i Rahmatu'llah of Sultanabad was one of the first to bring the new religion to Malayir and in the early 1860s converted a number of people, both in the town and in the villages of Upper and Lower Hamzihlu (42 km southeast of Malayir, pops. 350 and 310 respectively). The Baha'i populations in these villages disappeared over time, however, owing to persecutions and migrations (see p. 157).

Husayn-Quli Mirza (c. 1272/1855–1895) was a Qajar prince (his father, Imam-Quli Mirza, was a grandson of Fath-'Ali Shah) who is usually known by his poetic sobriquet of Mawzun. He was born in the village of Gamasa near Malayir which belonged to his father and he grew up in comfort and amidst wealth, having a share in the income from three villages. In 1297/1880 he travelled to Tabriz and was converted by the Baha'is there.[38] He established himself in Malayir and opened a wholesale grocery business in the bazaar. He gained such a reputation for honesty that merchants and landowners would lodge their important documents with him and he was entrusted with supervising a large charitable endowment in the town. In addition, he bravely taught the Baha'i Faith and succeeded in converting several members of his family and many others in Malayir, Tuysargan and the surrounding villages. Meetings were held at his home where, in addition to the Baha'is, some 40 to 50 Muslims would be present to hear about the Baha'i Faith. Mawzun had a charming personality and was well-liked by successive governors of the town. As a result, the Baha'is of Malayir felt relatively safe and it is reported that a few of them even openly displayed Baha'i symbols in their shops.[39]

A number of Jews of Malayir were also converted by Mawzun: Hakim Aqa Baba, Hakim Davud (a physician who had originally been from Tuysargan), and Mirza Ibrahim. Another Jew originally had the name Ilyas but, having converted to Islam, he became known as Mirza 'Ali Jadid and had apparently taken over a Jewish synagogue as his home. He became a Baha'i through Mawzun and used to hold Baha'i meetings in his home. In about 1882 Mirza Rayhan Rayhani, a visiting Jewish Baha'i, reports attending a Baha'i meeting in this home at which Jamal Burujirdi spoke

---

38 MH 2:511. Sulaymani's biography of Mawzun (MH 2:507–40) is based on accounts from two of Mawzun's sons as well as on a memoir by Ishraq-Khavari who also gives Tabriz as the location of Mawzun's conversion (MH 2:526). In one place Mazandarani states Mawzun became a Baha'i in Tabriz but gives the date as 1292/1875 (ZH 6:697); in another place he states that Mawzun was converted by Karbala'i Rahmatu'llah in the early 1860s (ZH 4:337).

39 MH 2:507–40; ZH 6:696–701.

and there were some 50 people present. Many Baha'is from Hamadan moved to Malayir at this time.[40]

Among those converted by Mawzun was Ustad 'Ali Zargar (goldsmith) and the two of them together, in 1306/1888, talked about the Baha'i Faith to Mirza Yusif Vujdani, who converted and went on to become a prominent teacher of the Baha'i Faith (*muballigh*; vol. 1:486–8).[41] Vujdani was among the entourage of his cousin Haji Sultan Muhammad ('Abdu'l-Muhammad) Mirza Sayf ud-Dawlih (c. 1852–1920), who was governor of Malayir and district in 1887–90 and of Hamadan in 1891–2 (see p. 200). Sayf ud-Dawlih was a brother of 'Ayn ud-Dawlih (who was later prime minister), a Sufi of the Safi 'Ali Shahi order and greatly opposed to the Baha'i Faith.[42]

When Sayf ud-Dawlih first arrived as governor in 1887, Mawzun had come to pay his respects and had recited one of his own poems before the governor in which he referred to Baha'u'llah's station. This angered the governor and he was waiting for a chance to move against Mawzun. His chance came in 1888, when a Qajar prince, Habibu'llah Mirza of Tuysar-gan, who had been converted by Mawzun and was a son of 'Ali-Quli Mirza, went to 'Akka to visit Baha'u'llah. On his return the other princes in the area plotted against him and refused to give him the rents he was due. The matter was taken before Sayf ud-Dawlih in Malayir and Mawzun pleaded the case eloquently. But the governor expressed his hostility towards the Baha'i Faith by ordering Mawzun to be bastinadoed severely, hoping that he would recant his faith, but he did not. He was held in prison for a time and eventually managed to secure his release by composing a poem in praise of the governor.[43]

In 1307/1889 in Malayir a mob broke into the home of one of the Jewish Baha'is, Hakim Davud, and ransacked the house, injuring his wife Maryam (known as Bilgis) and son Bulbul to such an extent that the latter died as a result of these injuries.[44] Sayf ud-Dawlih was evidently a harsh and unjust governor and in 1890 the people of the town arose against him and he was dismissed as governor, although he returned later.[45]

The clerics in Malayir were in a continuous struggle for power with

---

40   MH 2:515; Rayhani in Amanat, 'Negotiating Identities' 193–5.
41   MH 2:512–15.
42   See Ishraq-Khavari, *Hamadan* 266–7; Bamdad, *Tarikh* 2:99–102.
43   MH 2:507–22; ZH 6:698–700; Faizi, *'Abdu'l-Baha* 146–9.
44   ZH 6:700–1.
45   Bamdad, *Tarikh* 100.

successive governors of the town and the Baha'is were often the scapegoats caught in the middle. In 1310/1892 when one governor, Mirza Abu'l-Qasim Khan Nuri, had been dismissed and the new governor had not yet arrived, Shaykh Diya'u'd-Din Mujtahid and his brother Mulla Mahdi took advantage of the lack of authority in Malayir to plot a major persecution of the Baha'is there. They arranged with the head of the telegraph and post services that no one would be able to appeal for help. Mawzun was, however, able to slip away to Sultanabad and telegraph the shah from there. Orders were sent from the prime minister Amin us-Sultan to the new governor Muhammad Taqi Khan that if Shaykh Diya'u'd-Din did not desist he should be expelled from the town and this was enough to calm the situation.[46]

When Mawzun died in 1895 leaving a widow and young children, Mirza Isma'il Khayyat (tailor), who was originally from Kashan and had settled in Sultanabad, moved to Malayir to help look after the children; he eventually married Mawzun's widow. In 1903 the clerics were engaged in a power struggle with another governor named Nayyir ul-Mamalik. When news arrived of the 1903 anti-Baha'i pogrom in Isfahan and Yazd, the clerics saw it as a chance to initiate a persecution in Malayir and to discomfit the governor, who was, of course, responsible for maintaining order. The above-mentioned cleric Mulla Mahdi dressed two people in shrouds and paraded them through the streets of the town, preaching against the Baha'is. Mirza Isma'il Khayyat wrote to the governor but the latter was helpless; the situation was out of his control. He even gave a gift to the two shrouded men. In August a number of Jewish Baha'is who had come from Hamadan on business were attacked and seriously injured.[47] Some people attacked the shop of Ustad 'Ali Zargar in the Abu'l-Qasim Caravanserai one day and on the next arrested him and beat him, his nephew 'Abbas and Mirza Husayn Naqqash (painter) Burujirdi together with Murtada-Quli Mirza, Mahdi-Quli Mirza and Imam-Quli Mirza, sons of Mawzun, and put them all in the government prison. On 6 September 1903 a large crowd gathered in the town square for a recital of the sufferings of the Imams (rawdih-khani). During this, the mob was roused to the point that they set out for the

---

46 MH 2:524; ZH 6:701 states that the governor at this time was Sayf ud-Dawlih, but according to other sources he had been dismissed in 1890.
47 Report of Bassan to Alliance Israélite Universelle, dated 23 August 1903; archives of Alliance Israélite Universelle, Paris (I am grateful to Dr Daniel Tsadik for a copy of this document).

house of Mirza Isma'il and attacked it. They threw Mirza Isma'il from an upper floor window and then dragged him to a public square where they hacked him to death. They then demanded from the governor that Ustad 'Ali Zargar be handed over to them for a similar fate. The governor put them off by saying that he himself would execute Ustad 'Ali. Then by night he sent the prisoners out of town and they migrated to Hamadan. Ustad 'Ali, who was sent out five days after the others, was recognized by a group of people as he was travelling. They stripped him naked and threw him off a cliff, breaking his legs and teeth. He managed to drag himself all the way to Qazvin in this state and was brought back to health there, before moving to Hamadan. Many other Baha'is were attacked and some were forced to flee the town. On 21 Ramadan 1321 (11 December 1903), the holiest day of the month of the fast, Shaykh Diya'u'd-Din roused the mob to go to the cemetery, dig up the body of Mirza Isma'il and burn it.[48]

In 1911 the affairs of the area were once again in turmoil because of the rebellion of Salar ad-Dawlih (see fig. 81), a brother of Muhammad 'Ali Shah. Once more the people of Malayir rose against the Baha'is. On this occasion their target was the above-mentioned Habibu'llah Mirza. The latter appealed to the governor Sayf ud-Dawlih and even went to his house for sanctuary but the governor turned him away. He then tried to escape the town but was caught. The mob wanted to kill him there and then but some of the Qajar princes tried to save him by saying to the crowd that they needed to take him to the house of a cleric and obtain a *fatwa* first. So he was brought back to the town and taken to the house of Aqa Najafi, who refused to open the door to the mob. Thereupon a dervish named Mir Shayda brought his axe down on Habibu'llah Mirza's head and the rest of the mob beat him to death and burned his body. A young Baha'i, Mirza Javad Burujirdi, who was passing through the town, betrayed his emotions when he heard what had happened to Habibu'llah Mirza and was also beaten to death and his body burned.[49] Less than a month after this episode the town was captured by the forces of Salar ud-Dawlih and shortly after that Bakhtiyari forces retook the town. Many women were raped and many houses looted as a consequence of these events.

---

48   Faizi, *'Abdu'l-Baha* 150–5; ZH 7:222–3, 8a:284–5; Abizadih, Vaqayi' 590; Ishraq-Khavari, *Muhadarat* 221–2; he was called Siraj ush-Shuhada (lamp of the martyrs) by 'Abdu'l-Baha.

49   ZH 7:288–9; Avarih, *Kawakib* 2:234–7; Faizi, *'Abdu'l-Baha* 155–7; Hafizi, *Memoirs* 1:322.

It was in Malayir that 'Abdu'l-Hamid Ishraq-Khavari (1902–6 Aug. 1972, see fig. 86), who was to become one of the most eminent Baha'i scholars of the mid-20th century, became a Baha'i. He was born in Mashhad into a family of clerics (his great-grandfather had been custodian of the shrine of Imam Rida). He attended the religious colleges in Mashhad and then set off in 1922 on travels. In Qazvin later that same year he came across a former classmate, Sayyid Hidayatu'llah Shahab Firdawsi, who had in the meantime become a Baha'i, and this aroused Ishraq-Khavari's curiosity. Then he fell ill with typhoid and was treated by the Baha'i physician As'ad ul-Hukama,

86. 'Abdu'l-Hamid Ishraq-Khavari

who also tried to interest him in the Baha'i Faith. From Qazvin he went to various towns in Iran, in each place seeking out scholars in his main area of interest, mystical philosophy, before settling for a few years in a position of religious prominence in Malayir. The Baha'is of Malayir thought that he had the potential to become a Baha'i and determined to approach him. After one unsatisfactory encounter with the travelling Baha'i teacher (*muballigh*) Mirza 'Abdu'llah Mutlaq, he was befriended by a Malayir Baha'i, Muhammad Husayn Rabi'i, and eventually convinced of the truth of the Baha'i Faith during a visit in August 1927 by another *muballigh*, Mirza Yusif Vujdani.[50] When his conversion became known in Malayir, the town was in uproar and the Baha'i assembly decided it would be better for him to leave. He went to Burujird and then to Hamadan, where he taught at the Baha'i Ta'id school for two years.[51] There he married Sadru'l-Muluk Khanum, a daughter of Mahdi-Quli Mirza (d. c. 1937), the son of Mawzun, but she died soon afterwards following a medical accident in 1930.[52]

Haji Muhammad 'Ali Tuysargani became a Baha'i in Tehran and

---

50 Rastigar, *Sadr as-Sudur* 265–6; Molavi-Nejad, *Ishraq-Khavari* 136–53.
51 MH 9:8–85; Ishraq-Khavari, 'Dustan'.
52 MH 2:533.

returned to his home town. After a time, however, the religious leaders in the town forced his expulsion and he moved to Hamadan, where he died in 1344/1925 after being dragged into one of the religious colleges and beaten on the orders of Sayyid 'Abdu'l-Vahhab, the head of the college.[53] The Baha'i Faith was finally established in Tuysargan in 1927 when Haji Mirza Haydar 'Ali Sani'i Usku'i spent some time there and succeeded in converting two members of the prominent Sugand family, 'Abbas Khan and Vali Khan.[54]

Among those converted by Mawzun were a number of people in the villages around Malayir, including Mulla Khan Baba of the village of Jawzan (14 km southeast of Malayir), who was part of a gang of thieves and highwaymen prior to his conversion. A story is told of how, after becoming a Baha'i through Mawzun, he encountered at a Baha'i meeting Sayyid Ahmad Naraqi and recognized him as one of those from whom he had previously stolen a large quantity of goods. He hurried to collect the small amount of money that he had, returned to the meeting and offered it to the Naraqi merchant along with his apologies and regrets.[55]

In the village of Jurab (11 km south of Malayir, pop. 1,753 in 1952), a number of the residents became Baha'is, including some Jews, Mirza Rahim Big and his brother 'Abdu'l-'Azim Big, who was beaten to death on the orders of Sayf ud-Dawlih. Sayf ud-Dawlih put Na'ib Hidayatu'llah, a Baha'i, in charge of the village but later stripped him of all his wealth.[56]

It is not clear when the Baha'i Faith spread to the village of Avarzaman (27 km west of Malayir, pop. 150 in 1914) but there was a community there during the time of 'Abdu'l-Baha when 'Abdu'llah Mutlaq visited and debated with Haji Shaykh Musa, one of the leading clerics of the area. After the latter had been worsted in debate a number of people converted.[57]

Asadabad

Asadabad is a small town on the road between Kirmanshah and Hamadan (120 km east of Kirmanshah, pop. 5,190 in 1956). Its principal fame in Qajar history is as the home town of Sayyid Jamalu'd-Din Asadabadi

---

53   ZH 8b:891–2.
54   Ishraq-Khavari, *Hamadan* 168.
55   MH 2:516–17.
56   ZH 6:702; Abizadih, Vaqayi' 636–9.
57   MH 4:159–63.

'al-Afghani', the modernist and Islamic reformer, whom many at that time thought was a 'Babi'. There was some justification for this in that two of his closest associates when he lived in Istanbul were Azalis, Shaykh Ahmad Ruhi and Mirza Aqa Khan Kirmani. As a consequence and because there was no distinction in the public mind between Baha'is and Azalis (both groups were called 'Babis'), when a follower of 'al-Afghani' assassinated Nasiru'd-Din Shah in 1896, Baha'is were attacked in both Iran and in ex-patriot Iranian communities throughout the Middle East.

Nabil records meeting in Asadabad in 1283/1866 two Jewish Baha'i merchants who had been forced to leave Hamadan and had settled in Asadabad (see p. 181). Mazandarani records the names of four other Baha'is of Muslim background.[58] There must certainly have been Baha'i activity in Asadabad since Mirza Sharif Mustawfi, Sayyid Jamalu'd-Din's nephew, wrote to him from the town in 1884 urging him to write something against the Baha'is as he had noticed much propaganda activity and an increase in the number of the Baha'is.[59]

In the village of Sahnih, about halfway between Kirmanshah and Asadabad (pop. of about 1,000 in 1914 and about 6,000 in 1951), Haji Khudabakhsh (see p. 220) and his son Murad settled as merchants to escape persecution in Kirmanshah. They were, however, subjected to persecution and one day someone entered their business office and shot Murad dead. The governor of Kirmanshah, Farmanfarma, had the killer arrested and tried. The murderer was about to be executed when Khudabakhsh went onto the gallows, kissed the murderer, publicly forgave him and obtained his freedom. This action caused Khudabakhsh's wife Liya to leave him.[60]

In the village of Shirkhan (pop. 360 in 1951) in the Dinavar district to the northwest of Sahnih, the local chief of the Jalilvand Kurdish tribe, Khudadad Khan, became a Baha'i and brought several travelling Baha'i teachers to his village. Although this did not result in conversions immediately, in the next generation, some 20 people from this area, mostly notables, became Baha'is.[61]

---

58 ZH 6:720.

59 Mahdavi and Afshar, *Documents Inedit,* document 86, photograph 57, letter dated 15 Ramadan 1301/29 June 1884.

60 S. Mu'ayyad, 'Hajj Khudabakhsh' 77.

61 ZH 8b:756; interview with Mr Manuchehr Khodadad at Acuto, Italy, 2 July 2016.

Karand

This small town (pop. 3,000 in 1914; 4554 in the 1951) is situated 90 kilometres west of Kirmanshah close to the Iraqi border. When Tahirih passed
through it on her return from Iraq, she is said to have been feted by the inhabitants for three days and to have converted many people.[62] When Baha'u'llah
passed through the town in 1853, the governor Hayat-Quli Khan and the
people of the town expressed much friendliness towards the travellers. Karand
and the area to the northeast of town which is called Guran and is inhabited
by the Guran tribe of Ahl-i Haqq Kurds, was an area of much Babi activity.
In 1853 Timur of the Guran tribe of the village of Banyaran in Qal'ih-Zanjir
district, who had proclaimed the near advent of the Promised One and had
some 5,000 to 6,000 followers, was executed at Kirmanshah by the governor
Imam-Quli Mirza 'Imad ud-Dawlih.[63] Among those who converted to the
Babi religion were Timur Shah and Sayyid Barakat, who advanced claims
after the execution of the Bab. Timur Shah was an Ahl-i Haqq Kurd, whose
original name was Sayfur (or Fattah) but who took on this new name when
he claimed to be the return (raj'at) of the above-mentioned Timur of Banyaran.[64] Sayyid Barakat acknowledged the Bab as a Manifestation of God,
but Haji Mirza Haydar 'Ali Isfahani, who passed through Karand in about
1864, met Sayyid Barakat and was frustrated that he did not teach this to his
many followers.[65] In later years Karand had a succession of governors who
were Baha'is or sympathetic to the religion and the townspeople assisted
travelling Baha'is to such an extent that the people of the area called them
Baha'is.[66] Malik Niyaz Khan, the governor of the town during the ministry
of Baha'u'llah, was from the Ahl-i Haqq religious community and became
a Baha'i,[67] and during the time of 'Abdu'l-Baha, the governor Mirza Ishaq
Khan Haqiqi (see p. 223) became a Baha'i in about 1894.

The leader of the Ahl-i Haqq community in the Guran district, Sayyid
Faraj Gurani, was converted by Haji Tayfur (see fig. 84) in Sahnih but kept

---

62   Autobiographical account of Mirza Mustafa Baghdadi as translated by Mirza
     Abu'l-Fadl Gulpaygani in *Kashf ul-Ghita* 99.
63   Sipihr, *Nasikh ut-Tavarikh* 3:1180 (summarized in ['Abdu'l-Baha] *Traveller's
     Narrative* 2:184); Minorsky, 'Notes-2' 275–8, 291–3; Minorsky, 'Guran' 95;
     Amanat, *Resurrection* 86.
64   See Isfahani, *Bihjat* 37–9; Browne in ['Abdu'l-Baha], *Traveller's Narrative* 2:184n.
65   Isfahani, *Bihjat* 39–40.
66   Ishraq-Khavari, *Qamus Tawqi'* 105, 2:80–1.
67   ZH 6:695.

his allegiance secret.[68] Some members of the Guran tribe which populates this area also became Baha'is.[69] The border village of Qasr-i Shirin (21 km from the border; pop. 1,000 in 1914; 10,000 in 1951) was a place many Baha'is traversed on the road to Baghdad. Sayyid 'Abbas 'Alavi records that when he visited it in about 1930, the governor there was a Baha'i.[70]

The town of Sunqur (96 km northeast of Kirmanshah; pop. 10,000 in 1914) was visited by Mirza 'Abdu'llah Mutlaq in about 1918. There were already Baha'is in the town and he stayed with one of them, Mashhadi Nasru'llah Bazzaz. During his stay, Mutlaq talked with and converted the deputy governor for the area, Mu'tadid ul-Iyalih.[71]

Kurdistan

Kurdistan is a mountainous area in the west of Iran, north of Kirmanshah. The province was often called Ardalan in Qajar times. The Kurds are a fiercely independent people speaking a language that is related to Persian. Most of the Kurds in Iranian Kurdistan are Shafi'i Sunnis but there are also many Ahl-i Haqq among them, especially in the south of the area towards Kirmanshah. The capital of the province of Kurdistan is Sanandaj (also called Sinnih, 140 km north of Kirmanshah, 512 km west of Tehran; pop. 18,000 in 1868, 32,000 in 1914, 40,600 in 1956). The area exports carpets, sheep products and cereals. Sayyid Yahya Vahid Darabi is said to have taught the message of the Bab in this region.[72]

Kurdistan presented many difficulties to the Baha'is who wanted to spread the religion of Baha'u'llah there. Being Sunnis, the majority of Kurds have always had a degree of ill-feeling towards the Shi'i Iranians, as exemplified by the revolt of Shaykh 'Ubaydu'llah in 1880 (vol. 1:360–1, 418).[73] In 1313/1895 Kurds killed Shaykh Muhammad Taqi Hamadani, the leading Shi'i cleric in Sanandaj and burnt down his house.[74] Also, the Iranian Baha'is, being used to proving the Baha'i Faith on the basis of the

---

68 Ishraq-Khavari, *Muhadirat* 1:173–4; Muhammad-Husayni, 'Darvishan va 'Arifan' 18.
69 Among them was a Baha'i poet, Jalali Kirmanshahi, see Dhuka'i-Bayda'i, *Tadhkirih* 1:300–8.
70 MH 6:263.
71 MH 4:125.
72 DB 465.
73 ZH 5:249–51.
74 Qaraguzlu, *Hagmatanih ta Hamadan* 173–4.

Shi'i books of Islamic traditions, found it difficult to adapt their methods to a Sunni audience. Mirza Abu'l-Fadl Gulpaygani, who travelled to Kurdistan in the company of Haji Mirza Abu'l-Hasan Amin in the spring of 1888, came to be held in great esteem by the Sunni clerics of Sanandaj, especially by Shaykh Shukru'llah Kurdi, but did not consider it timely or wise to teach the Baha'i Faith among them.[75]

Among those Baha'is who settled in Kurdistan were Mirza Habibu'llah, a Jewish Baha'i physician from Hamadan who was learned in the Jewish scriptures, knowing both Hebrew and Chaldaean. He took up residence in Sanandaj but later moved to Ashkhabad, where he is said to have converted some 60 Polish Jewish soldiers who were stationed there.[76] There was also Mirza Asadu'llah, a physician from Isfahan, who moved to Sanandaj and established a family there.[77] Among those who travelled through Kurdistan in order to teach the Baha'i Faith were Fadil Shirazi and Sayyid Jalal, the son of Sina, together with Sayyid Hasan Mutavajjih (Hashimizadih).[78] The latter two were young men who had recently completed the teaching course of Sadr us-Sudur in Tehran (vol. 1:98) in about 1906. One result of their efforts was the conversion of Shaykh Muhammad Khatib, the Imam Jum'ih of Kurdistan. This man's father-in-law was a respected Sunni cleric of the town and arranged for the two young Baha'is to meet with the clerics of the town. At this meeting they were questioned and came out of it well, despite their relative ignorance of Sunni Islam. However, the opposition of some local religious leaders eventually grew to the point that their lives were under threat and they were ordered to leave town by the governor, Mirza Mahdi Khan Vazir Humayun.[79]

Another convert was Sayyid Mahdi Qavam Hamadani (1293/1876–1351/1932), who was the son of Sayyid Muhammad Rida Hamadani, a well-known cleric of the village of Isfandabad in Kurdistan. Although his father died when Sayyid Mahdi was young, he managed to obtain an education in Sanandaj and returned to his village both to farm and to be a mulla. He became a Baha'i in 1318/1900 and taught the Baha'i Faith to many others both in Kurdistan and beyond.[80] Other converts included

75 Mihrabkhani, *Gulpaygani* 151–2.
76 ZH 8b:894, 1061; Yazdi, *Tarikh 'Ishqabad* 181.
77 ZH 8a:140.
78 ZH8a:339; 8b:721.
79 MH6:53–8; ZH 8a:339; Mirza Mahdi Khan Vazir Humayun was a Baha'i (see pp. 90–1) and was probably trying to protect the two young men.
80 Dhuka'i-Bayda'i, *Tadhkirih* 3:226–9.

Dhu'l-Faqar Khan and Hakim Ibrahim.[81] One report states that in the 1890s the Baha'i community of Sanandaj included Baha'is from Jewish, Armenian Christian, Sufi, Iranian Shi'i and Kurdish Sunni backgrounds and among them were poets, musicians, merchants and government servants.[82]

87. Shaykh Faraju'llah Zaki al-Kurdi

Other Baha'i teachers who spent some time in Kurdistan at a later date were Mirza Muhammad 'Ali Khan Baha'i, who was there in 1922;[83] Haji Harun Akhavan, a converted Jew of Hamadan who came to Kurdistan on business in 1925 and began to speak about the Baha'i Faith, was poisoned and fell ill, dying shortly after his return to Hamadan;[84] 'Abdu'l-Hamid Ishraq-Khavari for three months in about 1940;[85] and Mirza Hasan Nushabadi, who spent some months in Sanandaj in 1942, resulting in some conversions.[86]

A number of the residents of the village of Qurvih, some 90 kilometres east of Sanandaj on the road to Hamadan (pop. c. 1,000 in 1914; 3,260 in 1952), became Baha'is in the time of 'Abdu'l-Baha.[87] In Bijar (70 km north of Sanandaj; pop. 10,000 in 1914), the centre of the area of Garrus, Mirza Musa, a well-known local preacher, was a Baha'i and quite open in his advocacy of his religion. Eventually, Shaykh Muhammad Hasan, the religious authority (*marja'*) in the area, declared him an apostate (*murtadd*) and he was forced to move to Adharbayjan. A number of other prominent people in the town were also Baha'is, including Darvish Ghulam-'Ali Rawshan (d. 1343/1924), Ahmad Najafiyan, Mirza Muhammad 'Ali Vakil ur-Ru'aya, Na'ib Muhammad Taqi, Yuzbashi Musa and Sharif Mawhibat.[88] Baha'i teachers also came to this town, including Mirza Mahdi Akhavan Safa and Mirza Habibu'llah Samimi in about 1906.[89]

---

81   ZH 8b:721. The names of other Baha'is resident in Kurdistan can be found in a series of letters addressed by 'Abdu'l-Baha to some of the Baha'is of Kurdistan in ILMA 85:26–55.
82   Gail, *Summon Up Remembrance* 89.
83   MH 8:368.
84   Abizadih, Vaqayi' 69.
85   MH 9:104.
86   MH 6:104.
87   ZH 8b:721.
88   ZH 8b:756–7.
89   MH 4:27.

One eminent Baha'i who was a Kurd from the village of Gilih in the district of Marivan (75 km west of Sanandaj) close to the Iraqi border was Shaykh Faraju'llah Zaki al-Kurdi Marivani (d. 1937, see fig. 87). He was the son of the village chief, 'Abdu'r-Rahim, and after studying at Sanandaj and at the A'zamiyyah religious college in Baghdad, he went on to study at the most famous religious college of the Sunni world, al-Azhar in Cairo. Here Shaykh Badru'd-Din introduced him to Mirza Abu'l-Fadl Gulpaygani and he became a Baha'i (as did his brother Shaykh Muhyi'd-Din al-Kurdi). As a result, he was expelled from al-Azhar. He started a bookstore and publishing company in Cairo that published many Baha'i books in Persian and Arabic, as well as many classical Islamic texts.[90]

---

90 Taken from an unpublished article 'The Road to Marivan' by Shaykh Faraju'llah's son-in-law Robert Gulick, Glendale, Arizona, 1970. Al-Kurdi's publishing company was variously called Matba'at us-Sa'adah and Matba'ah Kurdistan al-'Ilmiyyah, and he also sometimes published Baha'i books with his own name as publisher. See also Vejdani, 'Transnational Baha'i Print Culture' 509–10.

15

LURISTAN AND KHUZISTAN

Luristan and Khuzistan ('Arabistan) are the provinces in the southwest corner of Iran, Luristan being to the north of Khuzistan, on the border with Iraq; and 'Arabistan extending south to the head of the Persian Gulf. In ancient times this area was known as Elam and is mentioned in the Bible. Luristan and the eastern part of Khuzistan are mountainous and the tribespeople were mainly nomadic. The western part of Khuzistan forms a large plain at the head of the Persian Gulf.

Luristan

Luristan is a mountainous area south of Hamadan and Kirmanshah and north of Khuzistan. The Lurs are a nomadic tribe, speaking a dialect of Persian, and include the Bakhtiyari, Buyir Ahmad and Mamassani tribes. The closely-related Lak tribe inhabits the western part of the province. In the 19th century most of the rural population followed the Ahl-i Haqq religion. The capital of the area is Khurramabad (pop. 38,700 in 1956).

Vahid Darabi and Siyyid Basir Hindi, a blind Indian Babi, both taught

the Babi religion in Luristan and the latter was killed in this province by
the governor Ildirim Mirza in about 1851.[1] Haji Mirza Haydar 'Ali Isfahani was in Khurramabad for a short time in the 1860s teaching the Baha'i
Faith.[2]

Later, Mirza Abu'l-Qasim Hakim-bashi (his title indicates he was
probably physician to the governor) actively spread the Baha'i Faith and
succeeded in converting a number of people, among them Mirza Baqir
Khan (d. 1317/1899), the secretary (*munshī*) of the governor of Luristan,
Muzaffar ul-Mulk (governed 1881–6, see p. 203). Mirza Baqir Khan was
very open about his new beliefs and this caused the governor to send
someone secretly to his house and take all his papers and books. When
Mirza Baqir Khan returned home and realized what had happened, he
departed immediately for Tehran, on the advice of the Imam-Jum'ih, and
there he eventually became a secretary to the Sahib Divan and later to
Hishmat ud-Dawlih. Another convert was 'Abdu'n-Nabi ibn Azad Khan
(1283/1866– 1354/1935), who was from a leading and wealthy family of
the Lur tribe. But when he became a Baha'i at the age of 16, his mother
and brother deprived him of his inheritance and he was compelled to
leave for Tehran.[3] There was a small Baha'i community in Nahavand (pop.
26452 in 1951, including 2,000 Jews) on the road between Hamadan and
Burujird, with a few Jewish Baha'is, including Hakim Harun.[4] In about
1902 the Baha'i poet Binish Shirazi was in Luristan for a time spreading
the Baha'i Faith.[5]

Burujird

Burujird (140 km south of Hamadan; pop. 22,000 in 1905 and 49,200
in 1956) was a town that specialized in religion. One resident described
the town as consisting of one-third Tabataba'i Sayyids,[6] one-third clerics
and religious students (*ṭullāb*) and one third merchants and others. The
people of the town regarded it as a more important centre of religious

---

1   ZH 3:455–7, 468.
2   MH 1:17.
3   ZH 6:974–5.
4   Rayhani in Amanat, 'Negotiating Identities' 195.
5   Dhuka'i-Bayda'i, *Tadhkirih* 1:230.
6   Tabataba'i sayyids are descendants of Ibrahim at-Tabataba, a fourth-generation
    descendant of the second Shi'i Imam, Hasan.

learning than even Isfahan.[7] Sayyid Yahya Darabi (Vahid), one of the fore-most followers of the Bab, was the son of Sayyid Ja'far Kashfi, one of the prominent religious leaders of Burujird and a cleric of national impor-tance. Sayyid Yahya is stated to have preached the message of the Bab in Burujird between 1846 and 1848.[8]

A small number of Babis lived in Burujird and one of them, a physic-ian, informed Sayyid Jamal (Jamalu'd-Din) Burujirdi (d. 30 May 1911), a member of the important Tabataba'i family of clerics, about the Babi reli-gion, leading to him becoming a Babi in 1863 and then a Baha'i. He was, however, unable to withstand the hostility of his own family and others in Burujird and left for Isfahan and subsequently Tehran (vol. 1:20–5). He had succeeded in converting a few people in Burujird but these appear to have returned to Islam and no lasting community resulted.[9]

Haji Mirza Haydar 'Ali Isfahani spent a short time in Burujird teaching the Baha'i Faith in the 1860s and was thrown into prison in the town.[10] An early Baha'i is reported to have been the *khabbāz-bāshī* (chief baker of the governor).[11] Muhammad Hasan Khan of Kashan was a wealthy, influential man who owned property and held important positions in gov-ernment circles. He had become a Babi in Khurasan in the 1860s while working for the deputy governor Tahmasb Mirza there. Then he came to Burujird with Isma'il Mirza (son of Bahram Mirza) when he became gov-ernor of the town. The latter was a follower of Karim Khan Kirmani, the Shaykhi leader, and was very hostile to the Baha'i Faith. When he found out that Muhammad Hasan Khan was a Baha'i in about 1287/1870, he ordered that he be bastinadoed so severely that he died from the effects.[12] Mirza Husayn Naqqash, who was a native of Burujird, had been a follower of the Shaykhi leader Mirza Muhammad Baqir Hamadani and had been converted to the Baha'i Faith by Haji Mu'nis Qazvini. In 1319/1901 he returned to his home town with his brother-in-law Mirza 'Abdu'l-Husayn

---

7   ZH 8a:176.
8   DB 177, 465.
9   Rayhani reports meeting three of Burujirdi's converts in Tehran who stated that they had given up everything for the Baha'i Faith but, now that Burujirdi had come to Tehran, he would not have anything to do with them and they had rejected religion altogether (Amanat, 'Negotiating Identities' 186). Burujirdi's date of death is given incorrectly in vol. 1:20, 66.
10 Isfahani, *Bihjat* 24; MH 1:17.
11 Hafizi, *Memoirs* 2:116.
12 ZH 5:126.

Vahhaj, who had been converted by Karbala'i Darvish 'Ali Hamadani. They tried to teach the Baha'i Faith but an uproar ensued and they were expelled by the governor Salar ud-Dawlih (see fig. 81).[13]

No real Baha'i community was established in Burujird until about 1328/1910. At this time, Haji 'Abdu'r-Rahim, a merchant of Burujird, travelled to Rasht on business and there met Fadil Mazandarani. He became a Baha'i and returned to Burujird. At the same time, Mirza Ahmad Khan Naraqi, a Baha'i, was posted to Burujird in the government department for controlling opium. These two together managed to convert several others, including the two Avarigan brothers, Sayyid Hasan (1879–1943, see fig. 89) and Sayyid 'Ali Akbar (1881–?), and Mirza Hasan Niku. In 1911 Mirza Muhammad 'Ali Khan Baha'i was appointed to a senior position in the tax office for the Burujird, Nahavand and Malayir area. The clerics became alarmed, hurriedly ordered books from Hamadan and Iraq refuting the Baha'i Faith and set up classes to study them. Shaykh Husayn Najafi organized a large meeting at which many of the clerics of the town were present and Sayyid 'Ali Akbar Avarigan was questioned. The meeting ended in an uproar and the clerics petitioned both the governor and the newly-established Swedish-led gendarmerie to expel the Baha'is from the town, but were refused. For a time the situation eased for the Baha'is and there were regular meetings and many conversions. During the years of World War I, Aqa Husayn Tabataba'i (later known as Ayatu'llah Burujirdi, 1875–1962) returned to the town, having just obtained his certificates of completion of his studies (*ijazihs*) at Najaf. Wanting to make a name for himself, he brought in more than 50 armed Lur tribesmen and forced all the shops in the bazaar to close. He gave an ultimatum to the governor that this would continue until the well-known Baha'is left the town. After a couple of such episodes, the Avarigan brothers and Mirza Ahmad Khan left Burujird.[14]

The above-mentioned Mirza Hasan Niku (1880–Feb. 1963) was from the clerical class and had been a prominent supporter of the Constitutional Revolution. After his conversion in about 1910 he became an eloquent exponent of the Baha'i Faith. His father was a well-known cleric, and when he died in 1914 the other clerics in Burujird wanted to obtain control of

---

13   ZH 7:143–4; Ishraq-Khavari, *Hamadan* 141. In ZH 7:310, a date of 1916 is implied for this episode but this would appear to be incorrect as Abu'l-Fath Mirza Salar ud-Dawlih was governor of Burujird in 1900–6 and by 1916 was in exile.

14   ZH: 8a:174–98; MH 8:349.

the religious endowments (*awqāf*) that his father had controlled. So they accused Mirza Hasan Niku of being a 'Sufi and Babi' and drove him out of the town. He settled first in Sultanabad and then in Tehran. He travelled to India to spread the Baha'i Faith, but reports about his behaviour there caused 'Abdu'l-Baha to direct him to go to Egypt. In about 1922 he returned to Tehran and soon started consorting with Avarih. In about 1926, following Avarih, he left the Baha'i community and published a four-volume attack upon it, *Falsafih-yi Niku* (Tehran, 1927–46).[15]

In October 1917 (Muharram 1336), Aqa Sayyid Ibrahim Khabbaz (baker), who had been a Baha'i for only two years, was summoned to the governor Nusrat us-Sultan Gudarzi and ordered to recant but refused. This incurred the wrath of the governor and other notables of the area such as Dargham Gudarzi and some of the clerics of the town. A short time later he was shot and killed by Asad Husayn Kuhnih as he left

89. Sayyid Hasan Avarigan

his shop at night to return home. His house was then looted. His wife tried to obtain justice but both the government and the clerics refused this to her and even barred her from her inheritance from her husband.[16]

It was during the visit of 'Abdu'llah Mutlaq in 1924 that a local spiritual assembly was established.[17]

Khuzistan ('Arabistan)

This province lies in the southwest corner of Iran. The west of Khuzistan was inhabited by Arab-speaking tribes (and hence often called 'Arabistan) but the people in the east of the province around Bihbihan spoke Persian and Luri and the north was dominated by the Bakhtiyari tribe. During the 20th century with the discovery of oil, an increasing number of people from the rest of Iran moved to this province to work the oilfields. The

---

15 Nushabadi, 'Qa'im-Maqami'. There is a highly distorted biography of Niku by his son Ihsanu'llah Niku at the front of the first volume of *Falsafih-yi Niku* (Tehran: Farahani [1343]) from which one would think he had not been a Baha'i at all.

16 ZH 7:313; 8a:198–9.

17 *Akhbar Amri* year 41, no 7 (Aug. 1962) 342–3.

hot plains at the head of the gulf supported only desert agriculture except immediately around the rivers of the area, the Diz and Karun rivers. Shustar (Shushtar, Tustar, 26 km north of Ahvaz; pop. 15,000 in 1951) was the capital of this province but with increasing navigation on the Karun River as far as Ahvaz (937 km southwest of Tehran; pop. 120,098 in 1956), this city became the capital in 1910.

Being distant from the main centres of Babi activities, there were few converts in Khuzistan, except for Hindijan (also written as Hindiyan, see p. 245), which was sometimes counted as part of Fars and sometimes as part of Khuzistan. Mulla Hasan Khaza'i owned land in the village of Zaytan. He became a Babi and later a Baha'i. He moved to the village of Manyuha (25 km southeast of Abadan) where he succeeded in converting some 12 others. In 1314/1897 the Baha'is were persecuted and Mulla Hasan Khaza'i was arrested and imprisoned. He was eventually released on the intervention of his son-in-law. Sultan Muhammad Khan Abu'l-Virdi Shirazi, a Baha'i, moved to Ahvaz and became a confidant of Shaykh Khaz'al, the hereditary ruler of this province.[18]

Bihbihan

Bihbihan (349 km southeast of Ahvaz; pop. 24,000 in 1951) is a town situated only some 50 kilometres from the waters of the Gulf. Haji Mirza Haydar 'Ali Isfahani records staying in Bihbihan for six months in the 1860s. He says that he had hopes of being able to teach the Baha'i Faith there because there were a large number of Shaykhis in the town and he himself had originally been a Shaykhi. He managed to convert some Shaykhis and Sufis at this time including the son of the *kalantar* of the town but was then arrested, imprisoned and expelled.[19]

Tribes

There were no Baha'is among the tribespeople of this province until the time of 'Abdu'l-Baha. Then some conversions began to occur among the Buyir Ahmad tribe in the east of the Kuhkiluyih district, north of the town of Bihbihan. Once they had become Baha'is, they declined to arm themselves as the other tribespeople did and so were subjected to much harassment

---

18   ZH 6:137, 8a:263.
19   Isfahani, *Bihjat* 25.

90. Shaykh Salman (*right*) and
Abu'l-Hasan Bazzaz Shirazi (*left*).
The man standing in the middle
is not identified

from other tribespeople in the area. On one occasion, for example, a group
of tribespeople led by one of the notables of the area, who was related to
Sayyid Muhammad Ravanbakhsh, the chairman of the Baha'i Local Spiritual Assembly of Kata, attacked the Baha'is who were forced to flee into the
woods while their houses were looted. They appealed to the local government authorities in Bihbihan but were unable to obtain any justice.[20]

Among those Baha'is who either travelled to or migrated to Bihbihan
and the Kuhkiluyih district to spread the Baha'i Faith in the early years of
the 20th century were 'Abbas 'Ali Binish of Shiraz[21] and Mirza Fadlu'llah
Paymani of Nayriz.[22] According to Fadil Mazandarani who was writing in
the late 1930s, the number of Baha'is among the Buyir Ahmad tribe had
reached about 400, most of whom were farmers and herders, including
131 Baha'is in Kata (pop. 250 in 1951), 25 in Talkhab, 60 in Varih-Shur,
70 in Murgh-Char, and 40 in Katak.[23]

Hindijan area

Hindijan (or Hindiyan) is situated on the Hindiyan or Zuhra river and is
some 140 kilometres east of Khurramshahr and about the same distance

---

20   ZH 8a:146–7.
21   Dhuka'i-Bayda'i, *Tadhkirih* 1:230.
22   Rawhani, *Lama'at* 274.
23   ZH 8a:146–7.

southeast of Ahvaz (pop. 2,830 in 1951). Its people are mainly Arab-speaking but with Persian and Lur-speakers as well. From this area, Shaykh Salman (d. 1316/1898, his original name was Shaykh Khanjar, see fig. 90) had gone to investigate the religion of the Bab, returned and converted some 70 families of his tribe, the Afshars, living in the villages around Hindijan. Later, one of the Babis, Mulla Husayn Hindijani put forward a claim to leadership of the Babi community and gathered around himself some 40 disciples.[24] He then went to Basra and met Sayyid Muhammad Isfahani, Azal's associate. Through this link the majority of the Babis of the Hindijan area either became Azalis or remained Babis. However, Shaykh Salman travelled to Baghdad and became attached to Baha'u'llah. The other Babis in the Hindijan area attacked him for this and he was forced to leave the area. Most of the Azali and Babis of the area came under persecution from the clerics of the area and returned to Islam, although a few remained Babis up to recent times. Shaykh Salman returned to the area and succeeded in persuading some of them to become Baha'is. Shaykh Salman became an important figure in Baha'i history being Baha'u'llah's main courier between himself and the Baha'is of Iran from about 1853 to 1891, making annual journeys for this purpose. In the course of his journeys around Iran, during which he both distributed the tablets of Baha'u'llah for their intended recipients and picked up letters to Baha'u'llah, he was also given other tasks to perform by Baha'u'llah. Among his important tasks was to bring Munirih Khanum, the future wife of 'Abdu'l-Baha, to 'Akka. He was given the title 'the trustworthy courier' (*payk-i amin*).[25] 'Abdu'l-Baha described him thus:

> He had remarkable powers of endurance. He travelled on foot, as a rule eating nothing but onions and bread; and in all that time, he moved about in such a way that he was never once held up and never once lost a letter or a Tablet. Every letter was safely delivered; every Tablet reached its intended recipient.[26]

---

24   Azal, as cited by Browne in ['Abdu'l-Baha], *Traveller's Narrative* 2:331; Sayyid Mahdi Dahaji states that this man claimed leadership but not that he was 'He whom God shall make manifest' ('Risalih,' Browne manuscripts F.57, Cambridge University Library, p. 95). Dihaji is also insistent on correcting Browne's error in calling this man Sayyid Husayn.

25   ZH 6:888–91; Ishraq-Khavari, *Muhadarat* 2:1042–4; Muhammad-Husayni, *Tarikh* 62–7; 'Abdu'l-Baha, *Memorials* 13–16.

26   'Abdu'l-Baha, *Memorials* 15.

The work of Shaykh Salman in spreading the Baha'i Faith in this area was continued by a number of other Baha'i teachers, in particular Aqa Mirza Yahya Nuri Isfahani (d. 1341/1922), a physician whom Shaykh Salman persuaded to move to the area and settle. As a result of these activities, there was soon a flourishing Baha'i community. In 1905 Mirza Jalal, one of the Baha'is of the area, returned from visiting 'Abdu'l-Baha in 'Akka, bringing with him tablets for the other Baha'is of the area. This matter became well-known locally and the notables of the area complained to the governor. Mirza Jalal was arrested and his property looted. From the papers in his possession the identity of the other local Baha'is became known. The townspeople then wanted to arrest and loot the property of all the Baha'is. The Baha'is decided to defend themselves and gathered in one place. However, seeing that they would be unlikely to succeed, they took their families and livestock to a hill where they put up fortifications and successfully defended themselves. Eventually they sent a telegram to the governor of the province of 'Arabistan and obtained a decree for the release of Mirza Jalal and the safe return home for the Baha'is.[27]

The Baha'is were to be found not so much in Hindijan itself but in the smaller villages to the north, such as Safa'iyyih (20 km north of Hindijan; pop. 100 in 1951), Fili (2 km northwest of Safa'iyyih; pop. 50 in 1951), Chamtang (15 km north of Hindijan; pop. 240 in 1951), Chamtangu (15 km northeast of Hindijan; pop. 30 in 1951), Darihak (the home village of Shaykh Salman, 5 km northwest of Safa'iyyih; pop. 450 in 1951) and Jabrabad (8 km north of Hindijan; pop. 140 in 1951). The first four of these were either all Baha'i or mostly Baha'i villages. Fadil Mazandarani reports that there were two local assemblies and about 250 Baha'is in this area in the time of 'Abdu'l-Baha, but he may have been referring just to adult Baha'is.[28] In Safa'iyyih, a Baha'i school was established and a teacher called Mr Kuchiktan was recruited to teach. In the 1930s the school had six primary classes and about 30 pupils, some coming from Fili and a few being Muslims. At this time the village of Safa'iyyih had about 200 Baha'is.[29]

27 ZH 7:243–4.
28 *Asrar* 5:273; Interview Mr Hassan Songhorabadi in Luton on 19 June 2010.
29 Interview Mr Hassan Songhorabadi in Luton on 23 June 2010.

16

FARS

Fars is the principal province of southwest Iran. The west side of the province is taken up with the southern end of the Zagros mountains and is the domain of the large and powerful Turkish-speaking Qashqa'i tribe. In the eastern half of the province a tribal confederation called the Khamsih was formed by the government in 1861, mainly to counterbalance the strength of the Qashqa'is. In the south, the Zagros mountains fall away to a plain which is the coast of the Persian Gulf. The province is very dry, especially in its eastern half, but agriculture is possible with the help of irrigation, and cereals, vines, cotton, opium, grains and fruit were grown.

Shiraz

The capital of the province of Fars is Shiraz, the native city of the Bab and also of many famous poets, mystics and philosophers, such as Hafiz, Sa'di and Mulla Sadra. This city was for a brief time in the 18th century the capital of the founder of the Zand dynasty, Karim Khan Vakil, who built many of the large public buildings of the present city. It is situated on what became a main trade route of Iran in the 19th century, 935 kilometres south of Tehran, 500 kilometres south of Isfahan and 300 kilometres northeast of Bushihr. Its population was estimated at 35,000 to 40,000 (including about 2,000 Jews) in 1850.[1] According to a census carried out in about 1885, it had a population of 53,607 (25,284 males,

---

1   Abbot in Amanat, *Cities and Trade* 175; the report states 400–500 families of Jews, from which I have estimated 2,000 people. Thompson (1868) estimated the population of Shiraz as 25,000 with 1,500 Jews (in Issawi, *Economic History* 28, 32).

28,323 females),[2] although most estimates from the second half of the 19th century give lower figures (20,000 to 25,000);[3] it was estimated to have a population of 60,000 in 1905 and had 170,660 in the 1956 census. Shiraz was notorious for its faction-fighting, which occurred more frequently here than in other towns.[4] On certain days of the year it was customary for the *pahlavans* (champions) and members of the *zur-khanihs* (gymnasia) of each faction to lead the men of that quarter out into the streets and do battle with the rival faction. The quarters of the town were divided into two factions: five Ni'mati quarters (in the south and west of the city) and five Haydari quarters (in the north and east), with Jewish and Armenian quarters that were not counted as either.[5] The city was famous for its textiles and crafts, especially silver and inlaid work.

The main source for the history of the Baha'i Faith in Shiraz is the account written by Mirza Habibu'llah Afnan. It was prepared in response to the general request that went out in the 1920s from Shoghi Effendi through the Central Spiritual Assembly (Tehran) for a recording of local Baha'i histories. The Local Spiritual Assembly of the Baha'is of Shiraz asked Mirza Habibu'llah Afnan to prepare a history for Shiraz and Fars. His chronicle covers events up to 1909.

Shiraz witnessed the birth of the Babi movement. The Bab was born and brought up in the city. He first announced his mission to Mulla Husayn Bushru'i here on the eve of 23 May 1844, the event which both Babis and Baha'is looked to as the start of their calendar. The first disciples of the Bab, the Letters of the Living, gathered in Shiraz in the summer of 1844 until they were sent out by the Bab to spread the news of his claim. The Bab himself left on pilgrimage to Mecca on 10 September 1844 (26 Sha'ban 1260), returning to Bushihr on 15 May 1845. He then sent ahead of him his leading disciple, Quddus, who brought to Shiraz the Bab's instruction that there was to be an addition made to the call to prayer (*adhān*). When Mulla Sadiq Muqaddas tried to carry this out, he, Quddus, Mulla 'Ali Akbar Ardistani and Mulla Abu Talib were seized, severely beaten and expelled from the city (see fig. 92).[6]

2   Fasa'i, *Fars-Namih* 22.
3   Bémont, *Villes* 2:152.
4   Abbot reported weekly clashes in 1850 (Amanat, *Cities and Trade* 88, 175–6).
5   Fasa'i, *Fars-Namih* 22.
6   Although the account by Nabil (DB 145–6) states that only two Babis were punished and expelled from the city and Balyuzi (*The Bab* 77–8) reports three; a report of this episode that appeared in *The Times* of London on 1 Nov. 1845 (see

92. Report in *The Times* newspaper (1 November 1845, p. 4, col. 3) of the arrest and expulsion from Shiraz of four disciples of the Bab, the first published report of the Bab and the Babi movement.

The governor of Shiraz, Husayn Khan Ajudan-bashi, sent for the Bab in Bushihr and he was arrested on the Bushihr to Shiraz road. Back in Shiraz in June 1845, the Bab was set free, with his uncle Haji Sayyid 'Ali as guarantor. After a short time he was summoned to the Masjid-i Vakil, the principal mosque in Shiraz, to make a public recantation. His words on that occasion were sufficient to satisfy the authorities but he did not say

fig. 92) states that there were four Babis involved (BBR 69–70) and Hamadani (*Tarikh-i-Jadid* 202) names the fourth individual.

anything that would contradict his later full claim to be a Manifestation of God. In any case, it must have been a strange sort of recantation, since a considerable number of the Babis of Shiraz date their conversion from hearing the Bab on that day.[7] From further afield, a number of others who had heard of his claims came to investigate. Among the most important of these were Sayyid Yahya Darabi Vahid, who was asked by Muhammad Shah to investigate the matter; and the representative of Mulla Muhammad 'Ali Hujjat, one of the religious leaders of Zanjan. Both became Babis. On 23 September 1845 the Bab was re-arrested on the orders of the governor but, owing to an outbreak of cholera in the city, he was able to leave for Isfahan. After the departure of the Bab, his family members were persecuted by the authorities, despite the fact that none of them, except his wife, were Babis, while the Babi community kept a low profile.[8]

Matters were made much worse by the Babi upheaval in the town of Nayriz in 1850, which recurred in 1853. Following each of these two episodes a number of the Babis of Nayriz were brought as prisoners to Shiraz, and some of their womenfolk and children remained there. Also, after the Babi upheaval in Zanjan, the family of Hujjat, the Babi leader there, was brought to Shiraz and housed with a local dignitary, Abu'l-Hasan Khan Mushir ul-Mulk. After the attempt on the life of the shah in 1852, Aqa Muhammad Hadi Isfahani, a resident of Yazd who had fled to Shiraz after his father's house had been looted as a punishment for being one of the Babi companions of Vahid, was arrested and executed by the governor.[9]

The Afnan family

Among the prominent Baha'is of Shiraz were the members of the Bab's own maternal family, who took on the name given to them by Baha'u'llah, the Afnans. The Afnan family are the descendants of the three maternal uncles of the Bab: Haji Sayyid Muhammad (d. 1293/1876), who was an important merchant in Shiraz and Bushihr; Haji Sayyid 'Ali (1212/1797–executed 1850), who lived in Shiraz and whose only son died young; and Haji Mirza Hasan 'Ali, who lived in Yazd. The wife of the Bab, Khadijih

---

7   Afnan, *Ahd-i A'la* 164–9, 572–3.
8   On the period of the Bab in Shiraz, see Afnan, Tarikh 1–115 (trans. in Rabbani, 'The Bab in Shiraz' and *Genesis* 3–48); Afnan, *Ahd-i A'la* 29–71, 116–55; DB 50–96, 142–98; Amanat, *Resurrection* 109–254; Balyuzi, *The Bab* 15–39, 46–7, 76–105.
9   ZH 4:88.

93. Aqa Mirza Aqa Nuru'd-Din Afnan

Bigum, was his mother's paternal cousin and the Afnan family includes the descendants of Khadijih Bigum's two brothers and one sister: Haji Mirza Sayyid Hasan Afnan-i Kabir (c. 1810–1310/1892, see pp. 356–7 and fig. 134), who lived in Yazd and later in Beirut and 'Akka; Haji Mirza Abu'l-Qasim Saqqa-khanihi (1811–18 Nov. 1887, see fig. 105), an important merchant of Shiraz; and their sister Zahra Bigum (d. 11 Oct. 1889), who was married to a cousin of the Bab's father. The family was based in the Bazar-i Murgh quarter of Shiraz.[10]

Khadijih Bigum had been a follower of her husband and subsequently became a Baha'i. She was the only member of the family who was a Babi in the early 1850s. She then succeeded in converting, in about 1854, Aqa Mirza Aqa (c. 1842–20 Nov. 1903, see figs. 93 and 105), the 12-year-old son of her sister Zahra Bigum. His given name was Muhammad and he was named Nuru'd-Din by Baha'u'llah.[11] His home in Shiraz was, in later years, to become a major centre of Baha'i activities and the place where travelling Baha'i teachers would stay. His mother and father were the next to be converted.[12]

After the conversion of his own family in the late 1850s, Aqa Mirza Aqa set about trying to convince Haji Sayyid Muhammad, the uncle of the Bab, the senior member of the family, who protested that it seemed to him unlikely that the promised Qa'im had been his nephew. Aqa Mirza Aqa politely pointed out to him that his words were the exact ones used by Abu Lahab, the uncle of the Prophet Muhammad. Taken aback by this, Haji Sayyid Muhammad agreed to travel to Baghdad (on the pretext of a

---

10   Fasa'i, *Fars-namih* 2:45. Details of members of the Afnan family can be found in Faizi, *Khandan Afnan* and Shahidiyan, *Mansuban*.

11   See also Balyuzi, *Eminent Baha'is* 216–36.

12   Afnan, Tarikh 153–7 (trans. in Rabbani, *Genesis* 65–7); Faizi, *Khandan Afnan* 197–200.

pilgrimage to the shrines in Iraq and a meeting
with his sister, the mother of the Bab, who had
taken up residence in Iraq) to meet Baha'u'llah,
a trip which was undertaken in early 1861. Haji
Sayyid Muhammad returned from the journey
a convinced Babi (although his younger brother
Haji Mirza Hasan 'Ali, a resident of Yazd,
who had accompanied him, refused to meet
Baha'u'llah and was not converted at this time),
bringing with him Baha'u'llah's Kitab-i Iqan,
which had been written in answer to his questions. After this, Aqa Mirza Aqa concentrated

94. Haji Mirza Muhammad
'Ali Afnan

on the younger generation of the family. Haji Mirza Muhammad 'Ali
(1240 /1824–96, see fig. 94) and Haji Mirza Muhammad Taqi (Vakil ud-
Dawlih, see pp. 354–8 and fig. 133), the sons of Haji Sayyid Muhammad,
and Haj Sayyid Ja'far and Haj Sayyid Mahdi, the sons of Haji Mirza Hasan
'Ali, went to Baghdad and met Baha'u'llah, as a result of which they were
converted.[13] Next to be converted were two of the sons of Saqqa-khanihi,
the brother of the wife of the Bab: Aqa Sayyid [Muhammad] Husayn (see
fig. 105) and Mirza Abu'l-Hasan (see fig. 105).

The Afnans were an important family of wholesale merchants (*tujjār*) in
Shiraz and members of the family were spread widely to form an extensive
international trading network. Family members were stationed at Bushihr
(Haji Sayyid Muhammad, the maternal uncle of the Bab); Yazd (Haji
Mirza Hasan 'Ali; Haji Mirza Sayyid Hasan Afnan-i Kabir; and Haji Mirza
Muhammad Taqi Vakil ud-Dawlih, son of Haji Sayyid Muhammad);
Bandar 'Abbas (Mirza 'Ali, son of Saqqa-khanihi); Tehran (Haji Mirza
Sayyid Muhammad, son of Vakil ud-Dawlih, from 1311/1893); Shanghai
(Haji Sayyid Muhammad 'Ali, son of Haji Sayyid Muhammad; and Mirza
Ibrahim, son of Saqqa-khanihi); Beirut (Afnan-i Kabir and his sons);
Istanbul (Aqa Sayyid Ahmad, son of Afnan-i Kabir); Alexandria and Port
Sa'id (Aqa Mirza Aqa Nuru'd-Din, son of Zahra Bigum; and his sons, c.
1888 onwards, see figs. 93 and 105); Ashkhabad (Aqa Sayyid Ahmad, son

---

13   Afnan, Tarikh 1–115 (trans. in Rabbani, *Genesis* 67–70). According to ZH
     4:222, these four were the first to be converted by Baha'u'llah in Baghdad (on
     their way back from Mecca) in 1859 and they returned to Shiraz and persuaded
     Haji Sayyid Muhammad to meet Baha'u'llah in Baghdad. See also Rabbani,
     'Conversion'.

of Afnan-i Kabir; Vakil ud-Dawlih and his son, Haji Mirza Mahmud and others); and Bombay (Haji Sayyid Mirza and Sayyid Muhammad, sons of Afnan-i Kabir); Haji Sayyid Mahmud, son of Vakil ud-Dawlih; and Mirza Ibrahim, son of Saqqa-khanihi and other members of the family for varying lengths of time). In Bombay, the family set up a company of general merchants and commission agents under the company name of Messrs Haji Sayed Mirza and Mirza Mahmood Co. Also associated with this Afnan network were other Baha'i merchants, such as the two brothers Mirza Hasan and Mirza Husayn Nahri (see p. 20) in Isfahan, 'Ali Haydar Shirvani (vol. 1:52) in Tehran, and Haji Ghulam-Husayn Tajir Yazdi in Mashhad. Through this network they imported sugar from Russia, tea from India and porcelain from China. They exported tea to Central Asia and were also involved in exporting opium from Iran to India and China[14] until Baha'u'llah forbade it. They suffered some losses as a result of this but there were other factors creating an unfavourable trading environment. The European powers had arranged favourable terms for their merchants, which together with the fact that these merchants did not face the same extortions and corruption that Iranian merchants faced from governors and government officials, meant that Iranian merchants were increasingly unable to compete with the large European trading houses.[15] Therefore, the Afnan family, alongside many other merchant families in the 1870s, diversified into purchasing large estates in areas such as Istahbanat, either farming this themselves or becoming landlords.[16]

In 1891 the Afnan trading empire suffered a reverse. The false accusations of Muhammad 'Ali Isfahani, an Azali in Istanbul, led Shaykh Muhammad 'Ali Qazvini to commit suicide there in April 1891. Despite the fact that the accusations had been proved false to the satisfaction of the Iranian ambassador, Mirza Muhammad 'Ali Isfahani now accused Sayyid Ahmad Afnan of stealing papers and money from his office. The latter had already left for Beirut, so Isfahani sent the accusations on to there and broadcast them throughout Istanbul. Sayyid Ahmad returned to Istanbul and again proved the falsity of the accusation but the rumours had had their effect.

---

14 Faizi, *Khandan Afnan* 95; Mirza Sayyid Muhammad, the son of Haji Mirza Muhammad 'Ali, resident in Shiraz, was known as Mirza Aqa Taryaki – *taryak* being Persian for opium. See also Fasa'i, *Fars-namih* 2:45, where it is stated that most of the trade in opium from Isfahan, Yazd and Fars that went to China went through Haji Mirza Muhammad 'Ali Afnan in Hong Kong.

15 Floor, 'Merchants' 113.

16 Fasa'i, *Fars-namih* 2:45; Floor, 'Merchants' 112–14.

The Afnans' promissory notes were not accepted and their debtors recalled their debts, resulting in a collapse in confidence in the Afnan trading establishment and, effectively, bankruptcy. Various members of the family, such as Sayyid 'Ali, Haji Sayyid Mirza and Sayyid Muhammad, hurriedly sold property so as to recapitalize the business but it never regained the prestige that it had had. This sudden reversal of fortune had severe effects on the finances of the Baha'i community also, as the trading empire had been one way in which funds were transferred from Iran to 'Akka.[17]

Apart from the importance to Baha'u'llah of the adherence of these close relatives of the Bab, the Afnan family was important for the local prestige that it brought to the Baha'i community in cities such as Shiraz and Yazd, where, as a major wholesale merchant family, its members were among the notables of each city. Because of this, they were able to be of considerable assistance to the Baha'is, protecting some from persecution, assisting those who were poor or who had lost everything in the persecutions, giving employment to some (at least one of the Nayriz women Babis who came to Shiraz destitute found employment in the home of the Afnans[18]), providing some of the Baha'i retail merchants in the bazaar with capital or favourable terms (when Haji Abu'l-Hasan Bazzaz returned to Shiraz having had to leave after the 1283/1866 persecution, Aqa Mirza Aqa gave him a small shop in the bazaar and some capital to make a fresh start[19]), financing and accommodating travelling Baha'i teachers to come to Shiraz, making available large homes and gardens where the Baha'i community could meet and otherwise supporting the Baha'i Faith financially. They were careful, however, to protect their public image and to fend off the frequent accusations that were directed towards them by the more fanatical elements of the population. They would sponsor *rawdih-khanis* (recitations of the sufferings of the Imams) and *dastihs* (groups performing ritual mourning processions) and made generous donations to the coffers of the leading clerics in their quarter of the city.

Individual members of the Afnan family were also responsible for significant projects such as the building of the first house of worship in the Baha'i world in Ashkhabad and the establishment of the first Baha'i printing and publishing company, the Nasiri Press, which was established in Bombay and began to publish Baha'i books from about 1882 onwards. Aqa

---

17   Oral information from Mr Abu'l-Qasim Afnan in 1995.
18   Afnan, Tarikh 195 (*Genesis* 83).
19   Afnan, Tarikh 216–17 (*Genesis* 89).

Mirza [Muhammad] Hadi (1873–1955, see figs. 95 and 105), the son of Aqa Sayyid [Muhammad] Husayn (see fig. 105) and grandson of Saqqa-khanihi (see fig. 105), left Shiraz in 1316/1898 for 'Akka, where he married Diya'iyyih Khanum, the eldest daughter of 'Abdu'l-Baha, and became the father of Shoghi Effendi. A daughter of Saqqa-khanihi, Fatimih Sultan Bigum, became the mother of Muvaqqar ud-Dawlih, who was the father of the Hand of the Cause Mr Hasan Balyuzi; while another son of Saqqa-khanihi, Mirza Abu'l-Hasan (see fig. 105), had a daughter, Khadijih Khanum (Munavvar Khanum), who became the mother of Mr Hasan Balyuzi.

The claim of Baha'u'llah

Although Baha'u'llah was, before his open declaration, held in high regard in Shiraz as a result of the Kitab-i-Iqan, which was widely circulated among the Babis,[20] Sayyid 'Abdu'r-Rahim Isfahani, who had met Baha'u'llah in Baghdad, reports that when he raised the possibility that Baha'u'llah might be the one promised by the Bab ('He whom God shall make manifest') at a meeting of the Shiraz Babis held in the home of Aqa Mirza Aqa Rikab-saz, this was such a heresy in the estimation of his audience that he was physically attacked and had to be shielded by his host.[21] The first to bring the news of Baha'u'llah's claim to Shiraz was Nabil Zarandi in the autumn of 1866.[22] He stayed with Aqa Mirza Aqa Nuru'd-Din Afnan, whose son records that his father told him that one day Nabil asked Aqa Mirza Aqa to convene a gathering of all the Babis of the town and for them to bring whatever they had in the way of Babi writings. They met at the house of Mirza 'Abdu'l-Karim Kilid-dar (the key-holder, so called because he was the custodian of the Shrine of Shah Chiragh). After tea Nabil looked at all the writings they had brought and divided them into three piles. Then he addressed the gathering, lifting one pile and saying that these are the writings of the Bab. He put down that pile respectfully and lifted another pile, the writings of Baha'u'llah, saying that these are the writings of 'He whom God shall make manifest'. He proceeded to quote verses from the writings of the Bab saying that 'He whom God shall make manifest' would come soon and should be accepted by all Babis, while those who opposed him were only fit for hellfire. And as he said this, he lifted the third pile, probably

---

20   Afnan, Tarikh 164–5 (*Genesis* 69–70).
21   Anon., Tarikh Amri Isfahan 8; Rahmani Najafabadi, 'Sharh Ahval' 71.
22   Rafati, 'Nabil' 35–6; ZH 6:571–2, 855.

the writings of Azal, and said that therefore this third pile was fit only for the fire and then threw them into the fire (cf. his action in Mashhad, vol. 1:123). This caused an uproar in the room. Sayyid Muhammad the uncle of the Bab was furious and leapt to his feet, shouting, 'What sort of game are you playing? What is this all about? Do you think faith is like clover that you harvest one day and it grows again overnight?' Aqa Mirza Aqa calmed him down, saying that there must be good reason for Nabil's action and that Sayyid Muhammad had himself at first rejected the Bab until Baha'u'llah had produced the Kitab-i Iqan for him. It was agreed that this was a matter that required more study and consideration, and the meeting dispersed.[23]

Nabil left Shiraz after this meeting but Khadijih Bigum, the wife of the Bab, and Aqa Mirza Aqa accepted Baha'u'llah's claim immediately, while some of the family, such as Haji Sayyid Muhammad, took a little more persuading. In the same year, Haji Muhammad Ibrahim Muballigh (see fig. 135), who was related by marriage to the family and resident in Yazd, visited Shiraz, at which time he succeeded in converting all the remaining members of the Afnan family in Shiraz, except Haji Mirza Abu'l-Qasim Saqqa-khanihi, the brother of the wife of the Bab. During the visit of Haji Muhammad Ibrahim Muballigh to Shiraz, apart from members of the Afnan family, some 50 to 60 members of the Khayyat (tailor) clan originally from Kazirun were also converted. This led to an uproar in the town and Haji Muhammad Ibrahim had to depart, returning to Yazd, where he converted other members of the Afnan family (see pp. 356–7).[24]

After a spending a year in Yazd, Nabil Akbar came to Shiraz and stayed for 13 months, leading to further conversions, including Saqqa-khanihi.[25] The last of the Afnan family to convert was the mother of the Bab, who became a Baha'i in Karbala where she was living, shortly before her death in 1299/1881.[26]

The family of Hujjat Zanjani also converted and it was not long before

---

23 Afnan, Tarikh 168–74 (Genesis 71–4); the account of Nabil in Shiraz in MH 10:613–15 is not so dramatic.
24 Afnan, Tarikh 179–81 (Genesis 76–7); Balyuzi, Eminent Baha'is 224, indicates that the Khayyat clan became Baha'is as a result of the efforts of Aqa Mirza Aqa Nuru'd-Din, while family tradition holds that they first became attracted to the religion when they saw the Bab's address in the Masjid-i Vakil and were converted to the Baha'i Faith by Nabil in 1866 (email correspondence with Fariba Nadimi, 27 Nov., 14 Dec. 2015 and 8 Jan. 2016).
25 Afnan, Tarikh 184 (Genesis 79).
26 Faizi, Khandan Afnan 20–4; Shahidiyan, Mansuban 18–21.

95. Photograph taken in Haifa-'Akka area in about 1900. *Sitting, left to right:* Mirza Mahmud
Kashani, 'Abdu'r-Ra'uf (son of Mirza Muhammad-Quli), Mirza Muhsin Afnan, Mirza Hadi
Afnan (father of Shoghi Effendi), Zayn ul-Muqarrabin. *Standing, left to right:* Haji Mirza
Haydar 'Ali Isfahani, Jamal Effendi, Mirza Abu'l-Qasim Nazir Isfahani, Mishkin Qalam, Aqa
Rida Qannad Shirazi, Mirza Ja'far

all the Babis in Shiraz had become Baha'is. Only a certain Shaykh Muhammad Yazdi clung to Azal (although he had previously been a supporter
of Baha'u'llah), and he faced such hostility that he left for Yazd (see p.
352).[27] It is clear from the names of Baha'is given by Mazandarani that
many of the Baha'is of Shiraz were from among the retailers and artisans of
the bazaar. Among these names, designations such as *bazzāz* (cloth-seller),
khayyāt (tailor) and *'abā-dūz* (cloak-maker) indicate this.[28]

While visiting Shiraz from Yazd in 1298/1881, Sayyid 'Ali (see fig. 105),
the son of Afnan-i Kabir, asked his aunt, Khadijih Bigum, to arrange for
his marriage to Furughiyyih, a daughter of Baha'u'llah. Khadijih Bigum
agreed to do this on condition that, if successful, Sayyid 'Ali take her with
him to 'Akka – she longed to go and it was not possible for a woman to
make such a long journey without a male relative as escort. Although she

27   Afnan, Tarikh 174–7 (*Genesis* 74–5).
28   ZH 6:855–6, 861; see discussion of this in Cole, 'Religious Dissidence and
      Urban Leadership'.

was successful in arranging the marriage, Sayyid 'Ali let down his aunt and went off from Yazd for 'Akka via Ashkhabad, leaving her behind in Shiraz. She died shortly afterwards on 29 Dhu'l-Hijjih 1299/11 November 1882.[29] Sayyid 'Ali's marriage to Furughiyyih occurred in 1886 and his brother, Mirza Muhsin (1863–1927, see fig. 95), married Tuba Khanum (d. 16 Aug. 1959), the daughter of 'Abdu'l-Baha, in 1889.[30]

There were also a number of prominent Baha'is of Shiraz who resided outside Iran. Aqa [Muhammad] Rida Qannad Shirazi (d. 1912, see fig. 95) left Shiraz after the earthquake there in 1850 and settled in Karbala, becoming apprenticed to a confectioner (*qannād*). Through a fellow confectioner, Aqa Muhammad Husayn Qannad Isfahani, and a fellow Shirazi, Aqa Muhammad Karim Tajir, he became a Babi. He opened a small confectioner's shop with a fellow Babi, Mirza Mahmud Kashani (see fig. 95), and the two became like brothers. They accompanied Baha'u'llah on each stage of his exile and Aqa Rida became the steward of the households of Baha'u'llah and 'Abdu'l-Baha. Aqa Rida's son, Mirza Habibu'llah ('Ayn ul-Mulk), was educated in Paris at 'Abdu'l-Baha's expense and was at first an active Baha'i but later in life married a Muslim lady and pursued a diplomatic and political career that took him away from the Baha'i Faith. His son Amir-'Abbas Huvayda (Hoveyda) had no links to the Baha'i Faith but pursued a political career that culminated in him becoming prime minister of Iran in 1965 for 12 years.

The house of the Bab in Shiraz

Khadijih Bigum, the wife of the Bab, her sister and her sister's family remained very close over the years and were all involved in the fate of the house of the Bab in Shiraz, which Baha'u'llah came to designate as a place of pilgrimage. After the execution of the Bab in 1850, the mother of the Bab, who had lived in the house of the Bab in Shiraz, retired to Karbala, while Khadijih Bigum had felt unable to live in the house and had moved to the house of her half-sister, who was the wife of Haji Sayyid 'Ali, the executed uncle of the Bab. The house of the Bab had been put in the care

---

29 Afnan, Tarikh 235–41 (*Genesis* 96–8); Balyuzi, *Khadijih Bagum* 34–5; Ishraq-Khavari, *Rahiq-i Makhtum* 1:339–46.

30 The children of both these marriages failed to accept the authority of Shoghi Effendi and were expelled from the Baha'i community. Earlier, Sayyid 'Ali and Furughiyyih had sided with Mirza Muhammad 'Ali and were expelled by 'Abdu'l-Baha.

of a Muslim who had effectively taken possession of it and sold it on to someone else. As a result of this and of earthquake damage, the house of Bab had fallen into disrepair. Haji Sayyid Muhammad was persuaded by Aqa Mirza Aqa Nuru'd-Din Afnan, then still a boy, to reacquire the house and repair it. There was then a succession of Baha'i caretakers: 'Abdu'r-Razzaq, then Haji Abu'l-Hasan Bazzaz and then Mulla Aqa Buzurg Zarqani. During this time there were further earthquakes in Shiraz and the house suffered further damage.[31]

When in 1288/1871 Munirih Khanum, who was to become the wife of 'Abdu'l-Baha, was proceeding to 'Akka, she spent 15 days in the company of Khadijih Bigum in Shiraz. At this time, the latter sent a request to Baha'u'llah that the house of the Bab be repaired so that she could live there again. Baha'u'llah gave instructions that the house should be repaired in accordance with Khadijih Bigum's wishes. Since Khadijih Bigum could not bear to have the house exactly as it had been in the time of the Bab, considerable alterations were made in the course of the repair. This repair work was finished by 1290/1873. However, all the activity and the re-occupation of the house aroused hostile elements in the population and they reported this to the governor Farhad Mirza Mu'tamad ud-Dawlih. Two of the retinue of the governor, Abu'l-Hasan Khan Munshi-bashi and Mirza Zaynu'l-'Abidin Khan 'Aliyabadi, were Baha'is and brought news of this to the Baha'i community, whereupon it was decided that the house should be left untenanted for a few months until the commotion died down.[32]

After the death of Khadijih Bigum in 1882, her sister Zahra Bigum moved into the house. In 1302/1884 Baha'u'llah gave the custodianship of the house of the Bab to Zahra Bigum and her descendants.[33] Zahra Bigum lived in the house of the Bab for seven years until her own death in 1889. At that time Baha'u'llah summoned her son, Aqa Mirza Aqa Nuru'd-Din, who had left Shiraz in 1879 (see p. 267), had resided in Bombay for some years and then moved to Egypt (at first in Cairo and then in Port Sa'id) to come to 'Akka. Aqa Mirza Aqa called for his family to come from Shiraz, leaving behind his second son, Mirza Jalal, to look after the house of the Bab. They left from Port Sa'id for 'Akka on 24 Safar 1308/9 October

31   Faizi, *Khandan* 204–6.
32   Afnan, Tarikh 225–30 (*Genesis* 93–4); Faizi, *Khandan* 206–7.
33   Afnan, Tarikh 252–4 (*Genesis* 103). For the tablet of Baha'u'llah making this appointment, see Afnan, Tarikh 253 (*Genesis* 103); Faizi, *Khandan* 203.

1890.[34] In late 1311/early 1894, Aqa Mirza Aqa returned to Shiraz via Iraq, where he met with Mirza Hasan Shirazi (Mirza-yi Shirazi, 1815–95), the foremost Shi'i religious leader of the time, who was a paternal relative.[35]

Shortly after his return to Shiraz, Aqa Mirza Aqa went off to Abadih where he remained until 1316/1898 (see below under Abadih). At this time he went to visit 'Abdu'l-Baha in 'Akka, after which he stayed for a time in Port Sa'id where his sons, Mirza Buzurg (see fig. 105) and Mirza Habibu'llah, were established as merchants. Then, on the instructions of 'Abdu'l-Baha, the whole family returned to Shiraz, where they arrived in 1319/1901.[36] In 1903 'Abdu'l-Baha sent instructions for Aqa Mirza Aqa to rebuild the house of the Bab in accordance with its original design at the time of the Bab (as noted above, the wife of the Bab had made major alterations). This was in the midst of the disturbances caused by the reform movement in Iran (see p. 279) and several of the senior Baha'is of Shiraz advised postponing this project in view of the adverse conditions. But Aqa Mirza Aqa insisted on pushing ahead in view of 'Abdu'l-Baha's express instructions. Under the supervision of Aqa Mirza Aqa Mi'mar-bashi, the work was started on 8 August 1903. The existing structures were pulled down, the foundations of the original building were found and the building was reconstructed from these original foundations. This rebuilding and restoration caused much opposition, particularly from Sayyid Muhammad Kaziruni, a *mujtahid* who lived opposite the house. He threatened that one day he would return with a mob to destroy the house but he died that same night from an attack of colic. Owing to Aqa Mirza Aqa Nuru'd-Din's insistence on the urgency of the work, some 50 labourers were employed on the project. Within two months all the essential foundation work for the rebuilding of the house according to its original design had been completed. The work of rebuilding was almost complete when, in October of that year, Aqa Mirza Aqa fell ill. He died on 17 November 1903. It was providential that the Baha'is had pressed on with the rebuilding of the house of the Bab since only Aqa Mirza Aqa recalled its original layout and design.[37]

---

34 Afnan, Tarikh 297–307 (*Genesis* 120–3).

35 For an account of this meeting and Shirazi's profession of his secret allegiance to the Baha'i Faith, see Afnan, Tarikh 323–50 (*Genesis* 127–34); Balyuzi, *Eminent Baha'is* 251–60.

36 Afnan, Tarikh 350–1, 409–11, 416 (*Genesis* 134, 151–2).

37 Afnan, Tarikh 465–82 (*Genesis* 170–82); Faydi, *Khandan* 208–14; ZH 7:215–6, 8a:541–3.

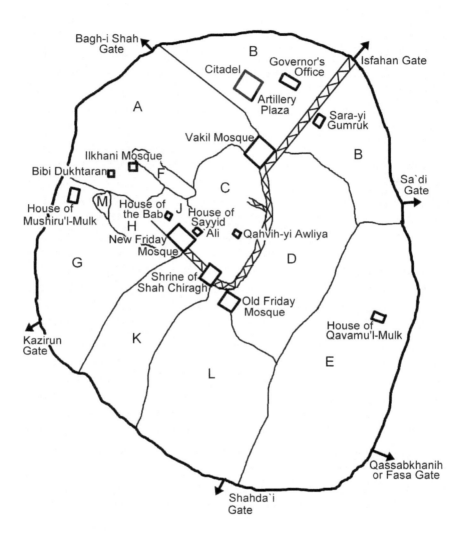

96. Map of Shiraz in the late 19th century. Buildings named in the text are shown. The quarters labelled A-E were the Haydari-khanih and the quarters G-L were the Ni'mati-khanih (see pp. 249, 263). F was the Jewish quarter and M the Armenian quarter. The hatched area is the bazaar. The Sara-yi Gumruk is where the Afnan family had their business offices.

The persecution of the Baha'is in Shiraz (1866–92)

One of the main source of problems for the Baha'is of Shiraz over many years was the long-standing enmity between the families of Mushir ul-Mulk and Qavam ul-Mulk. This enmity was partly due to the natural rivalry and competition for power between two prominent local families but also partly due to the historical phenomenon of faction-fighting in Iranian cities (between the Haydari-khanih faction and the Ni'mati-khanih faction). 'Ali Muhammad Khan, the second Qavam ul-Mulk (1829–13 December 1883), belonged to an established family of Fars notables, usually called the Hashimiyyih family, who were owners of extensive lands and had held the post of *kalantar* (mayor) of Shiraz in the family since 1812 (in 1801, the family had been almost wiped out on the orders of Fath-'Ali Shah).[38] They were the leading family of the Haydari-khanih and also head of the Khamsih tribal confederation. 'Ali Muhammad Khan's rival, Abu'l-Hasan Khan Mushir ul-Mulk (1811–1 December 1883, see fig. 97), was the *vazir* (official responsible for the collection of taxes) of the province of Fars for 30 years from 1262/1846.[39] His was the leading family of the Ni'mati-khanih.

The Afnan family lived in the Bazar-i Murgh quarter, one of the Haydari quarters of Shiraz, and were thus seen to be allied to the leader of the Haydari-khanih, Qavam ul-Mulk. As a consequence, the Baha'is incurred the enmity of Abu'l-Hasan Khan Mushir ul-Mulk, the head of the Ni'mati-khanih, despite the fact that one of the latter's wives, the daughter of Hujjat Zanjani, was a Baha'i. Mushir ul-Mulk took advantage of the alliance of the Afnans with the Haydari faction to discomfit his rival. In 1283/1866 he produced a lengthy list of 'Babis', headed by members of the Afnan family, and gave it to Sultan-Murad Mirza Hisam us-Saltanih, the new governor. The production of the list by Mushir ul-Mulk was calculated to embarrass Qavam ul-Mulk, who as *kalantar* (mayor) was responsible for public order and for controlling the enemies of the state. Qavam ul-Mulk, however, persuaded the governor that it would be unwise to arrest such a list of prominent citizens on no evidence. He even reminded the governor of an occasion when they had together attended a large commemoration of the martyrdom of Imam Husayn at the house of Saqqa-khanihi at which many of the poor of the quarter were fed and given presents. As mentioned

---

38   Churchill, *Persian Statesmen*, 22–4.
39   Bamdad, *Tarikh* 1:39–40.

97. Abu'l-Hasan Khan Mushir ul-Mulk

98. Muhammad Rida Khan,
the third Qavam ul-Mulk,
in 1902

99. Sayyid 'Ali Akbar Falasiri

100. Shaykh Yahya, Imam-Jum'ih
of Shiraz

above, the Afnans were careful to be patrons of such commemorations and to maintain an outward appearance of orthodoxy.[40]

The attitude of the Qavam ul-Mulk and Mushir ul-Mulk families towards the Baha'i community over the rest of the 19th century was to have many twists and turns. Mirza Habibu'llah Afnan records in his narrative history of the Baha'i Faith in Shiraz that on one occasion in 1903 he had a private conversation with Muhammad Rida Khan, the third Qavam ul-Mulk (1851–1907, see fig. 98), the son of 'Ali Muhammad Khan Qavam ul-Mulk.[41] Muhammad Rida Khan asked him about his visit to 'Akka and his meeting with Baha'u'llah. Afnan recounted for him the words of Baha'u'llah, spoken in 1891, commending the Qavam ul-Mulk family for the fact that they had not opposed the Baha'i Faith and had even supported it on occasion. Qavam ul-Mulk had been pleased with this.[42] As shall be seen, however, the friendship of the Qavam ul-Mulk family towards the Baha'is, since it was based on political expediency, was fickle. Moreover, towards the end of his life Mushir ul-Mulk's enmity towards the Baha'is was moderated under the influence of two Baha'is, Sayyid Isma'il Azghandi and Mulla Muhammad Manshadi (whose daughter he married), and it is said that he even became a Baha'i and wrote to Baha'u'llah.[43]

The enmity between Mushir ul-Mulk and Qavam ul-Mulk was not the only source of problems for the Baha'is of Shiraz. One of the important clerics of the town, Shaykh Husayn Nazim ush-Shari'ah (d. Oct. 1884), known to Baha'is and other inhabitants of Shiraz as Ẓālim (the tyrant),[44] had been an enemy of the Baha'is since the time of the Bab, while another cleric, Sayyid 'Ali Akbar Falasiri (1256/1840–Aug. 1901, see fig. 99), carried on the persecutions once the former died. These clerics were countered to some extent by Shaykh Abu Turab, the Imam-Jum'ih (d. 1272/1855), and his son and successor Haji Shaykh Yahya (d. 1919, see fig. 100), who tried

40 ZH 6:857–8; Afnan, Tarikh 184–90 (Genesis 79–81).
41 Bamdad, Tarikh 3:401–43.
42 Afnan, Tarikh 439–50 (Genesis 160–4).
43 Malmiri, Khatirat 96–7.
44 The Baha'is were not the only people to regard Shaykh Husayn as 'ẓālim' (tyrant). Mirza Hasan Fasa'i, the author of the Fars-namih, the best known Qajar history of Fars province (partly translated by H. Busse as History of Persia under Qajar Rule), takes up much of the first two pages of the first part of this history recounting Shaykh Husayn's appropriation of the village of Sahlabad in 1872, which belonged to Fasa'i, an act which he elsewhere calls a ẓulm (tyranny or injustice, see Fars-namih 1:2–3, 2:24, 44).

to mitigate the effects of these persecutions as far as they could.[45] This division may reflect to some extent rivalry and animosities that existed between the various groups of clerics in Shiraz. Shaykh Abu Turab is, for example, listed among the clerics who signed a judgement supporting Mirza Hasan Fasa'i in his suit against Shaykh Husayn Zalim.[46]

It was Shaykh Husayn who was responsible for the execution of three Baha'is. Aqa Mirza Aqa Rikab-saz (stirrup-maker) was active both in spreading the Baha'i Faith and in transcribing the scriptures. His wife denounced him as a 'Babi' to Shaykh Husayn, who was at first reluctant to accept her word, as Rikab-saz was one of his own retinue. However, when Rikab-saz refused to curse the Bab, Shaykh Husayn beat him and arrested him. Mushir ul-Mulk used the opportunity of the commotion resulting from this arrest to produce his list of Baha'is again and the governor Hisam us-Saltanih ordered their arrest. More than ten Baha'i traders, clerics and others were arrested, including Mulla 'Abdu'llah Fadil Zarqani, Mulla 'Abdu'llah Baka and Mirza Muhammad Khan Baluch. Most of these were released through the intercession of various dignitaries but there remained three whom Shaykh Husayn insisted should be executed. He issued a *fatwa* for their death and they were strangled in the presence of the governor. These were the aforementioned Aqa Mirza Aqa Rikab-saz and two tailors, Mashhadi Nabi and Muhammad Ja'far.[47]

---

45   Afnan, Tarikh 213 (*Genesis* 88); Balyuzi, *The Bab* 69, 233n1. As far as can be judged, the attitude of clerics towards the Babis and Baha'is did not follow the Haydari-Ni'mati divisions in the city.

46   Fasa'i, *Fars-namih*, 1:1–2.

47   ZH 5:134–6; 6:858–61; Afnan, Tarikh 191–219 (*Genesis* 82–90). The date for this event is uncertain. ZH gives the date as 1288/1871 and this is what is implied in Afnan, Tarikh. However, both these sources state that the governor at the time of the execution was Hisam us-Saltanih and he was governor from 1866 to early 1869 and from May 1874 to June 1875. That the execution occurred during Hisam us-Saltanih's first term would fit better with the fact that Mirza Baqir Shirazi was one of those arrested at this time since he is stated to have been executed in Kirman in 1871 (see pp. 434–5). There is, however, a report in February–March 1875 by the British consular agent in Shiraz of the execution on the orders of Hisam us-Saltanih of three 'Babis' without, however, naming them; *Vaqayi' Ittifaqiyyih* 26. The matter is made more complicated by the fact that Zill us-Sultan, who was governor from May 1869 to April 1874 (with a brief interlude September 1871–March 1872), states in his memoirs (Zill us-Sultan, *Khatirat* 1:324–5) that Aqa Mirza Aqa Rikab-saz was brought before him and he ordered the execution. He states that it was Haji Shaykh Mahdi Nuri and Haji Shaykh Muhammad 'Ali Mahallati who wrote the *fatwa* for the execution of Aqa Mirza Aqa Rikab-saz and that this execution was the first time that he had interacted with the Baha'is.

101. Muhammad Qasim Khan
Bayda'i

102. Sultan Uvays Mirza, Ihtisham ud-
Dawlih (later Mu'tamad ud-Dawlih)

In 1879, when news arrived in Shiraz of the execution in Isfahan of
the Nahri brothers, Mirza Hasan and Mirza Husayn (see pp. 20–2), there
was much talk in the town of a general movement against the Baha'is. This
was during the governorship of Farhad Mirza Mu'tamad ud-Dawlih, who
was much opposed to the Baha'i Faith. A meeting of the leading Baha'is
was held and it was decided that Aqa Mirza Aqa Afnan, who was the only
person well known as a Baha'i, should leave. Within 24 hours he was on his
way to Bushihr and thence to Bombay. His son Aqa Sayyid Aqa remained
behind and their house continued to be a centre for Baha'i activities.[48]

It was the *mujtahid* Sayyid 'Ali Akbar Falasiri who was responsible for
an episode that occurred in 1888. Muhammad Qasim Khan Bayda'i (see
fig. 101) was a prominent Baha'i who had been governor of Kazirun from
1292/1875 for three years[49] and then of Bihbihan for a few years. One of
his servants stole a couple of boxes from his strong-room. One was full of
jewels, which she hid, the other was full of writings which she threw out.
This latter box was found by the wife of a local official, Mirza Muhammad
Rida Mustawfi who, realizing that they were Baha'i scriptures, took the box
to Falasiri. The latter rushed to the Masjid-i Vakil, the principal mosque of
the town, and raised a hue and cry against Bayda'i. The latter went to the
governor, Sultan Uvays Mirza, Ihtisham ud-Dawlih (later became Mu'tamad
ud-Dawlih, c. 1839–93, see fig. 102), with whom he was on friendly terms.

48   Afnan, Tarikh 231–3 (*Genesis* 95–6); 'Ala'i, *Mu'assasih-yi Ayadi* 812–21.
49   Fasa'i, *Fars-namih*, 2:75.

The governor managed to trick Falasiri into giving him the box and took the opportunity to make it clear to Falasiri that he would brook no disorder in the town.[50]

Having been frustrated on this occasion, Falasiri took full advantage of the opportunity presented to him a few months later, in August 1888, when there were confrontations between the Baha'is and the Muslims in Sarvistan. Sayyid 'Ali Mushir us-Sadat was the main opponent of the Baha'is in Sarvistan. His cousin was the wife of Aqa Murtada Sarvistani, a Baha'i dyer, who prior to his conversion by Shaykh Muhammad 'Arab, had been much opposed to the Baha'i Faith. Owing to persecution and imprisonment when he became a Baha'i, Sarvistani moved to Shiraz. Mushir us-Sadat had Sarvistani arrested and taken before Falasiri, who had him beaten and sent to the governor, Ihtisham ud-Dawlih, to be imprisoned. Then Mushir us-Sadat forced Sarvistani's wife to marry him and had Karbala'i Hasan Khan, a prominent Baha'i landowner, and his brother, Karbala'i Sadiq Khan, arrested and brought before Falasiri. One source states that accusations were made that one of them had burned a Qur'an and the other had made his wife sleep with someone else.[51] These are typical of the sorts of accusations that have frequently been concocted against the Baha'is throughout Iran up to the present day. In 1307/1889 Falasiri gave a *fatwa* for the death of one of the prisoners, Karbala'i Hasan Khan, and he was poisoned the same night. Four months later Karbala'i Sadiq was killed. Aqa Murtada Sarvistani remained in prison.[52]

Falasiri also waged campaigns against Christians and Jews in Shiraz at this time and his confrontational stand against the government over the Tobacco Régie in April 1891 led to his exile to Iraq for a short time. During this exile he was responsible for urging Sayyid Jamalu'd-Din 'al-Afghani' to write to Mirza Hasan Mirza-yi Shirazi, the leading cleric of the Shi'i world, exhorting the latter to declare himself against the Tobacco Régie. Falasiri then went on to Samarra, where he used his close relationship with Mirza-yi Shirazi (he was the latter's son-in-law) to further advance the campaign

---

50 'Ali Aqa (later Muvaqqar ud-Dawlih) in Browne ['Abdu'l-Baha], *Traveller's Narrative* 2:410–11; Afnan, Tarikh 260–82 (*Genesis* 106–11); ZH 5:365–9.

51 Report for 12 July–14 Aug. 1888; PRO documents: FO 248 474; *Vaqayi' Ittifaqiyyih* 317–18.

52 'Abdu'llah Mutlaq in Ishraq-Khavari, *Muhadirat* 1:115–18; Afnan, Tarikh 278–82, 296–7 (*Genesis* 119–20, 111–13); Taju'd-Dini, Sharh-i Hal 32–53; ZH 6: 874 gives Mirza Ashraf Abadihi as the person who converted Aqa Murtada. Thabit (Tarikh 6) states that Karbala'i Sadiq died while being bastinadoed.

against the Tobacco Régie.[53] If, as has been suggested, the *fatwa* of Mirza-yi Shirazi banning the use of tobacco (the event which more than anything else caused the collapse of the Régie) was forged,[54] Falasiri must be a prime candidate for being the person involved at the Samarra end.

As a result of these activities and the incompetence of the Iranian government, far from Falasiri's exile being a cause of his humiliation, he returned to Shiraz with great glory and honour, in an even more powerful position to interfere with political matters. Among the

103. Rukn ud-Dawlih (Muhammad Taqi Mirza)

things that he did with his new-found power was to obtain the signatures of five of the clerics of Shiraz, including Shaykh Muhammad Tahir 'Arab, Mulla Ahmad Mahallati and Mirza Hidayatu'llah Dastghayb, for a *fatwa* for the death of Aqa Murtada Sarvistani. This *fatwa* was presented to the governor Muhammad Taqi Mirza Rukn ud-Dawlih (see fig. 103), and Sarvistani, after four years in prison, was publicly blown from a cannon outside the Maydan-i Tupkhanih (Artillery Plaza) in Shiraz on 4 October 1892 (see fig. 104).[55]

Rukn ud-Dawlih's governorship was already very unpopular owing to his injustices and corrupt practices and the people were also still agitated over the episode of the Tobacco Régie. Thus Sarvistani's execution triggered widespread discontent throughout the town. The British consular agent in Shiraz reported that a few days later a group of people attacked a policeman in the town shouting, 'Ask the governor why he blew an innocent

53 Tsadik, *Between Foreigners* 132–7; Bamdad, *Tarikh* 2:430–3; Keddie, *Sayyid Jamal al-Din* 342–55; Keddie, *Religion and Rebellion* 67–73.
54 Keddie, *Religion and Rebellion* 96 and n; N. Kirmani, *Tarikh-i Bidari* (5th ed.) 1:19.
55 Afnan, Tarikh 308–13 (*Genesis* 123–5); ZH 7:33–4 and n; Taju'd-Dini, *Sharh* 53–64; *Vaqayi' Ittifaqiyyih* 415.

104. Photograph said to be the execution of Aqa Murtada Sarvistani

man from a cannon? What sort of governing is this?'[56] Mirza Muhammad
'Ali Mujtahid, who had refused to sign the *fatwa,* wrote to Falasiri: 'Sayyid,
do you know what you have done? As a result of the sound of that cannon
today, you have become the cause of half of the town becoming Babis.
What a service you have rendered the noble religion of Islam!' And indeed,
a large number of people became Baha'is having had their attention first
drawn to the Baha'i Faith by witnessing the execution of Aqa Murtada
Sarvistani.[57] Rukn ud-Dawlih was dismissed as governor some five months
after the execution of Sarvistani.

The Baha'i community during the late 19th century

Following the threat of persecutions and the departure of Aqa Mirza Aqa
Afnan in 1879 (see p. 267), there was a lull in Baha'i activities in Shiraz, but
after a time, with the emergence of a new generation of leading Baha'is and
the arrival of travelling Baha'i teachers such as Mirza Asadu'llah Isfahani

56   *Vaqayi' Ittifaqiyyih* 416.
57   Afnan, Tarikh 313 (*Genesis* 125); ZH 5:373–4, 6:874–6; Thabit, Tarikh 4–5.

105. Photograph of Baha'is of Shiraz taken about 1881. *Seated at the rear in the portico on the far right*: Haji Mirza Abu'l-Qasim Saqqa-khanihi (the brother-in-law of the Bab and great-grandfather of Shoghi Effendi). *Front row, left to right*: Shaykh 'Ali Mirza (nephew of the Imam-Jum'ih); Mirza Abu'l-Hasan Afnan (the maternal grandfather of Mr Hasan Balyuzi); Mirza Mahdi Sabir; Mirza Buzurg Afnan; Sayyid Husayn Afnan (paternal grandfather of Shoghi Effendi); Aqa Mirza Aqa Nuru'd-Din Afnan. *Second row, left to right*: unknown; Mirza 'Ali Akbar (son of Sabir); Mirza Mahmud (son of Saqqa-khanihi), Haji Ghulam-Husayn Khan (a prominent Baha'i of Shiraz), Mirza Hadi Afnan (father of Shoghi Effendi), Mirza Sayyid 'Ali Afnan (see pp. 258–9), Mirza Muhammad Baqir Khan (Dihqan), Mirza Rahim (brother of Mirza Hadi Afnan). The three at the back are unknown

and Haji Mirza Haydar 'Ali, activities were resumed.[58] The former, who visited for two months at the end of 1882, encouraged the Baha'is to put into effect the instructions of the Kitab-i Aqdas and set up an assembly of consultation (*majlis-i shawr*). There is no evidence that this lasted for any length of time, however. In 1306/1888 the poet 'Andalib of Lahijan (vol. 1:351–3) moved to Shiraz, married, settled and became the main teacher of the Baha'i Faith in the town. E.G. Browne visited Shiraz in 1888 and described his interactions with the Baha'i community.[59]

Among the prominent Baha'is of Shiraz during the time of Baha'u'llah and 'Abdu'l-Baha, some of whom were influential in the town and could protect their fellow-Baha'is, were Muhammad Husayn Mirza Mu'ayyid

---

58   Afnan, Tarikh 233–5 (*Genesis* 96).
59   Browne, *Year* 326–69; Browne, *Selections* 37–84.

106. Mirza Aqa Khan Bashir us-Sultan, called by 'Abdu'l-Baha Bashir-Ilahi

107. Muvaqqar ud-Dawlih ('Ali Muhammad Khan)

us-Saltanih (see p. 199), a grandson of Tahmasb Mirza Mu'ayyid ud-Dawlih, who was head of the telegraph department in Shiraz from December 1897 to 1905;[60] Mulla Muhammad Husayn (d. 1878), who had met the Bab and became a tutor to the children of the Afnan family; his son Mirza Aqa Khan Bashir us-Sultan (1281/1864–28 July 1924; called by 'Abdu'l-Baha Bashir-Ilahi, see fig. 106), who was in charge of the post office in Yazd, then in Bushihr, then in Shiraz, and then in the whole province of Fars (for seven years), eventually going to Tehran in about 1919;[61] Ja'far-Quli Khan Amir-Panjih Mu'azzam ul-Mulk, who was in charge of the troops stationed in Shiraz (see pp. 279–80); Ahmad-Quli Khan Sarhang; Shaykh 'Ali Mirza, a nephew of the Imam-Jum'ih (see fig. 105); Mulla 'Abdu'llah Fadil Zarqani (see p. 318); Muhibb-'Ali Mirza; Haji Abu'l-Hasan Bazzaz (d. Aug. 1902, see fig. 90); his son Mirza Muhammad Baqir Khan (the progenitor of the Dihqan family, see fig. 105), who was a close confidant of Qavam ul-Mulk; and Mirza Husayn Khan Mu'tamad ud-Divan. The last named was also a close confidant of Muhammad Rida Qavam ul-Mulk, until they fell out in about 1903. Although 'Abdu'l-Baha tried to effect a reconciliation, they remained at odds. When in 1325/1907 Zill us-Sultan was appointed governor of Fars, the members of the Qavam ul-Mulk family were in exile and so Mu'tamad ud-Divan was appointed head of and had

60   Churchill, *Persian Statesmen*, 45–6.
61   ZH 6:865–7, 8a:563; Bashir-Ilahi, 'Bashir-Ilahi'; Bashir-Ilahi, *Alvah*.

financial responsibility for (*abwāb jam'ī*) the Khamsih tribes. He set out with a considerable force to collect the taxes due. However, the family and supporters of Qavam ul-Mulk plotted against him and on the way he was shot and killed by 'Askar Khan, one of the *kalantars* of the 'Arab tribe.[62] Another prominent Baha'i of Shiraz was 'Ali Muhammad Khan Muvaqqar ud-Dawlih (d. May 1921, also known as 'Ali Aqa, see fig. 107), a member of the Afnan family who was Consul-General of Iran in India for some years, then Foreign Office agent in Shiraz and Bushihr and later governor of Bushihr (1913–15). He had been educated in London and met Edward Granville Browne both there and in Shiraz. He played an important role in the Shiraz Baha'i community and 'Abdu'l-Baha commended the honest and capable manner in which he had governed Bushihr. When the British captured Bushihr in 1915 he was exiled to India. He returned in 1920 and was appointed as the government's Minister of Public Works in Tehran but died shortly after this.[63]

When Mirza Muhammad 'Ali, the half-brother of 'Abdu'l-Baha, brought his rebellion against 'Abdu'l-Baha into the open, a number of the Afnan family sided with him. Among these was Sayyid 'Ali Afnan, a son of Haji Mirza Hasan Afnan-i Kabir and a son-in-law of Baha'u'llah. He lived at Bahji where Mirza Muhammad 'Ali was headquartered. Sayyid 'Ali's sister Bibi Jan Bigum, who also lived at Bahji, and his two brothers, Sayyid Muhammad and Haji Sayyid Mirza, who ran the Bombay office of the Afnan trading company and who had been closely associated with Mirza Muhammad 'Ali when the latter visited India, sided with him but later the last named repented of this. Apart from these members of the Afnan family, there was Mirza Husayn Shirazi, who had accompanied Haji Mirza Haydar 'Ali on some of his travels in Iran, and arrived in Edirne with him in about 1867 and was sent with him to Egypt by Baha'u'llah. Here they were arrested in the winter of 1867–8 and exiled to Khartum for some 11 years. From this time on, Mirza Husayn was generally known as Khartumi. He returned to Iran and lived for a time in Shiraz, where E.G. Browne met him in 1888. He was a skilled calligraphist and in about 1889 he went to Bombay to assist with the production of Baha'i books there. A copy of Baha'u'llah's Kitab-i Aqdas in his handwriting was published there in about 1890. Also in Bombay for the same purpose was

---

62   Afnan, Tarikh 562–5 (*Genesis* 205–6).
63   Faizi, *Khandan*; 263–73; Shahidiyan, *Mansuban* 239–41; Rabbani, *Genesis* 349–52; Churchill, *Persian Statesmen* 61; 'Abdu'l-Baha, *Makatib* 3:238–41.

Mirza Muhammad 'Ali, the son of Baha'u'llah, and when he began plot-
ting against 'Abdu'l-Baha shortly after the passing of Baha'u'llah, Khartumi
followed him.[64] None of these partisans of Mirza Muhammad 'Ali lived in
Shiraz at this time, but they still maintained contacts with the Baha'is in
Shiraz and tried to use their influence. To counter this, 'Abdu'l-Baha sent
Aqa Mirza Aqa Afnan and his son Aqa Sayyid 'Ali from Egypt to Shiraz
in 1894.[65] There is no indication that anyone in Shiraz supported Mirza
Muhammad 'Ali.

In early 1896 Mirza Mahmud Furughi arrived in Shiraz from India.
Two of his fellow-travellers alerted the religious leaders of the town to the
arrival of a distinguished Baha'i and soon afterwards news reached them
of animated Baha'i meetings at which Furughi was speaking. Furughi was
arrested and held at the home of the Tufangdar-bashi (head rifleman).
Eventually the governor permitted Furughi to depart for Abadih.[66]

Haji Abu'l-Hasan Mirza, Shaykh ur-Ra'is (see fig. 20; and vol. 1:128–
31), a Qajar prince, settled in Shiraz in 1895. At first the clerics welcomed
him, for although he was a member of the Qajar family, he had undergone
a religious education. He gave addresses in the Shrine of Shah Chiragh
and the Masjid-i Naw and was such an excellent orator that soon he was
attracting large crowds, which did not please the clerics quite so much
since this was having an effect on their audiences. Shaykh ur-Ra'is continued, however, to establish himself in Shiraz, marrying two of his daughters
to sons of Shiraz notables, one to Mirza Abu'l-Qasim Fakhr ul-Ashraf, the
son of Fakhr ud-Dawlih, and one to the son of Haji Ahmad Khan Kurrani.
A bejewelled cane was even bestowed upon him by the shah in February
1897 and a great feast was held to mark the occasion.[67] At first the Baha'is
were unsure what to make of him since it was said that he was a Baha'i.
Soon, however, they realized that his preaching was in fact covertly con-
veying the Baha'i message and that in his private classes he was converting
a number of his students. So there collected around him a coterie of Baha'i
clerics, including Mulla 'Abdu'llah Fadil Zarqani.[68]

The first occasion on which Shaykh ur-Ra'is was publicly accused of

64   Isfahani, *Bihjat us-Sudur* 46, 64, 89–90; Balyuzi, *Eminent Baha'is* 121, 238–50;
     Browne, *Year* 360–9; Browne, *Selections* 41 and n, 74–83.
65   'Ala'i, *Mu'assasih-yi Ayadi* 817.
66   Afnan, Tarikh 350–60 (*Genesis* 135–6); ZH 6:84–5.
67   *Vaqayi' Ittifaqiyyih* 521.
68   Afnan, Tarikh 314–23 (*Genesis* 125–7); *Vaqayi' Ittifaqiyyih* 659; ZH 8a:210–13;
     Cole, 'Provincial Politics'.

being a 'Babi' was in September 1897, when the son of Shaykh Muhammad Tahir 'Arab, one of the *mujtahids* of Shiraz, accused him of this from
the pulpit of the Shrine of Shah Chiragh. The following night, supporters of Shaykh ur-Ra'is beat this man. Then a group of clerics went to the
governor Mirza Asadu'llah Khan Nazim ud-Dawlih and demanded the
expulsion of Shaykh ur-Ra'is, saying that if the governor did not expel
him, they would do the job themselves. The governor calmed them down
by saying he would see to the matter within ten days. But ten days later it
was Nazim ud-Dawlih himself who was dismissed and was leaving Shiraz.[69]
On another occasion in May 1900, a *rawdih-khan* who was a sayyid of
Sarvistan, began to accuse Shaykh ur-Ra'is of being a 'Babi' in the course
of his preaching. Shaykh ur-Ra'is accused the Imam-Jum'ih of putting this
man up to do this but the Imam-Jum'ih denied it.[70]

The Baha'i community during the early 20th century

On 8 January 1901, in the middle of the Islamic month of fasting
(Ramadan), a mob led by a cleric attacked the house of one of the prominent Baha'is, Mirza Jalal Zarqani. As he had been forewarned, he was
hiding in a neighbour's house, but the mob looted and ransacked his house
and dragged his wife before Sayyid 'Ali Akbar Falasiri. They wanted to forcibly marry her to a Muslim. Zarqani appealed to the governor Abu'l-Fath
Mirza Mu'ayyid ud-Dawlih but he did nothing. So Zarqani fled to Abadih
and sent a telegram to the government in Tehran. The prime minister,
Amin us-Sultan, replied that a new governor, Malik Mansur Mirza Shu'a'
us-Saltanih (1880–1920, see fig. 108, son of Muzaffaru'd-Din Shah), was
on his way and would deal with the matter. Shu'a' us-Saltanih collected
Zarqani in Abadih and arrived in Shiraz determined to set things right. He
gave orders that the cleric who had led the mob should be executed and
the other clerics involved should have their ears cut off. However, with
the intervention of Shaykh ur-Ra'is, these sentences were moderated and
the principal culprit was exiled from Fars. Zarqani's wife was freed and his
property returned.[71]

Upon his arrival in Shiraz as governor in February 1901, Shu'a' us-
Saltanih imposed his authority on the town and soon there was more order

---

69 *Vaqayi' Ittifaqiyyih* 533–4.
70 *Vaqayi' Ittifaqiyyih* 608.
71 ZH 7:141.

and calm than there had been for years. The Baha'is felt more confident and 'Andalib and Mirza Jalal Zarqani began a vigorous campaign of teaching the Baha'i Faith.[72] This, however, provoked a reaction from the clerics. At this time the country was in the throes of mounting demands for reform and there were disturbances in many parts. In Shiraz, those who wanted to raise some agitation in favour of reform found themselves in league with a number of the clerics who were alarmed by the teaching campaign of the Baha'is and also with those elements in the town who profited from disorder. They had their headquarters in the Shrine of Shah Chiragh and in the Masjid-i Naw and included such clerics as Mirza Ibrahim Mujta-hid Mahallati. The supporters of the governor were headquartered in the telegraph office and included Shaykh Yahya, the Imam-Jum'ih. Since the governor and Shaykh ur-Ra'is were both Qajars and close to each other, their opponents found it convenient to accuse both the governor and Shaykh ur-Ra'is of being 'Babis'. The clerics gathered at the Masjid-i Naw issued a *fatwa* declaring Shaykh ur-Ra'is to be an unbeliever and deserving of death.[73] Despite his previous support of the Baha'is, Muhammad Rida Khan Qavam ul-Mulk now found it opportune to be the leader of the opponents of the governor and thus the instigator of this anti-Baha'i cam-paign.[74] Part of the reason for Qavam's opposition to the governor was that the latter had laid claim to the Bazar-i Vakil and properties in that vicinity which Qavam considered to be his.[75]

The opponents of the governor forced the shops in the bazaar to close and put a crowd of women onto the streets chanting slogans: 'We don't want a Babi governor.' This situation lasted for four months and the Baha'is were under constant pressure throughout this time. Eventually, on 10 March 1902, a telegram came recalling the governor to Tehran and he left on 18 April.[76] At this point Qavam ul-Mulk put out the word that their objective had been the dismissal of the governor and there should be no further action against the Baha'is.[77] The new governor was Ghulam-Rida

---

72   Afnan 416–17 (*Genesis* 152).
73   *Vaqayi' Ittifaqiyyih* 665.
74   Afnan 428–30 (*Genesis* 156).
75   Bamdad, *Tarikh* 4:156.
76   Reports of Haydar 'Ali Khan Navvab, British agent in Shiraz, Shiraz News for 5–12 Mar., dated 12 Mar. 1902, and for 17–24 Apr., dated 24 Apr. 1902. PRO FO 248 773. *Vaqayi' Ittifaqiyyih* 664–5.
77   Afnan 430–2 (*Genesis* 157–8).

108. Shu'a' us-Saltanih (Malik Mansur Mirza)

109. Asif ud-Dawlih (Ghulam-Rida Khan)

110. 'Ala ud-Dawlih (Ahmad Khan)

Khan Asif ud-Dawlih[78] (see fig. 109) and on 10 August 1902 instructions came from Tehran that Shaykh ur-Ra'is was to leave for Karbala. He obtained permission to go by way of Isfahan (see pp. 36–7) and left on 26 August.[79] On another occasion in 1320/1902, when the 90-year-old Haji Abu'l-Hasan Bazzaz was passing near the house of Falasiri, some of the latter's students seized him. They took him before Falasiri, who personally beat him with his walking stick to such an extent that he died a short while later.[80]

The next governor, Mirza Ahmad Khan Qajar 'Ala ud-Dawlih (1852–1911, see fig. 110), was firm in imposing order on the town. When in June 1903 news arrived of the anti-Baha'i pogroms in Isfahan and Yazd, he acted swiftly to try to suppress any similar action in Shiraz. Despite his efforts, however, some of the clerics managed to rouse the populace and there was a commotion in the town. One of the leading clerics of the town, Mirza Ibrahim Mahallati, put out a written proclamation that anyone who managed to lay hold of a 'Babi' and kill him would have done an act of great religious merit (thavāb-i 'aẓīm). The governor gathered several of the leading local officials and consulted with them. Among those present were Qavam ul-Mulk, his son Habibu'llah Khan Biglarbigi, Muhammad Husayn Mirza Mu'ayyid us-Saltanih and Ja'far-Quli Khan Amir-Panjih. The result of this meeting was that the leading Baha'is were advised either to leave town or remain at home. Mirza Nasru'llah Bihishti Malik ul-Mutakallimin, who at this time was engaged with the Baha'i community but later joined the Azalis in agitating for the Constitutional Revolution (see pp. 31–2 and fig. 17), had been expelled from Isfahan and had been openly preaching about the Baha'i Faith in Shiraz for four or five months at this time. He was expelled from the town by the governor. Qavam ul-Mulk and his sons did their best to keep matters calm.[81]

The uproar in the town increased, however, and the bazaar was closed for four days. Word spread that on the fifth day, which was a Friday,

---

78 Cole states erroneously that this was Mirza 'Abdu'l-Vahhab Khan Shirazi Asif ud-Dawlih, an old enemy of Shaykh ur-Ra'is ('Provincial Politics of Heresy and Reform' 124), but he had died in 1887 and the title had been transferred; Bamdad, *Tarikh* 2:315. Afnan gives the name correctly (Tarikh 568, *Genesis* 207).

79 Report of British Agent in Shiraz, Shiraz News for 7–15 Aug., dated 15 Aug. 1902 and for 20–8 Aug., dated 28 Aug. 1902; PRO 248 773; *Vaqayi' Ittifaqiyyih* 680–1; ZH 8a:214.

80 Afnan, Tarikh 425–7 (*Genesis* 155–6).

81 *Vaqayi' Ittifaqiyyih* 707–8; Afnan, Tarikh 433–8 (*Genesis* 157–60).

there would be a general massacre of the Baha'is as had occurred in Yazd. The governor reprimanded Mahallati and then sent for Shaykh Yahya the Imam-Jum'ih and asked him to intervene. The latter, who, as noted above, had always done his best to maintain peace in Shiraz and protect the Baha'is, summoned all the people of Shiraz to Friday prayers in the Masjid-i Vakil in Shiraz. The people gathered, fully expecting Shaykh Yahya to issue a *fatwa* against the Baha'is. Instead, Shaykh Yahya, summoning all the *gravitas* of his position and his more than 80 years of age and, tapping the respect and affection the people had for him, preached a sermon designed to pacify the populace. He pointed out that the Qur'an says that if someone greets a Muslim with the word 'Salam', no Muslim has the right to say that that person is not a Muslim (Qur'an 4:94). He then went on to argue that this means that provided a person behaves as a Muslim, no Muslim has the right to call that person an unbeliever. He therefore went on to declare that, 'In our Shiraz, we have no Babis.' And he got the crowd to repeat this declaration after him three times. After that he urged the people to go to the bazaar and open up their shops and go about their business, which they did.[82]

As the demands for reform gathered momentum, however, conditions in Shiraz deteriorated and the Baha'is suffered. People took to carrying sticks and guns around with them and there were gunshots by night and uproar during the day. At the slightest pretext they would close the bazaar. This eventually led to the dismissal of 'Ala ud-Dawlih in February 1904 and the reinstatement of Shu'a' us-Saltanih. For a time the latter was able to maintain order in the town but once again the enmity of Qavam ul-Mulk brought about a coalition of forces against him. Once again the streets of Shiraz resounded to slogans accusing the governor and all his staff of being 'Babis'.[83]

In the event, the pretext that the clerics chose for action was that a Jew had built his house higher than a Muslim's. They gathered the mob in the Masjid-i Naw and urged them to attack the Jewish quarter. The Jewish quarter was situated not far from the Masjid-i Naw but between the two lay the house of the Bab. The Baha'is realized that the clerics would almost certainly take the opportunity to destroy the house of the Bab as they proceeded towards the Jewish quarter. Ja'far-Quli Khan Amir-Panjih, a Baha'i who was in charge of the troops stationed in Shiraz, had been ordered by

---

82   Afnan, Tarikh 455–61 (*Genesis* 165–9); ZH 7:214–15.
83   Afnan, Tarikh 510–14 (*Genesis* 186).

the governor to defend the Jewish quarter. He sent one of his servants, Mirza Husayn, who was a Baha'i, to the mob in the Masjid-i Naw to warn that if they approached the Jewish quarter he would order his troops to fire upon them. He had set himself up on the rooftop of the house of Mulla Rabi'a, a Jewish merchant, from which the house of the Bab was visible. As the mob approached, Ja'far-Quli Khan could observe some of them proceeding across the rooftops. They reached the house of the Bab and began to throw stones at the group of Baha'is who had gathered in the house. Ja'far-Quli Khan gave the order for a volley to be fired, and once the mob saw that he was serious about his task, they dispersed. However, the bazaar remained closed for three months until the governor was dismissed.[84]

At first no one was willing to take on the post of governor because of the disorderly state of the town but after three months 'Ala ud-Dawlih agreed to take on the task again. He entered the town with troops and restored order. In particular, he was firm towards the clerics, allowing them no opportunity to cause any mischief. As a consequence, there were some 18 months of peace for the town and for the Baha'is. As soon as the governor could sense that the mischief-makers were once again gathering strength, however, he immediately resigned.[85]

Again, no one could be found to take on the governorship, so eventually Qavam ul-Mulk was appointed. At first he was able with his local knowledge to control the various factions and troublemakers. However the Nuri clan in Shiraz had always been opposed to Qavam ul-Mulk and they now led the rising opposition to the governor. The Nuris had also been enemies of the Baha'is dating back to the days when several of them led the government forces against the Babis of Nayriz. Once more there was daily abuse and molestation of the Baha'is. Now, however, it was worse. In the past, when the abuse had been directed against the then governor, Qavam ul-Mulk had usually been on the side of those opposing the governor and therefore had been able to mitigate the attacks on the Baha'is to some extent but now the abuse was directed against Qavam ul-Mulk himself. Because one of the main members of Qavam ul-Mulk's staff, Mirza Muhammad Baqir Khan (Dihqan, son of Abu'l-Hasan Bazzaz), was a Baha'i, the mischief-makers were now saying that the Baha'is were trying to seize power, lead all the Muslims astray and make them Baha'is. Eventually matters deteriorated to the point that Qavam ul-Mulk was

84 Afnan, Tarikh 514–20 (*Genesis* 186–9).
85 Afnan, Tarikh 520–4 (*Genesis* 190–1).

dismissed and Ghulam-Husayn Khan Ghaffari was appointed governor in late 1906.[86]

In the midst of these troubles the Baha'is were faced with an additional problem when a certain Darvish 'Ali pretended conversion to the Baha'i Faith and then used his knowledge of the community to publicly denounce individual Baha'is. For example, he would stand outside the shop of a Baha'i and shout obscenities and curses at him. He would extort money from individual Baha'is by threatening to denounce them and then obtain money also from Muslims as a reward for his actions. His activities went on for four years until he died.[87]

In 1906 the Constitutional Revolution succeeded and Muzaffaru'd-Din Shah signed the Constitution. Immediately political parties and societies (*anjumans*) were created, some supporting the Constitution and some opposing it. Both sides accused the Baha'is of being among their opponents. Shortly after the Constitution was signed, Muzaffaru'd-Din died and Muhammad 'Ali Shah came to power, determined to annul the Constitution. He summoned Qavam ul-Mulk to Tehran and made him one of his key supporters. On his return, Qavam ul-Mulk began to work against the Constitution. Secret meetings were held and societies formed. Groups of people began to form, calling themselves *mujāhidīn* (holy warriors) to defend each side. The clerics were also divided, some supporting the Constitution and some opposing it. But whichever side they were on, in their preaching, they came increasingly to attack the Baha'i Faith, each side saying the *mujāhidīn* of their opponents were all Baha'is. Those opposing the Constitution would preach in the pulpits cursing the Baha'is and saying that they were the cause of the Constitution, that it was a fundamental teaching of theirs, that peace would never return to the country and Islam would not be safe until this 'evil and unbelieving sect' was rejected and defeated. The supporters of the Constitution would claim that the Baha'is were the defenders of autocratic government and that they should be extirpated so that the supporters of the autocracy would be frustrated and the foundations of Constitutionalism be firmly laid.[88]

It was at this time that Qavam ul-Mulk showed his fickle nature. Although he had recently, while in Tehran, contacted 'Abdu'l-Baha

---

86   Afnan, Tarikh 525–9 (*Genesis* 191–3).
87   Afnan, Tarikh 501–9 (*Genesis* 183–5).
88   Afnan, Tarikh 529–37 (*Genesis* 194–6).

111. Haji 'Ali Aqa Dhu'r-Riyasatayn (Vafa-'Ali Shah)

through Mirza Hasan Adib and professed friendship,[89] he now turned against the Baha'is. On one particular Thursday he summoned all of the notables, guild masters and people of Shiraz to the Masjid-i Naw. He then addressed them, saying it was necessary for them to know the source of the idea of the Constitution that had been foisted upon them. He then produced a copy of Baha'u'llah's book the Kitab-i Aqdas and proceeded to quote from the passage that speaks of the affairs of Iran being put into the hands of the people (*jumhūr un-nās*).[90] He then asked them whether they really wanted to bring about the constitutional government that Mirza Husayn 'Ali (i.e. Baha'u'llah) had promised his people. Did they not realize that everything they did to promote this matter brought upon them the curse of God and His Messenger?[91]

The supporters of the Constitution who were in the audience were not content to allow such assertions to pass unchallenged and they got up and replied, saying that Qavam ul-Mulk was merely trying to confuse and mislead people. The leading Constitutionalists met afterwards and discussed what to do. Haji 'Ali Aqa Dhu'r-Riyasatayn (d. 1336/1917, see fig. 111), who was a Sufi Ni'matu'llahi Shaykh with the Sufi name of Vafa 'Ali Shah,[92] stated that he was well-informed about the Baha'i community and was sure that they were not involved in any political affairs.[93] Afnan states that Dhu'r-Riyasatayn had attended Baha'i meetings and had read several

89 ILMA 84:336–7.
90 Kitab-i Aqdas, v. 93.
91 Afnan, Tarikh 537–41 (*Genesis* 196–8); Mr Hasan Balyuzi stated in an interview on 23 June 1977 that part of the reason for this action of Qavam ul-Mulk was his enmity towards Mu'tamad ud-Divan (see p. 272).
92 Bamdad, *Tarikh* 6:137.
93 Afnan, Tarikh, 542–4 (*Genesis* 198–9).

Baha'i books.[94] However, the party of Qavam ul-Mulk spread rumours to the effect that two of the leading Constitutionalists, Shaykh Muhammad Baqir Istahbanati and Dhu'r-Riyasatayn himself, were Baha'is. Then on 13 April 1907 a certain Ni'matu'llah Burujirdi shot Qavam ul-Mulk dead with a revolver. Since the assassin was killed on the spot by Qavam ul-Mulk's retinue, it was not possible to question him and ascertain his motives. Therefore a rumour went around that it was the Baha'is who had assassinated Qavam ul-Mulk. Shots were fired during the funeral of Qavam ul-Mulk and immediately afterwards two of the leading Constitutionalists, Shaykh Muhammad Baqir Istahbanati and Sayyid Ahmad Mu'in ul-Islam, were killed by the men of Qavam ul-Mulk, who then went around saying that the Baha'is had got their just punishment. Thus the Baha'is came to be blamed for every untoward event that occurred. After the two sons of Qavam ul-Mulk were exiled, there was some improvement in public security but the Baha'is continued to suffer, especially when a party called Ittihad-i Islam was set up specifically to attack the Baha'i community.[95]

There were at this time two important developments for the Baha'i community. The first was the arrival of instructions from 'Abdu'l-Baha strongly prohibiting any involvement in political parties and political manoeuvring.[96] This led to some problems for the Baha'is since some of the better informed supporters of the Constitution naturally expected the Baha'is to help them. The second was the arrival of instructions for the election of the Local Spiritual Assembly of Shiraz. This was elected on 16 June 1907. The members of the first assembly were Mirza Aqa Khan Bashir us-Sultan, Aqa Mirza Muhammad Baqir Khan (Dihqan), Aqa Sayyid Muhammad Husayn Afnan, Aqa Mirza Aqa Afnan, Mirza Buzurg Afnan, Mirza Habibu'llah Afnan, Mirza 'Ali Ashraf 'Andalib, Mirza Ali Muhammad Khan Muvaqqar ud-Dawlih and Haji Mirza Husayn 'Ali Yazdi 'Umumi.[97] As can be seen from this list, four of the members of the assembly are named Afnan and a fifth, Muvaqqar ud-Dawlih, was an Afnan on his mother's side, while the last named was married into the Afnan family. The assembly immediately took full charge of all Baha'i affairs in Shiraz. Among the matters it concentrated upon in its early years was to ensure that 'Abdu'l-Baha's injunction that the Baha'is should withdraw from all

94   Afnan, Tarikh 557 (*Genesis* 203 and n 326).
95   Afnan, Tarikh 542–55 (*Genesis* 199–202).
96   Afnan, Tarikh 556 (*Genesis* 202–3).
97   Afnan, Tarikh 560–1 (*Genesis* 204–5).

political involvement was carried out. The assembly met at the house of the Bab's uncle Haji Sayyid 'Ali (where the Bab had been born), which was purchased at this time by 'Ali Muhammad Khan Muvaqqar ud-Dawlih along with an adjacent house which was made into a meetinghouse for prayers (*mashriq ul-adhkar*).[98] Surprisingly, in view of developments elsewhere, no Baha'i school was established in Shiraz. Bashir us-Sultan did set up a school but there is no indication that this was a Baha'i establishment. Bashir us-Sultan was also the main intermediary for communications with 'Abdu'l-Baha.[99]

In 1909 Muhammad 'Ali Shah was deposed and the new regime appointed Asif ud-Dawlih as governor. He was a weak governor and the affairs of Fars fell into chaos. The powerful Qashqa'i tribe under its leader Sawlat ud-Dawlih (see fig. 124) had at first sided with the Constitutionalists, mainly because his arch-rival Qavam ul-Mulk, head of the Khamsih confederation of tribes, had sided with the shah. Then when the Bakhtiyari-led Constitutionalist forces triumphed, Sawlat ud-Dawlih formed an anti-government, anti-British alliance with Shaykh Khaz'al of Muhammarah in the south of Iran. The Baha'is suffered during this period of chaos but despite this, as a result of the arrival of two travelling Baha'i teachers, Tarazu'llah Samandari and Mirza 'Ali Akbar Rafsanjani, activities in the Baha'i community were at a high level and many were converted at this time.[100]

In about 1909 an illiterate Baha'i by the name of Hidayat of Sarvistan, a patcher, in conjunction with Amru'llah of Bavanat, claimed that 'Abdu'l-Baha had died and had appointed them jointly as his *khalifih* (successor). A number of people followed them until early 1920, when a number of pilgrims from Abadih came to Shiraz on their way back from visiting 'Abdu'l-Baha (see pp. 300–1). As a result, the falsity of these two men's claims became clear to their followers.[101]

In about 1900 there were some 120 to 150 Zoroastrians in Shiraz, mostly working in the Zoroastrian trading houses there; five of them were Baha'is. At this time Ardishir Hizari (1885–1981) of Yazd came to work for the Jahaniyan Company. He was an active Baha'i and used to take his

---

98   ILMA 52:424–5; 84:337, 418; ZH 8a:574.
99   Bashir-Ilahi, 'Bashir-Ilahi'.
100 Afnan, Tarikh 568–9 (*Genesis* 207).
101 Yazdi, Minahaj al-Ahkam 1:234; by December 1920 there were evidently a few
     left, whom Munir Nabilzadih persuaded of the error of their viewpoint; MH
     4:258.

friends to the teaching meetings that were held at the
home of Muhammad Baqir Khan Dihqan and in the
rear of the shop of Muhammad Hasan Bulur-furush.
By about 1909 there were 25 Zoroastrian Baha'is in
Shiraz.[102]

During World War I the Baha'is of Shiraz heard that
conditions were very hard for 'Abdu'l-Baha and the
Baha'is of Haifa and 'Akka. They decided to send Mirza
Fadlu'llah Banan (1891–2 March 1964, see fig. 112),
who was an employee of the British consulate, to 'Akka
with 3,000 *tuman*s in order to ameliorate the conditions
there. Banan travelled in 1915 via Bombay and Alexan-

112. Mirza
Fadlu'llah Banan

dria and succeeded in accomplishing this mission despite the dangers. He
was able, because of his influential position in the British consulate, to
protect the Baha'is. On one occasion Muhammad Baqir Hushyar, who
had just become a Baha'i, went to the *mujtahid* Shaykh Ja'far Mahallati
and publicly challenged him to respond to the Kitab-i Iqan. Mahallati had
Hushyar arrested but Banan used his influence with the governor 'Abdu'l-
Husayn Mirza Farmanfarma to have Hushyar released. Banan tried to get
a Baha'i girls' school started in Shiraz but the opposition to this was too
great. He did begin a magazine called *Fars*.[103]

In the late 1910s and early 1920s the head of the post office in Shiraz
was a Baha'i, Muhammad Rida Mirza of Isfahan (d. 1924). When a mob
attacked one of the employees of the post office who was a Baha'i, Mirza
Nasru'llah Jahrumi, as he walked through the bazaar in about 1921,
Muhammad Rida Mirza closed the post office and the telegraph office.
The merchants and business community were in uproar as they could not
function without these but Muhammad Rida Mirza refused to re-open
until the governor Husayn-Quli Mirza Nusrat us-Saltanih punished the
main attacker, saying that government officials must be free to walk about
the city without being attacked. Eventually, the governor ordered the arrest
of the main attacker and his beating in the main square of the town in
front of the citadel on Friday when large crowds would be present. As the
farrashes beat him, the man pleaded with Muhammad Rida Mirza first in
the name of the king but he paid no attention; then in the name of the

---

102 Faridani, *Dustan Rastan* 110; Hizari, 'Jinab-i Ardishir Hizari' 40–1; Khoshbin,
     Taraz Ilahi 1:302–3.
103 Gity Etemad, Biography of Fadlu'llah Banan.

souls of the prophets and still he paid no attention; finally in the name of 'Abbas Effendi ('Abdu'l-Baha) and promising not to attack the Baha'i Faith again; at this Muhammad Rida Mirza ordered the *farrashes* to stop.[104]

The protection of the Baha'is in Fars by powerful individuals who were not Baha'is continued. Shaykh Muhammad Hasan Dastghayb, one of the prominent clerics of the town, is reported to have been a believer in the Bab and an admirer of 'Abdu'l-Baha and, at the end of his life, to have come to believe in Baha'u'llah as well.[105] Other clerics were, however, opponents of the Baha'i Faith. Sayyid Abu Talib Mujtahid wrote a refutation of the Baha'i Faith, *Talibiyyih dar Radd-i Babiyyih*. After Mirza Munir Nabilza-dih, who was visiting Shiraz, demonstrated to him the errors in this book, Sayyid Abu Talib raised a disturbance in the town in December 1920–January 1921 that forced Nabilzadih to leave. Indeed, at one stage a mob gathered planning to storm the governor's residence and then carry out a general massacre of the Baha'is. But when the gendarmes fired a volley into the air, the mob dispersed.[106] It was probably also during this episode that a plan was made by some of the criminal elements of the town to attack and loot the shop of Aqa Muhammad Hasan Bulur-furush. The Baha'is heard of this and ten of the Baha'i youth stood in the corners of the square where the shop was situated. When the mob arrived, the youth charged it with sticks and stones and dispersed it, thus saving the shop from attack.[107]

It is difficult to form an estimate of the number of Baha'is in Shiraz by 1920. In 1920 it was being said that about one-third of the popula-tion of the town was Baha'i, which would mean 20,000 people.[108] This is too high a figure, but since there were no membership criteria, it may well have represented the total number of those attending Baha'i meet-ings or otherwise demonstrating that they were favourable towards the Baha'i Faith. Cole follows a statement by Bémont, who states that she was told by a leading Baha'i, presumably in the 1950s or 1960s when she did her research for her book, that the Baha'i community of Shiraz was the

---

104 ZH 8a:139; A.Q. Afnan, 'Dastan' 39–40.
105 Interview with Mr Hasan Balyuzi on 29 Aug. 1979.
106 MH 4:258–9; ZH 7:323.
107 'Andalib, vol. 22, no. 88 (2005) 6–8.
108 This figure is reported by Walter Smart (d. 1962), Oriental secretary at the British Legation in Tehran, from a meeting he had with Mirza Ishaq Khan Haqiqi. While the figure may have come from Haqiqi, Smart, who was well-informed about Iran, does not dispute it. Public Record Office FO 248 1279, file 'Bahais', paper 29.

largest Baha'i community of Iran, larger than Tehran.[109] This is not a credible statement. By this time there had been major migrations of Baha'is from all parts of Iran to Tehran and the numbers there were far greater than in Shiraz. Various Baha'i estimates of the number of Baha'is in Shiraz are about 200 to 300 in about 1925, and some 500 to 600 in 1935. They were spread throughout the city, though a large number lived in the Sa'diyyih district.[110]

Abadih

Abadih (pop. 6,000 in 1914; 8,264 in 1951) was a walled town in the north of the province of Fars on the main road between Isfahan (204 km to the north) and Shiraz (280 km to the south), situated to the east of the main chain of the Zagros mountains on a plain which was used by the Qashqa'i, a Turkish-speaking tribe, as their summer pasture. Originally it was a village located near present-day Sughad. The people moved the village to the present site in about 1730 under the guidance of a certain Husayn Sultan Harandi, who was from the village of Harand near Isfahan and was appointed *kadkhuda* or *kalantar* (headman) of Abadih by Nadir Shah. Subsequently, the village grew into a town which had its own deputy governor in Qajar times. The notables of Abadih were composed of two main clans, the Harandi, descended from Husayn Sultan Harandi, and the Kurji'i, descended from a cleric brought to Abadih from the village of Kurjih by Husayn Sultan. The two clans did not live in different quarters of the town and they intermarried. The grandson of Husayn Sultan, Aqa Yusif Khan Harandi, married Zulaykha, the sister of Manuchihr Khan Mu'tamad ud-Dawlih, the governor of Isfahan, who was the Bab's host there. The children of this marriage were successive *kalantars* of Abadih and some became Baha'is.[111] Many others from the Harandi clan also became Baha'is. Mulla Muhammad Husayn, the Imam-Jum'ih and leading cleric of Abadih, who became the main enemy of the Baha'is, was from the Kurji'i clan.

The Baha'i history of Abadih begins with the burial in this town in early

---

109 Bémont, *Les Villes d'Iran* 2:152; see Cole, 'Religious Dissidence' 123.
110 1925 estimate from Hasan Balyuzi in interview at his home on 20 October 1979; 1935 estimate from Mr Hasan Afnan, interview in London on 23 June 2004.
111 MH 2:214; Dihqan, Hadiqat ur-Rahman 1–11; this information was confirmed by Mr Ata Agah (personal communication, 18 July 2003). See also Introduction by Ghulam-'Ali Dihqan to Abadihi, *Vaqayi'* 4–12.

113. Mirza 'Ata'u'llah Khan Siraj ul-Hukama (*right*),
William Patchin (*left*), and between them Mirza
Muhammad Husayn (the eldest son of Siraj ul-Hukama)

1854 of the heads of exe-
cuted Babis of Nayriz, which
were *en route* to Tehran with
a group of captives from
Nayriz when orders arrived
that the heads were not to be
taken any further and were to
be buried at whatever point
these instructions reached
the party. Since the Muslims
of Abadih refused to allow
the heads to be buried in
the town's cemetery, they
were buried behind the old
ruined caravanserai where
the party of captives was
being housed.[112]

The Babi religion spread
to the Abadih area when
Mirza Ashraf settled in the
village of Dihdaq (5 km south of Abadih; pop. 600 in 1951) in about 1864
as a religious leader and married the daughter of the village chief (*kadkhuda*). He was born in Najafabad but had been driven from Najafabad by
the persecutions there (see p. 27). Although he was much respected by the
people of Abadih, he concealed his faith.[113]

While studying traditional medicine at a theological college, the
Madrasih Nimavard, in Isfahan, the son of Aqa Muhammad Husayn
Hakim-bashi of Abadih, Mirza 'Ata'u'llah Khan (1259/1843–14 Nov.
1913, see fig. 113), who was in 1318/1900 given the title of Siraj ul-
Hukama by the shah, heard of the Babi religion in 1861. His fellow student
Mirza Asadu'llah Hakim-Ilahi (the father of Aqa Husayn 'Ali Nur) led him
to Mirza Hasan Nahri and eventually he was converted. But he became
known as a Baha'i and was forced to leave Isfahan in about 1870 and
return to Abadih, where he began to teach the new religion to his friends.

---

112 Abadihi, *Vaqayi‘* 31–3; there is also mention in ZH 3:482–3 of a Babi named
      Haji Sayyid 'Ali Mihrijirdi who lived for a time in Abadih.
113 Ishraq-Khavari, *Muhadirat* 2:684; Abadihi, *Vaqayi‘* 33, 230–2; Mudarris, *Tarikh*
      215–21.

He used the pretext of not understanding parts of Baha'u'llah's Tablet to the Shah of Iran to ask his friend Mulla Muhammad Husayn Jinab to study the text with him. This resulted in the latter's conversion. Another person he spoke to about the new religion was his friend Karbala'i Muhammad Husayn (Ba'i), known as Da'i Husayn, who had been in Baghdad and heard of Baha'u'llah's expulsion from there. This man owned an extensive establishment in Abadih. He had a separate house for each of his two wives, one of whom was the sister of the Imam-Jum'ih of Abadih and became a Baha'i; the other

114. Haji 'Ali Khan

did not. Siraj ul-Hukama also converted his brother Mirza Ishaq who, however, died at a young age.[114] At this time Mirza Ashraf cast off his cloak of concealment and all these individuals began to teach the Baha'i Faith to others in Abadih.

Other prominent early converts were Mirza Husayn Khan (d. 1316/1898, a brother-in-law of Siraj ul-Hukama), and Haji 'Ali Khan (1835–1917, see fig. 114), who were both notables of Abadih and were on occasions appointed *kalantar* (mayor or governor) of the town. Because he was a Baha'i, the former was removed from being governor in April 1887

---

114 B. Agah, 'Sharh-i Ahval' 187–9; R. Agah, 'Mukhtasari' 23; ZH 6:876–7; Dhuka'i-Bayda'i, *Tadhkirih* 2:349–55; Abadihi, *Vaqayi'* 35–6. I have used the account of Siraj ul-Hukama's conversion given by his son Badi'u'llah Agah. Abadihi (*Vaqayi'* 34–5) states that Mulla Muhammad Husayn Jinab and Mirza Ishaq became Baha'is in Isfahan with Siraj ul-Hukama. Abadihi, Tarikh Abadih, MS A has all three becoming Baha'is in Isfahan (p. 9); MS B has only Siraj ul-Hukama and Jinab (p. 7). Although most accounts imply that Siraj ul-Hukama returned to Abadih in about 1863, I have suggested the date 1870 because B. Agah (p. 189) states that Siraj ul-Hukama became a Baha'i at about the same time as Mulla Kazim Talkhunchihi (see pp. 7–8); because B. Agah and R. Agah (pp. 189 and 23 respectively) state that the Tablet of Baha'u'llah to the Shah had arrived in Isfahan shortly before Siraj ul-Hukama's departure for Abadih; and because Ashraf, who fled Najafabad in 1864, was in the Abadih area for a number of years before Siraj ul-Hukama's return and the start of open teaching of the Baha'i Faith in Abadih (see p. 27).

and beaten, fined 1,200 *tumans* and imprisoned by Habibu'llah Khan Mushir ul-Mulk on the orders of Zill us-Sultan.[115] Haji 'Ali Khan returned to Abadih after being converted in Kashan by Haji Muhammad Isma'il Dhabih Kashani and marrying the latter's daughter, Bahiyyih (known as Bint Dhabih, see fig. 115), who was an effective teacher of the Baha'i Faith among the women of Abadih.[116] These prominent early converts were all members of the Harandi clan (see p. 287). Another prominent convert was Haji Muhammad Sadiq Khan Qashqa'i, whose father Lutf-'Ali Khan Sartip had been one of the commanders of the forces sent against the Babis of Nayriz.

In March 1878 Aqa Sayyid 'Abbas Hisam udh-Dhakirin (a *rawdih-khan*), in order to avoid repaying a debt that he owed to a Baha'i, Ustad 'Ali Akbar, accused him before the judge of the town, Haji Muhammad 'Ali (Haji Qadi), of maligning Islam. The judge ordered Ustad 'Ali Akbar to be whipped severely and thrown into prison and then tried but failed to arrest Karbala'i Hasan Khan Azad, a successful teacher of the Baha'i Faith and a poet. The judge sent a report to Farhad Mirza Mu'tamad ud-Dawlih, the governor of Fars, who ordered that Ustad 'Ali Akbar be sent to Shiraz. However the governor believed Ustad 'Ali Akbar's story and sent for Haji Qadi, whom he detained in Shiraz, meanwhile sending Ustad 'Ali Akbar back under his protection.[117]

In 1883 a number of the Baha'is were arrested and taken before a local cleric who ordered that they be bastinadoed and thrown into prison. Some of the Baha'is gathered together and were discussing what measures to take in response. When the cleric heard of this, he became frightened and apologized to the imprisoned Baha'is, saying that his action had been for their own protection in order to diffuse demands for more severe action. He urged them to return to the Baha'i community and calm the situation down.[118]

Because the town was on the road between Shiraz and Isfahan, it was visited by many Baha'i travelling teachers: Muhammad Khan Baluch

---

115 *Vaqayi' Ittifaqiyyih* 286; Fasa'i, *Fars-namih* 2:169; Abadihi, *Vaqayi'* 56–9; Dihqan, Hadiqat ur-Rahman 38–9; B. Agah 'Sharh' 190.
116 Abadihi, *Vaqayi'* 234–5.
117 Abadihi, *Vaqayi'* 48–52. ZH 5:93 places this episode in about 1869 but since the governor is here stated to be Farhad Mirza Mu'tamad ud-Dawlih, this would make 1878 correct, which is the date given in ZH 6:878.
118 ZH 5:329–30; Baha'i, Istintaqiyyih MS B 102–3 (in this latter account it is only one person who is bastinadoed and imprisoned).

(who brought the first copy of the Kitab-i Iqan to the town in the 1870s); Nabil Akbar Qa'ini (possibly 1882); Mirza Asadu'llah Isfahani (c. 1882); Sayyid Mahdi Dihaji (possibly 1883); and Haji Mirza Haydar 'Ali Isfahani (c. 1892). The number of Baha'is in the town grew rapidly and the new religion spread to some of the nearby villages also (see pp. 304–9). This alarmed the clerics, who began to plot together against the Baha'is. The first person upon whom they vented their wrath was Mirza Ashraf. As he was one of the clerical class, they felt he was the most culpable and he was forced to go into hiding. Eventually he left Abadih for a time, travelling to India in about 1884 but finally moving to Isfahan, where he was executed in 1888 (see pp. 27–8). One interesting development was the conversion of the Englishman in charge of the English telegraph office in Abadih, Mr William Patchin (d. 1910, see fig. 113).[119]

In 1895 Aqa Mirza Aqa Nuru'd-Din Afnan, recently returned from 'Akka, came to Abadih. April 1896 saw the arrival in Abadih of both Mirza Mahmud Furughi (vol. 1:184–7), on his way home from 'Akka, and Mirza Qabil Abadihi (see pp. 305–6), returning from Yazd. There was an upsurge in Baha'i activity as a result. A short time later, Furughi presided over a Baha'i marriage ceremony for Afnan's son, Aqa Sayyid Aqa, and the daughter of Da'i Husayn. Mulla Muhammad Husayn, the Imam-Jum'ih of Abadih, felt slighted that the marriage of two such important people had occurred without his officiating and was even more upset by the fact that a Baha'i marriage ceremony had taken place. A short while later, in May 1896, news came of the assassination of Nasiru'd-Din Shah. The religious leaders of Abadih, using the fact that the Baha'is were at first thought to be responsible for the assassination and the general sense of insecurity prevailing following it, concocted reports which they sent through Zal Khan Shirazi, the head of the telegraph office, to Rukn ud-Dawlih, the governor of Fars, stating that the Baha'is were arming themselves and planning to take over the town. It happened that Sayyid Yahya Khan Tafrishi Hishmat Nizam and a troop of soldiers from Hamadan arrived in Abadih at this time. Orders were sent from Rukn ud-Dawlih that they should arrest the leading Baha'is, so Hishmat Nizam attacked their houses. The Baha'is were warned, however, by Bibi Bigum Jan, who was a sister both of the Imam-Jum'ih and of the wife of Da'i Husayn, and some escaped. Furughi, Da'i Husayn and Haji 'Ali Khan were arrested. Because Furughi

---

119 *Bahai News* (later *Star of the West*), vol. 1, no 18, p. 6; Balyuzi, *'Abdu'l-Baha* 126–7 n58; Isfahani, *Bihjat* 271–2 (trans. *Delight* 122–3).

had a letter from Rukn ud-Dawlih saying that he should be treated well, he was expelled from the town. But the guards accompanying him towards Isfahan stripped him of everything he had and left him to perish in the wilderness. With great difficulty he managed to make his way back to Abadih and hide.[120]

In the meantime, the Imam-Jum'ih ordered a search for Qabil, who was eventually found in his father-in-law's house. He was severely beaten, taken before the Imam-Jum'ih and Hishmat Nizam and after an interrogation was bastinadoed. After an hour of being bastinadoed, the brother-in-law of the Imam-Jum'ih announced to the watching crowd that the Imam-Jum'ih had decreed that whoever of the crowd beat Qabil and spat on his face would have their sins forgiven. So the crowd also seized whatever sticks they could and carried out the Imam-Jum'ih's injunction.[121] After this, the Imam-Jum'ih and Hishmat Nizam planned a surprise raid on the house of Da'i Husayn in order to find the Afnans. This was again thwarted by Bibi Bigum Jan, the sister of the Imam-Jum'ih, who warned the Baha'is, and the Afnan men hid in a neighbour's house. Another plan to arrest the Afnan women and torture them to reveal the men's whereabouts was similarly thwarted. The warning of Bibi Bigum Jan enabled the Afnan women to escape to the house of the second wife of Da'i Husayn. She, however, was not a Baha'i and asked the Afnan women to leave before dawn the next morning. They were led by a servant to an upper room in the house of a peasant woman, which was dark and dank, and where they remained for a further day before their host asked them to leave. Finally they found refuge in the home of Mirza 'Ata'u'llah Khan Siraj ul-Hukama.[122]

The Afnan men in the meantime had been taken from their hiding place in a neighbour's house after one night and, accompanied by some armed Baha'is from the nearby village of Dirghuk, were taken to the hills where they were soon joined by many other Baha'is fleeing Abadih and Dirghuk. The armed men sent word to Da'i Husayn and Haji 'Ali Khan, who were still at this time in prison, and sought permission from them and from Nuru'd-Din Afnan to attack Abadih, free the prisoners and deal with the Imam-Jum'ih. They were, however, forbidden to do this and were urged to have patience; it was pointed out that such a course of action

---

120 Afnan, Tarikh 351–69 (*Genesis* 135–40); Abadihi, *Vaqayi'* 61–4; ZH 6:85–6, 7:91–3.
121 Abadihi, *Vaqayi'* 65–7.
122 Afnan, Tarikh 369–96 (*Genesis* 140–7); ZH 7:93n.

was against the Baha'i teachings and would nullify decades of effort by the Baha'is to reassure the government. After consultation it was decided to try to telegraph the prime minister in Tehran and Rukn ud-Dawlih in Shiraz and alert them to their plight. Some 300 to 500 of the Baha'i women of Abadih, Dirghuk and Himmatabad surrounded the telegraph station in Abadih and insisted that their complaint be sent. The head of the telegraph office, Zal Khan Shirazi, was, however, an enemy of the Baha'i Faith and not only did he fail to transmit their message but, on the contrary, sent false reports about them. So the Baha'is sent word to Mirza Muhammad Taqi Afnan Vakil ud-Dawlih (see pp. 354–8) in Yazd instead.[123]

At this time, on 22 May 1896, the Qajar prince Hisam us-Saltanih arrived in Abadih on his way to Bushihr, where he had just been appointed governor. Since he had known Mirza Husayn Khan from before, he took up residence in a garden belonging to Mirza Husayn Khan, who came down from the hills where he had been in hiding to attend upon the prince. On the day that Qabil was due to be executed, Hisam us-Saltanih sent for Qabil to be brought to his presence. The crowds followed, expecting to see Qabil executed. Instead Qabil argued his innocence in front of the prince and the latter set him free and reproached Hishmat Nizam for having thrown the town into turmoil and persecuted innocent people. As a result, Da'i Husayn and Haji 'Ali Khan were also freed, although they had to pay a 'fine' of 150 *tumans* each to Hishmat Nizam.[124]

Hisam us-Saltanih left Abadih on 24 May and immediately the Imam-Jum'ih and Hishmat Nizam began to plot a further attack on the Baha'is. That evening word reached Qabil of a plan to arrest him the following morning and put him to death immediately. Therefore Qabil left for Yazd straightaway. The next day Hishmat Nizam ordered a general attack on the Baha'is and a re-arresting of Qabil, Da'i Husayn and Mirza Husayn Khan. Those Baha'is had left but their houses and the houses of many other Baha'is were looted and a number of Baha'is tortured to get them to reveal the whereabouts of the wanted men. Qabil reached Yazd on 29 May and immediately went to Vakil ud-Dawlih with the news of events in Abadih. The latter was able to alert the prime minister to what was happening in Abadih and he in turn sent instructions to Rukn ud-Dawlih in Shiraz to restore order in Abadih. Rukn ud-Dawlih sent for Hishmat Nizam to come to Shiraz with his soldiers. Without the support of the

---

123 Afnan, Tarikh 396–405 (*Genesis* 147–9); Abadihi, *Vaqayi'* 67–8.
124 Afnan, Tarikh 407–8 (*Genesis* 150); Abadihi, *Vaqayi'* 68–9.

soldiers, the anti-Baha'i campaign in Abadih died down and the Baha'is were able to return to their homes.[125]

The enmity of the Imam-Jum'ih continued, however, and when in July 1896 'Askar Khan Surmaqi was killed by one of his enemies,[126] his nephew Khusraw Khan and other members of his family were persuaded by the Imam-Jum'ih to accuse the Baha'is of this murder. When Sa'id us-Saltanih, the agent (*pīshkār*) of the new governor, arrived near Abadih, Khusraw Khan went to him and accused Da'i Husayn, Haji 'Ali Khan, Mirza Husayn Khan and 'Abbas Khan of Dirghuk (see p. 305) of the murder of 'Askar Khan because he had assisted the Imam-Jum'ih in the attack on the Baha'is. Sa'id us-Saltanih ordered the arrest of these four Baha'is. They were sent to Shiraz, beaten and imprisoned for two months and only freed after they had paid 600 *tumans*.[127]

In January 1901 (during the month of Ramadan), Qabil was invited to the village of Vazirabad (see p. 305) and had within three days succeeded in converting several people. On 12 January a number of the Muslim notables of Vazirabad came to Abadih to complain to the Imam-Jum'ih there and the latter took their complaint to Mirza Faraj Khan Mir-Panj, the governor of Abadih. The latter had Qabil and his two companions brought to him and thrown into prison. At this time Da'i Husayn went boldly up to the governor and asked why the three had been arrested. The governor replied that they had been leading people astray, had been seen eating during the month of Ramadan and had trampled underfoot the laws of Islam regarding fasting and obligatory prayer. Da'i Husayn replied that it was God who had abrogated the Islamic laws and it had nothing to do with Qabil. If the Imam-Jum'ih had a complaint to make, he should make it to God, who had brought a new revelation into being and thus ruined his line of work. The governor was at first angry with this but after Da'i Husayn left, thought about it a great deal. The next day he summoned Qabil into his presence and questioned him about the new religion. Satisfied with Qabil's answers, he freed him. The Imam-Jum'ih was furious and set off with his son, Mirza Ahmad Shaykh ul-Islam, for Shiraz, determined to get the governor dismissed. The governor

125 ZH 8a:58–78. The whole of this 1896 episode is recorded in Afnan, Tarikh 397–409 (*Genesis* 135–50); see also Abadihi, *Vaqayi'* 59–72, the latter source is reproduced in MH 2:198–203; ZH 7:93–4, 8a:23–7.

126 Abadihi, *Vaqayi'* 73 and Abadihi, Tarikh Abadih, MS A 62 state that 'Askar Khan was killed by his nephew Khusraw Khan. Abadihi, Tarikh Abadih; MS B 56 states that the killer was Na'ib Khan Bakhtiyari.

127 Abadihi, *Vaqayi'* 73–5; ZH 7:101.

sent men to forcibly return them to Abadih and meanwhile he distributed some money among the sayyids and street roughs of the town so that when the two clerics re-entered the town, they were met by a hostile crowd who accompanied them all the way to their houses. Other Muslims from surrounding villages who had grudges against the Imam-Jum'ih joined the mob surrounding his house. Then word came from the governor that they should destroy the house. Since the Baha'is were not participating in this mob, the Imam-Jum'ih saw he had no choice but to appeal to the leading Baha'is of the town to save him and his property. These Baha'is went to the governor and the latter relented and dispersed the mob.[128]

In April 1901 a certain Asadu'llah Bayk of the Qashqa'i tribe resident in Qayrukazirin (100 km south of Shiraz) claimed that a descendant of the Imams named Shah 'Abdu'llah had come to him in a dream and told him where his grave was. He had a shrine built over this grave and then began to claim that Shah 'Abdu'llah was a deputy of the Hidden Twelfth Imam who was sending messages through Shah 'Abdu'llah to Asadu'llah. A cult soon built up around this man, especially among the Qashqa'i tribes people, and he appointed emissaries called *khalīfihs* as his representatives. Some of these *khalīfihs* came to an Imamzadih shrine in Husaynabad Bahman near Abadih. Crowds of thousands gathered around the shrine and a mass hysteria developed, with some people claiming that miracles had occurred and others that they had seen the Prophet Muhammad and the Imams in and around the shrine. The Imam-Jum'ih of Abadih saw this as an opportunity to attack the Baha'is and came out in support of the cult, saying that it proved that the Baha'i claim that the Bab was the Hidden Imam was false. He began to plan an attack on the Baha'is using the mass hysteria that was developing. Soon there were people walking around the town, chanting slogans against the Baha'is and beating them wherever they found them. One of the *khalīfihs* in the shrine wrote to Mirza 'Ali Khan, the leading Baha'i of the village of Kushkak, demanding that 17 of the Baha'is of the village be handed over. Mirza 'Ali Khan sent the letter to Muntasir ud-Dawlih, the governor of Abadih, who sent it on to Shu'a' us-Saltanih, governor of Fars. The latter dispatched Dargham ud-Dawlih,

---

128 Abadihi, *Vaqayi'* 78–86 (the episode is not recorded in MS B but only in Abadihi, Tarikh, MS A 73–84); MH 2:204–9; ZH 7:132–3. This appears to be the same episode that ZH 8a:588 dates to 1315/1897, although there it is stated that the initiative for the arrest of the three Baha'is came from a *fatwa* of Aqa Najafi of Isfahan.

a chief (*Īlbīgī*) of the Qashqa'i tribe to settle the matter. As Dargham ud-Dawlih approached the shrine in Husaynabad, he sent word that he had been sent by Shah 'Abdu'llah to defeat the 'Babis'. The people in the shrine rejoiced and welcomed the troops warmly, whereupon the latter turned on them and arrested a large number of men and women. Most were fined and released but 17 of the *khalīfihs* were taken off to Shiraz in chains, where they arrived on about 12 June 1901 and were imprisoned.[129]

In May 1903, when the persecutions of the Baha'is flared up in Isfahan, Mirza Hasan Adib fled from there to Abadih where he remained for six months; other Baha'i refugees from the persecutions in Isfahan and Yazd also arrived. Adib encouraged the Baha'is to elect the first Local Spiritual Assembly of Abadih, which was formed on 2 July 1903 in the house of Siraj ul-Hukama with ten members. A little while later, Mirza Qabil was expelled from Yazd during the anti-Baha'i pogrom there and came to Abadih. The upsurge in Baha'i activity caused a reaction among the clerics and one of them, Mulla 'Abdu'llah Va'iz Shirazi, began to preach against the Baha'is from the pulpit. The governor at this time was Mirza 'Ali Muhammad Midhat ul-Mulk who was certainly very sympathetic to the Baha'i Faith and may well have secretly been a Baha'i.[130] He sent a report to the governor of Fars, 'Ala ud-Dawlih, who ordered that Mulla 'Abdu'llah be sent to Shiraz. Midhat ul-Mulk at first consulted with the Baha'is so that they prepared themselves for any reaction and then showed Mulla 'Abdu'llah the orders that had arrived from Shiraz. The latter agreed to leave for Shiraz but then went to the house of the Imam-Jum'ih to seek his assistance. The latter's son, Mirza Ahmad, who held the title Shaykh ul-Islam, went out onto the streets and roused the people with shouts, proclaiming an attack on Islam had been launched and that it was the duty of every Muslim to defend their religion. He caused the bazaar to be closed and a large crowd gathered at the house of the Imam-Jum'ih. One Baha'i, Aqa 'Abdu'l-Hamid Isfahani (the son of Mulla Ja'far Gandumpakkun, the first Babi of Isfahan) was attacked in his shop and taken off by the mob, but Dr Muhammad Husayn Khan Diya' ul-Hukama Agah (1870–1955, a son of Siraj ul-Hukama)[131] and Aqa 'Ali Uvays (who had introduced

129 Abadihi, *Vaqayi'* 96–104; ZH 7:142–3; *Vaqayi' Ittifaqiyyih* 634, 639, 640, 642; on their arrival in Shiraz, it was given out that these *khalīfihs* were 'Babis' (*Vaqayi' Ittifaqiyyih* 642).

130 Dhuka'i-Bayda'i, *Tadhkirah* 2:32–3; ZH 7:217, 8a:470–1; Abadihi, *Vaqayi'* 104–12.

131 Dhuka'i-Bayda'i, *Tadhkirih* 1:57–62.

Mirza Qabil to the Baha'i Faith, see p. 305) rushed to his assistance and managed to free him. Diya' ul-Hukama shouted defiantly to the mob: 'Do you think that this is Isfahan or Yazd [where the mob had recently killed many Baha'is]? God is my witness! If you are intent upon committing evil then we will be forced to defend ourselves and within two hours we will have all of you bound in chains.' When the crowd saw a group of armed Baha'i youth coming towards them they speedily dispersed. Just at this time Midhat ul-Mulk, who had been outside the town, returned and arrested a number of the mob. They were later fined and released. A full report was sent to Shiraz and instructions arrived for the three clerics responsible, Mulla 'Abdu'llah, the Imam-Jum'ih and the Shaykh ul-Islam, to be sent to Shiraz. They were kept there for six months and then returned.[132]

Aqa Najafi was very concerned at the situation in Abadih and at reports of the governor's conversion to the Baha'i Faith and so he sent a group of clerics there from Isfahan. These attempted first to convince Midhat ul-Mulk of the falsity of the Baha'i Faith. The latter invited them to debate this openly with the Baha'is of the town. A public debate was organized and these clerics were confronted with Adib. They debated both proofs from the Traditions and rational proofs and the clerics from Isfahan were forced to acknowledge that Adib had bested them.[133]

Independent testimony of the power and influence enjoyed by the Baha'is of Abadih is provided by Arthur Hardinge, the British ambassador in Tehran, who was passing through on his way south in 1904. He stayed overnight with one of the Baha'is of the town and has left this account of his visit:

> That night we stayed at Abadeh, the first important town of Northern 'Fars', the 'Persia proper', and the birthplace of the old race of Farsis or Parsees. We were guests, in his house, of a local magnate, who, together with most of the gentlemen bidden to meet us at dinner, were all of them also very pleasant local notables. They were, it seemed, enthusiastic votaries of the fast-growing Babi sect, most of them being Behais, as distinct from Ezelis . . . The Behais, I think, were the more numerous of the two sects, and at Abadeh they constantly exchanged the salutation 'Beha el Abha' or 'The Most Majestic Majesty'. All were keen enthusiasts for their faith and bitter foes of the Persian Ulema or Priests, and at Abadeh, our host's

---

132 Abadihi, *Vaqayi'* 104–12; ZH 7:216–18, 8a:469–70.
133 ZH 8a: 470–3.

servants sat up late into the night with our Persian escort and other attend-
ants, endeavouring to convert them to Babism. They were not, however,
fanatical in their attacks on other creeds, especially on Christians, for they
revered, even more so than ordinary Moslems, the wondrous teaching and
miracles of Christ, although they held that Christianity was not a final
revelation but a mere preparation for further developments in the religious
evolution of the world. What struck me most was the resemblance which
their attitude seemed to bear to that of the Lollards in England, and the
Hussites in Bohemia, in their dislike of the rapacity and mainly worldly or
political aims of the Shiah priesthood.[134]

Following upon the election of the Local Assembly of Abadih in 1903
there were further developments in Baha'i community life over the next
few years. The land of the site of the burial of the heads of the Nayriz
martyrs (see p. 288) had been purchased by Mirza 'Ata'u'llah Khan Siraj
ul-Hukama in 1301/1883.[135] A suitable shrine called Ḥadīqat ur-Raḥmān
(the Garden of the All-Merciful) was built in 1326/1908 at this site, and
adjacent to this, a building was constructed by Haji 'Ali Khan in 1328/1910
which was at first called the *mashriq ul-adhkar* and later the Baha'i centre
(*hazirat ul-quds*), while the land around it became the Baha'i cemetery.[136]
Diya' ul-Hukama Agah built a public baths for the Baha'is in 1329/1911.
According to a tablet of 'Abdu'l-Baha, it was the first public baths in Iran to
be built in accordance with the decree of the Kitab-i Aqdas and therefore
had running clean water and showers instead of the stagnant and filthy
pools that were the traditional form in Iranian public baths.[137]

From its earliest years, a primary concern of the Abadih Baha'i community was the education of children and traditional schools (*maktabs*) were
established in the houses of several of the Baha'is. Girls' education was also
considered important and a Baha'i *maktab* for girls was set up by Qabil at
least as early as 1898, while some girls were educated privately.[138] Haji 'Ali
Khan established a boys' school in 1908, which at first was a traditional
maktab with one teacher and 24 pupils. When the *hazirat ul-quds* was

---

134 Hardinge, *Diplomat in the East* 304–5.
135 Dihqan, Hadiqat ur-Rahman 69; B. Agah, 'Sharh' 209, gives the date as Jamadi
     II 1306/Feb. 1889.
136 ZH 8a:586; Abadihi, *Vaqayi'* 113, 258–9.
137 Mazandarani, *Ma'idih* 5:32; Abadihi, *Vaqayi'* 113–14; Dhuka'i-Bayda'i, *Tadh-
     kirih* 4:59–60; Dihqan, Hadiqat ur-Rahman 17–18; ZH 8a:586.
138 ZH 8a:586; Abadihi, *Vaqayi'* 272; Dhuka'i-Bayda'i, *Tadhkirih* 2:95.

built in 1328/1910, the school moved into this. In 1911 the Baha'is hired 'Inayatu'llah Suhrab, a new teacher who was a graduate of the American school in Tehran and, with this, the Abadih school changed to a modern syllabus.[139] Haji 'Ali Khan is also said to have started a girls' school at this time. Unfortunately this initial impetus was lost when the girls' school was closed by the governor in 1913 and the boys' school was also closed, probably after the death of Haji 'Ali Khan in 1917.[140]

In 1912 the governorship of Abadih was given to a son-in-law of Mulla Muhammad Husayn the Imam-Jum'ih, Mirza Ahmad Khan Salar Nizam, who already had a record of persecuting the Baha'is in the Abarqu area (see p. 310). On one occasion, at the instigation of the Imam-Jum'ih and Shaykh ul-Islam, he arrested and had severely beaten an elderly Baha'i, Aqa Rida-Quli Baba-Muhammadi, on the pretext of having failed to show due deference when his carriage was passing. He was also responsible for persecution and the death of a Baha'i in Kushkak (see pp. 306–7).[141]

At the end of World War I, when Britain controlled much of southern Iran through its military unit the South Persia Rifles, Muhammad 'Ali Khan Qashqa'i, governor of Abadih, was dismissed by the British in 1918 and rose up against them, supported by Sayyid Sadiq Mujtahid. Muhammad 'Ali Khan succeeded in suborning Sultan Kazim Khan, who was one of the British officials in Abadih, as well as many others in that town. He wrote to the leaders of the Baha'i community saying that they had to join him or their property and lives would be in danger. The Baha'is explained that their beliefs forbade them from taking sides in this matter. This angered Muhammad 'Ali Khan and he promised to eliminate the Baha'is from any area that fell into his hands. On 28 June 1918 Muhammad 'Ali Khan's forces besieged Abadih and that night Sultan Kazim Khan and his co-conspirators betrayed many of the fortifications into the hands of the attackers. As a result, the next day Muhammad 'Ali Khan was able to take the town, except for the office of the British telegraph service, and he installed himself as governor. He immediately gave orders that the house of Aqa Sayyid Aqa Afnan, who had been employed by the British as an

---

139 *Star of the West*, vol. 1, no. 17 (19 Jan. 1911), p. 11; vol. 2, no. 2 (9 Apr. 1911), Persian section, p. 3; Abadih, *Vaqayi'* 113, 271–2; Anonymous, 'Shamih-iy dar barih-yi Madaris-i Baha'i Abadih - 1' 32–3.

140 Anonymous, 'Shamih-iy dar barih-yi Madaris-i Baha'i Abadih - 1' 33. Ghulam-'Ali Dihqan considers it unlikely that Haji 'Ali Khan started a girls' school, see Abadihi, *Vaqayi'* 273.

141 Abadihi, *Vaqayi'* 116–17; ZH 8a:586–7.

interpreter, should be looted and he himself gleefully put a copy of the Kitab-i Aqdas that they found there onto a bonfire. Within a few hours, however, he lay dying of cholera, which also took Sayyid Sadiq Mujtahid and many of the attacking force; the rest dispersed. But Sultan Kazim remained and continued to besiege the British telegraph office while threatening to destroy the Baha'i community as soon as he had finished off the British. Then, on 18 July, a British force arrived from Shiraz, defeated Sultan Kazim Khan's forces and drove them away. The British imposed a large fine on the townspeople because of their support for Sultan Kazim Khan but exempted the Baha'is from this. After the main British force left, however, Sultan Kazim Khan returned with the remnants of his force, reinforced by Qashqa'i tribesmen under Husayn Khan Kashkuli. Prior to his arrival, he announced that he intended to destroy the Baha'i community of Abadih. Most of the Baha'is fled the town but on his arrival Sultan Kazim Khan arrested Aqa Mirza 'Abdu'l-Vahhab, son of Aqa Mirza Aqa Afnan, and obtained 7,000 *tumans* from him; similarly he arrested and mulcted 300 *tumans* from Aqa Mirza Haji Himmatabadi and 1,200 *tumans* from the mother of Aqa Fathu'llah Kushkaki. Finding no other Baha'is whom he could mulct, he was about to loot the Baha'i houses when a force arrived under Ahmad Khan Sishbuluki and put Sultan Kazim Khan and his men to flight.[142]

In March 1919 a group of 18 Baha'is set off from Abadih to visit 'Abdu'l-Baha (with one child born on the way, this made 19 by the time they arrived, 11 males and 8 females, see fig. 115). Their leaving caused a stir in Abadih and the Muslims of the town telegraphed the clerics of Shiraz to try to have the party stopped. Two of the senior clerics of Shiraz, Aqa Sayyid Ja'far Mujtahid Mahallati and Aqa Sayyid Murtada Mujtahid, went to the governor, 'Abdu'l-Husayn Mirza Farmanfarma, about this but the latter refused to countenance any action, saying that this was just a result of rivalry between the Harandi and Kurji'i clans in Abadih. In Abadih itself the governor Shaykh Mahdi Khan, who was a Shaykhi, sided with the enemies of the Baha'is and they were preparing to annihilate the Baha'is once the pilgrims had been turned back from Shiraz. Instead, however, they received a stern telegram from Farmanfarma telling them to desist from their trouble-making.[143]

The party stayed two months in Shiraz, two months in Bombay and 70 days in Haifa. While the pilgrims were with 'Abdu'l-Baha, he impressed

---

142 Abadihi, *Vaqayi'* 123–7; ZH 7:313–14.
143 Abadihi, *Vaqayi'* 127–32, 265–71.

115. Women members and children of the family of 'Abdu'l-Baha with women pilgrims from Abadih, 1919. Middle row, seated left to right: Ruha Shahid (daughter of 'Abdu'l-Baha) with arm around Hasan Shahid (her son), Diya'iyyih Khanum (mother of Shoghi Effendi), Bahiyyih Khanum (Greatest Holy Leaf, sister of 'Abdu'l-Baha), Munirih Khanum (wife of 'Abdu'l-Baha), Tuba Khanum Afnan (daughter of 'Abdu'l-Baha), Munavvar Khanum Yazdi (daughter of 'Abdu'l-Baha) with Fu'ad Afnan (son of Tuba Khanum) leaning against her. Back row, left to right, women from Nayriz: Kayhan Qurban, Aftab Agah, Tal'at Vafa, Bint Dhabih, Hayya Agah, Jamaliyyih Agah, 'Attiyih Rawshan. Front row, seated on ground, left to right: Zahra Shahid (daughter of Ruha Khanum), Mihrangiz Rabbani (sister of Shoghi Effendi), Riyad Rabbani, child standing (brother of Shoghi Effendi), Maryam Shahid (daughter of Ruha), Nusratu'llah Dhabihi

upon them the importance of re-establishing the Baha'i schools in Abadih. The pilgrims returned in January 1920 and the Tarbiyat Schools for boys and girls were opened in Abadih later that same year. The schools built up to six primary classes at a time when the government school only had four classes and so those Muslims in the town who wanted their children to have further education had to enrol them at the Baha'i school. As the first cohort of children completed their six primary classes, new teachers were recruited and secondary school classes were added to the schools. Eventually Masih Khan Agah, who had studied at Beirut, was appointed head of the boys' school. He introduced a number of modern features, such as new textbooks, gymnastics classes and the wearing of a uniform, as well as establishing morning prayers and reducing the use of corporal punishment.[144]

The Tarbiyat School for girls was established by Tal'at Khanum Vafa (see fig. 115), the daughter of Siraj ul-Hukama, who had also been on that pilgrimage in 1919. She and her husband, Mirza 'Ali Khan Vafa, had desks and benches built and started the school in their own house. There was no other girls' school in the town and so Tal'at Khanum decided to encourage Muslim girls to attend the school also. She went to Mulla Muhammad Qadi and his brother, 'Amid ul-Islam, who were the sons of Haji Muhammad 'Ali (Haji Qadi) who been an enemy of the Baha'is (see p. 290). However, they were part of the Harandi clan and she persuaded them to send their daughters to the school. With this lead the other Muslim families in Abadih also sent their daughters to the school. In the early years there were some 37 pupils, 15 of whom were from Muslim families. The school eventually went up to class 9.[145]

In November–December 1920 Mirza Munir Nabilzadih, a travelling Baha'i teacher, visited Abadih and spoke to many people. The clerics of the town wanted to stir the people up against his teaching of the Baha'i Faith but the governor prevented this. Instead, it was decided that Nabilzadih would have a public debate with Mulla Muhammad, one of the leading clerics of Abadih, at the home of a notable of the town. The debate proceeded until Mulla Muhammad declared that in the Islamic Traditions it is stated that unbelief (*kufr*) would spread throughout the world before the return of the Twelfth Imam and he was convinced that the Baha'i Faith was this *kufr* and would spread throughout the world. Nabilzadih asked whether he really believed this and the mulla replied that he did. Then Nabilzadih asked, 'Are you really longing to see the day of the return of the Lord of Age (the Twelfth Imam)?' and the mulla replied, 'Of course I am.' Whereupon Nabilzadih said, 'Then you must give every assistance to the Baha'i Faith, for the quicker it spreads throughout the world, the quicker the Imam will come.' At this the mulla got up and left in a huff.[146]

The return of the above pilgrims also signalled a renewed vitality in the Baha'i community of Abadih and a number of new converts were

---

144 Abadihi, *Vaqayi'* 134–6, 272–4; Anonymous, 'Shamih-iy dar barih-yi Madaris-i Baha'i Abadih - 2' 31–3; Shahvar, *Forgotten Schools* 158.

145 Abadihi, *Vaqayi'* 275–81; Anonymous, 'Shamih-iy dar barih-yi Madaris-i Baha'i Abadih - 2' 33–4; Shahvar, *Forgotten Schools* 104, 158–9.

146 MH 4:256–7.

made. Among these was Haji Haydar 'Ali 'Attar of the Margir (snake-catcher) gang, whose members were among the enemies of the Baha'is. His former associates led by Haji Muhammad Ibrahim did not take kindly to his conversion and stirred up trouble against the Baha'is, attacking Haji Haydar 'Ali himself and his house on at least two occasions, once during Ramadan 1340 (May 1922) and again in Ramadan 1341 (May 1923). On this second occasion a new governor of Abadih, Nusrat ul-Mamalik, arrived in the town on 24 Ramadan (10 May 1923) about six days after the attack on Haji Haydar 'Ali and while the town was still in turmoil. Because he did not immediately impose order, the mob grew more bold in their attacks on the Baha'is. When they saw that the government was not going to defend them, some of the Baha'is decided to defend themselves. After some further attacks on the Baha'is over the next two days, the Local Assembly of Abadih summoned all the Baha'is of the town and the surrounding villages to the Hadiqat ur-Rahman and from there a delegation of 300 Baha'is went to the governor's office on 12 May to ask for action on his part. He promised to prevent further trouble and, as a consequence, the troublemakers put out peace feelers. Amanu'llah Khan, the head of the gendarmes stationed in the town, organized a meeting between the nine members of the Baha'i assembly and nine representatives of the main Muslim organization of the town on 13 May. An agreement was reached that both sides would refrain from any provocative or aggressive acts.[147]

Within a month, however, the agreement was broken when Aqa 'Ali Yazdi, a Baha'i who was a financial intermediary (*dallāl*) in arranging loans from the bank, tried to reclaim a debt owed him by one of the Margir gang. The latter began to abuse and beat him. Aqa 'Ali again accosted the debtor, which ended in a scuffle. On 11 June 1923 a mob collected, baying for the blood of Aqa 'Ali for having dared lay hands on a Muslim. They attacked the Baha'i centre at Hadiqat ur-Rahman and beat the caretaker there. The governor summoned the gangleaders and told them that he would deal with Aqa 'Ali but that they must disperse the mob. Aqa 'Ali went into hiding and things settled, but on the following day there were further episodes of abuse being hurled at Baha'is. The Muslims sent telegrams to Tehran, Shiraz, Qumm, Najaf and Karbala complaining of the Baha'is. A Baha'i in the nearby village of Himmatabad was also attacked. When the Muslims found that their telegrams had no result, the tumult

---

147 Abadihi, *Vaqayi'* 136–45.

gradually died down and after 15 days Aqa 'Ali was able to re-emerge and go about his business again.[148]

Florence Schopflocher, a Canadian Baha'i, records that when she visited Abadih in 1927, 'most of the leading men of the city are Baha'is, also those in the highest military circles and those holding municipal or government posts. Therefore we have an active progressive Baha'i community. The women are a little more advanced than most other cities in the East, and many of their sons and daughters have gone to the American College at Beirut, Syria, to study medicine and other professions.'[149]

Maurits Wagenwoort, a Dutch writer and traveller who was interested in the Baha'i community, recorded that when he passed through Abadih in April 1905 the town had a population of 6,000 of whom a thousand were Baha'is (17 per cent of the population). He recorded that he believed that the Baha'is formed the most prosperous segment of the town. He also reported a somewhat militant attitude among them. Wagenwoort, who had studied the Baha'i Faith with Haji Akhund and Ibn Abhar in Tehran, noted that, although it was against the teachings of the Baha'i Faith, the Baha'is of Abadih were excellent marksmen and, warned and alarmed by what had happened in Yazd two years before, were prepared to defend themselves against the Muslims of the town with rifles if necessary.[150] Wagenwoort's estimate of the number of Baha'is may well be on the low side, however. We have seen above that as early as 1896 there were some 300–500 Baha'i women available to besiege the telegraph office. Some of those women were from the surrounding villages, but given that not all the Baha'i women would be in a position to go to the telegraph office, it is likely that this represents a Baha'i population of 1,500 (i.e. about 25 per cent of the town's population). The delegation of 300 who went to the governor in 1923 would probably have been heads of families and that again would indicate a Baha'i population of at least 1,500.

Villages around Abadih

In the villages around Abadih there were considerable Baha'i communities also. In Himmatabad (1 km east of Abadih; pop. 950 in 1951), the first to become a Baha'i was a cousin of Siraj ul-Hukama, Aqa 'Ali Akbar.

---

148 Abadihi, *Vaqayi'* 145–9.
149 Schopflocher, 'Flying', 154.
150 De Vries, *The Babi Question* 72.

Five brothers who were notables of the village also
became Baha'is. A Baha'i travellers' hospice was
founded here in the early 20th century which served
also as a *hazirat ul-quds*.[151] In Dirghuk (1 km north
of Abadih; pop. 580 in 1951), 'Abbas Khan Dirghuki
was the first Baha'i and he and his three brothers
were among the notables of the village and powerful protectors of others who became Baha'is there. A
maktab (traditional school) for girls was established
in the village by Aqa Ahmad.[152] In Vazirabad (4 km
east of Abadih; pop. 58 in 1951), the first to become
a Baha'i was Mashhadi Husayn Ra'is, who was the

116. Qabil Abadihi

kadkhuda of the village, and others followed him. In later years Mulla
Mahdi Sughadi (c. 1836–1916), one of the respected clerics of Sughad
(14 km northwest of Abadih; pop. 500 in 1951), became a Baha'i. He was
the only Baha'i in the village and the people persecuted him relentlessly,
abusing him, beating him and destroying his crops. Despite being advised
to move away from the village, he persisted in staying and eventually a few
others were converted.[153] One of these was Mashhadi Murtada, who also
suffered much at the hands of the villagers.[154]

In 1881 Mirza 'Abbas, who took the pen-name Qabil and is generally
known as Qabil Abadihi (July 1863–December 1936, see fig. 116), of the
village of Idrisabad (1.5 km southeast of Abadih; pop. 534 in 1951), became
a Baha'i, having learned of the new religion through his Baha'i brother-in-
law Aqa 'Ali Uvays. The village mulla and *kalantar* conspired against him,
however, and on 5 July 1884 arrested him and took him off to the *kalantar*'s house where he was beaten and was about to be drowned when his
relatives stormed the house and rescued him. He went to live in Abadih,
leaving behind in the village several converts, including members of his
family. He was to become a noted travelling teacher of the Baha'i Faith,
going often to the Yazd area (where he was arrested and freed during the
1903 pogrom), and he was imprisoned and beaten on several occasions in

151 Abadihi, *Vaqayi'* 115–16; ZH 8a:586.
152 Abadihi, *Vaqayi'* 240–3, 272.
153 Abadihi, Tarikh Abadih, MS B 137–9; this and the next reference do not appear
     in MS A or the published book.
154 Abadihi, Tarikh Abadih, MS B 139–44; for later developments in this village and
     the two nearby villages of 'Abbasabad and Bahman, see M.T. Afnan, 'Hikayat'
     and Abadihi, *Vaqayi'* 162–5.

117. Mirza 'Ali Khan Kushkaki

the Abadih area, among them in 1896 (when he was given a thousand strokes of the cane), 1901 and 1903 (see accounts above). He visited 'Abdu'l-Baha with his nephew Mirza Nasru'llah Rawshan in 1317/1899 and with the large group of Abadih Baha'is in 1919–20. He was a poet and wrote several works about the Baha'i Faith: a book of proofs, a general history and local histories of Abadih and of several of the villages in the Yazd area (see Bibliography).[155]

In Kushkak (5 km west of Abadih; pop. 1,000 in 1951), the first Baha'i was Karbala'i Muhammad Salmani. Later Navvab Aqa Mirza Hidayatu'llah Khan, the *kalantar* of the village, and another notable, Mirza 'Ali Khan Kushkaki (see fig. 117), became Baha'is. The latter later founded a Baha'i travellers' hospice in the village, which served also as a *hazirat ul-quds,* and a local assembly was also established in the early 20th century (see below).[156] Baha'i children from the villages around Abadih used to go daily to the Baha'i schools in Abadih except for girls from Kushkak, which was a little more distant. Here what was in effect a branch of the main schools in Abadih was established, with teachers and senior students from the main schools coming out and teaching up to primary class 5, then the girls from the village would go to Abadih for class 6.[157]

As noted above, the governorship of Abadih was given to Mirza Ahmad Khan Salar Nizam (see pp. 299, 310) of Abarqu, a son-in-law of the Imam-Jum'ih, in 1912. The Imam-Jum'ih's son, the Shaykh ul-Islam, persuaded

---

155 Abadihi, *Vaqayi'* 53–6, 246–9; MH 2:182–234; ZH 6:879–86. In his history (*Vaqayi'* 53), Qabil says he became a Baha'i in December 1881, however in a poem (ZH 6:880), he says that he became a Baha'i in 1880.
156 Abadihi, *Vaqayi'* 115; ZH 8a:586.
157 Abadihi, *Vaqayi'* 279.

the new governor to take action against the Baha'is. The governor ordered four of his men to kill Mirza 'Ali Khan Kushkaki. On 23 August 1913 during the month of Ramadan, these four came to Mirza 'Ali's house and asked him to accompany them to the governor. As they walked away from the house, they drew out their guns and shot Mirza 'Ali Khan. He died later that day of his wounds. The Baha'is complained to Shiraz about what had happened and orders were sent that the murderers should be sent to Shiraz. Salar Nizam tried to get the family to forgo pressing the matter by offering them money but they refused. Instead, he sent money to the governor of Shiraz. After the culprits had spent six months in prison, the governor received more money from Salar Nizam and the men were freed and sent to Abarqu. Salar Nizam himself was also dismissed from his governorship and went to Abarqu. The Baha'is continued to press their complaint by telegraphing to Tehran. Salar Nizam was summoned to Tehran, and after nine months of fighting his case and spending 50,000 *tumans*, he eventually was able to return to Abarqu.[158]

In 1922–3 Abadih was much disturbed by anti-Baha'i persecutions (see p. 303). When these did not have the results desired by Haji Muhammad Ibrahim, the leader of the Margir gang, he and the gang turned their attention to trying to disrupt the good relations that had existed between the Baha'is and Muslims in Kushkak. They recruited two people from the village to spread accusations and try to raise trouble. The Baha'is did not rise to the bait however. Then a group from the gang came to Kushkak. They told the Muslims that they could not be said to be good Muslims while they mixed with Baha'is, who are *najis* (ritually impure), in the public baths and allowed Baha'i barbers to shave them. The two Baha'i barbers were prevented from working in the public baths. They got an order from the governor to allow them back into the baths but on 16 February 1924 the two were thrown out of the baths and beaten. They went back to the governor, who did nothing about this. This encouraged the mob, which now began to wander about the village abusing and attacking Baha'is. One of the local notables even offered a reward of 10,000 *tumans* for whoever would kill the two Baha'i barbers. A mob went on the rampage, looking for the two Baha'is. The Baha'is of the village barricaded themselves into an old fort and fought back to defend themselves. The Muslims of the village went to Abadih to try to raise a larger mob from there. Eventually

---

158 Abadihi, *Vaqayi'* 117–23; ZH 7:302.

Amanu'llah Khan Yavar, the head of the gendarmerie, threatened the mob, causing them to disperse. Amanu'llah Khan came to Kushkak to investigate the matter and the result was that he arrested 17 Baha'is and returned to Abadih. The mob attacked the other Baha'is of Kushkak, who then had to flee into the hills. The Baha'is of Abadih telegraphed to Shiraz and Tehran and eventually orders came for the prisoners to be freed. After 23 days in prison and being fined, the prisoners were released. It took some time for the Baha'is to return from the hills and for life in Kushkak to return to normal.[159]

In Surmaq (24 km southeast of Abadih; pop. about 5,000 in 1914 and 4,360 in 1951), a large village on the main road to Shiraz where a branch road to Yazd joins, there were a number of people who were much opposed to the Baha'i Faith, including 'Askar Khan Surmaqi and his nephew Khusraw Khan, who had assisted the Imam-Jum'ih of Abadih in the attack on the Baha'is in 1896 (see p. 294). Aqa Sayyid Ya'qub Surmaqi became a Baha'i and some of the people of the village planned to kill him on account of this. In the summer of 1893 a group headed by Khusraw Khan attacked Sayyid Ya'qub with clubs and knives when he left the village one day, eventually leaving him dead by the roadside. His sons and relatives appealed to the governor of Fars for justice and the case was sent to the governor of Abadih to determine, but the latter, after receiving a bribe, did nothing.[160] In Chinar (18 km southeast of Abadih; pop. 460 in 1951), Karbala'i 'Ali Khan and Mulla Amir were two brothers who brought many into the new religion. There was also Mulla Muhammad 'Ali, a notable of the village. During the persecution of the Baha'is of Abadih in 1896, Khusraw Khan attacked the Baha'is of the village of Chinar and looted the houses of Karbala'i Ali Khan and Mulla Amir.[161] Mirza Husayn Khan, the above-mentioned prominent Baha'i of Abadih, owned property in the Surmaq area and in particular in the village of Faydabad (2 km southeast of Surmaq; pop. 380 in 1951). After his death in 1316/1898, his brother 'Abdu'l-Karim Khan put a Baha'i, Aqa Sayyid Mirza, in charge of these properties. He resided in Faydabad and was quite open and fearless in promoting the Baha'i Faith in the area. This roused the wrath of Khusraw Khan and the other opponents of the Baha'i Faith in Surmaq and in early 1900 they attacked Aqa Sayyid Mirza, causing injuries that resulted in

---

159 Abadihi, *Vaqayi'* 149–55.
160 Abadihi, *Vaqayi'* 59–61; ZH 7:45–6.
161 Abadihi, *Vaqayi'* 37–8, 62–4, 73; ZH 7:101.

his death a short time later. Sometime after this, these opponents of the Baha'i Faith fell out among themselves. Khusraw Khan, in a bid for complete power in the Surmaq area, invited the other notables of the area to a banquet at his house and had them all murdered by his men after they had eaten. He in turn was shot dead by a robber a short time later.[162]

Abarqu and Isfandabad

The small town of Abarqu lies on the road between Yazd and Shiraz (218 km southwest of Yazd, 300 km northeast of Shiraz and 72 km east of Abadih; pop. 7,290 in 1951). The main crops grown in the area are grain and cotton and the main craft is the production of canvas fabric. This area was sometimes under the jurisdiction of the province of Yazd and sometimes of Fars.

There was no Baha'i community in Abarqu until 1949 but the Baha'i Faith was established in the nearby village of Isfandabad (25 km south of Abarqu; pop. 1,842 in 1951) in about 1886.[163] According to the oral tradition among the Baha'is of the village, three of the villagers, 'Ali 'Askar, Haji Ghulam-Rida and Haji 'Ali Biman, who owned shops in the village, went to Bavanat to purchase dried fruit and nuts from that area for their shops. While there, they were told about the Baha'i Faith and accepted the religion. They returned and about 20 people from the village were converted.[164] According to another account, it was Mulla Husayn from the village who went to Munj in the Bavanat area in the early 1890s, where he was employed by Sayyid Musa Yazdi (see below under 'Bavanat') to teach the children of the village and was eventually converted by him. He returned to Isfandabad to collect his wife and family and return to Munj but while he was back he succeeded in converting Aqa Sayyid Ja'far, Imam-Jum'ih and judge (qaḍi), and Ustad Zaman, and the three of them in turn converted some 60 in the village. Mulla Husayn returned to the village several times and the number of Baha'is grew. Meanwhile, Aqa Sayyid Ja'far went to Abadih where he obtained Baha'i books.[165]

In February 1901 a travelling Baha'i teacher, Mirza Mahmud Zarqani, came to Isfandabad and stayed at the house of Aqa Sayyid Ja'far. He began

---

162 Abadihi, *Vaqayi'* 76–8; ZH 7:130.
163 Ishraq-Khavari, *Taqvim* 106.
164 Oral interview Mrs Zibandih Shams-Isfandabadi (Khursandniya), at Skals, Denmark, 16 July 2006.
165 Malmiri, *Tarikh Yazd* 467; ZH 7:35–6.

to teach a number of the inhabitants of the village and this aroused the hostility of the clerics. Among those who attended the meetings was Haji Isma'il, the *kadkhuda* of the village. Although outwardly he expressed approval of what he heard, in secret he sent reports to Mulla (or Mirza) 'Abdu'l-Ghani, Mujtahid of Abarqu. The latter became enraged at these reports and pressured Mirza Ahmad Khan Salar Nizam, the governor of Abarqu, into sending some men to arrest Zarqani. By the time the men, under the leadership of Haji Asadu'llah Khan, arrived in Isfandabad on 17 March 1901, Zarqani had left for Yazd and so they arrested two of the Baha'is, Aqa Sayyid Ja'far and Ustad Muhammad Zaman Sabbagh (dyer), and with much beating and abuse dragged them back to Abarqu, where they were thrown into prison. On the day of Naw-Ruz, when the notables of Abarqu were gathered at the house of Mulla 'Abdu'l-Ghani to greet him, the discussion turned to the prisoners and Mulla 'Abdu'l-Ghani ordered that they be brought before him. Since they openly asserted that they were Baha'is, they were thrown back into prison and Mulla 'Abdu'l-Ghani issued a *fatwa* for their death. On 2 April 1901, the thirteenth day after Naw-Ruz, which is a traditional time for festivities, Salar Nizam ordered that the two men be publicly paraded through the town so that the whole population could partake in their execution. They were subjected to much torture including beatings, stabbings, having their ears cut off and being forced to eat them and having nails driven into their bodies. Eventually, after a whole morning of such torture, they both expired. Ustad Zaman's body was burned and his ashes scattered while Aqa Sayyid Ja'far's body was covered with rocks out in the wilderness.[166]

Mulla 'Abdu'l-Ghani and Haji Isma'il continued to campaign against the Baha'is of Isfandabad. Haji Isma'il grew fearful that Aqa [Muhammad] Rida (the brother of the above-mentioned Mulla Husayn, who was one of the first Baha'is of the village), who was famous for his bravery and fearlessness, would exact revenge on him for his part in the death of the two Baha'is, and so he obtained the permission of Salar Nizam to have Aqa Rida killed. By night on 1 September 1901 Haji Isma'il and a number of his men climbed the walls of Aqa Rida's house and shot him to death as he lay sleeping.[167] As a result of this campaign, several of the Baha'is, including Mulla Husayn, left the village, while other Baha'is withdrew to a fort at Asadabad to protect

---

166 MH 2:217–24; Afnan, 'Shuhada-yi Abarqu'; ZH 7:136–8; Abadihi, *Vaqayi'* 86–96.

167 Malmiri, *Tarikh Yazd* 470; MH 2:225; ZH 7:143, 144.

themselves. This level of pressure went on for two years. The Baha'is of Abadih protested to local and national governmental authorities. Da'i Husayn even telegraphed Muzaffaru'd-Din Shah, who was in Paris, all to no avail.[168]

In 1320/1902 Zaynab Khanum, the Muslim wife of one of the Baha'is, Aqa Husayn, poisoned and killed her husband. Shortly afterwards that same year the people of the village caught two Baha'is, Muhammad 'Ali and Husayn, in an isolated area and beat them such that Muhammad 'Ali died. On another occasion in late August or early September 1904, Haji Isma'il, together some of his men and a mob of some 50 people, followed four of the Baha'is – Ja'far (brother of the above mentioned Muhammad 'Ali); two brothers, Amru'llah and Aqa 'Ali; and one other – out of the fort of Asadabad to the land they cultivated at Valiyabad. Seeing the mob coming, the four Baha'is fled towards the walled village of Haruni, seeking refuge there, but Mulla Sayyid Hadi, the mulla of the village, ordered the gates of the village to be closed in the face of the Baha'is. So the four Baha'is ran for the nearby hills but were headed off by Haji Isma'il and some of his men on horses. Seeing no other recourse, the men lay in a ditch and brought out their guns. Haji Isma'il urged on the mob, reading out to them the *fatwa* of the Abarqu clerics, which included the promise of a hundred *tumans* and a cloak of honour from the clerics of Najaf to whomever brought them one of the Baha'is dead or alive. Then he thought of a deception to capture the men. He sent them a Qur'an in which he had signed and sealed a declaration to the effect that the men would come to no harm. The four Baha'is agreed to this. Then, as Haji Isma'il and his men approached the four Baha'is, he called out that everyone who was with him and was obedient to the command of Mulla 'Abdu'l-Ghani Mujtahid must shoot these wayward people. There was a hail of bullets and the four Baha'is fell. They finished off the two Baha'is who still showed signs of life and then burned the bodies.[169]

On another occasion, in the winter of 1904, Haji Isma'il led a night attack on the Baha'is sheltering in the fort of Asadabad. He had brought a ladder to scale the walls and planned to set upon the Baha'is and kill them all. But Kaka Sadiq, an elderly Baha'i, was awake, heard them coming and fired a gun in their direction, causing the attackers to disperse. The men of the Baha'i community held a hurried consultation and decided that

168 MH 2: 224–5; ZH 7:143; Malmiri, *Tarikh Yazd* 467–70.
169 ZH 7:144–5.

Haji Isma'il was not going to rest until he had killed all of them, including their women and children. They decided that the best plan was to counter-attack immediately. So they took the ladder that the Muslim attackers had discarded and set off for the fort of Haji Isma'il. There was then a battle which the Baha'is won, resulting in the death of Haji Isma'il and his nephew and many of his men. Shortly afterwards a cholera epidemic struck, resulting in the death of Mulla 'Abdu'l-Ghani.[170]

These two deaths did not spell the end of the troubles of the Isfandabad Baha'is, however. Haji Isma'il's brother, Mulla Baqir, now arose to avenge his brother. He wrote to both Murtada-Quli Khan, governor of Abarqu, and to Zill us-Sultan, in whose provincial jurisdiction the area lay. Murtada-Quli Khan came to Isfandabad and laid siege to the Baha'is in their fort. One of the besieged Baha'is succeeded in getting through the siege to Yazd, where he alerted Haji Mirza Mahmud Afnan to events in Isfandabad. The latter persuaded Jalal ud-Dawlih, governor of Yazd, to write to Murtada-Quli Khan and instruct him to withdraw from the siege. Mulla Baqir appealed again to Zill us-Sultan, who sent men to the village and arrested Aqa 'Ali Muhammad and Aqa Qasim, the brothers of Aqa Rida. They were taken to Isfahan where they languished in gaol for six months until Mirza Asadu'llah Khan Vazir intervened and paid a sum of money to obtain their release. The prisoners returned to Isfandabad. Some time later, Mulla Baqir paid a sum of money to Taqi, a servant of Aqa 'Ali Muhammad. Taqi crept up on Aqa 'Ali Muhammad and shot him dead while he lay asleep and then took refuge in the house of Mulla Baqir. The Baha'is were unable to obtain any redress for this and several of them moved away from the village afterwards.[171]

In about 1906 Mulla Baqir paid a bribe to Sardar Firuz Kamarkuhi who, with his Shahsivan cavalry, was in charge of the military in Fars, to send some of his horsemen to attack the Baha'is of Isfandabad. The Baha'is heard of this and fled the village, so when the horsemen arrived, the only Baha'i they found was Kaka Sadiq tending his land outside the village. They seized him and beat and tortured him to tell them where the other Baha'is were. But he remained silent on this. So they bound him and took him to Bavanat, where Sardar Firuz urged him to recant and to curse the Baha'i Faith. He refused to do this and, indeed, asserted that it was he and no one else who had killed Haji Isma'il. He was sent

170 ZH 7:146; MH 2:226.
171 Malmiri, *Tarikh Yazd* 470–1; MH 2:226–7; ZH 7:146–7.

in chains to Shiraz and thrown into prison there. Aqa Mirza Aqa Afnan went repeatedly to see the governor and spent money trying to obtain his release and to demonstrate that he was not guilty of any crime. Eventually the governor showed Afnan an order saying that Kaka Sadiq had to be sent to Tehran. He remained in prison there for some months before the Constitutional Revolution occurred and he was set free as a consequence of that. During the absence of Kaka Sadiq, Mulla Sayyid Hadi had urged his Baha'i wife to remarry. He repeated this so much that eventually she burst out saying, 'Do not do something that will cause me to beat you over the head.' Another action of the enemies of the Baha'is was to send out two men to Jiyan in the Bavanat area in 1913, where lived Aqa Abu'l-Qasim, whose two brothers Amru'llah and Aqa 'Ali had already been killed. When they found him, they shot him and buried his body under a pile of stones, then returned to Isfandabad. Similarly, Aqa 'Ali Muhammad left the village and moved to 'Azizabad. He was ill and his wife left him in the care of a certain Taqi while she went to obtain some milk. While she was away, Taqi shot 'Ali Muhammad. He was still alive when his wife returned and, before he died, forbade her to pursue his murderer.[172]

Bavanat and surrounding area

Bavanat is the name of an area in the east of the province of Fars (125 km southeast of Abadih and 140 km northeast of Shiraz). The main village of the area is Suriyan. Sayyid Yahya Darabi passed through Bavanat on his way to Nayriz and the Shaykh ul-Islam, Haji Sayyid Isma'il, and a considerable number of the population are reported to have become Babis.[173] The Afnans of Yazd (in particular, the sons of Haji Mirza Hasan 'Ali, the uncle of the Bab) came to own much property around Bavanat, particularly the villages of Munj (30 km southeast of Suriyan; pop. 484 in 1951), Khurrami (66 km west of Suriyan; pop. 1,851 in 1951), Bayan (82 km west of Suriyan; pop. 74 in 1951) and Tutak (48 km southeast of Suriyan; pop. 125 in 1951), which they owned. In these villages they made many improvements, for example, building public baths in Bayan and arranging for a Baha'i, Haji Mirza Husayn Mu'allim Yazdi, a Najaf- and Karbala-educated former cleric, to teach the children in Munj for some eight years

---

172 ZH 7:147–8, 226. The Baha'is of Isfandabad were to be subjected to another major persecution in 1950; see Afnan, *Bigunahan* 50–83.
173 DB 475–6.

from about 1885 to about 1893.[174] Haji Sayyid 'Ali Mihrizi, who had been forced to leave Mihriz, was for a time the agent of the Afnans in Munj.[175] Baha'i communities were established in the first three of these villages but the people of Tutak never became Baha'is and at times even acted against the Baha'is.[176]

As a consequence of the power of the Afnan family, this area became a relatively secure locality for Baha'is. Mulla Muhammad Sadiq Tafti (see p. 408) fled persecution in Taft and settled in Bavanat, where he converted over a hundred of the inhabitants to the Baha'i Faith.[177] During the anti-Baha'i pogrom in Yazd in 1903, the Afnans were able to summon riflemen from Bavanat to protect them in Yazd and then have them conduct Mirza Mahmud Zarqani and Aqa Muhammad Husayn Ulfat safely back to Munj.[178]

Bayan belonged to Haji Sayyid Mahdi Afnan. Khurrami, which had about 400 families and a population of about 1,400 in the late 19th century, was half owned by him. From about the 1880s Aqa Sayyid Musa Yazdi, the son of one of the companions of Sayyid Vahid Darabi, was the agent of the Afnans in Bavanat and taught many of the people there the Baha'i Faith.[179] Mirza Muhammad Tahir Malmiri (see pp. 359–60) spent ten years in the area from about 1885 onwards, after he had been forced to leave Yazd. In about 1897, after two years in Abadih, Malmiri arranged to rent Khurrami and Bayan from Sayyid Mahdi and he spent most of the year in Bavanat and the three harvest months in Khurrami until about 1901. Eventually Mustafa Big, who was responsible for guarding the roads in the area, became a Baha'i and brought into the Faith all of his family. Through him, Muhammad Hasan Khan, one of the notables of the area, and Mirza Husayn, *kadkhuda* of Khurrami, became Baha'is. Through the latter and his son, Mirza Mahmud, many of the inhabitants of the village became Baha'is.[180] Another of the notables who became a Baha'i was Aqa Muhammad Ja'far Khan, together with some 30 of his relatives.[181]

Hirat is an area east of Bavanat, about 200 kilometres south of Yazd

---

174 Malmiri, *Khatirat* 128; MH 6:405–8; Yazdi, *Tarikh 'Ishqabad* 430–3.
175 Malmiri, *Tarikh Yazd* 37–8. After Sayyid 'Ali Mihrizi had lived for a time in Munj, he settled near Abadih where he developed a farm called Jannatabad.
176 Malmiri, *Khatirat* 139, 225.
177 Malmiri, *Tarikh Shuhada* 232–3.
178 ZH 8a:565.
179 Rawhani, *Lamahat* 144–5.
180 Malmiri, *Khatirat* 125–32; MH 5:333–5.
181 Malmiri, *Tarikh Shuhahda* 384.

and about 100 kilometres north of Nayriz. After the first Nayriz upheaval in 1850, Sayyid Ja'far Yazdi, a Babi and prominent cleric of Nayriz, was sent under escort from that town. He stopped at Hirat and was asked to remain there, lead the prayers and be the religious authority in the area, which he did for five years.[182] The Afnans of Yazd, and in particular Vakil ud-Dawlih, came to own property in this area and a Baha'i community was established.[183] The village of Marvast (168 km south of Yazd; 160 km north of Nayriz; pop. 2,542 in 1951) was owned by Haji Mirza Aqa Afnan (a son of Haji Mirza Hasan 'Ali) and his son, Aqa Mirza Muhammad Javad, was resident to supervise affairs. There was a Baha'i community here and many of those fleeing persecution in Yazd came first to Marvast before going on to other places.[184] A tablet of 'Abdu'l-Baha from 1919 is addressed to 21 men of the village. If these were all heads of households, this would indicate a Baha'i community of about a hundred. This area is now part of the Yazd province.

Marvdasht

Marvdasht is the name of the plain on which the ruins of Persepolis are situated (some 50 km northeast of Shiraz beyond Zarqan and the Kur River). In this area there were several villages where Baha'i communities came into being during the time of Baha'u'llah and a number of the notables became Baha'is: in Firuzi (24 km from Zarqan; pop. 120 in 1914, 390 in 1951), Karbala'i Aqa Muhammad, the headman (*kadkhuda*), and his sons; in Fathabad (26 km from Zarqan; pop. 1,555 in 1951), Mirza Mahdi Khan, a local notable, Aqa Mahmud, the *kalantar*, and several clerics such as Mulla Abu'l-Qasim, Mulla Muhammad Sadiq, Mulla Muhammad Taqi and Mulla Muhammad Hasan; in Hajiyabad (44 km from Zarqan; pop. 1,092 in 1951), Mirza 'Ali Akbar Munshi; in Kushk (21 km from Zarqan; pop. 930 in 1951), Asad Khan Dabit (policeman) and his son. Also in this general area were Bandamir (14 km east of Zarqan; pop. 1,160 in 1951), where Muhammad Hashim Khan, the *kalantar*, and his son became Baha'is; and in Nasrabad Ramjird (35 km north of Zarqan; pop. 216 in 1951), were Haji Mulla Kazim, the *kalantar*, and his son Mulla

---

182 ZH 3:294.
183 Malmiri, *Khatirat* 134.
184 Malmiri, *Tarikh Shuhada* 340.

118. 'Abbas 'Ali Khan Binish (Diya' ush-
Shu'ara, Haqju)

Muhammad Hasan, who was poisoned by one of the clerics.[185]

One of the Baha'is of the Marvdasht area was 'Abbas 'Ali Khan who
had the pen-name Binish (Diya' ush-
Shu'ara, Haqju, 1284/1867–1940, see
fig. 118). He was born in 'Imadabad
(22 km north of Zarqan; pop. 691 in
1951) into a distinguished family. His
grandfather had been in Tehran visiting his brother, who was a surgeon to
the shah and had witnessed the executions of the Babis and in particular
of Sulayman Khan in 1852. He had
been much affected by this and Binish
heard this story from him. When he
was 13 he was married to a girl from
a Baha'i family. Through her, her
parents and Haji Mirza Haydar 'Ali
Isfahani, he was converted to the Baha'i Faith. His parents opposed him
and cut him off, so he left for Tehran. His father wrote to his relatives in
Tehran to apprehend him and return him to them. He therefore left for
Shiraz. After a time there, he fell foul of Muhammad Rida Khan Qavam
ul-Mulk and his house was looted. He was forced to set off on travels,
during which he taught the Baha'i Faith in many places, including India.
From 1906 for ten years he worked in government offices in Shiraz but
then the mullas plotted with the Qashqa'i tribal chiefs to have his house
in 'Imadabad looted and him dismissed from his position. From 1916 he
went into the service of Mirza Ibrahim Khan Qavam ul-Mulk and from
1918 he was made responsible for supervising the sons of Qavam while
they were studying in Beirut. He was a poet and also wrote a number of
treatises on the crafts of Iran.[186]

Qalat (33 km northwest of Shiraz; pop. 2,807 in 1951) was a large
village in which there were many Shaykhis. A group of them, when they
heard of the proclamation of the Bab in Mecca, went to the village of
Davan on the road to Burazjan to greet the Bab on his return. There they

185 ZH 6:894.
186 ZH 6:894–6, 8a:595; Dhuka'i-Bayda'i, *Tadhkirih* 1:228–35.

stayed with a Shaykhi cleric who showed them the book of Karim Khan Kirmani against the Bab (*Izhaq al-Batil*, composed in 1261/1845) and they decided against what they had proposed to do and returned to Qalat. Sayyid Baqir Saqqa'i of Qalat had been a water-carrier servicing the house of the Bab and had always defended the Bab against any who attacked the new religion. Later, in 1280/1863, Zill us-Sultan, who was at that time governor of Fars, arrested a number of the Shaykhi leaders and clerics of Qalat, accusing them of being Babis. He fined them and looted their houses. Then on the intervention of a number of notables, he relented and returned the fines to Shaykh 'Abdu'l-Husayn, the leading mulla of the village, who was supposed to return the money to those who had been fined. He, however, took the whole amount himself. This caused a great deal of dissension in the village and Mulla 'Ali Akbar, one of those who had been wronged, began to talk to two of the Baha'is of Shiraz, Haji Husayn Khayyat and Haji Ghulam-Husayn, and was converted. He then converted many others in the village, including Mulla Muhammad Rida and Mulla Ghulam-Husayn.[187]

Zarqan

Zarqan is a small town (some 35 km northeast of Shiraz; pop. about 3,500 in 1914 and 8,990 in 1956), which was at the completion of the first stage of the journey from Shiraz to Isfahan and therefore one of the main occupations in the town was that of muleteer, providing animals for those travelling on this road. A strong Baha'i community emerged here during the time of Baha'u'llah, including some of the notables of the town such as Haji Jamshid, the *kalantar* of the town, Mulla 'Abbas and Karbala'i Aqa Muhammad, another *kalantar* of the town, and his sons. Karbala'i Hasan, although illiterate, was an effective propagator of the Baha'i Faith.

Mulla 'Abdu'llah Baka (c. 1235–after 1875) received a religious education in Shiraz and returned to his home town where he was a cleric and a farmer. In about 1856 Mirza Hasan Va'iz Khurasani came to the town and converted Baka to the Babi religion. Baka in turn converted a number of people in the town, and when Baha'u'llah's claim became known, all the Babis of the town became Baha'is. On two occasions, the second being in the late 1870s, the clerics complained about Baka to the governor of Shiraz

---

187 ZH 6:897–8.

119. Fadil Zarqani (Mulla 'Abdu'llah)

and he was summoned to Shiraz. On both occasions he managed to obtain his freedom and return to Zarqan. He also taught the Baha'i Faith in other places around Fars.[188]

One of those who were taught the Baha'i Faith by Mulla 'Abdu'llah Baka was another Mulla 'Abdu'llah called Mulla 'Abdu'llah Fadil Zarqani (1257/1841–1327/1909, see fig. 119). His father was a builder but sent his son to Baka's *maktab* to become literate. Baka recognized the boy's aptitude and taught him Arabic and Persian literature as well. Fadil was also taught the Babi Faith by Baka and became a Babi at about the age of 18 in 1275/1858, later becoming a Baha'i. Fadil moved to Shiraz where he quickly mastered the Islamic sciences at the religious colleges there, becoming particularly adept at philosophy and mystical philosophy. He taught these subjects in Shiraz at the Madrasih Mansuriyyih, and when he was expelled from there as a Baha'i by its head Falasiri, he taught these subjects to a group of students in his own house. He was arrested as a Baha'i on several occasions. When Shaykh ur-Ra'is came to Shiraz and Shu'a' us-Saltanih became governor in 1901, these two compelled the Madrasih to take Mulla 'Abdu'llah back.[189]

Probably the most well-known Baha'i of Zarqan was Mirza Mahmud Zarqani (c. 1290/1873–October 1927, see fig. 120), who like his father was a maker of light summer shoes (*givih*). It appears he was born into a Baha'i family and he himself records that he became a Baha'i at the age of 16, taught by Nayyir and Sina, whom he then accompanied on some of their journeys. From 1896 he accompanied Mirza Haydar 'Ali Isfahani on his travels through Iran, then travelled through India from 1903 onwards and

188 ZH 6:864; Dhuka'i-Bayda'i, *Tadhkirih* 4:290–2.
189 ZH 6:863–4; Dhuka'i-Bayda'i, *Tadhkirih* 3:143–50; E.G. Browne met this man in Shiraz in 1888 and in *Year among the Persians* 354–60 there is a lengthy account of a discussion they had.

finally acted as a secretary for 'Abdu'l-
Baha and accompanied him on his
western journeys in 1912–13, resulting in a two-volume published diary
about that journey, *Bada'i' ul-Athar*.
He returned to India in 1914. After
the passing of 'Abdu'l-Baha, Shoghi
Effendi asked him to come to Haifa,
where he acted as secretary for a time
before returning to Iran.[190]

Mirza Jalal Zarqani, the son of
Mulla 'Abdu'llah Baka, was a close
companion of Haji Mirza Muhammad
Mu'addil ul-Mulk and went with the
latter when he was appointed by Zill
us-Sultan as his deputy as governor
of Yazd in 1302/1884. Mirza Jalal
then studied medicine in Tehran and

120. Mirza Mahmud Zarqani

returned to Zarqan, where he set up a medical practice as well as emulating
his father by preaching from the pulpit.[191] Later he moved to Shiraz where
he and 'Andalib conducted a vigorous campaign promoting the Baha'i Faith
in 1902, resulting in uproar in that city (see p. 276). In 1903, when news
arrived of the anti-Baha'i pogrom in Yazd, one of the religious leaders in
Zarqan, Mulla 'Ali Akbar, tried to rouse the people against the Baha'is in
the village and in particular against Ustad Ahmad Mulki-duz (shoemaker).
When news of this reached Shiraz, Mirza Jalal Zarqani decided to organize a
petition to the governor of the province, asking for freedom for the Baha'is.
The governor 'Ala ud-Dawlih was annoyed at this and sent word through
Qavam ul-Mulk that now was not the time for such petitions.[192] 'Abdu'l-
Baha wrote to a list of 57 Baha'is in Zarqan. Assuming these were heads of
families, there must have been of the order of 280 Baha'is in Zarqan.[193]

In the district of Zarqan is the village of Faruq (56 km northeast of
Zarqan; pop. 1,725 in 1951), where a small Baha'i community arose. The

---

190 MH 8:147–230; Dhuka'i-Bayda'i 4:183–6; ZH 8a:564–6. His diary of 'Abdu'l-
Baha's journey to the West in 1912–13 has been translated into English (see
Bibliography).
191 ZH 8a:566–7.
192 Afnan, Tarikh 434–6 (*Genesis* 159–60).
193 ILMA 84:432–3.

owner of the village, Haji Aqa, persecuted these Baha'is such that some of them migrated from the village, while the rest kept their beliefs hidden. In 1920 Haji Aqa's brother, Haji Ahmad, tortured and killed Aqa Mustafa, son of Haji Malik, one of the Baha'is of the village.[194]

Nayriz

The town of Nayriz (288 km southeast of Shiraz; pop. 7,500 in 1850,[195] 10,000 in 1914 and 15,391 in 1951) is situated at the south end of a large lake of the same name. The area is dominated by the 'Arab tribe, a Persian-speaking tribe (the name comes from the fact that the tribe originally migrated from Arabia in the 7th century during the Islamic conquest) that was part of the Khamsih federation of tribes in Fars. Agriculture in the area was carried on with irrigation by *qanats*; crops were mainly fruit, grains and opium.

There was a strong Babi community in Nayriz as a result of the conversion by Vahid in 1850 of some one-third of the population of the town. The town consisted of three quarters and the Chinar-Sukhtih quarter (also known as the Chinar-Shahi and, in the 20th century, the Pahlavi quarter) became mainly Babi. The first Babi upheaval in Nayriz had occurred in May–June 1850 and resulted in the deaths of Vahid himself and several hundred of the Babis of the town.

The immediate cause of the second upheaval was the relentless pressure under which the governor of the town, Mirza Zaynu'l-'Abidin Khan of the Shaybani branch of the 'Arab tribe, put the Babis. They sent people to Tehran to try to obtain some relief but this only made the governor more angry and caused the Babis more problems. On one occasion, Mirza Zaynu'l-'Abidin Khan succeeded in tricking the Babis and arresting all of the prominent male members of the community; however, they managed to free themselves again. Eventually hearing that the governor had ordered a general massacre of the Babis on Naw-Ruz 1853, the Babis decided that they had no recourse but to assassinate the governor. Although he was closely guarded, five of them managed to slip into the baths and kill him.

Following this, the Babis of the town fled to a nearby hill and set up defensive positions there. Thus followed what is called the second Nayriz upheaval in October–December 1853. In brief, some 400 Babi men took

---

194 ZH 7:322.
195 Abbott states 1,500 families (Amanat, *Cities and Trade* 180).

to the hills outside the town with their women and children and built barricades there from which they defended themselves successfully, at first against the force that was raised against them locally and then against some 3,000 troops that were sent against them with cannon from Shiraz. Eventually, however, the besieging army succeeded in killing 'Ali Sardar, the military leader of the Babis, and in inducing the remaining Babis to come down from the hills on promise of safety. They then seized hold of all the Babi men and women, killing some of the men and putting everyone else in chains. The episode resulted in the deaths of about 180 Babi men with about 180 men and 600 women being taken prisoner. Half the women and children were released and the remainder, together with all the men and the heads of the dead Babis, were sent to Shiraz, where four of the men were executed upon arrival. From Shiraz, some 73 of the men were sent on to Tehran with the heads of the executed Babis. The heads were buried (they were 203 in number), on the orders of the government, when the escorted prisoners reached Abadih. Some of the Babis died along the way and, on arrival in Tehran, some 15 were executed. The rest remained some two years in prison in Tehran, during which time some 23 of them died, leaving 13 who were released at the end of that time. Baha'i histories are silent regarding the fate of the Nayriz women that were brought to Shiraz but the British agent reports: 'Of the 300 women and maidens, all such as seemed fitting were taken by the Sirbaz [soldiers] and Government Servants. The rest being set at liberty are scattered about the city of Sheeraz, and seek their bread by begging.' Many of them eventually made their way back to Nayriz. The remaining male prisoners in Shiraz were set free and able to return to Nayriz in early 1272/late 1855.[196]

The community began gradually to rebuild itself. Mulla Muhammad Shafi' (1258/1842–1315/1897), whose father, grandfather and four uncles had all been killed in the two Nayriz upheavals, returned to Nayriz, having completed his studies in Shiraz under Shaykh Abu Turab, the Imam-Jum'ih. The latter thought so highly of Mulla Muhammad Shafi' that he gave him his granddaughter in marriage and appointed him to be Imam-Jum'ih of the Masjid-i Jami'-yi Kabir of Nayriz. He played a large part in

---

196 Details of these two Nayriz upheavals may be found in DB 465–9, 642–5; Rawhani, *Lama'at ul-Anwar* 30–56, 103–17; Faizi, *Nayriz Mishkbiz* 51–121; ZH 4:108–32; BBR 109–13, 147–52 (quotation from British agent, BBR 151). More recently, there have been two detailed studies in English of the Babi and Baha'i history of Nayriz: Rabbani, *The Babis of Nayriz*; and Ahdieh and Chapman, *The Awakening*.

consolidating the community after the traumas of the previous decade.[197] Among the other prominent Baha'is of Nayriz were two sons of Mulla 'Abdu's-Sami' Shirazi (who had been an eminent cleric in Shiraz and a tutor of the princes in the royal court). The first was Mulla Baqir, who had achieved the rank of *mujtahid*, married a niece of Shaykh Abu Turab, the Imam-Jum'ih of Shiraz, and was a leading cleric of Nayriz. He was converted by Sayyid Vahid Darabi but kept his allegiance secret and assisted the Babis in whatever way he could. The second son, Mulla Hasan Labshikari, who was appointed by Shaykh Abu Turab to supervise his properties in some of the villages of Fars and who had met the Bab, was more open about his beliefs. The sons of both these men were important Baha'is in Nayriz.[198]

As the community re-established itself, complaints began to be made by the Muslims of the town to Fath-'Ali Khan, the son of the assassinated governor Zaynu'l-'Abidin Khan, who had succeeded his father to the position of governor. During the second Nayriz upheaval, this man had led his relatives in demanding revenge for the assassination of his father. Fath-'Ali Khan sent men to kill Mulla Hasan Labshikari.[199] Mulla Muhammad Shafi' sensed that there was a possibility that the events of the previous two Nayriz upheavals would repeat themselves and so he arranged for two of the most courageous of the Babis to slip into the governor's bedroom and leave a knife at the head of the bed with a letter attached, saying that the Baha'is of Nayriz had no desire to take his life, otherwise they would have put this knife into him, but he should not try to attack them. Fath-'Ali Khan was frightened by this and decided to come to an accommodation with the Babis. He invited Mulla Muhammad Shafi' to a meeting and hammered out an understanding with him that meant that for some 46 years there were no major persecutions in Nayriz.

Mulla Muhammad Shafi' travelled to Baghdad and met Baha'u'llah in 1859. When Baha'u'llah's claim became known in Nayriz, he accepted immediately and the rest of the Babis of Nayriz followed suit. The Chinar-Sukhtih quarter thus became predominantly Baha'i. Two Nayriz Baha'is visited Baha'u'llah in Baghdad and became his companions-in-exile. One was Mirza Muhammad Taqi, a wealthy landowner of Nayriz who had participated in the upheavals, was given by Baha'u'llah the name Ayyub, and

197 Rawhani, *Lama'at* 124–32; ZH 6:870.
198 Rawhani, *Lama'at* 137–40; ZH 8a:579–80.
199 Rawhani, *Lama'at* 139.

lived in Baghdad for five years before his death.[200] The second
was Aqa Muhammad Ibrahim Amir, who accompanied
Baha'u'llah from Baghdad to Edirne and 'Akka.[201] A number
of travelling Baha'i teachers, such as Haji Mirza Haydar
'Ali Isfahani, Mirza Mahram Sidihi and Mirza Mahmud
Zarqani, came to Nayriz and were successful in converting
some of the Muslims of the town.

121. Mulla
Ahmad 'Ali

    Some Baha'is fleeing persecution elsewhere also came to
Nayriz and settled there. Among these was Mulla Ahmad
'Ali of Shiraz (1274/1857–1322/1904, see fig. 121), who had
had a religious education and was a *rawdih-khan*. He was
20 years old when he became a Baha'i in 1294/1877 and
was open about his new beliefs. He could no longer, therefore, work in Shiraz and so he moved to Nayriz, where he
opened a *maktab* and transcribed tablets for the Baha'is as well as occasionally performing a *rawdih-khani* for the Muslims of the town, who found
his performances compelling. In 1889–91 he went to India to spread the
Baha'i Faith there. While there he did the calligraphy for a publication
of a compilation of the writings of Baha'u'llah called the *Kitáb-i Mubín*.
Later, he also travelled around Iran.[202] Another was Karbala'i Husayn of
Istahbanat (see pp. 337–8). Some of the Nayriz Baha'is who had fled to
other towns gradually made their way back. Among these was Fatimih
Bigum (c. 1844–1300/1883). Her father, Sayyid Ja'far Yazdi, had been a
cleric and landowner of Nayriz and was closely connected to the governor.
He became a Babi, however, and was taken captive at the end of the first
Nayriz upheaval. After much torture and humiliation, he was freed and
took his family off to the Yazd area. Fatimih, who was six when the family
left Nayriz, grew up and married Haji Muhammad Isma'il, a merchant.
Then she decided to return to Nayriz with her husband and three young
children in about 1860. On the way they stopped at Qutruyih, where the
inhabitants greeted them warmly. However, news of their return to Nayriz
reached the governor, Fath-'Ali Khan, and he feared that Fatimih would
try to claim back the land which had belonged to her father and had been
taken over by Fath-'Ali Khan. He therefore sent orders for some of his
people at Qatruyih to kill Haji Muhammad Isma'il, which they did. When

200 Rawhani, *Lama'at* 76–8.
201 ZH 6:872–3.
202 Rawhani, *Lama'at* 279–81; ZH 6:870–1; 8a:579.

122. Sayyid 'Abdu'l-Husayn Lari (in
black turban) leading prayers

the Baha'is of Nayriz heard what had
happened, they sent armed men to rescue
Fatimih and her children and bring them
to Nayriz. Fatimih settled in the town
and brought up her children there. She
converted many women in the town and
deepened their knowledge of the Baha'i
Faith.[203] In 1325/1907 'Abdu'r-Rida, a
Muslim, got into an argument with his
mother Hajir, a Baha'i, over her beliefs
and in the middle of the argument he
pulled out a pistol and shot her dead.[204]

The Baha'is of Nayriz suffered greatly
during the Constitutional Revolution
and its aftermath in what is usually
called the third Nayriz upheaval.
After Muhammad 'Ali Shah overthrew
the Constitution in June 1908, the
forces opposed to him began to gather
strength. As the Constitutionalist forces began to advance on Tehran in
early 1909, there was disorder throughout Iran and a weakening of central
government. As a result, local leaders took the opportunity to consolidate
and extend their power and some also used the general disorder to enrich
themselves by plundering weaker neighbours. Sayyid 'Abdu'l-Husayn
Lari (1264/1848–1923, see fig. 122) was the foremost religious leader
in the Garmsir (uplands) area of Fars. His religious authority extended
over many towns and villages and people used to ascribe miracles to him.
Taking advantage of the disordered state of the country in early 1909, Lari
proclaimed himself the ruler of the Garmsir and upland region of Fars,
including Lar, Jahrum and Darab, and extending as far as Istahbanat and
Nayriz. He took over all the government offices, including the police, tax
and post. Because he was greatly opposed to Qavam ul-Mulk in Shiraz,
who supported Muhammad 'Ali Shah, he deemed himself a supporter of
the Constitution and indeed proclaimed himself the 'King of the Constitution' (Sulṭān-i Mashrūṭih) – although it was clear that his real aim was to
carve out a fiefdom for himself. His idea of the Constitution, as demonstrated

---

203 Rawhani, Lama'at 128, 132–4.
204 ZH 7:258, 8a:576.

in two published treatises and in his actions, was similar to that of Shaykh Fadlu'llah Nuri: that the Constitution should be defined by the Islamic *shari'ah* and administered by the clerics. So he set up a virtual dictatorship which he claimed was in accordance with the *shari'ah*, published a book of laws, and issued currency and postage stamps in his own name.[205] He appointed his close supporters to be in charge of each place in the area that he claimed. At this time there was a dispute between Sayyid Ashraf, the Shaykh ul-Islam of Nayriz, and the governor of the town, Mas'ud ud-Dawlih, son of Asif ud-Dawlih, who had married and then divorced the daughter of Sayyid Ashraf. Mas'ud ud-Dawlih wrote to Sayyid 'Abdu'l-Husayn Lari asking him to intervene in Nayriz. A further cause of the upheaval was the visit of two travelling Baha'i teachers, Mirza Tarazu'llah Samandari and Mirza 'Ali Akbar Rafsanjani. Their visit had resulted in an upsurge of Baha'i activity and had excited the opposition of the clerics in Nayriz.

Sayyid 'Abdul-Husayn Lari appointed Shaykh Dhakariya Kuhistani to take control of Nayriz and he advanced towards the town with a force of a thousand men. As he approached the town, he wrote to the Shaykh ul-Islam and the leading citizens of the town that they should submit to him, send him the town's leading opponents of Sayyid 'Abdu'l-Husayn and also expel all Baha'is from the town. The Nayrizis did not trust him, however, and prepared to defend themselves against him by going to the fortifications around the town. Shaykh Dhakariya camped close to one of the fortifications to the north of the town on 15 March 1909 and sent spies in to try to suborn the people defending this fortification. Two days later, he was able to take control of the Sayfabad quarter of the town, which is close to the Bazaar quarter, because most of the people there betrayed their fellow-townspeople and fell in with Shaykh Dhakariya. The Shaykh ul-Islam was also assisting Shaykh Dhakariya. After this, the Shaykh called for a truce and promised that he was only concerned with the opposing forces and the Baha'is and would leave everyone else alone. The people of the town agreed to leave the fortifications and return to their homes, whereupon the Shaykh promptly set about looting every house, including that of the Shaykh ul-Islam. The governor Mas'ud ud-Dawlih fled at this point and this left Shaykh Dhakariya free to turn his attention to the Baha'is.

On 17 March 1909 a *fatwa* arrived from Sayyid 'Abdul-Husayn Lari for a general massacre of the Baha'is, the looting of their property and the

---

205 Faizi, *Nayriz Mishkbiz*, 143; Afnan, Tarikh 572 (*Genesis* 208–9); Bamdad, *Tarikh* 2:257–8, 6:135–7; Zargari-nizhad, *Rasa'il Mashrutiyyat* 365–414.

demolition of their houses. On 20 March Shaykh Dhakariya advanced on the Chinar-Sukhtih quarter, the majority of the residents of which were Baha'is. He persuaded the Muslim inhabitants of that quarter not to join the Baha'is in defending it by declaring that he was only interested in eliminating the Baha'is from their town. Thus the Baha'is were left with only one fortification (*sangar*) in their hands, the fortification of the Masjid-i Jami'-yi Kabir. The Baha'is decided that there was no prospect of being able to defend the quarter effectively and so they decided to flee the town. The men in the fortification continued to hold the Shaykh's forces at bay for the whole of that day, while most of the rest of the Baha'is gathered what they could and fled to the hills to the south of Nayriz, a few hiding in the town. One Baha'i among the defenders was killed that day, and at dusk the Baha'is abandoned the fortification and fled.

Shaykh Dhakariya announced that the women and children under ten were to be left alone but anyone who brought a captured Baha'i man to the Shaykh would have a prize of 200 *tumans* and anyone who brought him the head of a Baha'i man would be given a hundred *tumans*. Therefore the next morning, 21 March 1909, a number of the riflemen of the Shaykh, together with townspeople to act as their guides, set off in pursuit of the Baha'is. In all, the Shaykh's men succeeded in finding some 17 Baha'is of Nayriz, either in the town or in the hills around. These were brought before Shaykh Dhakariya. Some of the townspeople interceded on behalf of some of those captured and offered to pay for their release. But Shaykh Dhakariya made it a condition of release that they deny their faith and they refused. An example of the manner of the death of these individuals is Mulla Muhammad 'Ali, who was captured with others and brought back to the town and interrogated. When he refused to recant his faith, Shaykh Dhakariya ordered his death. His throat was cut, and while he was still alive, a rope was tied around his ankles and he was dragged around the town until they reached the Chinar-Sukhtih quarter. Here his body was hung from a mulberry tree and burned. All 17 of those captured were killed on 21 March which, with the death on 20 March at the fortification, made 18 deaths in all.[206]

---

206 This account of the Nayriz episode of 1909 is based on Afnan, Tarikh 570–94 (*Genesis* 208–16; this source states there were 19 killed and seems to detail 20 persons killed); Rawhani, *Lama'at* 292–353; Faizi, *Nayriz Mishkbiz* 142–62; 'Alaqiband, Tarikh 268–9; ZH 8a:579–81. ZH 7:276–80 states that the killings were spread over five days. 'Abdu'l-Baha made a spiritual link between the sacrifice made by these 18 Baha'is and the entombment of the remains of the Bab on Mount Carmel, which also occurred on 21 March 1909; see Faizi, *Nayriz*

As for the Baha'is who had fled to the hills to the south of Nayriz, when news came to them of what the Shaykh was doing, it was decided that the men should continue their flight while many of the women and children returned to Nayriz. Some of the boys over the age of ten who were not able to walk a long way also slipped back into the town disguised as girls under a chador. The men, learning that Istahbanat (36 km southwest of Nayriz) was in the hands of Sayyid 'Abdu'l-Husayn Lari and would not be safe, made for Sarvistan. Word went around the fleeing groups of Baha'is to gather in the first instance at Runiz (60 km west of Nayriz; pop. 6,750 in 1951) where the Afnans had much property and where their representative was a Baha'i named Mir Muhammad Hasan Nayrizi. After 24 hours, because Runiz was not safe, they continued to Sarvistan, where there was a large number of Baha'is and they could find shelter. Word had been sent ahead to the Sarvistan Baha'is and they came out with food and warm clothing for the refugees, since there was still snow on the ground. One report states that 70 of the children died of hunger and deprivation during this episode.[207]

The Baha'i refugees, who numbered about 70 adults, remained in Sarvistan for two months, until a new governor, Saham ud-Dawlih, came to power in Fars. Mirza Muhammad 'Ali Khan Nasr ud-Dawlih (son of Qavam ul-Mulk) was sent with a large force to pacify the province. When he reached Sarvistan, the Baha'is presented him with a petition asking for redress for the wrongs done to them and for their safe return to Nayriz. He sent orders making Rida-Quli Khan Mushir Divan the new governor in Nayriz and instructing him to arrest the representatives of Sayyid 'Abdu'l-Husayn and to protect the Baha'is. At this point the Baha'is returned to Nayriz and began to try to rebuild their lives.[208]

The country was, however, in a state of increasing chaos at this time and the problems of the Nayriz Baha'is continued over the next few years. Sayyid 'Abdu'l-Husayn and Shaykh Dhakariya continued to attack them relentlessly. The latter sent a force under his brother Shaykh Abu'l-Hasan Kuhistani in the following year, 1910, but the whole town united against them and drove them off. In 1912 Shaykh Kamal Kuhistani took control of the town and extorted a large sum of money from the Baha'is; in 1913 'Ali Asghar Khan Dihkhayri did the same. In 1914 Hishmat us-Sultan came to

---

Mishbiz 142, 176.
207 'Alaqiband, Tarikh 269.
208 Rawhani, *Lama'at* 299.

Nayriz on behalf of the governor of the province, nominally to subdue the rebellious tribesmen of the area. He sent back false reports, claiming that the Baha'i quarter of the town (Chinar-Sukhtih) was in revolt, therefore had further troops and cannon sent to restore government control. All the inhabitants of the Chinar-Sukhtih quarter united, however, and drove his forces out of their quarter. Eventually Hishmat us-Sultan contented himself with obtaining a sum as blood-money for a soldier who had been killed in the fighting, and withdrew.[209] Sayyid 'Abdu'l-Husayn was finally defeated in 1333/1914.[210]

Hishmat us-Sultan was replaced as governor of Nayriz in 1915 by Amir Aqa Khan Mansur us-Saltanih Shaybani of the 'Arab tribe, who was a Baha'i, and this could have led to a respite for the Nayriz Baha'is had it not been for the activities of Amir Husayn Khan, a grandson of the former governor, Fath-'Ali Khan. Amir Husayn Khan tried to seize power in Nayriz and, being thwarted, retired to Darab where he obtained the assistance of the chiefs of the Baharlu tribe (one of the Khamsih confederation). In 1915 a force of Baharlu tribemen and some disaffected Nayrizis advanced on Nayriz, proclaiming that they would not leave a single Baha'i alive in the town. Muhammad Taqi Khan 'Arab, a captain in the army, a nephew of Mansur us-Saltanih and also a Baha'i, came to his uncle's assistance with some government troops. The two sides fought furiously for several days. One night, in a surprise raid, the Baharlu fighters gained possession of one of the quarters of Nayriz next to the Baha'i quarter and looted the houses there but were driven back the next day in intense hand-to-hand fighting. Eventually, realizing that they could not take Nayriz, the Baharlu tribesmen agreed to content themselves with some money and go.[211]

Paradoxically, with the advent of World War I and the resulting chaotic situation in Iran, the situation in Nayriz eased. With many of the notables of Fars engaged elsewhere, in the contest between Qavam ul-Mulk and the Qashqa'i leader Sawlat ud-Dawlih for example, the Baha'is of Nayriz under the governorship of Mansur us-Saltanih prospered. When Qavam ul-Mulk died in 1916, Mansur us-Saltanih was appointed chief (Ilkhani) of the Khamsih tribal confederation and his brother, Amir Salim Khan, became governor of Nayriz. During the World War the British created the South Persia Rifles to protect their interests in the south of the country

209 Rawhani, *Lama'at* 419–22.
210 Bamdad, *Tarikh* 2:258.
211 Rawhani, *Lama'at* 422–4.

and this also brought a great deal of security to that area, which relieved the pressure there had been upon the Baha'is of Nayriz. Then in 1918 there was a drought, which resulted in a famine. The Baha'is escaped the worst effects of the famine because they rallied around to help one another. Thus when the worldwide influenza epidemic hit Iran and carried off large numbers who had already been weakened by the famine, including about a quarter of the population of Nayriz, there were only a few deaths among the Baha'is.[212]

There were a number of conversions to the Baha'i Faith at this time. In 1918–19 Sayyid Ashraf, the Shaykh ul-Islam of Nayriz, who had invited Sayyid 'Abdu'l-Husayn to send his troops to Nayriz and thus had caused the third Nayriz upheaval in 1909, revealed that he had been deeply affected by what had happened. He had been studying the Baha'i books which had been looted from the Baha'i homes at that time and had become convinced of the truth of the Baha'i Faith. He made this revelation at Naw-Ruz, when, as was customary, a large number of Muslims and Baha'is called upon him to offer their respects and greetings for the new year. On this occasion he recited a poem he had composed about spring. He had written this such that its references to such Quranic verses as the coming of the Clear Evidence (Qur'an 98:1–4) and the 'meeting with the Lord' (Qur'an 13:2, etc.) and the occurrence of such phrases as the advent of the 'promised day' and a 'new creation', made it clear to the Baha'is that he was making a declaration of faith. The Muslims present, however, did not understand the significance of any of these references. Following on from this, the Shaykh ul-Islam had a number of private meetings with Shaykh Muhammad Husayn 'Ahdiyyih, the secretary of the local assembly, at which he confirmed his conversion.[213] Other converts at this time included Mirza 'Abdu's-Samad (d. 1926), who was *kadkhuda* (headman) of the Chinar-Sukhtih quarter where the Baha'is lived, and Dr Muhammad Muslih, who had moved to Nayriz from Shiraz in 1915.[214]

In 1921 the South Persia Rifles ceased to operate and the area became insecure again. Conditions were such that when Mirza Munir Nabilzadih, a travelling Baha'i teacher, wanted to proceed from Nayriz to Sarvistan in September 1921, a party of 20 armed Baha'is had to accompany him half the way, where they were met by another party of armed Baha'is from

212 Rawhani, *Lama'at* 425–7.
213 Rawhani, *Lama'at* 428–34.
214 Rawhani, *Lama'at* 435–8.

Sarvistan, who took him the rest of the way.[215] The visit of Nabilzadih to Nayriz and a number of conversions enraged the enemies of the Baha'is both in Nayriz and outside and a plot was hatched to attack the Baha'i quarter of the town on 10 Muharram, the day of 'Ashura, when the martyrdom of Imam Husayn is commemorated (2 September 1922). Mansur us-Saltanih learned of their plans and consulted with the Baha'i assembly and Nabilzadih. A decision was made for the Baha'is to buy whatever arms they could and for a force of 50 Baha'i youth to prepare themselves under the leadership of Nabilzadih to defend the community. On the day of 'Ashura, the Baha'is acted to prevent a mob gathering and so no attack occurred.[216]

A traditional school (*maktab*) was established in Nayriz by Mulla 'Ali Naqqash in one or two usable rooms in an old dilapidated religious college (*madrasih*) adjacent to the residence of the governor Fath-'Ali Khan in the Chinar-Shahi quarter. When in about 1920 the Baha'i teacher Natiq came to Nayriz, he saw that the government school only went up to the fourth year and so he arranged with the local spiritual assembly that Mirza Ahmad Khan 'Irfan (d. 1962) be appointed as the teacher of a small school (15 pupils) that would teach two more years of education using a modern curriculum. Mirza Ahmad Khan 'Irfan was very well educated, had become a Baha'i only seven years earlier and had then spent four years as a captain in charge of the South Persia Rifles force in Sirjan. Mirza 'Abdu's-Samad, who had received the title Vakil ur-Ru'aya (representative of the people), was very enthusiastic about this project and offered to hold the school in his own house and sent his own children to the school. Two years later, when Nabilzadih came to the town, he persuaded the local assembly to take this project forward and establish both a boys' and a girls' school, with about 80 pupils in each, called the Mithaqiyyih Schools. The boys' school was situated in the same place as the old *maktab*, which was refurbished by the local assembly, and teachers were employed. Mulla 'Ali Naqqash was the school supervisor. This school succeeded in gaining the support of the Muslims of Nayriz and was opened by Sayyid Abu Turab Mujtahid. The girls' school was situated in a location provided by Mash-hadi Zaynu'l-'Abidin Nurani. These schools were closed in 1934 as part of the general closure of the Baha'i schools throughout Iran. After this, so that the Baha'i children would not be deprived of education, the Baha'i

---

215 MH 4:260–1.
216 Rawhani, *Lama'at* 445–9; ZH 8a:577 appears to date this episode to Sept.–Oct. 1920.

Assembly of Nayriz asked Muhammad Hashim to teach the children, but after a time the government prohibited this as an illegal school. Eventually, the Baha'i children enrolled in the government school, where they were subjected to harassment.[217]

In 1923 a severe flood washed away most of Nayriz, including the Baha'i quarter. Shoghi Effendi alerted the Baha'i world of this and money poured in from around the world for the relief of the victims of the disaster. The Baha'is were able to rebuild their homes, strengthen flood defences, build a new *hazirat ul-quds* and establish a Baha'i cemetery. They also built at this time public baths with showers, which soon attracted most of the notables of the town. These events greatly added to the prestige of the Baha'i Faith. Many Baha'i travelling teachers came to Nayriz and there were further conversions, some among the tribespeople in the surrounding area.[218]

Sarvistan

Sarvistan is a large village (pop. about 1,500 in 1914, 3,250 in 1956) on the road between Shiraz (90 km to the northwest) and Nayriz (170 km to the southeast). According to the oral tradition in the Baha'i community of the village, before the declaration of the Bab, Karbala'i Sadiq Khan, the brother of Karbala'i Hasan Khan, who was *kalantar* (mayor) of the village and a landowner, had come to the conclusion as a result of his study of divination and prophecy that the advent of the Qa'im was near. When the Bab made his announcement in the Masjid-i Vakil in March 1845, several Sarvistanis were in the audience and brought back to the village news of the Bab. As a result of this, the two brothers mentioned above and five others became Babis. Sayyid Vahid Darabi stayed with Karbala'i Hasan Khan during one of his journeys and converted many.[219] At least one person from the town was among those who were involved in the first Nayriz upheaval in 1850.[220] Because of the prominent position of the two above-mentioned brothers, there was little opposition at first, despite the fact that they were openly teaching the new religion. Karbala'i Hasan Khan travelled to Baghdad and

217 Rawhani, *Lama'at* 439, 449–50; Mithaqi-Nayrizi, 'Madrasih'; Shahvar, *Forgotten Schools* 158.
218 Rawhani, *Lama'at* 450–4; ZH 8a:577; *Baha'i News Letter* (USA), no. 3, Mar. 1925, p. 2; no. 4, Apr. 1925, p. 3.
219 Taju'd-Dini, Sharh 16–18; Thabit (Tarikh 1–2) states that it was Vahid who first brought the news of the specific identity of the Bab to the village.
220 ZH 6:873.

met Baha'u'llah there. He also invited many prominent Baha'is to the village, including Mirza Ahmad Yazdi (see p. 351), who lived there from about 1866 to about 1888, and Shaykh Muhammad 'Arab. Opposition built up, however, and Karbala'i Hasan Khan was among the Baha'is arrested in Shiraz in 1875 (see p. 268).

After the episode of persecution in Tehran in 1883, the enemies of the Baha'is in Sarvistan were encouraged to increase their opposition. Leading the opposition was Aqa Muhammad 'Ali, who coveted the position of *kalantar* that Karbala'i Hasan Khan held. Matters quickly reached a point where there was a public confrontation and fighting. Fath-'Ali Khan, who was governing the province on behalf of Jalal ud-Dawlih (who had been appointed governor of Fars by his father Zill us-Sultan), sent an official, 'Ali Khan, to investigate. The latter fell in with the enemies of the Baha'is and sent back reports critical of them. He was ordered to arrest the troublemakers and he returned to Shiraz with four Baha'is. All four were bastinadoed and thrown into prison. One of them, a youth named Ghulam-'Ali, a grandson of Karbala'i Hasan Khan, had had the audacity to tattoo onto his arms the words:

> The face of Baha shines forth
>> Its brilliance brings me to life again.

His temerity earned him the cutting off of an ear. He was returned to prison with the other three, where they remained until Fath-'Ali Khan was dismissed after a five-year term.[221] In 1888 came the arrest of Karbala'i Hasan Khan and his brother Karbala'i Sadiq Khan, together with Aqa Murtada Sarvistani, and the execution of these three over the next four years (see pp.

---

221 Afnan, Tarikh 255–60 (*Genesis* 104–6); ZH 5:327–9. There is a somewhat different version of this episode (Baha'i, Istintaqiyyih MS B 101–2), where it is stated that as news of the arrest of the Baha'is in Tehran that year spread to Sarvistan, the Muslims there had taken this as a lead and attacked the Baha'is, killing one of them and then in further fighting the Baha'is killed one of the Muslims. Both parties came to Shiraz to lay a complaint with Fath-'Ali Khan. When the Muslims accused their opponents of being 'Babis', Fath-'Ali Khan retorted angrily that this was a matter of two factions in the town hostile to each other and there was no need to bring religion into it. One of the Baha'i youth was rude to one of Fath-'Ali Khan's retinue and had his ear cut off. Then 20 of the Baha'is and ten of the Muslims were imprisoned and the rest dismissed. After a time Fath-'Ali Khan fined the prisoners and, having obtained undertakings from them to keep the peace, released them.

123. Baha'is of Sarvistan. Among those mentioned in the text are, *seated second from left*,
Fath-'Ali Khan Kalantar; *seated fourth from left*, Aqa Haydar 'Ali

268–9). Ghulam-'Ali was also sought at this time but he escaped to Tehran.[222]

In 1909 the Baha'is of Sarvistan acted as hosts for two months to more than 70 Baha'is fleeing persecution in Nayriz (see p. 326–7). Writing about this episode, Mirza Habibu'llah Afnan comments that, unlike other places, the Muslims and Baha'is in Sarvistan got on well with each other, while Abu'l-Qasim Afnan states that Sarvistan was a relatively safe location for the Baha'is because the notables of the village were Baha'is.[223] Among these notables were Fath-'Ali Khan Kalantar (see fig. 123), Haji 'Abdu'l-Baqi and Aqa Ghulam-Rida, respectively the son-in-law and grandson of Karbala'i Hasan Khan, as well as Sayyid Jalalu'd-Din Vakil ur-Ru'aya, his brother Mir Ahmad, and Aqa Haydar 'Ali (see fig. 123).[224]

In 1912 there had evidently been some dispute among the Baha'is of Sarvistan since 'Abdu'l-Baha writes to them from America urging them to unity.[225] It is reported that during a visit by Mirza Munir Nabilzadih in September 1921, a Baha'i girls' school was established in the village.[226]

---

222 ZH 6:874.
223 Afnan, Tarikh 591–2 (*Genesis* 214–15); A.Q. Afnan, 'Dastan' 38.
224 Thabit, Tarikh 7–8.
225 *Makatib* 5:206–7.
226 MH 4:261.

It appears that the majority of the population of Sarvistan in the time of 'Abdu'l-Baha were Baha'is, with about a thousand Baha'is in Sarvistan itself and a large number in the adjacent Haftu quarter.[227]

Jahrum

In Jahrum (200 km southeast of Shiraz; pop. 4,500 in the town and another 14,000 on the outskirts in 1915[228] and 25,820 in 1951), a Baha'i community arose in the time of Baha'u'llah. One prominent cleric of this town was Shaykh Muhammad Fadil Jahrumi. Although it has been claimed that he was a Baha'i,[229] it appears that he was in fact a Babi.[230] Shortly after the death of Baha'u'llah, Haji Mirza Haydar 'Ali Isfahani came from Bombay to Jahrum accompanied by Mulla Husayn 'Ali Jahrumi. On this visit Mulla Husayn 'Ali was able to talk to many of the notables of the town and some 30 people became Baha'is. Mulla Husayn 'Ali then returned to Bombay, where he became a partisan of Mirza Muhammad 'Ali, with whom he had established close relations when the latter visited Bombay. He wrote many letters to Jahrum and elsewhere and published material in support of the latter's claims. He boasted to Mirza Muhammad 'Ali that the Baha'is of Jahrum would all follow him and he travelled to Jahrum in 1898 to this end but failed to gather any significant support and indeed faced such a hostile reception that he returned to Bombay. In about 1903 he travelled to 'Akka, pretending to be a seeker after truth in much the same way that Mirza Aqa Khan Kirmani had done in the time of Baha'u'llah (see p. 430).[231]

Tarazu'llah Samandari and Mirza 'Ali Akbar Rafsanjani visited in 1909 and began to teach the Baha'i Faith. At this time, however, the area was in turmoil as a result of the rebellion of Sayyid 'Abdu'l-Husayn Lari against Muhammad 'Ali Shah (see pp. 324–8) and the two Baha'is found themselves unable to return to Shiraz when they had finished in Jahrum. Amir

---

227 Interview on 27 November 2019 with Farham Sabet who has researched the history of the Baha'i community of Sarvistan and interviewed many of the older Baha'is there. See also tablet of 'Abdu'l-Baha addressed to 49 men of the village, ILMA 52:459–60.
228 Abbott in 1850 states 3,000 families (Amanat, *Cities and Trade* 183).
229 ZH 8a:575.
230 Interview with Mr Hasan Balyuzi, 25 June 1977, who was tutored in Arabic by this man in India.
231 Mazandarani, *Asrar* 3:51–2; Isfahani, *Bihjat* 292–3.

Aqa Khan Mansur us-Saltanih, a Baha'i (see
p. 328), sent four horsemen from Nayriz to
escort them as far as Sarvistan, where they
would be safe. It is reported that at this time
there were about 400 Baha'is in Jahrum
(nine per cent of the population).[232]

In 1911 there was an anti-Baha'i movement in Jahrum that resulted in arms being
taken up by both sides and the Baha'is bar-
ricading themselves in. The affair ended
with only four of the Baha'is being killed
but it would have been a far higher number
had it not been for the firm stance of resistance taken by the Baha'is.[233]

Sayyid 'Abdu'l-Husayn Lari, who was
responsible for the Baha'i deaths in Nayriz
in 1909 (see pp. 324–8), retired to Jahrum
after he had been defeated. In September

124. Sawlat ud-Dawlih (Isma'il
Khan)

1921 there was some anti-Baha'i commotion and the Baha'is of Jahrum
asked the Baha'is of Sarvistan to come armed to Jahrum to help protect
them and the situation calmed down.[234] Lari died in 1923 but his son,
Sayyid 'Ali Pishnamaz, continued his enmity towards the Baha'is. This
was a period of unrest in Fars. Isma'il Khan Sawlat ud-Dawlih (see fig.
124), the head of the Qashqa'i tribe, had created a coalition of anti-British,
anti-Qavam ul-Mulk forces in south Iran that had rebelled on several occasions since 1911. By 1926 Reza Shah was trying to bring the tribes in Iran
under control and it was in the interests of both Sawlat ud-Dawlih and
the Russian consul in Shiraz, Hugo Walden, for there to be further unrest.
Sawlat ud-Dawlih represented Jahrum in parliament and teamed up with
Sayyid 'Ali to create trouble in the town. There were simultaneous attempts
by Walden to stir up anti-Baha'i sentiments in Shiraz. In 1926 a certain
Sayyid Muhammad was sent from Shiraz to stoke up anti-Baha'i feeling in
Jahrum. During Ramadan, which fell in March–April in 1926, Sayyid 'Ali

232 A.Q. Afnan, 'Dastan' 38. A photograph of Baha'is in Jahrum taken in 1924 (H.
    Afnan, *Khatirat* 167) shows about a hundred male adults, which would equate
    to about 500 Baha'is in all.
233 KD 2:175–6.
234 MH 4:261.

began a particularly violent campaign of invective against the Baha'is from the pulpit. On 24 Ramadan (7 April) a mob went on the rampage as a result of which eight Baha'is were killed, many were severely beaten and left for dead and some 20 Baha'i houses were looted and burned. Although at first some 30 people including Sawlat ud-Dawlih were arrested and a trial was begun, several of those who were most active in pursuing the matter such as Amir Lashkar had to leave to attend the coronation of the shah in Tehran and at this point, all determination to pursue the matter evaporated. The accused in Shiraz were released and the shah pardoned Sawlat ud-Dawlih on the intervention of Mustawfi ul-Mamalik, his prime minister, and issued orders that no petitions from the Baha'is were to be accepted at any post or telegraph office. This episode was notable for the way in which the Baha'i communities in the rest of Iran both wrote to the government to appeal for help and justice and also sent financial and other help to the victims – it marks a stage in the emergence of a national Baha'i community.[235]

Istahbanat

A number of the inhabitants of Istahbanat (36 km southwest of Nayriz; pop. 5,000 in 1896[236]) had become Babis when Vahid Darabi passed close by the town in 1850 and some of them had taken part in the first Nayriz upheaval. It appears that a Babi community was established in this town, although some of the Babis did not later become Baha'is.[237] The sister of Vahid Darabi, Jahan Bigum, was resident in this town together with her husband, Haji Muhammad Isma'il Tajir Lari, and they became Baha'is. Their son Mirza Yusif Khan Vahid Kashfi Lisan-Hudur (1865–3 October 1959, see fig. 125) received an extensive education, including studies with his clerical relatives at Shiraz, Yazd and Isfahan and with the senior clerics of the shrine cities in Iraq. He learned something of the Baha'i Faith from Aqa Sayyid Ahmad and Aqa Sayyid Muhammad, two sons of Vahid Darabi, in Yazd and Kirman, and became a Baha'i in Mashhad in about 1886. He was appointed a teacher, first at the American missionary school in Tehran

---

235 BBR 465–72 (includes mention of appeals on behalf of the Jahrum Baha'is from the Baha'is of the United States and Canada, the British Isles, France, New Zealand and Iraq); Fu'adi, *Tarikh* 207.

236 Fasa'i, *Fars-Namih* 2:175.

237 The evidence (DB 478; ZH 3:477–8) indicates that a considerable Babi community came into being and in 1318/1900 the governor of the town is said to have been a Babi; *Lama'at* 283.

in 1307/1889, where he learned English, and later in 1310/1892 at the American missionary college at Urumiyyih. He visited Tabriz and was introduced to the Crown Prince Muzaffaru'd-Din Mirza, who gave him the title Lisan-Hudur. In 1902 he left Urumiyyih and travelled to visit 'Abdu'l-Baha in 'Akka. After this he proceeded to Egypt, Paris, London and parts of the United States, visiting Mirza Abu'l-Fadl Gulpaygani there and giving talks at Greenacre. After this two-year sojourn, he returned to Urumiyyih (vol. 1:426). In about 1921 he moved to Tehran where he worked at the Tar-biyat Baha'i School and then from 1925 as a translator for Arthur Millspaugh, an American financial consultant to

125. Mirza Yusif Khan Vahid Kashfi, Lisan-Hudur

the government. After this he became headmaster of the Baha'i schools in Qazvin. In 1933 he returned to Tehran. He acted as translator when the American Baha'is Martha Root (1929), Keith Ransom-Kehler (1934) and Mildred Mottahedeh (1938) and the New Zealand Baha'i Effie Baker (1930) visited Iran.[238]

No substantial Baha'i community came into existence in Istahbanat, however, although a number of inhabitants of the town did become Baha'is. Karbala'i Husayn Istahbanati (d. 1330/1912) was the son of a prayer-leader (*pishnamaz*) at one of the mosques in the town. He had studied the religious sciences at Karbala and had also taken the mystical path but was not content with either of these and became a maker of cloth shoes (*maliki-duz*). He heard of the Baha'i Faith in about 1893, questioned a Baha'i who came to Istahbanat, walked the 36 kilometres to Nayriz and studied the Baha'i Faith there weekly with Mulla Ahmad 'Ali until he was convinced. He then began to tell the people of the town openly about the Baha'i Faith. This aroused opposition from the town's clerics, Mulla Ja'far

238 MH 6:5–36; ZH 8a:567–9; *The Baha'i Magazine (Star of the West)*, 24 (1933) 43–6, 309–10; *Ahang-i Badi'*, year 10 (1954–5), no. 10, 22–6, no. 11, 18–23, no. 12, 15–21; *Akhbar-i Amri* year 116, no. 9 (1959) 305–15; Rawhani, *Lama'at* 68–74.

and Haji 'Ali Va'iz. Eventually in 1903 he was forced to flee Istahbanat and went to Nayriz. His wife, Qamar Sultan (known as Bibi Khanum), who remained behind, was placed in a difficult position and plans were made for her to remarry. She, however, loved her husband and sent word through her brother to him. A group of armed Nayriz Baha'is came to the vicinity of Istahbanat and sent word to the brother. Qamar Sultan and her brother come out to meet them and they all went off to Nayriz. In Nayriz, Karbala'i Husayn continued his trade of making cloth shoes and became a skilful teacher of the Baha'i Faith, converting several persons.[239]

239 Gulistanih, 'Bibi Buzurg'; Rawhani, *Lama'at* 281–4, 381; ZH 6:871.

17

PERSIAN GULF PROVINCES
(BUSHIHR AND LARISTAN)

This chapter includes Bushihr and Laristan on the northern coast of the Persian Gulf, which were sometimes separate provinces and sometimes part of Fars. Often, the governor of Bushihr would also be in charge of the Gulf ports of Iran. The climate of these areas is very hot and dry.

Bushihr

Bushihr is situated on a peninsula 290 kilometres southeast of Shiraz and was Iran's main port on the Persian Gulf during the 19th and early 20th centuries, handling the trade from British India and thus indirectly from Britain itself. It suffered some decline in the early 19th century as European merchants switched much of their trade to the northern route via Tabriz, and in the early 20th century as the route via Baghdad and Hamadan became more used. Bushihr was described as being very cramped and crowded and had a population of about 18,000 in 1868, 15,000 in 1914, and 18,400 in 1956. The Bab had spent about seven years in Bushihr as a merchant and other members of the Afnan family also traded there over the years.

Many high officials who came to this area were Baha'is, although the number of converts from among the local population does not seem to have been great. Husayn-Quli Khan Mafi (1248/1832–1326/1908; see fig.

127. Husayn-Quli Khan Mafi, Sa'd ul-Mulk,   128. Fadil Shirazi (Shaykh Muhammad
        later Niẓam us-Saltanih   Ibrahim Burazjani)

127 and vol. 1, fig. 129 and pp. 483–4) was a Baha'i who was given the title
Sa'd ul-Mulk and appointed governor of Yazd (1292/1874–1293/1875)
and then of Bushihr (1292/1875–1295/1878). He then worked in the
office of the prime minister, in charge of taking delivery of grain from
Crown lands until he was appointed governor of Bandar 'Abbas and Langih
and headed the customs for the province of Fars (1299/1881–1300/1882).
When he was given the title Nizam us-Saltanih in 1305/1887, his brother
Muhammad Hasan Khan (d. 1900) took over his title Sa'd al-Mulk.
He was also a Baha'i and succeeded his brother as governor of Bushihr
(1300/1882–1303/1885). He was then appointed governor of Bushihr
and all the Gulf ports (1305/1885–1308/1890, 1310/1892–1312/1894;
vol. 1:484). During their governorship no one was allowed to molest the
Baha'is, and when a mulla in Bushihr tried to do so in 1888, Muhammad
Hasan Khan issued an order for his expulsion and only withdrew this on a
promise of good behaviour.[1] Mirza 'Ali Muhammad Khan Muvaqqar ud-
Dawlih (1865–1921, see p. 273 and fig. 107) was the Foreign Office agent
in Bushihr in 1903 and then governor there, 1913–15.

---

1   'Ali Aqa (later Muvaqqar ud-Dawlih) in ['Abdu'l-Baha], *Traveller's Narrative*
     2:411.

Burazjan and Dashti

Burazjan is a small market town situated on the road between Bushihr (67 km to the southwest) and Shiraz (255 km to the northeast). The population grew from about 3,000 in the early 19th century to about 5,000 by its end. In 1911 it had decreased to 4,000 owing to political unrest in the area;[2] it's population was 9,826 in 1951.

The most prominent Baha'i to emerge from Burazjan was Shaykh Muhammad Ibrahim Burazjani, known as Fadil Shirazi (1863–19 September 1935, see fig. 128). After preliminary studies with his father, who was also a cleric, and in Shiraz, where Mushir ul-Mulk became his patron, Fadil went to Najaf in about 1885, where he completed his studies under Mulla Kazim Khurasani and other senior clerics and obtained a certificate of *ijtihad*. His studies were intermingled with periods of ascetic practices. He visited Mashhad in about 1888 and returned to Burazjan. Some years later he fell into conversation one day with a youth who was passing through on his way to visit 'Akka and who gave him the Kitab-i Iqan and other Baha'is scriptures to read. As a result of this encounter Fadil's demeanour changed. Rumours went around the town that he had become a Baha'i and an attempt was made to kill him. He therefore left for Najaf, where he taught Arabic and mystical philosophy for about two years. From there he went to 'Akka and met with 'Abdu'l-Baha and thus his conversion was complete. After four months he returned to Iran and spent many years travelling through the country to promote the Baha'i Faith, visiting, among other places, Rasht, Qumm, Sangsar and Shahmirzad during the ministry of 'Abdu'l-Baha, and Kurdistan in the time of Shoghi Effendi. He married Naw-Zuhur Khanum (1892–1949), the niece of Fa'izih Khanum (vol. 1:81–3), and became a teacher of Arabic at the Tarbiyat Baha'i School in Tehran. He also taught at the Baha'i schools in Hamadan for a short time (c. 1920–c. 1923); his wife was also a teacher, at the girls' school. In addition, he taught the Baha'i Faith at meetings in the evenings and wrote a few works.[3]

Karam-'Ali was a learned individual who taught at a small traditional school (*maktab*) in his home in the village of Nazar Aqa (18 km north of Burazjan; pop. about 700 in 1914, 870 in 1951). He was a Sufi dervish and it was presumably from a fellow dervish that he learned of the Baha'i Faith

---

2   Floor, 'Borazjan' 183–4.
3   MH 1:368–423; ZH 8a:569–71; see also Falahi-Skuce, *Radiant Gem*.

and began to recite Baha'i poetry in the streets and bazaars of the area. He visited 'Abdu'l-Baha in Port Sa'id in June 1913. Karam-'Ali was accused of being a Baha'i and, in about 1920, was killed by being thrown off a roof.[4]

The first Baha'i to reside in Burazjan was Hatim Butshikan (d. 1983) of Burujird, who moved into the town some time in the 1920s. He was a pharmacist who was successful in his profession and prospered despite suffering persecution for his religion.[5]

Of particular interest is the story of one of the family clans (*'ashirih* or *ṭā'ifih*) of Burazjan, the Dashti or Garmsari. According to their oral tradition, their ancestors migrated from Khurasan in Safavid times under the leadership of Shaykh Habibu'llah ibn Shaykh Sharaf Khurasani, who was a religious leader and Sufi shaykh admired by the king of that time, Shah 'Abbas I. He established a practice among his clan of night-long prayer vigils and a 40-day fast before Naw-Ruz. He also left behind a book called 'Kalam', which contains many prophecies. At first the clan occupied four villages, Arad, Bayram, Maz and Ashna in the west of Laristan, some 70–90 kilometres west of Lar (the shrine of Shaykh Habibu'llah is in Ashna). In the 18th century, either because of drought or problems with the predominantly Sunni people of that area, many of the clan moved to the Dashti area east and southeast of Bushihr (Khurmuj, Ahram and some of the nearby villages). From there in about 1913, some, under the leadership of Mulla Husayn Haqqdust, migrated to Burazjan, where they are called Dashti because they came from the Dashti area, whereas in Dashti they are called Garmsari. In Burazjan their occupations were *shīvih-kishī* (or *takht-kishī*, applying the hard sole of the traditional cloth shoe, *gīvih*) and weaving (*jūlāhī*), which appears to have been the traditional occupations of this clan. They built houses for themselves on land that they bought near a dried-out river. This area of the town thus became known as the Dashti quarter.[6]

Mulla Husayn Dashti (later Haqqdust, d. 28 Nov. 1951) was the spiritual leader of the Dashti clan in Burazjan and continued the practices of Shaykh Habibu'llah among them. From about 1914 when he met Darvish Karam-'Ali, a Baha'i from Shiraz, Haqqdust had a number of encounters

---

4   Fakhra, Tarikh Amr dar Burazjan 20–2; Memorandum from Hasan Rahimi, dated 24 July 2002; Zarqani, *Badayi' ul-Athar* 2:359.
5   Fakhra, Tarikh Amr dar Burazjan 25–8.
6   Memorandum from Hasan Rahimi, dated 24 July 2002; Fakhra, Tarikh Amr dar Burazjan 10–14; see also Farrashbandi, *Burazjan* 1: 206–10; Floor, 'Borazjan' 184. On Dashtis, Lorimer, *Gazetteer of the Persian Gulf* 206–8.

with Baha'is including Hatim Butshikan, Fadil Shirazi (in Tehran) and others. He eventually came to believe that the Baha'i Faith was the fulfilment of the prophecies of Shaykh Habibu'llah, and he and his brothers and sister became Baha'is some time before 1926.[7] One or two others of the clan became Baha'is at this time, including Haqqdust's brother-in-law, Mulla Ja'far Sha'irzadih. This was to be the start of a large number of conversions from this clan during the succeeding decades, both in Burazjan and in surrounding villages and small towns in the Dashti quarter where members of the clan resided, such as Ahram (54 km southeast of Bushihr, 44 km south of Burazjan; pop. 2,832 in 1951), Khurmuj (82 km southeast of Bushihr, 28 km south of Ahram; pop. 2,677 in 1951), and Faqih Sanan (Faqih Hasanan; 18 km southwest of Khurmuj; pop. 938 in 1951).[8]

Laristan

Laristan is the name of an area southeast of Fars adjoining the Persian Gulf. It is now divided between three provinces. The largest town of this province was Bandar 'Abbas (547 km south of Kirman; pop. 17,700 in 1956). Among the earliest Baha'is in Bandar 'Abbas were Haji Muhammad 'Avad and his brother Haji Muhammad in the time of Baha'u'llah. Although distant from most of the main centres of Baha'i activity, this area had a number of Baha'is in prominent positions. Among them were Sultan Muhammad Khan Abu'l-Virdi Shirazi, who was governor of Bandar 'Abbas (he later left government service and moved to Ahvaz; he was poisoned by his wife in Baghdad); Mirza 'Abdu'llah Khan Midhat ul-Vizarih (d. 1326/1908), who was the Foreign Office agent (*kārguzar*) in Bandar 'Abbas and built a caravanserai and public baths in the town as well as acquiring land for a Baha'i cemetery; the latter's son, Mirza 'Abbas Khan Amin ul-Vizarih (d. 1327/1909); Aqa Sayyid Hasan Natanzi, who worked for the customs; Ma'sum-'Ali Khan Farhat, who was in the service of the post office; and Mirza Hasan 'Ali Khan Shirazi (see fig. 129), who was head of the post office, first in Lar (1318/1900), then in Bandar Langih and finally in Bandar 'Abbas.[9] The latter had drawn upon himself the enmity of

---

7   The account in Fakhra (Tarikh Amr dar Burazjan 32) is contradictory, indicating both before 1926 and before 1933. It may be that the Darvish Karam 'Ali who was Mulla Husayn Dashti's first contact with the Baha'i Faith was the Karam 'Ali of Nazar Aqa mentioned previously.

8   Fakhra, Tarikh Amr dar Burazjan 36–9; *Baha'i World* 11:556–7.

9   ZH 6:897, 8a:582–5, 8b:854; Rasti, Tarikh 16–19.

129. Mirza Hasan 'Ali Shirazi

130. Sadid us-Saltanih Kababi
(Muhammad 'Ali Khan)

Haji 'Ali Karam Khan Shuja' Nizam, the governor, and Shaykh 'Ali Dashti, the religious leader of the town, and he was killed as he left work on 3 October 1918.[10] Aqa Javad, son of Aqa Husayn Yazdi, was poisoned and killed in 1904.[11] Mirza Muhammad Thabit-Sharqi of Yazd spent one year in Bandar 'Abbas successfully teaching the Baha'i Faith, but then Shuja' Nizam had him and some other Baha'is arrested, beaten and bastinadoed in 1917.[12] However, by 1339/1920 the governor was Mirza 'Abdu'l-Husayn Khan, the nephew of Muvaqqar ud-Dawlih, who was not a Baha'i but protected Siyavash Sifidvash and other Baha'is when, on disembarking from a ship from Bombay, they were attacked at the instigation of Haji Muslim, who was head of the municipal council (ra'is-i baladiyyih) in the town.[13] From the list given by Mazandarani, we may conclude that there were a minimum of 60 Baha'is in Bandar 'Abbas in about 1910 and that many of them were in the higher echelons of society.[14]

---

10   ZH 7:310, 8a:583–4 ; Rasti, Tarikh 20–1.
11   ZH 7:144.
12   MH 6:316–22.
13   Sifidvash, *Yar Dirin* 162–3; ZH 8a:585; Faizi, *Khandan* 273; Muhammad-Husayni, *Tarikh* 226.
14   ZH 8b:854.

Muhammad 'Ali Khan Sadid us-Saltanih Kababi Bandar-'Abbasi (1874–1941, see fig. 130), son of Sartip Ahmad Khan, who had been the agent of the Sultan of Masqat, was a prominent Baha'i in this area. He was the agent of the passport department of the Foreign Office of Iran in Bushihr from 1899 to 1903 and also acted for part of this time as the Foreign Office agent. He was then appointed Russian agent at Lingih.[15] He was a talented poet and the author of a number of important books on the history of the Gulf area.[16]

There were also Baha'i communities in Lar (366 km southeast of Shiraz, 259 km northwest of Bandar 'Abbas; pop. 8,000 in 1915 and 11,656 in 1951) and Bandar Lingih (688 km southeast of Shiraz on the Gulf coast; pop. 12,000 in 1915 and 9,404 in 1951), which Fadil Mazandarani visited in 1911.[17] The area was under the governorship of a Baha'i, Husayn-Quli Khan Mafi Nizam us-Saltanih (see above fig. 127 and pp. 339–40 and vol. 1:483–4) from 1299/1881 to 1300/1882. He was responsible for initiating the construction of a large quay which then enabled Bandar 'Abbas to become a major port and open up a new trade route for goods from Khurasan and Yazd to India.[18]

Haji Mirza Husayn Lari was a Baha'i merchant resident in the Red Sea port of Jiddah and the Iranian vice-consul there. He was able to assist those Baha'is who made the pilgrimage to Mecca as a way of going on to visit Baha'u'llah and 'Abdu'l-Baha in a prudent manner that did not alert the opponents of the Baha'i Faith in their hometown and excite their opposition. (Regarding his son-in-law Mirza Yahya Isfahani, see pp. 47–8.)

15   Churchill, *Persian Statesmen* 74.
16   Bamdad, *Tarikh* 6:243–4; ZH 8a:582; Rasti, Tarikh 48–53.
17   Mazandarani, *Amr va Khalq* 1:kaf.
18   *Sharaf*, no. 72 (Safar 1307) 1–3; *Sharafat*, no. 29 (Jamadi II 1317) 1–4.

18

YAZD

The province of Yazd lies in south-central Iran to the east of Isfahan. To the northwest is the great desert, the Dasht-i Kavir, and to the east is another desert, the Dasht-i Lut. This province is hot and dry; rain seldom falls in the summer, causing its few rivers to run dry. Rain and snow do, however, fall on the highest mountains in the area and some snow remains on the peaks all year round. Human habitation and agriculture is only possible through irrigation using *qanats* (more than 3,000 of these have been built in the province of Yazd[1]) to bring water from the surrounding hills. Most of the population, therefore, has to live around the edge of the central basin, close to the hills. The enterprise of building such extensive irrigation systems required a great deal of capital and this led to a social structure whereby a small number of landlords controlled large areas with many peasants working their land.

Yazd

The city of Yazd lies in a plain that runs northwest to southeast from Ardakan to Mihriz. The city is situated 300 kilometres southeast of Isfahan, and 340 kilometres northwest of Kirman. Yazd was, and to a large extent

---

1   Iraj Afshar, *Yazd-Namih* 1:213.

still is, a centre for textiles and for the production of glass and other goods. The main cash crops in the surrounding area were cotton and opium in the 19th century. In the late 19th century, however, the wealth of Yazd came mainly from trade. Yazd was a trading hub, with roads and regular caravans going towards Bandar 'Abbas (and on to India), Mashhad (and on to Central Asia), Isfahan and Tehran. Goods were imported from India, for example tea, dyes and spices; from Manchester, textiles and metal; and from Russia, sugar and kerosene oil. To these were added local products such as cotton, opium and textiles and all were then sent on north and south. European merchants increasingly dominated the Bushihr–Shiraz–Isfahan–Tehran trade route but the Bandar 'Abbas–Yazd–Tehran or Khurasan route remained in the hands of Iranian merchants mostly based in Yazd. There were about 250 to 300 export–import merchants in the city during the last half of the 19th century. The people of the area are Persian-speaking Iranians and the population of Yazd itself is famed for its piety and even its fanaticism. The city prided itself on its title of Dar ul-'Ibad (City of Worship). During the devastating heat of the summer, many of the wealthier residents retired to their farms and estates in the surrounding hills. The population of Yazd was given as 35,000–40,000 in 1850,[2] 40,000 in 1868,[3] 50,000–60,000 in 1900–13 (including 1,000 Zoroastrians and 1,000 Jews[4]) and 63,500 in 1956 (including 3,617 Zoroastrians and 1,337 Jews).

At the time in the 1920s when, on the instructions of Shoghi Effendi, histories of the various towns and provinces of Iran were being written, a history of the Baha'i community of Yazd was composed by Muhammad Tahir Malmiri but it only became available through publication when the present book was at an advanced stage of preparation and only a few references have been added from it. In the 1920s Qabil Abadihi wrote a Baha'i history of Yazd but it is only 19 pages long and deals with only one episode in the period that is covered by this book. He also wrote a number of histories of the villages around Yazd. Sayyid Abu'l-Qasim Bayda wrote a detailed history of the martyrs of Yazd. The material for this chapter is derived mainly from biographies (especially those in Malmiri's *Tarikh-i Shuhada-yi Yazd*) and general histories such as Mazandarani's *Zuhur ul-Haqq*.

---

2   Abbot in Amanat, *Cities and Trade* 79, 132.
3   Thomson, in Issawi, *Economic History* 28.
4   Sykes, cited in Adamec, *Historical Gazetteer* 1:691, gives a figure of 60,000 in 1900 with 1,068 Jews and 1,000 Zoroastrians (7,000 Zoroastrians in the surrounding villages); Sobotinski, in Issawi, *Economic History* 34, gives 50,000 in 1913.

Yazd was the residence of the Shaykhi leader Shaykh Ahmad al-Ahsa'i
from 1221/1806 to 1229/1814, although he made a number of journeys
during this period. While Shaykh Ahmad was in Yazd he stayed in the
home of Shaykh 'Abdu'l-Khaliq Yazdi, who later became a follower of the
Bab in Mashhad for a time (vol. 1:120 and n). It was while Shaykh Ahmad
was in Yazd that Sayyid Kazim Rashti was inspired through a dream to
join him and become his student. Shaykh Ahmad visited Yazd again in
about 1824. There was therefore a strong Shaykhi presence in Yazd and
the Shaykhi leader Haji Karim Khan Kirmani maintained an establishment there.

Mulla Sadiq Muqaddas was the first who openly proclaimed the
message of the Bab, from the pulpit of a mosque in Yazd in 1845. He was
assaulted and had to leave the town immediately; a similar fate befell one
of the Letters of the Living, Mulla Yusif Ardibili. Mulla Ahmad Azghandi,
a nephew of Sayyid Husayn Azghandi, one of the leading *mujtahids* of
Yazd, became a Babi in Khurasan and came to Yazd, where he managed to
assist Mulla Sadiq and Mulla Yusif when it became necessary.[5] Quddus also
passed through Yazd in that earliest period.

Also in about 1845 Sayyid Yahya Vahid Darabi, who had been born in
Yazd, came back there after he had met the Bab. Either on this visit or a
subsequent one in early 1850, Vahid's open preaching of the message of
the Bab brought a large number of people into the new religious community. Mazandarani lists some 27 notables of the town and the surrounding
villages who were converted at this time, including Mulla Muhammad
Rida Radi ur-Ruh and his brothers and Haji Mulla Mahdi 'Atri and his
family.[6] Vahid's activities in 1850 caused a great commotion in the city,
made worse by the activities of the main leader of one of the factions in
the town, Muhammad 'Abdu'llah, who appears to have had links with the
Shaykhi leader Muhammad Karim Khan Kirmani and who had come to
power in the town when it was in chaos after news arrived of the death
of Muhammad Shah in September 1848. He had restored order to the
town but had been much feared by successive governors and when one
of these, Aqa Khan Iravani (who was deputizing as governor on behalf of
Muhammad Hasan Khan Iravani), had one of Muhammad 'Abdu'llah's
supporters killed in 1849, the latter arose in revolt, sacked Iravani's house
and surrounded him in the citadel. Eventually Iravani prevailed and drove

---

5   DB 183–7.
6   ZH 3:470–1; Varqa, 'Sharh Ahval' 21.

Muhammad 'Abdu'llah and some 300 of his supporters out of the town. After this Muhammad 'Abdu'llah went into hiding, only to re-emerge when Vahid came to Yazd for the second time in early 1850. He supported Vahid and proclaimed himself a Babi. There was an open confrontation between the Babis and Iravani, and eventually Vahid was forced to leave the town.[7] Muhammad 'Abdu'llah was given amnesty by the next deputy governor, Shaykh-'Ali Khan, and then killed a short time later[8] (a brother of Muhammad 'Abdu'llah, Karbala'i Husayn, and another follower were with Baha'u'llah in the Siyah Chal in Tehran and later became Baha'is[9]).

At least five Babis were executed in Yazd in the period after the above events and when the orders for a general massacre of the Babis arrived in 1852 following the attempt on the life of the shah. Aqa 'Ali Akbar Hakkak Yazdi was ordered to recant by the governor and, despite the pleadings of his wife and child, refused to do so. He was blown from a cannon. Mirza Hasan Aqa Fadil, one of the *imam-jum'ihs* of the city, was arrested by Navvab 'Abdu'l-Hayy and sent to the governor. He was also blown from a canon when he refused to recant, as was Aqa Husayn Zanjani. Muhammad Sadiq Nassaj Yazdi was arrested by Navvab 'Abdu'l-Hayy, who had him beaten to death by the mob. Mulla 'Ali Turk, a *mujtahid* of Yazd, tried to use the situation to increase his power in the city. He denounced Mulla Baqir Ardakani as a Babi to the governor of Kirman, who was also in charge of Yazd. But when Ardakani was summoned to Kirman, the governor was so pleased with his manner and learning and the fact that he cured the governor's wife of stomach cramps that he released him. Mulla 'Ali also launched a campaign against another Babi cleric, Haji Mulla Mahdi, and tried to force his wife to divorce him. When Mulla 'Ali fell victim to a stroke, he stopped his campaign.[10]

Some of the more prominent Babis had to go into hiding during this period (see under Manshad below). Some Babis, however, recanted their faith out of fear of the order for a general massacre of the Babis that had been issued by the shah. Mulla Husayn ibn Mirza Sulayman, a *mujtahid* who had become a Babi and had even copied some of the Bab's works, was so fearful that he ordered Mulla 'Ali Naqi Rawdih-khan, a Babi, be

7   DB 466–75.
8   On the activities of Muhammad 'Abdu'llah (Muhammad the son of 'Abdu'llah), see Afshar, *Yazd-Namih* 226–8; BBR 106–9.
9   ZH 6:729–30.
10   ZH 3:481–2, 4:87; Malmiri, *Tarikh Shuhada* 9–15; Malmiri, *Tarikh Yazd* 31–7; this Mulla Mahdi is probably Mulla Mahdi 'Atri (see p. 365).

bastinadoed in order to ensure that he himself would not be accused; and indeed he went on to assume a respected place as a religious leader and gathered much wealth. Similarly, Haji Rasul Mihrizi, who had been one of the companions of Vahid, ordered that Haji Sayyid 'Ali Mihrizi, a Babi, be bastinadoed in order to protect himself.[11]

When news came that the Babi leadership had established itself in Baghdad after 1853, many of the Babis of the area travelled there. Several of these stayed while others returned bringing the news that rather than Azal, it was Baha'u'llah who had won their respect and admiration in Baghdad. Among these were Mulla Muhammad Rida Radi ur-Ruh Manshadi and Mirza Husayn (d. 1334/1915, son of the above-mentioned Haji Mulla Mahdi 'Atri and brother of Varqa). The former brought back the first copy of Baha'u'llah's Qasidih 'Izz Varqa'iyyih (the Ode of the Dove) to the Yazd area while the latter brought back Baha'u'llah's Hidden Words.[12] While in Baghdad in about 1858–9, Mirza Husayn had noted the increasing enmity being shown by Azal towards Baha'u'llah. Mirza Muhammad Tahir Malmiri recalls that he was about six or seven years of age when Mirza Husayn returned to Yazd in about 1858 (i.e. before Baha'u'llah had put forward any claim):

I remember well that it was three or four hours after sunset that there was a knock on our door. We responded and Aqa Mirza Husayn called out from behind the door 'Open the door, for Azal has gone to Hell.' My father was very disturbed, wondering who it was behind the door and what he was saying. He opened the door and saw that it was Aqa Mirza Husayn standing there, still in his travelling clothes, having come from Baghdad. My father said: 'What are you saying?' The reply came: 'Azal has been cast aside and Baha'u'llah is *Man Yuzhiruhu'llah* (He whom God shall make manifest).' So he began to explain the matter and gave details of Mirza Yahya's enmity and his betrayal.[13]

Thus when Baha'u'llah's claim became known, he already had a strong basis of support in the area. The first to bring news of Baha'u'llah's claim to the area was Mirza Ja'far Yazdi (d. 1309/1891). He arrived from Edirne in 1866 and announced that the one promised by the Bab had

---

11   ZH 4:87; Malmiri, *Tarikh Yazd* 37–8.
12   ZH 6:727, 729–30, 751–2.
13   Malmiri, *Khatirat* 39.

appeared, although he refused at first to
give the name. Then when the curiosity and eagerness of every Babi of Yazd
had been raised, he convened a large
meeting at which he named Baha'u'llah
as the one. Mirza Ja'far was a religious
scholar who had studied at Najaf, but
when he met Baha'u'llah in Baghdad he
abandoned the clerical garb. He accompanied Baha'u'llah on the various stages
of his exile as far as 'Akka. He was one
of those whom Baha'u'llah chose to
take the news of his claim to be the one
promised by the Bab to the Babi communities in Iran, being probably the
first to bring this news to Yazd, parts of
Khurasan and possibly Isfahan.[14]

132. Mirza 'Ali Muhammad Varqa,
son of Haji Mulla Mahdi 'Atri

Another who played an important
role in convincing the Yazd Babis of
Baha'u'llah's claim was Mirza Ahmad Yazdi (1220/1805–1320/1902),
who was from a family of Yazd notables, being the nephew of 'Abdu'r-
Rida Khan Biglar-Bigi who was the deputy-governor of Yazd and who in
1242/1826 had tried unsuccessfully to seize the governorship for himself.
Mirza Ahmad, however, turned his back on the wealth of his family and
became a wandering dervish, travelling to India before marrying and settling in Kashan. Having heard of the new religion, he travelled to Mashhad,
became a Babi there and met the Bab in Kashan. He went to Baghdad in
about 1858, where he met Baha'u'llah. He remained in Baghdad when
Baha'u'llah left and some time later set off for Edirne to visit Baha'u'llah
again. When he reached Istanbul in 1865, he received the Arabic Tablet
of Ahmad, which told him to propagate the new religion. He abandoned
his journey and set out for Iran. During his travels through Adharbayjan,
Tehran and Khurasan in 1865–6, he spoke to many Babis, suggesting
to them that Baha'u'llah may be He whom God shall make manifest,
the one foretold by the Bab. He faced a hostile reception to his words
in Tehran and in Dughabad (Furugh) in Khurasan; Mulla Muhammad

---

14   ZH 6:739–40; on him bringing the news to Yazd, see Blomfield, *Chosen Highway*
     61; Qummi, *Hizar Dastan* 121–2; for Khurasan, see ZH 6:23.

Furughi was so incensed that he hit him and broke his teeth, although, after studying the Bayan together, Furughi came to accept Yazdi's message. Yazdi was briefly arrested in Kashan and, after falling ill in Kirmanshah, he settled in Sarvistan in Fars from about 1866 to 1888. He then moved to Nayriz and Hirat in Fars briefly before settling in Munj in Fars for four years. In 1311/1893 he left for Kashan and settled in Tehran and Qazvin. He died in 1320/1902 at an age in excess of one hundred years.[15] Nabil Zarandi was also among the first to bring this news to Yazd in the summer of 1866 and others who came included Zayn ul-Muqarrabin, Nabil Akbar (Qa'ini) and Mulla Sadiq Muqaddas. It was not long before the majority of Babis had become Baha'is.

Of those Babis who did not become Baha'is, a small group of about six followed Mirza Ja'far Kaffash (cobbler) who put forward a claim to leadership and called his group the Kullu-Shay'is. Mirza Ja'far later moved to Karbala and withdrew his claims. He died in Yazd in 1309/1891 and no trace of his group remained, some of them having become Baha'is.[16] The only supporter of Azal in Yazd was Shaykh Muhammad Yazdi. He had been in Shiraz in the summer of 1866, when Nabil-i A'zam first brought the news of Baha'u'llah's claim to that city and had been the only person to raise any objections there. Finding himself without any support and fiercely opposed in Shiraz, he returned to his native Yazd. Here he mixed with the Baha'is, trying, without success, covertly to persuade them of the Azali position. In 1306/1888 Mirza Abu'l-Fadl Gulpaygani came to Yazd and held a debate with Shaykh Muhammad.[17] Unable to answer Gulpaygani, Shaykh Muhammad stormed out of the meeting and shortly thereafter moved to Istanbul, which had become a centre of Azali activity. He returned to Yazd in the early 1890s but since he was known as a 'Babi', he was unable to live there and moved to Karbala.[18] One person who wavered a while over Azal's claim was Mirza Muhammad Rida Tabib (physician), for whom Baha'u'llah later wrote the Tablet on the Practice of

---

15   Autobiographical account in Ishraq-Khavari, *Muhadarat* 2:653–61; ZH 6:790–1; Muhammad-Husayni, 'Muqaddamati tarikhi' 32–3; Malmiri, *Tarikh Yazd* 71–2. Ishraq-Khavari and Muhammad-Husayni state that he settled in Tehran, visited Qazvin but died in Tehran, while ZH states he moved from Tehran to Qazvin and died there.

16   ZH 6:854–5; Dihaji, *Risalih* 179–80; Browne, *Materials* 233; Gulpaygani, *Kashf ul-Ghita* 371.

17   Isfahani, *Gulpaygani* 281–94.

18   ZH 6:855; Balyuzi, *Baha'u'llah* 389–97.

Medicine (Lawh-i Tibb, often called the Tablet to the Physician), but Zayn ul-Muqarrabin spent some two years living at his house (about 1867–9) and eventually resolved his doubts.[19]

There were a number of skilled and very effective teachers of the Baha'i Faith resident in Yazd and the surrounding villages, such as Mulla Muhammad Rida Muhammadabadi, Mulla Muhammad Rida Radi ur-Ruh Manshadi, Mulla 'Abdu'l-Ghani Ardakani, Haji Muhammad Ibrahim Muballigh Shirazi, Haji Mirza Muhammad Afshar, Mirza Mahdi Akhavan Safa, Haji Mulla Muhammad Ibrahim Mujtahid Masalih-gu, Haji Muhammad Tahir Malmiri, Aqa Muhammad Husayn Ulfat and others. E. G. Browne, for example, testifies to the intensity and earnestness with which attempts were made to convert him while he was in that city in May 1888.[20] Many travelling Baha'i teachers also visited the town.[21] Nor, in general, were these efforts unsuccessful. At a meeting in Yazd as early as about 1878, 200 Baha'is (these would have been only the male Baha'is) were present.[22] This would represent a Baha'i population of at least one thousand in the city. By 1887 the Christian missionary agent Benjamin Badall was reporting that: 'the religion of Baha increases daily, and one of them said that since our last visit [in 1885] more than 400 men have become Baabis in Yezd alone, besides those in the surrounding villages.'[23]

One possible explanation for the fact that the Babi and Baha'i Faith spread so readily among the people of Yazd, despite their reputation for fiercely adhering to Islam, is the statement by one Yazdi writing in the

---

19   Malmiri, *Khatirat* 58–9; ZH 6:207n, *Tarikh Yazd* 131–2.
20   Browne, *Year* 431–47; interestingly, Gulpaygani reports that the Baha'is of Yazd thought that Browne had become a Baha'i, *Kashf ul-Ghita* 13–14.
21   For example Mirza Mahmud Furughi in 1896, 1899 and 1903 (ZH 8a:235, 237, 238; MH 3:459–63); Varqa (see fig. 132 and p. 366); Ibn Abhar in about 1895 and 1902–3 (ZH 8a:321, 323); Nayyir and Sina in 1894 (ZH 8a:331); Mirza Mahmud Zarqani in 1892, 1897 and 1900 (ZH 8b:564); Sayyid Asadu'llah Qummi in 1893 (ZH 8a:630); Shaykh Muhammad 'Ali Qa'ini for seven months in about 1898 (ZH 8b:1015); 'Alaviyyih Khanum Mahfuruzaki in 1903 (ZH 8b:815); Bibi Rawhaniyyih of Bushruyih stayed in Yazd for 15 years from 1903 (ZH 8a:226–7) and Mirza Qabil of Abadih, who visited Yazd and the surrounding villages annually for several years (ZH 8a:589–90; MH 2:182); he is especially credited with restoring the morale of the Yazd Baha'is after the 1903 pogrom, MH 2:183, 211. He wrote the Baha'i histories of several of the villages around Yazd (see Bibliography).
22   Malmiri, *Khatirat* 40–1.
23   *Bible Society Monthly Reporter*, Apr. 1887, 55–6, quoted in Momen, 'Christian Missionaries', 66.

early 20th century that the people of Yazd had tended towards the Akhbari school.[24] Thus a certain antagonism among the people of Yazd towards the Usuli school, that was rapidly becoming the established orthodoxy in Iran in the first half of the 19th century, would explain the welcome that they had given the founder of the Shaykhi school, Shaykh Ahmad al-Ahsa'i, when he had stayed in their city for eight years, and may well also partly explain the large number who were attracted to the Babi and, later, the Baha'i teachings. Of course, the strong Shaykhi presence in the city would itself have predisposed people towards the Babi and Baha'i Faiths. In any case, the conversions proceeded apace, spreading gradually to the various groupings in the city: the Sufis, the Shaykhis, and the Zoroastrians.

The Baha'i Faith, at least, in the initial stages, appears to have spread among three main groups in Yazd. The first was the clerical class, and among even the higher-ranking clerics. A number of *imāms* (prayer-leaders) of mosques and teachers at the religious colleges appear among the lists of those who became Baha'is. The second group is the merchant class, which was closely linked to the clerical class, and indeed several of the merchants among the list of Baha'is had also undertaken religious studies but had then chosen to become merchants. The third large group came from the guilded craftsmen and traders, a group which again had strong links with the religious classes.

The members of the family of the Bab, the Afnans (see pp. 251–6), who were resident in Yazd, comprised, it could be said, the premiere Baha'i family of the city.[25] Not only did they have prestige among the Baha'is because of their connection with the Bab, but they were also wealthy merchants and landowners and held a high position in Yazd society, enhanced by the fact that one of their number became a consular agent for Russia and therefore enjoyed Russian protection. There were three main branches of the Afnan family in Yazd. One was headed by Haji Mirza Hasan 'Ali (known as Khal-i Asghar, the youngest uncle of the Bab). A second was headed by Haji Mirza Muhammad Taqi Afnan (1246/1830–30 Aug. 1911, see figs. 133 and 136, a son of Haji Sayyid Muhammad, the Bab's eldest uncle), who moved to Yazd in 1854 and became the consular agent for Russia[26] in 1889 and was therefore called Vakil ud-Dawlih (representative

---

24   Navvab Vakil, *Khatirat* 263.

25   On the Afnan family in general, see Faizi, *Khandan Afnan* and Shahidiyan, *Man-suban*; on the Afnans in Yazd, see also Malmiri, *Khatirat* 59–65.

26   It appears that in the late 1880s the Afnans began to use Aqa 'Ali Haydar Shirvani (vol. 1:52) as their agent in Tehran. The latter was a Russian subject and used

133. Vakil ud-Dawlih (Haji
Mirza Muhammad Taqi
Afnan) holding a plan for
the Baha'i House of Worship
in Ashkhabad

134. Haji Mirza Hasan
Afnan-i Kabir

135. Haji Muhammad
Ibrahim Muballigh

136. Some of the Afnans of Yazd. *Seated, right to left*: Aqa Sayyid Aqa (son of Vakil ud-
Dawlih); Haji Mirza Aqa (son of Haji Mirza Hasan 'Ali); Vakil ud-Dawlih; Haj Sayyid Mahdi
(son of Haji Mirza Hasan 'Ali); Mirza 'Abdu'l-Husayn (son of Afnan-i Kabir). *Standing, right
to left*: Mirza Javad Afnan (son of Haji Mirza Aqa); Sayyid Muhammad (son of Vakil ud-
Dawlih?); Mirza Yusif; Sayyid 'Ali (son of Haji Sayyid Mahdi)

of the government). The third branch was headed by Haji Mirza Hasan (d. 1311/1893, see fig. 134), known as Afnan-i Kabir (the Great Afnan), a brother-in law of the Bab.[27] However, since there was widespread inter-marriage among the Afnans (for example, Afnan-i Kabir was married to a sister of Vakil ud-Dawlih and a daughter of Afnan-i Kabir was married to a son of Haji Mirza Hasan 'Ali), they acted as one family and all had their business offices in the Sara-yi Khajih, where other Baha'i merchants, such as Haji Muhammad Ibrahim Muballigh and Haji Muhammad Isma'il Gunduli, were also based. The Afnan family were important merchants with a widespread network of agents, importing and exporting goods along the lines described above for the merchants of Yazd.

Vakil ud-Dawlih (see fig. 136) and Haj Sayyid Mahdi (see fig. 136), the son of Haji Mirza Hasan 'Ali, were converted in about 1861–2 (after reading the Kitab-i Iqan in the case of Vakil ud-Dawlih) and visited Baha'u'llah in Baghdad at this time. The conversion of the rest of the Afnan family was the work of Haji Muhammad Ibrahim Muballigh (see fig. 135), who was also a Shirazi merchant resident in Yazd and whose sister was married to Haji Mirza Hasan 'Ali Afnan.[28] He had studied the religious sciences under Shaykh Muhammad Taqi Sabzivari and had excelled at these to the extent that the Shaykh gave him a certificate (*ijazih*) for being a *mujtahid*. Haji Muhammad Ibrahim did not, however, want to pursue a career as a reli-gious leader and returned to trade, which was the family occupation. He was converted in about 1863 and went to Shiraz three years later. In about 1867, after converting several members of the Afnan family in Shiraz (p. 257), Haji Muhammad Ibrahim returned to Yazd and began to teach the Afnan family there with the help of Mulla Muhammad Nabil Akbar Qa'ini and Mulla Sadiq Muqaddas. The younger members converted quickly, but Haji Mirza Hasan 'Ali refused to convert until Afnan-i Kabir was con-vinced. The latter had studied the Islamic religious sciences and was so

---

his connections in the Russian legation to obtain for Haji Mirza Muhammad Taqi the designation of Vakil ut-Tijarah (consular agent for trade) and Vakil ud-Dawlih-yi Rus (consular agent of the Russian Government; ZH 8a:430; Shavar et al., *Baha'is of Iran* 1:19). 'Abdu'l-Baha gave him the designation Vakil ul-Haqq (agent of the True One).

27 Malmiri, *Tarikh Yazd* 132–4, 138–9.
28 Faizi, *Khandan Afnan* 140; Shahidiyan, *Mansuban* 316, 340. Malmiri (*Tarikh Yazd* 52), ZH 6:788 and Ishraq-Khavari (*Muhadarat* 1:308) state that Haji Muballigh's sister was married to Haji Sayyid Mahdi, the son of Haji Mirza Hasan 'Ali. However, Faizi (*Khandan Afnan* 147) states that Haji Sayyid Mahdi was married to a niece of Haji Muballigh.

137. Mirza Mahmud Afnan

138. Mulla Muhammad Rida
Muhammadabadi Yazdi

learned in traditional medicine that he gave classes to the physicians in Yazd. Once he was convinced of the truth of the Baha'i Faith, Haji Mirza Hasan 'Ali signalled his acceptance. Haji Muhammad Ibrahim Muballigh was himself declared a unbeliever (*takfir*) by his erstwhile teacher Shaykh Muhammad Taqi Sabzivari and fled, going first to 'Akka and then settling in Bombay for eleven years before returning to Yazd.[29] Afnan-i Kabir migrated to 'Akka in 1881. He lived for a time in Beirut but returned to 'Akka in 1304/1886 (for the marriages of his sons, see pp. 258–9).

The Afnans had a powerful and influential position in the town. Vakil ud-Dawlih had a Russian flag flying over his house and was called locally the 'Agand' (agent).[30] No one, especially the governor of the town, wanted to risk offending the Russian government. Thus the Afnans were able to assist other Baha'is in Yazd and the surrounding villages when they were being persecuted. Frequently, indeed, Baha'is who were in danger of death would seek refuge in the homes of the Afnan family or would ask the Afnans to intercede with the governor for them. Vakil ud-Dawlih moved to Ashkhabad, arriving in October 1902, in order to build the Baha'i house

29   Malmiri, *Tarikh Yazd* 52; ZH 6:788–90; Balyuzi, *Eminent Baha'is* 229. Baha'u'llah addressed him as Muballigh (religious teacher) and Khalil, saying that he should be regarded as being a member of the Afnan family.

30   Tashakkuri-Bafqi, *Mashrutiyyat* 28, 30.

of worship there, but his son Mirza Mahmud (d. 1920, see fig. 137) took
over as the acting Russian consular agent and in that capacity was able to
offer a limited amount of protection to some Baha'is during the anti-Baha'i
pogrom of 1903. The Afnans also acquired extensive property in Bavanat
(see pp. 313–14), Rafsanjan (see p. 442) and elsewhere.

A somewhat colourful character was Mulla Muhammad Rida Muham-
madabadi Yazdi (see fig. 138), who had studied in the Madrasih Khan in
Yazd, becoming learned in all of the Islamic sciences as well as acquiring
knowledge of Shaykhism, Sufism and alchemy. He was introduced to the
Babi religion by his son-in-law who had known the Bab in Shiraz. Then
Sayyid Mahdi Dihaji showed him a copy of Baha'u'llah's poem Qasidih
'Izz Varqa'iyyih, which he had brought from Baghdad, and this convinced
Muhammadabadi that Baha'u'llah was the one promised by the Bab, even
though Baha'u'llah had made no claim at that time and Muhammadabadi
faced the censure of his fellow Babis for making such an assertion. When
Mirza Ja'far brought news of Baha'u'llah's claim to Yazd, Muhammadabadi
accepted immediately. He became known as a 'Babi' and the pressure upon
him increased to the point that he had to migrate to the Rafsanjan area,
near Kirman. Eventually however, due to the enmity of Murtada-Quli
Khan Nuri Vakil ul-Mulk, the governor there, he was forced to return to
Yazd in about 1286/1869. He was very open and outspoken in his teaching of the Baha'i Faith, on one occasion rebuking the *mujtahid* Shaykh
Muhammad Hasan Sabzivari for having failed to respond to Baha'u'llah
and, on another, giving him a copy of Baha'u'llah's book, the Kitab-i Iqan.[31]
As a consequence of his boldness, he was frequently beaten and imprisoned. When his father died, his brother accused Mulla Muhammadabadi
of being a Baha'i and managed in that way to obtain all the inheritance.
Muhammadabadi was bastinadoed and imprisoned on several occasions,
eventually expelled from Yazd in 1290/1873 (probably at the same time
as the other Baha'i persecutions of that year, see p. 365) and made his way
to Tehran. Here he made a living by writing letters for people at the Shah
Mosque (and for Manekji Sahib, see p. 96) and by writing out the works
of Baha'u'llah for the Baha'is. He was imprisoned in 1300/1882–3, when
his outspoken response to his questioners was in marked contrast to that
of the other Baha'is (vol. 1:39–41). After this he lived for three years in
the house of Haji Faraj and Fatimih Sultan (vol. 1:34, 70), teaching their

---

31   Yazdi, *Tarikh 'Ishqabad* 324; Malmiri, *Tarikh Yazd* 58; ZH 6:734.

children.[32] In 1896 he was in
Kashan, where the Baha'is had
to dissuade him from openly
debating the truth of the Faith
with Mirza Habibu'llah, the
main opponent of the Faith
in that town. When the assassination of Nasiru'd-Din Shah
occurred, he moved to Qumm.
In a gathering at the house of
Shaykh Mahmud, he chal-
lenged the host when the latter
asserted that Baha'is had assassinated Nasiru'd-Din Shah
and was arrested and sent to
Tehran. His guards on that
journey later attested to the fact
that, although they left him for
40 days while they chased some

139. Haji Muhammad Tahir Malmiri (or
Malamiri)

bandits, they returned to find him waiting for them in the caravanserai
where they had left him, despite the fact he was not bound in any way and
could easily have escaped. In prison in Tehran, he again refused to obtain
his freedom by concealing his beliefs and he died while still in prison. It is
said he had never told a lie in the whole of his life.[33] He was among four
persons named posthumously by 'Abdu'l-Baha as Hands of the Cause.

Among the prominent propagators of the Baha'i Faith to come from Yazd
was Haji Muhammad Tahir Malmiri (1856–1953, see fig. 139; Malmir or
Malamir is one of the quarters of Yazd), who followed the family trade of
weaving but also owned property in Madvar (6 km south of Mihriz). His
mother, Ma'sumih, had become a Babi through Sayyid Ja'far Yazdi who

32 ZH 6:449.
33 Qummi, Hizar Dastan, 117–23 (part of this is Muhammadabadi's own account
of how he became a Babi and then a Baha'i and this can also be found in *Ahang-i
Badi'* year 25 (1970–1) 102–4); Yazdi, *Tarikh 'Ishqabad* 324–8, 481–3; Malmiri,
Khatirat 48–52; Balyuzi, *Eminent Baha'is* 98–111; ZH 6:732–7; Rayhani in
Amanat, 'Negotiating Identities' 315–20. The account in ZH 6:449–51 implies
that he died at about the same time as the killing of Varqa and Ruhu'llah. This
would mean that his arrest must have occurred before the assassination of
Nasiru'd-Din Shah.

had in turn been converted by Vahid Darabi and she had in turn converted her husband and the rest of the family. Thus Malmiri was born into a Babi family and was well known as a Baha'i from his early days. He frequently had to go into hiding or to leave town whenever there was pressure building up either against him in particular or against the Baha'is generally. From about 1886 to about 1901, he was the agent of the Afnan family in Bavanat, Khurrami and Bayan and also spent two years in Abadih. He was responsible for the conversion of many Baha'is in Yazd and elsewhere and wrote a number of works including a history of the Baha'i community of Yazd, a history of the martyrs of Yazd and his own memoirs.[34]

Another leading Baha'i was Aqa Muhammad Husayn Ulfat 'Attar Yazdi (1853–1936, see fig. 140), a pharmacist who had been a leading Shaykhi in the town and taught classes on Shaykhi and Akhbari works. He became a Baha'i in about 1882 through Malmiri. On account of his successful teaching of the Baha'i Faith, he was arrested, imprisoned, beaten and fined on several occasions. According to Fadil Mazandarani, one major cause of the 1903 pogrom was Ulfat's propagation activities[35] and the first place that the mob headed for on the first day of that pogrom was his shop. He was not there and the Afnan family managed to smuggle him out of the town but his wife, Fatimih Sughra (see fig. 141), suffered badly. She was beaten and had her *chadur* and headscarf torn away in public. It is difficult for anyone not brought up in that culture to understand what it meant for a woman to have her face and hair exposed in public – it could perhaps be likened to being stripped naked in public. Malmiri tries to describe the enormity of this event for the family.

> That disaster that had befall his [Aqa Muhammad Husayn's] respected wife has not befallen anyone else. Indeed, martyrdom would have been easier to bear than the malicious gloating and the dishonouring of one's reputation. The question of the veiling of women was one that was held to be of great importance in Yazd. So much so that if the *rawdih-khans* (reciters of the tragedy of martyrdom of the Imam Husayn) had said that the Holy Family, after the events in the desert of Karbala and as they were being brought captive to Damascus, had been without veils, most of the people would have objected to this statement [even though it is what happened].

---

34   ZH 6:837–9; MH 5:300–75; all three books contain autobiographical material and all three have been published, see Bibliography.
35   ZH 6:840.

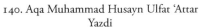

140. Aqa Muhammad Husayn Ulfat 'Attar   141. Fatimih Sughra
              Yazdi

They would have said that it is a lie; how could the family and wives of
Imam Husayn be without veils. And now the shamelessness of this mob
had reached such a stage that they had removed not just the *chadur* but
also the head-scarf from this respectable lady and had dragged her, with
her hair uncovered, all bloodied and covered with dirt, through the streets.
The shame of this disgraceful deed and the imprisonment in the house of
the *kadkhuda* was greater than martyrdom.[36]

So traumatized was Fatimih Sughra by this that she felt too ashamed to
remain in Yazd and she and her family moved away to Tehran. The episode
transformed her into a nervous woman for the rest of her life. In Tehran,
Ulfat continued propagating the Baha'i Faith, making occasional journeys
around Iran.[37]

    Haji Mirza Muhammad Afshar was one of the prominent merchants of
Yazd and owned much property in the Mihriz area. He was also a scholar
and had a large library. Some years after he became a Baha'i he wrote a

---

36   Malmiri, *Khatirat* 102.
37   ZH 6:839–41; Malmiri, *Khatirat* 99–102, *Tarikh Yazd* 69–70; Momen, *Momen
     Family* 7–81.

book of Baha'i proofs, the *Bahr ul-'Irfan* (The Ocean of True Understanding, Bombay; no date of publication is given but it was about 1890), which may have been the first book of Baha'i proofs to have been published. He then visited Baha'u'llah in Bahji. He brought his two brothers, Haji Muhammad Sadiq and Haji Muhammad Husayn, into the new religion. He appears to have lived in Shiraz for a time in the 1890s but returned to Yazd. These brothers were such prominent people in Yazd that during the 1903 anti-Baha'i pogrom, Navvab Vakil and some of the clerics of the town made certain that the mob did not attack their houses.[38] Mirza Muhammad Afshar also converted his son-in-law, Haji Muhammad Isma'il Gunduli, a wealthy merchant whose father had come from Khurasan. Despite the fact that an attempt was made on his life, Gunduli was outspoken as a Baha'i. He was one of the main people being sought by the mob during the 1903 anti-Baha'i pogrom. He managed to hide while his house was looted and taken to pieces and while the men who had been sent by the governor to guard it took their share of the spoils.[39]

Mirza Muhammad Rida Kirmani, a *mujtahid* of Yazd, had met the Bab and was a Babi and later a Baha'i. He kept his belief so secret that neither the other Baha'is nor even his own family knew. Then on his deathbed in 1885, he told his son Shaykh Zaynu'l-'Abidin Abrari (1864–1936) to go to Vakil ud-Dawlih and investigate the Baha'i Faith. Shaykh Zaynu'l-'Abidin, who was a teacher at the Madrasih Musalla Safdar Khan, became a Baha'i but when his brothers found out, he had to leave Yazd. He went eventually to Najaf where he studied under Sayyid Kazim Tabataba'i Yazdi (c. 1831–1919), one of the foremost Shi'i scholars of the time, and obtained a certificate of *ijtihad*. He worked for a time as an Imam-Jum'ih in Najaf and then returned to Iran in 1317/1899. He went at first to Khurasan and later settled in Barfurush (Babul), Mazandaran, but fell into the pattern of spending the winter months in Mazandaran and the summer months in Khurasan and Tehran, teaching the Baha'i Faith. He moved to Tehran in 1905 and taught for a time at the branch of the Baha'i Tarbiyat School that was at Sabr Qabr Aqa, and later at the main school. In 1912 he moved to Barfurush to teach at the Sa'adat Baha'i School there and then to Sari to be the headmaster of a newly opened Baha'i school there. This school

---

38   ZH 6:809; Malmiri, *Khatirat* 34–5, *Tarikh Yazd* 108–9; Malmiri, *Tarikh Shuhada* 167. The grandson of Muhammad Sadiq Afshar, Dr Iraj Afshar, was a prominent Iranian scholar of history.

39   ZH 8b:928–31; Malmiri, *Khatirat* 35–7; Malmiri, *Tarikh Shuhada* 158.

later became a government school but Abrari continued to teach there until he retired. During the time he was a teacher at these schools by day, most nights he attended meetings to teach the Baha'i Faith.[40]

Numerous others from all walks of life also became Baha'is. At the upper levels of society, these ranged from government officials, such as Iskandar Khan, who was deputy governor for a time and governor from 1288/1871 to 1290/1873,[41] to religious leaders, such as Aqa Shaykh Sadiq[42] who taught at the Madrasih Shafi'iyyih and the above-mentioned Haji Shaykh Zaynu'l-'Abidin Abrari. These individuals had to keep the fact that they were Baha'is hidden

142. Ustad 'Ali Akbar Banna Yazdi

and they did not mix with the other Baha'is. Despite this, the latter two became known as Baha'is and were forced to leave their positions.

There were also many merchants, tradesmen and skilled workers who became Baha'is. One of these, Ustad 'Ali Akbar Banna (builder, 1845–1903, see fig. 142), is said to have converted as many as 300 persons in the Yazd area. As a consequence he was much persecuted by the local clerics and arrested by the governor. Benjamin Badall, an Armenian who was in the employ of the British and Foreign Bible Society, visited Yazd in early 1884 and in his report calls Ustad 'Ali Akbar the 'head Babi' in Yazd. Baha'u'llah's well-known work Tajalliyat was written to him. He was among the first Baha'is to move to Ashkhabad, arriving there in April 1884. He began by working for the Afnan family building houses and shops in this rapidly growing town. In 1886 he visited Baha'u'llah and in 1887 he completed a building for the Baha'is of Ashkhabad to use as a meeting-place on a corner of the land that was later used for the house of worship. In 1888 he visited Yazd for six months before returning to Ashkhabad and in 1311/1893, he again visited 'Akka and while there, under the instructions of 'Abdu'l-Baha, he drew up the designs for the house of worship in Ashkhabad. When work on this began in October 1902, he supervised the first six months of its building before he was killed on a visit to Yazd during the anti-Baha'i pogrom of 1903.[43]

The Baha'is in Yazd were well-organized. Baha'i meetings were held in the homes of the wealthier Baha'is who had large houses. Larger meetings were held in a number of gardens owned or rented by these wealthy families outside the town, especially one called Salsabil rented by Vakil ud-Dawlih, where Baha'i travelling teachers would also stay. Another place where meetings were held was a farm called Mahmudi, owned by Haji Mirza Mahmud Tajir Isfahani and his nephew Haji Mirza Hasan 'Ali Isfahani.[44] Browne describes attending two such meetings in 1888, at which 'Andalib was present.[45] Ibn Abhar, who visited Yazd in 1902 and 1903, established the local spiritual assembly there.[46] Haji Mirza Mahmud Afnan (c. 1272/1855–1336/1917), the eldest son of Vakil ud-Dawlih, did not go into the family business of trade but dedicated himself to working for the Baha'i community. Dawn prayers (*mashriq ul-adhkar*), which were instituted during Ibn Abhar's visit in 1902–3, were held in his house every day.[47] The above-mentioned merchant Haji Muhammad Isma'il Gunduli had two buildings in his walled complex, one of which he put one aside for a community *mashriq ul-adhkar*.[48] In the Vaqt va Sa'at Quarter a group of nine Baha'is would take it in turn to have nightly *mashriq ul-adhkar* in their house.[49]

As mentioned above, Yazd was well-known throughout Iran as being rather fanatical in its Islam. Therefore there was always an atmosphere of repression towards the Baha'is of the city. At first, matters were moderated by the fact that several of the leading religious figures in Yazd were indifferent to the new religion while others were supporters or even secret

43   MH 3:549–615; ZH 6:833–6; 8b:995, 1029–34; Malmiri, *Khatirat* 117–18; Malmiri, *Tarikh Shuhada* 150–7; Dhuka'i-Bayda'i, *Tadhkirih* 1:195–216; Ishraq-Khavari, *Muhadarat* 2:1113; *Bible Society Monthly Reporter*, July 1884, p. 124. His descendants took the family name Shahidi (from *shahid*, meaning 'martyr').
44   Malmiri, *Tarikh Yazd* 48–9.
45   *Year among the Persians* 436–8.
46   vol. 1:500; ZH 6:336; however Malmiri (*Khatirat* 61, *Tarikh Yazd* 134) states that the local assembly was set up by Sayyid Ahmad Afnan, who came to Yazd in 1898.
47   Malmiri, *Khatirat* 61–3, *Tarikh Yazd* 135; ZH 5:520; 8a:323–4.
48   Malmiri, *Tarikh Shuhada* 158; Malmiri, *Khatirat* 37.
49   Malmiri, *Tarikh Shuhada* 291.

believers, like Aqa Sayyid Abu'l-Qasim Mujtahid, Mirza Muhammad Rida Mujtahid Kirmani (see p. 362), Mulla Muhammad Baqir Mujtahid Ardakani (see p. 413) and Shaykh Sadiq Chavush (who taught at the Madrasih-yi Shafi'iyyih and was a Baha'i).⁵⁰ However, as the older generation of clerics died, religious leadership in Yazd fell into the hands of the *mujtahid* Shaykh Muhammad Hasan Sabzivari and his son Shaykh Muhammad Taqi Sabzivari who together with Mirza Sayyid 'Ali Mudarris and the two sons of Mulla Muhammad Baqir Mujtahid Ardakani, Mulla Husayn and Mulla Hasan, were much opposed to the Baha'is. In these later years, only two of the major clerics of Yazd were protective of the Baha'is, Sayyid 'Ali Ha'iri and Sayyid Husayn Sultan ul-'Ulama (one source states the latter was a secret convert)⁵¹ but they were no match for the vehemence with which the Sabzivaris pursued the Baha'is.

From about 1290/1873 onwards the persecutions intensified. In that year, there were some 200 Baha'is at a large and noisy celebration of the holy day of Ridvan at the house of Haji Mulla Mahdi 'Atri (d. 1297/1879), who was learned in the Islamic, natural and occult sciences, and had been arrested on several occasions on account of his open teaching of the Baha'i Faith. Such a large meeting of Baha'is had never been held in Yazd before and the following day, Shaykh Muhammad Hasan Sabzivari had 'Atri severely beaten. A complaint was made by 'Atri's son to the governor and since nothing happened, Sabzivari felt confident enough to continue to arrest, fine and beat other Baha'is in the town. It was only the refusal by the *mujtahid* Mulla Muhammad Baqir Ardakani, who was secretly a Baha'i (see p. 413), to sign a *fatwa* against Haji Mulla Mahdi 'Atri that saved the latter's life, although he was compelled to leave Yazd.⁵² He and his sons Mirza Husayn (d. 1334/1915; vol. 1:418) and 'Ali Muhammad Varqa (killed 1896; see fig. 132; vol. 1:67–8, 372, 462–4), the progenitor of the Varqa family, moved to Adharbayjan. Another son, Mirza Hasan moved to the village of Harabarjan (near Marvast on the way to Nayriz), where he remained until he died.

A daughter of 'Atri, Bibi Tuba remained in Yazd but had a hard life with her husband dying young, a son being murdered and she being left to raise

---

50 Malmiri, *Tarikh Yazd* 70–1.

51 MH 7:346. However in about 1897, it is reported that Ha'iri was saying that the Baha'i Faith was nonsense and was challenging the Baha'is to an open debate. Eventually Mirza Mahmud Furughi came to Yazd to take up the challenge but Ha'iri pleaded illness and did not meet him. MH 3:459–63.

52 'Abdu'l-Baha, *Memorials* 84–5; ZH 6:748–50; Malmiri, *Khatirat* 39–44; Varqa, 'Sharh-i Ahval' 22.

three children alone.[53] Another of the Baha'i women, Bibi Fatimih Mahd-i Ulya, was denounced as a 'Babi' by her husband, who took some of her Baha'i books to the governor as evidence. But the governor at this time, about 1873, was Iskandar Khan, who was secretly a Baha'i and ignored this. So her husband went to the clerics and obtained a divorce, although in later years he became a Baha'i and regretted his actions. She did not marry again and raised her three children as Baha'is. At times she hid in her house Baha'is who were being sought.[54]

In 1879, when news of the killing of the Nahri brothers in Isfahan (see pp. 18–23) reached Yazd, there was nearly an uprising against the Baha'is and a number of prominent Baha'is hurriedly left town in order to pacify the tumult.[55] In January 1881 Mirza Asadu'llah Isfahani visited Yazd. He found the Baha'is there having gatherings for dawn prayers but the intense pressure upon them made it impossible to establish other institutions there such as the communal fund. It was decided that the Afnan family would establish such a fund among themselves.[56]

'Ali Muhammad Varqa (see fig. 132) returned to Yazd from Tabriz in 1883, at a time when Zill us-Sultan was the governor. The latter was in Tehran and had appointed Ibrahim Khalil Khan Tabrizi to govern Yazd for him. As Varqa was now married to the daughter of an important member of the court of the crown prince in Tabriz, he was able to bring with him letters of recommendation from friends and family of the governor. As a consequence, Varqa gained access to the governor's circle and was able to propagate the Baha'i Faith among the notables of the town for about 20 months. Then Shaykh Muhammad Hasan Sabzivari wrote letters of complaint to Mulla 'Ali Kani, a prominent religious leader in Tehran (see Index of vol. 1), who sent them on to the shah. The shah ordered Varqa's arrest and Zill us-Sultan instructed that he be sent to Isfahan, to await his arrival there (see p. 24).[57] Also in 1301/1883, Aqa 'Ali Akbar, an 18-year-old Baha'i was killed by a man whom he had prevented from attacking another Baha'i. The killer was executed by Ibrahim Khalil Khan.[58]

---

53   Malmiri, *Khatirat* 43–4; Malmiri, *Tarikh Yazd* 46–50.
54   Malmiri, *Tarikh Yazd* 47–8.
55   ZH 6:838; MH 5:304–5.
56   Asadu'llah Isfahani, *Yad-dasht-ha* 48.
57   ZH 5:330–1, 6:752–3; Baha'i, *Istintaqiyyih* MS B 103–4; MH 1:257; Malmiri, *Khatirat* 42; Varqa, 'Sharh-i Ahval' 23–4; Balyuzi, *Some Eminent Baha'is* 78–80; Malmiri, *Tarikh Yazd* 48.
58   ZH 6:807.

In the summer of 1886 an episode of persecution was precipitated, according to a Tehran newspaper, by the activities of a teacher of the Baha'i Faith identified as Darvish Hakkak. It is not clear from Baha'i sources who this individual was but it may have been Haji Qalandar (see p. 197).[59] The dervish was expelled from Yazd. At this time, attention was turned to six Baha'is who had previously been arrested in Manshad (see p. 410). Shaykh Hasan Sabizvari demanded their death and even wrote to Mulla 'Ali Kani in Tehran to try to get instructions for their execution sent from there. But Haji Mirza Muhammad Mu'addil ul-Mulk (a nephew of Mushir ul-Mulk of Shiraz) who was governing Yazd on behalf of Zill us-Sultan wrote to the latter who instructed they be sent to him in Isfahan. The prisoners were sent in chains on foot to Isfahan and two of their women-folk accompanied them because of fears for their health; Fatimih Bigum, the 28-year old sister of Aqa Sayyid Muhammad 'Ali Hunza'i, walked barefoot alongside her ailing brother for the whole journey, bearing the weight of his heavy chains on her shoulders. As they walked along, they rattled their chains to beat an accompaniment while they sang these verses:

> The tresses of the hair of the Friend are the chains of misfortune's snare
>   Whoso is not entrapped therein, knows not our state
> Not every hand nor foot nor head measures up to these shackles
>   The chains and fetters of these shackles are worthy of the people of Baha.

After three months' imprisonment in Isfahan (see p. 25) and the presentation by Fatimih Bigum of a petition to Zill us-Sultan, they were set free.[60]

The first culmination of these persecutions was the episode of the Seven Martyrs of Yazd in 1891. According to Baha'u'llah and 'Abdu'l-Baha, this episode had its origins in events that occurred far away in Tehran, where one of Zill us-Sultan's confidants, Haji Sayyah (see fig. 12), had been arrested

---

59   Gulpaygani, *Rasa'il* 351.
60   ZH 5:255–6 places this episode in the year 1298/1881 and Malmiri in 1300/1882–3 (*Tarikh Shuhada* 544–9), however Mu'addil ul-Mulk was deputy governor between 1302 and 1304 (Afshar, *Yazd-Namih* 215). Moreover, some letters of Mirza Abu'l-Fadl Gulpaygani, written in Isfahan in late 1303 (late 1886), refer to the arrival of the prisoners in Isfahan and their release. Gulpaygani, *Rasa'il* 351–2, 363–4, 369, 371, 377–9; see also ZH 5:371n and insert, 6:831–3; Yazdi, *Tarikh 'Ishqabad* 298–300; Malmiri, *Tarikh Yazd* 63, 65–6. According to Malmiri (*Tarikh Shuhada* 548), all six of these men and Fatimih Bigum were later killed, one in 1891 and the rest in the anti-Baha'i pogrom of 1903.

143. Jalal ud-Dawlih (Sultan Husayn Mirza)

on suspicion of being involved in the movement clamouring for reform. Zill us-Sultan, terrified that his schemings to overthrow the shah would be uncovered, wrote from Tehran to his son, Jalal ud-Dawlih (1870–1913, see fig. 143), who governed Yazd on his behalf, to set afoot a persecution of the Baha'is in order to divert attention.[61] Support for this account of events comes from a British diplomatic report that describes Zill us-Sultan writing to the shah about this incident and boasting about his ardour in suppressing the Baha'is and protecting the interests of both Islam and the state.[62] A number of other reasons for the execution of these seven Baha'is has been suggested. One Baha'i writer has suggested that, since Zill us-Sultan had sent Haji Sayyah to Baha'u'llah in 'Akka hoping to obtain support for his claims to the throne and Baha'u'llah had refused this, the executions were in revenge for this refusal.[63] Another Baha'i writer makes the accusation that the arrests in Tehran at this time (vol. 1:53–4) were made by Kamran Mirza primarily in order to extract money from those arrested and that Jalal ud-Dawlih initiated the action in Yazd hoping for the same result.[64] There is support for this account in the memoirs of Haji Sayyah, who states that when some political activists were arrested in Tehran, Kamran Mirza had said that those arrested (which included Haji Sayyah) were all 'Babis' and that many were arrested merely to extract

---

61   See Baha'u'llah's account in Ishraq-Khavari, *Ma'idih Asmani* 4:124–34, and
      Rahiq-i Makhtum 1:283–9; Afnan Tarikh 443–5 (*Genesis* 161–2); 'Abdu'l-Baha
      gives much the same details in a letter to E.G. Browne, *Materials* 295–6; see also
      BBR 357.
62   BBR 357–8.
63   MH 1:262; this is supported by Baha'u'llah's account, see footnote 61.
64   'Alaqiband, Tarikh 357–8.

money from them.[65] These explanations do not, of course, exclude each other.

In any case, Jalal ud-Dawlih had no difficulty in persuading Shaykh Muhammad Hasan Sabzivari and his son Shaykh Taqi to initiate a persecution of the Baha'is. From time to time some of the Baha'is would visit mosques during important festivals so as to show that they were not antagonistic to Islam. On 2 May 1891, which was 23 Ramadan, the night on which Shi'is celebrate the first revelation of the Qur'an (Laylat al-Qadr), two Baha'is entered the Mir Chaqmaq Mosque. When this was reported to Shaykh Muhammad Hasan Sabzivari, he ordered their arrest. A number of other Baha'is were arrested and their property looted, some were beaten and seven were publicly executed on 18 May 1891 on the judgement of five of the town's clerics and on the orders of the governor. The seven are named as Mulla Mahdi Khavidaki (Khavidak is 18 km southeast of Yazd; pop. 1,200 in 1951), Mulla 'Ali Sabzivari (vol. 1:164–5), Aqa 'Ali (of the Kazargah quarter), Aqa Muhammad Baqir, Aqa 'Ali Asghar (of the Fahadan quarter) and two brothers, Aqa 'Ali Asghar and Aqa Hasan, sons of Aqa Husayn Kashi. Then at the instigation of the clerics, Jalal ud-Dawlih took another Baha'i, Haji Mulla Muhammad Ibrahim Masalih-gu, who had been a very effective teacher of the Baha'i Faith, into the wilderness on about 23 May and, taking the first shot himself, ordered his retinue to continue shooting until their prisoner was dead. Quite apart from the Baha'is that were killed in that episode, there was widespread harassment and looting of Baha'i property. Shaykh Muhammad Hasan Sabzivari and his son Shaykh Muhammad Taqi Sabzivari took the opportunity to send word to everyone whom they knew or suspected as Baha'is saying that unless they received a suitable bribe, they too would be exposed as Baha'is and executed.[66] About four months later, on 3 October 1891, Haji Mulla Muhammad 'Ali Dihabadi, an 80-year-old who had been one of the leading clerics of Ardakan and had been forced to leave there and 'Izzabad, was shot dead in Yazd on the decree of some of the clerics (see also pp. 420 and 403 below).[67]

After the first executions on 18 May 1891, several other Baha'is were

---

65 Sayyah, *Khatirat* 343, 352.
66 Browne, *Materials* 304–8; Malmiri, *Tarikh Shuhada* 32–61, *Tarikh Yazd* 73–95; BBR 301–5, 357–8; Baha'i, 'Gushih-iy az Tarikh'.
67 Malmiri, *Tarikh Shuhada* 61–6, *Tarikh Yazd* 100–3; Yazdi, *Tarikh 'Ishqabad* 147–9; ZH 5:431; Navvabzadih, *Ardakan* 75–6.

arrested and three Europeans who were present in Yazd intervened on their behalf before the governor and offered to pay for the release of Haji Mulla Muhammad Ibrahim Masalih-gu. The Europeans were Cornelius Prins, a Dutch merchant who had just opened the Yazd branch of J.C.P. Hotz and Son; Captain Henry Vaughan, a British officer of the Indian Staff Corps, who was surveying Iran and had just arrived in Yazd two days after the Baha'i executions; and someone named Arthur.[68] Unfortunately these interventions did not prevent the execution of Masalih-gu, but their reports to Tehran did result in strongly-worded orders being sent from Tehran that caused Jalal ud-Dawlih to prevent further deaths and no doubt played a part in his dismissal a short time later.[69] These interventions by Europeans were mentioned by Baha'u'llah in a passage addressed to *The Times* of London in which he described this episode.[70]

Zoroastrian conversions

When the Arab Islamic armies defeated the Persian Empire in the 7th century and imposed the rule of Islam on the country, many Zoroastrians fled to the Yazd area. There continued to be a large population of Zoroastrians in Yazd for several centuries, although many emigrated to India, founding the Parsi community there. By 1854, however, a census of the Zoroastrians in the town of Yazd yielded 1,379 persons (289 men, 412 women and 678 children), with 4,919 in the villages around Yazd.[71] In 1900 there were reckoned to be a thousand Zoroastrians in the city of Yazd and 6,000 in the villages around Yazd.[72] The Zoroastrians in the villages were all peasant farmers, while those in the town included a number of merchants and priests. In Yazd and Kirman, the Zoroastrians were obliged to wear yellow robes which immediately distinguished them from the rest

---

68   MH 4:388–9; for a fuller account of these interventions, see BBR 301–5, De Vries, *Babi Question* 30–7.
69   Malmiri (*Tarikh Yazd* 170–1) states that Haji Muhammad Husayn Turk of Manshad (see p. 410) went to Tehran and stopped the carriage of the shah and wept and complained so bitterly that Jalal ud-Dawlih was dismissed.
70   Quoted in White, 'Baha'u'llah and the Fourth Estate', p. 977.
71   Census by Manekji Sahib (vol. 1:16, 27), Gobineau, *Trois Ans en Asie* 108; Abbott (1850) estimated 200 families in the city (which would be equivalent to about 1,000 persons) and 640 families in eight villages around the city (about 3,200 persons); Amanat, *Cities and Trade* 137.
72   Adamec, *Historical Gazetteer* 1:691, citing Sykes.

of the population.[73] By the beginning of the
20th century, the Society for the Ameliora-
tion of the Condition of the Zoroastrians in
Persia, based in Bombay, had founded four
schools in Yazd and four in the surrounding
area, in which a total of 500 boys but no
girls were taught.

One of the most interesting developments in the history of the Baha'i Faith in
Yazd was the conversion of a comparatively
large number of Zoroastrians. The first Zoroastrian conversions occurred in Kashan (see
pp. 100–1). One of these Kashan converts
Kaykhusraw Khudadad (Payman, see fig. 41)
moved back to Yazd and was publicly known
as a Baha'i.[74] But there was no great number
of new converts until Mulla Bahram (Akhtar-
Khavari, 1859–1349/1930, see fig. 144 moved

144. Mulla Bahram (Akhtar-
Khavari)

from Kashan to Yazd and became a Baha'i in about 1885 (see p. 101). Since
he had a thorough knowledge of Zoroastrian prophecies, he, together with
some Baha'is of Muslim background such as Haji Qalandar, Mulla 'Abdu'l-
Ghani and Haji Muhammad Tahir Malmiri developed a successful approach
to the Zoroastrians of Yazd and some of the villages around.[75]

The relations between the Baha'is and Zoroastrians in Yazd is described
as being cordial by Browne, who visited the city in 1888 and was in close
contact with both groups there:

> In the last chapter I have spoken chiefly of the Zoroastrians; in this I pro-
> pose to say something concerning my dealings with the Babis of Yezd, of
> whom also I saw a good deal. And first of all a few words are necessary as
> to the relations subsisting between the votaries of these two religions, the
> oldest and the newest which Persia has produced. Their relations to one
> another are of a much more friendly character than are the relations of

73   Browne, *Year* 395.
74   'I. Sifidvash, *Pishgaman* 58–9; Faridani, *Dustan Rastan* 37–8. It is not recorded
     when he returned to Yazd and this may have been after Mulla Bahram's
     conversion.
75   ZH 6:842; Malmiri, *Khatirat* 112–14, 118.

either of them towards the Muhammadans, and this for several reasons. Both of them are liable to persecution at the hands of the Muhammadans, and so have a certain fellow-feeling and sympathy. Both of them are more tolerant towards such as are not of their own faith than the Muhammadans, the Zoroastrians, as already said, regarding 'the virtuous of the seven climes' as their friends, and the Babis being commanded by Beha to 'associate with men of all religions with spirituality and sweet savour', and to regard no man as unclean by reason of his faith.[76]

The cordial relations noted by Browne did not last, at least as far as the Zoroastrian priests were concerned. In 1891, after the episode of the Seven Martyrs of Yazd, some of the Zoroastrians became fearful that the Baha'i converts would drag the Zoroastrian community into the ongoing persecutions of the Baha'is. Dastur Tirandaz, the chief Zoroastrian priest of Yazd, summoned some 12 Zoroastrian Baha'is from Maryamabad and tried unsuccessfully to pressure the Baha'i converts to revert to their former religion.[77] A similar fear of dragging the Zoroastrians into the Baha'i persecutions was probably behind Arbab Jamshid's letter to the Zoroastrian Council (Anjuman-i Nasiri). When a Muslim Baha'i, Ghulam-Husayn Banaduki, had been killed on the orders of Shaykh Muhammad Ja'far Sabzivari (a brother of Shaykh Muhammad Taqi Sabzivari) on 1 June 1898,[78] Mulla Bahram wrote a letter of protest to Prime Minister Amin us-Sultan. The latter had ordered Sabzivari's expulsion from Yazd and had shown a copy of the orders he had sent to Yazd to Jamshid Arbab, thinking to gain the latter's approbation. Jamshid Arbab wrote an angry letter to the Zoroastrian Council, as a result of which Mulla Bahram was forced to resign from it.[79]

By the late 1890s, the Zoroastrian priests were regularly harassing the Zoroastrian Baha'is. After a minor affray on the city streets, Dastur Tirandaz went to the governor, Jalal ud-Dawlih and had some of the Zoroastrian Baha'is arrested. The Baha'is raised a complaint through a Baha'i, Bashir us-Sultan (see p. 272 and fig. 106), who was then head of the post office in

---

76   Browne, *Year* 431–2. For the quotation from Baha'u'llah, see *Gleanings* 95.
77   MH 4:395–6; Stiles, 'Zoroastrian Conversions' 78.
78   Malmiri, *Tarikh Yazd* 110–15; Malmiri, *Tarikh Shuhada* 66–73.
79   'I. Sifidvash, *Pishgaman* 79; ZH 8b:964–5; Faridani, *Dustan Rastan* 42; S. Sifidvash, *Yar Dirin* 37 seems to indicate that the episode of the letter to Amin us-Sultan may have been related to disturbances following the arrival in Yazd of Mirza Mahmud Furughi.

the town, and the matter died down. Then a number of Zoroastrian priests who were renting some properties from Mulla Bahram invited some local thieves to rob the furnishings of the place, after which they accused some of the Zoroastrian Baha'is of being the robbers.[80] In about 1898 Dastur Tirandaz and Dastur Namdar, having failed to overcome Nush Gushtasp and Jamshid Khudadad of Qasimabad village (see p. 399) in argument, decided that only force would overcome the Baha'is and so they went to Jalal ud-Dawlih and asked him to halt the activities of the Baha'is. When he declined to involve himself in what he considered an internal affair of the Zoroastrian community, the priests sent orders that the Zoroastrians were to have no contact with Baha'is and that if anyone saw a Zoroastrian being converted to the Baha'i Faith, they should intervene and prevent this. This caused hostility among some Zoroastrians towards the Baha'i converts to increase.[81]

When Mulla Bahram's daughter died in about 1898, the Zoroastrians priests refused to allow the body to be taken to the *dakhmih*, the open structures where the Zoroastrians leave their dead. As the Baha'i community had not at this time established its own funeral arrangements and had no cemetery, this led to a problem which was only resolved when the priests relented under pressure from Dinyar Kalantar, the 'mayor' of the Zoroastrian community (who was sympathetic towards the Baha'is).[82]

Although individuals such as Mulla Bahram had succeeded in converting some of the Zoroastrians of Yazd and these had then converted their own family members, these conversions were mostly in the villages around Yazd and were not openly announced. Thus, for example, despite mixing intimately with the Baha'is and Zoroastrians of Yazd when he was there in 1888, E.G. Browne's only comment ('some few at least of the Zoroastrians are not indisposed to recognise in Behā [Baha'u'llah] their expected deliverer, Shāh Bahrām') indicates that he did not realize the extent of the Zoroastrian conversions.[83] The first open teaching of the Baha'i Faith among the Zoroastrians of Yazd was carried out by Hurmuzdiyar Khudabakhsh Haqpazhuh (1871–1951, see fig. 145). In 1909, he married Kharman Majzhub (see fig. 146) and established a house in Khalaf Khan

---

80 ZH 7:121–2.
81 Faridani, *Dustan* 131.
82 MH 4:397–400.
83 Browne, *Year* 432. He appears to have thought that only one Zoroastrian had converted, and that in Kirman. See also 'I. Sifidvash, *Pishgaman* 141–2.

145. Hurmuzdiyar Khudabakhsh Haqpazhuh

146. Kharman Haqpazhuh

'Ali, the Zoroastrian quarter of Yazd. Here he had regular meetings where he would invite the Zoroastrians of the town to meet with Baha'i teachers such as Mulla 'Abdu'l-Ghani. As a result of these meetings many Zoroastrians were converted.[84] Also attending these meetings were a number of Zoroastrian women. Haqpazhuh's own wife Kharman was the first Zoroastrian woman to become a Baha'i and she converted many other women, holding regular meetings for them in her house.[85] At this time many of the Zoroastrian converts moved to other parts of Iran. Some moved on account of the pressure exerted upon them as a consequence of having become Baha'is. Shahpur Mihrshahi, for example, left Yazd for Rafsanjan on account of this.[86] However, Zoroastrian merchants and businessmen were expanding all over Iran at this time and, for example, Ardishir Hizari moved to Shiraz to work for the Zoroastrian Jahaniyan company.[87] Many moved to Tehran, which was rapidly become a major centre of Zoroastrian commerce and prosperity.

The division in the Zoroastrian community in Yazd became acute

---

84   'I. Sifidvash, *Pishgaman* 141–2.
85   'I. Sifidvash, *Pishgaman* 142, 146–8; Faridani, *Dustan* 179–84.
86   Faridani, *Dustan* 70.
87   Faridani, *Dustan* 110.

and came into the open in 1914 when Siyavash Sifidvash (vol. 1:61, 507–9, see fig. 147) returned to Yazd from Tehran, following the sudden collapse of Arbab Jamshid's business empire (vol. 1:61–2). Sifidvash had been studying the Zoro-astrian scriptures and had come to the conclusion that parts of the Zoroastrian scriptures referring to the coming of the Promised One had been deleted from the texts then being circulated. He had written a series of booklets detailing the omissions in each of the important Zoroastrian texts and had published these by gelatin printing. These book-lets had had a wide distribution and had resulted in a public condemnation of them by the Zoroastrian priests (*dastūrs*)

147. Siyavash Sifidvash

in Yazd, shortly before Sifidvash's arrival in Yazd.[88] The *dasturs* even wrote to the Muslim clerics suggesting they make a common cause together against the Baha'is and kill them.[89]

Shortly after Sifidvash's return to Yazd, the anniversary of his father's death came round. He sent the customary *vadirīn* (a basket of fruit to be blessed by the priests) and asked that they recite the Farvardīn Yasht of the Avesta (dedicated to the Fravashis) as was the normal practice.[90] They refused to do this. He appealed to the head priest (*dastūr dastūrān*) and received a curt reply, saying that the priests would not perform this cere-mony for one who was openly stating that he was a Baha'i.[91] Following this the Zoroastrian priests roused the people to such an extent that Sifidvash felt it necessary to write to the governor Mu'adid us-Saltanih in June 1914 to ask for protection.[92] Then in the next year (1915), the priests refused to perform the marriage ceremony of a Baha'i couple, Mihraban Tashakkur

---

88   S. Sifidvash, *Yar Dirin* 90–7; Faridani, *Dustan* 88–9; Muhammad-Husayni, *Tarikh* 222.
89   S. Sifidvash, *Yar Dirin* 97; Muhammad-Husayni, *Tarikh* 223.
90   See Jackson, *Zoroastrian Studies* 59–60; Boyce, *Stronghold of Zoroastrianism* 39–40, 161.
91   S. Sifidvash, *Yar Dirin* 97–8.
92   S. Sifidvash, *Yar Dirin* 98–9.

148 Firuz Tirandaz   149. Ustad Javanmard Shirmard

(Sifidvash's brother) and Farangis Hushangi. The Baha'is appealed to the Zoroastrian council, the Anjuman-i Nasiri, which, after negotiations with the priests had failed, authorized the wedding to be performed without priests, arguing that there was nothing in the Zoroastrian scriptures that decreed that the ceremony had to performed by a priest. As a consequence, the ceremony was performed with Firuz Tirandaz (Firuzmand, 1884–1968, see fig. 148), a lay person, performing the marriage service and Isfandiyar Ardishir carrying out the other ceremonies such as the *ābzūr* (libation).[93] After this wedding, Dastur Tirandaz and Dastur Namdar went to the *mujtahid* Hujjat ul-Islam Mir Sayyid 'Ali Labkhandigi saying that a 'Babi', Firuz Tirandaz, had interfered with their priestly functions by performing the marriage ceremony and they asked for a *fatwa* of death against him. Mir Sayyid 'Ali turned them away saying that if Firuz Tirandaz was an

---

93   S. Sifidvash, *Yar Dirin* 101–6; Faridani, *Dustan* 88–9; Muhammad-Husayni, *Tarikh* 223; Stiles, 'Zoroastrian Conversions' 82–3. All these sources indicate that this controversy arose after Sifidvash returned to Yazd following the downfall of Arbab Jamshid's business empire in 1914. Malmiri (*Tarikh Yazd* 500–1), however, reproduces the text of three letters dated Aug.-Sep. 1912, from Sifidvash to Dastur Namdar about this matter. On the Zoroastrian wedding ceremony, see Boyce, *Stronghold of Zoroastrianism* 173–4.

unbeliever performing marriage ceremonies, then they were the same.[94] This event was the first split that occurred between the Zoroastrian Baha'i converts and the Zoroastrian community.

At about the same time, the priests threatened to refuse burial to the mother of Siyavash, who was very ill. As a result the Baha'is set aside some land owned by Isfandiyar Gushtasp Qasimabadi as a cemetery in December 1914. In 1918–19 there was further trouble when the Zoroastrian priests urged some of their people to attack the Baha'i cemetery repeatedly, pulling down its walls and opening graves.[95] Later a new cemetery was established at Mahdiyabad on land donated by Haji Sayyid Mahdi Afnan.[96]

Among the more eminent of the Zoroastrian converts was Ustad Javanmard (1844–1928, see fig. 149). He had attended the traditional elementary school (*maktab*) set up by Manekji Sahib in Yazd in about 1854 and had been among the first batch of pupils taken by Manekji in 1865 from Yazd to the new secondary boarding school that he established in Tehran.[97] After completing his schooling in Tehran, he returned to Yazd where he taught at the Zoroastrian *maktab* for 13 years until 1885–6, when, on a trip to India, he persuaded a wealthy Parsi to build a modern school in Yazd, of which he became the headmaster. He was introduced to the Baha'i Faith by Aqa Muhammad 'Alaqiband, and converted after speaking to Varqa in 1302/1884. He then wrote to Baha'u'llah asking seven questions which were answered in a well-known work of Baha'u'llah called the Tablet of the Seven Questions (Lawh-i Haft Pursish), in which Baha'u'llah addresses him as *Shīr-mard* (lion man), which he then took as his surname. Being the headmaster of the Zoroastrian school, he had a prominent position in the Zoroastrian community and was on the community's council, the Anjuman-i Nasiri. His conversion to the Baha'i Faith caused him to be persecuted by the Zoroastrian priests and eventually to be dismissed from his position as headmaster. After the assassination of Mastir Khudabakhsh

---

94 S. Sifidvash, *Yar Dirin* 106–7; Muhammad-Husayni, *Tarikh* 223.
95 S. Sifidvash, *Yar Dirin* 109–20; Malmiri, *Tarikh Yazd* 499, 503; Letter of Mirza Azizu'llah Varqa to Sir Percy Cox, 20 Apr. 1919, PRO FO 248 1271.
96 Malmiri, *Tarikh Yazd* 531.
97 It is said in most sources (Mihrabkhani, *Sharh-i Ahval* 61; Faridani, *Dustan-i Rastan* 52, 211; Stiles, 'Zoroastrian Conversions', 71; Fischer, 'Social Change' 36) that he had had Mirza Abu'l-Fadl Gulpaygani as a teacher at this school, but this is unlikely since Javanmard would have been finished at this school by 1872 or 1873 and Gulpaygani did not start to teach there until about 1877.

(1865–1918; see below), Javanmard was in danger as the Zoroastrian priests had condemned him to death. He therefore left for Tehran for some three years before returning to Yazd. He was possibly the first Zoroastrian to openly stop wearing the *kushtī* and *sidrih* (the traditional Zoroastrian sacred cord and shirt) from at least as early as 1902, and his funeral in 1928 is said to have been the first fully Baha'i funeral among the Zoroastrian Baha'is.[98] Another influential Zoroastrian of Yazd to become a Baha'i was Arbab Gudarz Mihraban, who was converted by Nush. He was a wealthy and influential merchant who protected the Zoroastrian Baha'is on several occasion when they were threatened by the priests.[99]

Although Manekji Sahib had established councils (*anjumans* or *panchyats*) in Yazd and Kirman in 1854 after the Indian Parsi model, as a way of countering the power of the Zoroastrian priests who tended to block all reforms, these did not receive government recognition until 1890. The first official council in Yazd, the Anjuman-i Nasiri, was set up in 1891 by Manekji Sahib's successor, Kaykhusrawji Sahib, and included several Baha'is such as Ustad Javanmard Shirmard, Mulla Bahram Akhtar-Khavari, Kaykhusraw Khudadad, Arbab Gudarz Mihraban, and Firuz Tirandaz (Firuzmand). According to Mulla Bahram, Baha'is and close sympathizers of the Baha'is made up the majority of the 19 lay members of the council.[100]

Mastir Khudabakhsh had been educated in India and returned to Yazd in 1884. He taught in the Kaykhusravi School and became one of the leading Zoroastrians of Yazd and head of the Zoroastrian council there, the Anjuman-i Nasiri. He never formally became a Baha'i but his writings show that he was very sympathetic and accepted most of the claims of Baha'u'llah.[101]

---

98 ZH 6:848–51, 8b:969–70; Faridani, *Dustan* 51–6; 'I. Sifidvash, *Pishgaman* 63–71; Malmiri, *Tarikh Yazd* 512–16; some of the details about the early life and conversion differ in Javanmardi, 'Ustad Javanmard Shirmard'.
99 Faridani, *Dustan* 68–9.
100 MH 4:404; see list of members and those who were either Baha'is or sympathizers in 'I. Sifidvash, *Pishgaman* 56–7. There were four priests on the council as well, making the total composition of the council 23; for general information on the Zoroastrian Anjumans, see M. Kasheff, 'Anjoman-e Zartoštīān', *Encyclopædia Iranica*.
101 See, for example, a letter that Khudabakhsh wrote on 4 December 1897, in *'Andalib* vol. 10, no. 40 (Fall 1991) 26–31. He had sheltered three Baha'is of Muslim background during the 1903 persecution in his own home and had defended the Zoroastrian Baha'is over issues such as the burial of their dead; 'I. Sifidvash, *Pishgaman* 88–9. Although some Baha'is have claimed him as a Baha'i, it is clear from 'Abdu'l-Baha's words ('I. Sifidvash, *Pishgaman* 88; ZH 7:316) that he regarded him as a sympathizer rather than a believer.

Because of this, he was attacked and reviled by the more conservative faction. The split between the conservative Zoroastrians and the reform element who were sympathetic to the Baha'is came to a head in 1918, when the conservative faction hired a certain Firaydun Rustam from Kirman to assassinate both Khudabakhsh and one of the leading Zoroastrian Baha'is, Firuz Tirandaz. The assassin succeeded in killing Khudabakhsh but not Tirandaz.[102]

Later events in Yazd

At the time of the passing of Baha'u'llah in 1892, Haji Mirza Haydar 'Ali Isfahani was in Yazd and he, together with Vakil ud-Dawlih, worked hard to establish the authority of 'Abdu'l-Baha. The supporters of Mirza Muhammad 'Ali found only one person who sided with them – Haji Sayyid Mirza, a son of Afnan-i Kabir, who was in Bombay and returned to Yazd. He had no effect, however, and even his wife, Sarih Sultan Bigum, a daughter of Haji Mirza Abu'l-Qasim Saqqa-khanihi, and children cut their ties with him. Eventually, he reverted to supporting 'Abdu'l-Baha in about 1901.[103] It was also during this stay in Yazd, or rather in the Afnan's summer residence in Dih-bala, that Haji Mirza Haydar 'Ali Isfahani wrote his book of proofs of the Baha'i Faith *Dala'il ul-'Irfan*, which was published in Bombay in 1895.[104]

At the very beginning of the ministry of 'Abdu'l-Baha, Aqa Muhammad Rida Muhammadabadi,[105] a young merchant and poet, who had been condemned to death for being a Baha'i by Mirza Sayyid 'Ali Mudarris and Shaykh Muhammad Taqi Sabzivari, was shot dead near the main bazaar on the day before his wedding, 7 June 1893 (see pp. 403–4). There was a further murder of a Baha'i, Haji Muhammad Husayn Qarashahi, in 1312/1894,[106] and of Aqa Muhammad Husayn Saghiri-saz (the maker of shagreen, a type of leather) Yazdi, in about 1897.[107] Ustad Ghulam-Husayn

---

102 Faridani, *Dustan* 57–66; 'I. Sifidvash, *Pishgaman* 87–9; Malmiri, *Tarikh Yazd* 504–8.
103 Faizi, *Khandan Afnan* 73–4; Shahidiyan, *Mansuban* 2301; ZH 8b:895 gives this man's relationships incorrectly. It may be that this man reverted to supporting 'Abdu'l-Baha at the same time that his brother Sayyid 'Ali did in 'Akka in 1903.
104 Isfahani, *Bihjat* 270.
105 This Aqa Muhammad Rida Muhammadabadi should not be confused with Mulla Muhammad Rida Muhammadabadi (see pp. 358–9).
106 ZH 7:47.
107 ZH 7:104.

Takhtkish (maker of cloth shoe soles) Banaduki (or Banatuki) came from Banaduk to Yazd in connection with his trade. In the bazaar, one of the traders who owed him money began shouting that he was a Baha'i in order to avoid repaying his debts. A crowd gathered and took him to Sayyid Husayn Mujtahid but he did not want to have anything to do with the matter and refused to see them. He was then taken before Shaykh Muhammad Ja'far Sabzivari, a brother of Shaykh Muhammad Taqi Sabzivari, who brought together a number of clerics and issued a joint *fatwa* for his death. Then, on 12 June 1897 Ustad Ghulam-Husayn was set upon by the mob and beaten and stabbed to death. Shaykh Muhammad Ja'far was expelled from the city.[108] A couple of years later, following complaints from the citizens of Yazd, the leading clerics of the shrine cities in Iraq issued a *fatwa* condemning Shaykh Muhammad Taqi Sabzivari, leaving him isolated and bereft of influence in the city.

In 1900 a commotion began in the bazaar when a certain Javad had a business disagreement with a Baha'i merchant, Haji Sayyid Hashim Kaffash. Javad began cursing the Baha'i Faith and went to a senior cleric, Mirza Abu'l-Hasan Mudarris, accusing Sayyid Hashim of blasphemy against Islam. Mirza Abu'l-Hasan gathered some of the town's clerics together at the Madrasih Musalla Safdar Khan and they were in the process of signing and sealing a judgement condemning Sayyid Hashim to death, when Mahdi-Quli Mirza Saham ul-Mulk, the governor of Yazd who was sympathetic to the Baha'is (and according to one account, a secret believer), arrived, dispersed the crowd that had gathered in expectation of an execution and upbraided the clerics.[109]

The anti-Baha'i pogrom of 1903

In 1903 there was a much more serious episode that can only be described as an anti-Baha'i pogrom. For one entire month a blood-thirsty mob went on the rampage through the streets of Yazd and in the nearby villages killing Baha'is wherever they found them and looting and destroying their property. Yazd was famous for the fanaticism of its population but

---

108 Sources agree that this episode occurred on 11 Muharram, but ZH 7:102–3 gives the year as 1315, rendering a date of 12 June 1897; while Malmiri (*Tarikh Shuhada* 66–72) gives the year as 55 BE rendering a date of 1 June 1898; ZH 8b:964–5 gives only 1315/1897.

109 ZH 6:821; Malmiri, *Tarikh Yazd* 123–4.

it is difficult to discern exactly why such an exceptionally violent episode
should have occurred at this time. Certainly there were tensions in the
country over the call for constitutional reform and frustration with the
reactionary prime minister Amin us-Sultan, but these tensions were no
greater than at other times both before and after this episode. There had
just been an anti-Baha'i outburst in Isfahan and this had excited the populace in Yazd. But the Isfahan episode was typical of many such events in
that city. Some Baha'i historians maintain that Mushir ul-Mamalik (who
was *mustawfi* and *vazir* of Yazd and according to one account a Shaykhi
and an enemy of the Baha'is[110]) plotted with the governor Jalal ud-Dawlih
to stir up some trouble against the Baha'is in order to mulct the Baha'is
of some money, but still this was a regular experience for the Baha'is of
Iran.[111] The episode coincided with the arrival of a new Imam-Jum'ih from
the shrine cities of Najaf and this individual was keen to make a name for
himself and so he instigated the upheaval,[112] but again this was not out of
the ordinary – Baha'is were frequently scapegoated whenever clerics felt
they needed to make a point or to make a name for themselves.

Perhaps somewhat more convincing as a cause of the violence of this
event is the picture that emerges from a Muslim writer who was an eyewitness to these events, Sayyid Muhammad Radavi, Navvab Vakil. The
memoirs of Navvab Vakil need to be treated with caution as they are self-
serving and in places distorted (for example, he tries to maintain that he
was uninvolved in persecuting the Baha'is, whereas Baha'i sources state
that he was one of the chief instigators of persecutions[113]), nor does his
chronology correlate well with that in the contemporary sources or the
Baha'i histories (but this may be because he was writing his memoirs years
later). The events that he considers caused this episode of persecution are
of interest, however, since they must presumably reflect what the Muslim
population of Yazd was thinking and saying, particularly that portion of
the population that was inimical to the Baha'is. He says that the chain of
events leading up to this episode began when two Baha'i military officers

---

110 ZH 7:170.
111 ZH 6:298–9; 8a:172; 'Alaqiband, Tarikh 413–14.
112 'Abdu'l-Baha appears to consider this the main factor, see *Makatib* 3:130.
113 On Navvab Vakil's claim, see his *Khatirat* 268, 269–73; Mazandarani however
     lists him among the enemies of the Baha'is (ZH 6:727), and indeed states the
     whole family were anti-Baha'i (ZH 7:170). Avarih states that he was a Shaykhi, a
     follower of Karim Khan Kirmani, and looked on laughing while the crowd were
     tormenting the wife of Aqa Muhammad Husayn Ulfat, *Kavakib* 2:124.

were appointed to head the troops stationed in Yazd: Mirza Muhammad Khan Mir Panj and his brother Jahan Shah Khan Mir Akhur. He says that these brothers began to talk to the prince governor Jalal ud-Dawlih about the Baha'i Faith and eventually brought along the prominent Baha'i teacher Ibn Abhar to speak to the governor. Navvab Vakil says that Jalal ud-Dawlih became a Baha'i as a result of these meetings. He cites as evidence of this the fact that he had changed the name of the estate of Tah-dast that he had bought outside Yazd to 'Abbasabad (said to be in honour of 'Abdu'l-Baha) and that he put nine entrance porches on the palace he had built there.[114] Unlikely as it seems at first, there is some support in the Baha'i sources also for the view that Jalal ud-Dawlih had become a Baha'i. After the episode of the Seven Martyrs in 1891, Jalal ud-Dawlih had been dismissed from his post but was re-appointed the following year. During this second term as governor, he had been protective of the Baha'is. Mazandarani writes that Jalal ud-Dawlih's first contact with the Baha'is was when Ibn Abhar, the well-known Baha'i travelling teacher, visited Yazd in about 1896 and that when Jalal ud-Dawlih was in Tehran after his second dismissal, he was in contact with Ibn Abhar again. When he went to Yazd to take up his post as governor for a third term in 1902, he sent for Ibn Abhar. Mazandarani confirms the assertion that Jalal ud-Dawlih became a Baha'i.[115] In any case, the important point is that this was what the people of the town thought had happened.

Nabilzadih has suggested that news of the start of the building of the first Baha'i house of worship in Ashkhabad reached Iran at this time and had infuriated the clerical class, leading to the upheavals of 1903.[116] Another rumour that is said to have gone around the town with the arrival in Yazd in the spring of 1903 of Ustad 'Ali Akbar Banna, the designer and supervisor of the Baha'i house of worship in Ashkhabad, was that he had come to Yazd to build a house of worship there.[117] Certainly word of the persecutions that had erupted in Rasht and Isfahan that year would have excited the mob. Also pertinent is the rapid growth of the Baha'i Faith in

114 This is how I have translated a phrase which is not easily understood: 'kiryas-i 'imarat-i 'abbasabad ra . . . nuh tarak [or tark] qarar dad' (Navvab Vakil, Khatirat 259).

115 ZH 6:334, 7:170, 8a:172; Jalal ud-Dawlih later met 'Abdu'l-Baha in France and England, ZH 8a:174; Balyuzi, 'Abdu'l-Baha 346; Jasion, 'Abdu'l-Baha in the West 411.

116 MH 4:235.

117 Malmiri, Tarikh Shuhada 151, Tarikh Yazd 145–6; MH 3:584; KD 2:119.

Yazd, as reported, for example, by the Christian missionary agent Benjamin Badall in 1887 (see p. 353). During Ibn Abhar's four-month stay in Yazd in the period immediately before the outbreak of this 1903 pogrom, it is reported that meetings of 700 to 800 people were being held and 40 to 50 people at a time were converting at these meetings.[118] Some of the most successful of these meetings, in terms of ensuing conversions, were the ones that were held almost every day in the home of two brothers, Aqa Muhammad Rida and Aqa Muhammad Ja'far.[119] Then on one occasion, Navvab Vakil states, a sayyid was bastinadoed by the prince for striking a Baha'i and this sayyid went about accusing the prince of supporting the Baha'is. This caused a great deal of agitation in the town.[120] One can see that, if it was circulating in the town that large numbers of people were becoming Baha'is and that even the prince governor had become a Baha'i and was actively supporting them, it may well have been that the clerics were alarmed and felt an urgent need to strike back forcefully against these advances of the Baha'i Faith.

Despite the above factors as explanations of cause, one is still somewhat at a loss to explain the severity and ferocity of the pogrom when it broke out. Scenes were enacted on the streets of Yazd that have rarely been seen in the history of humanity, despite its worst excesses. Day after day for a month, a reign of terror gripped the city. Systematically and thoroughly, the mob attacked the house of every known Baha'i in the town. Where they found the owner of the house in, they dragged him into the street and put him to death, usually in a frenzy of blows and stabs, but sometimes by shooting, slitting the throat or abdomen or cutting off the head. Even women and children were not spared the beatings and death. The house was then looted of anything that could be moved. Whatever could not be moved was destroyed. Even the door frames and windows were removed from some houses.[121]

The episode began with the arrival in the city of Sayyid Ibrahim who had been studying at Najaf and was now returning to take up the post of his deceased father as Imam-Jum'ih. He had been passing through Isfahan on

---

118 Malmiri, *Khatirat* 135; according to MH 4:547, Ibn Abhar spent a year in Yazd on this visit but this probably refers to the whole journey which included a visit to Rafsanjan and Kirman also.

119 Malmiri, *Tarikh Shuhada* 182–3.

120 Navvab Vakil, *Khatirat* 259–62.

121 Details of these killings were recorded by Sayyid Abu'l-Qasim Bayda (*Tarikh-i Bayda*). A shorter account was published in Malmiri, *Tarikh Shudada Yazd*.

his way back from Najaf when the episode of persecution erupted there in May 1903 (see pp. 38–41). He had witnessed the terrorizing and killing of the Baha'is there and consulted with Aqa Najafi. It appears that he decided that the best way of making his mark and establishing his authority in Yazd upon his arrival was to initiate a campaign against the Baha'is. He sent word ahead that he was bringing with him a *fatwa* against the Baha'is from Sayyid Kazim Yazdi, one of the leading *mujtahids* of Najaf, and from other *mujtahids*. One account states that he even claimed to be bringing a piece of paper written in green ink that had emerged from the well at Samarra decreeing a general massacre of the Baha'is (the implication of this is that it was a decree from the Hidden Imam who is supposed to have gone into hiding in this well). However no one ever saw any of these documents. Sayyid Ibrahim arrived in Yazd on 12 June 1903 and immediately began to describe and praise what he had seen in Isfahan, inciting the crowd that had come to greet him on his arrival.[122]

The violence began on the next day, 13 June 1903. Since this was the day (17 Rabi' ul-Avval) that Shi'is celebrate the birth of the Prophet Muhammad and people would in any case have come, as custom dictated, to greet the new Imam-Jum'ih, the crowd attending at the house of Sayyid Ibrahim was unusually large. Sayyid Ibrahim therefore took the opportunity to preach against the Baha'is and gave orders to the mob to arrest four of the most active Baha'is: Aqa Muhammad Husayn Ulfat, Aqa Muhammad Ja'far,[123] Mulla 'Abdu'l-Ghani and Haji Muhammad Isma'il Gundali Khurasani. They found none of those four and so they began to attack the other Baha'is in the city. On that first day, a number of doors of Baha'i houses were burned and some Baha'i shops looted. The next day they attacked the house of Mirza Muhammad Halabi-saz (tinsmith) and dragged him and his wife out into the streets. They removed his wife's veiling to shame her publicly and then the husband was attacked with a butcher's meat cleaver and wounded so severely that he died later the same day. On the next day the governor took measures to restore calm in the town. For a week the city was calm but the governor's men were weak in their enforcement of the peace and many even hinted to the mob that they were on their side. The news of the attacks in Yazd spread to the surrounding villages, setting off attacks and looting there: in Ardakan (see pp.

---

122 Malmiri, *Tarikh Shuhada* 81–3; ZH 7:170–1.
123 This is probably the Aqa Muhammad Ja'far in whose house meetings for the propagation of the Baha'i Faith were being held as mentioned above.

419–20), where two were killed on 17 June, and in Taft (see p. 408) where five were killed, on 21 June. When news of these killings reached Yazd, it re-ignited the passions of the mob and the killing and destruction broke out again in the town on Friday 26 June, while it continued and spread throughout the villages.[124]

There is not room here to detail all of the killing, looting and burning that went on over this period. The frenzied nature of the attacks can perhaps best be described by a sample of vignettes from European eyewitnesses. The first is from Dr Henry White, a British missionary doctor, who witnessed the deaths of Aqa 'Ali (of the Chahar-Minar quarter) and Mash-hadi Hasan Na'ib Shatir, the head footman of the Prince Governor, on the day that the attacks were renewed in Yazd:

> However, on Friday, June 26, just as I had finished my morning work at the hospital, an urgent message came to me to go to see a man who had been assaulted by a mob. I went off at once and at the opposite end of Yezd found my patient. He was a young man, a small manufacturer, and had evidently been severely and savagely dealt with by a mob. He had several large wounds on head, neck, and body, caused by a knife or sword, and was very faint with loss of blood, almost unconscious in fact, and the prognosis was bad. I began to stitch up the wounds, and before I had finished the mob began to howl round the house. Soon a battering-ram was brought to break the door in, and finally naphtha was poured on it and it was fired. The shouts of the mob got louder and louder, like the roar of an angry wild animal. Then the door gave way and with a rush the house was stormed. It was an exciting moment; my patient died of shock and another man was killed in the house. No one touched me; one man shouted out, 'We have no work with foreigners,' and, much to my annoyance, one huge Sayyid came up and kissed me. I pleaded for the women and I think they were all uninjured; certainly none were wounded in any way. Seeing that I could do no more, I rode home.[125]

The second is from another British missionary, Napier Malcolm:

> The attacks were often made by men who had lived for a long while in close companionship with the Behais, knowing them all the time to be

---

124 Malmiri, *Tarikh Shuhada* 81–130; ZH 7:170–6; BBR 386.
125 White, 'How Babis died for their Faith in Persia' 275–6, in BBR 389.

members of the sect, and yet consorting and eating with them freely. Holes were bored in the heads of some of these poor wretches with awls, oil was then poured into the hole and lighted. Other forms of torture were used about which one cannot write. Women and children were very seldom actually killed, but were fearfully ill-treated, and sometimes left to die of starvation. It was reported that in one of the villages Babi children died within full sight of villagers, after waiting for days under the trees where their murdered parents had left them . . .

. . . a soldier found a Yezdi who was dragging about another man, and trying to make out whether he was really a Behai. 'You see,' he said, 'I have been a wicked man all my life, and have never said my prayers or done any other *savabs* [pious acts], so, unless I can do a big *savab*, I shall certainly go to Hell. If this man is a Babi, I mustn't let him go, for if I kill an infidel of course I shall go straight to Heaven.'[126]

A third comprises extracts from the diary of an English missionary, Miss Jessie Biggs:

On Tues. June 23 our head-servant (a Babi [Aqa Muhammad Husayn Akhavan Safa]) told us of more deaths in town, and for the first time, he himself seemed nervous, and asked, if necessary, would we shelter his wife and children – and other relations. This man's father-in-law [Mulla 'Abdu'l-Ghani Ardakani] is a leader and teacher among the Babis, and he was very frightened for him . . . On Wed. June 24, our servant's father-in-law and brother-in-law . . . came and stayed in our servants' compound with our servants. At this time we ourselves were not at all apprehensive, indeed we were going about our usual work in town and never dreamt of all that was going to happen. We saw and heard nothing of these 2 men and gave them very little thought . . .

Things all seemed fairly quiet to us till Friday June 26. That day, at the invitation of Mr Eldrid, the Vice-Consul here, most of us went out for the day to a Persian garden. We left town at 6 a.m. because of the heat. In the evening, as we neared Yezd, Dr White came to meet us bringing us news of great disturbances in town since noon. He told us of his own experiences that day, and how 8 at least whom we knew well were either killed or badly hurt. The news touched home very closely, for some of our

126 Malcolm, *Five Years* 88, 89, 104, in BBR 390–1.

converts were amongst the number and we feared for the others. Also we did not know where this might end if the Prince had lost so much power. He has been looked on as a very strong Governor till now. When we ladies got in, our man told us, his wife and 3 little children, his mother (aged 60) and her sister (80) and also a sister and another brother-in-law were all here taking refuge. It was a terrible realisation to see these poor things creeping up out of our cellar. First one and then another, the little children and the baby in arms and the poor old woman of 80. They all looked so scared and terrified, even the little children who are usually so merry with us, did not speak a word . . . It seems at midday they fled from their house in a panic of fear, leaving their food half-cooked and bringing the children half-dressed. Now it was that the 2 men in the other compound began to trouble us, for we knew the older man had many enemies, and had been through a great deal of persecution before tho' we were not really apprehensive of the immediate danger for any of them . . .

Sat. June 27. We took dispensary as usual. At the finish one of our 2 women converts was brought in badly hurt during yesterday's mob. One of her sons, a Babi, had gone as usual to a small weaving factory close by, and some one told her he was in danger. With this she hastened to him but got into the house only to see him killed before her eyes. In her efforts to protect him she got badly beaten on her head and arm and leg, one finger broken and dislocated and another nearly cut off. We dressed her wounds, and did all we could for her. She was so brave and patient but fainted with pain and exhaustion. One of her brothers was killed and also a small child only a few months old. These people do not know what they do in their frenzy . . .

We next heard the crowd was getting furious, and the Sayids were urging them not to care for the Prince or the Shah, but to get the men. All this made us realise, that we were in some danger now, and if the crowd got scent of where the men were, we did not know what would happen. Mr Malcolm and Dr White both said if the mob came, there was nothing for it but to give the men up. Mr Malcolm kindly went and spoke to the men on this matter and they quite agreed that the mob, if irresistible, would have to be turned into the servants' compound and thus the women and children who were still sheltering in our cellar would be saved. It was wonderful to see the old man's composure, as he sat smoking a 'Qalian' and waiting for death. He seemed as tho' he gloried in the thought of

martyrdom. Then the afternoon began to wear away. Our hospital doorkeeper who had been with us all day in refuge said he would fly to the
desert as he knew of holes he could hide in. Our other Babi man implored
us to let him go to Shiraz, at nightfall, as he had relations and friends there,
and could send for his wife etc. later. Mr Eldrid wrote down to us saying
that if he expressed a wish to go, he ought to do so and the other 2 men
should be got off at nightfall also . . .

Sunday June 28 . . . A command has also gone forth that searching of
homes is to stop, and that any Babi found is to be taken up to the Castle
and there judged. The judgement seems simply to make the prisoner curse
the Bab, which if he refuses to do, is punished by death, probably being
blown from a cannon's mouth. Their modes of killing these poor hunted
Babis have been dreadful. Some have been beaten and stoned to death,
others shot over and over again, and others cut to pieces . . .

Monday June 29. We admitted an old woman about 70, well known to
Miss Stirling, into our hospital. She had a bad knife or sword cut to the
elbow joint and other hurts. We heard further reports of deaths. Today our
poor hospital doorkeeper came back to us. He is in a pitiful plight, but we
had to get rid of him at nightfall again . . .[127]

Thus even the friends of the Baha'is became too frightened to hide them.
The English Christian missionaries, having hidden a number of Baha'is in
their homes at the start of the outbreak, insisted on their leaving once the
pogrom had gone on for a few days and was intensifying.[128] Other Baha'is
who called on friends and neighbours for help and shelter would usually
find it refused out of fear of the actions of the mob, although a few did
shelter Baha'is. Those who survived, especially the women and children,
suffered greatly and an unknown number died of the deprivations they suffered rather than being directly killed by the mob. They often could find
no help from friends or relatives. Fatimih Sughra, the wife of Muhammad
Husayn Ulfat, after their house had been looted and rendered uninhabit-
able, found she could not even get food or shelter for her children from
her Muslim relatives who lived in the same housing complex. Her children
had to sleep in the open air and the next day she had to go out of the

---

127 Church Missionary Society Archives, quoted in BBR 392–5.
128 BBR 393–5.

house to find food. Upon her return, it was the women of the neighbourhood who had been her friends and often visited her house who attacked her with knives and scissors, dragged her into the street and pulled off her *chadur* and headdress.[129] Another woman, Sakinih Sultan, aged 17, having had 16 members of her family and her husband killed and left to look after her three children by herself, was told by her neighbours that if she cried a tear or let out a moan of distress, they would cut her to pieces.[130]

Some of the Baha'is fled the town with no provisions for a journey. For several months, groups of fleeing Baha'is could be found roaming the countryside and seeking refuge in the towns and villages around Yazd. In some places these refugees were treated sympathetically while in others they were subjected to attacks as fierce as that which they had fled in Yazd. Some of these refugees wandered for many miles. Sayyid Muhammad 'Ali Jamalzadih, who was to go on to become the 'father of the modern Persian short story', records how as a boy of about eight years old he was being taken from Isfahan to Tehran in the year 1903 (his family themselves fleeing from Isfahan, accused of being Baha'is). En route near Kashan, they entered the village of 'Aliyabad (12 km north of Kashan and about 375 km from Yazd):

In that village, we encountered a large group of men and women, young and old, who were lying half-dead, their colour pale, their legs swollen, and their condition extremely pitiful, in the shade of the walls. They were crying out in hunger and thirst and out of anguish and desperation. We discovered that they were from Yazd and because, with the encouragement of the governor Jalal ud-Dawlih, a severe outbreak of Babi-killing had erupted, these people, having no helper or protector from the bigoted persecution of their hard-hearted fellow-citizens, had set out across the desert on foot. My mother, on witnessing the sad condition of these helpless people became very distressed and started calling out . . . I, in turn, seeing my mother tearful, began to cry and soon some of the village women who had come out to see the Babis and to look at us and our carriage began to weep too.[131]

---

129 Author's interview with and tape-recording of Khadijih Ulfat, the daughter of Fatimih Sughra, an eyewitness as a young woman of these events, summer 1970, Tehran.
130 MH 9:483.
131 Jamalzadih, *Sar u tah* 104.

It would appear that Jalal ud-Dawlih became thoroughly frightened by the vehemence of the mob and the fact that he was considered a supporter of the Baha'is. At one point a mob of 4,000 people was chanting slogans linking the governor to the 'Babis':

> Qabā-yi ābī nimīkhaym.   Hakim-i Bābī nimīkhaym
> (We don't want a blue cloak.   We don't want a Babi governor)[132]

Consequently, Jalal ud-Dawlih turned against the Baha'is and in order to shore up his Islamic credentials even ordered the execution of some of the them.[133] He also took the opportunity presented by the persecutions to renege on a contract that he had with Mulla Bahram and some Baha'i contractors and not pay them for work they had done on his estate at 'Abbasabad (see p. 400).

The count of those killed in this 1903 pogrom usually puts the number at 81 deaths, by counting up the names recorded in Malmiri's detailed account of these events, *Tarikh Shuhada-yi Yazd*. This figure, however, underestimates the death-toll. Although Malmiri gives an account of each of those directly killed in this episode, the count of 81 deaths does not include those whose deaths were indirectly caused by it. His own three children, for example, died of thirst and heat as they fled Yazd in mid-summer.[134] The above account by Jamalzadih indicates that there must have been many more such deaths. Another example is the elderly mother of Ustad Husayn of Manshad, who was beaten and stoned while trying to protect her son and died 20 days later.[135] In all, the reports indicate that between 80 and 195 Baha'is were killed in Yazd and the surrounding towns and villages during this episode[136] and that the number of those who

---

132 Navvab Vakil, *Khatirat* 267; Tashakkuri-Bafqi, *Mashrutiyyat* 29, gives a slightly different vowelling probably more accurately reflecting the Yazdi accent:
     Qabā-yi ābī namūkhim.   Hakim-i Bābī namūkhīm
133 Tashakkuri-Bafqi, *Mashrutiyyat* 30.
134 Malmiri, *Khatirat* 225.
135 Rabbani and Astani, 'Manshad' 25.
136 The lower estimates come from counting the individual killings recorded by Malmiri, *Tarikh Shuhada* 80–591; Bayda (*Tarikh* 613–15) describes 84; a higher estimate of 140 comes from Navvab Vakil, *Khatirat* 257, 268; an estimate of 150 was contained in a letter of a Yazd cleric Shaykh Ja'far Yazdi (Majd ul-Islam, *Tarikh Inhilal Majlis* 225); a figure of 170 comes from Haji Sayyid Mahdi Afnan, as reported by 'Abdu'l-Baha, *Makatib* 3:139 and [Isfahani], *Bahai Martyrdoms* 26; the figure of 195 comes from Isfahani, *Bihjat* 394; see also BBR 385–402.

died indirectly as a result of the episode was much greater than that. Most of these were in the town of Yazd, but in addition, there were 9 killed in Taft, 29 in Manshad (including one woman), 4 in 'Abbasabad, 4 in Hunza (including one woman) and 12 in Ardakan (see pp. 419–20). The Zoroastrian Baha'i converts were largely spared in this episode.

Eventually the mob ran out of steam. Probably all the well-known Baha'is had either been killed or had fled and their houses had been looted (most of the Baha'is of the town probably kept their Baha'i identity hidden). Jalal ud-Dawlih eventually summoned up the courage to take a stand. He sent a message to Sayyid 'Ali Ha'iri Mujtahid that if the clerics of the town did not reign in the mob, he would leave the town and send a message to the government to dispatch the army to suppress this revolt against authority. This scared Ha'iri sufficiently to preach in the main mosque of the town, urging the people to cease the violence and that Baha'is should not be killed on the streets but brought before him to judge. He also sent word to the main preachers and *rawdih-khans* of the town to do likewise, although some of the clerics such as Sayyid Ibrahim Imam-Jum'ih continued to urge the people to attack the Baha'is.

In Tehran, the reaction to the pogrom against the Baha'i was muted. None of the European powers were prepared to intervene with the shah. Vladimir Ignatyev, who worked for the Russian consular service in Iran, reported to Baron Rosen in Moscow: 'It is taken for granted that neither Russia nor England have any reason to support the Babis and it seems inconceivable to me that such a reason would ever (in the foreseeable future) be found.'[137] The central government was also reluctant to act. But eventually, alarmed by the anarchy on the streets of a major town, the central government sent a force of a thousand soldiers under Huzhabr us-Saltanih to Yazd. By the time of their arrival order had mostly been restored but they punished one or two of the ringleaders of the rioters and this had a further calming effect on the townspeople, such that some of the Baha'is in hiding felt able to emerge.[138] Jalal ud-Dawlih himself was dismissed from his post.

---

137 Ioannesyan, *Development* 119.
138 Tashakkuri-Bafqi, *Mashrutiyyat* 30–1 (including report of a speech by Sayyid 'Ali's son Sayyid Abu'l-Hasan Ha'irizadih in the Iranian Parliament on 15 Sept. 1955); Navvab Vakil, *Khatirat* 269; ZH 8b:920; BBR 391.

Events after the 1903 pogrom

Among those who suffered in this pogrom was the Akhavan Safa family. In 1303/1885, Aqa Muhammad Husayn was the first of five brothers, sons of Mulla Muhammad Baqir of the Bandar quarter of Yazd, who became Baha'is along with their three sisters (the oldest brother was a cleric in the shrine cities of Iraq and did not become a Baha'i). During the anti-Baha'i pogrom of 1903 the oldest of the Baha'i brothers, Aqa Muhammad (1876–1903, who had become a Baha'i only a year previously) was killed, together with their sister's son (the latter's body was dragged through the streets, fuel oil was poured over it and it was set on fire). Their house was ransacked and looted. Three other brothers were attacked and only saved from death by the intervention of the *kadkhuda* of the Chahar-Minar quarter in one case and the deputy *darughih* in another instance. They sheltered for a few days with the above-mentioned Dr White but when he turned them out, they had nowhere to go. For the next few days they went from place to place finding refuge wherever they could. It was presumably after this event that 'Abdu'l-Baha addressed the other four brothers as Akhavan Safa (the Brethren of Purity), which they took as their family name.

The youngest of the Akhavan Safa brothers, Mirza Mahdi (d. 1919, see fig. 150), was a weaver (*sha'rbaf*). After the 1903 pogrom he went to Tehran and became a pedlar in the bazaar. He joined the Baha'i teachers' classes of Sadr us-Sudur (vol. 1:98). He was first sent by Sadr us-Sudur to Hamadan and Kirmanshah with Mirza Habibu'llah Samimi and then went on to Baghdad and 'Akka in 1907. For the rest of his life (about 12 years) he was continually travelling from place to place in Iran as well as Turkistan and the Caucasus (in summer 1916 – spring 1917) propagating the Baha'i Faith. Most of this time he was accompanied by one of a number of people, such as Mirza Hasan Rahmani Nushabadi (see p. 138), who were learning from him the skills of being a Baha'i religious teacher (*muballigh*). Unlike most of the other teachers, he was not well educated but he had committed large portions of the Baha'i scriptures to memory and when speaking to those who were enquiring about the Baha'i Faith, he was able to string these passages together as though they were his own words.[139] In this way he was able to speak even to learned clerics. He was reported to have had an attractive personality and a radiant appearance

---

139 MH 4:4; Subhi also describes this, although he paints a negative picture of it (*Khatirat* 292–3).

that made some call him an angel. As
he travelled around, he made special
efforts to build up Baha'i institutions,
such as local assemblies, dawn prayers
(*mashriq ul-adhkar*), nineteen day
feasts, payment of Huququ'llah, and
the establishment of Baha'i schools,
in every town or village he visited. He
was also very skilled at healing rifts in
the community and resolving disputes.
'Abdu'l-Baha instructed Haji Amin
to pay Akhavan Safa's expenses out of
the funds at his disposal. He died in
Isfahan.[140]

After the overthrow of Muhammad
'Ali Shah in 1909, there was a brief
period (from October 1909 for a year)
of improvement in the condition of the
Baha'is of Yazd during the governorship

150. Mirza Mahdi Akhavan Safa

of Sardar Jang and his deputy Mudabbir ud-Dawlih. The latter was noted
for his justness and in particular forbade anyone from using religion as a
pretext for attacking another person.[141]

Mirza Muhammad Bulur-furush (seller of crystalware, 43 years old)
had became a Baha'i in 1915 and was so enthusiastic about the new religion that he was soon widely known as a Baha'i. On 2 May 1917 a mob
dragged him from his shop to a cleric, Aqa Sayyid Yahya, at the Madrasih-
yi Khan. When he refused to recant his new belief, he was thrown out of
an upstairs window and beaten to death by a mob of some 2,000 people.[142]
In 1920 Aqa 'Ali Akbar, a Baha'i baker of Yazd, went for the summer up to
the village of Dih-bala in the hills surrounding Yazd, where he baked bread
for the local people. There he was accosted by Aqa Ghulam-Husayn Yazdi,
who was displeased that a 'Babi' was selling bread that had been rendered
impure by his touch. When Aqa 'Ali Akbar answered calmly that no one

140 MH 4:4–91; ZH 8b:924–6; Rastigar, *Sadr us-Sudur* 60–1; Malmiri, *Tarikh Yazd*
     142–3.
141 'Alaqiband, Tarikh 405–7.
142 Malmiri, *Tarikh Shuhada* 598–612, *Tarikh Yazd* 493–7; BBR 443; MH
     6:311–12.

was forcing him to buy this bread, Aqa Ghulam-Husayn became abusive and violent, eventually kicking Aqa 'Ali Akbar in the side, which caused him to collapse and die a few hours later.[143]

Because of the persecutions, many of the Baha'is of this town moved to other areas, especially to Ashkhabad and to the Haifa-'Akka area. Baha'is from Yazd formed almost one-third of the Baha'i emigrants to Ashkhabad[144] and included such persons as Haji Muhammad Taqi Afnan and Ustad 'Ali Akbar Banna Yazdi (see pp. 354–8, 363). One migrant from Yazd, Haji Mirza Husayn Qannad, moved to Samarqand in 1305/1887 and set up a Baha'i traveller's hospice there which continued for 34 years.[145] Between 1907 and 1916 some 15 of the farming families of Zoroastrian background from Mahdiyabad and other villages moved to 'Adasiyyih in the Jordan valley where 'Abdu'l-Baha helped them to establish a thriving agricultural settlement.[146]

Despite the persecutions, the Baha'i Faith spread in Yazd. Indeed, Captain Henry Vaughan, who chanced to be in Yazd a few days after the episode of the Seven Martyrs in 1891, states that he was told that 'these persecutions would give a great impetus to the movement, and that each death caused numerous converts'.[147] Following the 1903 pogrom Napier Malcolm, a British missionary resident in Yazd, wrote: 'There is, of course, no doubt that the horrors of the past three weeks will make Behaiism a much greater force in Yazd than it has hitherto been.'[148] Ustad 'Ali Akbar Banna, who was himself to fall a victim to the 1903 pogrom, in writing an account of Ustad 'Ali Chit-saz, states that prior to the episode of the Seven Martyrs of 1891, he had been circumspect and had not attracted any attention as a Baha'i but after this event he came out into the open about his beliefs and began to tell those around him of them.[149] Malmiri writes that far from people being frightened away by the severity of the persecution in 1903, the months and years after this episode saw many people enquiring about the Baha'i Faith and converting, even in quarters of the town where there had not previously been Baha'is.[150] Similarly many

---

143 ZH 7:320–1; Malmiri, *Tarikh Yazd* 481–3.
144 Momen, 'Baha'i Community of Ashkhabad' 296.
145 ZH 6:827.
146 Poostchi, "Adasiyyih: A Study in Agriculture and Rural Development'.
147 BBR 301.
148 *Church Missionary Intelligencer* (Oct. 1903) 768; BBR 390n.
149 Yazdi, *Tarikh 'Ishqabad* 188.
150 Malmiri, *Khatirat* 150–1.

Baha'is of Yazd are recorded as having first had the Baha'i Faith brought to their attention through these killings.[151]

Later events in Yazd

Despite these severe persecutions, the Baha'i community of Yazd continued to grow and develop. Although there had been a *maktab* (traditional school) for girls established in a house owned by and adjacent to the house of Vakil ud-Dawlih and run by the three unmarried sisters of Shaykh Sadiq Chavush (see p. 365) since the early 1890s,[152] eventually a need for modern schools was felt among the Baha'is. Various individuals with communal help set up four schools in the city, three of which were for girls. Having been widowed at an early age without children, Hajiyyih Bibi Sughra (c. 1880 – 6 Nov. 1972) persuaded her relatives to allow her to go to Tehran where she lived with a Baha'i family and attended school. When she graduated from school, she returned to Yazd where she set up, with support from the Baha'i community, the Tarbiyat-i Dushizihgan School for girls in 1911. In 1919 the school was recognized as a government school, the first recognized girls' school in Yazd, and went up to the 9th class. The Hushangi School was set up in 1921 primarily for the Zoroastrian Baha'i girls by Sifidvash using property donated for this by his uncle Arbab Hushang Hushangi. The headteacher was Gulchihr Khanum Faridani. The Tahdhib School for girls was set up in 1927 by Aqa Muhammad 'Ali Tahdhib and Sultan Nik-A'in in the house of Mirza Yahya Ra'fati. The teachers were Ruhangiz and Vafa Yazdaniyan and lessons were given up to the sixth class. The Tawfiq School for boys was set up by the local assembly in 1927 with Khusraw Haqpazhuh as headmaster.[153] Later the Baha'is built modern public baths, Ḥamām-i Shirkat, with shower facilities which became well-known for its cleanliness and was used by many of the government officials and physicians of the town.[154]

---

151 See, for example, the accounts of some of the Zoroastrian converts above and the biographies of many of the Baha'is of Yazd to be found in Yazdi, *Tarikh 'Ishqabad*.

152 Malmiri, *Tarikh Yazd* 71.

153 Merrit-Hawkes, *Persia* 144–5; 'I. Sifidvash, *Pishgaman* 151–5; Hidayati 'Madrasih-yi Dukhtaranih' 29–31; Anon, 'Hajiyyih Bibi Sughra'; Faridani, 'Madaris-i Baha'i dar Yazd'; Malmiri, *Tarikh Yazd* 149–50; Shahvar, *Forgotten Schools* 170–3.

154 Afnan, *Bigunahan* 15.

151. Haji Abu'l-Qasim Shaydanshaydi   152. Mirza Muhammad Thabit-Sharqi

Among the prominent Baha'i teachers to emerge from the city in this latter period were Haji Abu'l-Qasim Shaydanshaydi (1882–1972, see fig. 151) and Mirza Muhammad Thabit-Sharqi (1310/1892–1961, see fig. 152). These two friends were well-known reciters of poetry lamenting the martyrdom of the Imam Husayn (*nawḥih-khāns*) and were much in demand at sessions of *rawdih-khani* (recitals of the sufferings of the Imams) in Yazd. They entered into discussions with Haji Va'iz Qazvini, Haji Muhammad Tahir Malmiri and others. In 1914 this led to a meeting at which four of the prominent clerics of Yazd debated with Malmiri and Mirza Abu'l-Qasim Nayrizi. When the clerics were worsted in the debate, they left saying they would consult their books and bring them to a further debate – but this never happened. As a result, Thabit-Sharqi, Shaydanshaydi and two others became Baha'is. When news of this broke in Yazd, there was much agitation, especially against Thabit-Sharqi and Shaydanshaydi, and danger of a general uprising against the Baha'is. The Spiritual Assembly of Yazd determined that they should leave the city, and so they left for Kirman. After seven months they returned but in a short time there was further agitation against them and the clerics sent a letter to the governor saying that if these two are not expelled, there would be disturbances in the city. They left for Manshad for four months. After this, both of them spent much of the rest of their lives travelling around both within Iran and outside, teaching the Baha'i Faith, until illness prevented it.[155]

Another prominent religious teacher (*muballigh*) to emerge from Yazd was Aqa 'Abdu'l-Husayn Dhabihi, whose father and 16 other relatives were killed in the 1903 anti-Baha'i pogrom. He began by propagating the Baha'i Faith in the villages around Yazd but after visiting Shoghi Effendi in Haifa in 1932, he travelled more extensively around Iran and in 1971 in Afghanistan. He was also caretaker of the house of Baha'u'llah in Takur for more than 10 years.[156]

There appears to be no reliable estimates of the number of Baha'is in Yazd. Cornelius Prins thought that a report of 12,000 to 14,000 made to him in 1891 was 'slightly exaggerated'.[157] The figure of 5,000 Baha'i households (25,000 Baha'is) appears in a report sent to 'Abdu'l-Baha in 1903 but this probably applies to the towns and villages around Yazd as well as to the town itself.[158] In all, an estimate of 8,000 to 10,000 by 1903 would not seem to be excessive (some 16–20 per cent of the population of the town).

Zoroastrian villages around Yazd

The conversions in the villages around Yazd appear to have started in earnest from the 1880s onwards. One group of villages in which conversions occurred was clustered closely around Yazd and their inhabitants were mostly Zoroastrians. Mulla Bahram, who was instrumental in initiating the Zoroastrian conversions in Yazd, was himself from one of these villages, Maryamabad (2 km northeast of Yazd; pop. 2,018 in 1955). Here he converted members of his own family, the *kadkhuda* (headman), Rustam Khursand,[159] and others. A school was established there with Ustad Shahriyar as teacher.[160] Later Mulla Bahram took up residence in the nearby village of Mahdiyabad (3 km east of Yazd; pop. 653 in 1955). This village was established in about 1884, when Sayyid Mahdi of the Afnan family,

---

155 MH 6:294–344, 8:394–508; Malmiri, *Khatirat* 152–7; BW 15:509–10.
156 MH 9:482–568.
157 De Vries, *Babi Question* 31.
158 Report sent to 'Abdu'l-Baha, see *Makatib* 3:137; trans. Rabbani, "Abdu'l-Baha's proclamation' 62 and [Isfahani], *Bahai Martyrdoms* 17.
159 'I. Sifidvash, *Pishgaman* 76; cf Malmiri, *Khatirat* 113, which gives a slightly different account of Khursand's conversion.
160 Malmiri, *Tarikh Yazd* 531; Shahvar, *Forgotten Schools* 173–4.

acting in concert with Vakil ud-Dawlih and Haji Husayn dug a *qanat* to this location and encouraged a number of Zoroastrian families to move there.[161] Apart from Mulla Bahram, another who converted many of the families in this village was Ustad Mihraban Rasti, who was a teacher in the Zoroastrian school in Yazd.[162] Of the 70 Zoroastrian families that made up the village, all but three eventually converted.[163] Because Yazd was too far away for the girls of Mahdiyabad to attend school there, a school for girls was established in the village in a house donated by Mihraban Rustam Dinyar.[164] The Yazd Baha'is often held large meetings with several thousand people present in the property of the Afnans in Mahdiyabad, since they could do this easily there whereas it would entail danger in Yazd itself. Prayers and tablets would be chanted and *āb-ghūsht* (meat soup) would be served. Muslim and Zoroastrian Baha'is would eat from the same dish and this in itself was the cause of some Zoroastrian conversions.[165] In Maryamabad, one of the Baha'is, Nushirvan Khurshid, was subjected to much persecution and refused to recant his beliefs. He even dared to make a complaint to the authorities. In about 1917 his eight-year-old orphaned grandson, Ardishir, was kidnapped, taken to a garden where he was beaten and suffocated.[166] Also in Maryamabad, on 29 April 1920, Aqa Husayn, the 45-year-old son of Shahbaz, was working in the fields when Haji Rajab, known as Siyah Khan, approached him and beat him over the head with a large spade he was carrying. Aqa Husayn fell and soon died. A group of Muslims who were nearby witnessed the event and neither helped nor informed anyone. Although the Baha'is tried to have the killer arrested, he was protected by the notables of the area and was sent elsewhere by them.[167]

In Khurramshah (3 km south of Yazd; pop. 1,715 in 1955), the *kadkhuda*, Biman Jivih (1872–1940, see fig. 153) began to actively teach the Faith after his return from India. He converted his wife Shirin (see fig. 154), the daughter of Mihraban Vakil ur-Ru'aya (a title that indicates that the government regarded him as the representative of the Zoroastrians)

---

161 Hizari, Vaqa'i' 12.
162 Faridani, *Dustan* 212–13; Rasti, 'Ustad Mihraban Rasti'.
163 Oral communication from Vahid Bihmardi, Acuto, Italy, July 2003.
164 Faridani, *Dustan* 213, 260; Malmiri, *Tarikh Yazd* 510–11; Shahvar, *Forgotten Schools* 174.
165 Hizari, Vaqa'i' 12–13.
166 ZH 7:313.
167 ZH 7:321–2.

153. Biman Jivih

154. Shirin Jivih

and they held Baha'i meetings in his home. A number of the Zoroastrians of the village were converted and a local spiritual assembly elected.[168] In the late 1910s the above-mentioned Shirin, the wife of Biman Jivih, began to educate the girls of the village.[169] In the Zoroastrian village of Qasimabad (6 km southwest of Yazd; pop. 544 in 1951), two brothers, Shah Siyavash and Shah Kavus, became Baha'is in about 1892. They were joined in 1895 by Nush Gushtasp, a poet (d. 1338/1919), and Jamshid Khudadad (d. 1349/1930), a physician, both of whom had returned from India, having become Baha'is there through Mirza Mahram.[170] Soon word spread in the village that some 30 Zoroastrians had become Baha'is in Yazd, and that this religion had also spread to Qasimabad. Five Baha'i families were forced to move to Mahdiyabad and the families that remained were subjected to cursing and stone-throwing.[171]

In about 1902 the governor of Yazd Jalal ud-Dawlih, who had purchased some barren land in the Pish-i Kuh district about 55 kilometres

---

168 Faridani, *Dustan* 199–204.
169 'I. Sifidvash, *Pishgaman* 178.
170 Malmiri, *Tarikh Yazd* 511–12; Mazandarani, *Asrar* 4:464.
171 Faridani, *Dustan* 129.

south of Yazd in about 1896, decided to build a farm and summer residence there, which he called 'Abbasabad (see p. 382).[172] He asked Mulla Bahram to supervise the work necessary to bring water to the site and turn it into arable land. Mulla Bahram was unwilling to do this but Jalal ud-Dawlih exerted pressure through Ardishirji Sahib, the head of the Zoroastrian Council (Anjuman), and Haji Mirza Mahmud Afnan until he consented. He sold everything he had and moved to this farm together with some 15 of the Baha'i Zoroastrian families. They constructed a road to the site, made water channels (qanats), created fields and built houses for themselves. They had just about completed their work of bringing the area under cultivation and were about to ask for the recompense they were due under their contract when the anti-Baha'i pogrom of 1903 occurred. Jalal ud-Dawlih was frightened by the fact that many of the townspeople accused him of siding with the Baha'is. Thus he sent some of his officials to 'Abbasabad to force the Baha'is to leave the hamlet so that he would not be accused of sheltering them. These officials also beat Mulla Bahram until he surrendered to them the contract that had been made whereby Jalal ud-Dawlih had promised to compensate Mulla Bahram, who had sunk all his capital into this project.[173] Although years later in Tehran, Jalal ud-Dawlih, after receiving a letter from 'Abdu'l-Baha, did give some reparation to Mulla Bahram, it was only a fraction of what he owed.[174] Several Muslim Baha'is had also moved to 'Abbasabad to be shopkeepers and provide other services. Four of these were killed in the 1903 pogrom.[175]

In the Ashkadhar (Ashkidhar) district to the northwest of Yazd on either side of the road to Ardakan, there were several villages with Baha'i communities. In Husaynabad[176] (24 km northwest of Yazd; pop. 984 in 1951), news of the Baha'i Faith arrived in about 1883 and some of the Zoroastrian inhabitants of the village were curious but no reliable information could be obtained. In 1887 a Baha'i of Muslim background visited the village and

---

172 It is said that Jalal ud-Dawlih tried to entice the Baha'is to come and work his land by claiming that he had call 'Abbasabad after 'Abdu'l-Baha (see p. 382). His purchase of the property in about 1896 is recorded in Afshar, Yazd-Namih 229.

173 MH 4:417–20; Malmiri, Tarikh Yazd 161–2, 234–46.

174 MH 4:425–31.

175 Malmiri, Tarikh Yazd 234–9.

176 It appears that Husaynabad was founded by Husayn Khan Ajudan-bashi, who was the governor of Shiraz at the time of the Bab. He was governor of Yazd for four years prior to becoming governor of Shiraz in 1844; Adamec, Historical Gazetteer 1:240, Bamdad, Tarikh 1:428.

attracted the attention of Jamshid Bahram (1866–1947) and his family when he asked to visit their home (something that no Muslim would do) and recited one of Baha'u'llah's prayers. Then in 1891 Anushirvan Mihraban, one of the Zoroastrians of the village, witnessed the episode of the Seven Martyrs of Yazd and this prompted him and Jamshid Bahram to seek out Mulla Bahram who was living in Mahdiyabad at that time. They became Baha'is, returned to the village and began to teach others. Soon, assisted by some travelling Baha'i teachers such as Mirza Mahdi Akhavan Safa and Mirza Qabil Abadihi, a number of the Zoroastrian villagers became Baha'is and opposition inevitably arose among the Zoroastrian priests (*dasturs*), especially Dastur Namdar of Yazd, who was himself from Husaynabad. The Baha'is were called unbelievers and apostates and Anushirvan Mihraban was called the 'Ahriman (the Zoroastrian equivalent of the devil) of the Age' and the 'Stealer of People'. But despite this, most of the Zoroastrians of the village were converted. After Anushirvan Mihraban and Jamshid Bahram went to visit 'Abdu'l-Baha in 1909, they returned with a redoubled enthusiasm to establish Baha'i institutions in the village. In 1328/1910, a local spiritual assembly of the Baha'is of the village was elected and in 1332/1913 a Baha'i cemetery and baths were established in the village.

Haji 'Ali, one of the Muslim inhabitants of Husaynabad, began a campaign to persecute the Baha'is in the village, but when he failed in his scheme to have some of the leading Baha'is killed, he began to investigate the Baha'i Faith and was eventually converted in about 1915. He faced severe pressure in the village and on several occasions was captured and only narrowly escaped death. Several other Muslims eventually converted also. In 1337/1918 the local assembly started a small school for the Baha'i children of the village and asked Haji 'Ali to be the teacher. In 1918 the Baha'is of the village, encouraged by a visiting Baha'i teacher, Mirza Mahdi Akhavan Safa, decided to build a *mashriq ul-adhkar* (Baha'i house of worship) in the village. They collected money, purchased suitable land and over the next few years built a large building for this purpose. In later years when Shoghi Effendi gave general instructions that in each Baha'i locality there should be a *hazirat ul-quds* (Baha'i centre) for the meetings of the Baha'is, this building was renamed as the Hazirat ul-Quds of Husaynabad.[177]

Isfandiyar Qubad states that in 1953 the village of Husaynabad had

---

177 All information about this village is from Qabil Abadihi, Tarikh Amri Husaynabad, except where indicated. See also ZH 8b:953–6; Anvari, 'Jamshid Bahram'; Malmiri, *Tarikh Yazd* 535; Faridani, *Dustan* 96–104.

200 Baha'is (20 per cent of the population),[178] which is interesting, since this is almost exactly the same number as that given a century earlier by Manekji for the number of Zoroastrians in this village.[179] Indeed, some accounts state that all the Zoroastrians resident in this village became Baha'is,[180] while other accounts state that only one Zoroastrian family did not convert.[181] Whereas previously the Zoroastrians in this village had grown thousands of kilograms of grapes to be turned into wine, by 1900 they had completely stopped this activity and there was no wine to be found in any of the Baha'i houses.

Other villages in the Yazd area

In other villages in the Ashkadhar district the Baha'is were mainly converts from Islam. In 'Aliyabad (26 km northwest of Yazd; pop. 387 in 1951) the Baha'i community arose as a consequence of the move there in about 1306/1888 by 'Ali Akbar Khabbaz Yazdi, who had suffered severe persecution and was no longer able to remain in Yazd. Later two other Baha'is and a Zoroastrian convert moved to the village and conversions occurred among both the Muslims and the Zoroastrians. One of the members of the family that owned the village, Aqa Mahdi, the son of Aqa Muhammad Husayn Haji Abu Turab, was a Baha'i and his brothers were friendly towards the Baha'i Faith.[182] In 1953 the population of the village was 387 and 60 of these were Baha'is.[183]

In Mahdiyabad-i Rustaq[184] (35 km northwest of Yazd; pop. 485 in 1951), Qubad states that in 1953 this village had 61 Baha'is (i.e. 12.5 per cent of the population).[185] The first Baha'i of this village was Aqa Husayn son of Haji Ahmad, who was converted in 1889 by the above-mentioned 'Ali Akbar Khabbaz Yazdi who was resident in 'Aliyabad.[186] In 'Izzabad (32 km north-

---

178 Qubad, *Khatirat* 133.
179 Gobineau, *Trois Ans en Asie* 2:108. Manekji gives 99 adults and 107 children.
180 Malmiri, *Tarikh Yazd* 535; ZH 8b:938.
181 Sifidvash, *Pishgaman* 93; Anvari, 'Jamshid Bahram' 58.
182 Abadihi, Tarikh Amri 'Aliyabad, 2–6; ZH 8b:952–3.
183 Population statistic from Razmara, *Farhang* 10:137; number of Baha'is from Qubad, *Khatirat* 134.
184 This Mahdiyabad is called Mahdiyabad-i Rustaq to differentiate it from Mahdiyabad, the Zoroastrian village 3 km from Yazd mentioned previously, which is sometimes referred to as Mahdiyabad-i Humih.
185 Qubad, *Khatirat* 135.
186 Abadihi, Tarikh Amri 'Izzabad, Sharafabad va Mahdiyabad 3; ZH 7:129, 8b:957; Malmiri, *Tarikh Yazd* 101.

west of Yazd; pop. 1,170 in 1951), Haji Mulla Muhammad 'Ali Dihabadi, who had been expelled from his own village and from Ardakan, set up a school and converted two prominent villagers, Haji Mulla Muhammad Rida and Aqa Mirza Asadu'llah Vazir 'Izzabadi and others, all of whom remained covert Baha'is. But Dihabadi was expelled from the village (see p. 369) and it was not until the above-mentioned Aqa Husayn of Mahdiyabad came to 'Izzabad and converted Aqa Rajab-'Ali 'Izzabadi in 1900 that there was open teaching of the Baha'i Faith.[187] On 29 April (10 Muharram) 1901, Haji Ahmad, the second Baha'i of the village, was attacked by a mob emerging from the Husayniyyih of 'Izzabad and narrowly escaped death.[188]

Other villages were Sharafabad (34 km northwest of Yazd), where conversions began in 1330/1911;[189] Firuzabad (12 km northwest of Yazd), where the leading Baha'i, Aqa Husayn 'Ali, a doctor and a nephew of the Sufi leader Safi 'Ali Shah, was attacked and killed in 1923;[190] Allahabad (15 km northwest of Yazd), 'Asrabad (23 km northwest of Yazd) and nearby Ja'farabad (pops. 626, 1145, 633, 189, and 286 in 1951 respectively). In these villages all the converts were Muslims and, over the years, they faced much persecution and threats of death instigated by the local clerics; several were killed.[191] Qabil Abadihi played an important role in spreading the Baha'i Faith in this area which he visited yearly. A local assembly was established in 'Izzabad, Sharafabad and Mahdiyabad-i Rustaq in 1332/1913–14.[192]

There were also Baha'i communities in many other villages around Yazd such as Kuchih-buyuk (2 km south of Yazd; pop. 1,972 in 1951, see account of Isfandiyar from this village under 'Taft' below), Nasrabad (2 km east of Yazd; pop. 1,238 in 1951) and Muhammadabad (12 km south of Yazd; pop. 2,418 in 1951). In Muhammadabad, Aqa Muhammad Rida (c. 1857–93), who was from the leading family of Muhammadabad and himself an accomplished poet and a landowner, became a Baha'i and many others in the village also converted. Thus the village was divided between Aqa Muhammad Rida and his supporters, including the Baha'i families, and Haji Sayyid Javad Jamal and his brothers, who headed those opposed to him. Seeing that Aqa Muhammad Rida was gaining the upper hand,

---

187 ZH 6: 807–8, 7:129, 8b: 957; Abadihi, Tarikh Amri 'Izzabad, Sharafabad va Mahdiyabad 3; Malmiri, *Tarikh Yazd* 100–1.
188 Malmiri, *Tarikh Yazd* 184.
189 Abadihi, Tarikh Amri 'Izzabad, Sharafabad va Mahdiyabad 17–18; ZH 8b:959.
190 ZH 8b:956–7; Malmiri, *Tarikh Yazd* 193–5.
191 ZH 8b:956–60.
192 ZH 8b:960.

Sayyid Javad obtained a *fatwa* from the leading clerics of Yazd and ordered three men to kill him. They did this while Aqa Muhammad Rida was in Yazd buying some goods on 17 June 1893, the day before his wedding. Following this assassination, 1,500 of the residents of Muhammadabad came to Yazd demanding justice and sending telegrams to Isfahan and Tehran. As a result, the head of the assassins was arrested and executed and the house of Sayyid Javad pulled down.[193]

About 35 kilometres southeast of Yazd is the village of Khavidak (pop. 1,200 in 1951). One of the mullas in the village, Mulla Mahdi Khavidaki, became a Babi and subsequently a Baha'i. He converted others in the village and made a point of inviting any visiting Baha'is, such as Haji Amin in 1300/1882 and Mirza 'Ali Muhammad Varqa in 1306/1888, to come and stay with him in the village and to teach the Baha'i Faith there. His activities soon aroused opposition and he was among the seven Baha'is executed in Yazd in 1891 (see p. 369).[194]

In some of these villages such as Muhammadabad, the Baha'is were predominantly from a Muslim background, while in other villages, such as Maryamabad and Husaynabad, the Baha'is were predominantly from a Zoroastrian background. In some there was a mixed community. When the first Local Spiritual Assembly of 'Aliyabad was elected in 1341/1922, five of its members were from Muslim background and four from Zoroastrian.[195]

Taft

There is a range of mountains to the southeast of Yazd. The district between Yazd and the mountains is called Pish-i Kuh (in front of the mountains); the district in the mountains is called Miyan-Kuh (in the midst of the mountains) and the district beyond is call Pusht-i Kuh (behind the mountains). The main town in the Pish-i Kuh district is Taft (25 km southwest of Yazd on the road to Shiraz; pop. 5,000, of which some 600 were Zoroastrians, in 1879;[196] 7,500 in 1905 and 7,100 in 1951). Being at a higher elevation, it is much more pleasant than Yazd in the summer and many notables of Yazd had estates around Taft, where they grew fruit. The town

---

193 Malmiri, *Tarikh Shuhada* 73–8, *Tarikh Yazd* 103–8; ZH 6:794–5; 7:36; 8b:904–6; 'Alaqiband, Tarikh 413–14. See p. 379 and note 105.
194 ZH 6:786–7.
195 Abadihi, Tarikh-i Amri 'Aliyabad 17–18; ZH 8b:954.
196 Schindler cited in Adamek, *Historical Gazetteer* 1:78–9.

had 17 quarters, four of which were inhabited by Zoroastrians. Browne states that the town was divided into two by a river bed, the north part being inhabited by Zoroastrians and the south by Muslims.[197] In Rahatabad, one of the Zoroastrian quarters, Hurmuzdiyar Khudabakhsh was the first Zoroastrian in Taft to become a Baha'i. Through his efforts, most of the Rahatabad Zoroastrians became Baha'is.[198] A Zoroastrian Baha'i convert, Isfandiyar Kuchihbuyuki (a nephew of Kaykhusrawji Sahib, the Zoroastrian agent), was sent by the Zoroastrian Council, the Anjuman-i Nasiri, to Taft to open a school in the Zoroastrian temple there. On account of his being a Baha'i, he was opposed by the Zoroastrian priest and some of the Zoroastrians there. Eventually they joined forces with a Muslim mob and, in about 1900, shot Isfandiyar dead.[199] Ustad Mihraban Rasti (1879–1939) was another Baha'i who came from Yazd to teach at the Zoroastrian school in Taft.[200] Many Zoroastrians left Taft, as there were no possibilities for them there except to become farmers, and went to India, where some of these migrants became Baha'is.[201]

There were also Muslim converts in Taft, including several important Muslim clerics. Among these were three brothers whose grandfather had been a Shaykhi who had corresponded with Shaykh Ahmad al-Ahsa'i.[202] The first brother was Shaykh Muhammad 'Ali who was *imam-jum'ih* in two of the mosques in Taft. He became a Baha'i and visited Baha'u'llah in 'Akka. The second brother, Shaykh Muhammad Taqi, also became a Baha'i.[203]

The third brother was Shaykh 'Abdu'l-Husayn (Avarih, later Ayati, 1288/1871–1372/1953, see fig. 155), who at first opposed the Baha'i Faith greatly and was instrumental in driving his brother Shaykh Muhammad 'Ali out of the town (and taking over his posts at the two mosques) in about 1895, but was eventually converted in 1901 by Fadil Yazdi. Avarih was unable to remain in Taft when it became known that he was a Baha'i and he left for Ardistan, where he taught in a Baha'i *maktab* there. After

---

197 Browne, *Year* 394.
198 Faridani, *Dustan* 211, 307–10.
199 ZH 7:129–30, 8/2: 938–9, Faridani, *Dustan* 339–41; Malmiri, *Tarikh Yazd* 508–9.
200 Faridani, *Dustan* 211–14; Rasti, 'Ustad Mihraban Rasti'.
201 See accounts of the Zoroastrian Baha'is of Taft in Faridani, *Dustan* 314, 327, 329.
202 See statements made by Avarih in KD 1:85–6.
203 Malmiri, *Tarikh Shuhada* 412.

155. Avarih ('Abdu'l-Husayn Ayati)

Ardistan, he lived for a time in Tehran, in Kirmanshah in 1919–20 and after this in Baku. He was a well-known teacher of the Baha'i Faith and wrote a history of it, *al-Kawakib ud-Durriyyih*. He was one of those summoned to Haifa in 1922 for consultation after the passing of 'Abdu'l-Baha and he then travelled to Britain at the request of Shoghi Effendi. Both in Baku and London he caused disquiet among the Baha'is when he was seen behaving inappropriately towards young women. When he returned from that trip, he went to Egypt to arrange for the publication of his history. As the publication of this was proceeding, he tried, in collaboration with an Armenian Baha'i named Fa'iq Effendi, to get an Arabic translation of this book published as well but the Central Assembly in Egypt did not consider this advisable. Avarih then bypassed the Central Assembly and obtained permission from the Local Spiritual Assembly of Kawm as-Sa'adah. When this became known, there was uproar and dissension in the Egyptian Baha'i community and a report was sent to Haifa. From Egypt, Avarih went to Haifa (when Shoghi Effendi was absent) and on to Lebanon, causing dissension there also. He was also writing letters to his Baha'i acquaintances in Iran which were so discordant that they were reported to Haifa. Eventually Bahiyyih Khanum, who was in charge of the affairs of the Baha'i Faith in the absence of Shoghi Effendi, was forced to write to the Baha'is of Baghdad warning them about him. 'Abbas Ayman was instructed to drive him from Baghdad to Tehran without stopping in any of the main towns where he might meet with the local Baha'is.[204] In Tehran, Avarih began to associate with enemies of the Baha'i Faith. Eventually, in about July 1924, Bahiyyih Khanum sent a message to the Baha'is of Iran expelling Avarih from the Baha'i community.[205] He managed to gain employment as a journalist on the Tehran newspaper *Sitarih-yi Iran*. At one stage he approached the Central Spiritual Assembly stating that he wished to repent. He was

---

204 Momen, *Ayman/Iman Family* 57–8.
205 *Akhbar Amri* year 42, no. 5 (July 1963) 321.

instructed to write a letter. He wrote
some poetry and this was forwarded
to Shoghi Effendi, who replied that he
must write a full account of his actions.
This he declined to do. After a time, Dr
Sa'id Khan Kurdistani persuaded Dr
Samuel Jordan the head of the American
Protestant College in Tehran to finance
Avarih, who now changed his surname
to Ayati, to write a refutation of the
Baha'i Faith and to publish it. This came
out as a vitriolic and abusive three-vol-
ume attack on the Baha'i Faith called
Kashf ul-Hiyal (published in 1928). Following this, Avarih was financed to edit
and write for a journal called *Namak-
dan,* which was published from 1929 to
1936.[206]

156. Fadil Yazdi ('Ali Mumtazi)

'Ali Mumtazi, Fadil Yazdi (1290/1873–1960, see fig. 156), was born in
the village of Nadushan (70 km northwest of Taft) but after he completed
his studies under Aqa Najafi in Isfahan, he was asked to be *imam-jum'ih*
of the Ghiyathabad Mosque in Taft in about 1900. He became interested
in the Baha'i Faith after reading two anti-Baha'i works and asked one of
the Baha'is for a Baha'i book. He was given the Kitab-i Iqan and then
Gulpaygani's book *Fara'id* and was convinced by these. With his conversion, there was a wave of conversions in the Ghiyathabad quarter of the
town where he was the religious leader. He and Avarih were close friends
and when Fadil became a Baha'i after reading the Baha'i books, he brought
Avarih into the Baha'i Faith with him. In 1903 Fadil was forced to leave
his post and moved eventually to Tehran, from where he made numerous

---

206 *Kashf ul-Hiyal,* 3 vols., Tehran, 1326 Sh./1947; ZH 8b:961–4, 977–8; *Da'irat
    ul-Ma'arif Tashayyu'* 1:241–2; Abizadih, Vaqayi' 161–9; Muhammad-Husayni,
    Hadrat Bab 56–8; Bamdad, *Tarikh* 5:140–1. Ishraq-Khavari has recorded that
    when he first became a Baha'i, the superintendent of the school where he was
    teaching was very surprised and told him that he had once spoken to a Baha'i
    religious teacher named Avarih in Sultanabad. He had offered Avarih wine and
    got him drunk, whereupon Avarih said to him: 'Do not believe what I have said
    to you about the Baha'is . . . I only say these things because of the money which
    I get from them' (MH 9:75).

journeys to teach the Baha'i Faith, especially in the south and centre of Iran.[207] Another cleric, Mulla Muhammad Sadiq Tafti and his brother, Mulla Muhammad 'Ali, also became Baha'is. They were forced to leave Taft and first settled in Bavanat, where Mulla Muhammad Sadiq converted over a hundred people, and then in Yazd.[208]

In the anti-Baha'i pogrom of 1903 Taft was one of the main places where the persecutions occurred. Indeed, after the first killing in Yazd, the prince governor Jalal ud-Dawlih had almost restored calm when the persecutions broke out in Taft and it was news of this that re-kindled the fire in Yazd.[209] When news of the first killing in Yazd reached Taft, a number of people got together and began to plot a movement against the Baha'is there. Word of this reached Jalal ud-Dawlih and he sent an official to Taft to urge all of the notables of the town to maintain order. After his departure, however, the plotting began again, led by Mirza Muhammad 'Ali Amir. He gathered a number of the notables and ruffians of the town in a garden in the Garmsir quarter and made an agreement that they would all stand together if there were any consequences from their actions. After drinking a great deal of alcohol all that night, this group came in the early morning of 21 June to the Ghiyathabad quarter. There they shot to death the first Baha'i they encountered, Aqa 'Abdu's-Samad. The attackers then fled and sent word to the other quarters in Taft that they had been attacked by the Baha'is. This lead to the gathering of a mob that attacked the Baha'i houses, resulting in the death of five other Baha'is on that day and three others over the next nine days, all from a Muslim background.[210]

One of the active Baha'is whom the Muslims tried unsuccessfully to kill in 1903 was Aqa Mahdi Hunza'i. They kept him in their sights, however, and one day in 1907, when Hunza'i set out for Yazd, they lay in wait for him outside the town and ambushed him. When his body was found, it had 75 knife wounds.[211] Qubad states that in 1953 the town had 150 Baha'is (2 per cent of the population).[212]

207 ZH 8b:973–8; MH 7:342–8.
208 Malmiri, *Tarikh Shuhada* 232–3.
209 Malmiri, *Tarikh Shuhada* 394–5, *Tarikh Yazd* 56–7.
210 Malmiri, *Tarikh Shuhada* 393–432, *Tarikh Yazd* 211–33.
211 ZH 7:259.
212 Qubad, *Khatirat* 143.

Manshad and surrounding villages

Beyond Taft, the main town in the Miyan-Kuh district is Mihriz but the main centre of Baha'i activities was the village of Manshad (some 55 km south of Yazd, 27 km west of Mihriz; pop. 2,867 in 1951). Mulla Muhammad Rida Radi ur-Ruh Manshadi (c. 1818–1284/1867) and his three brothers were converted when Vahid had preached in Yazd in March 1850. Their father, Mulla Haji Muhammad, an influential *mujtahid* of the village, also became a Babi and participated in the Yazd episode of 1850. The rest of the family was also converted. After the attempted assassination of the shah in 1852, Radi ur-Ruh spent four and a half years in hiding in the caves of the hills around Manshad. He also visited Baha'u'llah in Baghdad. He was a skilled physician and his fame aroused jealousy in some. Eventually Mirza Muhammad Taqi Mujtahid gave a judgement condemning him for unbelief (*kufr*) and decreeing his death. Radi ur-Ruh's skill protected him for a time but then Haji Rasul the bailiff (*ḍābiṭ*) and governor of Manshad and Miyan-Kuh, summoned him to Mihriz, with the ruse that there was a sick person there who needed treatment. There he murdered Radi ur-Ruh with poison.[213]

Another famous Babi and later Baha'i of Manshad was Haji Shah Muhammad Manshadi, known as Amin ul-Bayan. He was a sheep-herder and sheep-dealer and became a Babi through Radi ar-Ruh. He visited Baha'u'llah in Baghdad and then, when Baha'u'llah put forward his claim, Haji Shah Muhammad sold everything he had, gave each of his four daughters a portion, took the rest with him to Edirne and offered it all to Baha'u'llah. At this time Baha'u'llah made him the first Trustee of the Huququ'llah. In this capacity he travelled extensively and was killed in 1880 in Miyandu'ab by the rebels of Shaykh 'Ubaydu'llah (vol. 1:26, 360–1, 418, 422).[214]

In 1299/1881 Navvab Radavi visited Manshad from Yazd and, together with Sayyid Mirza, the Imam-Jum'ih of Manshad, launched an attack on the Baha'is, in which five of them were beaten and many houses looted. Many of the Baha'is fled the village. Sayyid [Muhammad] Taqi Manshadi (c. 1824–1909) was expelled from Manshad at this time and settled in Yazd. A short time later he travelled to visit Baha'u'llah in 'Akka and remained. He opened a small shop in Haifa. Here he took care of the needs of the pilgrims and became an intermediary for correspondence with 'Abdu'l-Baha

---

213 Malmiri, *Tarikh Shuhada* 18–22, *Tarikh Yazd* 41–2; ZH 6:728–30.
214 ZH 6:740–2; Malmiri, *Tarikh Yazd* 44–5.

from about 1894 onwards. Because of his role, he was in danger during the Commission of Investigation in about 1905 and 'Abdu'l-Baha instructed him to move to Port Sa'id in Egypt, where he continued to be an intermediary for 'Abdu'l-Baha's correspondence.[215]

Many others in Manshad became Babis and later Baha'is. Among them were three brothers, Haji Zaynu'l-'Abidin, Haji Muhammad Husayn and Aqa Hasan, who were among the wealthier inhabitants of the village and whose father had migrated from Adharbayjan, thus they were known as 'Turk'.[216] During the 1299/1881 attack on the Baha'is mentioned above, the first two of the brothers were beaten. Haji Muhammad Husayn Turk made his way with three others to Isfahan. Here he petitioned Zill us-Sultan, who agreed to send orders to Ibrahim Khalil Khan, his deputy in Yazd, to intervene on behalf of the Baha'is of Manshad. This, however, only excited greater hostility and Sayyid Mirza, the Imam-Jum'ih of the village, alleged that three Baha'is had tried to assassinate him, thus reigniting the persecution. One of the Baha'is, Sultan Ibrahim, used to collect brushwood to sell to the public baths for their fires. He was seized and thrown into a cellar. Here he was visited by a number of clerics who, since it was 21 Ramadan (the night of the revelation of the Qur'an, 6 August 1882) and any religious act on that night is more meritorious, beat Sultan Ibrahim. Many others joined in until Sultan Ibrahim was unconscious. He was sent in chains to Yazd but then freed.[217]

In 1884 Mulla Muhammad Mujtahid, who had studied in Najaf for 12 years and received certificates of *ijtihad* from Mirza-yi Shirazi and Mulla Isma'il Sadru'd-Din Isfahani, was a *mujtahid* and a *pish-namaz* (prayer-leader) in Manshad and had religious leadership throughout the Miyan-Kuh and Pusht-i Kuh districts, became a Baha'i. He announced his conversion, left his position in the mosque and became a builder. However the clerics of Manshad wrote to Shaykh Muhammad Hasan Sabzivari who in turn complained to the deputy governor Mu'addil ul-Mulk. Officials were sent to Manshad in 1886 and six Baha'is arrested and sent to Yazd (for their subsequent fate, see pp. 367 and 25). Mulla Muhammad himself was eventually killed in the 1903 anti-Baha'i pogrom.[218]

---

215 'Abdu'l-Baha, *Memorials* 54–7; ZH 6:815–16, 8b:913; the latter source seems to indicate that he moved to Haifa after 1903.
216 Yazdi, *Tarikh 'Ishqabad* 449.
217 Yazdi, *Tarikh 'Ishqabad* 453–63; ZH 5:263–6.
218 Malmiri, *Khatirat* 104–9, 112, *Tarikh Shuhada* 446–8, *Tarikh Yazd* 61–3, 167–8; MH 5:325–6, 331.

Many of the people of Manshad were followers of a Sufi Shaykh known as Shaykh Manshadi, who had been informed about the Baha'i Faith by Mulla Muhammad Nabil Akbar. Although he did not become a Baha'i, when he was leaving Manshad on one occasion and his followers asked what they should do in his absence, he told them they should associate with the Baha'is. As a consequence, many of them became Baha'is.[219] Edward Stack of the Indian civil service visited Manshad in the first half of 1881. He was told, 'As for the village people [of Manshad], they are Bâbîs . . .'[220]

When the anti-Baha'i pogrom of 1903 occurred and Mirza Muhammad Halabi-saz was killed in Yazd, Jalal ud-Dawlih sent a troop of soldiers to Manshad to maintain order. But suddenly on 25 June, the leader of the troop received a message from Jalal ud-Dawlih and they hurried back to Yazd in the middle of the night. After this, a certain Muhammad Sadiq Na'imabadi took the lead in plotting against the Baha'is, supported by Muhammad the Kalantar. The next day, a sayyid was said to have been attacked as he walked along the road and left unconscious – despite the fact that the doctor attending him could find not a mark on him. On 27 June Na'imabadi raised a hue and cry against the Baha'is. Haji 'Ali Muhammad, a notable of the village who was a Baha'i, tried to calm the crowd but only succeeded temporarily. Seven Baha'is were killed on that first day and the killing went on for almost three weeks, resulting in the deaths of some 28 men and one woman.[221]

The Baha'is of Manshad were under continual pressure from the Muslims in the village and there were several further episodes of harassment and persecution.[222] In 1953 there were about 300 Baha'is in the village (i.e. about 10 per cent of the population).[223]

About ten kilometres northwest of Manshad is the village of Banaduk (pop. 2,761 in 1951). Aqa Sayyid 'Ali the prayer-leader (*pish-namaz*) of the

---

219 MH 3:565–6.
220 Stack, *Six Months*, 1:282–3. In fact, Stack mistakenly calls Manshad 'Manshar' and repeats the allegation that they have 'have community of wives and daughters'.
221 Malmiri, *Shuhada* 432–85, 487–94, Malmiri, *Tarikh Yazd* 386–428; KD 2:129–36. There is also an eyewitness account of these events in Manshad: Manshadi, *Sharh Shahadat*.
222 Some of these are reported by Malmiri, *Khatirat* 190–4. When he visited them in 1953, Qubad reports that, at that time, the Baha'is were prevented from going to the public baths and there was talk of expelling them from the village (*Khatirat* 138).
223 Qubad, *Khatirat* 137.

village became a Baha'i and converted the rest of his family. He was unable to continue to live in Banaduk and retired to the village of Arnan, but a Baha'i community was established in Banaduk.[224] During the 1903 anti-Baha'i pogrom one of the Baha'is of the village was killed.[225] In the village of Hunza (7 km north of Banaduk; pop. 1,674 in 1951), Fatimih Bigum and her brother Aqa Sayyid Muhammad 'Ali, who were involved in the 1886 arrests in Manshad (see pp. 367 and 25), were both killed during the 1903 pogrom along with two others.[226]

Beyond Manshad in the Pusht-i Kuh district of Yazd is the village of Sakhvid (about 75 km southwest of Yazd; pop. 355 in 1951). The governor of the Pusht-i Kuh and Miyan-Kuh districts, Sadiq Khan Sakhvidi, was a covert Baha'i and used to help and associate with the Baha'is as much as he could.[227] Hurmuzak (5 km west of Sakhvid) is a hamlet in the Pusht-i Kuh district. One of the Baha'is of Yazd, Aqa Muhammad Isma'il Gazar, was a part-owner of the lands on which the hamlet was built and he used to spend the summer months there with his family. He spoke with the inhabitants of the hamlet about the Baha'i Faith. In 1319/1901 he invited the Baha'i teacher Qabil Abadihi to Hurmuzak. As a result of this visit, 'Ali Rida, his wife and six sons became Baha'is and eventually all the people of the hamlet, which consisted of some six families, became Baha'is. During the anti-Baha'i pogrom in Yazd in 1903, a group of people came from Sakhvid looking for Aqa Muhammad Isma'il but he was hidden by friends. Some houses were looted and a number of Baha'is were arrested and had money extorted from them.[228]

Ardakan (Ardikan)

Ardakan (62 km northeast of Yazd; pop. at the end of the 19th century was probably over-estimated at 15,000[229] and in 1951 was 11,270) is a small town on the road from Yazd to Kashan and Tehran and at the edge of the

---

224 MH 5:343; Malmiri, *Khatirat* 161.
225 Malmiri, *Tarikh Shuhada* 494–8.
226 Malmiri, *Tarikh Shuhada* 535–72, *Tarikh Yazd* 429–46.
227 Malmiri, *Tarikh Yazd* 148.
228 Abadihi, 'Tarikh Amri Hurmuzak' 1–6; Malmiri, *Tarikh Yazd* 148. Hurmuzak was the location of a further episode in 1955 when, following Muhammad Taqi Falsafi's instigation on the radio, a mob attacked the hamlet and killed seven Baha'is; see Labib, *Seven Martyrs*.
229 Adamek *Historiccal Gazetteer* 1:47, quoting Sykes, who says that he thinks this figure given him by local people was an over-estimate.

central desert of Iran, the Dasht-i Kavir. The Baha'i community in this town dates back to the Babi period, when several important figures such as Quddus and Vahid Darabi visited the town and some were converted.[230] Some of those converted such as Mulla Muhammad Baqir Ardakani (see p. 365), who had studied at Isfahan and Najaf and was a *mujtahid* and *imam-jum'ih* in the town, and another *mujtahid* Aqa Muhammad Ardakani (1834–1919), hid their belief and did not associate with the Babis and Baha'is. The sons of the former were even enemies of the Baha'i Faith (see p. 365).[231] More important for the history of the Baha'i Faith were such individuals as Haji 'Abdu'l-Husayn, known as Haj Navvab (1277/1860–1940), whose sister was the wife of Sadr us-Sultan (see p. 417) and whose father-in-law was the deputy governor of Ardakan. He was subjected to much persecution but his position in society was such that the enemies of the Baha'i Faith were not able to have him killed.[232] Another was Mulla Rajab-'Ali (1819–26 Sept. 1887) who had obtained his certificate of *ijtihad* in Isfahan and returned to a position of religious leadership in Ardakan. He became a Babi and later a Baha'i and was persecuted by Haji Abu'l-Hasan, one of the notables of the town. He was involved in several conversions, including those of Haji Amin, who had married his sister, and Mulla 'Abdu'l-Ghani (see below).[233]

Perhaps the most well-known Baha'i to emerge from Ardakan was Haji Abu'l-Hasan Ardakani (c. 1248/1832–28 May 1928, see fig. 157). He became a Babi in about 1851 through Mulla Rajab-'Ali, his father-in-law, Shatir Rida and Radi ur-Ruh Manshadi, and later became a Baha'i. Since his wife's family was among the most respected of the Babi families, he was able to travel through Iran meeting the established Babi families and informing them about and converting them to the Faith of Baha'u'llah. He was appointed to assist Amin ul-Bayan in the collection of the Huququ'llah. In 1286/1869 he accompanied Amin ul-Bayan to 'Akka, being the first to

230 DB 182, 465.
231 On Mulla Muhammad Baqir, see Navvabzadih, *Ardakan* 50–3. This has some important differences with ZH 3:481–2 and this is explained by the author. Regarding Aqa Muhammad there is some confusion since Navvabzadih (*Ardakan* 57) says that he was known as Mulla 'Abdu'l-Karim, but Mulla 'Abdu'l--Karim was Aqa Muhammad's father (see http://www.ghoolabad.com/index2. asp?cat=d&id=17; accessed 29 July 2019). It may be that Mulla 'Abdu'l-Karim became a Babi secretly when Vahid and Quddus visited the town and his son (who was 16 on Vahid's last visit) was later also a crypto-Baha'i (*Ardakan* 153).
232 ZH 8b:917–21.
233 ZH 6:742–3, 818; Navvabzadih, *Ardakan* 63–70.

157. Haji Amin (Abu'l-Hasan Ardikani)

establish contact with the exiles there, but they were unable to enter the city and only met with Mirza Aqa Jan, to whom they handed over the money they had brought. On a second journey the following year, he was able to see Baha'u'llah in the public baths in 'Akka. When Amin ul-Bayan was killed in 1879, Haji Abu'l-Hasan was appointed the Trustee (*amin*) of the Huququ'llah and became known as Haji Amin, making numerous journeys to 'Akka in fulfilment of this responsibility. He had no money or possessions of his own and ate and lived very simply, staying with Baha'is in each locality. He used to visit every Baha'i house in each area, regardless of whether the occupant had the money to contribute to the Huququ'llah or not. He was trusted by successive heads of the Baha'i Faith to give out receipts to people and sometimes even to spend the money based on his own judgement of what would benefit the Baha'i Faith. He was imprisoned in Tehran and Qazvin for two years in 1891–3 (vol.1:53–5) and was arrested on a number of other occasions. He married Gulbaji Khanum and had four surviving daughters. Shoghi Effendi named him posthumously as one of the Hands of the Cause.[234]

Another prominent Baha'i of Ardakan was Mulla 'Abdu'l-Ghani Ardakani (c. 1835–1917). He was born in the village of Tarkabad, near Ardakan, and followed Sufism for a while. After being the prayer-leader in the village for a time, he moved to Ardakan and became the *imam-jum'ih* in one of the mosques in the town. He was introduced to the new religion by Mulla Rajab-'Ali, read some of the writings of the Bab and became a Babi. When he first obtained a copy of the Hidden Words, he assumed that its author must be Mirza Yahya Azal and became a supporter of him. Later he became a Baha'i through Mulla Rajab-'Ali in 1295/1878. He then resigned from his position as *imam-jum'ih*. When for the third time in 1309/1891 his house was attacked and he was beaten until close to death,

---

234 Balyuzi, *Eminent Baha'is* 263. ZH 6:742–8, 8b:901–3; Samandar, *Athar* 200–2; Sulaymani, 'Haji Abu'l-Hasan Amin'; Navvabzadih, *Ardakan* 70–2.

he left Ardakan for Yazd, where he taught the children of the Afnan family
Arabic and later had a grocery, where he used to teach the Baha'i Faith to
his customers. When this became too dangerous, he remained at home
and the other Baha'is of Yazd would bring people to him to teach. Many
Muslims and Zoroastrians in Yazd became Baha'is as a result of his efforts.
During the anti-Baha'i pogrom of 1903 he was one of the main targets of
the mob. He hid with his son-in-law, who was a servant living in the compound of the English missionaries, while the mob thought he had been
taken to the citadel and they besieged that (see pp. 386–8). Although there
was no real danger to the English missionaries, he was asked to leave the
compound at nightfall and he went off into the wilderness, where he had
several other adventures before the pogrom died down.[235]

Among the other prominent Baha'is of Ardakan were: Shatir Rida, a
baker, who after becoming a Babi left with his brother for Baghdad, where
they took up residence near Baha'u'llah and were joined by their father;
Aqa Muhammad 'Ali Hakim-bashi, a skilled physician and calligrapher;
Aqa Sayyid Rida Va'iz (d. 1309/1892), a notable orator, who was forced to
leave for Kirman when his conversion became know; and Mulla Husayn
Va'iz.[236]

Persecutions of the Baha'is in Ardakan increased gradually over the
years and a number of Baha'is died as a result of the beatings and mistreat-
ment they received, while others were forced to move away. On 30 June
1868, for example, during the annual celebrations that are held in Shi'i
communities commemorating the death of the Caliph Omar on 9 Rabi'
ul-Awwal, the clerics instigated a mob, led by Mirza Husayn, son of the
town's *kalantar* Isma'il Big, and Khanlar Mirza, that went around the town
shouting abuse outside the homes of the Baha'is. They attacked the house
of Abu Turab, the son-in-law of Shatir Rida, and dragged him off to be
beaten and imprisoned by the *kalantar*. He remained imprisoned for three
days and each day was paraded around the town and beaten. It took him
six months to recover from his injuries and he then left for Sabzivar. Six
other Baha'is were captured and beaten, kicked and stamped on so severely
that one of them, an elderly man, Aqa Gul-Muhammad, died and his
body was then dragged around the streets. Most of the Baha'is managed to
escape into the countryside while their houses were looted. Other Baha'is

---

235 MH 3:63–113; ZH 6: 818–21; Navvabzadih, *Ardakan* 73–5, 84–92; Malmiri,
      Tarikh Yazd 120–1.
236 Navvabzadih, *Ardakan* 54–5, 72–3.

were then imprisoned and two of them, Ustad Kazim Khan Jalal and Mulla Hasan Kamlaqi (who had become a Babi after meeting Vahid in Yazd), died as a result of beatings they received.[237] On a later occasion, Aqa Hashim, the son of Ustad Kazim Manqal-saz (brazier-maker), was being taken by a crowd of ruffians to the house of Mulla Mirza Muhammad Mujtahid. He was hit on the back of the neck so forcefully that he collapsed and died a few days later.[238]

In 1892, there was a cholera epidemic in the town and one of the prominent Baha'is, Ustad Muhammad Haddad died and was buried. Three days later, at the instigation of the clerics of the town, some people dug up the corpse, poured paraffin over it and burnt it. After this there was an upheaval in the town against the Baha'is and some of the more well-known ones were arrested, beaten and taken before the governor, who fined them and released them. After this episode, however, some of the Baha'is found that they were under relentless pressure and were forced to migrate elsewhere. Also as a result of this episode, the body of Ustad Muhammad was buried on some land that he owned and when in following years the Muslim clerics forbade Baha'is being buried in the town cemetery, this land became the Baha'i cemetery.[239]

The main enemies of the Baha'is in the town were the religious leaders, especially Shaykh 'Ali Mujtahid (1255/1839–1337/1918), Haji Mulla Muhammad Diya' ul-'Ulama (also Sultan ul-'Ulama, 1280/1863–1336/1917) and Mulla 'Ali Asghar Majd ul-'Ulama.[240] Another cleric of Ardakan, Sayyid Isma'il (d. 1317/1899), wrote an anti-Baha'i polemic called *Ibtal Madhhab at-Ta'ifa ad-Daliyyih al-Babiyyih* (The Refutation of the School of the Misguided Babi Sect, published in Isfahan in 1313/1895), which was written so badly that Aqa Muhammad, a cleric of Ardakan, commented that it would probably help the Baha'i cause, rather

---

237 Yazdi, *Tarikh 'Ishqabad* 203–4; Navvabzadih, *Ardakan* 96–8; Malmiri, *Tarikh Yazd* 117–18; Ishraq-Khavari, *Muhadarat* 1:556; ZH 5:207–8, 8b:898–9; Shoghi Effendi, *God Passes By* 200.

238 Navvabzadih, *Ardakan* 99.

239 Navvabzadih, *Ardakan* 100–2; ZH 5:431–2; Malmiri, *Tarikh Yazd* 118–20.

240 Malmiri, *Tarikh Shuhada* 577–8; Navvabzadih, *Ardakan* 129–30, 139–42; KD 2:145–6, 147; ZH 8b:920. Majd ul-'Ulama wrote a refutation of the Baha'i Faith named *Hadiyat ul-Mahdawiyyah fi Radd at-Ta'ifah ul-Baha'iyyah* (published in Isfahan in 1902). Although referring respectfully to Gulpaygani, the author quotes passages from *al-Fara'id* that do not exist (Mihrabkhani, *Gulpaygani* 401–3; postscript to Gulpaygani, *al-Fara'id* 438).

than hinder it.[241] One of the quarters of Ardakan, called Charkhab, which was renowned in the town for the arrogance and overweening nature of its inhabitants, was also particularly hostile to the Baha'is.[242]

After the death of the above-mentioned Mulla Rajab-'Ali, his sons became one of the most prominent families of Ardakan, as both landowners and clerics. His eldest son, Aqa Shaykh Mahdi, assumed his father's position of religious leadership in the town. In the episode of persecution that occurred in 1312/1894, he received a blow that caused him to become blind in one eye. He died on a journey back from Mashhad.[243] After his death, his brother Aqa Shaykh Baqir rose to great prominence among the notables of the town. Indeed his influence extended beyond the town. He travelled often to Yazd and Tehran and was in contact with high government officials. As a consequence, he was able to protect the Baha'is in Ardakan to a great extent. He was at first given the title Sadr ul-'Ulama and later Sadr us-Sultan and he is often referred to as Sadr Ardakani. As a result of his prominence other members of his family also rose to prominence and his elder brother, Aqa Shaykh Husayn, was given the title Mu'tamad ush-Shari'ah and his younger brother, Aqa Shaykh Rida (who married a daughter of Haj Amin), became Nizam ush-Shari'ah, while his sister's son, Aqa Sayyid Asadu'llah, received the title Diya' ush-Shari'ah. With his prominence, Sadr us-Sultan became the object of the envy and hatred of other clerics in Ardakan, and Diya' ul-'Ulama and Majd ul-'Ulama even collected the signatures of many of the clerics of Ardakan and Yazd (including Aqa Sayyid Murtada Mudarris and Shaykh Muhammad Taqi Sabzivari in Yazd) to a *fatwa* decreeing the death of Sadr us-Sultan on account of his being a Baha'i. Copies of this declaration were printed and put up on walls in Yazd and Ardakan.[244]

In the summer of 1312/1894 Sadr us-Sultan invited Majd ul-'Ulama, Diya' ul-'Ulama and several other clerics to his garden at Sayf outside the town. They first went to see Aqa Shaykh Mahdi, the eldest brother of Sadr us-Sultan. As they were leaving there, Nizam ush-Shari'ah arrived on a horse, greeted them and urged them to proceed to Sayf before the day became too warm. Instead, they chose to take offence at the fact that he had not got down from his horse when addressing them. They returned

---

241 Navvabzadih, *Ardakan* 153–67.
242 Navvabzadih, *Ardakan* 128–31.
243 Navvabzadih, *Ardakan* 65.
244 Navvabzadih, *Ardakan* 126–31.

to the Charkhab quarter and roused a mob to anger over the imagined insult. They then proceeded to Sadr us-Sultan's garden at Sayf and beat everyone there with chains and sticks and destroyed the place. They took everyone back to the house of Majd ul-'Ulama. On the way, however, they encountered one of the notables of the town, who insisted they hand over Sadr us-Sultan to his care. Majd ul-'Ulama then wrote a report to Yazd full of lies, to the effect that they had heard that gambling and wine-drinking was going on and had sent some men to investigate and that these men, upon seeing the sins that were being committed there, immediately took steps to break up the proceedings and arrest those present. Sadr us-Sultan lost no time, however, in going to Yazd and speaking to the deputy governor Mirza Muhammad Vazir. The latter sent men to Ardakan who arrested those responsible and fined them heavily. Majd ul-'Ulama and Diya' ul-'Ulama fled to Yazd, where some of Sadr us-Sultan's servants, without Sadr us-Sultan's knowledge, found Diya' ul-'Ulama in the bazaar and beat him severely. Sadr us-Sultan went towards Tehran and came across Majd ul-'Ulama in Isfahan. Here Aqa Najafi brokered a peace between the two men, on the condition that Majd ul-'Ulama swore an oath that he would not seek to harm Sadr us-Sultan again. It was at this time that Sadr us-Sultan went on to Tehran where he obtained the title Sadr us-Sultan (he had previously held the title Sadr ul-'Ulama).[245] The clerics in Ardakan were thus forced to hold back their actions for a time but they continued to plot against the Baha'is. One of their actions was to send a certain 'Abbas ibn Muhammad into the Baha'i meetings, pretending to be interested in the new religion and meanwhile gathering the names of all the Baha'is of the town.[246]

A few years later, Diya' ul-'Ulama exerted great pressure on Jalal ud-Dawlih and managed to obtain from him the concession to collect taxes from the Ardakan area. Majd ul-'Ulama was greatly distressed by this, knowing that he would now not be able to get away with avoiding taxes as he had in the past. He came to Sadr us-Sultan and implored him to do something about this. The latter saw that, with Diya' ul-'Ulama's greed, this situation was a disaster for the people of Ardakan and so he sent his nephew, Mirza Muhammad Husayn Rastigar to Mushir ul-Mamalik, who was responsible for tax-collection in the province of Yazd, and urged the cancellation of the concession to Diya' ul-'Ulama. Sadr us-Sultan had enough influence in Yazd to be able to achieve his purpose and the

---

245 Navvabadih, *Ardakan* 126–35.
246 Navvabadih, *Ardakan* 245–6.

concession was cancelled. Needless to say, Diya' ul-'Ulama was incensed at Sadr us-Sultan's action and moved to Yazd, where he awaited an opportunity to wreak revenge on him.

Diya' ul-'Ulama's chance for revenge came when the anti-Baha'i pogrom of 1903 in Yazd began. He immediately wrote to Shaykh 'Ali Mujtahid in Ardakan urging the killing of Sadr us-Sultan and, in order to ensure his compliance, he also gifted him some considerable land with pistachio trees growing on it and promised him money if his object were achieved. Diya' ul-'Ulama also wrote to others in Ardakan urging the same course of action and telling them to gather around Sayyid 'Ali and press him to carry this out.

When news of the first killing in Yazd arrived in the town, many of the enemies of the Baha'is gathered and started to plot. The clerics issued *fatwas* and on about 17 June, a mob took to the streets of Ardakan chanting abuse at the Baha'is and seeking them out. They came across one 60-year-old Baha'i, Aqa Muhammad Hasan, returning from the fields, dragged him to the middle of the town and set upon him, beating him to death. They then attacked the house of 'Abdu'n-Nabi Naddaf (cotton-carder, 70 years old) and killed him also. Sadr us-Sultan did what he could to restore calm to the town and prevent the escalation of the violence. He telegraphed Jalal ud-Dawlih, who in turn sent instructions to the governor of Ardakan, Mirza 'Abdu'l-Karim Khan. On several occasions when Sadr us-Sultan heard that Baha'is were in the hands of particular gangs of ruffians in the town, he sent word to the gang-leader and managed to save these Baha'is from harm. He even went in person to Yazd to try to get Jalal ud-Dawlih to act. Jalal ud-Dawlih promised to do so but in fact did very little. After Sadr us-Sultan's return to Ardakan, there was some semblance of calm restored but beneath the surface the clerics were still stirring up trouble. Majd ul-'Ulama continued to visit Sadr us-Sultan and appeared to be on his side, but was actually plotting against him with the other clerics. On 27 June, emboldened by news of the killing of Baha'is in Taft, the mob took to the streets again. They attacked the homes of Aqa Muhammad Ibrahim (85 years old) and Aqa Mirza Muhsin Ashkudhari (70 years old) and killed them both.[247]

---

247 Navvabzadih, *Ardakan* 242–62; Malmiri, *Tarikh Shuhada* 572–7, *Tarikh Yazd* 447–9. Malmiri states that all four were killed on 24 June when news of the killings in Taft reached Ardakan. I have followed Navvabzadih's chronology, since on balance, it is more likely to be correct as he quotes dated telegrams that Sadr us-Sultan sent to Yazd.

The mob then turned their attention to Sadr us-Sultan, who, after his return from Yazd, had taken his family to his estate, called Sadrabad, outside the town. On 27 June at about midday, a mob of some 2,000 led by Shaykh 'Ali Mujtahid headed for Sadrabad. Although the Baha'is numbered some 30 persons, were well-armed and could have defended themselves, they chose not to fire on the mob as it approached. Sadr us-Sultan went up to Shaykh 'Ali and spoke to him, but Shaykh 'Ali's only response was to strike Sadr us-Sultan across the face and then signal his companions to beat him until he fell to his knees whereupon one of those present shot him dead. Following this the mob set upon his two brothers and his nephew, as well as four from among the family and retainers and killed them.[248]

Navvabzadih comments that the people of the villages around Ardakan are so prejudiced and hostile to the Baha'i Faith that only a handful of people have ever become Baha'is in these villages. One of these was Haji Mulla Muhammad 'Ali Dihabadi, who was forced by persecution to move from his village of Dihabad (12 km south of Ardakan) to Ardakan, and again forced to move to 'Izzabad and Yazd, where he was killed in 1891 (see above pp. 403 and 369).[249]

Na'in

Na'in is a small town about mid-way on the road between Yazd and Kashan, where a road branches off to Isfahan (169 km northwest of Yazd, 140 km east of Isfahan, 212 km southeast of Kashan; pop. 5,000 in 1905 and 6,235 in 1954). The area produces grain and cotton and the town itself was famous for producing the best quality cloaks ('abās) worn by the religious classes. One of the followers of Shaykh Ahmad al-Ahsa'i, Haji 'Abdu'l-Vahhab, was a leading religious figure in this town and became known as

---

248 Navvabzadih, *Ardakan* 273–346; Malmiri, *Tarikh Shuhada* 577–91 Malmiri, *Tarikh Yazd* 449–54; KD 2:144–8. Following an attack on the Baha'is of Yazd in 1951, Sayyid Muhammad Rida Khatami (who was the son of Sayyid Isma'il, the above mentioned author of *Ibtal Madhhab*, and who had played a small role in the 1903 persecutions) together with his son Sayyid Ruhu'llah led an attack on the Baha'is of Ardakan resulting in the expulsion of all 300 and the looting and destruction of their houses. The latter's son, Sayyid Muhammad Khatami, was later president of Iran, 1997–2005. Navvabzadih, *Ardakan* 396–416; Faridani, *Dustan* 324.

249 Navvabzadih, *Ardakan* 75–6.

Pir-i Na'in (the prominent Iranian family of Pirniya are descended from him). As a result of this, the majority of the population, including all of its notables, were Shaykhis and in 1897 when the Shaykhi leader Mirza Muhammad Baqir Hamadani was forced to leave Hamadan (see p. 202 and n), he settled in Na'in. Haji Hasan Na'ini, a student of Haji 'Abdu'l-Vahhab, was stirring up expectation of the near advent of the Twelfth Imam in this town in the years before the Bab's ministry.[250] Shaykh Abu'l-Qasim Mazgani (see pp. 130–1) who later became a Babi and Baha'i had earlier been a follower of Haji Hasan. Despite this early millennialist groundwork and Shaykhi background, the town does not appear to have responded favourably to the Babi movement. Although a certain Mirza Muhammad Baqir Na'ini became a Babi in the first few months after the start of the ministry of the Bab, this was in Mashhad and there is no mention in the histories of a Babi community being established in Na'in nor any people from Na'in listed among the Babis at Shaykh Tabarsi. In the early 1860s, Haji Mirza Haydar 'Ali Isfahani, who was himself of a Shaykhi family, challenged the Shaykhi leadership in the town by reading to them the Qur'an, which they had asked him to recite, intermingled with verses of the Bab and then pointing out to them that they had not detected any difference. He had to go into hiding and flee the town.[251]

Since it was on a major road, the town was visited by many Baha'is and gradually a small community emerged. Among those who became Baha'is was Aqa Mirza 'Ali Muhammad Nazim udh-Dhakirin and his two brothers. In about 1901 they were attacked and badly beaten. In 1337/1918 the two sons of Haji Mulla Zaynu'l-'Abidin, a *rawdih-khan* of the town, became Baha'is. The younger son, Mirza Habibu'llah, began to talk about his new beliefs very openly and aroused opposition. One day he was seized by a mob in the nearby village of Muhammadiyyih and thrown from an upper storey and then beaten to death. In the autumn of 1921 a Baha'i merchant, Haji Muhammad 'Ali, was killed by one of the town ruffians named 'Ali.[252]

In Anarak (75 km northeast of Na'in; pop. 2,173 in 1951), which was famous for the coal mines in the area, a number of residents became Baha'is. The first two of these, Husayn, son of Najaf-'Ali, and Mashhadi Ja'far, who after he became a Baha'i took the name of Mirza 'Ali Muhammad,

---

250 DB 7–9; Faizi, *Nuqtih-yi Ula* 25n.
251 Isfahani, *Bihjat* 19–20.
252 KD 2:240; ZH 7:318–19, 425.

migrated to Ashkhabad in 1311/1893 and some four others followed later. Some of these subsequently returned. Another early Baha'i, Haji Baqir and his sons migrated to Shahrud.[253] This latter migration may well have been in about 1910 when many of the residents of Anarak fled to Shahrud as a result of the depredations of Na'ib Husayn Kashi (see pp. 115–17).[254]

253 ZH 8a:316; Yazdi, *Tarikh 'Ishqabad* 542–3.
254 Naraqi, *Kashan dar Junbish Mashrutih* 101.

19

KIRMAN

This province forms the southeast part of Iran. In the northwest of Kirman province lies a desert, the Dasht-i Lut, and between this and the parched coastal plain of Baluchistan agriculture is only possible around small oases or by the use of *qanats*. The Baluchi people are ethnically Iranian but speak their own dialect of Persian and are Sunnis. Other tribal groups are Shi'is.

Kirman

The town of Kirman (Kerman) lies in southeast Iran (1,100 km southeast of Tehran) on the edge of the great central desert, which forms much of the province. The town had five quarters within the city walls and three outside (including a Zoroastrian quarter).

The town is famous for its carpets and goat's wool products, while the countryside produced cotton and, in the 19th century, opium. The town had been devastated as a result of being captured by the forces of the first Qajar monarch, Agha Muhammad Shah, in 1794. It was given over to the victorious army to do as they wished for three days, after which the Qajar monarch demanded that his men bring him 7,000 eyes removed from the inhabitants of the town.

In religious terms, Kirman has always been a place where fringe religious movements and religious minorities have found a home. Zoroastrianism clung on there after it had been eliminated from most of Iran. The Isma'ili doctrine had had a strong foothold in Kirman since the 11th century when the Hamidu'd-Din Kirmani was the leading Isma'ili propagandist in Iran. This Isma'ili influence continued into the 18th century, when the ruler of Iran, Karim Khan Zand, appointed the Isma'ili Imam Abu'l-Hasan 'Ali governor of Kirman. The latter's grandson, Hasan 'Ali Shah, the first Aga Khan (1804–81), was appointed governor of Kirman in 1835 by Muhammad Shah but came into conflict with the prime minister Haji Mirza Aqasi and, after a military defeat, Hasan 'Ali Shah left Iran for India in 1841.[1] Hasan 'Ali Shah evidently had some relationship with the Babi movement and Baha'u'llah later sent Haji Niyaz Kirmani to India with a message for him. Unfortunately, Haji Niyaz was delayed and only reached India after Hasan 'Ali Shah's death in 1881.[2] Kirman was also the headquarters of the Ni'matu'llahi Sufi order and its founder, Shah Ni'matu'llah Wali (d. 1431), is buried in the nearby village of Mahan. In addition, Kirman is one of the main centres for the Shaykhi movement in Iran. When Sayyid Kazim Rashti died in 1843 without naming a successor, one of the main claimants to leadership of the Shaykhi movement was Haji Muhammad Karim Khan (usually abbreviated to Haji Karim Khan) Kirmani (1810–71, see fig. 159), whose father, Ibrahim Khan Zahir ud-Dawlih had been governor of Kirman from 1218/1803 to 1240/1824 and had restored the town to some measure of prosperity after its sacking in 1794. Muhammad Karim Khan had studied under Sayyid Kazim and then returned to Kirman in 1253/1837. He was vehemently opposed to the Bab and wrote one of the first refutations of the Babi religion (*Izhaq al-Batil*, 1261/1845), as well as later opposing the Baha'is. His residence was in the village of Langar (34 km southeast of Kirman) and most of the Shaykhis in Kirman lived in the southeast part of the town.

Possibly as a result of this heterodox admixture, the town was not very highly thought of by Iranians. The *Gazetteer of Persia* (1914) stated, 'The moral standard of the town is very low, lower it is said than that of any other portion of Persia'; venereal disease was 'rampant', with 75 per cent of the population having syphilis and gonorrhoea; and opium-smoking was 'almost universal', with even girls of 13 and 14 years of age indulging in the habit.[3] The town was reckoned to have a population of 25,000 in 1850

---

1   Daftari, *Short History of the Ismailis* 195–6.
2   ZH 6:920–1.
3   Adamec, *Historical Gazetteer*, 4:350.

and 30,000 in 1868.[4] In 1902–3 Kirman was reckoned to have a population of 50,000 divided thus: 37,000 Shi'is, 6,000 Shaykhis, 1,200 Sufis, 3,000 Baha'is, 60 Azalis, 1,700 Zoroastrians, 160 Jews and 20 Hindus.[5] The population in 1956 was 62,157.

A history of the Baha'i community of Kirman appears in some lists of manuscripts but I have not been able to locate a manuscript of this work. The material for this section comes mainly from biographies and general histories such as Mazandarani's *Zuhur ul-Haqq*.

The Babi movement found it difficult to become established in the town of Kirman owing partly to the intense opposition of the Shaykhi leader Haji Karim Khan Kirmani. Quddus was the first to attempt to bring the new religion to the town but he was driven from it by the opposition of Haji Karim Khan.[6] He was followed by Mulla Sadiq Muqaddas and Mulla Yusif Ardibili, who also met the same fate.[7] However, the Imam-Jum'ih of Kirman, Haji Sayyid Javad Shirazi (d. 1287/1870), a paternal relative of the Bab who had come to Kirman in about 1246/1830 and been appointed Imam-Jum'ih in 1253/1837,[8] did his best to mitigate the activities of Haji Karim Khan and protect the Babis and later the Baha'is.[9]

The Shaykhis of Kirman

The Shaykhi leaders kept up the pressure on the Babis over the following years, partly as a way of establishing their own orthodoxy, which had been thrown into doubt when their founder Shaykh Ahmad al-Ahsa'i had been declared an unbeliever by Mulla Taqi Baraghani in Qazvin in 1824. They instigated several episodes of persecution of the Babis and Baha'is over the years. In 1269/1852 a certain Mulla Ghulam-'Ali Rawdih-khan Isfahani,

---

4 Abbot (1850) in Amanat, *Cities and Trade* 83, 148; Thomson (1868) in Issawi, *Economic History* 28.
5 *Gazetteer* 1905, 4:347–9; these estimates are probably from Sykes, *Ten Thousand* 195, since the figures given there are almost identical; cf Sobotsinskii (in Issawi, *Economic History* 32), who also gives the figure of 50,000 for the total population for 1913. Percy Sykes was British Consul in Kirman 1894–9.
6 DB 180–2.
7 DB 187.
8 Kirmani, *Tarikh Kirman* 486; Nazim ul-Islam Kirmani, *Tarikh Bidari* 9–10; see a somewhat different account of Sayyid Javad in Himmat-Kirmani, *Tarikh Mufassal* 449.
9 DB 180–2, 187; Balyuzi, *The Bab* 33; Mashhuri, *Rag-i Tak* 1:193–4; Izadinia and Naziri, *Ard-i Kaf va Ra* 186–90.

Shaykhi leaders of Kirman. *Left*: 159. Haji (Muhammad) Karim Khan Kirmani;
Right: 160. Haji Muhammad Khan Kirmani

who had participated in the Nayriz upheaval and had fled from there to
Yazd, was driven out of Yazd by the hostility of the clerics there and moved
to Kirman. The clerics of Yazd informed the Kirman clerics of the presence
of a Babi in their midst. One day one of Mulla Ghulam-'Ali's servants stole
some of his Babi books and took them to Haji Karim Khan, the Shaykhi
leader. This provided the firm evidence that was needed and Haji Karim
Khan wrote to the governor, Muhammad Hasan Khan Sardar Iravani, who
arrested Mulla Ghulam-'Ali and executed him.[10]

Following the death of Haji Karim Khan on 6 November 1871, there
was a dispute over the succession between two of his sons, Haji Muhammad Rahim Khan and Haji Muhammad Khan (d. 1906, see fig. 160). In
1878 there was a major anti-Shaykhi upheaval in Kirman which went on
for over a year and at the end of this time Haji Muhammad Rahim Khan
was expelled from the town, thus ending the succession dispute in Haji
Muhammad Khan's favour.

Mulla Kazim, the son of Ustad Yusif Banna (builder), a learned and
respected Shaykhi, became a Baha'i through reading some of the Baha'i

---

10   ZH 6:901; Himmat-Kirmani, *Tarikh Mufassal* 276–7; Kirmani, *Tarikh Kirman*
     401n, quoting from *Nasikh ut-Tawarikh* (3:1220).

scriptures and through a dream. One day he stood up at the assembly that was held daily at the home of the Shaykhi leader in Langar and boldly proclaimed the new religion. He was soundly beaten and died some time later.[11] Another prominent Shaykhi who converted was Karbala'i Husayn 'Ali Baqqal (grocer). His wife stole some of his books and took them to the Shaykhi leader Haji Muhammad Khan. The latter sent word to the governor of Kirman, Vakil ul-Mulk, who ordered Karbala'i Husayn 'Ali Baqqal be arrested, bastinadoed and to have his ears nailed to the gate of the citadel square. All his property was taken from him and he died some time later in great poverty and hardship.[12] There were even two members of Karim Khan's own family who became Baha'is: Yusif Khan and 'Isa Khan, the sons of Haji Isma'il Khan, a brother of Karim Khan.[13]

The Azalis of Kirman

The difficulty for Baha'is caused by the presence of the Shaykhis was compounded by the presence in Kirman of a strong Azali group. Although their numbers were not great, they were influential in the town and were vehement in their enmity towards the Baha'is. The leading Azali was Mulla Muhammad Ja'far Kirmani Shaykh ul-'Ulama (Tahibaghilalihi, 1241/1825–1311/1893, see fig. 161), a prominent Islamic scholar and a teacher at a religious college. He was the son of a trader in the Kirman bazaar who studied under the Shaykhi leader Muhammad Karim Khan Kirmani and became a Shaykhi. When Mulla Sadiq Muqaddas came to Kirman, Mulla Muhammad Ja'far became a Babi and thus incurred the enmity of Muhammad Karim Khan. Later, when news of the claim of Baha'u'llah reached Kirman, he sided with Azal. Muhammad Karim Khan instigated his imprisonment for a month during the governorship of Khan Baba Khan Iravani (i.e. during the period 1268/1851–1274/1857).[14] In about 1869 he was expelled from Kirman and spent some time in Mashhad before returning. He concealed his Babi beliefs and acted as an Islamic

---

11   ZH 6:900–1; Browne, *Year* 509–10; according to Browne, Mulla Kazim was a boy of 15, but since Browne confirms the prefix to his name as being 'Mulla', it seems more likely that Mazandarani's assertion that he was a learned and respected member of the Shaykhi community is correct.
12   ZH 6:902.
13   Nabili, 'Ard-i Kaf va Ra' 151–2.
14   Bamdad, *Tarikh* 3:329–30, 6:274n; ZH 3:401–2; Nabavi Razavi, *Tarikh-i Maktum* 91–9.

religious leader for the Tahibaghilalih quarter in the centre of Kirman. Baha'u'llah condemns him strongly for his support for Azal.[15] Through him a number of others became Azalis, including two of his students: his son, Shaykh Ahmad Ruhi (c. 1272/c. 1856–96,[16] see fig. 162), and Mirza 'Abdu'l-Husayn Bardsiri known as Mirza Aqa Khan Kirmani (1270/1853–96, see fig. 163). The latter was the son of Mirza 'Abdu'r-Rahim Bardsiri (or Mushizi) of the Ahl-i Haqq and his mother was a granddaughter of Mirza Muhammad Taqi Muzaffar 'Ali Shah, a Ni'matu'llahi Sufi shaykh. They were a wealthy land-owning family in the Bardsir area.

Haji Mirza Haydar 'Ali Isfahani records an interesting conversation that he had with Shaykh Ahmad Ruhi. Shaykh Ahmad had concocted what he claimed to be a tablet of Baha'u'llah and sent it to the Baha'is of Rafsanjan. At this meeting, Shaykh Ahmad boasted to Haji Mirza Haydar 'Ali of having deceived the Baha'is of Rafsanjan:

> I responded: 'God, who is aware of our innermost secrets, does not allow anyone to be in any doubt or uncertainty. They (the Baha'is of Rafsanjan) saw through your forgery and they concocted a reply and sent it so that it would be clear to you that they are able to discern [genuine] Divine verses and that you are drowning in an ocean of the bitter waters of perplexity. "And thus was he who disbelieved confounded" (Qur'an 2:258).'
>
> And he [Shaykh Ahmad Ruhi] openly denied all of the prophets and with great deal of indignation and anger said: 'I neither want to speak of nor hear about any religion.'
>
> I replied: 'Praised be to God that I have not overstepped the bounds of courtesy and friendship while you have turned fairness into injustice.'
>
> We discussed some other matters and then I got up to go out and the

---

15 Baha'u'llah says that he is the true 'Ja'far-i Kadhdhab' (Ja'far the liar), not the brother of Hasan al-'Askari, the eleventh Shi'i Imam, who denied the existence of the Twelfth Imam and whom Shi'is had for a thousand years called by this name; Mazandarani, *Asrar* 5:21.

16 Some sources give Shaykh Ahmad's birth as 1263/1847 (Adamiyat, *Andishih-ha* 2; Mirza Muhammad Qazvini in the introduction to Kirmani and Ruhi, *Hasht Bihisht*, p. *bih*) which would make him seven years older than Mirza Aqa Khan. I have preferred the later dates of 1272 or 1273 given by Browne (1272, *Persian Revolution* 414), Nazim ul-Islam Kirmani (1272, *Tarikh Bidari Iraniyan* 13), Kirmani, *Tarikh Kirman* 430n (1273) and, as an alternative, by Mirza Muhammad Qazvini in the introduction to *Hasht Bihisht* (p. *bih*, 1272), as it makes him just two or three years younger than Mirza Aqa Khan, and since Mirza Aqa Khan married the older of two daughters of Azal, I suspect he was the older of the two.

Shaykh accompanied me. In the vestibule of the house, he said: 'I have one astute word to say to you. If [the revelation of] verses is proof, then I also have verses. And if having a pervasive influence is proof, then I have influenced many.'

I said: 'So, you yourself are a law-giver and law-maker and have been sent by God to carry out His decrees?'

He said: 'Yes, inwardly and in secret. Yes, I myself have revealed verses, and a *shari'ah* and a law (*qānūn*), but outwardly I teach in the name of the Bab. When I have prepared people, I will reveal my laws, commands and prohibitions.'

I said: 'Now you are being truthful and sincere and talking from your heart in saying that in reality you have no faith in prophethood and consider the Divine commands to be man-made laws and have no belief in a Divine ruler and creator. All you are interested in is to take measures for your own power and leadership. And because you saw that this mighty Cause is victorious and protected, you realized, indeed you saw and understood that, by dishonesty, deception and determination in your worldly desires, you would not be able to achieve in this mighty Cause the complete leadership that is your chief goal and soul's desire. Therefore, seeing that Azal has no personality nor any intelligence, you pinned your hopes on becoming his illusive heir and reprehensible "mirror" and you are teaching in the name of the Bab . . .'[17]

Mirza Aqa Khan left Kirman for Isfahan in 1301/1883 after falling out with the governor of Kirman, 'Abdu'l-Hamid Mirza Nasir ud-Dawlih (see p. 438). Shaykh Ahmad Ruhi joined him in Isfahan the following year and the two participated in circles where social and political reform was much discussed. In late 1885 they moved to Tehran but were unable to remain there on account of being pursued by Nasir ud-Dawlih. Towards the end

---

17   Isfahani, *Bihjat* 240–1. It is difficult to know when this meeting occurred. The chronology of *Bihjat us-Sudur* is not always clear and the author often recounts episodes relating to several visits to a particular town all together in one place. Thus although this episode comes chronologically at about 1889 in the narrative, it must have occurred on an earlier trip to Kirman since Shaykh Ahmad left Kirman in about 1883–4. Alternatively, it may be that it was Shaykh Ahmad's father, Mulla Ja'far, whom Isfahani met and he has mistakenly used Shaykh Ahmad's name. Certainly at the beginning of this account it says that the person whom he visited was teaching Imam 'Ali's *Nahj ul-Balaghah*, and that seems more likely to have been Mulla Ja'far.

of 1886 they therefore left for Istanbul. Within a few months of their arrival there, they travelled to Cyprus to visit Azal. Here Mirza Aqa Khan and Shaykh Ahmad married two of Azal's daughters, Safiyyih and Tal'at (daughters of Badri Jan Tafrishi), respectively.

The two wives soon fell out with their husbands and returned to Cyprus. At this time, Shaykh Ahmad Ruhi left Istanbul for Baghdad, while Mirza Aqa Khan undertook a pilgrimage to Mecca and lived in Damascus and Aleppo. In the course of this time, Mirza Aqa Khan received permission to visit Baha'u'llah in 'Akka.[18] According to Mazandarani, the reason for this visit was to try to persuade Baha'u'llah to support the schemes of Sayyid Jamalu'd-Din 'Afghani' (Asadabadi).[19] When Baha'u'llah refused to do this, Mirza Aqa Khan turned against him, and when both he and Shaykh Ahmad Ruhi had returned to Istanbul (by 1889), they jointly authored an attack on the Baha'i Faith, the *Hasht Bihisht*, as well as writing articles in the newspaper *Qanun*. Mirza Aqa Khan also wrote *Fasl ul-Khitab fi Tarjumati Ahwal ul-Bab* (The Decisive Discourse on the Circumstances of the Bab), *'Aqa'id-i Shaykhiyyih va Babiyyih* (The Beliefs of the Shaykhis and Babis) and *Khulasat ul-Bayan* (Summary of the Bayan).[20] In 1895, a few months after their wives returned to them, the shah managed to prevail upon the Ottoman authorities to arrest these two, together with their associate Mirza Hasan Khan Khabir ul-Mulk, and they were kept at Trebizond. After the assassination of Nasiru'd-Din Shah in 1896, they were handed over to the Iranian authorities and executed in Tabriz.[21]

Shaykh Ahmad Ruhi had three brothers, Shaykh Abu'l-Qasim, Shaykh Mahdi Bahr ul-'Ulum and Shaykh Mahmud Afdal ul-Mulk (d.

---

18   Ishraq-Khavari, *Rahiq-i Makhtum* 1:750.

19   ZH 6:907–8. However, it should be noted that 'al-Afghani' (Asadabadi) was only in Istanbul in 1869–71, before Ruhi and Kirmani arrived there, and in 1892–7 after the passing of Baha'u'llah (Keddie, *Sayyid Jamal al-Din*). It may be, however, that Ruhi and Kirmani were already working in support of Asadabadi's ideas before his arrival in Istanbul in 1892.

20   Momen, *Browne* 485; Adamiyyat, *Andishih-ha* 52; 'Abdu'l-Baha in *Ma'idih* 5:21; some of these may be different titles for the same book. According to a letter from Kirmani to Mirza Malkam Khan, the second book was written at the behest of Mirza Husayn Sharif Kashani, the son of the Azali leader in Kashan, Mulla Muhammad Ja'far, who then double-crossed him (Balyuzi, *Birawn* 85–6, see also Adamiyyat, *Andishih-ha* 52).

21   Adamiyat, *Andishih-ha* 1–35; Himmat-Kirmani, *Tarikh-i Mufassal* 386–98; Bayat, *Mysticism* 140–2, 157–61; Balyuzi, *Browne* 18–28; Browne, *Persian Revolution* 93–5, 409–15; ZH 6:905–10; Ishraq-Khavari, *Rahiq-i Makhtum* 1:738–55; Dawlatabadi, *Hayat* 1:64–7; Amini, *Rastakhiz-i Pinhan* 285–356.

Azalis of Kirman: *Top left*: 161. Mulla (Muhammad) Ja'far Kirmani. *Top right*: 162. Shaykh
Ahmad Ruhi. *Bottom left*: 163. Mirza Aqa Khan Kirmani. *Bottom right*: 164. Mirza Ahmad
Kirmani at the time of his arrest in 1896

1330/1912), as well as one sister, Bibi Buzurg (Mutahhirih), who were also
Azalis and highly involved in politics. Bibi Buzurg was married to another
leading Azali, Mulla Yusif.[22]

A somewhat strange figure was Mirza Ahmad Kirmani (see fig. 164).
He was a well-educated individual who was at first a Shaykhi. He was so

---

22   Bastani-Parizi, *Vadi Haft Vad* 1:361–2; Kar, 'Huma Ruhi'.

well thought of by the Shaykhi leader Haji Muhammad Khan Kirmani
that he was permitted to address the Shaykhis from the pulpit in Langar,
near Kirman, where they were headquartered. He was then converted to
the Baha'i Faith by Nabil Akbar when the latter was in Kirman (possibly in
1873, vol. 1:233). He spoke about the Baha'i Faith so openly from the pulpit
that Haji Muhammad Khan sent a complaint to Tehran. Mirza Ahmad
Kirmani was arrested and sent to Tehran in about 1875, where he spent a
year in prison before returning to Kirman. After this, he appears to have
become somewhat deranged. His wild and unpredictable behaviour can to
some extent be explained by the fact that at this time he became addicted
to large quantities of alcohol and drugs. He would frequently attack the
Baha'i Faith and yet repeatedly wrote letters of repentance to Baha'u'llah.
He aligned himself with the Azalis at times and at others made claims for
himself. He travelled through Iran in the 1880s spreading chaos and vexa-
tion among Baha'i communities in places such as Faran (vol. 1:208), Rasht
(vol. 1:336) and Barfurush through his contradictory actions.[23] He also
visited Istanbul where he joined up with the Azalis. Eventually he moved
to Tehran, put forward certain religious claims of his own[24] and became a
supporter of the reform movement. In 1891, at the height of the turbu-
lence caused by the activities of Sayyid Jamalu'd-Din 'al-Afghani', he wrote
and distributed leaflets against the government which appeared to be by
the Baha'is, thus leading to the arrest of Haji Amin and Haji Akhund (vol.
1:53–5).[25] Mirza Rida Kirmani, the assassin of Nasiru'd-Din Shah, stayed
with him immediately before he shot the shah in 1896. Mirza Ahmad then
fled Tehran for Hamadan. Here he persuaded a certain Sayyid Hasan to
claim to be the Imam Mahdi. The two of them were arrested and Mirza
Ahmad died in prison in Tehran in about 1314/1896.[26]

---

23   ZH 6:910–20. In the town of Faran, for example, having ascended the pulpit and
     preached against the Baha'i Faith for a month, he then proclaimed that should
     Baha'u'llah claim that his proof is that he raised a son such as 'Abdu'l-Baha, none
     could refute this evidence; Ishraq-Khavari, *Qamus Tawqi' 105*, 2:312–3. He
     wrote a treatise supporting the Azali position which is published as the third part
     of *Tanbih an-Na'imin* (an Azali book which was later published in Tehran, n.d.).
     MacEoin has mistakenly attributed this to Shaykh Ahmad Ruhi (*Sources* 27n).
24   Ishraq-Khavari, *Qamus Tawqi' 105*, 2:311–12.
25   Tablet of Baha'u'llah quoted in Balyuzi, *Birawn* 229.
26   Browne, *Persian Revolution* 78, 405–6; Bamdad, *Tarikh* 1:99–100, 339 and
     pictures at back of vol. 6; Ishraq-Khavari, *Qamus Tawqi' 105*, 2:310–13; ZH
     6:915–17; Yazdi, *Tarikh 'Ishqabad* 483–4, 495. See also Baha'u'llah words about
     him in Ishraq-Khavari, *Rahiq-i Makhtum* 1:288.

165. Photograph taken in Port Saʻid: Left to right: Haji Niyaz Kirmani,
Mirza Ahmad Sohrab (*standing*), Mirza Ahmad Yazdi (who married
Munavvar Khanum, the daughter of ʻAbduʼl-Baha)

Mirza Mahdi Akhavan Safa records that a delegation of eight Azalis, led by a certain Mulla Salih, came to dispute with him during his visit to Kirman in about 1911. When they were defeated in argument, they left saying that they would return with a more learned member of their group but failed to do so.[27]

The Sufis of Kirman

A number of the Sufis of the Kirman area converted to the Bahaʼi Faith. The best known of these was Haji ʻAvad Kirmani, the son of Darvish ʻAvad-ʻAli Kirmani, who became a Babi in 1280/1863. He was arrested at the same time as Mirza Baqir Shirazi (see p. 435) but managed to escape and left Iran, eventually making his way to ʻAkka. Here took the name Haji Niyaz Kirmani (see fig. 165). Later he moved to Egypt, where he was one of the leading Bahaʼis and converted a number of Sufis and others.[28]

27   MH 4:69.
28   Mazandrani, *Asrar* 5:21; Muhammad-Husayni, ʻDarvishan va ʻArifanʼ 17.

166. Edward Granville Browne

The Baha'i community of Kirman

The Baha'i community of Kirman had many difficulties. In addition to the strength of the Azali and Shaykhi communities, the Baha'is were also faced with the problem of some anti-nomian Baha'is who were somewhat dissolute, freely partaking of opium and alcohol, as was the custom of many of the townspeople. Professor Edward G. Browne (1862–1926, see fig. 166), who was in Kirman in the summer of 1888, describes meetings at which intoxicated Baha'is made wild statements which any other Baha'i would have found obnoxious.[29] It is of interest to note that Browne's Baha'i acquaintances in Yazd appear not to have held a high opinion of the Kirman Baha'is and tried to dissuade Browne from going there. With the presence of the Shaykhi leadership, the strong Azali element and such Baha'is, it is not difficult to see the reason for Baha'u'llah's reproachful address to Kirman in the Kitab-i Aqdas. Elsewhere he writes of the need for some Baha'i with intelligence and prudence to settle there on account of the adverse factors in the town.[30]

Mirza Baqir Shirazi was a Baha'i, whose sister Fatimih was one of the wives of Azal. He travelled from Shiraz to Edirne, became aware of the situation between Baha'u'llah and Azal, and sided with Baha'u'llah. He was a excellent calligrapher and during the six or seven months that he spent in Edirne he was transcribing 2,000 verses a day. On his return to Shiraz, he was imprisoned there for four months at the time that Aqa Mirza Aqa Rikab-saz was executed, and was then exiled from the town. He moved to Kirman, where he managed to convert a number of the Shaykhis and thus incurred the wrath of the Shaykhi leadership, who denounced him to the governor, Murtada-Quli Khan Vakil ul-Mulk. He was expelled by the governor and moved to Sirjan. The wife of his landlord in Sirjan secretly

---

29   See, for example, the interchanges in Browne, *Year* 501, 534–9.
30   Kitab-i-Aqdas, v. 164; Mazandarani, *Asrar* 5:21.

sent some of his Baha'i books to the Shaykhi leadership in Kirman as proof of his being a Baha'i. He was
arrested with two other Baha'is and taken to Kirman.
Here Sayyid Javad Shirazi, Imam Jum'ih, for whom
Mirza Baqir had executed a Qur'an in his fine calligraphy, managed to arrange for the Baha'i prisoners
to escape but Mirza Baqir was caught and executed
(1288/1871).[31]

One figure associated with Kirman is Sayyid
Javad Karbala'i (see fig. 167), about whom there is
some controversy since the Azalis have claimed that
he was one of them. Indeed, Shaykh Ahmad Ruhi
and Mirza Aqa Khan Kirmani succeeded in convincing E.G. Browne that the *Hasht Bihist*, which they
had written to advance the claims of Azal, was the
work of Karbala'i. Karbala'i was from the eminent
Tabataba'i family and a grandson of Sayyid Mahdi

167. Sayyid Javad
Karbala'i

Bahr ul-'Ulum, one of the leading figures of the Shi'i world at the end of
the 18th century. He himself had studied under the leading clerical figures
in the Shi'i shrine cities. He met Shaykh Ahmad al-Ahsa'i, studied under
Sayyid Kazim Rashti and became one of the most respected figures of the
Shaykhi school. He had travelled to India and Mecca and lived and taught
in both places for a time. He was a friend of the family of the Bab and so
knew the latter from childhood. He accepted the new religion as soon as
he heard about it in Karbala in 1844 and went to Shiraz, where he stayed
for a time while the Bab was there. He then returned to Karbala and was
there when Baha'u'llah visited in 1851–2. Sayyid Javad Karbala'i was three
years in Sabzivar, where he met with the famous philosopher Mulla Hadi
Sabzivari, and he also spent some time in Mashhad, where he stayed at
the Madrasih Dawdar. He associated with only one or two of the Baha'is
there, but they were in doubt as to him being a Baha'i. Karbala'i later
moved to Tehran in about 1876 where he lived in the house of a Baha'i,
Mirza Asadu'llah Isfahani, and where Mirza Abu'l-Fadl Gulpaygani learned
much from him when he first became a Baha'i. In 1299/1881 Karbala'i was
warned by his close friend Mirza Husayn Khan Mushir ud-Dawlih that his
name was on a list of Baha'is that had been submitted to the shah and so

---

31   ZH 5:144, 6:867–9; Mazandarani, *Asrar* 5:21–2; Yazdi, *Tarikh 'Ishqabad* 335–7.
     Shoghi Effendi, *God Passes By* 171.

he moved to Kirman. Here he was, at first, welcomed by the Shaykhis and invited to lecture at their religious college, the Madrasih Zahir ud-Dawlih. Later, when they realized he was a Baha'i and was actively promulgating the Baha'i Faith from their madrasih, he left the college and set up classes in his home where he taught philosophy and the Islamic sciences. Shaykh Ahmad Ruhi and Mirza Aqa Khan Kirmani may have been taught by him in these classes and he may well have also given some private classes on the writings of the Bab that they attended. However, he was very much a Baha'i and would have had nothing to do with the contents of the *Hasht Bihisht*. When he became too old and feeble to live by himself, one of the Baha'is of Kirman, 'Ali Rida Khan Mahallati I'tidad ul-Vuzara (see p. 177), invited him into his house, where he remained until his death in about 1883. Baha'u'llah is most emphatic that Karbala'i was one of his followers.[32]

'Ali Rida Khan Mahallati, who was the postmaster in Kirman, had become a Baha'i through the teaching of Sayyid Javad Karbala'i at the Madrasih Zahir ud-Dawlih, as had his father-in-law, a merchant named Mirza Hasan Hirati. The latter's wife, Shahrbanu Khanum (also known as Karbala'i Khanum, d. 1306/1888), a poetess who wrote under the name Hamamih (dove), noticed her husband going out every night and followed him to the Madrasih, where she stood outside the door, listened to their conversations and was converted as a result. The couple later moved to Tehran (vol. 1:33).[33]

Muhammad Tahir Malmiri visited Kirman in 1879 and wrote that at that time Baha'i meetings were being held regularly at the house of Mirza Nazar-'Ali, a merchant.[34] Edward Granville Browne remained in Kirman for some two and a half months in the summer of 1888. During his stay he

---

32   ZH 3:238–44; Gulpaygani, *Kashf* 55–64; Fu'adi, *Tarikh* 82–3; Muhammad-Husayni, *Hadrat-i Bab* 666–73; Izadinia and Naziri, *Ard-i Kaf va Ra* 190–5. Although Fu'adi indicates that Karbala'i left Mashhad directly for Kirman in order to teach the Baha'i Faith there at the instruction of Baha'u'llah, it seems likely that Karbala'i's stay in Sabzivar and Mashhad were before he moved to Tehran, since Gulpaygani says that he met with Karbala'i throughout the period 1292/1875–1299/1881 in Tehran. Considering that Karbala'i died in about 1883, this would not leave sufficient time for the events that are stated to have occurred in Sabzivar, Mashhad and Kirman. Furthermore, a note from Gulpaygani (ZH 6:30n) indicates Karbala'i came from Khurasan to Tehran. For Baha'u'llah on Karbala'i, see Ishraq-Khavari, *Ma'idih Asmani* 7:215, 8:4.

33   ZH 6:469; Arbab, *Akhtaran* 1:119–21; Dhuka'i-Bayda'i, *Tadhkirih* 1:270–7.

34   Malmiri, *Khatirat* 74.

became addicted to opium and
was only able to extract himself
from this situation with the greatest difficulty. It was in Kirman
that Browne became acquainted
with Azalis for the first time.
Among them was a brother of
Shaykh Ahmad Ruhi, Shaykh
Mahdi Bahr ul-'Ulum (see fig.
168), whom Browne describes
as the chief Azali in Kirman.[35]
Another was their brother-in-
law Mulla Yusif. A third was
Shaykh Mahdi Qummi, who
was a confidant of the governor
and very knowledgeable about
the Babi and Baha'i religions.

168. Shaykh Mahdi Bahr ul-'Ulum

Browne regarded Shaykh Mahdi Qummi as an Azali but others described
him as a free-thinker and materialist.[36] There were also individuals who
acknowledged the truth of the Bab but were undecided between Azal and
Baha'u'llah. Such a person was Muhammad Ja'far Mirza, a Qajar prince
who was head of the telegraph office.[37]

Browne's description of the Baha'is he met in Kirman is revealing.
Among the characters he met was Ustad 'Ali 'Askar Nukhudbiriz (whom
Browne calls Usta' Akbar the pea-parcher in his book), son of 'Ali Dhu'l-
Faqar. Ustad 'Ali 'Askar was described by Haji Mirza Haydar 'Ali, who
came to Kirman shortly after Browne, as being one of the leading Baha'is
of Kirman, 'illiterate but articulate, eloquent, bold, fearless and stout-
hearted'[38] and by Mazandarani as having converted many.[39] Browne,

---

35   Although Mulla Muhammad Ja'far Kirmani (see p. 427) was still alive, Browne
     did not meet him and it may be that he was too old by this time to be the effec-
     tive leader.

36   Browne, *Year* 477–8, 486–7, 492–3, 542, 572; Browne, *Diary* 404, 450.

37   Browne, *Year* 582.

38   Isfahani, *Bihjat* 235–6; his name is given as Ustad 'Ali Asghar here but since both
     Mazandarani and Browne give it as 'Askar (ZH 6:901; Browne in *Diary* 414 and
     no. 200 in list at end of diary) or 'Ali 'Askar (Mazandarani, *Asrar* 5:24), I have gone
     with the latter. Browne conceals the identity of those Baha'is and Babis he met in
     Iran in his book (*Year* 500) but gives the true names in the diary of his journey.

39   ZH 6:901–2.

however, describes him as addicted to opium and prone to making wild, exaggerated statements, especially when under the influence of opium.[40] Another Baha'i whom Browne met in Kirman was Shaykh Sulayman Sultanabadi, who was in the service of Mirza Rahim Khan Burujirdi, the *farrash-bashi* (head-attendant of the governor). Shaykh Sulayman had been involved in the Sultanabad persecution of 1864 (see pp. 158–9) and told Browne about it. He was also addicted to cannabis and alcohol and prone to wild talk.[41] These antinomian Baha'is associated freely with the Azalis of the town while the more orthodox Baha'is did not.

More orthodox among the Baha'is of Kirman at the time of Browne's visit were the above-mentioned Mirza 'Ali Rida Khan Mahallati I'tidad ul-Vuzara and his father-in-law Mirza Hasan Hirati. Another Baha'i, Haji Muhammad Rahim (d. 1333/1915), a merchant and landowner, was learned and skilled in propagating the Baha'i Faith.[42] Browne also met a lady (unnamed) who was described to Browne as being very learned, who was called 'Mulla' and who, Browne says, was regarded as a return of Tahirih.[43] It may be that she is the same person as Bibi Fatimih of Rafsanjan, who was a skilled teacher of the Baha'i Faith and a poetess. She was married to Muhammad Karim Khan, the *kalantar* (mayor) of Rafsanjan, and Rakhsarih, her daughter from a previous marriage, was married to Nasir ud-Dawlih, the governor of Kirman (see below).[44]

In the decade following the visit of Browne, the Baha'i Faith grew in Kirman both in numbers and in the regard with which it was held by the citizens of the town. This was particularly so during the governorships of 'Abdu'l-Hamid Mirza Nasir ud-Dawlih (d. 1892, governor 1298/1881–92, see fig. 169) and his brother 'Abdu'l-Husayn Mirza Nusrat ud-Dawlih Farmanfarma (1858–1938, governor 1892–3, see fig. 170),[45] who were impartial in religious disputes and paid no attention to the accusations of the Azalis, Shaykhis or *mujtahids* such as Haji Shaykh Muhammad Taqi Mujtahid of Rafsanjan. Baha'i travelling teachers who visited Kirman

---

40   See, for example, Browne, *Year* 501, 520 and especially 573.

41   Browne, *Year* 482, 520–1, 562–6.

42   ZH 6:902.

43   Browne, *Year* 567–8.

44   ZH 6:904; Dhuka'i-Bayda'i, *Tadhkirih* 2:147–8. On his list of those he met, which he kept in his diary, Browne names her as 'Haji Bibi'. Bibi Fatimih's family name was Tahiri and it may be this that made Browne think she was regarded as a return of Tahirih.

45   ZH 6:246, 904; ZH 8b:733.

169. Nasir ud-Dawlih ('Abdu'l-Hamid   170. Farmanfarma ('Abdu'l-Husayn Mirza
              Mirza)   Nusrat ud-Dawlih), taken in 1916

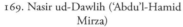

during this period, such as Haji Mirza Haydar 'Ali in 1888 and 1891, and
Nayyir and Sina in 1892, were able to teach the Baha'i Faith freely, and
many Azalis and Shaykhis became Baha'is. Haji Mirza Haydar 'Ali notes
that the Baha'is of Kirman would bring people to him who had expressed
an interest in the Baha'i Faith and almost all of these became Baha'is. He
comments, however, that the people of Kirman have a particular charac-
teristic: most are not constant in their belief:

> For example if a person were to stay in Kirman for just two months, some
> 200–300 people would declare their belief and by the end of the two
> months matters would be at the stage of 'they enter into the religion by
> troops'. But since the people are Shaykhis or Sufi dervishes or orthodox
> legalists (qishrī – and these last have even less regard for the shari'ah than
> the Sufi dervishes), they adhere to the outward form of religion solely for
> the sake of earning a living and material benefit. And so they are a false
> and wayward people. However much a person who enters the town may
> try to act prudently and conceal himself and be careful, it is not possible
> to remain there more than two months. And after one has left, those souls

who accepted the Faith become dervishes, dissolute and debauched and even atheists and irreligious individuals to such an extent that it is then impossible to guide them aright. This has become an acquired trait of the people of Kirman on account of the intercourse and mixing of these three religious groups.[46]

One who converted at this time was Mirza 'Ali Naqi Khan Isfahani, who held the rank of *sarhang* and was the head of the telegraph office. He was converted by Haji Mirza Haydar 'Ali in 1891 and subsequently was head of the telegraph office in Kashan, achieving the rank of *sartip*.[47]

Ibn Abhar visited Kirman in 1903 and managed to convert many of the Azalis to the Baha'i position.[48] However, there continued to be a community of Azalis in Kirman in later years.[49] Despite the anti-Baha'i pogrom in the neighbouring province of Yazd in 1903, the situation in the city of Kirman remained calm. In 1323/1905 there was a major anti-Shaykhi riot in Kirman. Its instigator was a certain religious leader named Shaykh Bahrayni, who was at one stage arrested by the governor Rukn ud-Dawlih and sent away to a village. However, a large mob surrounded the government citadel and Rukn ud-Dawlih was forced to allow Shaykh Bahrayni to resume his preaching. This eventually led to an anti-Shaykhi riot. The Baha'is do not appear to have been involved in this episode.[50]

Another who visited Kirman was the blind Baha'i teacher Haji Va'iz Qazvini. During his visit in 1909 the people of the town were roused against him and he was forced to flee the town by night.[51] During his stay in Kirman, his host was Karbala'i Asadu'llah Saqat-furush (seller of small goods). His wife, however, betrayed him and took some Baha'i writings he had to Sayyid 'Ali Mujtahid, who ordered that all Karbala'i Asadu'llah's property should be taken. He was subsequently stabbed to death on 12 June 1927.[52]

---

46   Isfahani, *Bihjat* 247; quotation from Qur'an 110:2.
47   Isfahani, *Bihjat* 258; Muhammad-Husayni, *Tarikh* 297–8.
48   'Abdu'l-Baha in Ishraq-Khavari, *Ma'idih Asmani* 5:19 and Ishraq-Khavari, *Rahiq-i Makhtum* 1:750.
49   See, for example, the reference to Azalis at a meeting in 1922, MH 9:271. There continue to be some Azalis in Kirman to the present day (information from a Baha'i resident of Kirman).
50   Himmat-Kirmani, *Tarikh-i Mufassal* 353–7.
51   MH 5:134–5.
52   ZH 7:266–7, 8b:737–8; MH 6:235–57.

Despite these obstacles, a number of conversions to the Baha'i Faith occurred in the city and the community did grow. A few of the Shaykhis and Zoroastrians[53] of the town became Baha'is as did some others, including Haji Davud Mizrahi, a Jew of Kirman who had gone to Palestine to study Judaism and was converted as a result of meeting 'Abdu'l-Baha there in 1921.[54] The community purchased a Baha'i centre in about 1917.[55] A picture of the Local Spiritual Assembly of Kirman in 1933 shows that at least six of the members were of Zoroastrian origin.[56] In the 1920s and 1930s a Baha'i kin-

171. Mirza 'Ali Adhari

dergarten was established in this town. As noted above, Sykes, who was British Consul in Kirman, 1894–9, reckoned that the Baha'is numbered 3,000 or six per cent of the population of the town in the early 1900s.[57]

Mirza 'Ali Adhari (c. 1895–?, see fig. 171) was born in Kirman. His grandfather was Mulla Abu'l-Muhsin Anari, a *mujtahid* in the village of Anar. His father was also a cleric. Adhari was given a religious education but when his father died, he opened a shop. In 1913 he became a Baha'i while on a visit to his uncle in Merv, who was a Baha'i. He married this uncle's daughter and remained in Merv and Tashkent. In 1922 he decided to devote himself to propagating the Baha'i Faith and returned to Iran. He travelled around the provinces of Khurasan, Kirman and Yazd for nine

---

53   ZH 8b:744.
54   *Ahang Badi'* no. 12, year 26, 388–90; Izadiniya and Naziri, *Amr-i Mubarak* 209–12.
55   MH 4:83.
56   *'Andalib* vol. 17, nos. 67–8 (1988) inside back cover.
57   This figure seems somewhat high but may well represent the circle of those interested in the Baha'i Faith at the height of the turmoil which led to the Constitutional Revolution. In one tablet Baha'u'llah names 47 Baha'is of Kirman and this may well represent the heads of the leading Baha'i families there. Eleven of these names are of Zoroastrian origin; Mazandarani, *Asrar* 5:23–4.

months. He then accompanied Mirza Hasan Nushabadi for six months in the Qa'inat area of Khurasan, learning from him much about teaching the Baha'i Faith. Later he continued this work on his own in Khurasan until 1926, with occasional journeys to visit his family in Merv and Ashkhabad. From 1928 until 1938 he travelled throughout Iran on the instructions of the Central Assembly and later the National Spiritual Assembly of Iran; from 1938 to 1942 he was engaged in taking a census of the Baha'is of Iran. In 1942 he moved to Kabul in Afghanistan, where he stayed until 1947. After this he returned to Iran and both travelled within the country and was in charge of Baha'i publications. In 1968 he moved to Pakistan and travelled around that country.[58]

Rafsanjan

Rafsanjan, which had previously been known as Bahramabad, is situated on the road between Kirman and Yazd (123 km west of Kirman, 253 km south of Yazd; pop. 5,000 in 1914 and 14,700 in 1951). The crops of the area include cotton and pistachio nuts. Mulla Sadiq Muqaddas passed through the town in 1845 and delivered a letter of the Bab to Haji Aqa Ahmad Mujtahid, who lived part of the time in Rafsanjan and part in Kirman. Although the latter did not accept the Bab, he and his descendants did not oppose the new religion.[59]

The Shaykhis were strong in this town and when Haji 'Abdu'r-Rahim Qannad Yazdi (whose son, Mirza Ahmad Yazdi, see fig. 165, later became a son-in-law of 'Abdu'l-Baha) was forced to leave Yazd and tried to settle in Rafsanjan in about 1873, the Shaykhi governor of the town, Isma'il Khan (a brother of Karim Khan, the Shaykhi leader), had him beaten, fined and expelled.[60]

A strong Baha'i community emerged here, however, at a later date. Aqa Muhammad 'Ali Yazdi (1247/1832–1312/1895) moved to the town in order to look after the properties of Haji Mirza Muhammad Taqi Afnan Vakil ud-Dawlih. He already had relatives in the village of Hasanabad (12 km northwest of Rafsanjan; pop. 270 in 1951), the Tahiri family, who were notables of the area and Shaykhis. He married one of them, Shahrbanu Khanum, and settled in that village. Little by little Aqa Muhammad 'Ali

---

58   MH 9:242–308; ZH 8b:736.
59   Fallah, 'Tarikh Mukhtasar' 66–7; Imani, Tarikh.
60   Malmiri, *Khatirat* 45–6; Imani, Tarikh 53–4.

established himself as a merchant and one of the most prominent citizens of Rafsanjan such that even the governor of the town was beholden to him. Because of his prominence in the town, several eminent Baha'i teachers such as Haji Mirza Haydar-'Ali and Shaykh Muhammad 'Arab were able to teach openly here despite the opposition of the leading cleric of town, Haji Shaykh Muhammad Taqi Mujtahid, and two of the landowners of the area, Haji Yusif and Haji 'Abdu'l-Vahhab. Gradually the conversions to the Baha'i Faith increased, first Yazdi's own family, then the whole of the village of Hasanabad and also many in Rafsanjan.[61] E.G. Browne visited Yazdi here in August 1888. During the 1891 persecution of Baha'is in Yazd, Yazdi was able to give shelter to some of the Baha'is of Yazd who had fled the city, although there was considerable agitation in Rafsanjan itself and a few of the Baha'is had to leave the town for a time.[62]

The period of the governorships in Kirman of Nasir ud-Dawlih and his brother Farmanfarma (1881–93, see p. 438) were particularly fruitful and prosperous for the Baha'is of Rafsanjan. The former even married Rakh-sarih Khanum, the daughter of one of the most active of the Baha'i women of Rafsanjan, Bibi Fatimih, who composed poetry under the pen-name of Darvishih. Although the governor of Rafsanjan itself, 'Ali Naqi Khan, a nephew of Karim Khan Kirmani, was at heart inimical to the Baha'is, he was unable to show this hostility because of the position taken by these two governors of Kirman and because he owed Yazdi money. Haji Shaykh Muhammad Taqi Mujtahid did try to instigate persecution of the Baha'is but Farmanfarma acted firmly and had him exiled to Isfahan for a time. Sometime in about 1892 Haji Mirza Haydar 'Ali Isfahani visited for the third time, and on this occasion, Yusif Khan, the son of the former governor and a nephew of Karim Khan Kirmani, and most of his family who were resident in 'Aliyabad, were converted. The brother of Aqa Muhammad 'Ali Yazdi, Aqa Muhammad Hasan (c. 1832–1910), heard of his brother's new religion and came from Mashhad where he was a cleric to try to persuade his brother of the error of his path. After a long period of debate and investigation, he also became a Baha'i, returned to Mashhad

---

61   Isfahani, *Bihjat* 234; Browne, Diary 429; Imani, Tarikh 106–8.
62   Browne, *Year* 593–6; Isfahani, *Bihjat* 234; ZH 6:903–4, 8b:734; Fallah, 'Tarikh Mukhtasar' 68–9; Dhuka'i-Bayda'i gives him the title Malik ut-Tujjar, which would indicate he was the head and official representative of the merchants of the town (*Tadhkirih* 2:147). Malmiri, *Tarikh Yazd* 157–8 states that Aqa Muhammad 'Ali Yazdi was the grandson of a Jewish rabbi who had converted to Islam in the early years of the 19th century.

and converted their sister also. Brother and sister then returned to Rafsanjan and assisted in the spread of the Baha'i Faith there.[63]

After the passing of Baha'u'llah, Mirza Husayn Khartumi, who had
visited Rafsanjan with Haji Mirza Haydar 'Ali and was now one of the supporters of Mirza Muhammad 'Ali's rebellion against 'Abdu'l-Baha, made
an effort to influence the Baha'is of Rafsanjan. The numerous letters he
wrote to the Baha'is of the town had no effect but when Ustad Muhammad Haddad went to Bombay on his way to 'Akka, Khartumi met him
there and managed to recruit him to Mirza Muhammad 'Ali's side. He
returned to Rafsanjan and persuaded a small number of others, mainly
from among his own family, to follow this path. Disagreements also broke
out among the Baha'is of Rafsanjan about the station of 'Abdu'l-Baha. In
1314/1896 Mulla Ahmad 'Ali (see p. 323 and fig. 121) came from Nayriz
and spent some time in Rafsanjan resolving these disagreements, and Haji
Mirza Haydar 'Ali Isfahani also spent four months in Rafsanjan. By the
time of Ibn Abhar's visit in 1903, only Ustad Muhammad Haddad and his
son-in-law remained partisans of Mirza Muhammad 'Ali.[64]

Despite the favourable circumstances, there were episodes of persecution in Rafsanjan, especially in the time of 'Abdu'l-Baha. In 1310/1892
two Baha'i shopkeepers, Aqa Mirza Ja'far and Aqa Habibu'llah, who were
teaching the Baha'i Faith openly, were set upon and beaten by a number
of the Muslims of the town and then taken before the deputy governor,
Husayn Khan, the son of the above-mentioned Isma'il Khan. They were
severely bastinadoed. Aqa Muhammad Husayn, the postmaster at Rafsanjan, who was a Baha'i, informed Aqa Muhammad 'Ali Yazdi of what had
happened and the latter telegraphed the governor of Kirman, Nasir ud-
Dawlih, who dismissed Husayn Khan. Despite this, the two shopkeepers
were forced to leave the town and they migrated to Khurasan.[65]

Mulla Husayn Arbab (d. 1317/1899), a prominent cotton merchant
of the town, became a Baha'i and when he began to teach others about
the new religion, the clerics created an uproar and reported him to the
governor. He was arrested and when he refused to recant his faith, he was
bastinadoed and his shop and storehouse of cotton burned. As a result,
he was forced to flee Rafsanjan for Ashkhabad with his three sons in

---

63   Fallah, 'Tarikh Mukhtasar' 69–71.
64   ZH 8b:732–3; Fallah, 'Tarikh Mukhtasar' 73; Imani, Tarikh 58–9.
65   ZH 7:35; Imani, Tarikh 56–8.

1314/1896.[66] A number of others from Rafsanjan fled to Ashkhabad after suffering persecution. Ustad 'Ali Akbar Najjar Rafsanjani (d. 1331/1913) had been converted in 1307/1889 by Mulla Ibrahim Mas'alihgu of Yazd. Ustad 'Ali Akbar's wife, Umm Kulthum (d. 1918), and daughter Bibi Sakinih, had at first opposed him greatly before finally themselves converting. He was beaten on the orders of the governor Muhammad Taqi Khan, a brother of the Shaykhi leader Muhammad Karim Khan, and moved to Ashkhabad, where Bibi Sakinih married Sayyid Mahdi Gulpaygani (see p. 176).[67]

172. Gawhartaj Khanum Thabit
(Rafsanjani, Sirjani)

Another Bibi Sakinih, together with her husband, Karbala'i Yusif, and their daughters Gawhartaj and Bilqis, fled to Ashkhabad in 1322/1904 after much persecution. When Bibi Sakinih had been converted at the age of 14 by her uncle, her mother had been so angry that she had pulled fistfuls of her daughter's hair out and beaten her. Eventually, however, she became convinced herself and converted. Gawhartaj Khanum (c. 1890–1958, see fig. 172), the elder daughter of Bibi Sakinih and Karbala'i Yusif, was an accomplished poet. She married Ustad Qadr in Ashkhabad but her husband died when she was only 21 years old. They had a daughter, Ishraqiyyih, who in later years was head of the Baha'i Vahdat-i Bashar Girls' School in Kashan. Gawhartaj married a second time, to Mirza Muhammad Thabit Maraghihi (vol. 1:410–11), in 1919 and together they travelled through Central Asia spreading the Baha'i Faith. When Thabit became the head of the two Baha'i kindergartens in Ashkhabad (one was Persian language and the other Turkish), Gawhartaj assisted with this. After their expulsion from Ashkhabad, she accompanied her husband on his travels to towns and villages in the area of Kirman, Shiraz, Isfahan and Sultanabad, where Thabit died. In each place Gawhartaj would teach the women literacy and the Baha'i Faith while he

---

66   ZH 6:904–5; Yazdi, *Tarikh 'Ishqabad* 518–20.
67   ZH 8b:734–5.

taught the men. After her husband's death Gawhartaj continued this work, settling in Yazd for a time as the head of the Baha'i school in Mahdiyabad and then moving to Isfahan and finally in 1953 to Nayriz where she taught mainly women but also some men. After a year and a half, however, she fell ill and left for Tehran, where she remained until her death.[68]

As a result of the visits of travelling Baha'i teachers, many in Rafsanjan became Baha'is. One of these was Aqa Muhammad Rida Yazdi, who was a *rawdih-khan* and grocer. He became a Baha'i in 1309/1891, and although he tried to keep his conversion a secret, he soon became known as a Baha'i. Haji Shaykh Muhammad Taqi Mujtahid raised a campaign against him. His shop was burned down and a complaint against him was made to the Shaykhi governor of Rafsanjan, Mirza Muhammad Khan Mustawfi, a bitter enemy of the Baha'is, who had him bastinadoed and fined. Another complaint was sent, this time to the governor of Kirman, who had him and two other Baha'is arrested and imprisoned in Kirman for a time in 1897 before fining and releasing them.[69] A later governor of Rafsanjan, Muhammad Husayn Khan Raf'at us-Sultan, however, became a Baha'i and welcomed Mirza Mahmud Zarqani when he visited in 1318/1900 .[70]

In 1903 Ibn Abhar stayed for a time in Rafsanjan both on his way to Kirman and on his way back. Shaykh Muhammad Taqi Mujtahid roused a mob to attack the house where Ibn Abhar was staying but Yusif Khan and his three sons arrived armed from 'Aliyabad to forestall this. Anxious to prevent bloodshed, 'Ali Naqi Khan, the governor of Rafsanjan, managed to persuade the mob to disperse. He asked Ibn Abhar to leave and so he moved to Hasanabad where he arranged the formation of a local spiritual assembly.[71] Shortly afterwards, when news of the anti-Baha'i pogrom in Yazd reached Rafsanjan and some of the refugees from there also arrived, Shaykh Muhammad Taqi Mujtahid incited a mob to attack the Baha'is. Although instructed by the governor of Kirman, Zafar us-Saltanih, to prevent any disturbance, 'Ali Naqi Khan instructed the Baha'is and the refugees to flee to the hills, and in their absence allowed the mob to loot their houses. Most of the Baha'is had fled the town but the mob found Ustad Mirza Parihduz Davarani, one of the local Baha'is who was a cobbler, killed him

---

68   Dhuka'i-Baydai (*Tadhkirih* 3:245–52) calls her Sirjani. But her second husband, Thabit Maraghihi (*Dar Khidmat* 229) calls her parents Rafsanjani. See also ZH 8b:735–6; Anonymous, 'Gawhartaj Khanum Thabit'.
69   ZH 8b:738; Fallah, 'Tarikh Mukhtasar' 73–4; ZH 7:101; Imani, Tarikh 56–7.
70   Fallah, 'Tarikh Mukhtasar' 74.
71   Fallah, 'Tarikh Mukhtasar' 74–5; ZH 8a:324; MH 4:544–5.

and burned his body. They also beat many of
the Baha'is, and the governor and *mujtahid*
extorted much money from them. Eventually, however, Zafar us-Saltanih sent a force
to Rafsanjan, restored order and dismissed
the governor. He took Shaykh Muhammad
Taqi Mujtahid to Kirman to punish him but
the clerics there intervened on his behalf.[72] In
about 1910 Mirza Mahdi Akhavan Safa visited
Rafsanjan, Hasanabad and the village of Rah-
matabad just on the outskirts of Rafsanjan (to
the northeast) where Aqa Muhammad Sadiq
and his son Mirza 'Abbas Khan Tahiri, both
Baha'is, lived. He reports meeting an Azali
there called Haji Khan and a follower of Mirza
Muhammad 'Ali called Ustad Muhammad.[73]
In early 1921 Mirza 'Abdu'llah Mutlaq visited
Rafsanjan. During his visit he converted the

173. Mirza 'Ali Akbar Rafsanjani

merchant Aqa Mirza 'Ali Mu'avin ut-Tujjar and spoke at length to others.[74]

Mirza 'Ali Akbar Rafsanjani (1297/1880–1921, see fig. 173) became
a Baha'i in 1315/1897. His education had been cut short when he was
12 by the death of his father and he had started work as an apprentice
to a builder. From this he saved enough to open a shop selling pens and
paper in the bazaar. His piety and honesty attracted the attention of one
of the Baha'is in the bazaar who succeeded in talking to him about the
Baha'i Faith and converting him. He in turn began to teach others and
this caused opposition to him to arise in the bazaar. He was forced to leave
Rafsanjan after the persecutions that erupted in 1903 following on from
the anti-Baha'i pogrom in Yazd. He went to Tehran where he attended the
class for Baha'i teachers that were being held in Tehran by Sadr us-Sudur
and in 1905 began to travel with Tarazu'llah Samandari throughout Iran
as a travelling Baha'i teacher (*muballigh*). He had a good memory for the
scriptures of the Baha'i Faith and a beautiful voice for chanting them and
this made him a very effective teacher of the Baha'i Faith. In 1911 he was

---

72   Fallah, 'Tarikh Mukhtasar' 76; Faridani, *Dustan* 217; ZH 6:336, 7:218–20;
     Imani, Tarikh 61–2.
73   MH 4:65.
74   MH 4:153–7.

summoned by 'Abdu'l-Baha to Paris and sent on a trip through Germany and England teaching the Baha'i Faith, with Lutfu'llah Hakim as his translator. In about 1916 he returned to Iran. He contracted tuberculosis and isolated himself from everyone, refusing offers of help so that he would not spread the disease. After a time in Tehran he returned to Rafsanjan and lived with his Muslim family until his death.[75]

In the late 1910s a preacher named Sayyid Yahya Muhammadabadi Yazdi used to come to Rafsanjan in the month of Ramadan and preach there, usually inciting violence against the Baha'is in his sermons. In Ramadan 1919 (June), as a result of this incitement, a Baha'i was shot one night by two assassins but only wounded. A pattern of problems for Baha'is emerged during the months of Muharram, Safar and Ramadan, when Muslim susceptibilities were at their highest, and continued in subsequent years.[76]

Other towns and villages in Kirman province

There were several important Baha'i communities in the villages in the north of the province which were sometimes accounted part of the province of Yazd. The village of Anar (148 km south of Yazd and 203 km north of Kirman; pop. 2,000 in 1914 and 2,800 in 1951) had a small community of Baha'is. Here a prominent local notable and cleric, Aqa Muhammad Ja'far, visited Dihaj and was converted by Sayyid Mahdi Dihaji. When he tried to spread the new religion in Anar, he excited the opposition of Mirza Sulayman Khan, a cleric who was head of the Khajih clan in the village, and Shaykh Nasru'llah, the custodian of a local shrine. There was a clash between the men of each side and some of the Baha'is of Dihaj came to Anar to support Aqa Muhammad Ja'far. Following this and a visit from Ibn Abhar and Haji Mirza Haydar 'Ali, there were many conversions. Mirza Sulayman Khan and Shaykh Nasru'llah sent a complaint to Kirman and Muhammad Ja'far was summoned to that town. Here he was interrogated by the above-mentioned Haji Aqa Ahmad Mujtahid, who sent him back to Anar.[77] Since the village was on the road between Yazd and Kirman, many other prominent Baha'i teachers visited it.[78] By

75 ZH 8b:738–44; Khoshbin, *Taraz Ilahi*, 1:334–6.
76 Fallah, 'Tarikh Mukhtasar' 78–9.
77 Imani, Tarikh 37–40.
78 For example, Ibn Abhar (with Aqa Mirza Haji Aqa Rahmaniyan Sangsari) in

the 1920s the number of Baha'is in Anar was over 70, the most prominent members being Aqa Sadr, who was a notable of the town; Shaykh
Muhammad 'Ali; Amin ur-Ru'aya; Aqa Muhammad Ja'far, who gave his
house for the use of the Baha'is; and a *sarhang* who was head of the post
and telegraph office.[79]

In the same region is Dihaj (150 km south of Yazd and 45 km west of
Anar; pop. 2,265 in 1951). According to the oral tradition of the Baha'i
community there, the religion was first brought to the village by a certain
Darvish Hasan Ja'far, who managed to convert a few of the local peasant
farmers. Someone reported to Sayyid 'Ali Akbar, a notable of the village,
that some of the villagers had left Islam, were meeting in secret and were
planning to corrupt the village. Sayyid 'Ali Akbar asked to be informed
when these people next met. He went to their meeting and listened to
them for a time. They were reading a tablet of Baha'u'llah from a piece of
paper. At the end, he picked up the piece of paper, put it in his pocket and
left. A few days later he summoned the Baha'is to his house. They went,
fearing that they might be condemned to death. Sayyid 'Ali Akbar said to
them that what was on this piece of paper was clearly divine and asked
them who wrote it. They replied that the author was Baha'u'llah and spoke
about his claims. Sayyid 'Ali Akbar then became a Baha'i and several other
notables of the village also converted, thus making the village a comparatively safe place for the Baha'is. Even one of the clerics of the village, Mulla
Sadri, became a Baha'i.[80] Sayyid 'Ali Akbar Dihaji travelled widely teaching the Baha'i Faith and visited 'Akka many times. He was well known as
a Baha'i but was protected by the fact that during the course of his travels
he had managed to acquire British citizenship in India. He died some time
before 1882 in Tehran on his way back from 'Akka.[81]

Another prominent Baha'i from this village was Sayyid Mahdi Dihaji
(1836–1339/1920, see fig. 174), who was an uncle of Sayyid 'Ali Akbar.
He became a Babi in 1268/1851 and lived for a time in Baghdad while
Baha'u'llah was there. He visited Baha'u'llah in Edirne in 1867, after
which he was directed to live in the house of Baha'u'llah in Baghdad for a

1902, MH 4:546; Mutlaq in 1921, MH 4:153; Thabit-Sharqi and Shaydan-
shaydi in about 1925, and the latter again in 1936, MH 6:304–5, 8:441–5, 494;
Mirza Hasan Rahmani Nushabadi in 1926, MH 6:100; Nabilzadih in 1928,
MH 4:298.

79   MH 4:153, 6:304–5, 8:441–5.
80   Interview with Mr Jalal Mahmudi, Skalsa, Denmark, 16 July 2006.
81   ZH 6:815; Malmiri, *Khatirat* 57–8, *Tarikh Yazd* 128–9.

174. Sayyid Mahdi Dihaji,
photograph taken in Edirne in
about 1867

while. He fled Baghdad just before the Baha'is there were exiled to Mosul in 1868. Later he established himself in 'Akka and made trips from there to Iran to teach the Baha'i Faith. Baha'u'llah gave him the title Ismu'llah ul-Mahdi (the Name of God the rightly-guided). He arrived in Tehran in 1300/1882 and was among the Baha'is arrested there that year (vol. 1:35–50). He used to travel under the name of his nephew, the above-mentioned Sayyid 'Ali Akbar, in order to benefit from British protection. At first, after the passing of Baha'u'llah, he supported 'Abdu'l-Baha and even wrote a treatise against Mirza Muhammad 'Ali. He went to 'Akka, wanting to marry his son to 'Abdu'l-Baha's daughter, and when he failed to achieve this, he went over to the side of Mirza Muhammad 'Ali in mid-1910, writing a treatise attacking 'Abdu'l-Baha. Towards the end of his life, a local man tricked him out of all his money and he was left destitute.[82]

Also from Dihaj was Mulla Muhammad 'Ali Dihaji, who played a role as one of Baha'u'llah's couriers. He travelled backwards and forwards annually some ten times, leaving with the pilgrims going on the Hajj to Mecca. He was killed in Kashan in 1307/1889 when some people in the caravanserai in which he was staying on his tenth return trip found out he was a Baha'i.[83]

In about 1916 Aqa Muhammad Ja'far and Aqa Muhammad Baqir Hafiz were each independently killed while walking outside the village.[84] Another Baha'i nephew of Sayyid Mahdi Dihaji was Sayyid Habibu'llah (1875–1910), whose sister's husband, Mirza Ahmad, was the governor of Dihaj and much opposed to the Baha'i Faith. In about 1918 Mirza Javad, one of Mirza Ahmad's men, shot Sayyid Habibu'llah dead. The Baha'is

---

82   ZH 6:782–4; 8b:900–1; Ishraq-Khavari, *Rahiq-i Makhtum* 1:755–7; Dihaji, *Risalih* 259; see BBR 293–5 and Isfahani, *Gulpaygani* 142, for his use of his nephew's British citizenship.
83   ZH 6:739; Avarih, *Kavakib* 1:447; Malmiri, *Tarikh Yazd* 129.
84   ZH 7:311.

prevailed upon Sardar Jang Bakhtiyari, the governor of Yazd, to arrest Mirza Ahmad but he was soon free again after paying a bribe.[85]

After the defection of Sayyid Mahdi Dihaji, the Baha'i community in Dihaj was in disarray and some of the Baha'is became inactive. Then Firaydun Jamshid Zal (1874–1929), who had been a Zoroastrian priest (*dastur*) before he became a Baha'i, moved to Dihaj from Manshad. Ostensibly this was to open a shop and earn a livelihood but his actual motive was to revive the community. In this he succeeded and eventually a local spiritual assembly was elected and regular meetings were held. On several occasions the rowdy elements in the village harassed Firaydun Jamshid Zal and stole from him but on 15 May 1929, five people crept into his house and killed him. After exertions by his family and payments made to officials, the killers were arrested but even the ringleader Murad-Quli spent only four years in prison.[86] From a list of 50 people addressed in a tablet of 'Abdu'l-Baha to this community, it can be estimated that there were about 250 Baha'is in the village.

Sirjan (Sa'idabad) is a small town about 110 kilometres southwest of Rafsanjan and about halfway on the road between Kirman and Nayriz. Living here were three brothers, whose father, Sayyid Mahdi Mujtahid, had moved from Yazd to Sirjan in 1844 and set up as a religious leader there. No information is available about the eldest brother, Sayyid Javad. The second brother, Sayyid Hasan (d. 1332/1914), was also a cleric and became a Baha'i as a result of meeting Sayyid Muhammad and Sayyid 'Ali Akbar, the son and grandson respectively of Vahid Darabi. Although cautious at first, hiding his new belief, he became bolder after visiting Baha'u'llah. He put aside his clerical functions in the community and began to propagate the Baha'i Faith. This made him the target of abuse and ill-treatment to such an extent that he became virtually housebound. The third son, Sayyid Yahya (c. 1861–late summer 1908), also received a clerical training and was noted for his fine calligraphy. He rejected life as a cleric, however, and set up as a merchant in a caravanserai. Owing to his honesty and natural abilities, he prospered and became one of the notable and respected figures of the area, particularly as he had a tendency to defend the weak and poor against the tyranny of

---

85   ZH 7:315, 8b:924; Malmiri, *Tarikh Yazd* 129–30; the latter source states that Mirza Ahmad, the governor, had in fact been a Baha'i at one stage, but love of leadership led him to oppose the Baha'is and to bring about Sayyid Habibu'llah's death.

86   Faridani, *Dustan* 208–10.

governors and officials. This trait, however, also earned him the enmity of those in power, such as the governor, Haji Mirza Davud Khan. Sayyid Yahya learned of the Baha'i Faith from his brother, was soon convinced of its truth and began teaching it to others. His work as a merchant took him to different places such as Rafsanjan and Bandar 'Abbas.

In 1326/1908, after Muhammad 'Ali Shah's coup d'etat, there was much disorder in the area and three local notables tried to overthrow Haji Mirza Davud Khan and two of his associates, the *kalantar* and the Ra'is ut-Tujjar (head of the merchants), by inviting them to a party and assassinating them. The *kalantar* was killed but the governor survived the attempt and the would-be assassins fled. The post of *kalantar* was filled by Sayyid Husayn Rashid us-Sultan, the brother of the previous *kalantar*. Finding that the real culprits had fled, Rashid us-Sultan, in conjunction with the governor, accused Sayyid Yahya of complicity and arrested him. This was for several reasons: first, the governor was anti-Constitutionalist and believed the Baha'is to be the main supporters of the Constitutionalist cause; second, the above-mentioned enmity towards Sayyid Yahya; and third, the hope of extorting money from him. When friends of Sayyid Yahya appealed to the provincial governor in Kirman, an official was sent to investigate and freed Sayyid Yahya. The *kalantar* became afraid that Sayyid Yahya would write an official complaint, which would ruin him, and so he arranged for some of his men to kill Sayyid Yahya in a way that could not be traced to him. The next day some men called at the house of Sayyid Yahya, dragged him to the marketplace and began to accuse him of being a 'Babi'. The people of the bazaar knew Sayyid Yahya well and were reluctant to be involved, so the *kalantar's* men went around forcing the shop-owners to close, thus causing more disorder. The rabble of the town joined in and soon a mob was stabbing and beating Sayyid Yahya to death.[87]

Nuq is a district to the north of Rafsanjan. Mulla Muhammad Rida Muhammadabadi (see pp. 358–9) established himself in Shamsabad (38 km northwest of Rafsanjan; pop. 160 in 1951) in this area in the 1860s. Although he managed to get on well with the governor, Isma'il Khan, when the latter's son Murtada-Quli Khan Vakil ul-Mulk succeeded him,

---

87   MH 5:77–111; KD 2:174; ZH 8b:736–7, 7:256–7 gives a substantially different account of the death of Sayyid Yahya, asserting that it was the result of the preaching of Mulla Muhammad 'Ali Nasir ul-Islam, who had been brought to Sirjan by Haji Davud Khan and who incited the mob to attack Sayyid Yahya. See also references to the killing of Sayyid Yahya in letters of 'Abdu'l-Baha in MH 4:553–6 and ILMA 79:54, 84:332–3, 85:351–2.

he arrested Muhammadabadi, who had to return to Yazd.[88] Then Vakil ud-Dawlih Afnan sent Aqa 'Ali Naqi to Nuq as his agent for the supervision of his properties and he settled in Isma'ilabad (45 km northwest of Rafsanjan; pop. 400 in 1951). There were no conversions in Isma'ilabad, however, until Aqa Muhammad Husayn Ta'iri moved here from Yazd and converted many.[89] In 1903, following the anti-Baha'i persecutions in Yazd, Aqa Muhammad, son of Aqa Bakhsh 'Ali of Shahrabad, was returning home from Jalalabad (15 km northwest of Rafsanjan; pop. 160 in 1951), when he was set upon, beaten and paraded through Jalalabad. The attackers were going to kill him but he was saved by a friend.[90]

In the village of 'Aliyabad (48 km northwest of Rafsanjan; pop. 160 in 1951), also in the Nuq area, Aqa Muhammad 'Ali Banna Yazdi was attacked one night at the instigation of some of the notables of the area and was strangled to death with his own shawl. However hard the Baha'is of Kirman tried to have the murderer caught, their efforts came to nothing.[91]

Further away from Kirman, Haji Mirza Haydar 'Ali reports that there were many Baha'is in Shahrbabak (85 km southwest of Rafsanjan; pop. about 10,000 in 1914). He reported that when he visited them in about 1888, they were smoking opium and he had to try to gradually wean them from this habit.[92] In the village of Khabraqta' from 1315/1897, a community was established by Mulla Fath-'Ali.[93] There were also Baha'is in Chatrud (54 km north of Kirman; pop. 3,000 in 1951) and in Ravar (200 km north of Kirman; pop. 2,500 in 1951), where 'Abbas Khan Nakhi'i Huzhabr us-Sultan and Haji Mirza Lutfu'llah were the leading Baha'is and where a local assembly was established.[94] In the village of Bahramjird (50 km west of Bam; pop. about 500 in 1914, 35 in 1951) a number of people became Baha'is.[95] In Khabis (later renamed Shahdad, 108 km east of Kirman; pop. 5,000 in 1914 and 3,584 in 1951), Mu'in udh-Dhakirin, a reciter of *rawdihs*, pretended secretly to be a Baha'i, but in fact betrayed those he found were Baha'is.[96]

---

88   Fallah, 'Tarikh Mukhtasar' 67–8; Imani, Tarikh 35.
89   Imani, Tarikh 36.
90   ZH 7:218, 8b:745.
91   ZH 7:320.
92   Isfahani, *Bihjat* 234.
93   ZH 8b:745.
94   ZH 8b:754–5.
95   ZH 8b:745.
96   MH 8:454–7.

175. Muhammad Khan Baluch

Baluchistan (Sistan)

There were very few Baha'is in Baluchistan in the period covered by this book. During the time of Baha'u'llah, the most prominent Baha'i from Baluchistan was Muhammad Khan Baluch (d. 1330/1912, see fig. 175). He was from a prominent family of Baluchistan who were often appointed governors of the area and he himself was governor for a time. He was also a dervish, however, who heard of the Baha'i Faith in the course of his travels. He went to 'Akka and became a Baha'i after meeting Baha'u'llah. He then returned home, converted his family and then set off travelling again. For a time he acted as Baha'u'llah's courier (he went at least six times backwards and forwards before 1879). He died in 'Akka.[97]

---

97   ZH 6:921–2; KD 1:447; Malmiri, *Khatirat* 74–5; for his arrest in Shiraz, see
     Afnan, Tarikh 206–12 (*Genesis* 86–8), where it is stated he was a British citizen,
     but it appears that this was merely a stratagem to obtain his release.

GLOSSARY

ābdār: literally 'water-carrier'; denotes a servant who is responsible for seeing to personal needs. Can be translated as 'butler'.

Ahl-i Ḥaqq: a Shīʿī Islamic religious community that is accused by its enemies of raising the first Shīʿī Imām ʿAlī to the level of divinity. Hence they are derogatorily called ʿAliyuʾllāhīs. They call themselves Yārsān.

andarūn: inner, private apartments of a home where the women of the household live.

Āqā: master or mister. A title of courtesy used as an address for men or prefixed to a man's name; sometimes used to denote seniority or importance.

ʿĀshūrā: commemoration of the martyrdom of Imām Ḥusayn on the tenth day of the Muslim month of Muḥarram. In Iran it is customary to hear recitals of the martyrdom (*rawḍih-khānī*) after which bands of men march through the streets beating their chests (*sīnih-zanī*), whipping themselves (*zanjīr-zanī*) or cutting their foreheads (*qummih-zanī*).

Azal, Azalī: Mīrzā Yaḥyā (1831–1912), the half-brother of Bahāʾuʾllāh, was given the title Azal by the Bāb and claimed to be the successor of the Bāb. He opposed and attacked Bahāʾuʾllāh and the Bahāʾīs. An Azalī is a follower of Azal.

bastinado: a torture frequently inflicted in Qājār Iran whereby the feet are held in the air tied to poles and the soles of the feet are beaten with rods, sometimes resulting in permanent injury.

Bībī: A title of courtesy and respect prefixed to the name of many Iranian women, especially grandmothers.

Big or Bayk: used after a person's name in Iran to denote someone of high standing in the community, usually a landowner or military officer. Also an Ottoman rank.

bīglarbīgī: see *kalāntar*.

bīrūnī: outer apartments of a house where guests are entertained and business is transacted (see ***andarūn***)

chādur: a sheet of cloth that Iranian women pull over their head scarf and then across the lower part of the face, thus fulfilling Islamic requirements that a woman should not be seen by any male who is not her husband or close relative.

dārūghih: loosely translated as police chief. Appointed in large towns by the *kalāntar* to be in charge of public order and the control of crime. He had *farrāshes* (see below), *na'ibs* (see below) and *kishīkchīs* (night watchmen) under him to assist with his duties.[1]

darvīsh: dervish, usually means a wandering Sufi mystic who would generally beg for alms.

dastūr: Zoroastrian high priest.

farrāsh: footman, assistant (***farrāsh-bāshī***, head footman). Refers to the paid employee of any public official or notable whose task was to carry out the orders of his master, often involving compelling others to do his master's wishes.

farsakh (farsang): unit of measurement of distance in Iran. It was the distance that a laden mule could travel in an hour and varied from five to eight kilometres (three to five miles).

fatwā (fatvā, fetwa): a ruling by a cleric, typically a *mujtahid*, on a point of religious law, usually in judgement on a specific case laid before him.

ḥadīth: report of a saying of the Prophet Muḥammad which was transmitted orally over a number of generations and then written down. In this book, the word 'Tradition(s)' (with capital T) translates this word.

---

1   Floor, 'The Police in Qajar Persia'.

Ḥājī: designation of any Muslim who has performed the Ḥaj, the pilgrimage to Mecca

Ḥakīm: physician, doctor; sometimes also more generally applied to a philosopher.

Hand of the Cause: an honour bestowed by the head of the Baha'i Faith, designating certain individuals and charging them with promoting the propagation and protection of the Baha'i Faith.

ḥaẓīrat ul-quds: a designation that came into Baha'i use during the leadership of Shoghi Effendi for the meeting place of a local Baha'i community. It would usually also house the offices of the local spiritual assembly; see *mashriq ul-adhkār*.

He whom God shall make manifest: see *Man Yuẓhiruhu'llāh*

Ḥuqūqu'llāh: a religious tax instituted by Bahā'u'llāh as a personal obligation. It is calculated as 19 per cent of one's wealth and thereafter 19 per cent of any increase in one's wealth after all the basic necessities of life have been paid for and all debts taken into account. Certain items such as one's residence and furnishings are exempt and it only comes into operation once a minimum threshold of wealth or increase in wealth, equivalent to the value of 19 *mithqāls* (69.192 grammes or 2.22456 troy ounces) of gold, has been passed. It is paid to the head of the religion for use at his discretion.

Ḥusayn: name of the third Shī'ī Imām, martyred at Karbalā in 680 AD.

Ḥusayniyyih: a building in which the martyrdom of the Imām Ḥusayn is commemorated.

ijāzih: written statement given by a *mujtahid* to one of his students affirming the latter's knowledge and competence to practice *ijtihād* or to teach.

ijtihād: the process of striving to arrive at judgements on points of religious law using certain principles of jurisprudence, developed by the Uṣūlī school within Shi'ism.

***Imām,* Imām-Jumʻih**: An *imām* is a member of the *ʻulamā* who leads the Friday congregational prayers. Each mosque will have an *imām* or *imām-jumʻih* but most cities also had an Imām-Jumʻih appointed by the government to the main mosque of the city (although in practice the post usually became hereditary). Imām is the title given by Twelver Shīʻīs to the 12 descendants of the Prophet Muḥammad whom they regard as having been the rightful successors to the Prophet.

kadkhudā: headman of the village, responsible for public order and collecting taxes. He was answerable to the local governor or the owner of the village. Each quarter of a town also had a *kadkhudā*, appointed by the *kalāntar*, with similar responsibilities.

kalāntar: often translated as mayor; he was the local official responsible for maintaining order in the town and for ensuring that taxes were collected. He would fix the prices and ensure the quality of necessities, such as bread, in the bazaar and often also ran a court in which he judged commercial and other cases. He also represented the people in voicing their grievances to the shah or the governor. He was responsible for appointing the *kadkhudā*, headman, of each of the town's quarters, and also appointed the *dārūghih* (see above) and *muhtasib* (bazaar police). In some towns such as Tabriz, this post was called *bīglarbīgī* and the *kalāntars* were in charge of quarters of the town (i.e. were equivalent to the *kadkhudā*). In rural areas, a *kalāntar* was sometimes appointed to be in charge of a *bulūk* or group of villages.[2]

khalīfih: (literally successor or deputy). This term is applied by Sunnīs to the successors of the Prophet Muḥammad (Caliphs). It is applied more generally within some religious groups, especially Sufi orders, to the vicegerent or appointed successor of the present leader.

kufr: unbelief; to be neglectful or disdainful of the bounty that God has bestowed on humanity through the appearance of the Prophet Muḥammad and the revelation of the Holy Qur'ān.

Letters of the Living (*Ḥurūf-i Ḥayy*): title given by the Bab to the first 18 people who came to believe in him after the declaration of his mission in 1844.

---

2   Floor, 'The Office of Kalantar in Qajar Persia' and Floor 'kalantar' in *Encyclopædia Iranica*.

lūṭī, lūṭīgarī: the two terms *lūṭīgarī* and *awbāsh* were frequently used interchangeably and thus often referred to the same people. Insofar as there was a difference between them, the *lutigari* referred to groups organized around the *zūr-khānih* (gymnasia) and professing certain ideals of *javānmardī* (loosely translated as chivalry): truthfulness, honesty, protecting the weak and opposing oppression; while the *awbāsh* referred to the criminal and low-life elements that exist in the poorer quarters of any town or city. In practice, however, the line between 'Robin Hood' and robber was not clear-cut and the two usually merged. In relation to the persecution of the Baha'is, it refers to a certain element in the population of each city that was often poor and unemployed and therefore dependent on the patronage of the clerical class or local notables. They could thus easily be incited to form a mob and attack a person or a house, either as repayment for their patron's favours or in anticipation of loot. In this book, references to ruffians and criminal elements are usually translations of *lūṭī* and *awbāsh*. (*Lūṭīgarī* also sometimes referred to troupes of musicians and entertainers but is not used thus in this book).[3]

madrasih: religious college, where students would prepare to become clerics (*'ulamā*). These ranged from small institutions, usually in the home of a local cleric, to the large establishments at Najaf and Karbalā, where the leading clerics of the Shī'ī world would teach advanced students. In the 20th century this word has come to be applied to modern secondary schools.

maḥallih: one of the quarters of a town.

maktab: small informal primary school, often set up in the home of a cleric, where elementary literacy, memorization of the Qur'ān, religious education and some Persian poetry would be taught to children. Those who showed promise would then go on to the *madrasih*.

Man Yuẓhiruhu'llāh: 'He whom God will make manifest': refers to a messianic figure, prophesied repeatedly in the writings of the Bāb, who would institute a new revelation which would be the fulfilment of the religion of the Bāb.

---

3   Floor, 'The Lutis'; Arasteh, 'Character, social organization and social role of the Lutis'. There is some question over the origin of the word 'Luti'. Some have asserted that it is derived from the biblical figure Lot and refers to the homosexuality said to have been common among this group, while there are other claims that this is a generic term for the gypsies who entered Iran from India.

marja' ut-taqlīd: title used mainly in the 20th century to designate leading mujtahids who are to be followed in their rulings. See *mujtahid*.

mashriq ul-adhkār: literally, the dawning-place of the remembrance or recitation [of the names of God]. This refers both to gatherings of the Baha'i community at dawn to say prayers and to the building in which this activity occurs. Many Baha'i communities in Iran in the time of 'Abdu'l-Bahā built or adapted existing houses for use as a *mashriq ul-adhkār*. Later Shoghi Effendi restricted the use of this term to buildings purpose-built to a specific design (none of which have ever been erected in Iran). The buildings previously called *mashriq ul-adhkārs* in Iran were renamed *ḥaẓīrat ul-quds* and became community meeting places and, often, also offices for the local spiritual assembly.[4]

Mīrzā: when used before a name (e.g. Mīrzā Ḥusayn), it denoted someone who is literate and thus of some social standing. When used after a name (i.e. Ḥusayn Mīrzā) it denotes a prince. As a noun it means a secretary.

muballigh: literally, propagator; teacher of the Baha'i Faith. This was the designation given to a number of learned Baha'is who taught the Baha'i Faith to others. Most of these individuals travelled around Iran under the instructions of the Baha'i institutions or head of the Baha'i Faith but some cities had resident *muballighs*.

Muḥarram: first month of the Islamic lunar year. The martyrdom of the Imām Ḥusayn occurred on 10th Muḥarram and the first ten days of Muḥarram are dedicated to mourning rituals. Since Baha'is joyfully celebrate the births of the Bāb and Bahā'u'llāh on 1st and 2nd Muḥarram, this is often a cause of tension between the two communities.

mujtahid: a member of the senior level of the clerical class, who has studied to the point where he can give independent judgements in religious law. In Shī'ī theory (of the majority Uṣūlī school), everyone who has not done sufficient study to become a *mujtahid* must choose a *mujtahid* and follow him in all matters of holy law. In contemporary Iran, *mujtahids* are called ayatu'llāhs.

Mullā/mulla: used both as a prefix to a name and as a noun, it denotes a person who has attended a *madrasih* and received a religious education.

---

4   See 'Mašreq al-Aḏkār' in *Encyclopædia Iranica*.

musāfir-khānih: traveller's hospice, guest house. Many Baha'i communities had a guest house in which to lodge travelling Baha'i teachers. In many places this building was also the Baha'i school or *hazīrat ul-quds*.

mustawfī: accountant, financial controller.

nā'ib: deputy; often used for a deputy governor. Many governorships in Iran were given to individuals who would not actually go to the region of their governorship but would appoint a deputy to go there and govern on their behalf. When used on its own or in front of a name (e.g. Nā'ib Ḥusayn) in the early 20th century, it designated officials appointed by the *dārūghih* in a city to keep order and pursue criminals, or individuals appointed by the governor to carry out his orders.

Nineteen Day Feast: a meeting of the Baha'i community on the first day of each Baha'i month (i.e. every 19 days). This practice originated with the Bāb and was then developed by Bahā'u'llāh, 'Abdu'l-Bahā and Shoghi Effendi.

pahlavān: athletes or strongmen who would exercise in a particular gymnasium (*zūr-khānih*) and form a fraternity with the other members of that place. They would do body-building exercises and compete with each other in wrestling competitions. They would lead the men of their quarter in processions during 'Āshūrā and also lead the street-fighting between the different quarters of the city that was common in some Iranian towns; see '*lūṭī*'.

pīshnamāz: prayer-leader in a mosque; also called an *imām*.

qanāt: a system of underground canals for irrigation and providing water to towns. Underground channels, often 15 kilometres or more, are dug deep into the hills to collect water that has seeped into the soil and carry it to a town or rural settlement for agriculture.

qirān: a unit of currency, a silver coin. Ten *qirāns* equalled a *tumān* (see below); 20 *shāhīs* equalled a *qirān*. Each *shāhī* was equal to 50 *dīnārs*.

rawḍih-khān: (pronounced rowzeh-khaan in Persian), reciter of the story of the martyrdom of the Imām Ḥusayn. These would have received clerical training to a low level but were skilled at raising the emotions of their audience. They were in high demand during the early part of the Muslim month of Muḥarram when the martyrdom of the Imām Ḥusayn is commemorated. These recitals (*rawḍih-khānī*, often shortened to just *rawḍih*) would be held in a private home, a mosque or in buildings specially built or set aside for the purpose.

Riḍā: (pronounced, in Persian, Rezaa), title given to the eighth Shī'ī Imām, whose given name was 'Alī. His shrine is at Mashhad.

sarhang: colonel.

sartīp: brigadier-general.

sayyid: descendant of the Prophet Muhammad.

Sharī'ah: the holy law of Islam that is based on the Qur'ān and the Sunnā (the practice of the Prophet Muhammad as recounted in orally transmitted Traditions). In Shī'ī Islam, the exercise of deriving answers to the problems of daily life from these two sources through a number of specialized procedures is called *ijtihād* and is carried out by *mujtahids*. In Qājār Iran, most people put themselves under the guidance of or referred disputes to a *mullā*, a lower level member of the clerical class, who would deal with most matters and refer only difficult questions to the *mujtahid*. Important people could access the *mujtahid* directly but would be expected to hand over a sum of money for the privilege.

Shaykh: general title of respect given to a leader or elder. In Iran, this title tends to be restricted to religious and tribal leaders.

Shaykh ul-Islām: refers to a clerical post that many cities had. In Safavid times, the holder of the post was the head of the *Sharī'ah* court in the city but by Qājār times it had become largely hereditary and honorary.

Shaykhī: a follower of Shaykh Aḥmad al-Aḥsā'ī who, together with Sayyid Kāẓim Rashtī, was the founder of a movement that preceded and in many ways paved the way for the Bāb. Many of the early Bābīs and Baha'is were former Shaykhīs. But equally, the later Shaykhīs were often much opposed to the Bābī and Baha'i religions.

Spiritual Assembly (*maḥfil-i rawḥānī*): councils elected to govern the Baha'i community in an area. The Central Spiritual Assembly (*maḥfil-i rawḥānī-yi markazī*) of Tehran performed this task for Tehran as well as representing the Baha'is of Iran to the national government. After the period covered by this book, in 1934, the Central Spiritual Assembly became the National Spiritual Assembly of Iran.

tablet: Baha'i terminology used as translation of the word *lawḥ*, meaning any writing of Bahā'u'llāh or 'Abdu'l-Bahā.[5]

tājir: wholesale merchant, import-export merchant.

takfīr: a formal judgement by a cleric that someone is an infidel.

takyih: place where religious recitals or theatrical performances of the story of the martyrdom of the Imām Ḥusayn take place. Can also be used for a retreat or home for Sufis.

tumān: the standard unit of money, ten *qirāns* (see above) were equal to one *tumān*.

Year	One pound sterling in *tumāns*	1 *tumān* in 2018 money (using retail price index):
1860	2.2	£4.15 ($5.25)
1870	2.6	£3.57 ($4.47)
1880	2.7	£3.61 ($4.49)
1890	3.5	£3.14 ($3.84)
1900	5.1	£2.13 ($2.58)
1910	5.4	£1.90 ($2.29)

To give some idea of its value, in 1900 an unskilled labourer could expect to earn about one *qirān* a day or about three *tumāns* a month, while a skilled labourer, such as a mason or carpenter, could expect two and a half to four *qirāns* a day.[6]

---

5   See under 'Lawḥ' in *Encyclopædia Iranica*.

6   Chart created using Issawi, *Economic History* 343–5 (note that Issawi's table is using *qirāns* rather than *tumāns*); Officer, 'Five Ways to Compute the Relative Value of a UK Pound Amount'; Officer and Williamson, 'Computing "Real Value" Over Time'. For wages, see Issawi, *Economic History* 40–2.

tuyūl: translated as fiefdom. This was an area the taxes of which were transferred to an official in lieu of his remuneration or to a prince or someone the government wished to honour. That person would then be effectively the governor of the area and could appoint officials who would rule the area and collect taxes for him.

'ulamā: literally, the learned; the Islamic learned class that took on many priestly functions. In the present book the word 'cleric' has been used to refer to these people. Members of this class will often have the word 'Mullā' in front of their name. *Mujtahids* were the highest level of this class in Qājār Iran.

vā'iz̧: preacher; usually a cleric who is not attached to a mosque and therefore preaches in the open air or is invited as a guest preacher to a mosque.

vazīr: minister. In Qājār Iran, each province would have a governor and a *vazīr*. The latter was usually responsible for ensuring taxes were collected. From the late 1850s onwards, Iran moved slowly towards cabinet government and ministers (*vazīrs*) were appointed with responsibilities for various areas of government.

zūr-khānih: gymnasium. A building where muscle-building exercises and wrestling took place. It was also a social institution where a closely-knit fraternity would be established which would then form an alliance providing the 'muscle' for factions in the town that sought power; see also '*lūṭī*' and '*pahlavān*'.

BIBLIOGRAPHY

All manuscript items below are in the Afnan Library, unless otherwise indicated. All dates of publication are Common Era (CE/AD), except where indicated otherwise: BE – Badí' era (Bahá'í); AHQ – Islamic lunar; AHS – Islamic solar; SH – Sháhansháhí (the calendar introduced for a few years by Muḥammad Riḍá Sháh Pahlaví).

Abbreviations of publications frequently cited in the footnotes

BBR Momen, Moojan. *The Bábí and Bahá'í Religions, 1844–1944: Some Contemporary Western Accounts*. Oxford: George Ronald, 1980.

DB Nabíl [Zarandí]. *The Dawn-Breakers: Nabíl's Narrative of the Early Days of the Bahá'í Revelation* (trans. and ed. Shoghi Effendi). Wilmette, IL: Bahá'í Publishing Trust, 1970.

EIr *Encyclopædia Iranica*. (ed. Ehsan Yarshater). vols. 1–4. London: Routledge & Kegan Paul, 1985–9; vols. 5–, Costa Mesa, CA: Mazda, 1992–. All articles available at www.iranicaonline.org (accessed 29 Jan. 2020).

ILMA Intishárát-i Lajnih-yi Millí-yi Maḥfaẓih-yi Áthár va Árshív-i Amr. Photocopied collection of the manuscripts in the National Baha'i Archives of Iran. 105 volumes. Available at: http://www.afnanlibrary. org/docs/persian-arabic-mss/inba/ (accessed 29 Jan. 2020).

KD Ávárih, 'Abdu'l-Ḥusayn. *Kavákib ud-Durriyih*. 2 vols. Cairo: as-Sa'ádah, 1923.

MH Sulaymání, 'Azízu'lláh. *Maṣábíḥ-i Hidáyat*. 9 vols. Tehran: Mu'assasih-yi Millí-yi Maṭbú'át-i Amrí, 104 BE/1947–132 BE/1976; vol. 10, unpublished TS.

ZH Mázandarání, Asadu'lláh Fáḍil. *Táríkh-i Ẓuhúr ul-Ḥaqq*. 9 vols.: vol. 3, Tehran, n.d.; vol. 4, Hofheim: Bahá'í-Verlag, 2011; vol. 8 (parts 1 and 2), Tehran: Mu'assasih-yi Millí-yi Maṭbú'át-i Amrí, 131–2 BE; vols. 5, 6, 7, 9, undated MSS. in private hands.

Ābādihī, Qābil. [Tārīkh-i Amr]. Untitled general history of the Bābī and Bahā'ī Faiths. MS, completed 85 BE/1928. 164 pp.

— Tārīkh-i Amrī-yi Ābādih. Completed in 1926; MS A, dated Sharaf 82 BE/January 1926, 178 pp.; MS B, Sha'bān 1344/February 1926. 148 pp. Published as *Vaqāyī'-yi Amrī-yi Ābādih* (ed., intro. and appendices by Ghulām-'Alī Dihqān). Hofheim: Bahā'ī-Verlag, 2007.

— Tārīkh-i Amrī-yi 'Aliyābād. MS, written 83 BE/1926. 21 pp.

— Tārīkh-i Amrī-yi Hurmuzak. MS, written 1926. 10 pp.

— Tārīkh-i Amrī-yi Ḥusaynābād. MS, completed 83 BE/1926. 71 pp.

— Tārīkh-i Amrī-yi 'Izzābād, Sharafābād va Mahdiyābād. MS, completed 1925. 35 quarto pp.

'Abdu'l-Bahā, *Makātīb-i 'Abdu'l-Bahā*, 8 vols. 1–3. Cairo: Maṭba'ah Kurdistān al-'Ilmiyyah 1910–22; vols. 4–8. Tehran: Mu'assisih-yi Millī-yi Maṭbū'āt-i Amrī, 121–34 BE/1964–76.

— *Memorials of the Faithful*. Wilmette, IL: Bahā'ī Publishing Trust, 1971.

— *Muntakhabātī az Makātīb-i Ḥaḍrat-i 'Abdu'l-Bahā*, vol. 4. Hofheim: Bahā'ī-Verlag, 2000.

— *Selections from the Writings of 'Abdu'l-Bahā*. Haifa: Bahā'ī World Centre, 1978.

['Abdu'l-Bahā]. *A Traveller's Narrative Written to Illustrate the Episode of the Bāb* (trans. E.G. Browne). 2 vols. Cambridge: Cambridge University Press, 1891.

Abīzādih, 'Abdu'llāh. Nigāhī bih Vaqāyī'-yi Tārīkhī-yi Amr dar Ustān-i Hamadān. MS, completed September 1986. 655 pp. In private hands.

Adamec, Ludwig. *Historical Gazetteer of Iran*. 4 vols. Graz: Akademische Druck-u. Verlagsanstalt, 1976–89.

Ādamiyyat, Firaydūn. *Andīshih-hā-yi Mīrzā Āqā Khān Kirmānī*. Tehran: Ṭahhūrī, 1346/1967.

Afary, Janet. *The Iranian Constitutional Revolution, 1906–1911: Grassroots Democracy, Social Democracy and the Origins of Feminism*. New York: Columbia University Press, 1996.

Afḍal ul-Mulk (Mīrzā Ghulām-Ḥusayn). *Safarnāmih-yi Iṣfahān* (ed. Nāṣir Afshārfar). Tehran: Vizārat-i Farhang va Irshād-i Islāmī, 1379 AHS/2000.

Afnān, Abu'l-Qāsim. *'Ahd-i A'lā: Zindigānī-yi Haḍrat-i Bāb*. Oxford: Oneworld, 2000.

— 'Dāstān-i Kutak Khurdan-i Mīrzā Naṣru'llāh Jahrumī', *Payām-i Bahā'ī*, no. 182 (Jan. 1995) 37–40.

— 'Shuhadā-yi Abarqū', *Payām-i Bahā'ī*, no. 189 (Aug. 1995) 28–30.

Afnān, Ḥabibu'llāh. *Khāṭirāt-i Mīrzā Ḥabibu'llāh Afnān* (comp. Maryam Afnan). Hofheim: Bahā'ī-Verlag, 2011.

— 'Tārīkh-i Amrī-yi Shīrāz'. MS, covers events up to 1909. 602 pp. Trans. as *The Genesis of the Bābī and Bahā'ī Faiths in Shirāz and Fārs* (trans. Ahang Rabbani). Leiden: Brill, 2008.

Afnān, Muḥammad. ''Abu'l-Ḥasan Mīrzā Shaykh ur-Ra'īs', *'Andalīb*, year 16, no. 63 (Summer 1997) 39–46, 52.

Afnān, Muḥammad Taqī. 'Ḥikāyat-i Ḥazīratu'l-Quds-i Sughād', *Payām-i Bahā'ī*, no. 201 (Aug. 1996) 15–16, 27.

Afroukhteh, Dr Youness. *Memories of Nine Years in 'Akkā*. Oxford: George Ronald, 2003.

Afshār, Īraj. *Yazd-Nāmih*, vol. 1. Tehran: Intishārāt Farhang-i Īrān-Zamīn, 1371/1992.

Agāh, Badī'u'llāh. 'Sharḥ-i Aḥvāl-i Sirāj ul-Ḥukamā Avvalīn Muṣaddiq-i Amr-i Bahā'ī dar Ābādih', *Āhang-i Badī'*, year 5, no. 9 (Mashiyyat 107 BE/September 1950) 187–91; year 5, no. 10 ('Ilm 107 BE/October 1950) 207–10, 215, 220.

Agāh, Rahbar. 'Mukhtaṣarī dar Sharḥ-i Aḥvāl-i Mīrzā 'Aṭā'u'llāh Sirāj ul-Ḥukamā Avval Man Amana-yi Ābādih', *Payām-i Bahā'ī*, no. 123 (Feb. 1990) 23–5.

Āhang-i Badī'. Periodical published by the Bahā'ī community of Iran. Tehran: vols. 1–32 (1946–78).

Ahdieh, Hussein, and Hillary Chapman. *Awakening: A History of the Bābī and Bahā'ī Faiths in Nayrīz*. Wilmette, IL.: Bahā'ī Publishing Trust, 2013.

Akhbār-i Amrī. Periodical published by the Bahā'ī community of Iran. Tehran: vols. 1–57 (1921–78).

'Alā'ī, 'Abdu'l-'Alī. *Mu'assasih-yi Ayādī-yi Amru'llāh*. Tehran: Mu'assasih-yi Millī-yi Maṭbū'āt-i Amrī, 130 BE/1973.

'Alāqiband Yazdī, Hāj Āqā Muḥammad. *Tārīkh-i Mashrūṭiyyat*. MS, issued as vol. 2 of ILMA. Breaks off while recording events of 31 October 1910. 477 pp.

Algar, Hamid. *Religion and State in Iran 1785–1906*. Berkeley: University of California Press, 1969.

d'Allemagne, Henry René. *Du Khorassan au pays des Backhtiaris: trois mois de voyage en Perse*. 4 vols. Paris: Hachette, 1911.

Amanat, Abbas (ed.). *Cities and Trade: Consul Abbott on the Economy and Society of Iran, 1847–1866*. Oxford Oriental Monographs no. 5. London: Ithaca Press for the Board of the Faculty of Oriental Studies, Oxford University, 1983.

— *Resurrection and Renewal: The Making of the Babi Movement in Iran, 1844–1850*. Ithaca: Cornell University Press, 1989.

Amanat, Mehrdad. *Jewish Identities in Iran: Resistance and Conversion to Islam and the Baha'i Faith*. London: I.B. Tauris, 2011.

— 'Negotiating Identities: Iranian Jews, Muslims and Baha'is in the Memoirs of Rayhan Rayhani (1859–1939)'. PhD thesis. University of California, Los Angeles, 2006.

Amānat, Mūsā. Abnā-yi Khalīl-i Kashānī: Bahā'īyān-i Kalīmī-nizhād. MS, Los Angeles, 1998. 438 pp.

— 'Aḥibbā-yi Kalīmī-tabār-i Kāshān', *Payām-i Bahā'ī*, nos. 236–7 (Jul.–Aug. 1999) 49–53, 66–70.

— Bahā'īyān-i Furqānī-yi Kāshān. MS, Los Angeles, 1998. 390 pp.

— *Bahā'īyān-i Kāshān* (ed. Noura Amanat-Samimi). Madrid: Fundacion Nehal, 2012.

— 'Kayfiyat-i Iqbāl-i Yahūdiyān-i Hamadān bih Diyānat-i Bahā'ī', *Payām-i Bahā'ī*, no. 210 (May 1997) 19–24; no. 215 (Oct. 1997) 22–4; no. 216 (Nov. 1997) 28–32; no. 217 (Dec. 1997) 24–8.

'Amīdu'l-Aṭibbā Hamadānī, Mīrzā Yaḥyā. 'Tārīkh-i Amrī-yi Rasht'. MS, completed in Rabi' I 1345 AHQ/Sept. 1926. 78 pp.

al-Amīn, Ḥasan. *Mustadrakāt A'yān ush-Shī'ah*. 10 vols. Beirut: Dār at-Ta'arruf li'l-Maṭbū'āt, 1408 AHQ/1987–1410 AHQ/1989.

al-Amīn, Muḥsin. *A'yān ush-Shī'ah*. 11 vols. Beirut: Dār at-Ta'arruf li'l-Maṭbū'āt, 1406 AHQ/1985.

Amīnī, Tūraj. *Rastākhīz-i Pinhān: Bāzgushāyī-yi nisbat-i Āyīn-hā-yi Bābī va Bahā'ī bā jaryān-i rawshanfikrī-yi Īrān*. Spånga, Sweden: Baran, 2012.

'Andalīb. Periodical published by the Bahā'ī community of Canada. Thornhill, ON: vols. 1– (1981–).

Anonymous. 'Risālih-yi Istidlāliyyih-yi Āqā Mīrzā Maḥmūd Kāshānī', *'Andalīb*, no. 71 (Summer 1999) 61–5.

Anonymous. 'Shammih-iy dar bārih-yi Madāris-i Bahā'ī-yi Ābādih', *Payām-i Bahā'ī*, no. 164 (Jul. 1993) 31–3; no. 166 (Sep. 1993) 31–4.

Anonymous. 'Sharḥ-i Aḥvāl-i Ḥājiyyih Bībī Sughrā'. *Āhang-i Badī'*, year 28, nos. 7–8 (1973–4) 28–9.

Anonymous. 'Sharḥ-i Ḥāl va Khadamāt-i Gawhartāj Khānum Thābit', *'Andalīb*, vol. 5, no. 19 (Summer 1986) 58, 67.

Anonymous. Tārīkh-i Amrī-yi Iṣfahān. MS, completed in late 1930. 71 pp.

Anonymous. Tārīkh-i Amrī-yi Sangsar. MS, completed 1311 AHS/1932. 33 pp.

Anvarī, Nūru'd-Dīn. 'Sharḥ-i Ḥāl-i Jamshīd Bahrām Ḥusaynābādī', *'Andalīb*, vol. 17, no. 65 (Winter 1997) 57–60, 43.

Arbāb, Furūgh. *Akhtarān-i Tābān*, vol. 1. Delhi: Mir'āt, 3rd printing, 1999; vol. 2, Delhi: Mir'āt, 1990.

Arjumand, Ḥāj Mahdī. *Gulshan-i Ḥaqāyiq*. [Tehran]: n.p., n.d.

Āvārih, 'Abdu'l-Ḥusayn. *al-Kavākib ud-Durriyih*. 2 vols. Cairo: as-Sa'ādah, 1923. Abbreviated as KD.

Ayman, Iraj. 'Ḥāj Mihdī Arjmand', in Moojan Momen (ed.). *Scripture and Revelation*. Oxford: George Ronald, 1997.

Bāb, The. *Livre de Sept Preuves* (trans. A.-L.-M. Nicolas). Paris: Maisonneuve, 1902.

The Bahā'ī World. vols. 1–12 (1925–54). Wilmette, IL: Bahā'ī Publishing Trust, rpt. 1980.

Bahā'ī, 'Alī Aṣghar. Istinṭāqiyyih-yi Ṭihrān. Work written c. July 1883. MS A, written by Ḥājī Āqā Burūjinī, dated 1333 AHQ/1914, 77 pp.; MS B, undated, no scribe indicated. 145 pp. (Text of MS A ends on p. 80 of MS B.)

Bahā'ī, Mīrzā Muḥammad 'Alī Khān. 'Gūshih-iy az Tārīkh'. *Ahang-i Badī'*, year 26 (1350 AHS/1971), no. 12, pp. 381–8.

Bahā'u'llāh. *Epistle to the Son of the Wolf.* Wilmette, IL: Bahā'ī Publishing Trust, 1988.

— *Gleanings from the Writings of Bahā'u'llāh.* Wilmette, IL: Bahā'ī Publishing Trust, 1983.

— *The Kitāb-i-Aqdas.* Haifa: Bahā'ī World Centre, 1992.

— *Kitāb-i Badī'.* Prague: Zero Palm Press, 148 BE/1992.

— *Mā'idih-yi Āsmānī,* see Ishrāq-Khāvari.

— *Majmū'ih-yi Maṭbū'ih-yi Alvāḥ.* Wilmette, IL: Bahā'ī Publishing Trust, rpt. 1978.

Bakhash, Shaul. *Iran: Monarchy, Bureaucracy and Reform under the Qajars: 1858–1896.* London: Ithaca Press and Middle East Centre, St Anthony's College, 1978.

Bakhtiyārī, Sardār A'sad. *Khāṭirāt* (ed. Īraj Afshār). Tehran: Saṭīr, 1372/1993.

Balyuzi, H. M. *'Abdu'l-Bahā: The Centre of the Covenant of Bahā'u'llāh.* Oxford: George Ronald, 2nd ed. with minor corr. 1987.

— *The Bāb: The Herald of the Day of Days.* Oxford: George Ronald, 1973.

— *Bahā'u'llāh: The King of Glory.* Oxford: George Ronald, 1980.

— *Edward Granville Browne and the Bahā'ī Faith.* Oxford: George Ronald, 1970. Translated into Persian and revised by the author, *Idvārd Giranvīl Birawn va Diyānat-i Bahā'ī* (ed. Moojan Momen). Hofheim: Bahā'ī Verlag, 2016.

— *Eminent Bahā'īs in the Time of Bahā'u'llāh: With Some Historical Background.* Oxford: George Ronald, 1985.

— *Khadījih Bagum.* Oxford: George Ronald, 1981.

Bāmdād, Mahdī. *Tārīkh-i Rijāl-i Īrān.* 6 vols. Tehran: Zavvār, 1347 AHS/1968–1351 AHS/1972.

Bashīr-Ilāhī, 'Abdu'l-Ḥusayn. 'Sharḥ-i Ḥāl-i Mutaṣā'id ila Allāh Mīrzā Āqā Khān Bashīr-Ilāhī', *Āhang-i Badī'*, year 29, no. 325 (Mar.–Apr. 1974/131 BE) 38–46.

Bashīr-Ilāhī, Nāṣir. *Alvāḥ Nāzilih bih I'zāz-i Mīrzā Āqā Khān Bashīr us-Sulṭān Mulaqqab bih Bashīr Ilāhī.* Ellicott City, MD: privately published, 2010.

Bassett, James. *Persia: Eastern Mission.* Philadelphia, PA: Presbyterian Board of Education, 1890.

Bāstānī-Parīzī, Muḥammad Ibrāhīm. *Vādī Haft Vād*, vol. 1. Tehran: Anjuman-i Āthār-i Millī, 2535 SH/1977.

Bayat, Mangol. *Iran's First Revolution: Shi'ism and the Constitutional Revolution of 1905–1909*. New York: Oxford University Press, 1991.

— *Mysticism and Dissent: Socioreligious Thought in Qajar Iran*. Syracuse, NY: Syracuse University Press, 1982.

Bayḍā, Āqā Sayyid Abu'l-Qāsim. *Tārīkh-i Bayḍā* (ed. Siyamak Zabihi-Moghaddam). Hofheim: Bahā'ī-Verlag, 2016.

Bémont, Fredy. *Les Villes d'Iran: des cités d'autrefois a l'urbanisme contemporain*. 2 vols. Paris: privately published (?), 1969–73.

Blomfield, Lady [Sara Louise]. *The Chosen Highway*. Oxford: George Ronald, rpt. 2007.

Boyce, Mary. *A Persian Stronghold of Zoroastrianism*. Oxford: Clarendon Press, 1977.

Brookshaw, Dominic Parviz, and Seena B. Fazel (eds.). *The Baha'is of Iran*. Routledge Advances in Middle East and Islamic Studies, vol. 12. London: Routledge, 2008.

Browne, Edward Granville. [Diaries kept during his journey in Iran 1887–8]. Pembroke College Library, Cambridge (now digitized at https://cudl.lib.cam.ac.uk/view/MS-LC-II-00073; also 74 and 75, accessed 16 Sep. 2019).

— *Materials for the Study of the Bābī Religion*. Cambridge: Cambridge University Press, 1918.

— *The Persian Revolution, 1905–1909*. Cambridge: Cambridge University Press, 1910.

— *Press and Poetry of Modern Persia*. Cambridge: Cambridge University Press, 1914; Los Angeles: Kalimāt Press, rpt. 1983.

— *Selections from the Writings of E. G. Browne on the Bābī and Bahā'ī Religions* (ed. Moojan Momen). Oxford: George Ronald, 1987.

— *A Traveller's Narrative*. See ['Abdu'l-Bahā]. *A Traveller's Narrative*.

— *A Year Among the Persians*. Cambridge: Cambridge University Press, new ed. 1926.

Century of Light. Haifa: Bahā'ī World Centre, 2001.

Churchill, George P. *Persian Statesmen and Notables: Biographical Notices*. Confidential publication. Calcutta: Office of the Superintendent of Government Printing, 1906.

Cole, Juan R. I. 'The Provincial Politics of Heresy and Reform in Qajar Iran: Shaykh al-Rais in Shiraz, 1895–1902'. *Comparative Studies of South Asia, Africa and the Middle East*, 22/1&2 (2002) 119–29.

— 'Religious Dissidence and Urban Leadership: Bahais in Qajar Shiraz and Tehran'. *Iran: Journal of the British Institute of Persian Studies* 37 (1999) 123–42.

Curzon, George Nathaniel. *Persia and the Persian Question*. 2 vols. London: Longman Green, 1892; London: Frank Cass, 2nd printing, 1966.

Daftari, Farhad. *A Short History of the Ismailis*. Edinburgh: Edinburgh University Press, 1998.

Dāʾirat ul-Maʿārif-i Tashayyuʿ (ed. Aḥmad Ṣadr Ḥaj Sayyid Javādī, Kāmrān Fānī and Bahāʾ ud-Dīn Khurramshāhī), vols. 1–. Tehran: Bunyād-i Islāmī-yi Ṭāhir, 1366 AHS–/1986–.

Ḍarrābī, ʿAbduʾr-Raḥīm Kalāntar. *Tārīkh-i Kāshān* (ed. Īraj Afshār). Tehran: Amīr Kabīr, 2536 SH/1977.

Dawlatābādī, Yaḥyā. *Ḥayāt-i Yaḥyā*, vol. 1. Tehran: Ibn Sīnā, 1st ed., n.d.

De Vries, Jelle. *The Babi Question You Mentioned: The Origins of the Bahāʾī Community of the Netherlands, 1844–1962*. Leuven: Peeters, 2002.

Dehqan, Mustafa. 'Notes on a Bahāʾī Polemic against Ahl-i-Haqq'. *Oriente Moderno*, 88 (2008) 137–41.

Dhukāʾī-Bayḍāʾī, Niʿʿmatuʾllāh. *Tadhkirih-yi Shuʿarā-yi Bahāʾī-yi Qarn-i Avval-i Badīʿ*. 4 vols. Tehran: Muʾassisih-yi Millī-yi Maṭbūʿāt-i Amrī, 122–7 BE/1965–70.

Dihgān, Ibrāhīm. *[Kār-nāmih yā Daw Bakhsh Dīgar az] Tārīkh-i Arāk*, vol. 3. Arak: Chāpkhānih Mūsavī, 1345/1966.

Dihkhudā, ʿAlī Akbar. *Lughatnāmih*. CD. Tehran: Intishārāt-i Dānishgāh-i Tihrān, 2nd ed. 1377 AHS/1998.

Dihqān, Ghulām-ʿAlī. Ḥadiqat ur-Raḥmān, photocopy of MS. 1988. 137 pp. In private hands.

Encyclopædia Iranica (ed. Ehsan Yarshater). vols. 1–4, London: Routledge & Kegan Paul, 1985–9; vols. 5–, Costa Mesa, CA: Mazda, 1992–; all articles available at www.iranicaonline.org (accessed 29 Jan. 2020). Abbreviated as EIr.

Faizi (Fayḍī), Abuʾl-Qāsim. *Bih Yād-i Dūst*. Wilmette, IL: National Spiritual Assembly of the Bahāʾīs of the United States, 1998.

Faizi (Fayḍī), Muḥammad ʿAlī. *Ḥayāt-i Ḥaḍrat ʿAbduʾl-Bahā*. repr. Langenhain: Bahāʾī-Verlag, 1986.

— *Khāndān-i Afnān, Sadrih-yi Raḥmān*. Tehran: Muʾassisih-yi Millī-yi Maṭbūʿāt-i Amrī, 127 BE/1970.

— *Nayrīz-i Mishkbīz*. Tehran: Muʾassisih-yi Millī-yi Maṭbūʿāt-i Amrī, 130 BE/1973.

— *Nuqtih-yi Ūlā*. Tehran: Muʾassisih-yi Millī-yi Maṭbūʿāt-i Amrī, 132 BE/1975.

Fāʾizih Khānum. Untitled Treatise and autobiographical account. MS, dated 18 Jamadi II 1342 AHQ/26 January 1924. 242 pp.

Falahi-Skuce, Houri. *A Radiant Gem*. Victoria, BC: privately published, 2004.

Fallāḥ, Muḥammad. 'Tārīkh-i Mukhtaṣar-i Diyānat-i Bahāʾī dar Rafsanjān', *ʿAndalīb*, year 22, no. 86 (2004) 66–80.

Farīdānī, Suhrāb. *Dūstān-i Rāstān: Tārīkh-i Ḥayāt va Khadamāt-i Bahā'iyān-i Pārsī*. 2 vols. Hofheim: Bahā'ī-Verlag, 2002.

— 'Sharḥ-i Mukhtaṣarī dar bārih-yi Madāris-i Bahā'ī dar Yazd', *'Andalīb*, year 10, no. 37 (Winter 1991) 35–6.

Farkhā, Firishtih. *Tārīkh-i Amr dar Burāzjān*. Thesis. Tehran: Mu'assisih-yi Ma'ārif-i 'Ālī-yi Amr, 1997. 124 pp.

Farrāshbandī, 'Alī-Murād. *Tārīkh va Jughrāfiyā-yi Burāzjān yā Sangar-i Mujāhidīn*. 2 vols. Shiraz: Chāpkhānih-yi Aḥmadī, 1336/1957.

Farrukhyār, Ḥusayn. *Mashāhīr-i Kāshān*. Kāshān: Nashr-i Rāsikh, n.d. [c. 1994].

Fasā'ī, Mīrzā Ḥasan. *Fārs-nāmih*. 2 vols. in 1; lithograph 1314/1896; Tehran rpt. [1965]. Much of the first volume is translated as *History of Persia under Qajar Rule* (trans. Heribert Busse), Persian Heritage Series. New York: Columbia University Press, 1972.

Fischel, Walter. 'The Bahai Movement and Persian Jewry', *The Jewish Review* (London), 7 (Dec.-Mar. 1934) 47–55.

Fischer, Michael. 'Social Change and the Mirrors of Tradition: The Bahā'īs of Yazd', in *The Bahā'ī Faith and Islam* (ed. H. Moayyad). Ottawa: Association for Bahā'ī Studies, 1990, pp. 25–55.

Floor, Willem. 'Borāzjān: A Rural Market Town in Bushire's Hinterland', *Iran, Journal of the British Institute of Persian Studies*, vol. 42 (2004), 179–200.

— 'The Lūṭīs: A social phenomenon in Qājār Persia: A Reappraisal'. *Die Welt des Islams*, new series 13/1–2 (1971) 103–20.

— 'The Merchants (*tujjār*) in Qājār Iran', *Zeitschrift der Deutschen Morgenländischen Gesellschaft* 126 (1976) 101–35.

— 'The Office of Kalāntar in Qājār Persia', *Journal of the Economic and Social History of the Orient*, 14/3 (Dec. 1971) 253–68.

— 'The Police in Qājār Persia', *Zeitschrift der Deutschen Morgenländischen Gesellschaft*, 123 (1973) 293–315.

Fu'ādī (Bushrū'ī), Ḥasan. Manāẓir-i Tārīkhī-yi Nihḍat-i Amr-i Bahā'ī dar Khurāsān. TS, completed 1931, 1954. 461 pp. Published as *Tārīkh-i Diyānat-i Bahā'ī dar Khurāsān* (ed. Mīnūdukht Fu'ādī). Darmstadt: Aṣr-i Jadīd, 2007.

Furūghī, Mīrzā Muḥammad 'Alī. *Sharḥ-i Vaqāyī'-i Amrī dar Narāq*. Tehran: Lajnih-yi Nashr-i Āthār-i Amrī, 106 BE/1950.

Gail, Marzieh. *Summon Up Remembrance*. Oxford: George Ronald, 1987.

Gazetteer of Persia. 4 vols. Compiled by MacGregor et al. in the Intelligence Branch of the Quarter-Master General's Dept. Simla: Printed at the Government Central Printing Office, 1885–1905.

Gazetteer of Persia. 4 vols. Prepared by the General Staff, Headquarters. Simla, India: Government Press, 1910–18.

Geula, Arsalan. *Iranian Bahā'īs from Jewish Background: A Portrait of an Emerging Community*. Claremont, CA: privately published, 2008.

Ghani, Ghassem (Qāsim Ghanī). *Yād-dāsht-hā*, vol. 1. London: Cyrus Ghani, 1980.

Gidney, William Thomas. *The History of the London Society for Promoting Christianity Amongst the Jews*. London: London Society for Promoting Christianity Amongst the Jews, 1908.

Gobineau, Joseph Arthur, Comte de. *Religions et Philosophies dans l'Asie centrale*. Paris: Gallimard, 10th ed., 1957.

— *Trois Ans en Asie*. 2 vols. Paris: Bernard Grasset, 1922.

Gulistānih, Māhmihr. 'Dāstān-i Bībī Buzurg', *Payām-i Badī'*, year 19, nos. 219–20 (Apr.–May 2001) 52–63; no. 221 (Jun. 2001) 28–38.

Gulpāygānī, Mīrzā Abu'l-Faḍl. *Kashf ul-Ghiṭā* (completed by Sayyid Mahdī Gulpāygānī). Ashkhabad, n.d.

— *Rasā'il va Raqā'im* (ed. Rūḥu'llāh Mihrābkhānī). Tehran: Mu'assisih-yi Millī-yi Maṭbū'āt-i Amrī, 134 BE/1977.

Gulzār, Luṭfu'llāh. Untitled Baha'i History of Zavārih. MS, undated. 24 pp.

Guy, Walter B. 'A Jewish Martyr', *Star of the West*, vol. 20 (1930) 374–5.

Ḥabībābādī, Muḥammad 'Alī Mu'allim. *Makārim ul-Āthār*. 5 vols., vols. 1 and 2 in 1 vol. Isfahan: Kamāl, 1362 AHS/1983; vols. 3–5, Isfahan: Idārih-yi Kull-i Farhang va Hunar-i Ustān-i Iṣfahān, 1351 AHS/1973–1352 AHS/1973.

Habibi, James. A Very Brief Life Story of my Grandparents. MS. 3pp.

Ḥāfiẓī, Ḥājī Yuḥannā. Tārīkh-i Zindigī-yi Ḥājī Mīrzā Yuḥannā. 2 vols. TS, c. 1950. 419 pp. Trans. as Hafizi, Yuhanna Yahya. *Memoir: A Family's Life in Iran, 1850–1950* (trans. Jamshid Javid). 2 vols.; privately published, 2011.

Hairi, Abdul-Hadi. *Shi'ism and Constitutionalism in Iran*. Leiden: Brill, 1977.

Hamadānī, Mīrzā Ḥusayn. *The Tārīkh-i-Jadīd or New History of Mīrzā 'Alī Muḥammad the Bāb*. Cambridge: Cambridge University Press, 1893.

Hamadānī, Mīrzā Mahdī Ṭabīb-i. Tārīkh-i Hamadān va Rasht. MS. Contains events up to 1921. 172 pp.

Ḥaqīqat, 'Abdu'r-Rafī' (Rafī'). *Tārīkh-i 'Irfān va 'Ārifān-i Īrānī*. Tehran: Kūmish, 1375/1996.

Hardinge, Arthur. *A Diplomat in the East*. London: Jonathan Cape, 1928.

Harper, Barron. *Lights of Fortitude: Glimpses into the Lives of the Hands of the Cause of God*. Oxford: George Ronald, 1997.

Hidāyatī, Rūḥangīz. 'Madrasih-yi Dukhtarānih-yi Hūshangī Yazd va Daw Madrasih Dīgar', *Payām-i Bahā'ī*, no. 155 (Oct. 1992) 29–31.

Himmat-Kirmānī, Maḥmūd. *Tārīkh-i Mufaṣṣal-i Kirmān*. Kirmān: Furūsh-gāh-i Himmat, 1350/1972.

Ḥirzu'd-Dīn, Muḥammad. *Ma'ārif ur-Rijāl*. Qum: Manshūrāt-i Maktabih-yi Āyatu'llāh al-'Uzmā al-Mar'ashī al-Najafī, 1405/1984.

Hizārī, Ḥabīb. 'Jināb-i Ardishīr Hizārī', *'Andalīb*, year 18, no. 70 (Spring 1999) 40–3.

Hizārī, Rashīd. Vaqāyī'-yi Tārīkhī. MS, 1980. 157pp. In private hands.

Hobsbawm, Eric. *Bandits*. London: Weidenfeld and Nicolson, 1969; revised ed. 2000.

Hunarfar, Luṭfu'llāh. *Ganjīnih-yi Āthār-i Tārīkhiyyih-yi Iṣfahān*. Isfahan: Kitābfurūshī-yi Thaqafī, 1344/1965.

Īmānī, Ṭaybiyyih. 'Tārīkh-i Amrī-yi Rafsanjān az Buduw Ẓuhūr tā Sāl-i 1362 Hijrī Shamsī'. Thesis. Mu'assisih-yi Ma'ārif-i 'Alī, Iran. 1379/2000. 238 pp.

Intishārāt Lajnih-yi Millī-yi Maḥfaẓih-yi Āthār va Ārshīv-i Amr: photocopied collection of the manuscripts in the National Bahā'ī Archives of Iran, 105 volumes. Available at: http://www.afnanlibrary.org/docs/persian-arabic-mss/inba/ (accessed 29 Jan. 2020).

Ioannesyan, Youli. *The Development of the Babi/Baha'i Communities: Exploring Baron Rosen's Archives*. London: Routledge, 2013.

Iṣfahānī, Mīrzā Asadu'llāh. Yād-dāsht-hā. MS completed c. 1300 AHS. 135 pp.

Iṣfahānī, Ḥājī Mīrzā Ḥaydar 'Alī. *Bihjat uṣ-Ṣudūr*. Hofheim: Bahā'ī-Verlag, 2002, partly trans. as *Stories from the Delight of Hearts* (trans. A.Q. Faizi). Los Angeles: Kalimāt, 1980.

[Iṣfahānī], Hadji Mirza Heidar Ali. *Bahai Martyrdoms in Persia in the year 1903* (trans. Youness Khan [Afrūkhtih]). Chicago: Bahai Publishing Society, 1904 (the authorship of this is wrongly attributed to Ḥājī Mīrzā Ḥaydar 'Alī Iṣfahānī; it is in fact by 'Abdu'l-Bahā).

Ishrāq-Khāvarī, 'Abdu'l-Ḥamīd. 'Dūstān Sharḥ-i Parīshānī-yi Man Gūsh Kunīd'. *Āhang-i Badī'*, year 27, nos. 1–2 (1972–3) 10–18.

— *Ganjīnih-yi Ḥudūd va Aḥkām*. New Delhi: Bahā'ī Publishing Trust, rpt. 1980.

— *Mā'idih-yi Āsmānī*. 9 vols. Tehran: Mu'assisih-yi Millī-yi Maṭbū'āt-i Amrī, 121–9 BE/1964–72.

— *Muḥāḍarāt*. 2 vols. Tehran: Mu'assisih-yi Millī-yi Maṭbū'āt-i Amrī, 120–1 BE/1963–4.

— *Nūrayn Nayyirayn*. Tehran: Mu'assisih-yi Millī-yi Maṭbū'āt-i Amrī, 123 BE/1966.

— *Qamūs-i Tawqī'-i Manī'-i Mubārak-i Sanih-yi 105 Badī'*. 2 vols. Tehran: Mu'assisih-yi Millī-yi Maṭbū'āt-i Amrī, 118 BE/1963.

— *Raḥīq-i Makhtūm*. 2 vols. Tehran: Mu'assisih-yi Millī-yi Maṭbū'āt-i Amrī, 130 BE/1973.

— *Taqvīm-i Tārīkh-i Amr*. Tehran: Mu'assisih-yi Millī-yi Maṭbū'āt-i Amrī, 126 BE/1969.

— *Tārīkh-i Amrī-yi Hamadān* (ed. Vahid Rafati). Hofheim: Bahā'ī-Verlag, 2004.

— *Yādgār*. Dundas, ON: Association for Bahā'ī Studies in Persian, 1994.

Issawi, Charles. *The Economic History of Iran 1800–1914*. Chicago: Chicago University Press, 1971.

I'timād us-Salṭanih (Muḥammad Ḥasan Khān). *Rūznāmih-yi Khāṭirāt-i I'timād us-Salṭanih*. Tehran: Amīr Kabīr, 1377 AHS/1998.

Īzadīniyā, Farūq and Farzād Naẕīrī. *Amr-i Mubārak dar Arḍ-i Kāf va Rā'*. n.p.: Adel, n.d.

Jackson, A.V. Williams. *Zoroastrian Studies*. New York: Columbia University Press, 1928.

Ja'farī, Yaḥyā. Pā-varaqī dar bārih-yi dhayl-i ṣafḥih-yi 349 jild-i shishum Kitāb-i Ẕuhūr ul-Ḥaqq. 1998. 4 pp. Copy in author's possession.

Jamālzādih, Sayyid Muḥammad 'Alī. *Khāṭirāt-i Sayyid Muḥammad 'Alī Jamālzādih* (ed. Īraj Afshār and 'Alī Dihbāshī). Tehran: Shahāb Thāqib and Sukhan, 1378/1999.

— *Sar u tah-i yik karbās* (ed. 'Alī Dihbāshī). Tehran: Sukhan, 3rd ed., 1389/2011.

Jasion, Jan. *'Abdu'l-Bahā in the West: A Biographical Guide of People associated with His Travels*. Paris: Éditions bahā'īes France, [2012].

Kār, Mihrangīz. 'Humā Rūḥī: Avvalīn Dabīr-i Kull-i Sāzimān-i Zanān-i Īrān'. http://www.iran-emrooz.net/index.php?/zanan/more/17355/ (accessed 28 Aug. 2019).

Kasheff, Manouchehr. 'Anjoman-e Zartoštīān', *Encyclopædia Iranica* (see above).

Keddie, Nikki. *Sayyid Jamal al-Din 'al-Afghani'*. Berkeley: University of California Press, 1972.

— *Religion and Rebellion in Iran: The Iranian Tobacco Protest of 1891–1892*. London: Frank Cass, 1966.

Khoshbin, Parivash Samandari. *Ṭarāz-i Ilāhī*, vol. 1. Hamilton, ON: Mu'assasih-yi Ma'ārif-i Bahā'ī, 2002.

Khusravī, Muḥammad Riḍā. *Tughyān-i Nāyibīn dar Jariyān-i Inqilāb-i Mashrūṭiyyat-i Īrān*. Tehran: Intishārāt Bih-Nigār, 1368/1989.

Kirmānī, Aḥmad 'Alī Vazīrī. *Tārīkh-i Kirmān (Salāriyyih)* (ed. Muḥammad Ibrāhīm Bāstānī-Parīzī). Tehran: Kitāb-hā-yi Īrān, 1340.

Kirmānī, Aḥmad Majd ul-Islām. *Tārīkh-i Inḥilāl-i Majlis*. Isfahan: Intishārāt-i Dānishgāh-i Iṣfahān, 1972.

Kirmānī, Nāẓim ul-Islām. *Tārīkh-i Bīdārī-yi Irāniyān* (ed. 'Alī Akbar Sa'īdī Sīrjānī). 1st ed., Part 1: 3 vols. in 1 vol. [Tehran]: Bunyād-i Farhang-i Īrān, 1346 AHS/1967. Also used 5th ed., vol. 1, Tehran: Paykan, 1376/1997.

Labīb, Muḥammad. Khāṭirāt-i Shast-Rūzih. 1976. Photocopy of typescript in the author's possession. 371 pp.

— Majmū'ih-yi Muṣavvar: 'Ahd-i A'lā (Sanih 1 tā 9 Badī'). Photocopy of typescript in author's possession. 2 vols. 1,160 pp.

— *The Seven Martyrs of Hurmuzak* (trans. Moojan Momen). Oxford: George Ronald, 1981.

Levy, Habib. *Tārīkh-i Yahūd-i Īrān.* 3 vols. [Tehran]: Berukhim, 1954–60; abridged trans.: *Comprehensive History of the Jews of Iran: The Outset of the Diaspora* (abridged and ed. Hooshang Ebrami and trans. George W. Maschke). Costa Mesa, CA: Mazda, 1999.

Litvak, Meir. *Shi'i Scholars of Nineteenth Century Iraq: The 'Ulama' of Najaf and Karbala'.* Cambridge: Cambridge University Press, 1998.

Lorimer, John G. *Gazetteer of the Persian Gulf, 'Oman, and Central Arabia.* 2 vols. in 6. Calcutta: Superintendent Government Printing, 1908–15.

Mahdavi, Asghar, and Iraj Afshar. *Documents Inedit concernant Seyyed Jamāl-al-Dīn Afghānī.* Tehran: Université de Tehran, 1342/1963.

Majd ul-Islām. See Kirmānī, Aḥmad Majd ul-Islām.

Malcolm, Napier. *Five Years in a Persian Town.* London: John Murray, 1908.

Malik-Khusravī, Muḥammad 'Alī. *Tārīkh-i Shuhadā-yi Amr.* 3 vols. Tehran: Mu'assasih-yi Millī-yi Maṭbū'āt-i Amrī, 130 BE.

Malikzādih, Mahdī. *Tārīkh-i Inqilāb-i Mashruṭiyyat-i Īrān.* 7 vols. Tehran: Sukhan, 1383 AHS/2004.

— *Zindigī-yi Malik ul-Mutakallimīn.* Tehran: Shirkat-i Nasabī-yi 'Alī Akbar 'Alamī, 1325 AHS/1946.

Malmīrī, Ḥājī Muḥammad Ṭāhir. *Khāṭirāt-i Mālmīrī.* Langenhain: Lajnih-yi Nashr-i Āthār-i Amrī bih Zabān-i Farsī va 'Arabī, 1992.

— *Tārīkh-i Shuhadā-yi Yazd.* Pakistan, 2nd printing, 135 BE/1978.

— *Tārīkh-i Amrī-yi Yazd.* Bundoora, Vic., Australia: Century Press, 2013.

Manshādī, Sayyid Muḥammad Ṭabībī. *Sharh Shahādat-i Shuhadā-yi Manshād.* Tehran: Mu'assasih-yi Millī-yi Maṭbū'āt-i Amrī, 127 BE/1970. Trans. Ahang Rabbani and Naghmeh Astani. 'The Martyrs of Manshad', *World Order* 28/1 (Fall 1996) 21–36.

Mashhūrī, Dilārām (Fāḍil Ghaybī). *Rag-i Tāk.* 2 vols. Vincennes, France: Khavaran, 2nd printing, 1378/1999.

Māzandarānī, Asadu'llāh Fāḍil. *Amr va Khalq.* 4 vols. Langenhain: Lajnih-yi Nashr-i Āthār-i Amrī bih Zabān-i Fārsī va 'Arabī, 1986.

— *Asrār ul-Āthār.* 5 vols. Tehran: Mu'assasih-yi Millī-yi Maṭbū'āt-i Amrī, 124–9 BE/1967–72.

— *Tārīkh-i Ẓuhūr ul-Ḥaqq,* vol. 3. Tehran: n.p., n.d.; vol. 4. Hofheim: Bahā'ī-Verlag, 2011; vol. 8 (parts 1 and 2). Tehran: Mu'assasih-yi Millī-yi Maṭbū'āt-i Amrī, 131–

2 BE; vols. 5, 6, 7, 9, undated MS. In private hands. All vols. abbreviated as ZH.

Mihrābkhānī, Rūḥu'llāh. Nāmih-yi Zindigī, vol. 1. MS, c. 1950. 142 pp. In private hands.

— Zindigānī-yi Mīrzā Abu'l-Faḍl-i Gulpāygānī. Langenhain: Bahā'ī-Verlag, 1988.

The Ministry of the Custodians, 1957–1963: An Account of the Stewardship of the Hands of the Cause. Haifa: Bahā'ī World Centre, 1992.

Minorsky, V. 'The Gūrān', Bulletin of the School of Oriental and African Studies 11 (1943) 75–102.

— 'Notes sur le secte des Ahlē-Haqq – deuxième partie', Revue du monde musulman 40–1 (1921) 205–302.

Mīthāqī-Nayrīzī, Jalāl. 'Madrasih-yi Bahā'ī-yi Nayrīz va Khāṭirāt-i Ayyām-i Kūdakī', 'Andalīb, year 9, no. 35 (Summer 1990) 64–5.

Molavi-Nejad, Saleh (ed.). Ishrāq-Khāvarī, Zindigī, Āthār va Khāṭirat. Madrid: Fundacion Nehal, 2009.

Momen, Moojan. The Ayman/Iman Family. Los Angeles: Privately published, 2002.

— The Bābī and Bahā'ī Religions, 1844–1944: Some Contemporary Western Accounts. Oxford: George Ronald, 1980. Abbreviated as BBR.

— 'The Baha'i Community of Ashkhabad: Its Social Basis and Importance in Baha'i History', in Cultural Change and Continuity in Central Asia (ed. S. Akiner). London: Kegan Paul, 1991, pp. 278–305.

— 'The Baha'i Community of Iran: Patterns of Exile and Problems of Communication', in Iranian Refugees and Exiles since Khomeini (ed. Asghar Fathi). London: Mazda Publications, 1991, pp. 21–36.

— 'Early Relations between Christian Missionaries and the Bahā'ī Faith', in Studies in Bābī and Bahā'ī History, vol. 1 (ed. Moojan Momen). Los Angeles: Kalimāt, 1982, pp. 49–82.

— An Introduction to Shi'i Islam: The History and Doctrines of Twelver Shi'ism. New Haven and London: Yale University Press; Oxford: George Ronald; New Delhi and Bombay: Oxford University Press, 1985.

— The Momen (Ulfat) Family History. Nyon, Switzerland: Privately published, 2018.

— 'Social Basis of the Bābī Upheavals in Iran (1848–53): A Preliminary Analysis', International Journal of Middle East Studies 15 (1983) 157–83.

Mu'ayyad, Ḥabīb. Khāṭirāt-i Ḥabīb, vol. 1. Hofheim: Bahā'ī-Verlag, 1998.

— Sharḥ-i Shahādat-i Jināb-i Mīrzā Ya'qūb Mutaḥḥidih. Tehran: Lajnih-yi Millī-yi Nashr-i Āthār-i Amrī, 100 BE/1943.

Mu'ayyad, Ḥishmat. 'Na'īm-i Sidihī va Shi'r-i ū', 'Andalīb, year 23, no. 90 (2006) 34–49.

Mu'ayyad, Surūsh. 'Ḥājj Khudābakhsh Mu'ayyad-i Kirmānshāhī', 'Andalīb, no. 73 (2000) 75–8.

Mudarris (Jānimī Najafābādī), Fatḥu'llāh. Tārīkh-i Amrī-yi Najafābād. MS in the handwriting of Muḥammad 'Alī Malik-Khusravī, undated. 52 pp. Published as *Tārīkh-i Amr-i Bahā'ī dar Najafābād* (ed. Vahid Rafati). Darmstad: 'Aṣr-i Jadīd, 2004.

Mudarrisī-Ṭabāṭabā'ī, Ḥusayn (ed.). *Qumm-nāmih*. Qumm: Intishārāt Kitābkhānih-yi 'Umūmī-yi Āyatu'llāh ul-'Uzmā Najafī-Mar'ashī, 1364 AHS/1895.

Muḥammad-Ḥusaynī, Nuṣratu'llāh. 'Darvīshān va 'Ārifān', *Payām-i Bahā'ī*, no. 162 (May 1993) 17–19.

— *Ḥaḍrat-i Bāb*. Dundas, ON: Institute for Bahā'ī Studies in Persian, 1995.

— 'Muqaddamat-i tārīkhī-yi nuzūl-i Lawḥ-i Mubārak-i Aḥmad', *'Andalīb*, vol. 2, no. 6 (Spring 1983) 32–9.

— 'Tārīkh-i Ardistān va Alvāḥ-i Haḍrat-i Fatḥ-i A'zam', *'Andalīb*, year 22, no. 86 (2004) 57–65.

— *Tārīkh-i Amr-i Bahā'ī dar Shahr-i Qumm*. Darmstadt: 'Aṣr-i Jadīd, 2005.

Munjadhib, Mahtā. Mukhtaṣarī az Tārīkh-i Amr Allāh dar Māzgān. Thesis. Mu'assisih-yi Ma'ārif-i 'Ālī-yi Amr, 162 BE/2015, revised 175 BE/2018.

Nabavī Raḍavī, Miqdād. *Tārīkh-i Maktūm*. Tehran: Pardīs Dānish, 1393/2014.

Nabīl [-i A'zam Zarandī]. *The Dawn-Breakers: Nabīl's Narrative of the Early Days of the Bahā'ī Revelation* (trans. and ed. Shoghi Effendi). Wilmette, IL: Bahā'ī Publishing Trust, 1970. Abbreviated as DB.

— *Mathnavī*. Hofheim: Bahā'ī-Verlag, 2nd ed. 1995.

Nabīlī, Nāṣir. 'Arḍ-i Kāf va Rā', *Safīnih-yi 'Irfān* 13 (2012) 133–72.

Nādirī, Bahiyyih. 'Sharḥ-i Zindigānī-yi Bahiyyih Khānum-i Nādirī bih Qalam-i Khud-i Īshān', *Payām-i Bahā'ī*, no. 349 (Dec. 2008) 36–40; no. 350 (Jan. 2009) 18–23; no. 351 (Feb. 2009) 48–53.

Na'īmī, Muḥsin. 'Tarjumih-yi Ḥāl-i Ḥaḍrat-i Na'īm', in Muḥammad Na'īm, *Aḥsan at-Taqvīm ya Gulzār-i Na'īm* (ed. 'Abdu'l-Ḥusayn Na'īmī). Delhi: Privately published, 1958, pp. 21–54 of Introduction.

Narāqī, Ḥasan. *Kāshān dar Junbish Mashrūṭih-yi Īrān*. Tehran: Chāp Mash'al Āzādī, 2535 SH/1976.

— *Tārīkh-i Ijtimā'ī-yi Kāshān*. Tehran: Mu'assisih-yi Muṭāli'āt va Taḥqīqāt-i Ijtimā'ī, 1340 AHS/1961.

Navā'ī, 'Abdu'l-Ḥusayn. *Sharḥ-i Ḥāl-i 'Abbās Mīrzā Mulk-Ārā*. Tehran: Bābak, 2nd ed. 2535 SH/1976.

Navvāb Vakīl, Sayyid Muḥammad Raḍavī. *Khāṭirāt-i Navvāb Vakīl*. Tehran: Gītā, 1999.

Navvābzādih Ardakānī, Ṣadrī. *Amr-i Bahā'ī dar Ardakān* (ed. Vahid Rafati). Hofheim: Bahā'ī-Verlag, 2009.

Netzer, Amnon. 'Conversion of Iranian Jews to the Bahā'ī Faith: Early Period', *Irano-Judaica* 6 (2007) 232–65.

Nicolas, A.-L.-M. *Livre de Sept Preuves. See under* The Bāb.

— *Massacres des Babis en Perse.* Paris: Adrien Masionneuve, 1936.

— *Seyyèd Ali Mohammed dit le Bâb.* Paris: Dujarric, 1905.

Nuqabā'ī, Ḥisām. Tārīkh-i Iqbāl va Īmān-i Kalīmiyān va Zardushtiyān bih Amr-i Bahā'ī. MS, c. 1980. In private hands.

Nūr, Āqā Ḥusayn 'Alī. Tārīkh-i Iṣfahān va Muhājirat az Iṣfahān bih Ṭihrān. MS, dated Safar 1346/August 1927. 33 pp.

Nūr, 'Izzat. *Khāṭirāt-i Muhājirī az Iṣfahān dar Zamān-i Shahādat-i Sulṭān ush-Shuhadā and Maḥbūb ush-Shuhadā.* Tehran: Mu'assisih-yi Millī-yi Maṭbū'āt-i Amrī, 128/1971.

Nūshābādī, Ḥasan. 'Rajul-i Rashīd: Mukhtaṣarī az Sharḥ-i Ḥayāt-i Amrī-yi Jināb-i Mīrzā Āqā Khān-i Qā'im-Maqāmī', *Āhang-i Badī'*, year 28, nos. 9–10 (1973–4) 18–39.

Officer, Lawrence H. 'Five Ways to Compute the Relative Value of a UK Pound Amount, 1270 to Present', MeasuringWorth, 2008. https://www.measuringworth.com/calculators/ukcompare (accessed 8 Dec. 2020).

— and Samuel H. Williamson, 'Computing "Real Value" Over Time with a Conversion between U.K. Pounds and U.S. Dollars, 1830 to Present', MeasuringWorth, 2009. https://www.measuringworth.com/calculators/exchange/ (accessed 8 Dec. 2020).

Official Handbook of the Tribes and Personalities of Western Persia. Baghdad: Government Press, 1918.

Poostchi, Iraj. "Adasiyyih: A Study in Agriculture and Rural Development', *Baha'i Studies Review* 16 (2010) 61–105.

Qarāguzlū, Ghulām-Ḥusayn. *Hagmatānih tā Hamadān.* Tehran: Iqbal, 1369/1990.

Qubād, Isfandiyār. *Khāṭirāt.* Mu'assisih-yi Millī-yi Maṭbū'āt-i Amrī, 131/1974.

Qūchānī, Muḥammad. 'Pidar bih ravāyat-i pisar'. *Shahrvand* 49 (Khurdād 1387/May–June 2008). http://www.ensani.ir/fa/content/49406/default.aspx (accessed 5 Aug. 2019).

Qummī, Sayyid Asadu'llāh. Hizār Dāstān. Undated MS. 324 pp.

Rabbani, Ahang. "Abdu'l-Baha in Abu-Sinan: September 1914–May 1915', *Baha'i Studies Review* 13 (2005) 75–103.

— "Abdu'l-Baha's Proclamation on the Persecution of Baha'is in 1903', *Baha'i Studies Review* 14 (2008) 53–67.

— 'The Bab in Shiraz: An Account by Mirza Habibu'llah Afnan', *Baha'i Studies Review* 12 (2004) 91–127.

— The Babis of Nayriz: History and Documents. https://www.academia.edu/634955/ The_Babis_of_Nayriz (accessed 14 Dec. 2019).

— 'The Conversion of the Great-Uncle of the Báb', *World Order*, vol. 30, no. 3 (Spring 1999) 19–38.

— (intro. and trans.). 'Ponder Thou upon the Martyrdom of Hájí Muhammad-Ridá: Nineteen Historical Accounts'. http://bahai-library.com/pdf/r/rabbani_martyr dom_haji_muhammad-rida.pdf (accessed 10 Dec. 2014).

Rafʿat, Yadu'lláh. 'Ridá Qulí Khán Sarvar ush-Shuhadá', *Áhang-i Badíʿ*, year 27, no. 3–4 (1972–3) 29–37.

Rafati, Vahid. 'Nabíl-i Aʿzam-i Zarandí'. *Khúshih-há-iy az Kharman-i Adab va Hunar* 7 (1996) 29–57.

— *Payk-i Rástán*. Darmstadt: ʿAsr-i Jadíd, 2005.

Rahmání, Sháh Khalílu'lláh Big. 'Amr-i Bahá'í dar Fárán', in Rafati, Vahid. *Fárán-i Hubb: Amr-i Bahá'í dar Fárán*. Hofheim: Bahá'í-Verlag, 2012, 281–455.

Rahmání Najafábádí, ʿAtá'u'lláh. 'Sharh-i Ahvál-i Áqá Sayyid ʿAbdur-Rahím Isfahání (mulaqqab bih Ismu'lláh ur-Rahím)', *'Andalíb*, year 23, no. 89 (2005) 68–74.

Rasooli, Jay M. and Cady H. Allen. *Dr Saʿeed of Iran*. Pasadena, CA: William Carey Library, 1957.

Rástí, Bihzád. *Táríkh-i Nufúdh va Intishár-i Amr-i Bahá'í dar Bandar ʿAbbás*. Thesis. Muʾassisih-yi Maʿárif-i ʿÁlí, Iran, 163 BE/2006.

Rástí, Kaykhusraw. 'Ustád Mihrabán Rástí', *'Andalíb*, year 16, no. 61 (Winter 1966) 46–9.

Rastigár, Nasru'lláh. *Táríkh-i Hadrat-i Sadr us-Sudúr*. Tehran: Muʾassisih-yi Millí-yi Matbúʿát-i Amrí, 108 BE/1951.

Rawhání-Nayrízí, Muhammad Shafíʿ. *Lamaʿát ul-Anvár*. 2 vols. in 1. Bundoora, Vic. Australia: Century Press, 2002.

Razmárá, Husayn ʿAlí, and Sartíp Nawtásh. *Farhang Jughráfiyá'í-yi Írán*, 10 vols. Tehran: Dá'irih-yi Jughráfiyá'í-yi Sitár-i Artish, 1327/1948–1332/1953.

Rúz-Námih-yi Vaqáyiʿ-yi Ittifáqiyyih, vol. 1. Tehran: Kitábkhánih-yi Millí Jumhúrí-yi Islámí-yi Írán, 1372 AHS/1993.

Sadeghian, Saghar. 'Minorities and Foreigners in a Provincial Iranian City: Baha'is in the Russian Consulate of Isfahan in 1903', *Journal of Persianate Studies* 9 (2016) 107–32.

Sádiqiyán, ʿInáyatu'lláh. 'Sharh-i Hál-i Jináb-i Ha'ím Isháq Abrár', *Payám-i Bahá'í*, no. 294 (May 2004) 48–50.

Sádiqzádih, Badru'l-Mulúk. *Nufúdh va Paydáyish Amr dar Shahridá*. Thesis. Muʾassisih-yi Maʿárif-i ʿÁlí. Iran: Isfahán, February 2007.

Safá'í, Ibráhím. *Asnád-i Barguzídih*. Tehran: Bábak, 2535 SH/1977.

— *Nāmih-hā-yi Tārīkhī.* Tehran: Bābak, 2535 SH/1977.

Sahim, Haideh. 'Jews of Iran in the Qajar Period: Persecution and Perseverance', in *Religion and Society in Qajar Iran* (ed. Robert M. Gleave). London: RoutledgeCurzon, 2005, 293–319.

Saʿīdī, Nīkā. Tārīkh-i Nufūdh Amr dar Ardistān. Thesis. Muʾassisih-yi Maʿārif-i ʿĀlī, Iran, 2002.

Salmānī, Ustād Muḥammad-ʿAlīy-i-. *My Memories of Bahāʾuʾllāh* (trans. Marzieh Gail). Los Angeles: Kalimāt Presss, 1982.

Ṣamadānī, Muḥsin. 'Āghāz-i Amr-i Ilāhī dar Hamadān', *ʿAndalīb*, year 23, no. 90 (2006) 74–80.

Samandar, Kāẓim. *Āthār-i Qalamī-yi Jināb-i Shaykh Muḥammad Kāẓim Samandar va Baʿḍī Āthār-i Mutafarriqih* (ed. Rūḥuʾllāh Samandarī). Hofheim: Bahāʾī-Verlag, 2011.

Sayyāḥ, Ḥamīd (ed.). *Khāṭirāt-i Ḥājj Sayyāḥ.* Tehran: Amīr Kabīr, 1359/1980.

Schopflocher, Florence. 'Flying in Spiritual and Material Atmosphere', *The Bahaʾi Magazine: Star of the West*, vol. 18, no. 5 (Aug. 1927) 150–4.

Shahīdiyān, Amīnuʾllāh. *Mansūbān-i Āstān-i Ṭalʿat-i Aʿlā (Khāndān-i Afnān).* Bundoora, Vic., Australia: Bahāʾī Distribution Services, 2009.

Shahriyārī, Hishmatuʾllāh. 'Nufūdh-i Amr-i Muqaddas-i Bahāʾī dar Zavārih', *Āhang-i Badīʿ* 9/4 (Tīr 1333/146 BE/1954) 18–21; 9/5 (Murdād 1333/146 BE/1954) 14–20, 25. Updated with further research and republished as 'Nufūdh-i Āʾīn-i Bahāʾī dar Qariyih-yi Zavārih va Sharḥ-i Ḥāl-i Pidar va Pisar-i Shahīd', *Payām-i Bahāʾī*, no. 229 (Dec. 1998) 40–5; no. 230 (Jan. 1999) 46–51.

Shahvar, Soli. *The Forgotten Schools: The Bahaʾis and Modern Education in Iran, 1899–1934.* London: I.B. Tauris, 2009.

Sharīfī, Gloria. 'Mishkīn Qalam', *Payām-i Badīʿ*, no. 89 (May 1990) 24–8.

Shoghi Effendi. *God Passes By.* Wilmette, IL: Bahāʾī Publishing Trust, rev. ed. 1974.

Sifidvash, ʿInāyat-Khudā. *Tani chand az Pīshgāmān-i Parsī-nizhād dar ʿAhd-i Rasūlī.* Dundas, ON: Association for Bahaʾi Studies in Persian, 1999.

Sifidvash, Siyāvash. *Yār-i Dīrīn.* Tehran: Muʾassasih-yi Millī-yi Maṭbūʿāt-i Amrī, 132 BE/1976.

Sipihr, Mīrzā Taqī Lisān ul-Mulk. *Nāsikh ut-Tavārīkh* (ed. Jamshīd Kiyānfar). 3 vols. Tehran: Asāṭīr, 1377 AHS/1998.

Smith, Peter. 'The American Bahaʾi Community, 1894–1917: A Preliminary Survey', in Moojan Momen (ed.) *Studies in Bābī and Bahāʾī History*, vol. 1. Los Angeles: Kalimāt Press, 1982, pp. 85–223.

Stack, Edward. *Six Months in Persia*, 2 vols. London: Sampson Low, Marston, Searle and Rivington, 1882.

Stern, Henry A. *Dawnings of Light in the East*. London: Charles H. Purday, 1854.

Stileman, Charles H. 'A Week with the Babis', *The Church Missionary Intelligencer*, vol. 44, no. 543 (July 1893) 512–16.

Stiles (now Maneck), Susan. 'Early Zoroastrian Conversions to the Bahā'ī Faith in Yazd, Iran', in *From Iran East and West* (ed. Juan Cole and Moojan Momen). Los Angeles: Kalimāt Press, 1984, pp. 67–93.

Subḥī, Faḍlu'llāh Muhtadī. *Khāṭirāt-i Inḥiṭāṭ va Suqūṭ* (ed. 'Alī Amīr Mustawfiyān). Tehran: Nashr-i 'Ilm, 1384/2005.

Suhā, Manūchihr Ṣadūqī. *Tārīkh-i Ḥukamā va 'Urafā-yi Muta'akhirīn-i Ṣadr ul-Muta'alihīn*. Tehran: Anjuman-i Islāmī-yi Ḥikmat va Falsafih-yi Īrān, 1359 AHS/1980.

Sulaymānī, 'Azīzu'llāh. 'Ḥājī Abu'l-Ḥasan Amīn', *Āhang-i Badī'*, year 28, no. 11–12 (1973–4) 31–40.

— *Maṣābīḥ-i Hidāyat*. 9 vols. Tehran: Mu'assasih-yi Millī-yi Maṭbū'āt-i Amrī, 104–32 BE/1947–1976; vol. 10, unpublished TS. All vols. abbreviated as MH.

Sulṭānī, Muḥammad 'Alī. *Tārīkh-i Mufassal-i Kirmānshāhān. Jughrāfiyā-yi tārīkhī va tārīkh-i mufassal-i Kirmānshāhān*. vols. 3 and 4. Tehran: Suhā, 1373.

Sykes, Percy M. *Ten Thousand Miles in Persia or Eight Years in Iran*. London: John Murray, 1902.

Taherzadeh, Adib. *The Revelation of Bahā'u'llāh*, vol. 3. Oxford: George Ronald, 1983.

Tāju'd-Dīnī, Mihrangīz. *Sharḥ-i Ḥāl Shahriyār-i Dayār-i Inqiṭā' Shahīd Āqa Murtaḍā Sārvistānī*. Thesis. Shiraz: Mu'assisih-yi Ma'ārif-i 'Alī, 1375/1996.

Tashakkurī-Bafqī, 'Alī Akbar. *Mashrūṭiyyat dar Yazd*. Tehran: Markaz-i Yazd-shināsī, 1377/1998.

Tavāngar, 'Alī. 'Yādī az Bahā'īyān-i Shahābād-i Arāk', *Payām-i Bahā'ī*, no. 210 (May 1997) 25–6, 28.

Thābitī, Ḥabīb. 'Sharḥ-i Ḥāl-i Jināb-i Ḥakīm Āqā Jān, Avval man Amana-yi Kalīmiyān', *'Andalīb*, year 13, no. 50 (Spring 1994) 62–5.

Thābitī, Ḥabību'llāh. *Vārithān-i Kalīm: Tārīkh-i ḥayāt va khadamāt-i aḥibbā-yi kalīmī-yi Hamadān*. Bundoora, Vic., Australia: Century Press, 2004.

aṭ-Ṭihrānī, Āghā Buzurg (Muḥammad Muḥsin). *adh-Dharī'ah ilā Taṣānīf ush-Shī'ah*. 25 vols. Tehran and Najaf: distributed through author, 1355/1936–1398/1978.

Tsadik, Daniel. *Between Foreigners and Shi'is: Nineteenth Century Iran and its Jewish Minority*. Stanford Studies on Jewish History and Culture. Stanford: Stanford University Press, 2007.

Ṭulū'ī, Dhawqiyyih and Ya'qūb Ṭulū'ī. 'Sharḥ-i Aḥvāl-i Jināb-i Hāshim Sajjād ('Āshūr Ghayyūr)', *'Andalīb*, vol. 16, no. 61 (Winter 1996) 54–8.

Uskū'ī, Mīrzā Ḥaydar 'Alī Ṣanī'ī. *Tārīkh-i Amrī-yi Ādharbāyjān*. Parts 1 and 2 were completed in 83 BE/1926; part 3 is undated. MS A, 111+25+26 pp.; MS B, written by Muḥammad ʿAlī Malik-Khusravī. 141 pp.

Ustādī, Riḍā. *Yād-Nāmih-yi Āyatuʾllāh al-ʿUzmā Arākī*. Tehran: Anjuman-i ʿIlmī, Farhangī va Hunarī-yi Ustān-i Markazī, 1375/1996. http://www.hawzah.net/fa/ Book/View/45232/17537 (accessed 5 Aug. 2019).

Vaḥīd-Ṭihrānī, Mehrangīz. Memorandum on Sayyid Ḥasan Mutavajjih. MS. In private hands.

Vaqāyīʿ-yi Ittifāqiyyih (ed. ʿAlī Akbar Saʿīdī Sīrjānī). Tehran: Nashr-i Naw, 1361/1982.

Varqā, Mahdī. ʿSharḥ-i Aḥvāl va Shahādat-i Jināb-i Varqā va Rūḥuʾllāhʾ. *Khūshih-hā-iy az Kharman-i Adab va Hunar* 5. Landegg, 1994, 21–33.

Vejdani, Farzin. ʿTransnational Bahaʾi Print Culture: Community Formation and Religious Authority, 1890–1921ʾ, *Journal of Religious History*, 36 (2012) 499–515.

Vujdānī, Ashraf. Athmār-i Shish Shajar. Privately published, 1992.

Walcher, Heidi. ʿFace of the Seven Spheres: The Urban Morphology and Architecture of Nineteenth-Century Isfahan (Part Two)ʾ. *Iranian Studies*, vol. 34 (2001), pp. 117–39.

— *In the Shadow of the King: Zill al-Sultān and Isfahān under the Qājārs*. London: I.B. Tauris, 2008.

Waterfield, Robin. *The Christians in Persia*. London: George Allen and Unwin, 1973.

White, Roger. ʿBahāʾuʾllāh and the Fourth Estateʾ. *The Bahāʾī World*, vol. 18, pp. 975–9.

Wills, Charles J. *The Land of the Lion and the Sun or Modern Persia*. London: Ward Lock, new ed., 1891.

Wilson, Samuel G. *Bahaʾism and Its Claims*. New York: AMS Press, rpt. 1970.

— *Persia: Western Mission*. Philadelphia: Presbyterian Board of Publication, 1896.

Yaghmāʾī, Iqbāl. *Shahīd-i Rāh-i Āzādī: Sayyid Jamāl Vāʿiz-i Isfahānī*. Tehran: Tūs, 2537 SH/1978.

Yazdī, Ustād ʿAlī Akbar Bannā. ʿTārīkh-i ʿIshqābādʾ. MS published as vol. 94 of ILMA, c. 1903. 407 pp. Now published as *Tārīkh-i ʿIshqābād* (ed. Vahid Rafati). Hofheim: Bahāʾī Verlag, 2015.

Yazdī, Fāḍil. Manāhaj ul-Aḥkām. 2 vols. MS, published as vols. 5–6 of ILMA.

Zargarī-nizhād, Ghulām-Ḥusayn. *Rasāʾil Mashrūṭiyyat*, vol. 1. rpt. Tehran: Kavīr, 1377.

Zarqānī, Maḥmūd. *Badāyīʿ ul-Āthār*. 2 vols. rpt. Hofheim: Bahāʾī-Verlag, 1982. Trans. as *Maḥmūdʾs Diary* (trans. Mohi Sobhani with Shirley Macias). Oxford: George Ronald, vol. 1, 1998; vol. 2, forthcoming.

Zayn, Nūruʾd-Dīn. Khāṭirāt-i Ḥayāt dar Khidmat-i Maḥbūb. TS, 2 vols. 866 pp.

Ẓill us-Sulṭān, Masʿūd Mīrzā. *Khāṭirāt Ẓill us-Sulṭān* (ed. Husayn Khadīv-Jam). 3 vols. Tehran: Asāṭīr, 1365 AHS/1986.

INDEX

This index is alphabetized word for word; thus **ʿAlī Zargar** precedes **ʿAliyābād**. Hyphenated names are considered as two separate words; thus **ʿAbdu'l-Vahhāb** precedes **ʿAbdu'llāh**.

The following connecting letters are ignored for the purpose of alphabetization: al-, ad-, -i, ud-, ul-, un-, ur-, us-, ut-, uz-, udh- and -yi, as are apostrophes and *ʿayn* ('). Thus **Amīn us-Sultān** precedes **Amīn ul-Vizārih**.

The words **and, at, in, of, the** and **to** are also ignored. The letters **ʿA, Ā** and **ʿĀ** are alphabetized as **A**.

As there were no surnames in Iran for most of the period covered by this book, most individuals are indexed under their given names. Those with titles given them by the Qājār state or the Bahāʾi leadership are indexed under their titles. A few individuals whose surnames are clear are indexed under their surnames. In these last two cases, the person's given name is alphabetized next, ignoring any prefix such as Mīrzā and Sayyid. Hence **Ṣadr ul-ʿUlamā, Sayyid Jaʿfar** precedes **Ṣadr ul-ʿUlamā, Mīrzā Mahdī**.

As so many Iranian names are very similar, to assist the reader the index is designed to give as much information about the identity of individuals as needed to identify that person. Hence entries may include the following elements in this order: the person's given name, occupation, town of origin, prefixed title (such as Ḥājī and Mīrzā) and, in parentheses, the town of residence (occasionally preceded by alternative names and titles). For example: **Ḥusayn Naʿlband Kāshānī, Ustād (Ḥusayn Bābī; Tehran)**.

Note that where Karbalāʾī and Mashhadī occur as a prefix to a name, they denote that a person has been on pilgrimage to Karbala or Mashhad (cf. Ḥājī) and not that the person is from one of these cities.

Names of small towns or villages are followed in parentheses by the name of the province or district in which they are located. Additional information about significant localities can be found under these entries: baths, public; cemeteries and graves; Christians/Christianity; *ḥaẓīrat ul-quds*; Jews/Judaism; *mashriq ul-adhkār* (house of worship); schools; Shaykhis/Shaykhism; Spiritual Assembly; telegraph/telegraph office; *and* women.

Where there are multiple page numbers for an index entry, numbers in *italics* indicate the significant pages for that entry. Page numbers in **bold** indicate an illustration, map or chart related to that entry.

Lightning Source UK Ltd.
Milton Keynes UK
UKHW050849291221
396207UK00003BA/25